WITHDRAWN

"Emperor Dead"

*and Other
Historic American
Diplomatic Dispatches*

In 1881 the American minister to Russia, John Foster, reported the death of Czar Alexander II in a telegram that read, in its entirety, "Emperor dead."

"Emperor Dead"

and Other Historic American Diplomatic Dispatches

Edited by Peter D. Eicher
With a Foreword by Ernest R. May

An ADST-DACOR Diplomats and Diplomacy Series Book

Congressional Quarterly Inc.
Washington, D.C.

For the men and women of the U.S. Foreign Service
who have been my friends and colleagues
in many lands through many years,
and among them especially Stephanie, who has shared
my odyssey to the farthest outposts of the world

Copyright © 1997 by the Association for Diplomatic Studies and Training, Washington, D.C.

All rights reserved. No part of this publication may be reproduced or transmitted in any form or by any means, electronic or mechanical, including photocopy, recording, or any information storage and retrieval system, without permission in writing from the publisher.

Printed in the United States of America

Illustration credits: pp. 1, 77, 141—Library of Congress; pp. 193, 403—Bettman; p. 247 National Park Service; p. 303 Theodore Roosevelt Collection, Harvard College Library; p. 361 *Chicago Tribune*

Library of Congress Cataloging-in-Publication Data

"Emperor dead" and other historic American diplomatic dispatches /
   [edited by] Peter D. Eicher
   p.   cm.
   Includes index.
   ISBN 1-56802-249-2
   1. United States—Foreign relations—Sources. I. Eicher, Peter D.
E183.7.E47 1996
327.73—dc20

96-44314

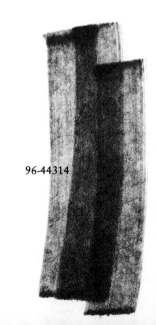

Contents

Series Note		*xiv*
Foreword		*xv*
Preface		*xvii*
Introduction		1

I. The Early National Period: 1776–1815 — 23

Year	Title	Author	Page
1776	In the Beginning . . .	Silas Deane	25
1780–1781	Prisoner in the Tower	Henry Laurens	29
1781	Wolf at the Door	Benjamin Franklin	31
1783	Establishing Broad Relations	Benjamin Franklin	32
1783	Franklin on Peace	Benjamin Franklin	33
1785	Thirteen Ministers for Thirteen States?	John Adams	34
1785	John Adams Meets George III: "An Epoch in . . . History"	John Adams	36
1786	Jefferson Urges War against the Barbary States	Thomas Jefferson	38
1786	Trade with China	Samuel Shaw	39
1789–1794	The French Revolution	Gouverneur Morris, Thomas Jefferson, James Monroe	42
1793	Help for American Captives in Algiers: "Twelve Cents a Day"	David Humphreys	50
1797	Bribery in Paris: The XYZ Affair	Charles Cotesworth Pinckney et al.	52
1798	Pirates in New Orleans	Daniel Clark Jr.	54
1798	Naval Tensions with Britain: American Fleet Captured Off Havana	George C. Morton	57
1801	Tripoli Declares War: "Our Flag-staff Was Chopped Down"	James Leander Cathcart	58
1802, 1810	Napoleon: "A Spoilt Child of Fortune"	Robert R. Livingston, Jonathan Russell	59
1803	Bargaining for Louisiana	Robert R. Livingston	60
1803	Transfer of Louisiana	Daniel Clark Jr.	64

1805	Napoleon Victorious: "A Very Favorable" Situation for the United States	James Monroe	66
1806	The British Move into Africa: The Cape of Good Hope	John Elmslie	68
1808	Threatened by the Dey of Algiers	Tobias Lear	69
1813	Napoleon's Retreat from Moscow	John Quincy Adams	71
1814	Treaty of Ghent Signed	John Quincy Adams et al.	73
1815	Waterloo	Henry Jackson	75

II. Years of U.S. Expansion: 1816–1860   77

1818	Description of Oregon and California	John B. Prevost	79
1819	Assisting an American Seaman Stranded in Bermuda	W. R. Higinbothom	82
1820–1821	The Acquisition of Florida	John Forsyth, Andrew Jackson	82
1821	Surrender of Lima to San Martín: "South America . . . Forever Free"	Michael Hogan	84
1821	Independence of Mexico	James Smith Wilcocks	85
1824	Suppression of the Slave Trade	Richard Rush	90
1824	Pirates of the Caribbean	Thomas Randall	92
1827	Consular Service on the Western Frontier: "The Indians Stole My Horses"	David Dickson	93
1828–1829	The Demise of Greater Colombia	William Henry Harrison	94
1830	The French in Algeria: "Fear and Blood"	Henry Lee	97
1830	France's July Revolution: "One of the Most Wonderful . . . in the History of the World"	William G. Rives	98
1831	Preserving the Peace	Martin Van Buren	100
1835	War in South Africa	Isaac Chase	102
1838	Savagery in Tahiti: "Twelf Wounds, Five upon My Head"	Jacob Antoine Moerenhaut	103
1840	Prelude to the Opium War	Peter W. Snow	105
1840	Napoleon's Remains Go Home	William Carrol	107
1842	"Texians" to Arms as Mexicans Invade	Joseph Eve	107
1842	The French Seize Tahiti	Samuel Blackler	109
1843	Insurgents Take Madrid	Washington Irving	111
1843	Arabian Horses for President Tyler	Richard P. Waters	113
1846	The Acquisition of New Mexico: "Our Country Has Acquired without Bloodshed a Province"	Manuel Alvarez	113

1847	The Treaty of Guadalupe Hidalgo: Expanding the Country without Instructions	Nicholas P. Trist	116
1848	Recognizing the Republic of Venice	William A. Sparks	117
1851	Gold and Opportunity in Australia	James H. Williams	119
1853	Guerrilla Warfare in Southeast Asia: The British in Burma	Charles Huffnagle	121
1853	First Visit to the Interior of China	Humphrey Marshall	122
1854	First Attempt to Annex Hawaii	David L. Gregg	126
1854	The Ostend Manifesto	Pierre Soulé et al.	128
1855	British Ignorance of U.S. Politics	James Buchanan	129
1855	A Consular Case: "Assault with Intent to Commit Murder"	Nathaniel Hawthorne	131
1857	The Indian Mutiny: "India Is Held by the Sword"	Charles Huffnagle	134
1858	Emancipation of the Russian Serfs	Francis S. Claxton	136
1858	Nicaragua: An Incident en Route to the Capital	Mirabeau B. Lamar	138

III. The Civil War Era: 1861–1867   141

1861	Reactions to the American Civil War	Charles J. Faulkner, George W. Morgan, John Appleton, George M. Dallas, William Preston, Joseph A. Wright, Thomas Corwin, John P. Brown	143
1861	The Death of Cavour, Hero of Italian Unification	Romaine Dillon	148
1862	Confederates Chained in the Consulate	James de Long	149
1862	The *Monitor* and the *Merrimac*: A Swedish Victory?	J. S. Haldeman	152
1862	Bureaucratic Mysteries in Japan	Robert H. Pruyn	153
1862–1864	The Confederate Raider *Alabama*	Charles Francis Adams, James E. Harvey, Thomas Adamson Jr., Walter Graham, William L. Dayton	154
1862	Foreign Recruits	Charles Boernstein	159
1862	A Diplomatic Blunder: Garibaldi and the Civil War	Theodore Canisius, William H. Seward	160

1862	The Ottoman Empire: A Public Execution	Edward Joy Morris	163
1862	China's First Flag	Anson Burlingame	164
1862	The Emancipation Proclamation: Turning the Tide in Europe	James S. Pike	165
1863	Turmoil in the Balkans	John Lothrop Motley	166
1863	Japan: Legation Destroyed, No Fire Insurance	Robert H. Pruyn	168
1863	Discovery of the Source of the Nile	William S. Thayer	169
1864	Tunisia's Tax Revolt	Amos Perry	171
1864	Progress in Russia	Cassius M. Clay	172
1864	Karl Marx Congratulates Abraham Lincoln	Charles Francis Adams	173
1865	Lincoln Assassinated	Abraham Hanson, S. Wells Williams	175
1865	Pestilence and Conflagration in Constantinople	Edward Joy Morris	176
1865	Pope Pius IX Comments on World Affairs: "Anything but Satisfactory"	Rufus King	178
1866	The Fenian Invasion of Canada	Freeman N. Blake	179
1866	Insurrection in Spain: "My House Was Hit by One Cannon Ball"	John P. Hale	182
1866	The Austro-Prussian War: Moving toward a German Empire	John Lothrop Motley	183
1866	The Continents United: The Transatlantic Cable	John Bigelow	185
1866	Arresting a Lincoln Conspirator	Charles Hale	186
1867	The Purchase of Alaska: "Seward's Folly"	Cassius M. Clay	187
1867	The Saga of Maximilian	Marcus Otterbourg, E. L. Plumb	188

IV. A Period of U.S. Isolation: 1868–1882   193

1868	Eyewitness to a Hara-Kiri	Robert B. Van Valkenburgh	195
1868	A Grave Robber in Korea	George F. Seward	197
1868	Earthquake: "Ecuador Is in Ruins"	Alvin P. Hovey	199
1871, 1874	Stanley and Livingstone	Francis R. Webb	201
1871	A Prussian Victory: "Paris Seems . . . to have Died"	Elihu B. Washburne	202
1871	The Paris Commune	Elihu B. Washburne	204
1871	Indian Depredations: "Murdering and Marauding Savages" on the Mexican Border	William Schuchardt	208

Year	Title	Author	Page
1873	Earthquake in San Salvador: "A Terrific Reverberation, which Baffles Description"	Thomas Biddle	210
1873	The Shah of Persia: "Studded All Over with Diamonds, Rubies"	George Bancroft	212
1873	Slaves for the Harem: Helpless Women and Eunuchs	George H. Boker	213
1875	Anti-Jesuit Riots in Argentina	Thomas O. Osborn	215
1875	A Court Occasion in Athens: Dancing with the Queen	John Meredith Read	217
1875	Eyewitness to an Attempted Revolution in Bolivia: "A Memorable Day"	Robert M. Reynolds	218
1877	Unearthing the Arms of Venus de Milo	John Meredith Read	220
1877	Freeing a Slave in Egypt	Elbert E. Farman	220
1877	Shooting at the Moon in Constantinople: "A Curious Custom"	Horace Maynard	222
1878	The Royal Court of Spain: Pageantry and Tragedy	James Russell Lowell	223
1879	Cleopatra's Needle: An Obelisk for New York	Elbert E. Farman	228
1879	A Plague of Grasshoppers in the Caucasus	Wickham Hoffman	229
1879	Morocco: Inspiring Terror among the Rebels	Felix A. Mathews	230
1879	The German-Austrian Alliance	Andrew D. White	230
1880–1886	French Conquests in Africa	John Smyth, Levi P. Morton, Robert M. McLane	233
1880–1881	Czar Assassinated	Wickham Hoffman, John W. Foster	236
1880	The Consulate in Bangkok: In a "Disgraceful Condition"	John Singleton Mosby	238
1881	Lima Surrenders to Chilean Forces	Isaac P. Christiancy	239
1881	Immigration and Epidemic in Hawaii	James M. Comly	241
1881	Pogroms in Russia: "More Worthy of the Dark Ages than of the Present Century"	John W. Foster	242
1881	A Memorial for President Garfield	Lew Wallace	244

V. The Late Nineteenth Century: 1883–1897 — 247

Year	Title	Author	Page
1883	The Steamship *Aurania*: "The Most Remarkable Ship that Has Ever Been Built"	Bret Harte	249
1883	The Siamese Royal Elephant Hunt	John A. Halderman	251

Year	Title	Author	Page
1883	Eruption of Krakatau	Stewart Hatfield Jr.	253
1883	Antiforeign Riots in Canton: "An Interesting Day"	Charles Seymour	255
1884	Early Vladivostok: "Caviar and Vodka"	John A. Halderman	257
1884	Accepting the Statue of Liberty	Levi P. Morton	258
1885	Korea: Execution of Revolutionists	George C. Foulk	260
1885	The Central American Union: A Month of Turmoil	H. Remsen Whitehouse, Henry C. Hall	261
1885	Conditions in Central Africa	W. P. Tisdel	263
1886	End of Arab Power in East Africa	E. D. Ropes Jr.	267
1887	The Trans-Siberian Railroad	Charles Denby Jr.	268
1888	The Rothschilds at the Court of Vienna: "A Great Sensation"	Alexander R. Lawton	269
1888	Slavery: Down but Not Out	Charles Denby Jr., Thomas J. Jarvis	270
1889	The Birth of International Organizations	Boyd Winchester	272
1889	New Constitution for Japan: "The Most Important Political Event in the History of the Empire"	Richard B. Hubbard	274
1889	Revolution in Brazil: "The Most Remarkable . . . in History"	Robert Adams Jr.	276
1890	A Sacred and Curious Gift from Japan: A Rope of Human Hair	John F. Swift	278
1890	Revolution and War in Central America	Lansing B. Mizner	279
1890	Conditions in Haiti: "Full of Promise"	Frederick Douglass	281
1891	Civil War in Chile	Patrick Egan	283
1891	A Chinese Emperor's Daily Routine: "More Work than Any Other Sovereign"	Charles Denby Jr.	284
1892	Famine in Russia: "The Distress . . . Can Hardly Be Overstated"	Charles Emory Smith	286
1893	Punishment in Persia: Eighteen Lashes for Insulting an American	Watson R. Sperry	287
1893	Hawaii: A U.S. Protectorate	John L. Stevens	289
1893	Riots in Peru: Bullet in Leg but Archives Saved	John Hicks	291
1894	The Mosquito Reservation: "American to the Core"	Lewis Baker	292
1894	Troubles in Baghdad	John C. Sundberg	294
1894	The Sino-Japanese War	Charles Denby Jr.	298
1894	An Arrest on the Mexican Border	Reuben D. George	299
1896	Shah of Persia Assassinated	Alexander McDonald	300

VI. Emergence of the United States as a World Power: 1898–1919   **303**

Year	Title	Author	Page
1898	The *Maine*	Fitzhugh Lee	305
1898	Anti-American Riots in Spain	R. M. Bartleman	308
1898	The Battle of Manila Bay	Oscar F. Williams	310
1898–1900	The Great Gold Rush	James C. McCook	312
1900	The Boer War: "The Afrikander . . . Is to Be the Ruling Race of South Africa"	W. Stanley Hollis	315
1900	The Boxer Rebellion: The Siege at Peking	Edwin H. Conger	318
1901	End of an Era: The Death of Queen Victoria	Joseph H. Choate	322
1901	Greece: Rioting against a Vulgar Bible	Charles S. Francis	323
1901	First Nobel Prizes	William W. Thomas Jr.	325
1902	Universal Suffrage Riots in Belgium	Lawrence Townsend	327
1902	Establishing the Rhodes Scholarship	Joseph H. Choate	328
1903	Lawlessness in Lebanon: "Beirut Is Unsafe"	G. Bie Ravndal	329
1904	Kurdish Outlaws: "Love of Blood and Pillage"	Richmond Pearson	330
1906	Unrest in Moscow	Samuel Smith	332
1906	A Nobel Prize for President Roosevelt	Herbert H. D. Pierce	336
1908	Atrocities in the Congo	James A. Smith	338
1908	Constitutional Government in Turkey	John G. A. Leishman	340
1914–1917	Crisis with Mexico	William W. Canada, Philip C. Hanna, William P. Blocker	342
1914	Assassination of Archduke Franz Ferdinand	Frederic Courtland Penfield	346
1914	Europe on the Brink of War	James W. Gerard, Frederic Courtland Penfield, Myron Timothy Herrick, Walter Hines Page, Huntington Wilson	346
1914	Germany Victorious	Brand Whitlock, Walter Hines Page, James W. Gerard	349
1915	The Political Process in Haiti	Arthur Bailly-Blanchard, Robert Beale Davis Jr.	351
1915	Human Shields at Gallipoli	Henry Morgenthau	352
1915	Armenian Genocide	Henry Morgenthau	353
1915	An Ambassador's Observation: "The Whole German People Is Dangerously Mad"	James W. Gerard	356

1917	The Zimmermann Telegram	Walter Hines Page	357
1917	The Russian Revolution	North Winship	358

VII. The World in Upheaval: 1920–1945   361

1921	Sun Yat-sen Elected President of China	Ernest B. Price	363
1922	Nicaragua: The U.S. Minister Quells a Revolution	John Edward Ramer	364
1923	Earthquake in Japan	Earle R. Dickover	366
1925	Revolt in Damascus	James Hugh Keeley	367
1927	Besieged by a Chinese Mob	John Van A. MacMurray	368
1927	The Kellogg-Briand Pact: A Protocol to Outlaw War	Sheldon Whitehouse	369
1930	An Early Nazi Victory: Banning a Movie	Frederic Mosley Sackett	370
1931	Views on Japan's Invasion of Manchuria	Nelson T. Johnson	372
1932	Communist Uprising in El Salvador	William J. McCafferty	373
1933	The Reichstag Fire: The Nazi Ascent to Power	Frederic Mosley Sackett	374
1933, 1934	The National Socialist German Workers' Party: Seeking to Dominate the Globe	George S. Messersmith, Douglas Miller	377
1933	Batista Seizes Power in Cuba	Benjamin Sumner Welles	380
1934	Establishing Relations with the Soviet Union	William C. Bullitt	382
1934	Nazis Assassinate the Austrian Chancellor	George S. Messersmith	385
1936	The Italian Invasion of Ethiopia	Cornelius Van H. Engert	386
1936, 1938	The Spanish Civil War	Herschel V. Johnson, Claude G. Bowers	388
1940	Great Britain on the Verge of Defeat	Joseph P. Kennedy	391
1940	The Fall of France	William C. Bullitt	393
1941	Early Warning of Pearl Harbor	Joseph C. Grew	397
1942	Gandhi and Civil Disobedience	George R. Merrell	398
1945	Suing for Peace	Herschel V. Johnson	399

VIII. The Cold War: 1946–1964   403

1946	Progress in Honduras	John D. Erwin	405
1946	Revolution in Bolivia: Chance for Democracy	Joseph Flack	406
1948	Churchill on the Soviets: "Raze Their Cities"	Lewis Williams Douglas	407
1948	The Birth of Israel	Thomas C. Wasson, William C. Burdett, John J. Macdonald	408

1948	The Berlin Airlift	Robert Daniel Murphy	413
1949	China Goes Communist	John Leighton Stuart, John Moors Cabot, Edmund Clubb	414
1949	Indonesian Independence	Stephen Chapin	417
1950	Tito Comments on His Revolution	George V. Allen	418
1950	The Perón Regime: "One of the Most Dramatic . . . Experiments in the History of the World"	Stanton Griffis	420
1950	Riots in South Africa	Bernard C. Connelly	422
1950	The Korean War	John J. Muccio	424
1951	Establishing a Mission in Kuwait	Enoch S. Duncan	426
1953	The Mau Mau Revolt	Edmund J. Dorsz	427
1954	Dien Bien Phu: The French Defeated in Vietnam	Robert McClintock	430
1955	Two Views of the Chinese Communists	Winthrop W. Aldrich, John Foster Dulles	432
1955	Military Tensions in China	Karl L. Rankin	435
1956	The Suez Crisis	Edward B. Lawson, Raymond A. Hare	436
1956	The Hungarian Uprising	Edward T. Wailes	439
1957	*Sputnik*	Llewellyn E. Thompson Jr.	441
1959–1960	Castro and Communism in Cuba	Daniel M. Braddock, Philip W. Bonsal	442
1961	The Berlin Wall	Edwin A. Lightner Jr.	449
1961	Vietnam: A "Powder Keg"	W. Averell Harriman	451
1963	Fomenting a Coup d' État in Vietnam	Henry Cabot Lodge	453
1964	The Gulf of Tonkin Incident	Maxwell D. Taylor	456

Index 459

The ADST-DACOR Diplomats and Diplomacy Series

In 1995 the Association for Diplomatic Studies and Training (ADST) and Diplomatic and Consular Officers, Retired (DACOR) created a book series to increase public knowledge of the involvement of American diplomats in the events of world history. For 220 years an extraordinary group of men and women have represented the United States abroad—for better and for worse—under all kinds of circumstances. What they did, how they did it, and why are not well known by their fellow citizens. The ADST-DACOR Diplomats and Diplomacy Series thus seeks to demystify diplomacy by bringing to the rest of us the story of those who conduct our foreign relations.

No better book could have launched this series than Peter D. Eicher's *"Emperor Dead" and Other Historic American Diplomatic Dispatches*. The dispatches tell their own story—of remarkable Americans most of whom served their country "well and faithfully," in the words of the ambassadorial oath. Together with Mr. Eicher's scene-setting introductions, these dispatches provide insight into the historical circumstances and human side of how the United States over two centuries has related to the world around it.

> Stephen Low
> ADST President
>
> Robert H. Miller
> DACOR President

Foreword

"What exactly do diplomats do?" This question is not an easy one to answer. To respond that diplomats "mostly write letters and attend parties" seems not only flip but too much like replying "not much worthwhile." That, however, is far from the truth.

In fact, the activities described in *"Emperor Dead" and Other Historic American Diplomatic Dispatches*—representation and reportage—are of enormous importance and value to the health and well-being of the United States and its citizens, both at home and abroad. As for the diplomats themselves, not many federal employees have day-to-day functions that are as demanding and useful as those fulfilled by America's foreign representatives, for diplomats' letters or cables home weigh—much more than those of journalists—what is happening abroad that can be of immediate danger or yield immediate gain to American citizens. In appearing publicly abroad, these representatives are assumed to embody the qualities of their country. In contrast, a business leader usually symbolizes a company or an industry. A scholar or athlete or performer symbolizes at least in part the international community comprising members of his or her profession. But a diplomat, even if only a junior consul, *is* the United States.

"Emperor Dead" and Other Historic American Diplomatic Dispatches helps greatly to substantiate the seriousness of the statement "diplomats write letters." By means of excerpted dispatches dating back to the American Revolution, the book depicts American representatives abroad noticing and calling attention to events, opportunities, and historical achievements about which people at home needed urgent knowledge. As Peter D. Eicher points out in his perceptive introduction, this reportage changed as telegraph lines and transoceanic cables speeded up communication, as proliferating news media made comprehensive reportage of events less necessary—at least from places where newspapers or networks located foreign bureaus—and as matters of concern to Americans multiplied and broadened. Yet diplomatic reporting has remained vital for its analysis, its perspective on events, and its important confidential information. Moreover, it provides a fascinating window on two centuries of world history. Of all this, the volume provides wonderful illustration.

In addition to illustrating what diplomats do and what roles they play in reporting or even shaping history, the volume should be useful to diplomats themselves. The best samples here, not only from Franklin,

Jefferson, and the Adamses but also from more recent foreign representatives such as Llewellyn Thompson, Averell Harriman, and Joseph C. Grew, also set high standards for present-day foreign representatives.

Finally for all readers—citizens and professionals alike—this collection of historical documents shows that the past is worth studying not only for its mistakes but for its examples worth imitating. It also calls attention to the truth that everything—even diplomacy—undergoes change. For the courageous men and women serving their country abroad, however, the mission, perils, and challenges remain much the same.

>Ernest R. May
>Charles Warren Professor of History,
>Harvard University

Preface

In many ways the men and women who have served the United States in diplomatic and consular assignments abroad have reflected all that is American—our hopes and our prejudices, our confidence and our bluster. In other ways, they have been a breed apart—individuals who chose to leave the familiar comfort and safety of their homes for the uncertainty and adventure of foreign shores. But there is another important way in which this group of Americans has made itself unique: they have left a detailed written account of their experiences. Thus they not only have forged history but also have written it. Indeed, their dispatches provide an unparalleled record of the American view of the world over the past two centuries. They have witnessed and recorded history's great events; often they have been key actors. They have endured and reported on war, riot, plague, and famine. They have described and commented on people, places, customs, and changing social and political norms around the world. Their reports trace not only the history of foreign lands, but also the emergence of the United States from backwater to world power and the changing American perceptions that accompanied this transformation. Their reports chronicle America's diplomatic experience in its most human form, while providing an often startling kaleidoscope of the events and personalities that have shaped the modern world.

For those researching American diplomatic dispatches, it is hard to avoid feeling overwhelmed. The sheer volume of historical dispatches is staggering, certainly in the millions. The points of origin span the globe, many of them from place names that no longer exist—Alexandretta, Aspinwall, Batavia, Christiania, the "Mosquito Reservation," Pest, Point de Galle, Yedo. And the issues covered in these dispatches are as diverse as the history of the past two centuries. Logical patterns are difficult to discern. We tend to study history in systematic progressions, focusing on the development of specific countries, ideas, policies, or issues. This approach makes events easier to understand, but it distorts the complexities of world affairs and the reality that foreign developments do not occur in orderly patterns. While a consul in Canton might be experiencing and reporting a siege by antiforeign rioters, his counterpart in Glasgow might be calmly penning a dispatch on the latest developments in shipbuilding; both of these examples from the year 1883 can be found in this collection. In the same year the State Department received other dispatches on subjects as diverse as the crowning of a king of Hawaii, a revolution in Haiti, the reception of the first American minister in Persia, and a volcanic eruption in the East Indies. And 1883 was not an atypical year.

Although America's view of the world often has tended to be Eurocentric, U.S. diplomatic reporting has been produced in a more equitable manner, mirroring the world's diversity. The dispatches in this volume were selected to reflect the variety, richness, and broad geographical scope of American diplomatic reporting and to strike a balance among events and developments in different parts of the world and in different time frames. The broad scope of the dispatches serves as a reminder that while Americans may focus on one set of issues, entirely different problems may preoccupy the people of other countries. During the American Civil War, for example, U.S. representatives rightly tended to concentrate on foreign reactions to the conflict but did not limit their reporting to this issue. Dispatches from the years 1862–1863 in this collection describe turmoil in the Balkans, political transformation in Japan, and the discovery of the source of the Nile.

Selecting the Dispatches

The broad and inclusive nature of American diplomatic reporting mandated use of an extremely selective approach to choosing material for this volume. Most of the dispatches were chosen for their content—that is, the preponderance of documents in this collection describe particularly significant or interesting historical events of the first two centuries of American diplomacy. The collection includes dispatches on such key historical international developments as the French Revolution and the Napoleonic era, the independence of Latin America, the colonization of Africa, the emergence of Japan, wars and insurrections in all parts of the world, the Russian Revolution, the rise of the Nazis, the establishment of the People's Republic of China and the state of Israel, and the cold war.

A number of the dispatches were selected because of the prominence of their authors—among them, presidents, statesmen, and literary figures. In some instances, both the event and the author were prominent, resulting in a dispatch of particular significance—for example, James Monroe's report on the French Revolution's Reign of Terror and John Quincy Adams's analysis of Napoleon's retreat from Moscow.

A third criterion for the selection of dispatches was the importance in American history of the events they describe. The collection thus begins with the first American diplomatic dispatch and moves through the American Revolution, the XYZ affair, the Barbary Wars, the Louisiana Purchase, the Treaty of Ghent, the Ostend Manifesto, the Civil War, the sinking of the *Maine* and the battle of Manila Bay, the world wars, and Vietnam.

This volume also includes a particularly interesting and often overlooked set of important American historical documents: consular reporting from U.S. representatives in foreign territories later to become part of the United States. U.S. Consul Daniel Clark, for example, reported in 1798 on problems with pirates in Spanish New Orleans. In 1818 envoy John Prevost provided one of the earliest official descriptions of Oregon and California. Several early U.S. representatives reported to Washington from Mexican Texas and later from the Republic of Texas. Manuel Alvarez provided a unique perspective of the Mexican War from his post as consul in Santa Fe. Throughout the second half of the nineteenth century American consuls in Honolulu reported on developments in the Kingdom of Hawaii. From his post in the Yukon Territory's Dawson City, James McCook reported home on the discovery of gold in Nome, Alaska.

Many other dispatches in this collection were selected because they describe particularly unusual, interesting, horrific, or amusing events, even if the events did not touch on the most important issues of their day. Thus the collection includes dispatches recounting grave robbing in Korea, Indian depredations on the Western frontier, elephant hunting with the king of Siam, an eyewitness report of a hara-kiri, the supposed discovery of the arms of Venus de Milo, and other curiosities. Several of the more dramatic dispatches in the volume recount natural disasters: the eruption of Krakatau; earthquakes in San Salvador, Japan, and Ecuador; famine in Russia; epidemics in Constantinople, Honolulu, and Baghdad. Many of the authors themselves fell victim to epidemics and other disasters while serving abroad. Finally, a few dispatches were selected as representative examples of common types of consular and diplomatic correspondence. These include accounts of assistance to seamen, an important responsibility of early American representatives abroad, and reports of gifts received from foreign dignitaries or governments.

The collection ends with events in the early 1960s because of declassification constraints. Most diplomatic correspondence through that time has been declassified; of that, a small percentage has been published by the State Department or others. Most dispatches of the past three decades, however, remain sealed to the public on national security grounds. Declassification rules are established by presidential executive orders designed to safeguard the confidentiality of sensitive information. The classification systems are fairly complex and have been modified from time to time. President Jimmy Carter instituted an accelerated declassification schedule for many documents. Under President Ronald Reagan, a new executive order required officers drafting dispatches to cite a specific, future date on which the documents would be declassified. In practice, however, a great many documents have been exempted from early or automatic declassification. In the Reagan and Bush years, for example, rather than assigning a specific declassification date, drafters routinely labeled their dispatches "OADR," or "originating agency determination required," meaning the documents would not be automatically declassified on a specific date but would have to be reviewed at some unspecified, future time for a determination whether they could be declassified and released. A new executive order issued by President Bill Clinton in October 1995 attempted to tighten classification rules by requiring drafters to classify each paragraph of a document separately and to cite a reason for classifying each document. Despite such efforts to restrict classification, however, much diplomatic reporting remains unavailable to the public for thirty years or more after it is written. Individuals can petition the State Department for release of classified documents under the Freedom of Information Act, but the process can be lengthy and there is no guarantee that the documents requested will be made available. Although a substantial number of documents have been released in this manner, there is no readily accessible, comprehensive collection of recent dispatches comparable to what is available for the years prior to 1964. To have included random, more recent dispatches in this volume on an as-available basis would have risked distorting the collection's overall balance of geographic regions, time frames, and great events. Dispatches for events since the early 1960s offer a rich area for future research and publication.

Usage

Over the years the term *despatch*—rather than the now more familiar *dispatch*—has most commonly been used to refer to diplomatic reporting. *Despatch* was used exclusively throughout the eighteenth and nineteenth centuries. In the early years of the twentieth century, the term *dispatch* began to appear interchangeably with *despatch* but never replaced it in standard diplomatic usage. *Despatch* is the form still used in most official publications of the U.S. Department of State and the National Archives, but *dispatch* is used in this volume because it is a form more familiar to most readers. This being said, with the advent of modern communications, both terms have been largely set aside and neither is used frequently in today's State Department. Messages from embassies and other U.S. missions abroad are now generally referred to as *telegrams* or *cables*—although most have been sent for years through satellite channels rather than by cable. As an indication of the volume of present-day reporting, batches of diplomatic dispatches are now usually called *traffic*. One of the first daily tasks of many Foreign Service personnel overseas and in Washington is to scan the morning traffic. Many modern dispatches never make it to paper at all; they are created and transmitted electronically, then read on computer screens.

The spelling, capitalization, punctuation, and grammar in the dispatches in this volume appear as they do in the originals. The single exception is the omission of the long "s" favored by correspondents and printers before 1800. Although strict adherence to the originals results in some inconsistencies and occasionally in some curious forms, it provides the reader with a completely accurate picture of the original dispatch. It also sometimes helps to provide a glimpse of the era and of changing writing styles and social usage. Some authors, for example, freely used terms or expressed views that are now considered offensive or derogatory.

Ellipses have been used to indicate all instances in which text has been deleted from the original documents. A number of the original dispatches were far too lengthy to include in this volume in their entirety. In other instances the authors touched on many events in a single dispatch, although only one or two might be of particular historical interest. Some original dispatches included obscure references which were omitted when their inclusion would have tended to diminish the clarity of the broader text. In a few cases, portions of the hand-written original manuscripts were illegible and could not be included.

Sources

The final repository for U.S. diplomatic papers is the U.S. National Archives, which contains the definitive, master collection of the millions of pages of reporting from around the world over the past two centuries. It is still possible for scholars to peruse the original letters penned by our envoys abroad. Many of the dispatches are bound neatly into aging volumes. Some documents, frustratingly, have gone astray and no longer can be found. Happily, however, diplomatic records are among those the National Archives has placed on microfilm for easy accessibility. Most dispatches from the early days of the Republic through the first years of the twentieth century are available on microfilm; a few sets continue into the 1940s. The microfilm of the original dispatches, which usually were handwritten, can make for difficult reading. John Hedges's *Diplomatic Records, A Select Catalog of National Archives Microfilm Publications* (Washington, D.C.: National Archives Trust Fund Board, National Archives and Records Administration, 1986) provides a detailed list of the record groups available on microfilm and instructions on how to locate them. Most of the dispatches in this volume were taken directly from the originals in the National Archives; many have never been published before.

Among published sources of dispatches, the most complete is *Foreign Relations of the United States* (Washington, D.C.: Government Printing Office), a series now prepared by the Office of the Historian of the Department of State. The first volume in this series appeared in 1861 as *Message of the President of the United States to the Two Houses of Congress at the Commencement of the Second Session of the Thirty-Seventh Congress* (Washington, D.C.: Government Printing Office, 1861). The two volumes for 1862 were entitled *Papers Relating to Foreign Affairs* (Washington, D.C.: Government Printing Office, 1862). Volumes were published under various titles until 1870, when the series took the name *Papers Relating to the Foreign Relations of the United States* (Washington, D.C.: Government Printing Office). Initially, volumes were published fairly promptly after the end of each year but by the early years of the twentieth century publication had begun to lag behind. In 1947, beginning with the volumes covering the year 1932, the series was renamed *Foreign Relations of the United States: Diplomatic Papers* (Washington, D.C.: Government Printing Office). The present title, *Foreign Relations of the United States*, came into use in 1969, beginning with the volumes covering 1946.

At first the series comprised one or two volumes a year, or occasionally more, which consisted almost entirely of diplomatic dispatches. In the second decade of the twentieth century the number of volumes published yearly was expanded substantially to cover the events of World War I and its aftermath. Since the 1930s, several volumes have been published each year, and the volumes have begun to include internal papers of the State Department and other agencies in addition to diplomatic reporting. The most recent volumes are arranged by presidential administration. Twenty-five volumes are planned to cover the three Kennedy years; seventeen of these volumes had appeared by mid 1996. Two of thirty-five planned volumes on the Johnson administration had been released by the same time. As of this writing, 369 volumes have been published, plus various indexes and microfiche supplements. This series has been a primary source for the more recent dispatches in this book, particularly those from the twentieth century.

Other collections of dispatches are useful but far more restrictive. For the earliest years of the Republic, an excellent collection is *The Diplomatic Correspondence of the American Revolution*, edited by Jared Sparks (Boston: Nathan Hale and Gray and Bowen, 1829), which includes the writings of Silas Deane, Benjamin Franklin, John Adams, John Jay, and others. *American State Papers, Documents, Legislative and Executive of the Congress of the United States* (Washington, D.C.: Gales and Seaton, 1832, and later editions) includes many interesting early dispatches. Another good early collection is *State Papers and Publick Documents of the United States* (Boston: Thomas B. Waite, 1819), which was published in several multivolume editions under the patronage of Congress. Other early congressional reports also have sometimes included the texts of diplomatic dispatches; for example, the dispatch in this collection on the presentation of a pair of Arabian horses to President John Tyler by the sultan of Muscat is from Document 256 of the Twenty-eighth Congress, House of Representatives (Washington, D.C.: Blair and Rives, 1844). A small collection of very interesting dispatches is included in the *Report on the Diplomatic Archives of the Department of State, 1789–1840* (Washington, D.C.: Carnegie Institution, 1906). Also useful and interesting is Jonathan Elliot's *The American Diplomatic Code*

(Washington, D.C.: Jonathan Elliot, Junior, 1834), which incorporates a diplomatic manual and a wealth of other information in addition to a selection of early dispatches.

A few very specialized volumes of dispatches also have been published. For example, in 1881 the House of Representatives ordered the publication of *Reports from the Consuls of the United States on the Commerce, Manufactures, etc., of their Consular Districts* (Washington, D.C.: Government Printing Office, 1881), a six-hundred-page collection of dispatches on trade and commercial conditions around the world. In 1914 the Senate ordered the publication of a *Diplomatic History of the Panama Canal* (Washington, D.C.: Government Printing Office, 1914), a compendium of diplomatic correspondence on the canal negotiations and related events. The *American Journal of International Law* issued a lengthy special supplement in 1917 entitled *Diplomatic Correspondence between the United States and Belligerent Governments Relating to Neutral Rights and Commerce* (New York: Oxford University Press, 1917), consisting entirely of documents provided by the Department of State, most of them diplomatic dispatches. Material from these collections has not, however, been included in this volume.

The collected papers of prominent statesmen provide another useful source of dispatches. For example, Albert Smyth's *The Writings of Benjamin Franklin* (New York: Macmillan, 1906) includes examples of Franklin's diplomatic dispatches. Similar compilations exist for other American diplomats. One with an unusual twist is Virginia Mason's *The Public Life and Diplomatic Correspondence of James M. Mason* (New York: Neale Publishing, 1906). Mason served as commissioner in London for the Confederate States of America during the Civil War. Such collections have a special value for those interested in a particular individual or period. Because the dispatches they contain often are available in the National Archives, these works have not been drawn on for the dispatches in this volume.

Numerous other, more recent collections of documents on the history of American foreign relations have included a few dispatches. Unlike those collections, however, this volume provides the texts of diplomatic dispatches from all time frames and geographic regions for their own historical value and as a window into the history of American diplomacy.

Acknowledgments

This book was made possible by the separate support and efforts of the Una Chapman Cox Foundation and the Association for Diplomatic Studies and Training. The Cox Foundation sponsored a sabbatical fellowship that enabled me to break away from the day-to-day rigors of Foreign Service duty long enough to delve into the rich and colorful past of American diplomacy. To Ambassador Roy Atherton, executive director of the foundation, I offer my special thanks. The Association for Diplomatic Studies and Training deserves full credit for bringing this manuscript to publication. I thank the association's president, Ambassador Steve Low, for his leadership and Publishing Adviser Margery Boichel Thompson for her confidence and perseverance, as well as her skill in guiding the final stages of preparation of the manuscript. Phil Gochenhaur, wherever he may be, was a valuable research assistant who uncovered several of the more interesting dispatches in the collection. Shana Wagger, acquisitions editor at CQ Books, provided essential professional advice and counsel in preparing the manuscript for publication. Sabra Bissette Ledent undertook the gargantuan task of editing the collection and offered many helpful suggestions that much improved the final product. Finally, but not least, this book would not have been possible without the constant support of my wife, Stephanie, who spent countless hours typing, proofreading, and encouraging me in its production.

            Peter D. Eicher
            Washington, D.C.

Introduction

The large black marble plaques at each end of the State Department's flag-bedecked diplomatic lobby bear the names of some of the members of the U.S. Foreign Service who have lost their lives in heroic or tragic circumstances abroad.

Introduction

When Silas Deane sat down by candlelight in his Paris apartment on the evening of August 18, 1776, quill pen in hand, to complete a lengthy letter to members of the American Continental Congress, he hardly could have imagined that he was playing out the first scene in what would become one of the world's great traditions of diplomatic reporting. Deane's letter was the first American diplomatic dispatch, or official communication, from an appointed representative abroad. It was awaited eagerly by Deane's correspondents in Philadelphia, the seat of Congress, who knew that the success of the revolution to which they had just pledged their lives, fortunes, and sacred honor would depend substantially on whether they could obtain assistance from abroad, and particularly from France. Deane sent good news. He had been received by the French foreign minister and had succeeded in obtaining military supplies to ship home.

Deane's first dispatch, which leads off the collection in this volume, is little remembered, but it tells one of the most dramatic stories in the annals of American foreign policy. It recounts a dangerous venture into the unknown, a delicate mission to tell a new nation's story and to win support in a foreign land. It describes an uncertain undertaking in which an American representative abroad would change history. Deane's dispatches may have, for better or worse, guided the fortunes and policies of a nation.

Yet one of the most interesting aspects of Deane's story is not that it stands apart from other American diplomatic endeavors, but that it fits into their consistent pattern. The very factors that made Deane's mission so potentially significant—the danger, the unknown, the effort to win friends, the ability to influence the course of history, and even the report home—are the same factors that would characterize thousands of American diplomatic undertakings in the years ahead. In this sense, Silas Deane's mission was special only in having been the first. He would be followed in the role of U.S. representative abroad by heroes and scoundrels, by intellectuals and fools, by envoys of brilliance who would captivate the royal courts of Europe and by lesser individuals who would be captivated by the brilliance of those courts, by representatives whose dispatches home would be touched with eloquence and insight and by others who could barely compose a sentence, by some of the best-remembered Americans and by some long forgotten.

American Representatives Abroad: The Authors

Silas Deane's successors over the next two centuries would become involved in issues and places as varied as the globe itself. While their reporting provides fascinating insights into history, they themselves are a noteworthy group. Taken as a whole, it would be difficult to find a more colorful or interesting collection of individuals.

In looking back at the country's diplomats, the average American might think first of Silas Deane's better-known contemporaries—Benjamin Franklin, John Adams, Thomas Jefferson, James Monroe, and others from the list of America's distinguished Founders. In fact, early American envoys often were among the most prominent and capable Americans. At one point it even seemed that the standard career progression for an American president was from diplomat abroad, to secretary of state, to president. Half of the first eight presidents followed this pattern (Jefferson, Monroe, John Quincy Adams, and Martin Van Buren), while several others (John Adams, William Henry Harrison, and James Buchanan) served at least briefly as U.S. representatives abroad and one (Andrew Jackson) served as a commissioner. Dispatches from each of these presidents are among those found in this collection.

John Quincy Adams was one advocate of sending only the best Americans to represent the United States at foreign courts. The ideal diplomat, he wrote,

> should have an education in classical learning and in the knowledge of general history, ancient and modern. . . . He should be well versed in the principles of ethics, of the law of nature and nations, of legislation and government, of the Civil Roman Law, of the law of England and the United States, of the public law of Europe and in the letters, memoirs and histories of those great men who have heretofore shone in the diplomatic order. . . . He should be active, attentive and industrious, and, above all, he should possess an upright heart and an independent spirit, should be one who decidedly makes the interest of his country, not the policy of any other nation nor his own private ambition or interest, or those of his family, friends, and connections, the rule of his conduct.[1]

By the mid-nineteenth century, however, the United States was so caught up in domestic concerns that affairs abroad no longer were regarded as vital to the national interest, and overseas experience no longer was viewed as a critical qualification for the presidency. George Bush, who served as U.S. ambassador to the United Nations from 1971 to 1973 and chief of the U.S. Liaison Office in China from 1974 to 1975, was the first president since James Buchanan to have served the United States as chief of a diplomatic mission abroad.

U.S. envoys have included the best and worst America has to offer. Franklin, Jefferson, and John Quincy Adams stand at the pinnacle of

American representation. Some of their successors were equally distinguished, but others were rogues or scoundrels who embarrassed themselves and their country abroad. Some have demonstrated unusual courage or eloquence. U.S. representatives have included explorers, adventurers, professors, authors, soldiers, politicians, businessmen, thieves, millionaires, and paupers. Historically, they are a fascinating collection of individuals—a far cry from their striped-pants stereotype.

Each of the authors of dispatches in this volume has an interesting personal story, which often is not reflected in the official correspondence. James Leander Cathcart, for example, was just a lad when he was captured by pirates off the coast of North Africa in 1785 and pressed into slavery. He spent more than ten years as an Algerian slave, slowly working his way up through a complex hierarchy from clerk of the galley slaves to chief Christian secretary to the ruler. After finally gaining his freedom, Cathcart served successively as American consul in Algiers, Tunis, Madeira, and Cadiz. Samuel Blackler, assigned in 1839 as consul to the Kingdom of Otaheite (now Tahiti), illegally peddled gin to thirsty seamen far from home. Queen Pomare complained to President John Tyler about Blackler's bootlegging activities, asserting that he used the consulate to shelter lawbreakers, that he drew his sword against local officials, and that he violated the laws against adultery and fornication "before our eyes, without shame, and in defiance of us."[2] But Tyler was not responsive; Blacker remained consul until his death. Pierre Soulé, a fiery former senator from Louisiana, offended his Spanish hosts in the 1850s with repeated public bellicose rants that the United States should annex the Spanish colony of Cuba. The impetuous Soulé made himself notorious in Spanish social circles by dueling with and maiming the French ambassador over a supposed insult to Soulé's wife about the low-cut dress she wore to a French embassy party. Soulé's exploits led the *New York Herald* to comment, "We wanted an Ambassador there, we have sent a matador."[3]

At the dawn of the twentieth century, one of the most unusual American outposts abroad was the U.S. consulate in the Yukon's Dawson City during the Klondike gold rush. The activities of American consul James McCook reflected the pandemonium of the time and place. During an evening of carousing with dance hall queen Diamond-Tooth Gertie, McCook reportedly handed out money and gold nuggets to the bar girls, scuffled on the floor with other saloon customers, and capped off the night by pinning an American flag to the seat of his pants and inviting the saloon's proprietor to give it a swift kick.[4]

These roguish types notwithstanding, many American representatives have been individuals of considerable distinction or accomplishment, if not always of international experience. Mirabeau B. Lamar, a U.S. representative to Costa Rica and Nicaragua in the mid-1850s, had earlier served as president of the Republic of Texas (1838–1841). Frederick

Douglass, the one-time slave who rose to be an adviser to President Abraham Lincoln and one of America's leading orators and voices of conscience, capped his distinguished career with an appointment as minister and consul general to Haiti in 1889. Elihu Washburne, a member of Congress from Illinois and secretary of state, showed unusual bravery and compassion during the Prussian occupation of Paris and the Commune that followed in 1871. America's foremost man of letters in the second half of the nineteenth century was arguably James Russell Lowell, who served successively as minister to Madrid and to London. His dispatches are among the most touching and beautifully written of those submitted by American envoys. Henry Morgenthau, a New York financier, worked valiantly as ambassador to Turkey (1913–1916) to alleviate suffering during the Armenian genocide and the early years of the First World War. American businessman Joseph P. Kennedy served as ambassador to Great Britain (1938–1940) at the outset of World War II and urged that the United States stay out of the conflict. Dispatches from each of these envoys are included in this collection.

Also notable among American representatives abroad were some other of the nation's best-known authors and literary figures. Those whose dispatches appear in this volume include Washington Irving (Madrid), Nathaniel Hawthorne (Liverpool), Lew Wallace (Constantinople), and Bret Harte (Glasgow).

While the talents and accomplishments of American representatives were varied, envoys tended, until well into the twentieth century, to be drawn from a very narrow stratum of American society. The typical American representative overseas belonged to a well-to-do East Coast family. Until the 1920s American representatives abroad were exclusively male, with a single, unauthorized exception. In 1863 Mrs. Ebenezer Eggleston reported from Cadiz, Spain, that her husband the consul had left post on extended travel and that she was taking charge of the consulate in his absence. The State Department did not take issue with her action. The first woman to head a U.S. diplomatic mission was Ruth Bryan Owen, daughter of Secretary of State William Jennings Bryan; she served as minister to Denmark in the 1930s. In 1949 Eugenie Anderson became the first woman to be appointed a U.S. ambassador—also to Denmark.

In contrast to the total absence of women, a few African Americans did serve in the early foreign service. Although the best known is Frederick Douglass, he was not the first. William Liedesdorff became vice consul in San Francisco in 1846, during the final months before the United States wrested California from Mexico. Liedesdorff was appointed by the American consul in Monterey, California, Thomas Larkin, and was never officially acknowledged by the State Department. Ebenezer Bassett became the first black to win an official overseas appointment when he was named minister resident and consul general to Haiti in

1869. Richard Greener, the first black graduate of Harvard, was appointed consul in Bombay in 1898. An outbreak of bubonic plague in India kept Greener from taking up his post, but he was reassigned as commercial agent in Vladivostok, where he served for seven years. The first Asian American appointed to a foreign affairs position was Joseph Heco, who also was one of the first Japanese to be naturalized as an American. Heco served from 1862 to 1871 as part of the consulate staff in Kanagawa (now Yokohama).

Service Abroad

Although until the twentieth century there was no professional career foreign service, many U.S. representatives abroad did a creditable job of promoting and protecting American interests, and most at least muddled through without causing too much damage or embarrassment to their country. Early American envoys faced unpleasant and often dangerous conditions at their assigned posts while laboring under unfavorable terms of service. Travel was slow and unreliable; foreign ports usually were unhealthy; and the American flag did not always command respect. Many American envoys fell victim to war, accident, or disease; many never returned to their homes. Walter Stapp, an early consul in Pernambuco (now Recife), Brazil, once commented that one of his predecessors resigned before even leaving for post on hearing how difficult life in Brazil could be. Four others, Stapp continued, "have left their bones to bake in these fearfully hot sands, without a slab of stone or a stick of wood to point the stranger to their graves."[5]

Nor were such instances rare. The diplomatic lobby of today's Department of State is a large and impressive hall colorfully bedecked with the flags of almost two hundred countries in which the United States has envoys stationed. At each end of the lobby is a large black marble plaque bearing the names of some of those who lost their lives in heroic or tragic circumstances abroad. The first name on the plaque is that of William Palfrey of Massachusetts, a one-time member of the Sons of Liberty, aide-de-camp to George Washington, and paymaster of the Revolutionary Army. Palfrey was appointed by the Continental Congress as the first American consular officer. He was assigned to join Benjamin Franklin in France, where his duties were to include obtaining supplies for the American army, outfitting warships and privateers, disposing of naval prizes, and handling other shipping problems. Palfrey set sail in December 1780 aboard the *Shellelagh*, but neither he nor the ship were ever heard from again. His brief epitaph on the memorial plaque is one of many that reads simply "lost at sea." The second name on the plaque is Joel Barlow, a prominent Connecticut man of letters and America's first epic poet. In 1796 Barlow negotiated the release of ninety American seamen held hostage by the dey of Algiers, some for as long as eleven years. Later appointed American minister to Paris during the Napoleonic Wars (1804–1815), Barlow faced the pressing task of trying to lift French restrictions on American commerce—an issue high on the American agenda but low on Emperor Napoleon Bonaparte's list of priorities. Because the emperor had gone east to direct French military operations in Russia, Barlow traveled to Vilna, Lithuania, at the invitation of the French foreign minister for what might be a crucial appointment with Napoleon. The American minister did not know, however, that Napoleon and his forces already were in retreat from Moscow, leaving hundreds of thousands of soldiers dead and dying in the winter snows of western Russia and Poland. Thus Barlow found himself on a futile winter trek across central Europe in a tiny carriage that offered no protection from the elements. Barlow contracted severe pneumonia. On Christmas Day 1812, he slipped into a coma, lingered through the night, and died the next morning in the tiny Polish village of Zarnowiec.

Palfrey and Barlow are but the two first names on a plaque that lists well over a hundred U.S. envoys. Each story seems more interesting or tragic than the last. The causes of death record the panoply of dangers that faced American envoys: lost at sea, exposure, yellow fever, murdered, cholera, epidemic, coast fever, tropical fever, African fever, drowned saving life, smallpox, malaria, volcano, earthquake, hurricane, gunfire, exhaustion. Twenty-eight names on the plaque represent the first century of American diplomacy, after which the numbers rise geometrically. Two-thirds of the deaths listed date from the past fifty years; half date from the past twenty-five years. But the list on the plaque is far from comprehensive. Through quirk or accident of omission, most of the hundreds who have died while serving their country in foreign affairs positions abroad are not listed.

Even putting aside the possibility of an untimely death, the conditions of service abroad for the first century and a half of American diplomacy were close to abysmal. Diplomatic officials received small salaries based on their assigned post, with appointees to Paris and London at the top of the scale. Consular officers received no salaries at all until 1856. Consuls initially were permitted to retain the fees they collected for performing their official duties. At some ports bustling with American shipping, this made for a comfortable living. In Liverpool, for example, consular fees brought author Nathaniel Hawthorne about $15,000 a year, far more than he had ever earned from his writings and enough to support his family in style, with sufficient savings left over to live in Europe for three years after he left office. Hawthorne's situation was unusual, however, and most American consuls had to resort to other pursuits to support themselves. Many early consuls were wealthy, well-respected traders who used their consular positions to enhance the prestige of already-thriving businesses. Others had what DeBenneville Keim, a U.S. Treasury Department inspector who traveled much of the world in 1870–1871 to investigate conditions at American consulates, termed "peculiar and diverse occupations."[6] Keim reported that he had heard so many credible tales about how consuls supported themselves that he would hesitate to discount any story. Perhaps Keim had heard the story of the American consul in the eastern Mediterranean who kept a saloon across the street from the consulate and reportedly greeted his visitors with "What will it be, gentlemen, a cocktail or an invoice?"

American envoys who tried to survive on meager diplomatic salaries or consular fees often fared badly. One such envoy was John Porter Brown, who sometimes is regarded as the first "regional specialist" in American diplomacy. Brown spent his entire adult life as an envoy to the Ottoman Porte in Constantinople (now Istanbul), beginning at age eighteen. He became fluent in Turkish, Arabic, and Farsi, and served successively as the American legation's translator, consul, consul general, and secretary of legation. Upon his death in 1872, Brown was so impoverished after forty years in government service that his widow could not afford to travel back to the United States. The Ottoman sultan, out of respect for Brown's work and for the United States, paid for her ticket back to America.

Conditions did not improve much when low consular salaries were authorized in midcentury. Appointees were still required to pay their own passage to post and back. A consul to Batavia, Dutch East Indies (now Jakarta, Indonesia), in 1863 found that his $1,000 yearly salary was barely enough to pay for his one-way transportation. He arrived in Batavia almost penniless and within months the American community in the remote port had to solicit contributions to send him home. Not until 1906 did Congress appropriate funds to cover the expense of sending envoys abroad (it authorized an allowance of five cents a mile). Well into the twentieth century, envoys were responsible for finding their own lodging and office space, with those at even the most important posts strapped for funds and hard-pressed to locate new premises to suit their wallets. A well-known political cartoon portrayed U.S. Ambassador to England Joseph Choate clinging forlornly to a lamppost as a London bobby enjoined him to go home. "I have no home," Choate is pictured to reply. "I am the American Ambassador!"[7]

Diplomats, Consuls, and Protocol

Understanding historical foreign affairs dispatches requires a brief background in diplomatic usage. Over the years American representatives have sported a bewildering array of titles. Generally, American diplomatic titles have conformed to the practice set out at the 1815 Congress of Vienna. The senior diplomatic rank, it was agreed, would be ambassador or, more properly, ambassador extraordinary and plenipotentiary. Although the U.S. Constitution provided specifically for the appointment of ambassadors, Americans of the eighteenth and nineteenth centuries found the title too pretentious and reminiscent of nobility to be suitable for representatives of a democracy. Not until 1893 did the United States begin to confer the title of ambassador on selected representatives; the first was Thomas Bayard, a former secretary of state assigned as ambassador to London. The highest rank conferred on American representatives before that time was the only slightly less pretentious "envoy extraordinary and minister plenipotentiary," commonly shortened to "minister." In descending order of precedence, other titles conferred on chiefs of diplomatic missions were minister plenipotentiary, minister resident, commissioner, chargé d'affaires, and agent. Diplomatic ranks below chief of mission have included minister, counselor, secretary of embassy or legation (sometimes subdivided into first, second, and third secretaries), and attaché. To complicate the issue further, an array of titles without clear order of precedence has been given to individuals assigned specific, sometimes short-term, duties: commissioner, treaty negotiator, special negotiator, special diplomatic agent, confidential agent, and in more recent years, representative, permanent representative, and ambassador at large. This list, for all its length, is not comprehensive. When an ambassador was appointed to a foreign country, the U.S. office there was normally termed an embassy; when a minister was the highest official, the office was called a legation.

Any of these diplomatic ranks meant that an individual was accredited formally to a foreign government, entitled to do business with that government, and immune from the laws of that country. The particular rank and title accorded to American envoys sometimes affected their ability to operate effectively; in some instances, an American chief of mission with a low rank would have difficulty gaining access to senior host government officials. In addition, an envoy's title determined where he or she stood in the larger order of precedence within the diplomatic community. Since the United States did not confer the title of ambassador until 1893, American ministers up to that time were ranked lower than the ambassadors of far smaller and less important countries. Some American representatives were irritated at always finding themselves placed at the end of the receiving line or the foot of the banquet table by virtue of their inferior diplomatic rank.

For almost 150 years, American diplomats were outnumbered overseas by another category of foreign affairs official—consuls. Unlike diplomatic officials, who dealt primarily with governments, consular officers were charged primarily with the protection of American citizens abroad and with matters related to commerce. The earliest American consular instructions concentrated heavily on the protection of American seamen in foreign ports, calling them a "class of our fellow citizens, whose habits of life require a kind of guardianship of their persons and interests in foreign countries, but, at the same time, a strict vigilance over their conduct."[8] Consuls were authorized to expend up to twelve cents a day to support destitute seamen and could require American ships to take stranded seamen aboard and return them to the United States for a charge of not more than ten dollars.

Over the years, consular functions became extremely complex. Consuls who took their work seriously became expert on such arcane matters as commercial regulations and citizenship laws. In the Middle East and China, consuls acquired judicial powers over American citizens; consular courts and even consular jails were established.

Although consulates could not be established without the concurrence of foreign governments, consuls were not formally accredited to governments because they were to transact most of their business with citizens of their own country. In some instances, consuls received an exequatur—a kind of commission—from the sovereign of their host government granting them certain privileges and immunities, usually including immunity from prosecution for acts carried out in their official capacities.

While embassies and legations normally could be established only in capital cities, consulates could operate almost anywhere—in capitals, commercial centers, remote outposts, and even colonial possessions. Because commercial affairs and shipping matters were so high on the consular list of responsibilities, consulates were established most often at ports, although consuls were appointed for major inland cities as well.

Consular officials had their own order of precedence, separate from that of diplomatic officers. Titles varied somewhat over the years. Legislation passed by Congress in 1856, for example, established a consular precedence list that included agent and consul general, followed by consul general, consul, vice consul, deputy consul, consular agent, commercial agent, vice commercial agent, and consular clerk.[9] In theory, the consular service and diplomatic service were entirely separate in their duties and functions. In practice, however, there often was substantial overlap. A few individuals were given appointments in both services at once, with titles such as "secretary of legation and consul" or "minister and consul general," but such combined titles were rare. Overlaps in function were more common. In the Barbary States of North Africa, for example, American consuls were specifically vested with diplomatic powers, in part because American leaders did not deem those piratical regimes worthy of full diplomatic representation and in part because the Barbary rulers were still nominally subservient to the Ottoman sultan. In small countries where the United States had no diplomatic representative, consuls often found themselves taking on diplomatic functions. This was certainly true in the Pacific Islands, where some American consuls came to play major political roles in promoting Western takeovers. In almost all parts of the world, however, American consuls at least occasionally became involved in political affairs, despite strict instructions "scrupulously to abstain from all participation whatever, direct or indirect, in the political concerns of the countries to which they are appointed."[10] One example that appears in this collection was the action of William Sparks, consul in Venice when the city rebelled against Austrian rule and declared itself a republic in 1848. Sparks was so taken with the new government and its democratic spirit that, without checking with Washington, he took it upon himself to recognize the new republic on behalf of the United States. Sparks died a few months later as Austrian troops were besieging the city before recapturing it.

In Latin America especially, American consuls seemed likely to become embroiled in political affairs. The 1834 consular instructions gave a special warning to consuls in the "republics of South America and the United Mexican States." Because of the "disturbed and unsettled conditions" in those areas, consuls were asked to "forbear intermeddling" in the political or local affairs of the states

> in the smallest degree whatever. . . . In their letters, even to this Department, upon such subjects, they [consuls] will . . . [avoid] all unnecessary reflections or criticism upon the characters or conduct of individuals; and they will, on no occasions, give publicity, through the press, to opinions or speculations injurious to the public institutions of those countries, or the persons concerned in the administration of them."[11]

Despite such warnings, however, consuls as well as diplomats were expected to submit dispatches on political developments. The 1834 instructions, although warning consuls to avoid meddling, told them to consider it a "duty to report, freely and seasonably, to their own government, all important facts which may come to their knowledge, through authentic channels, touching the political conditions" of the country to which they were assigned.[12] Many of the best examples of political reporting in American diplomatic archives were filed from consulates.

Although both diplomats and consuls reported to the Department of State, the diplomatic and consular services remained separate until 1924, when they were combined by the Rogers Act into the Foreign Service of the United States.

Even today, the U.S. Foreign Service preserves the distinction between diplomatic and consular functions and titles, a distinction made necessary in part by the international treaties that govern the placement and immunities of each. In practice, however, American career diplomats often rotate routinely among different functions; all U.S. career diplomats are expected to gain some consular experience.

The Home Front: Growth of the State Department and the Foreign Service

The ultimate destination of most American diplomatic dispatches, the Department of State, has developed a great deal since the birth of the Republic. Silas Deane directed his early dispatches to a five-member committee of the Continental Congress, chaired by Benjamin Franklin, which dubbed itself the Committee of Secret Correspondence. Congress later renamed the group the Committee of Foreign Affairs and voted the committee a budget of seventy dollars a month, which it used to hire revolutionary thinker and writer Thomas Paine as its secretary, making him, in a sense, America's first domestic-based foreign affairs bureaucrat. After the defeat of British forces at Yorktown in 1781, Congress established the Department of Foreign Affairs and named Robert Livingston as the first secretary of foreign affairs. Livingston hired two secretaries, a clerk, and a translator of French, and established a small office at 13 South Sixth Street in Philadelphia.

The department at times seemed as peripatetic as its representatives abroad. Between 1790 and 1799, before Washington, D.C., was established as the nation's capital, the department moved to five different locations. A yellow fever epidemic in Philadelphia in 1793 actually caused the department to close down entirely.

After the adoption of the Constitution in 1789, Congress gave the Department of Foreign Affairs additional responsibilities over domestic matters and renamed it the Department of State. State's domestic duties included safeguarding the seal of the United States, managing the mint, issuing patents and copyrights, administering the census, supervising federal attorneys and marshals, recording sales of public lands, overseeing territorial affairs, and handling correspondence between the federal government and the states. As the U.S. government grew over the years, most of the State Department's domestic duties were transferred to other agencies.

In 1790 President George Washington appointed Thomas Jefferson as the first secretary of state, recalling him from a four-year stint as U.S. minister to France. Drawing on the Constitution's provision empowering the president to "appoint Ambassadors, other public Ministers and Consuls," Washington named diplomatic representatives to five European countries: France, Spain, England, the Netherlands, and Portugal. In addition, he assigned consuls or vice consuls to eighteen cities in Europe, North Africa, the Caribbean, and as far afield as China.

In its early years, the United States rapidly emerged as one of the world's foremost commercial countries. Yankee traders plied the seas, and rural as well as urban Americans recognized that their prosperity depended to a considerable extent on foreign trade. Under these circumstances, the growth in official American representation abroad was rapid. By

1800 the number of consulates already had risen to seventy. Because consuls received no salaries and were expected to support themselves through private business and consular fees, there were no budgetary restraints to limit appointments. With the development of the spoils system in the early 1800s, the distribution of consular commissions seemed an ideal, cost-free way to increase political patronage.[13] Thus the number of consular appointments had skyrocketed to 437 by the outbreak of the Civil War in 1861; no respectable foreign port was without its American consul. During the same period, the number of U.S. diplomatic missions—those formally accredited to do business with foreign governments—rose to thirty-three. Much of this growth was attributable to the independence of Latin America and the appointment of ministers to most of the new Latin American republics.

The breadth of American representation abroad by 1860 was somewhat deceptive. Although the United States boasted thirty-three diplomatic missions, their total Washington-appointed staffs numbered only forty-five. Most American legations were officially one-person operations; only the most important had diplomatic secretaries assigned to assist the minister. In most instances, ministers and consuls had to use their own funds to hire private secretaries or clerks to assist them. Consuls often appointed vice consuls to represent the United States in nearby cities where there was no consul, but such appointments were not always reported to Washington. Some ministers were assisted by young men of prominent families who went abroad at their own expense to work without salary at American legations for the sake of educational or professional experience. Often given the title attaché, these individuals were recognized by foreign governments as part of the American diplomatic establishment. As late as 1900, the largest American embassy in the world—in Paris—boasted a total staff of just seven people, including the ambassador and the janitor.

The growth of the State Department in Washington did not match the expansion of American representation overseas. In the 1850s the department still had just seven clerks to deal with its 470 offices abroad. Supervision of overseas posts was necessarily minimal. The single laborious task of hand copying correspondence overwhelmed the department's resources. Mail from many consulates simply went unanswered.

During the Civil War (1861–1865), the size of the Department of State and the number of American consular posts expanded rapidly, reflecting efforts to prevent foreign recognition of the Confederacy and to track blockade runners and the movements of Confederate privateers. President Abraham Lincoln's appointments of able representatives to the major courts of Europe—most notably Charles Francis Adams to Great Britain—showed his recognition of the importance of foreign affairs to the war effort. As America turned inward after the war, the diplomatic establishment also contracted. Nevertheless, by 1865 the department's longtime offices next door to the White House had grown overcrowded. The next year, in a step that showed the lack of priority accorded to the Department of State during Reconstruction, the whole staff was moved uptown to occupy "temporary" quarters in a rundown building previously home to the Washington orphan asylum. This remained State's home for nine years. The congressional response to overcrowding was to reduce the department's newly enlarged personnel complement from forty-eight clerks to thirty-one.

Through the rest of the nineteenth century, while most of America looked inward, the American foreign affairs establishment resumed its slow growth. By 1890 the number of diplomatic posts abroad had risen to forty-one and consular posts had reached an all-time high of 760, largely because of the continued prevalence of the spoils system. Overseas positions were among those regularly handed out to political cronies, regardless of qualification, much to the detriment of the efficient practice of diplomacy. In some instances, assigning an incompetent to an overseas mission was regarded as a useful way to remove an annoyance from Washington. In the Department of State the spoils system probably peaked during the administration of Ulysses S. Grant (1869–1877), although it continued under his successors and has not been eliminated even today. Grant gave supporters a card to carry to the State Department designating the bearer as a loyal supporter worthy of a consular or diplomatic assignment; Secretary of State Hamilton Fish would then confer the appointment to a specific post. This unbridled system of appointment without regard to qualification, together with the lack of adequate supervision of overseas posts and difficult conditions of service, led to endless instances of personal and financial abuse.

The depths to which the American consular system had sunk by the mid-nineteenth century were evident from the report of official inspector DeBenneville Keim in 1872. Keim commented at some length on the unusual personalities he encountered at American posts overseas: "I have heard so much of the souvenirs of coarse habits and vulgar humor . . . that a compilation of this information would make an exceedingly entertaining report, even if it were not very pleasing to our keen sense of national pride."[14] Keim reported problems of mismanagement or fraud at virtually every consulate he visited. Not a single consulate he encountered had a complete set of record books as required by regulation. He found abuses in the collection and recording of fees, in the exercise of judicial powers, in the assistance rendered to Americans in distress, and in the services accorded to American shipping and seamen. He also observed officials selling the protection of the American flag and issuing illegal passports. Keim marveled at the "ingenuity displayed by consular officers . . . in defrauding the Government and grasping gains from various outside sources as well."[15] Much of the abuse he attributed to the constant replacement of officials incident to the spoils system. Although Keim noted some efficiently managed consular posts staffed by dedicated and honest officers, his ultimate appraisal was starkly negative: "If all could be told of the consular service of the United States, as illustrated in the conduct of its officers, the excess of bad over good would be so great that the most cold and indifferent citizen would blush for the name of his country."[16] In fairness, it must be noted that Keim mainly visited remote consulates and investigated only the consular side of the American establishment overseas, not commenting on the diplomatic missions.

At the dawn of the twentieth century, the Spanish-American War led to the emergence of the United States as an imperial power with far-flung territorial possessions. This forceful American entry onto the world scene signaled the need for a larger and stronger diplomatic presence. The domestic U.S. foreign affairs complement began to grow geometrically. Between 1898 and 1920 the department's domestic personnel multiplied tenfold, to a then-mammoth 708. By that time, however, World War I (1914–1918) had marked the emergence of the United States as the world's most powerful nation and had demonstrated to the satisfaction of most Americans the value of a strong diplomatic establishment. The U.S. leadership role after World War II (1939–1945), the increasingly complicated and specialized nature of foreign affairs in the modern world, and the emergence of dozens of new nations led to a continued expansion of the State Department's duties and responsibilities.

Today's State Department deals with problems and issues that Silas Deane scarcely could have imagined—the United Nations, nuclear proliferation, foreign assistance, refugees, narcotics control, satellite communications; the list is as varied as today's world. Reports on international events, whether conveyed by instantaneous telegram, fax, telephone, or in the traditional diplomatic pouch, flood into the State Department building at the rate of hundreds every hour. Still, among these communications are many that would seem familiar to Deane, Franklin, and the other founders of American diplomacy. The traditional dispatch may have changed form, but its essence of conveying important or interesting information on developments in faraway places remains constant.

The Development of Diplomatic and Consular Reporting

Reporting always has been one of the major responsibilities of U.S. envoys abroad, but a systematic approach to reporting took some time to develop. The first American diplomats reported home sporadically. For all the importance of American diplomatic activity in Paris during the American Revolution, envoys sometimes were lax in letting the government know what they were up to. In December 1780, for example, James Lovell of Congress's Committee of Foreign Affairs wrote to Benjamin Franklin in Paris, chiding him because the committee has "had no letter from you since that of May last," six months earlier![17]

When Thomas Jefferson became the first secretary of state in 1790, he instructed all American diplomats abroad to report home once or twice a month. His instructions to consuls required them to report every six months on the extent of American shipping at their ports and to file additional reports on "such political and commercial intelligence as you may think interesting to the United States."[18] Jefferson's instructions formalized a pattern of diplomatic and consular reporting that American envoys already had begun to adopt without specific instructions. As U.S. minister in Paris during the early stages of the French Revolution, Jefferson himself had followed the precedent set by Silas Deane, reporting at length on political developments in France, including a remarkable dispatch on the storming of the Bastille which appears in this volume. As secretary of state, his instructions to U.S. envoys added a formal element to American diplomatic and consular reporting by ensuring that even in times of relative quiet official Americans abroad would continue to report in detail on important developments in their countries of assignment. To Jefferson, therefore, can be traced the development of a system of more consistent and comprehensive reporting by U.S. officials abroad. The result was a burgeoning collection of American dispatches from around the world reporting on everything from political unrest to commercial opportunities and travel conditions.

The disparate reports were clearly well received in Washington, for they led to ever-expanding requests for more of the same. Instructions of 1805 asked American envoys to report "as the occasion is suitable" on conditions in foreign ports; duties; fees for lights, anchorage, and piers; and quarantine regulations. Envoys also were to report on "epidemical disorders" abroad and were authorized to spend up to ten dollars a year obtaining scientific and medical publications on disease for transmission home.[19] In 1815 Secretary of State James Monroe asked his envoys to send "from time to time, information of all military preparations, and other indications of war, which may take place in your ports." Monroe also put consular reporting on a more regular schedule, requiring consuls to report at the end of June and December details on all American ships that had visited their ports in the previous six months.[20] Still, the frequency of reporting was not strictly enforced and representatives in distant ports sometimes felt no need to comply with the instructions. Earlier, in 1807, the American consul in La Guaira, Venezuela, had been dismissed for not having filed a single report in seven years.[21] Other envoys seemed not to want to bother the department with local developments—Jacob Moerenhaut, an early consul in the South Pacific, actually apologized for troubling the department with so many letters when he wrote twice in a three-month period.[22]

The 1833 consular instructions substantially expanded reporting responsibilities, requiring immediate reports from abroad on any laws or regulations in any way affecting the commerce of the United States. The instructions went on to say that consuls

> are expected, once in three months at least, to write to the department, if it be for no other purpose than that of apprising the department of their being at their respective posts. They are not required to write oftener, unless in emergent cases, or where interest of business points out the propriety of more frequent communication. In their correspondence, they will note all events that bear upon the commerce of the country with the United States, and of our navigation, the establishment of new branches of industry in the extent of their consulate, and the increase and decline of those before established; they will make such suggestions as, in their opinion, may lead to the increase of our commerce or navigation, and point out those which have a contrary effect, with the means that appear proper for avoiding them. Samples of manufactures, and specimens of produce which appear to be valuable articles either of export or import, if not generally known, should be sent, if not too bulky, with the consular letters. . . .[23]

The American Diplomatic Code for 1834 reminded American ministers and other diplomatic agents that among their most important duties was "that of transmitting . . . accurate information of the policy and views of [the government] to which [they are] accredited, and of the character and vicissitudes of its important relations with other Powers."[24] In addition, diplomats were urged "to transmit information of every kind, relating to the Government, finances, commerce, arts, sciences, and condition of the nation . . . which may be useful to the United States."[25] Since dispatches from ministers were bound in volumes after their receipt in Washington, the instructions gave precise requirements for the format of dispatches:

> [D]espatches should be regularly numbered; and . . . should be written on paper of the same dimensions, 13 1/4 inches long, 8 1/4 broad, and a margin of at least 1 1/4 inch around all its borders, for stitching, and cutting off the edges, without injury to the text. . . . Minute as these particulars appear, they are found to be very essential to the good order and convenience of business in the Department of State.[26]

As the years went by, requests for reporting of all types continued to increase, stretching the capabilities and resources of American representatives abroad. In 1879, for example, new instructions asked for reports from all posts showing the humidity of each foreign country during each month of the year. Legations also were required that year to submit detailed reports on the amount of currency in use and the amount minted each year, while consulates were to file weekly reports on sanitary conditions in every major port.[27] This trend toward more and more detailed reporting has continued to the present day, with many American embassies now required to submit dozens of reports every year on subjects ranging from foreign holidays, to human rights, to narcotics. In recent years efforts have been made occasionally to reduce the amount of reporting required of embassies in order to enable them to concentrate on the issues they judge to be of the greatest importance. In the face of declining resources and personnel in 1995, for example, the State Department eliminated a number of reports previously required from embassies. Still, every embassy is required to file an annual "reporting plan" projecting the key analytical reports it expects to submit in the coming year. In addition, all embassies are expected to engage in an active program of "spot reporting" and analysis of breaking developments. These reports arrive at the Department of State by the thousands every day. As in the past, the most interesting dispatches usually are not those formally required, but those written spontaneously to report on events or developments of special interest.

With the development of more rapid communications, the style of some diplomatic dispatches began to change. When President Lincoln was assassinated in 1865, the news took two weeks to reach Europe by steamship and forty days to make its way to the American legation in Peking. Within a year, however, the successful laying of the transatlantic cable led to virtually instantaneous communications between Washington and the major capitals of Europe. For a short period it seemed as if the traditional, detailed, slow-moving diplomatic dispatch might be on the way to extinction. This was not to be the case, however. Diplomatic instructions of 1897 specified that "the use of the telegraph at the expense of the Government is not permitted in the ordinary business of a mission or in communicating with the Department of State, except when justified by the importance and urgency of the case or under instructions from the Department."[28] Until well into the twentieth century, in fact, the Department of State continued in such fashion to discourage the use of telegrams to communicate. When telegrams were used, they normally were limited to a single short sentence or two. In 1870, for example, the consul in Paris reported simply, "Prussians within 28 miles. I shall remain in Paris to guard our interests."[29] In 1881 the American minister in St. Petersburg reported a major event in a telegram that read, in its entirety, "Emperor dead."[30] While such telegrams had their usefulness, they could not substitute for lengthier and more thoughtful analyses of events, which continued to be submitted by letter. Even the typewriter was slow in gaining acceptance; at many overseas posts dispatches were laboriously handwritten until the twentieth century. Eventually, though, telegraphic dispatches became longer and began to supersede other types of reports. Today, virtually all dispatches of whatever length are submitted electronically.

The advent of the telegram and of more sophisticated communications systems also changed the style of dispatches. The effort to save funds and space on telegrams resulted in a more cryptic, telegraphic writing style in which articles, pronouns, prepositions, and even verbs frequently were omitted. The resulting communications often lacked the flair and eloquence of earlier dispatches. The telegraphic style continued to be used by some drafters into the 1970s and 1980s. Fortunately, advanced telecommunications systems have enabled present-day dispatch writers to revert to full sentences.

Modern communications also altered the content of dispatches. With the advent of instantaneous international news coverage of events, major developments no longer had to be reported immediately by diplomatic dispatch. Now key foreign events often are monitored from Washington on live television. Other major developments usually are reported first by telephone to the State Department Operations Center. Still, diplomatic reporting remains vital for analysis and policy recommendations, for putting events into perspective, for providing information on countries, regions, and events of little interest to the international media, and for reporting private discussions and confidential information.

The Cycles of History

Many members of today's Foreign Service would feel a strong sense of familiarity with the activities of their nineteenth-century predecessors, or even with those of Silas Deane. It is true that today communications are faster, issues are more complex, the world in many ways is a more dangerous place, and America as a superpower is far more involved in developments abroad than it has ever been before. But much remains unchanged. The young diplomat or consul still packs a lifetime into a suitcase and goes abroad to face unfamiliar circumstances, uncertainties, and possible danger. The ambassador or minister still ponders the weighty issues that can mean war or peace for the United States.

Two centuries ago Silas Deane picked up a quill pen to compose his dispatches. Today's envoy is more likely to sit in front of a word processor, but his or her dispatches to the State Department often will reflect startlingly familiar themes and issues. Thomas Jefferson's 1786 dispatch from Paris urging war with the piratical Barbary States could just as easily have been written to urge war with Iraq after its 1990 invasion of Kuwait. David Humphreys's 1793 instruction to a consul to provide care for distressed Americans in Algiers would seem familiar to any consular officer today. Charles Huffnagle's 1853 report on war in the jungles of Southeast Asia could have been written as easily about the American experience in Vietnam as about the British in nineteenth-century Burma. Japanese politics are no less mystifying to Americans today than they were 130 years ago when Robert Pruyn wrote from Tokyo about the difficulties of understanding local political relationships. Indeed, decades-old dispatches often read as if they were today's headlines: in 1863 the American minister in Vienna reported that arms shipments to Serbia threatened stability in the Balkans; in 1903 the American consul in Lebanon reported that "Beirut is unsafe"; in 1904 a minister in the Middle East reported problems with the Kurdish minority; in 1915 the minister in Haiti reported a revolution; in 1932 the minister in El Salvador reported a communist uprising. All of these dispatches and many more await the reader in the pages ahead.

Perusal of America's diplomatic archives brings on an astounding sense of déjà vu. If history does not actually repeat itself, it seems at least to travel in cycles and to hold lessons for the future. Reading diplomatic dispatches, even selectively, produces a deeper understanding of the mechanics of history, of America's place in the world, and of the men and women who took it there.

America's diplomats have not been the most representative group of its citizens, but they have spanned its broadest spectrum. From frontier explorer to ivory tower philosopher, from charlatan to philanthropist, from swashbuckler to statesman, they have taken the worst and the best of American culture and mores abroad with them as America's messengers to the world. And, through two centuries of dispatches, they have brought the world home to America's shores.

Notes

1. Ann Luppi, ed., *American Diplomacy and the Foreign Service* (Washington, D.C.: American Foreign Service Association, 1989), 3.
2. Letter from Chief Paratia to the President of the United States, August 18, 1841, State Department Consular Despatches, Tahiti.
3. Thomas Baily, *A Diplomatic History of the American People* (New York: Appleton-Century-Crofts, 1964), 292.
4. Pierre Berton, *The Klondike Fever* (New York: Carlo and Graf, 1958), 325–326.
5. David F. Trask, "A Short History of the U.S. Department of State," U.S. Department of State Publication, Washington, D.C., 1981, 13.
6. DeBenneville Randolph Keim, *A Report to the Hon. George S. Boutwell, Secretary of the Treasury, upon the Condition of the Consular Service of the United States of America* (Washington, D.C.: Government Printing Office, 1872), 80.
7. Baily, *Diplomatic History*, 12.
8. "General Instructions to Consuls, &c.," U.S. Department of State, Washington, D.C., 1834, 22.
9. Keim, *Report to the Hon. George S. Boutwell*, 191.
10. "General Instructions to Consuls, &c.," 26.
11. Ibid., 26–27.
12. Ibid., 26.

13. The term *spoils system* is actually drawn from the comments of Secretary of State William L. Marcy (1853–1857), a defender of political patronage. He is known for his remark "to the victor go the spoils." The practice of wholesale patronage appointments had begun during the presidency of Andrew Jackson (1829–1837).
14. Keim, *Report to the Hon. George S. Boutwell,* 180.
15. Ibid., 183.
16. Ibid., 184.
17. Letter of December 21, 1780, from Lovell to Franklin, quoted in Jared Sparks, *Diplomatic Correspondence of the American Revolution,* vol. 3 (Boston: Nathan Hale and Gray and Bowen, 1829), 184.
18. David Patterson, unpublished manuscript on the history of the Department of State through 1989, Office of the Historian, U.S. Department of State, Washington, D.C., chap. 1, 16.
19. Circular letter to consuls and vice consuls, in "Consular Instructions. Standing Instructions to Consuls and Vice Consuls of the United States; 1815," U.S. Department of State, Washington, D.C., 16.
20. Ibid., 1.
21. Trask, "Short History of the U.S. Department of State," 5.
22. Dispatch from Jacob Moerenhaut to Secretary of State John Forsyth, May 4, 1836, State Department Consular Despatches, Tahiti.
23. "General Instructions to the Consuls and Commercial Agents of the United States," U.S. Department of State, Washington, D.C., 1833, 37.
24. Jonathan Elliot, *The American Diplomatic Code* (Washington, D.C.: Jonathan Elliot, Junior, 1834), 391.
25. Ibid.
26. Ibid., 393.
27. U.S. Department of State, *Papers Relating to the Foreign Relations of the United States* (Washington, D.C.: Government Printing Office, 1879), xxix.
28. "Instructions to the Diplomatic Officers of the United States," U.S. Department of State, Washington, D.C., 1897, 37.
29. Dispatch from John Meredith Read to Secretary of State Hamilton Fish, September 12, 1870, State Department Consular Despatches, Paris.
30. Dispatch from John W. Foster to Secretary of State William M. Evart, March 13, 1881, in *Papers Relating to the Foreign Relations of the United States* (Washington, D.C.: Government Printing Office, 1882), 1008.

PART I

The Early National Period: 1776–1815

The storming of the Bastille, a state prison in Paris, on July 14, 1789, marked the beginning of the French Revolution. Thomas Jefferson, U.S. minister to France at the time, reported the dramatic event.

1776 In the Beginning . . .
Dispatches from Agent of Congress in France Silas Deane to the Committee of Secret Correspondence

Silas Deane, a member of the Continental Congress from Connecticut, was commissioned by Congress to travel to France on "commercial and political" business, making him the first American sent abroad on behalf of the combined thirteen colonies. He arrived in Paris two days after Congress adopted the Declaration of Independence on July 4, 1776, but he did not learn of the event until some weeks later. Deane was instructed to obtain military supplies and explore the possibility of French political and military assistance to the colonies, duties that Benjamin Franklin assumed when he arrived in Paris six months later.

Deane remained as one of three American commissioners in Paris (with Franklin and Arthur Lee) until early 1778, when he was recalled under a cloud concerning his financial dealings. The congressional investigation of his affairs was inconclusive, but Deane was not reimbursed for large financial claims against Congress.

The first of these three dispatches is the earliest ever submitted by an official American representative overseas. In the second dispatch Deane reports on his presentation of the Declaration of Independence to the French court, and in the third on his success in what was to prove a very important recruiting effort.

The First Dispatch

Paris, August 18, 1776

. . . I left that city [Bordeaux] on the last of June, and arrived here the Saturday following. . . . I spent at Angouleme a day in viewing what, as to manufactures alone, deserves attention on the journey; the foundery for cannon, where the greatest part of those used in the kingdom are manufactured. The cannon are cast solid, after which they are put as in a turner's lathe, and bored out, and the outside smoothed and turned at pleasure; they can bore and complete a twelve pounder in one day in each lathe, which takes four men only to work; the workmen freely showed me every part of their furnace and foundery. . . .

M. Dubourg told me that the ministers would not see me, as they meant to be quite secret in any countenance they gave the United Colonies. . . . I showed him my commission, and told him I was determined to apply; for every circumstance, in my opinion, was favorable instead of otherwise. On this he wrote a letter to Count de Vergennes, asking liberty to introduce me the Thursday following, on which day I went to Versailles, and though the letter had not been delivered to his excellency, yet he gave us immediate admission. Fortunately his chief secretary spoke English well, by which means I had an opportunity of conversing freely with him on the subject of my commission for two hours, and was attentively and favorably heard by him, and was asked many questions, which shows that the American disputes had been, and still were a principal object of attention. I pursued nearly the line marked out by my instructions, stating . . . that I was purchasing a large quantity of manufactures for which I expected to pay the money, and that I should want a quantity of military stores, for which remittances would be made. That I doubted not the Colonies had before this declared independency, and that I should soon receive instructions in consequence, more full and explicit; that in the mean time they were very anxious to know how such a declaration would be received by the powers in Europe, particularly by France, and whether, in such case, an ambassador would be received from them, &c.

To which he replied, that the importance of the American commerce was well known, . . . for which reason the court had ordered their ports to be kept open and equally free to America, as to Britain. That, considering the good understanding between the two courts of Versailles and London, they could not *openly* encourage the shipping of warlike stores, but no obstruction of any kind would be given. . . . That I was under his immediate protection, and should I meet with any difficulty, either from their police, with the rules of which he supposed me unacquainted, or from any other quarter, I had but to apply to him and every thing should be settled. That as to independency, it was an event in the womb of time, and it would be highly improper for him to say any thing on that subject, until it had actually taken place. . . .

I most sincerely thanked him for his protection and assistance so generously offered. . . .

After many questions . . . he put this, in which I thought he seemed interested,—whether, if the Colonies declare an independency, they would not differ among themselves? To this I replied, that the greatest harmony had as yet subsisted, and I had no grounds to doubt it in future; that the common danger, which first drove them into measures, which must end in such a declaration, would subsist, and that alone was sufficient to ensure their union. . . .

It is by no means probable that Europe will long remain in a state of peace; the disputes between Portugal and Spain are on the point of producing an open rupture; the former relies on England; the latter will look to this kingdom, and has already applied to this Court on the subject. Nothing but the division of Poland has taken the king of Prussia's attention off from the injustice done him by Great Britain, at the close of the last war. He has now completed his part of the extraordinary work, and I am well informed, listens with pleasure to the dispute between the United

Colonies and Great Britain. He is ambitious of becoming a maritime power, and is already in possession of the capital ports on the Baltic; but without commerce it is impossible to effect the design, and no commerce can put him so directly in the road as the American. . . . In case of a war in Europe, France, Spain and Prussia might be brought into one interest, and the emperor of Germany is too closely connected with his majesty of France to take part against them, after which Great Britain, having her whole force employed in America, there could be nothing on the one hand to prevent Spain and France from reducing Portugal to a submission to the former, nor from Prussia and France subduing and incorporating into their own dominions Hanover, and the other little mercenary electorates, which lie between them, and which for several centuries have been one principal cause of every war that has happened in Europe.

. . . Not to enlarge on this plan at present, I have only to suggest, that an application to the king of Prussia will do no harm, and may be attended with good and great consequences. . . .

. . . I was directed to apply for arms and clothes for 25,000 men, and for 100 field pieces, with ammunition and stores in proportion. This I wished to get of the ministry direct, but they evaded it, and I am now in treaty for procuring them, through the agency of Mons. Chaumont and Mons. Beaumarchais, on a credit of eight months, from the time of their delivery. If I effect this, as I undoubtedly shall, I must rely on the remittances being made this fall and winter without fail, or the credit of the Colonies must suffer. . . .

Without intelligence from April to this time, leaves me quite uncertain and extremely anxious about the line of conduct now pursuing by Congress, and consequently I cannot, without further intelligence and instructions, proceed in my negotiation either with safety or honor. The resolution of Congress of the 15th of May, is not considered by the ministry as a declaration of independence, but only a previous step, and until this decisive step is taken, I can do little more to any purpose. . . . I must therefore urge this measure, if not already taken, and that the declaration be in the most full and explicit terms. . . .

Thus I have in a minute, possible a tedious detail, mentioned every thing material on my mind, which has occurred since my arrival, and submit the whole to the wisdom and candor of the honorable Congress, observing that I had gone to the extent of my instructions, and . . . I have been successful beyond my expectations. . . .

. . . I am with the highest esteem and respect for the honorable Congress and their committee of Secret Correspondence, &c.

                                        Silas Deane

"Declaration of Independency" Presented to France

Paris, 28th November, 1776

Gentlemen,

... A copy of yours of the 8th of July, I received, though the original never came to hand. This letter also enclosed the *Declaration of Independency* with instructions to make it known to this and other powers of Europe; ... I received it the 7th inst. though the vessel which brought it had but 38 days passage from Salem. This letter was very far from relieving me, as it enclosed what had been circulated through Europe for two months before, and ... your orders, were expressed in the style of any common affair. ... As the United States of America, by this act, introduce themselves among the established powers, and rank with them, it must of course be expected that at the first introduction, or the announcing of it, some mode more formal, or if I may so say, more respectful, would have been made use of, than simply two or three lines from the committee of congress. ...

As the copy was dated the eighth of July I took occasion to observe, that the honorable Congress had taken the earliest opportunity of informing this Court of the declaration of their Independency, and that the variety of important affairs before Congress, with the critical situation of the armies in their neighborhood, and the obstructions of their commerce, had prevented that intelligence which had been wished for, but that the present served to shew the early and principal attention of the United States to this Court. ... To this I was answered, unless France by a public acknowledgement of your Independency makes war on Great Britain in your favor, what service can such acknowledgment be of to the United States? You are known here, our ports are open, and free for your commerce, and your ships are protected in them, and greater indulgencies allowed than to any other nations. ... The United States can receive the same succors and assistance from France without, as well as with, such an open acknowledgment, and perhaps much more advantageously. ...

I was further told that the Swiss Cantons, though in every respect free and independent States for several centuries, had not to this hour been acknowledged as such by any public act of any one power in Europe, except France, and that neither the Revolution in the United Provinces or Portugal had been attended with any such acknowledgement, though the powers of Europe in both cases lent their aid. I replied that I would not urge a formal acknowledgment, as long as the same ends could be

obtained, and without the inconveniences hinted at; besides, as I daily expected further instructions I would reserve myself until their arrival.
   . . . I . . . am, with great truth and sincerity,

                                                        Silas Deane

Recruiting Lafayette

                                              Paris, December 6, 1776

Sir,

. . . The desire which the Marquis de la Fayette shows of serving among the troops of the United States of North America, and the interest which he takes in the justice of their cause makes him wish to distinguish himself in this war, and to render himself as useful as he possibly can; but not thinking that he can obtain leave of his family to pass the seas, and serve in a foreign country till he can go as a general officer, I have thought I could not better serve my country, and those who have intrusted me, than by granting to him in the name of the very honorable Congress the rank of Major General, which I beg the States to confirm to him, to ratify and deliver to him the commission to hold and take rank, to count from this day, with the general officers of the same degree.

   His high birth, his alliances, the great dignities which his family holds at this Court, his considerable estates in this realm, his personal merit, his reputation, his disinterestedness, and above all his zeal for the liberty of our provinces, are such as to induce me alone to promise him the rank of major general in the name of the United States. In witness of which I have signed the present, this 7th of December, 1776. . . .

                                                        Silas Deane

1780–1781 Prisoner in the Tower
Dispatches from U.S. Minister to the Netherlands Henry Laurens

Henry Laurens, once president of the Continental Congress, was commissioned as minister to the United Provinces and the Low Countries (now the Netherlands) in 1780 to assess the possibility of a treaty of friendship and to negotiate a loan. En route, his ship was captured by a British frigate. Laurens was conducted to Great Britain and imprisoned in the Tower of London. In the first of these two dispatches Laurens reports his capture and his unsuccessful attempt to destroy his papers, among them a draft treaty with the Netherlands that prompted the British to declare war on that country. The second dispatch reports his treatment in the Tower.

The British chose to treat Laurens as a state prisoner charged with treason rather than a prisoner of war and therefore, unlike other captives, not subject to exchange. Laurens was finally freed shortly after writing the second dispatch, by which time word had just reached London of the American victory at Yorktown, which effectively marked the end of Great Britain's efforts to retain control of its colonies. Laurens's condition had so deteriorated by the time of his release that he was unable to stand without crutches. After his release, Laurens went on to join Benjamin Franklin, John Jay, and John Adams in negotiating the treaty of peace between Great Britain and the United States.

Capture

To the Committee of Foreign Affairs

> *Vestal*—British Frigate
> St. John's, Newfoundland,
> September 14, 1780

Gentlemen,

I had the honor of writing . . . from on board the *Mercury* packet, the 23d. . . . On the 3d instant, the *Vestal* came in view, and after a pursuit of some five or six hours, Captain George Keppel took possession of the packet. Mr. Young, Captain Pickles, and myself, were conducted on board this ship, and yesterday we arrived here.

Certain papers, among which were all those delivered to me by Mr. Lovell, and the board of Admiralty, fell into Captain Keppel's hands. These papers had been enclosed in a bag, accompanied by a considerable weight of iron shot, and thrown overboard, but the weight proved insufficient for the purpose intended. Admiral Edwards, Governor of this Island, and commander of the stationed squadron, has ordered me to England in the sloop of war *Fairy*, under the command of Captain Keppel. . . .

I should be wanting in justice, and indeed deficient in common gratitude, were I to omit an acknowledgment of Captain Keppel's kindness to myself and to everybody captured in the *Mercury*. . . .

> I have the honor to be, &c.
>
> Henry Laurens

Confinement

To the President of Congress

Tower of London,
December 20, 1781

Sir,

Almost fifteen months have I been closely confined, and inhumanly treated, and even now have not a prospect of relief. The treaty for exchange is abortive. There has been langour, and there is neglect somewhere. If I merit your attention, you will no longer delay the only speedy and efficacious means for my deliverance. Enter this if you please, and what it may produce, on your Secret Journal, and pardon the omission of ceremony.

I am, full of love and respect for you,

Henry Laurens

1781 Wolf at the Door

Dispatch from U.S. Minister to France Benjamin Franklin to
U.S. Minister to the Netherlands John Adams

American representatives abroad have complained consistently through the years of insufficient funding to carry out their missions. Seldom, however, was the situation more desperate than for the ministers in Europe during the American Revolution.

Passy, Feb. 22, 1781

Sir,

I received the Letter your Excelly did me honour of writing to me the 15th Inst. respecting Bills, presented to you for Acceptance drawn by Congress in favour of N. Tracey for 10,000£ Sterling payable 90 Days Sight; and desiring to know if I can furnish Funds for the Payment.

I have lately made a fresh & strong Application for more Money. I have not yet received a positive Answer. I have however two of the Christian Graces, Faith & Hope. But my Faith is only that of which the Apostle Speaks, the Evidence of things not seen. For in Truth I do not see at present how so many Bills drawn at random on our Ministers in France, Spain & Holland, are to be paid. Nor that anything but omnipotent Necessity can excuse the Imprudence of it. Yet I think Bills drawn upon us by the congress ought at all Risques to be accepted. I shall accordingly use my best Endeavours to procure Money for their honourable Discharge against they become due, if you should not in the meantime be provided; and if those Endeavours fail, I shall be ready to break, run away, or go to prison with you, as it shall please God. . . .

—With great Respect,
I have the honour to be
Sir,

B. Franklin

P.S. Late Advices from Congress mention that Col. Laurens is coming over as Envoy Extraordinary to this Court & Col. Palfray as Consul General. They may be expected every day.

1783 Establishing Broad Relations
Dispatch from U.S. Minister to France Benjamin Franklin to the President of Congress

After the conclusion of a formal peace treaty between the United States and Great Britain in 1783, many of the countries of Europe and North Africa lined up to establish relations with the newly independent United States. Benjamin Franklin, the senior American representative abroad, found himself the recipient of approaches from all parts of Europe and beyond. In this dispatch, dated just three days after the signing of the peace treaty with Great Britain, Franklin describes some of the diplomatic activity surrounding American's emergence as a recognized member of the international community.

Passy, September 13, 1783

Sir:

. . . In a former letter I mentioned . . . obtaining a treaty between us and the Emperor of Morocco. We have since received a letter from a person who says . . . he is sent by the Emperor to be the bearer of his answer to the United States, and that he is arrived in Spain on his way to Paris. He has not yet appeared here, and we hardly know what answer to give him. I hope the sending a Minister to that Court, as recommended in my last, has been taken into consideration, or at least that some instructions respecting that nation have been sent to your Minister in Spain, who is better situated than we are for such a negotiation.

The Minister from Denmark often speaks to me about the proposed treaty. . . . No commission to sign it, nor any instructions from Congress relating to it, are yet received; and though pressed, I have not ventured to do any thing further in the affair.

I forward herewith a letter to the Congress from the city of Hamburg. I understand that a good disposition towards us prevails there, which it may be well to encourage.

No answer has yet been given me from the Court of Portugal, respecting the plan of a treaty concerted between its Ambassador here and me. . . .

I send also a copy of a note I received from the Pope's Nuncio. He is very civil on all occasions, and has mentioned the possibility of an advantageous trade America might have with the ecclesiastical State, which he says has two good ports. . . .

This Court continues favorable to us. . . .

With great esteem &c.,

Benjamin Franklin

1783 Franklin on Peace

Dispatch from U.S. Minister to France Benjamin Franklin to British Treaty Negotiator David Hartley

Benjamin Franklin served as U.S. minister to France until 1785 and was one of the three U.S. peace commissioners who negotiated the treaty ending the Revolutionary War. The British negotiator who eventually signed the peace treaty was David Hartley, long one of Franklin's many close friends in Europe. In this letter to Hartley, Franklin acts without instructions in floating the idea of a formal peace compact among Britain, France, and the United States.

Passy, October 16, 1783

My dear friend,

. . . What would you think of a proposition, if I should make it, of a compact between England, France, and America? America would be as happy as the Sabine girls, if she could be the means of uniting in perpetual peace her father and her husband. What repeated follies are those repeated wars! You do not want to conquer and govern one another. Why then should you be continually employed in injuring and destroying one another? How many excellent things might have been done to promote the internal welfare of each country; what bridges, roads, canals, and other useful public works and institutions, tending to the common felicity, might have been made and established with the money and men foolishly spent during the last seven centuries by our mad wars in doing one another mischief! You are near neighbors, and each have very respectable qualities. Learn to be quiet, and to respect each other's rights. You are all Christians. One is *the most Christian King,* and the other *defender of the faith.* Manifest the propriety of these titles by your future conduct. "By this," says Christ, "shall all men know that ye are my disciples, if ye love one another." Seek peace, and ensure it.

Adieu, yours, &c.

Benjamin Franklin

1785 Thirteen Ministers for Thirteen States?
Dispatch from U.S. Minister to the Court of Great Britain John Adams to Secretary of Foreign Affairs John Jay

American diplomacy under the Articles of Confederation faced very special challenges. Among them, the powers of Congress to speak for the states were sharply limited. Foreign governments—already uncomfortable dealing with a republic—were further confused by the divisions within the American federal system. In this dispatch John Adams, just appointed as the first U.S. minister to the court of Great Britain, outlines his difficulties with a British government that questions his authority to speak for all thirteen states. Adams offers strong arguments for increasing the power of Congress to conduct foreign affairs. He also predicts America's emergence as "the greatest Power on earth." The dispatch was written from France shortly before Adams took up his duties in London.

Auteuil, near Paris,
May 8, 1785

Sir:

. . . The British Cabinet have conceived doubts whether Congress have power to treat of commercial matters, and whether our States should not separately grant their full powers to a Minister. I think it may be taken for granted that the States will never think of sending separate Ambassadors, or of authorizing directly those appointed by Congress. The idea of thirteen Plenipotentiaries meeting together in a congress at every Court in Europe, each with a full power and distinct instructions from his State, presents to view such a picture of confusion, altercation, expense, and endless delay, as must convince every man of its impracticability. Neither is there less absurdity in supposing that all the States should unite in the separate election of the same man, since there is not, never was, and never will be a citizen whom each State would separately prefer for conducting the negotiation. It is equally inconceivable that each

State should separately send a full power and separate instructions to the Ministers appointed by Congress. What an heterogeneous mass of paper, full of different objections, various views, and inconsistent and contradictory orders must such a man pull out of his *porte feuille* from time to time to regulate his judgment and his conduct! He must be accountable, too, to thirteen different tribunals for his conduct: a situation in which no man would ever consent to stand, if it is possible, which I do not believe, that any State should ever wish for such a system. . . . Yet it is plain . . . that the British Cabinet have conceived a different opinion. . . .

It is very possible that the Cabinet of St. James may decline even entering into any conferences at all, upon the subject of a treaty of commerce, until the powers of Congress are enlarged. . . .

We ought to attend to considerations of strength and defence. Our situation is different from some of the Powers of Europe, who have neglected their own defence. Switzerland is situated so, that if she should be attacked by one neighbor, she would infallibly be defended by two others. . . . Holland, attacked by France, found a friend in England; when attacked by England, France supported her. . . . But what are Switzerland and Holland, small Powers limited by nature, so that they never can be great, to the United States of America, destined, beyond a doubt, to be the greatest Power on earth, and that within the life of man. This is so well known, that instead of being overlooked among the Powers, like Holland and Switzerland, we shall be more an object of jealousy than any other upon earth. All the Powers know that it is impossible for any, the proudest of them, to conquer us; and therefore, if we should be attacked by any one, the others will not be fond of undertaking our defence. . . . It behooves the United States, then, to knit themselves together in the band of affection and mutual confidence, . . . and I am much afraid we shall never be able to do this, unless Congress are vested with full power . . . of forming treaties of commerce with foreign Powers.

With great esteem, &c.,

John Adams

1785 John Adams Meets George III: "An Epoch in . . . History"

Dispatch from U.S. Minister to the Court of Great Britain John Adams to Secretary of Foreign Affairs John Jay

The reception of the first U.S. minister in London two years after the end of the American Revolution was a moment of high emotion. John Adams, the first accredited U.S. representative to Great Britain, would hold the position for three years. Adams was deeply concerned about what kind of reception awaited him at the British court. While American representatives were being well received elsewhere in Europe, it was not clear that the same would be true in London. Adams was therefore much relieved when his reception was cordial. American interest in the event was sufficient that Adams thought it necessary to describe in detail the ceremony and tension surrounding his presentation to King George III. This excerpt from his dispatch begins with his arrival at the palace.

           Bath Hotel, Westminster,
           June 2, 1785

Dear Sir,

. . . When we arrived in the Ante-Chamber . . . of St. James's, the master of the ceremonies met me and attended me, while the Secretary of State went to take the commands of the King. While I stood in this place, where it seems all Ministers stand upon such occasions, always attended by the master of ceremonies, the room very full of Ministers of State, Bishops, and all other sorts of courtiers, as well as the next room, which is the King's bed-chamber, you may well suppose I was the focus of all eyes. I was relieved, however, from the embarrassment of it by the Swedish and Dutch Ministers, who came to me and entertained me in a very agreeable conversation during the whole time. Some other gentlemen, whom I had seen before, came to make their compliments to me, until the Marquis of Caermarthen returned and desired me to go with him to his Majesty. I went with his Lordship through the levee room into the King's closet. The door was shut, and I was left with his Majesty and the Secretary of State alone. I made the three reverences, one at the door, another about half way, and the third before the presence, according to the usage established at this and all the northern Courts of Europe, and then addressed myself to his Majesty in the following words:
"Sir: The United States of America have appointed me their Minister Plenipotentiary to your Majesty. . . . I have the honor to assure your Majesty of their unanimous disposition and desire to cultivate the most friendly and liberal intercourse between your Majesty's subjects and their citizens, and of their best wishes for your Majesty's health and happiness,

and that of your royal family. The appointment of a Minister from the United States to your Majesty's Court will form an epoch in the history of England and of America. I think myself more fortunate than all my fellow-citizens in having the distinguished honor to be the first to stand in your Majesty's royal presence in a diplomatic character. . . ."

The King listened to every word I said with dignity, but with an apparent emotion. Whether it was the nature of the interview, or whether it was my visible agitation (for I felt more than I did or could express) that touched him, I cannot say; but he was much affected, and answered me with more tremor than I had spoken with, and said:

"Sir: The circumstances of this audience are so extraordinary, the language you have now held is so extremely proper, and the feelings you have discovered so justly adapted to the occasion, that I must say that I not only receive with pleasure the assurance of the friendly dispositions of the United States, but that I am very glad the choice has fallen upon you to be their Minister. . . ."

I dare not say that these were the King's precise words, and it is even possible that I may have in some particular mistaken his meaning, for although his pronunciation is as distinct as I ever heard, . . . he was much affected, and I was not less so, and therefore I cannot be certain that I was so attentive, heard so clearly, and understood so perfectly as to be confident of all his words or sense. . . . I retreated, stepping backward as is the etiquette, and, making my last reverence at the door of the chamber, I went my way.

The master of the ceremonies joined me the moment of my coming out of the King's closet, and accompanied me through the apartments to my carriage. I have been thus minute as it may be useful to others hereafter. . . .

There are a train of other ceremonies to go through. The Queen, and visits to and from Ministers and Ambassadors, which will take up much time, and interrupt me in my endeavors to obtain what I have at heart—the object of my instructions. It is thus the essence of things are lost in ceremony in every country of Europe. We must submit to what we cannot alter. Patience is the only remedy.

With great respect, &c.,

John Adams

1786 Jefferson Urges War against the Barbary States
Dispatch from U.S. Minister to France Thomas Jefferson to
Vice President John Adams

U.S. negotiations with the Barbary States of Algiers, Tripoli, and Tunis were carried out under the direction of the U.S. minister in Lisbon. The 1785 treaty with Algiers required the United States to pay those states ransom for captured sailors, give them presents, and provide an annual tribute to the dey, the Algerian ruler. Thomas Jefferson, who was minister in Paris at the time, was not involved in the negotiations but objected to buying peace. In this dispatch Jefferson outlines his reasons for preferring war with Algiers to submitting to its piratical demands.

After becoming president in 1801, Jefferson did go to war with Tripoli. He eventually concluded a largely unsatisfactory peace that provided for "presents" but no tribute. Congress declared war on Algiers during President James Madison's administration (1809–1817). The peace of 1816 eliminated all ransom, tribute, and presents and required the dey to pay reparations to the United States.

Paris, July 11, 1786

Dear Sir,

Our instructions relative to the Barbary States . . . required us to proceed by way of negotiation to obtain . . . peace. . . . I acknowledge I very early thought it would be best to effect a peace through the medium of war. . . .

I shall trouble you with my reasons. Of the four positions laid down in your letter, . . . I agree to the three first, which are, in substance, that the good offices of our friends cannot procure us a peace without paying its price; that they cannot materially lessen that price; and that paying it, we can have peace in spite of the intrigues of our enemies. As to the fourth, that the longer the negotiation is delayed the larger will be the demand, this will depend on the intermediate captures. If they are many and rich, the price may be raised; if few and poor, it will be lessened. However, if it is decided that we shall buy a peace, I know no reason for delaying the operation, but should rather think it ought to be hastened. But I should prefer the obtaining it by war.

1st. Justice is in favor of this opinion. 2d. Honor favors it. 3d. It will procure us respect in Europe; and respect is a safeguard to interest. 4th. It will arm the Federal head with the safest of all the instruments of coercion over its delinquent members. . . . 5th. I think it least expensive. . . . I ask a fleet of one hundred and fifty guns, the one half of which shall be in constant cruise. This fleet built, manned, and victualled for six months, will cost four hundred and fifty thousand pounds sterling. Its annual expense will be . . . forty-five thousand pounds sterling a year. . . . Were we to charge all this to the Algerine war, it would amount to little more than we must pay if we buy peace. But as it is proper and necessary that we should establish a small marine force, (even were we to buy a peace from the Algerines,) . . . that force, laid up in our dockyards, would cost us half as much annually as if kept in order for service. . . . 6th. It will be as effectual. . . . About forty years ago the Algerines having broken their treaty with France, this Court sent Monsieur de Massiac with one large and two small frigates. He blockaded the harbor of Algiers three months, and they subscribed to the terms he proposed. If it be admitted, however, that war, on the fairest prospects, is still exposed to uncertainties, I weigh against this the greater uncertainty of the duration of a peace bought with money from such a people. . . .

So far I have gone on the supposition that the whole weight of this war should rest on us. But, 1. Naples will join us. . . . 2. Every principle of reason assures us that Portugal will join us. . . . I suppose, then, that a convention might be formed between Portugal, Naples, and the United States, by which the burthen of the war might be quotaed on them, according to their respective wealth; and . . . Algiers should subscribe to a peace with all three, on equal terms. This might be left open for other nations to accede to, and many, if not most of the Powers of Europe . . . would sooner or later enter into the confederacy for the sake of having their peace with the piratical States guaranteed by the whole. . . .

These are the reasons which have influenced my judgment on this question. . . . You make the result different from what I do. The same facts impress us differently. . . . As I have nothing to say in the decision, [I] am ready to proceed heartily on any other plan which may be adopted, if my agency should be thought useful. . . .

I add nothing . . . on any other subject, but assurances of the sincere esteem and respect, with which I am, &c.,

Th. Jefferson

1786 Trade with China

Dispatch from U.S. Consul in Canton Samuel Shaw to Secretary of Foreign Affairs John Jay

Samuel Shaw, a Boston merchant, first distinguished himself as a soldier in the Revolutionary Army, earning the rank of major. In 1784, after the war, he undertook what was reputed to be the first American trading visit to China, aboard the Empress of China. *Shaw's account of his travels much impressed the Continental Congress, which conveyed to him their "peculiar satisfaction at the successful termination of the enterprise." In 1786*

Shaw was elected by Congress as consul to Canton; up to that time only two other American consuls had been named, both to France. President George Washington reappointed Shaw in 1790, making him the first consular appointment under the new Constitution. Shaw remained consul for the rest of his life, residing at Canton and making numerous trading voyages around the Orient, including a stop at Batavia (now Jakarta, Indonesia). In 1794, at age thirty-nine, he died near Cape Town, South Africa, en route home to Boston.

> Canton, in China,
> December 31, 1786

Sir,

I have the honor to avail myself of this opportunity, which the return of our ship to America affords me, for communicating to you such information respecting the commerce carried on with China by the other nations of the world, as my situation and circumstances, after a second voyage to this country, have enabled me to obtain....

No Europeans are suffered to remain at Canton throughout the year. After their ships are gone, and they have settled their accounts with the Chinese, they repair to Macao, where they continue till the arrival of their ships the next season, when they return to Canton.

As soon as a ship, whether public or private, arrives at Whampoa, a fiador or security must be engaged before she can discharge any part of the cargo. This person is one of the principal merchants, and generally him with whom the trade is made, though it does not hinder from dealing with others. He is answerable to the custom-house for payment of the Emperor's customs of entrance, which average between four and five thousand dollars a ship. Besides this tax, there are duties on every other article whether of import or export....

The trade on the part of the Chinese is conducted by a set of merchants, who style themselves the cohoang, a word expressing our idea of a trading company. This cohoang consists of ten or twelve merchants, who have the exclusive privilege of the European and country trade, for which they pay a considerable sum to Government....

Each ship and factory must also have a comprador. This is a person who furnishes provisions and other necessaries, for which he contracts at certain prices....

Besides a fiador and comprador, each ship must also have a linguist. ... This person is absolutely necessary, as he is employed in transacting all business with the custom-house, which is in the city where no European can be admitted—provides boats for loading and unloading and is always at call....

The factories at Canton, occupying less than a quarter of a mile in front, are situated on the bank of the river.... The limits of the

Europeans are extremely confined; there being, besides the key, only a few streets in the suburbs, occupied by the trading people, which they are allowed to frequent. Europeans, after a dozen years' residence, have not seen more than what the first month presented to view. They are sometimes invited to dine with Chinese merchants, who have houses and gardens on the opposite side of the river; but even then no new information is obtained. Every thing of a domestic concern is strictly concealed, and though their wives, mistresses, and daughters, are commonly there, never one of them is visible.

The Europeans at Canton do not associate together as freely as might be expected; the gentlemen of the respective factories keeping much by themselves, and excepting in a few instances, observing a very ceremonious and reserved behavior. At the Danish factory there is, every Sunday evening, a concert of music, performed by gentlemen of the several nations, where every body attends that it pleases. This is the only occasion where there appears to be any thing like a general intercourse. On the whole, the situation of the Europeans is not enviable; and considering the length of time they reside in this country, the restrictions to which they must submit, the great distance they are from their connections, the want of society, and of almost every amusement, it must be allowed that they dearly earn their money.

Much has been said respecting the knavery of the Chinese, particularly those of the trading class; but there is no general rule without exception. The small dealers are, many of them, indisputably rogues, and require to be very narrowly watched. But the merchants of the cohoang are a set of as respectable men as are commonly found in other parts of the world. They are intelligent, exact accountants, punctual to their engagements; and, though not worse for being well looked after, value themselves much upon maintaining a fair character. . . .

The ships employed in this trade are, on an average, seven hundred tons each. . . . The present season the list is as follows: twenty-nine English, five Dutch, one French, two Spanish, two Danish, one Swedish, five American for Europe and America, twenty-three English country ships (trading between India and China) . . . and five Portuguese from Macao to Europe. . . .

The inhabitants of America must have tea, the consumption of which will necessarily increase with the increasing population of our country. And while the nations of Europe are, for the most part, obliged to purchase this commodity with their ready money, it must be pleasing to an American to know that his country can have it on more easy terms, and that the otherwise useless produce of its mountains and forests will in a considerable degree supply him with this elegant luxury. The advantages peculiar to America in this instance are striking, and the manner in which her commerce has commenced and is now going on with this country, has not a little alarmed the Europeans. . . . Such are the advantages which America derives from her ginseng. . . .

The ship in which I have made my second voyage to China stopped at Batavia, the capital of the Dutch establishments in India. We were well received there, and allowed to trade on the same terms as other nations . . . . A profit may be sometimes made on merchandize carried from Batavia to Canton. No doubt similar advantages might result to the Americans in circuitous voyages to China, by the coasts of Malabar and Coromandel, and through the Straits of Malacca.

On the whole, it must be a most satisfactory consideration to every American, when he finds that his country can carry on its commerce with China under advantages, if not in many respects superior, yet in all cases equal with those possessed by any other people. . . .

Should these remarks be found in any degree interesting to my country, it will afford me the most heartfelt satisfaction. . . .

I have the honor to be, &c.,

Samuel Shaw

1789–1794 The French Revolution
Dispatches from U.S. Representatives in Paris

The startling events of the French Revolution were reported in vivid detail by some of America's most distinguished statesmen. Thomas Jefferson was concluding his term (1785–1789) as U.S. minister to France when the revolution broke out. Before returning to the United States to become the first secretary of state, he submitted a remarkable dispatch on the storming of the Bastille, a state prison in Paris. Jefferson was joined in Paris by Gouverneur Morris, who was appointed by President George Washington in 1789 as a U.S. executive agent in Europe and in 1792 as minister to France. Morris remained at this post through the worst of the "Reign of Terror," even when most other foreign diplomats left the city. A friend to King Louis XVI and the monarchists, Morris was recalled in 1794 at the request of the French. He was succeeded by James Monroe, who was able to report the fall from power of Maximilien Robespierre, an ardent revolutionary whose brief leadership witnessed some of the worst excesses of the terror. The execution of Robespierre marked a turning point in the revolution, which led ultimately to a military takeover, as foreshadowed in Monroe's dispatch. These dispatches record some of the most critical events of the tumultuous period.

The Revolution Begins

From U.S. Executive Agent in Europe Gouverneur Morris to Secretary of Foreign Affairs John Jay

Paris, July 1st, 1789

My Dear Sir:

I am too much occupied to find time for the use of a cipher, and in effect the Government here is so much occupied with its own affairs, that in transmitting to you a letter under an envelope there is no risk. This, however, I am pretty certain will go safe. The States General have now been a long time in session, and have done nothing.... [T]he nobles deeply feel their situation. The King [Louis XVI], after siding with them, was frightened into an abandonment of them. He acts from terror only.

The soldiery in this city, particularly the French guards, declare they will not act against the people. They ... now ... parade about the streets drunk.... Some of them have in consequence been confined, not by the force, but by the adroitness of authority. Last night this circumstance became known, and immediately a mob repaired to the prison. The soldiers on guard unfixed their bayonets and joined the assailants. A party of dragoons ordered on duty to disperse the rioters, thought it better to drink with them, and return back to their quarters. The soldiers, with others confined in the same prison, were then paraded in triumph to the Palais Royal, which is now the liberty pole of this city, and there they celebrated, as usual, their joy. Probably this evening some other prisons will be opened: for *liberté* is now the general cry, and authority is a name, not a real existence.... [I]n effect, the sword has slipped out of the Monarch's hands, without his perceiving a tittle of the matter.

All these things in a nation, not yet fitted by education and habit for the enjoyment of freedom, give me frequently suspicions, that they will greatly overshoot their mark, if indeed they have not already done it. Already some people talk of limiting the King's negative upon the laws. And as they have hitherto felt severely the authority exercised in the name of their princes, every limitation of that authority seems to them desirable. Never having felt the evils of too weak an Executive, the disorders to be apprehended from anarchy make as yet no impression.

... My opinion is, that the king, to get fairly out of the scrape in which he finds himself, would subscribe to any thing. And truly, from him, little is to be expected in any way. The Queen [Marie Antoinette], hated, humbled, mortified, feels, and feigns, and intrigues, to save some shattered remnants of the royal authority; but to know that she favors a measure is the certain means to frustrate its success.

... The best chance which royalty has, is, that popular excesses may alarm. At the rate at which things are now going, the King of France must soon be one of the most limited monarchs in Europe.

I am, &c.

Gouverneur Morris

Storming of the Bastille
From U.S. Minister to France Thomas Jefferson to Secretary of Foreign Affairs John Jay

Paris, July 19, 1789

Dear Sir,

I am become very uneasy lest you should have adopted some channel for the conveyance of your letters to me, which is unfaithful. I have none from you of later date than November the 25th, 1788. . . .

The scarcity of bread . . . is still threatening, because we have yet two or three weeks to the beginning of harvest, and I think there has not been three days' provision beforehand in Paris for two or three weeks past.

. . . On the 11th . . . troops, to the number of about twenty-five or thirty thousand . . . were posted in and between Paris and Versailles. . . . The news of this . . . began to be known in Paris about one or two o'clock. In the afternoon, a body of about one hundred German cavalry were advanced and drawn up in the *Place Louis XV.,* and about two hundred Swiss posted at a little distance in their rear. This drew the people to that spot, who naturally formed themselves in front of the troops, at first merely to look at them, but, as their numbers increased, their indignation arose. They retired a few steps, posted themselves on and behind large piles of loose stones, collected in that place for a bridge adjacent to it, and attacked the horse with stones. The horse charged, but the advantageous position of the people, and the showers of stones obliged them to retire, and even quit the field altogether, (leaving one of their number on the ground.) The Swiss in their rear were observed never to stir. This was the signal for universal insurrection, and this body of cavalry, to avoid being massacred, retired towards Versailles. The people now armed themselves with such weapons as they could find in armorers' shops and private houses, and with bludgeons, and were roaming all night through all parts of the city, without any decided and practicable object. The next day the . . . mob, now openly joined by the French guards, forced the prison of St. Lazare, released all the prisoners, and took a great store of corn, which they carried to the corn market. . . . On the 14th they sent one of their members (Monsieur de Corny, whom we knew in America) to the *Hotel des Invalides,* to ask [for] arms. . . . It was remarkable that not only the Invalides themselves made no opposition, but that a body of five thousand foreign troops, encamped within four hundred yards, never stirred. Monsieur de Corny and five others were then sent to ask arms of Monsieur de Launai, Governor of the Bastile. They found a great collection of people already before the place, and they immediately planted a flag of truce, which was answered by a like flag hoisted on the parapet. The deputation prevailed on the people to fall back a little, advanced themselves to make the demands of the Governor, and in that instant a discharge from the Bastile killed four people of those nearest to the Deputies. The Deputies retired; the people rushed against the place, and almost in an instant were in possession of a fortification, defended by one hundred men, of infinite strength, which, in other times, had stood several regular sieges, and had never been taken. How they got in, has, as yet, been impossible to discover. Those who pretend to have been of the party, tell so many different stories as to destroy the credit of them all. They took all the arms, discharged the prisoners, and such of the garrison as were not killed in the first moment of fury, carried the Governor and Lieutenant Governor to the *Greve,* (the place of public execution,) cut off their heads, and sent them through the city in triumph to the Palais Royal.

. . . At night the Duke de Liancourt forced his way into the King's bedchamber, and obliged him to hear a full and animated detail of the disasters of the day in Paris. He went to bed deeply impressed. The decapitation of M. de Launai worked powerfully through the night on the whole aristocratical party, in so much that in the morning those of the greatest influence on the Count d'Artois represented to him the absolute necessity that the King should give up everything to the States. This according well enough with the dispositions of the King, he went about eleven o'clock, accompanied only by his brother, to the States General, and there read to them a speech, in which he asked their interposition to reestablish order. Though this be couched in terms of some caution, yet the manner in which it was delivered made it evident that it was meant as a surrender at discretion. He returned to the chateau afoot, accompanied by the States. They sent off a deputation, the Marquis de la Fayette at their head, to quiet Paris. He had the same morning been named commander-in-chief of the *Milice Bourgeoise.* . . . Tranquillity is now restored to the capital; the shops are again opened; the people resuming their labor; and if the want of bread does not disturb our peace, we may hope a continuance of it. The demolition of the Bastile is going on, and the *Milice Bourgeoise* organizing and training. The ancient police of the city is abolished by the authority of the people; the introduction of the King's troops will probably be proscribed, and a watch or city guards substituted, which shall depend on the city alone. But we cannot suppose this paroxysm confined to Paris alone. The whole country must pass successively through it; and happy if they get through it as soon and as well as Paris has done.

I went yesterday to Versailles, to satisfy myself what had passed there; for nothing can be believed but what one sees, or has from an eye witness.... The churches are now occupied in singing *"de profundis"* and *"requiems"* for the repose of the souls of the brave and valiant citizens who have sealed with their blood the liberty of their nation....

I have the honor to be, &c.,

Th: Jefferson

The Reign of Terror

From U.S. Minister to France Gouverneur Morris to Secretary of State Thomas Jefferson

Paris, 10th September, 1792

Dear Sir:

... We have had one week of unchecked murders, in which some thousands have perished in this city. It began with between two and three hundred of the clergy, who had been shut up because they would not take the oaths prescribed by law, and which, they said, was contrary to their conscience. Thence *these executors of speedy justice* went to the Abbaye, where the persons were confined who were at court on the tenth. These were despatched also; and, afterwards, they visited the other prisons. All those who were confined, either on the accusation or suspicion of crimes, were destroyed. Madame de Lamballe was (I believe) the only woman killed, and she was beheaded and embowelled; the head and entrails were paraded, on pikes, through the street, the body dragged after them. They continued, I am told, at the Temple, till the Queen looked out at this horrid spectacle.

Yesterday the prisoners from Orleans were put to death at Versailles. The destruction began here about five in the afternoon, on Sunday, the second instant. A guard had been sent, a few days since, to make the Duke de la Rochefoucault prisoner. He was on his way to Paris, under their escort, with his wife and mother, when he was taken out of his carriage and killed. The ladies were taken back to La Roche Guyonne, where they are now, in a state of arrestation. Monsieur de Montmorin was among those slain at the Abbaye. You will recollect that a petition was signed by many thousands to displace the Mayor, on account of his conduct on the twentieth of June. The signing of this petition is considered as a sufficient proof of the crime of feuillantisme, and it was in contemplation with some to put all those who were guilty of signing that petition to death. This measure seems, however, to be suspended, (for the present at least) but as there is no real executive authority, the plan may be easily resumed, should it suit the views of those who enjoy the confidence of that part of the people who are now active.

> I am, very dear sir,
> very sincerely yours,
>
> Gouv. Morris

Execution of Louis XVI

From U.S. Minister to France Gouverneur Morris to Secretary of State Thomas Jefferson

Paris, 25 January 1793

Sir,

The late King of this Country has been publicly executed. He died in a manner becoming his dignity. Mounting the scaffold he expressed anew his forgiveness of those who persecuted him and prayed that his deluded people might benefit by his Death. On the scaffold he attempted to speak but the commanding officer Santerre ordered the drums to be beat. The King made two unavailing efforts but with the same bad success. The Executioners threw him down and were in such haste as to let fall the axe before his neck was properly placed so that he was mangled. It would be needless to give you an affecting narrative of particulars. I proceed to what is more important having but a few minutes to write by the present good opportunity.

The greatest care was taken to prevent an affluence of people. This proves a conviction that the majority was not favorable to that severe measure. In effect the greatest of the Parisian citizens mourned the fate of their unhappy Prince. I have seen grief such as for the untimely death of a beloved parent. Everything wears an appearance of solemnity which is awfully distressing. . . .

If my judgement be good, the testament of Louis the Sixteen will be more powerful against the present rulers of this country than an army of an hundred thousand men. You will learn the effect it has in England. I believe that the English will be wound up to a pitch of enthusiastic horror against France which their cool and steady temper seems to be scarcely susceptible of.

. . . I consider a war between Britain and France as inevitable. The Continental powers opposed to France are making great and prompt efforts, while on this side I as yet see but little done to oppose them. There is a treaty on foot (I believe) between England and Austria whose object is the dismemberment of France. I have not proof but some very leading circumstances. Britain will I think suspend the blow till she can strike very hard, unless indeed they should think it advisable to seize the moment of indignation against late events for a Declaration of War.

> With sincere esteem I am
> my dear sir
> your obedient servant,
>
> Gouv. Morris

Execution of Marie Antoinette

From U.S. Minister to France Gouverneur Morris to President George Washington

Paris, October 18th, 1793

My Dear Sir,

... The present Government is evidently a despotism both in principle and practice. The Convention now consists of only a part of those who were chosen to frame a constitution. These, after putting under arrest their fellows, claim all power, and have delegated the greater part of it to a *Committee of Safety*. ... It is an emphatical phrase in fashion among the patriots that *terror is the order of the day*. Some years have elapsed since Montesquieu wrote that the principle of arbitrary governments is *fear*.

The Queen was executed the day before yesterday. Insulted during her trial and reviled in her last moments she behaved with dignity throughout. This execution will, I think, give to future hostilities a deeper dye and unite more intimately the allied Powers. ...

But whatever may be the lot of France in remote futurity, and putting aside the military events, it seems evident that she must soon be governed by a single despot. Whether she will pass to that point through the medium of a triumvirate or other small body of men seems as yet undetermined. I think it most probable that she will. A great and awful crisis seems to be near at hand. ...

> I am, &c.
>
> Gouverneur Morris

Fall of Robespierre

*From U.S. Minister to France James Monroe to
Secretary of State Edmund Jennings Randolph*

Paris, August 11, 1794

Sir:

On the 31st ultimo I arrived at Havre, and, on the 2d instant, at this place.

. . . I heard, at Havre, of the crimes and execution of Robespierre, St. Just, Couthon, and others of that party, and should have written to you on the subject, from that port, but that I knew I could give only the current report, varying, perhaps, in every sea port town, and which might reach you before my letter. I hastened, therefore, to Paris, in the hope of acquiring there immediately more correct information of facts, as well as of the causes which gave birth to them; but, even yet, I suspect I am on the surface only, for it will take some time to become well acquainted with the true state of things on a theatre so extensive and important.

That Robespierre and his associates merited their fate is a position to which every one assents. It was proclaimed by the countenances and voices of all whom I met and conversed with from Havre to Paris. In the latter place, where the oppression was heaviest, the people seemed to be relieved from a burthen which had become insupportable. It is generally agreed that, from the period of Danton's fall, Robespierre had amassed in his own hands all the powers of the Government, and controlled every department in all its operations. It was his spirit which ruled the committee of public safety, the Convention, and the revolutionary tribunal. . . . Robespierre, therefore, had become omnipotent. It was his spirit which dictated every movement, and particularly the unceasing operation of the guillotine. Nor did a more bloody and merciless tyrant ever wield the rod of power. His acts of cruelty and oppression are, perhaps, without parallel in the annals of history. It is generally conceded that, for some months before his fall, the list of prisoners was shown him, every evening, by the president of the revolutionary tribunal, and that he marked those who were to be the victims of the succeeding day, which order was invariably executed. Many whole families, those under the age of sixteen excepted, were cut off, upon the imputation of conspiracies, &c. but for the sole reason that some members had been more friendly to Brissot, Danton, &c. or had expressed a jealousy of his power. His oppression had, in fact, gained to such a height that a convulsion became unavoidable. . . .

. . . It will be observed, by those who wish to form a just estimate of the future course and fortune of this revolution, that, from its commencement to the present time, no person ever raised himself to power but by the proof he had furnished of his attachment to the cause, by his efforts to promote it; and that, from the moment doubts were entertained of the solidity and purity of his principles, did his influence begin to decline in equal degree. This was seen in the instances of Lafayette, Dumouriez, Brissot, Danton, and finally, Robespierre himself; two of whom, though popular generals, were abandoned by the armies they commanded; the former compelled to seek refuge in a foreign country, and the latter in the camp of the enemy; and the others, though eminent in the civil department, were, upon like charges, condemned by the public voice to the same fate. In fact, the current of sentiment and principle has been such, that no character or circumstance has been able to obstruct its course; on the contrary, it has swept every thing before it. . . .

It may be asked: Is there any reason to hope that the vicious operation of the guillotine will be hereafter suspended? May not factions rise again, contend with and destroy each other as heretofore? To this I can only answer, that the like is not apprehended here, at least to the same extent; that the country from Havre to Paris, and Paris itself, appears to enjoy perfect tranquillity; that the same order is said to prevail in the armies, who have addressed the Convention, applauding its conduct, and rejoicing at the downfall of the late conspirators. . . .

But . . . what will become of the army at the end of the War? Will it retire in peace, and enjoy in tranquillity that liberty it has so nobly contended for; or will it not rather turn its victorious arms against the bosom of its country? These are great and important questions, and to which my short residence here will not permit me to give satisfactory answers. . . .

With respect to the state of the war, I can only say, in general, that the armies of France have prevailed over the combined forces every where. . . .

I shall write you again in a few days, and I hope to inform you of my reception. For the present, therefore, I shall conclude, with assurances of the great respect and esteem with which I am, &c.

James Monroe

1793 Help for American Captives in Algiers: "Twelve Cents a Day"

Instructions from U.S. Commissioner to the Dey and
Regency of Algiers David Humphreys to U.S. Consul in Alicante
Robert Montgomery

From the earliest days of the consular service, a primary responsibility of American consuls has been to assist American seafarers in trouble in foreign ports and to aid other Americans in distress. In the final decade of the eighteenth century and the early years of the nineteenth century, some of the most beleaguered Americans were those captured and held for ransom by the Barbary States of North Africa. In 1793 the U.S. minister to Portugal, David Humphreys, was appointed concurrently as special negotiator with Algiers, which was holding a number of Americans captive. Since the United States had no regular representative in Algiers at the time, Humphreys instructed Robert Montgomery, who, although not American, served for thirty years as U.S. consul in Alicante in southern Spain, to provide assistance to the imprisoned Americans.

Alicant, December 1, 1793

Sir:

In the application of that part of the money, the property of the United States of America, received by you from me, which is designed for relieving the necessities of the citizens of the United States who are prisoners in Algiers, and for defraying the contingent expenses which have been or may be inevitably incurred on the subject of Algerine affairs, you will be pleased to be guided by the following general principles, viz:

In the first place, in order to hide the nakedness, and screen from the inclemency of the season, the poor American prisoners in Algiers, you will have the goodness to provide for each one of them a comfortable suit of clothing, nearly in conformity to the estimate which has been made out for the purpose, unless the captains should choose rather to receive the amount in money, in which case you will comply with their wishes.

Secondly, you will please transmit, regularly, by way of subsistence, and for all other personal expenses, eight dollars a month to each of the captains, six dollars a month to each of the mates, and at the rate of twelve cents a day to each of the mariners.

Thirdly, you will please to repay whatever moneys may have been advanced by the consul general of Sweden at Algiers, or his brother Pierre Eric Skjoldebrand, Esq. to relieve the pressing necessities of the citizens of the United States lately captured and carried into Algiers; also such other sums as may become indispensably necessary.

Fourthly, you will please to keep accurate accounts of your disbursements, and obtain as correct vouchers as the nature of the circumstances will admit; in order that there may hereafter be as little obscurity, trouble, and delay, in the final settlement, as possible.

Fifthly, the residue of the property of the United States, deposited by me in your hands, you will please to retain safely in your care, until you may receive further directions from the Secretary of State. . . .

Given at Alicant, this 1st day of December, 1793.

D. Humphreys

1797   Bribery in Paris: The XYZ Affair
Dispatch from U.S. Envoys to France Charles Cotesworth Pinckney, John Marshall, and Elbridge Gerry to Secretary of State Timothy Pickering

Tensions between the United States and France flared in the final decade of the eighteenth century as American relations with Great Britain were normalized and President John Adams (1797–1801) sought to maintain neutrality in the conflict between Britain and France. Relations with France boiled over in 1797 when French foreign minister Talleyrand refused to receive a U.S. delegation unless it first paid a substantial amount in bribes. The American envoys considered the idea but declined, in part because they did not have the necessary funds available. The incident came to be known as the XYZ affair, since the American envoys used the letters as code names for their French intermediaries. The envoys' report home caused a furor in the United States and gave rise to the slogan, "Millions for defense, but not one cent for tribute!" This dispatch reports the attempted extortion in remarkably matter-of-fact terms.

Paris, October 6, in the 22d
year of American independence

Dear Sir,

... [T]he morning of October the eighteenth Mr. W. ... called on general Pinckney, and informed him, that a Mr. X. who was in Paris ... was a gentleman of considerable credit and reputation ... and that we might place great reliance on him. ... Mr. X. called on general Pinckney, and after having sat some time ... whispered him, that he had a message from Mr. Talleyrand to communicate, when he was at leisure. General Pinckney immediately withdrew with him into another room; and when they were alone Mr. X. said, that he was ... very desirous that a reconciliation should be brought about with France; that to effectuate that end, he was ready, if it was thought proper, to suggest a plan, confidentially, that Mr. Talleyrand expected would answer the purpose. General Pinckney said he should be glad to hear it. Mr. X. replied, that the directory, and particularly two of the members of it, were exceedingly irritated at some passages of the President's speech, and desired that they should be softened; and that this step would be necessary previous to our reception: and that besides this, a sum of money was required for the pocket of the directory and ministers, which would be at the disposal of Mr. Talleyrand: and that a loan would also be insisted on. Mr. X. said, if we acceded to these measures, Mr. Talleyrand had no doubt that all our differences with France might be accommodated. On inquiry, Mr. X. could not point out ... the quantum of the loan, but mentioned that the douceur [gratuity] for the pocket was twelve hundred thousand livres, about fifty thousand pounds sterling. General Pinckney told him, his colleagues and himself, from the time of their arrival here, had been treated with great slight and disrespect; that they earnestly wished for peace and reconciliation with France; and had been entrusted by their country with very great powers to obtain these ends, on honourable terms: that with regard to the propositions made, he could not even consider of them before he had communicated them to his colleagues. . . . After a . . . consultation, . . . it was agreed, that general Pinckney should call on Mr. X. and request him to make his propositions to us all; and . . . that he should be requested to reduce the heads into writing. . . . Mr. X. . . . consented. . . . He said his communication was not immediately with Mr. Talleyrand, but through another gentleman, . . . this proved to be Mr. Y.

. . . On the morning of the 20th Mr. X. called and said, that Mr. Y., the confidential friend of Mr. Talleyrand, instead of communicating with us through Mr. X would see us himself . . . at seven o'clock, in general Marshall's room. . . . At seven Mr. Y. and Mr. X. entered; and the first mentioned gentleman . . . immediately stated to us the favourable impressions of that gentleman towards our country. . . . He was willing to aid us in the present negotiation by his good offices with the directory, who were, he said, extremely irritated. . . . Mr. Talleyrand . . . had authorized his friend Mr. Y. to communicate to us certain propositions, . . . if we would engage to consider them as the basis of the proposed negotiation, he would intercede with the directory to acknowledge us, and to give us public audience. . . . Mr. Y. dilated very much upon . . . the satisfaction he said was indispensably necessary as a preliminary to negotiation. "But, said he, gentlemen, I will not disguise from you, that this satisfaction being made, the essential part of the treaty remains to be adjusted: il faut de l'argent—il faut beaucoup d'argent:" *you must pay money, you must pay a great deal of money.* He spoke much of . . . honor and . . . republican pride of France: and represented to us strongly the advantages which we should derive from the neutrality thus to be purchased. . . . Concerning the twelve hundred thousand livres little was said; that being completely understood, on all sides, to be required for the officers of government, and therefore needing no further explanation. . . . We asked whether we were to consider it as certain, that without a previous stipulation to the effect required, we were not to be received. He answered, that Mr. Talleyrand himself was not authorized to speak to us. . . .

Mr. Y. . . . said that Mr. Talleyrand and himself were extremely sensible of the pain we must feel in complying with this demand; but that the directory would not dispense with it: that therefore we must consider it as the indispensable preliminary to obtain our reception; unless we could find the means to change their determination. . . . On being asked to suggest the means, he answered, money; that the directory were jealous of its own honour and . . . that this honour must be maintained in the manner before required, unless we substituted in the place of those reparations something perhaps more valuable, that was money . . . thirty-two millions of florins of Dutch inscriptions, worth ten shillings in the pound. . . . We asked him whether the fifty thousand pounds sterling, as a douceur to the directory, must be in addition to this sum. He answered in the affirmative. . . .

We committed immediately to writing the answer we proposed, in the following words: "Our powers respecting a treaty are ample: but the proposition of a loan in the form of Dutch inscriptions, or in any other form, is not within the limits of our instructions. . . ." Mr. Y. observed that we had taken no notice of the first proposition, which was . . . the disavowal . . . [of] the President's speech. We told him that we supposed it to be impossible . . . that such a proposition could require an answer: that we did not understand it as being seriously expected; but merely as introductory to the subjects of real consideration. . . .

He said that we should certainly not be received; and seemed to shudder at the consequences. We told him, that America had made every possible effort to remain on friendly terms with France; that she was still making them: that if France would not hear us; but would make war on the United States; nothing remained for us, but to regret the unavoidable necessity of defending ourselves. . . .

We parted with mutual professions of personal respect. . . .

We have the honor to be, &c.

Charles Cotesworth Pinckney
J. Marshall
E. Gerry

1798 Pirates in New Orleans

Dispatch from Acting U.S. Vice Consul in New Orleans Daniel Clark Jr. to U.S. Border Commissioner Andrew Ellicott

After emigrating to New Orleans in his youth, Daniel Clark amassed a fortune as a trader, becoming one of the most influential residents of the city. He acted as U.S. vice consul beginning in 1798, was appointed consul in 1802, and served until the transfer of Louisiana to the United States in December 1803. He later was elected as the new territory's first representative to Congress. In 1807 Clark seriously wounded the governor of Louisiana, his political rival, in a duel.

As consul, Clark dealt not only with pirates but also with frontier Indian problems and settler intrigues. At the same time he was urging the

United States to take Louisiana by force from Spain. In this dispatch Clark appeals for help from the nearest U.S. official in dealing with the privateers who still plagued the Caribbean of his day.

New Orleans, 7th August 1798

Sir,

I shall make no apology for addressing you on the present occasion, and requesting from you the most efficacious support, confident that you will look upon it as a duty to assist me in my endeavors to be serviceable to the Citizens of the U.S., and protect their shipping & property from the piratical depredations of the French Privateers, who again begin to infest this quarter and have lately sent for this port the three following Prizes:

The Ship *Mars* of New York . . .
Schooner *Apollo* of Charleston . . .
Schooner *Lunbury Packet* of New York . . .

These vessels, whose cargoes consist of mahogany & logwood, have been captured by the Schooner *Creole*, Francis Michel Commander, bearing a French Commission, fitting out on the Island of Cuba, chiefly manned with Spaniards, and on pretext of falling under the late decree of the French Directory ordering all vessels to be seized laden with British Manufactures.

The Captains of the American captured vessels arriving in town last night . . . immediately applied to me to take their affairs in hand which I have complied with, and shall give them every assistance. . . .

In hopes that your patronage and interference on the part of the U.S. with this Government may have its due weight, and cause justice to be administered, I apply to you . . . to remonstrate with the Government on the countenance afforded to Pirates, and procure more . . . protection to the Americans than they have hitherto met with.

. . . Francis Michel who commanded the Sloop *Hennique* when she first arrived here [last year] . . . acknowledged himself a Pirate and a forger of Commissions and . . . with a simple copy of this forged commission . . . brought in here . . . four . . . vessels which with their cargoes were sold but for which I procured security to be answerable to the owners when the legality of the captures was decided on.

It may be necessary to remark that the tribunals of this country declare themselves incompetent to judge of the validity of prizes, and only meddle so far as to order security to be given, when they permit vessels' cargoes to be disposed of as the captors think proper.

In this business however the most shameful partiality in favor of the French and neglect of the Americans takes place. . . . The Captains . . . were immediately turned ashore, refused their clothes and papers, left without the means of subsistence, and afterwards when it suited the views of the Privateer's men they were permitted to make prisoners a second time in the Streets of Orleans of the Citizens of the U.S.... This last circumstance has not escaped the notice of Government as it is public and notorious here, but is winked at for reasons best known to the Officers of Government.

This... same Michel... is now here Commander of the Privateer *Creole*.... [I shall] demand of the Spanish Government to arrest him as a Pirate and seize his new Prizes....

[Spanish] Governor Gayoso [of Louisiana] has I believe no cordial goodwill towards the French but seeing how every thing is regulated by their nod in Spain he will be entirely cautious of giving them the least cause of offense.... You will render your country an essential service [if] you will... force him to do justice... and impress him with the fear of his conduct being made the ground of a complaint from the Executive of the U.S. to the Court of Spain. I should have forwarded these remarks to the Secretary of State... but for seeing the delay and time necessary to have his answer and take measures in consequence would defeat the purpose by giving Michel who proposes staying here but a few days time to transact his business and depart. I entertain the most sanguine hopes that a pointed demand from you on the subject may procure his arrest, more attention to my demands in favor of the Citizens of the U.S., and by throwing difficulties in the way of the condemnation of American vessels may entirely discourage privateering and break the Cruise of the Schooner *Creole*, as I was fortunate enough to effect last year with respect to the Sloop *Hennique* which was sold to defray the expenses.

I have myself no personal interest in soliciting your interference nor anything to gain....

The ship *Mars*, one of the three vessels lately taken has not yet got in and I entertain the pleasing hope that she may yet be met with and retaken by the American armed ship *Star*....

May I request the favor of an answer... on a subject of so much importance and which will afford you a new opportunity of rendering another service to your country. I remain, with esteem, etc.

Daniel Clark

1798 Naval Tensions with Britain: American Fleet Captured Off Havana

Dispatch from Acting U.S. Consul in Havana George C. Morton to Secretary of State Timothy Pickering

One of the major issues of U.S. foreign policy from the time of independence through the War of 1812 was the right of neutral shipping. American merchantmen fell victim to British and French vessels, both of which were authorized by their governments to prey on neutrals trading with the other. A related issue was impressment, the British practice of forcibly taking seamen—ostensibly British nationals but very often naturalized Americans—from American ships. While American merchantmen were the most frequent victims, crew members of American warships were not always immune from impressment. This dispatch reports significant British depredation of American shipping.

Havana, 18th Nov. 1798

Sir,

By the delegation of Daniel Hawley, Esq. I am at present acting as consul of the United States in this district, with which he will most probably have acquainted you. It imposes upon me the mortifying task of informing you, sir, of the partial capture of an American fleet, under the convoy of the Baltimore sloop of war, —Phillips, Esq. commander, by a British squadron, off this harbour, accompanied with circumstances rather grating to the feelings of Americans, and by no means analogous to that good harmony which seems to subsist between the two governments.

  . . . [British] Commodore Loring ordered . . . 55 men out of the Baltimore, "on board of his ship, previous to any proposal of exchanging the natives of one nation for those of the other; and retained five of the hands as being British subjects, without giving an equal number of Americans, whom he *acknowledged* to have on board."

George C. Morton

1801 Tripoli Declares War: "Our Flag-staff Was Chopped Down"

Dispatch from U.S. Consul in Tripoli James Leander Cathcart to Secretary of State James Madison

James Leander Cathcart had among the most unusual backgrounds of any American diplomat. In 1785 the young man was aboard an American ship captured by the dey of Algiers. Pressed into slavery, he spent over a decade in captivity, much of it at hard labor on public works, before gaining his freedom when the United States agreed to pay tribute to Algiers. Cathcart was appointed consul in Tripoli in 1797, then served successively as consul in Algiers, Tunis, Madeira, and Cadiz, totaling more than twenty years as a U.S. envoy abroad. In this brief dispatch Cathcart reports the onset of war with Tripoli, which was to continue intermittently for several years.

Tripoli, in Barbary,
May 16, 1801

Sir:

This evening (10th May,) at six, P.M. Hadgi Mahomude la Sore . . . came to the American house, and told me not to be alarmed, for the Bashaw had sent him to inform me that he declared war against the United States, and would take down our flag-staff on Thursday, the 14th instant; that, if I pleased to remain at Tripoli, I should be treated with respect, but, if I pleased, I might go away. I sent my compliments to the Bashaw, and informed him that it was my positive instructions not to remain an instant after a declaration of war took place, and that I should charter a vessel to-morrow, if possible.

Thursday, 14th, at one, P.M. Hadgi Mahomude la Sore came to inform me that the chavux were coming to take our flag-staff down.

. . . At a quarter past two they effected the grand achievement, and our flag-staff was chopped down six feet from the ground, and left reclining on the terrace. Thus ends the first act of this tragedy. I hope the catastrophe may be happy.

I have the honor to be your
obedient servant

J. Cathcart

1802, 1810 Napoleon: "A Spoilt Child of Fortune"
Dispatches from U.S. Representatives in Paris

Graduating forty-second in his class of fifty-one at a Parisian military academy, Napoleon Bonaparte (1769–1821) rose to the rank of general by age twenty-six. After a series of spectacular military successes in Italy and Egypt, Napoleon returned to Paris in 1799 and seized control of the government of France in a coup. Naming himself first consul, Napoleon ostensibly ruled as a member of a triumvirate, but the real power lay in his hands. In 1802 the French people voted him consul for life, and in 1804 he crowned himself emperor. Until 1813 Napoleon ruled with great success, bringing most of Europe under French control.

From his earliest days in power Napoleon totally dominated the French government. A series of American ministers in Paris complained bitterly of the difficulties of doing business in a country governed by an often capricious absolute ruler.

"One Man Is Every Thing"
From U.S. Minister to France Robert R. Livingston to Secretary of State James Madison

Paris, September 1, 1802

Sir:

... There never was a Government in which less could be done by negotiation than here. There is no people, no Legislature, no counsellors. One man is every thing. He seldom asks advice and never hears it unasked. His ministers are mere clerks; and his Legislature and counsellors parade officers. ... The extreme hauteur of this Government to all around them will not suffer peace to be of long continuance.

I am, sir, &c. &c.

R. R. L.

"No Policy but His Power"
From U.S. Chargé d'Affaires in France Jonathan Russell to Secretary of State Robert Smith

Paris, 4th Decem 1810

Sir:

... The strange influence, which the Emperor exercises over those whom he employs, appears to merge all they may possess of suavity of benevolence in a zeal to execute his unbending will. He has no favorite or confident—he neither loves or trusts those whom he finds it necessary to use but considering himself alone and concentrating within himself all his affections and all his projects he braves and he despises the opinions of others. His Ministers and his Marshals approach him—not to give their counsel but to receive his orders. The most intrepid among them shrink from his regard and a word from him confounds alike their wisdom and their courage. He has no policy but his power—and to make this power felt and feared he is obliged often to display it in acts of oppression and injustice. . . . Indeed the awe which all about him manifestly feel is inconceivable to those who are not familiar with the excesses and extravagancies of a man possessed of absolute power and actuated by violent and unmanagable passions. Our relations with a country governed in this way must, I fear, at best be precarious and uncertain. . . . [W]hat security can we have for the permanency of any arrangement which depends on the single will of a spoilt child of fortune who regards neither the sanctity of principle or the decency of forms. . . .

The free and negligent manner in which this letter is written will be sufficient to advise you that it is private and confidential.

> I remain
> faithfully and respectfully
> Sir
> Your very Hble Servt
>
> Jona Russell

1803 Bargaining for Louisiana

Dispatches from U.S. Minister to France Robert R. Livingston to Secretary of State James Madison

Robert Livingston's reports of American negotiations with France for the purchase of Louisiana—a territory extending from the Mississippi River to the Rocky Mountains and from the Gulf of Mexico to Canada—bring to mind an Eastern bazaar, with offers and counteroffers on both the amount of territory for sale and its price. The largest real estate deal in history was concluded on April 30, 1803, after barely three weeks of serious discussion. The American negotiators exceeded their instructions by agreeing to pay 60 million francs and to assume another 20 million francs in claims of American citizens against France, for a total equivalent to about $15 million.

"Our Wishes Extended Only to New Orleans"

Paris, April 11, 1803

Dear Sir:

... [French foreign minister] M. Talleyrand asked me this day, when pressing the subject, whether we wished to have the whole of Louisiana. I told him no; that our wishes extended only to New Orleans and the Floridas; that the policy of France, however, should dictate (as I had shown in an official note) to give us the country above the river Arkansas, in order to place a barrier between them and Canada. He said, that if they gave New Orleans the rest would be of little value; and that he would wish to know "what we would give for the whole." I told him it was a subject I had not thought of; but that I supposed we should not object to twenty millions, provided our citizens were paid. He told me that this was too low an offer; and that he would be glad if I would reflect upon it and tell him to-morrow. I told him that, as . . . [Special Negotiator James] Monroe would be in town in two days, I would delay my further offer until I had the pleasure of introducing him. . . . I think that, if we succeed, it would be good policy to exchange the west bank of the Mississippi with Spain for the Floridas, reserving New Orleans. Perhaps, however, I am too sanguine in my expectations: we will not, therefore, dispose of the skin till we have killed the bear. . . .

I shall see the minister again to-morrow, in order to sound him more fully before we offer any thing formal on Mr. Monroe's arrival. . . .

I am, dear sir, with the most respectful consideration.

Your most obedient
humble servant,

R. R. Livingston

A Bargaining Session

Paris, April 13, 1803, midnight

Dear Sir:

I have just come from the Minister of the Treasury. Our conversation was so important, that I think it necessary to write it, while the impressions are strong upon my mind. . . .

. . . While we were taking coffee he [Treasury Secretary Marbois] came in; and, after being some time in the room, we strolled into the next room, when he told me . . . that he thought I might have something particular to say to him, and had taken the first opportunity to call on me. I saw that this was meant as an opening to one of those free conversations which I had frequently had with him. . . . This led to long discussions of no moment to repeat. We returned to the point: he said, that . . . the Consul [Napoleon] told him . . . "Well, you have the charge of the Treasury; let them give you one hundred millions of Francs, and pay their own claims, and take the whole country." Seeing, by my looks, that I was surprised at so extravagant a demand, he added that he considered the demand as exorbitant, and had told the First Consul that the thing was impossible; that we had not the means of raising that. The Consul told him we might borrow it. I now plainly saw the whole business: first, the Consul was disposed to sell; next, he distrusted Talleyrand, on account of the business of the supposed intention to bribe, and meant to put the negotiation into the hands of Marbois, whose character for integrity is established. I told him that the United States were anxious to preserve peace with France: that, for that reason, they wished to remove them to the west side of the Mississippi; that we would be perfectly satisfied with New Orleans and the Floridas, and had no disposition to extend across the river; that, of course, we would not give any great sum for the purchase; that he was right in his idea of the extreme exorbitancy of the demand, which would not fall short of one hundred and twenty-five millions; that, however, we would be ready to purchase, provided the sum was reduced to reasonable limits. He then pressed me to name the sum. I told him that this was not worth while, because, as he only treated the inquiry as a matter of curiosity, any declarations of mine would have no effect. If a negotiation was to be opened, we should (Mr. Monroe and myself) make the offer after mature reflection. This compelled him to declare, that, though he was not authorized expressly to make the inquiry from me, yet, that, if I could mention any sum that came near the mark, that could be accepted, he would communicate it to the First Consul. I told him that we had no sort of authority to go to a sum that bore any proportion to what he mentioned; but that, as he himself considered the demand as too high, he would oblige me by telling me what he thought would be reasonable. He replied that, if we would name sixty millions, and take upon us the American claims, to the amount of twenty more, he would try how far this would be accepted. I told him that it was vain to ask any thing that was so greatly beyond our means. . . . He admitted the weight of all this: "But," says he, "you know the temper of a youthful conqueror; every thing he does is rapid as lightning; we have only to speak to him as an opportunity presents itself, perhaps in a crowd, when he bears no contradiction. When I am alone with him, I can speak more freely, and he attends; but this opportunity seldom happens, and is always accidental. Try, then, if you cannot come up to my mark. Consider the extent of the country, the exclusive navigation of the river, and the importance of having no neighbors to dispute you, no war to dread." I told him that I considered all these as important considerations, but there was a point beyond which we could not go, and that fell far short of the sum he mentioned.

... Thus, sir, you see a negotiation is fairly opened, and upon ground which I confess I prefer to all other commercial privileges; and always to some a simple money transaction is infinitely preferable. As to the quantum, I have yet made up no opinion. The field opened to us is infinitely larger than our instructions contemplated; the revenue increasing, and the land more than adequate to sink the capital, should we even go the sum proposed by Marbois; nay, I persuade myself, that the whole sum may be raised by the sale of the territory west of the Mississippi, with the right of sovereignty, to some Power in Europe, whose vicinity we should not fear. ... We shall do all we can to cheapen the purchase; but my present sentiment is that we shall buy. Mr. Monroe will be presented to the minister to-morrow, when we shall press for as early an audience as possible from the First Consul. I think it will be necessary to put in some proposition to-morrow: the Consul goes in a few days to Brussels, and every moment is precious.

I am, dear sir, with the most respectful consideration, your most obedient, humble servant.

Robt. R. Livingston.

Close to a Deal

Paris, April 17, 1803

Sir:

I have an opportunity to give you a relation of what has passed since my letter of the 13th. On the 14th I called upon Mr. Monroe, to present him to the minister.... Before we went we examined our commission ... with which I am not quite satisfied. The commission contains power only to treat for lands on the east side of the Mississippi. You will recollect that I have been long preparing this Government to yield us the country above the Arkansas, because I saw the effect of their holding and giving encouragement to settle it would draw off a prodigious population from our side of the river, and form such a connexion between the inhabitants of the Western country and these new settlers who would be their relations and friends, as would be extremely dangerous. In my private negotiations with Joseph Bonaparte, I had urged every reason that I could think of to induce them to give us the country; and those reasons have had their effect. I am, therefore, surprised that our commission should have entirely lost sight of the object. Mr. Monroe, however, agrees with me that we will proceed as well as we can....

The next day, Mr. Monroe and myself, after spending some time in consultation, determined to offer fifty millions, including our debts: we presumed it would be best only to mention forty in the first instance. This I accordingly did, in a conference I had on the 15th with M. Marbois. He expressed great sorrow that we could not go beyond that sum, because he was sure that it would not be accepted, and that perhaps the whole business would be defeated, which he the more feared, as he had just received a note from the minister, indicative of the Consul's not being quite pleased that he had so greatly lowered his original proposition. He said that he saw our situation, and he knew that there was a point beyond which we could not go with safety to ourselves or the President; but he wished us to advance to that point.... The next morning, which was yesterday, I again called to see him. He told me that he had been to St. Cloud; that the Consul received his proposition very coldly....

I dined with the Second Consul yesterday; and in the evening M. Marbois came in. I took him aside, and asked him if any thing further had passed: he said not; but, that as he was to go to St. Cloud the next day, it was possible that the Consul might touch upon the subject again; and that, if he did not, I might consider the plan as relinquished; and that, if I had any further proposition to make, it would be well to state it. I then told him, that on further conversation with Mr. Monroe, we had resolved to go to the greatest possible length, and that we would give fifty millions....

I am, dear sir, with much esteem and respect, your most obedient, humble servant.

R. R. Livingston

1803 Transfer of Louisiana
Dispatch from U.S. Consul in New Orleans Daniel Clark Jr. to Secretary of State James Madison

Although France and the United States agreed to the terms of the Louisiana Purchase in April 1803 (see "Bargaining for Louisiana," p. 60), the actual transfer was not completed until December. Part of the delay stemmed from the reluctance of Spain, which still controlled Louisiana, to return the territory to France. The U.S. consul in New Orleans, Daniel Clark, played a pivotal role in assuring a smooth transition from Spanish to French to U.S. rule in the tense final weeks of 1803. In this dispatch he reports the impending transfer from Spain to France and his fears that French-Spanish tensions in New Orleans will boil over. To deal with the threat, Clark organized and captained a U.S. volunteer force to keep order in the city. American troops arrived three weeks later to take possession of Louisiana.

New Orleans,
29 November 1803

Sir:

I had the honor of advising under date of the 28th that a conference was to be held at the Government House in the course of the Morning between the French and Spanish Commissioners—it took place, and the authority of the Prefect to take possession of the Province being deemed sufficient he intends tomorrow taking the reins of government into his hands. I waited on him yesterday at noon at his request and he communicated his Plans with the names of the Persons he designed to fill the different Offices civil and military. As his intentions had been manifested to the Governor before I saw him, it was too late to attempt dissuading him from his purpose, but he made no difficulty in making such Changes among the administrative Officers as I thought necessary. He means by a solemn act to take possession and with the Militia to garrison the Forts and take charge of the public Offices. To command them he has appointed a particular Friend of mine, who when first applied to refused the appointment and gave me advice of it, suspecting that some treachery was intended—when I found the Prefect resolved on his Scheme I advised my friend to accept the command being better pleased to see it in his hands than in those of a Person in whom I could not confide. A Municipality consisting of a Mayor, two Assistants or *adjoints,* a Greffier or Secretary and 8 Members among whom are to be 3 Americans are likewise to be appointed. The customhouse he wished to place under the charge of the Vice Consul, who thinking the exercise of any Office under him incompatible with his duty to the U. S. will not accept it, and I presume he will cast his Eyes on some other American to fill that place. With the revenue of the customhouse he proposes to pay the Militia and the charges attending taking possession of the country. . . . I do not see these preparations with pleasure altho' I firmly believe he means to act honestly towards the U.S. I am fearful of Events which it may be impossible to guard against or controul and dread the consequences that may ensue. A Fete is to be given at his House on the night of the day on which he takes possession, and as it will at the same time gratify his ruling Passion and humble the Spaniards whom he would run all risks to mortify, it will increase the fermentation of the public Mind which is already but too apparent. . . . The Prefect read to me the first Sketch of a Proclamation which he means to issue, and it tends entirely to tranquilise the People and attach them to our Government. I wish however that this Experiment of his were not to be attempted as it will give the lower Classes a hankering for a French government and will arouse that Spirit which I have long attempted to subdue. I shall give advice of his measure to the Commissioners by this day's Express, and when the Prefect is in possession will dispatch another to hasten their arrival; in the mean time I shall be careful to do that only which I think most prudent in the present posture of affairs.

> I remain very respectfully
> Sir
> Your most obedt Servt.
>
> Daniel Clark

1805 Napoleon Victorious: "A Very Favorable" Situation for the United States

Dispatch from U.S. Minister to Great Britain James Monroe to Secretary of State James Madison

After spending two years as U.S. minister to France, James Monroe spent more than four years as American minister at the Court of His Britannic Majesty during the Napoleonic Wars (1804–1815) that engulfed Europe. In this dispatch Monroe reports the latest victories of the French armies and ponders whether Emperor Napoleon Bonaparte is operating under some master plan for the conquest of Europe or is merely seizing the opportunity to advance farther after each successive military victory. Monroe assesses that the war in Europe, by pitting America's potential enemies against each other, has benefited American security.

> Cheltenham,
> December 11, 1805

Sir:

The delicate state of health which my family has enjoyed of late, attributable, as is supposed, in a great measure, to the atmosphere of London, induced me to come here last week. . . .

By late accounts from the continent, it appears that the French have entered Vienna almost without opposition, the Austrian and Russian armies having left it open to them. . . . Thus the campaign seems to be hastening to its crisis. . . . It will soon be seen whether the Emperor of France has been drawn on, without system, by the brilliancy of his success against [Austrian] General [Karl] Mack, to hazard more than an able and prudent commander ought to have done, or, having in view the accomplishment of a vast object, his movements, combined with those of General [André] Masséna in Italy, were judicious, and conformable to a plan wisely laid down in the commencement. . . . Whatever may have been the motive of the Emperor of France to take his present position, it is certainly a daring and hazardous one. It gives, in plain terms, the defiance to Europe; and, if Prussia takes part against him, he may be considered as fairly pitted against Europe; for the Powers that are on his side are not volunteers in the cause. . . . It remains to be seen whether, in case he succeeds by completely vanquishing the armies opposed to him, he will be able to make a prudent use of his victories, for the purpose of consolidating and securing his own power; and of course whether his victories are to prove of any solid and permanent advantage to him. It may, perhaps, require greater talents in the present state of the world, in respect to that object, to turn such victories to the best account, than, at the head of the veteran armies of France, to gain them.

The situation of the United States, in respect to all these Powers, is, in every view, a very favorable one. So circumstanced are they, respectively, that while we have the means of doing each irreparable injury, all are interested in preserving the relations of peace and friendship with us; and none have it in their power to do us comparatively equal harm. As things now stand, each of the parties forms a complete counterpoise to the other, in a way best adapted to its own safety, and to our interest. Victorious by land, France has scarcely a ship at sea, and is, therefore, interested in the prosperity of our commerce. Victorious at sea, Great Britain finds herself compelled to concentrate her force so much in this quarter, with a view to her own security, that she would not only be unable to annoy us essentially in case of war, but even to protect her commerce and possessions elsewhere which would be exposed to our attacks. As to Spain, she ought not, perhaps, to be considered as a party to this controversy. If she were asked in which scale her interest lay, which party she wished to prevail, her friends or her enemies, she would most probably be at a loss to decide. I think it must be her interest that neither should succeed; but that the scales should stand suspended as they now are. If her enemies succeeded completely, she would be undone; and the same thing would happen if her friends did. Thus it appears that from none of these Powers have we any serious danger or injury to apprehend in the present state of affairs; nor, from what I can see, is it likely that we soon shall have. While the Powers of Europe are contending against each other, none of them can venture to break with us, in consideration of such motives as the just pretensions and claims of our Government may furnish; and by many causes they seemed to be destined to remain in that state some years longer, or at least in one of great jealousy and rivalry of interest, which may produce the same effect. . . .

I am, sir, with great respect and esteem, your very obedient servant,

James Monroe

1806 The British Move into Africa: The Cape of Good Hope

Dispatch from U.S. Consul in Cape Town John Elmslie to Secretary of State James Madison

The Dutch established the first permanent European settlement at the Cape of Good Hope in 1652. When French forces overran Holland a century and a half later, the British briefly seized Dutch colonies to keep them from falling into French hands. The colonies, including the Cape of Good Hope, were later returned to the Dutch Republic. During the Napoleonic Wars (1804–1815), the process was repeated. The French again marched into Holland and the British again seized the Cape, but this time with more permanent effect. John Elmslie, who served for a decade as American consul in Cape Town, witnessed the Dutch capitulation in 1806. In this dispatch he describes the raising of the British flag over "the castle"—the Dutch fort at Cape Town—and the retreat of a small Dutch force to make a brave but futile last stand in the mountains.

Cape Town 18th Jany. 1806

Sir:

I have the honor to inclose for the information of Government the Articles of Capitulation of the Cape of Good Hope to His Britannick Majesty's forces under the command of Major-General Sir David Baird. The British fleet consisting of 57 sail of ships of war & transports arrived in Table Bay the 4th instant & in the course of a few days the troops were landed & according to reports to the number of 15,000 men, little opposition being given to their landing on the part of the Dutch. On the 6th, the Governor, General Janssens marched out with his small army in order to oppose the British forces. On the 8th between 7 & 10 o'clock a.m., an engagement took place which ended in the defeat of the Dutch. General Janssens however has retreated with a small part of his army to a strong pass named Hottentots Holland Cloof. The British troops marched on to Cape Town. On the morning of the 9th when the English were within a few miles of the lines, the Commandant of the castle sent a boat with a flag of truce to the British Commander . . . offering to capitulate, upon which the British General came to town, & the inclosed Articles of Capitulation were signed. The English troops took quiet possession of the lines the same evening, and on the 10th at 4 o'clock p.m. the British flag was hoisted on the Castle. General Janssens with his small party, not above five hundred men, still hold out & no doubt will give the British Government a good deal of trouble, but General Baird is determined should General Janssens not accept the terms offered him by Brig. General Beresford who is marched out with a large detachment of the

English army to oblige him by force of arms. General Janssens probably wishes to imitate Leonidas & if his troops are equally heroic as the Grecian, most certainly is in possession of a second Thermopylae. A short time will determine the event. As there is a vessel to be dispatched to England tomorrow I embrace the opportunity to forward the enclosed Gazettes. All foreign vessels are at present detained among which are several Americans. As the British General has been much engaged since the capture I have not as yet had an opportunity of paying respects, or to learn whether foreign Consuls are to be received at the Cape.

> I have the honor to be,
> most respectfully
> Sir
> your obedient servant
>
> John Elmslie

1808 Threatened by the Dey of Algiers

Dispatch from U.S. Consul General in Algiers Tobias Lear to Secretary of State James Madison

Tobias Lear served for a decade as George Washington's private secretary before beginning his diplomatic career. After a brief tour of duty in Haiti, Lear took up residence in Algiers, where he served as consul general from 1803 to 1812—a period that fell within the most difficult years of U.S. relations with the Barbary States of North Africa. (See "Jefferson Urges War against the Barbary States," p. 38, and "Help for American Captives in Algiers," p. 59.)

> Algiers, March 28, 1808

Sir:

It is with regret I have to inform you, that our affairs here wear a different aspect from what they did when I had last the honour of writing to you. On the 16th instant, the dey sent me a message by my drogerman, that I should pay immediately sixteen thousand dollars for eight of the subjects of his regency, said to have been destroyed on board the American schooner Mary Ann, captured some time since, by one of his frigates, as mentioned in my former letters. I returned for answer, that I had not yet received any authentick advices of this business, and could therefore say nothing about it. The dey then sent me word, that he would wait the arrival of the courier from Alicante, by which I might receive some information.

But on the 24th, (the courier not having yet arrived) the drogerman informed me, that the dey had sent for him, and ordered him to tell me, that if I did not pay the money before night, I should be sent to prison in chains. I ordered him to return immediately to the dey, and say that I could not pay the money, without the order of my government, as it was an affair out of the usual course of our business here, and that I was ready to meet the event. He brought me word, that the dey would see me the next day at noon, on the subject.

He accordingly sent for me at noon on the 25th. When I entered the palace, I met Mr. Ulrick, the Danish consul, who was descending from an audience of the dey. He was seized by a Chaoux, who carried him through the streets, in the most indignant manner, to the slave prison, where he was loaded with an enormous chain; the reason assigned for which was, that he had been called upon for his biennial presents, which he declared he could not make, without having time given him, as the vessel containing it, and annuities for the regency, had been taken by the English. On meeting the dey, he demanded from me immediate payment for the persons before mentioned, together with an additional two thousand dollars for the boy said to have been carried in the schooner to Naples. I told him, with firmness, that I could not pay it without the orders of my government, as it was an extraordinary case, and requested time to write and receive an answer; but was answered, that if it was not paid immediately, I knew what the consequence would be. I replied, that let the consequence be what it might, I should not pay it. I was then ordered to leave his presence. On descending to the area of the palace, where the Danish consul had been seized, I expected the same compliment which he had met with, and was *prepared* for it; but finding no one to molest me, I left the palace and returned to my own home, where I supposed the orders would be sent to have me arrested; but the day passed without my hearing any thing more of the matter. In the evening I met the French and Swedish consuls (the others being at their gardens) and we agreed to send for the other consuls the following morning, to concert measures for the liberation of the Dane. At noon we met at the Danish consul's house, with our respective drogermen, and proceeded to the palace, where we had an audience of the dey; who, after some conversation, agreed to release the Danish consul from his chains, at the intercession made for him. From thence we went to the marine (where the consul had been sent to work with the *other* slaves, carrying a chain of 40lbs. weight) to receive and conduct him to his house.

While we were with the dey on the business before mentioned, he asked me, in presence of the consuls, if I did not intend to pay the money. I answered him as I had done the day before; to which he made the same reply; and I remain in daily expectation of experiencing the effects of this refusal; which is dictated by a sense of duty, and a conviction that the honour of my country demands such conduct from me. I make no comments on the unpleasantness of my situation. My government and my country will consider it, and do what is right respecting it. . . .

Notwithstanding all I have stated, it is *possible* that the dey may not proceed to extremities towards me, or commit hostilities on our commerce and citizens. . . . But I have thought it my duty to guard as much as possible against the evil, by giving notice to our vessels which may be in this sea, as well as those in the Atlantick; for, at present, there is nothing to prevent their cruisers from passing the straits. . . .

With sentiments of the highest respect, and most sincere attachment, I have the honour to be, sir, &c.

Tobias Lear

1813 Napoleon's Retreat from Moscow
Dispatch from U.S. Minister to Russia John Quincy Adams to Secretary of State James Monroe

John Quincy Adams has been variously described as America's first "career diplomat" and as its greatest diplomat. He served successively as U.S. minister to the Netherlands, Prussia, Russia, and Great Britain before returning to Washington to become secretary of state and president. Adams penned this dispatch while serving as the first U.S. minister accredited to Russia. It was written about six weeks after French emperor Napoleon Bonaparte's disastrous retreat, just as the full scope of the defeat was becoming known. Adams comments on events in Paris and elsewhere as well as at the Russian court, analyzes the impact of the retreat on both Russia and France, and predicts with accuracy the likely consequences for Napoleon.

St. Petersburg, 2 February 1813

Sir,

. . . The Catastrophe of the French armies has been more complete than the imagination of the most sanguine of their Enemies ever anticipated, and as terrible as the most inveterate could have desired. Their losses by the most moderate computations exceed three hundred thousand men.

The Emperor Napoleon personally succeeded in making his escape, and travelling with equal secrecy and rapidity, without guards, without attendants, accompanied only by the Duke of Venice and passing under his name reached Paris late at Night on the 18th Decr. . . . During his absence, and while he was yet in the Career of victory, a formidable conspiracy against his Government had been defeated only by a premature attempt to accomplish its object. When the disasters of his armies had become too great to admit of concealment, they were partially acknowledged in a Bulletin which was published just before his arrival at Paris, and which produced symptoms of popular fermentation threatening the stability of his authority. The project of restoring the throne of France to the House of Bourbon is again strenuously urged in the English Ministerial papers; that of reducing France to its ancient limits as when governed by the Bourbons, though less distinctly avowed, is inseparably connected with it. They are both naturally favoured here, and certainly at no period since the commencement of the French Revolution have the Circumstances of the times given greater appearance of plausibility to the design.

The war in its progress has been extremely destructive and distressing to Russia, but its result has been not only to deliver her entirely from that terror of the French Power, which had spread itself so universally over the whole Continent of Europe, but place in the hands of Russia herself that predominant influence which France had been so long and so perseveringly striving to establish. It is scarcely possible but that henceforth Russia should be the arbitress of Europe *by Land*. Her loss of Human lives in this dreadful struggle has probably been greater than that of France. Her loss of property has certainly been more considerable. But her losses have not been in the sinews of her strength. Those of France have been in the vitals of her military power. The spell of the Emperor Napoleon's name is not yet totally dissolved. His friends yet cherish a vague and general hope, and his Enemies feel an involuntary fear that his transcendent *Genius* (so they term it) will yet burst forth, chain down Fortune at his feet, and range the world again, conquering and to conquer. I see no substantial ground for such a hope or such a fear. The highest probabilities now are that his fall will be as great as his elevation has been extraordinary, and with regard to his Genius, if it ever surpassed that of other Generals and Statesmen, it has most assuredly deserted him in the undertaking, and in the execution of the Russian War. . . . That he may still maintain his authority in France it would be presumptuous to deny. That he may again collect armies and win battles is altogether possible. . . . But in the tenour of human history, when Fortune has once turned her back upon those to whom she has been most lavish of her favours, she never takes them to her arms again. . . .

> I am with great respect
> Sir,
> Your very humble and obedt. Servt.
>
> John Quincy Adams

1814 Treaty of Ghent Signed

Dispatch from U.S. Plenipotentiaries John Quincy Adams, James A. Bayard, Henry Clay, Jonathan Russell, Albert Gallatin to Acting Secretary of State James Monroe

The War of 1812, a conflict unpopular among many Americans and Britons, erupted largely over maritime disputes between the United States and Great Britain. During the Napoleonic Wars (1804–1815), the United States profited considerably by shipping supplies to both sides. But this policy brought the United States into conflict with Great Britain. The conflict was heightened by the British policy of impressment, or the practice of forcibly taking suspected British sailors from American ships.

The United States and Britain also were at loggerheads in the American West after it was discovered that the British had been supplying weapons to hostile Indians. In 1812 the United States finally declared war, even though two days before the declaration Great Britain, unknown to the United States, had altered its maritime policies.

After two years of inconclusive fighting, the combatants signed the Treaty of Ghent, which ended the war and restored the situation to exactly what it had been before the conflict, with no territorial advances on either side. Other issues in contention at Ghent were the status of fisheries and the status of navigation on the Mississippi River. The American negotiators were led by John Quincy Adams. They also included Henry Clay, one of the prominent "War Hawks" who had petitioned for war, and Albert Gallatin, who had been vehemently opposed to the conflict. This dispatch reports the conclusion of the peace treaty.

Ghent, December 25, 1814

Sir:

We have the honor of transmitting, herewith, one of the three copies of the treaty of peace between Great Britain and the United States, signed last evening by the plenipotentiaries of His Britannic Majesty and by us.

The papers, of which copies are likewise now forwarded, will exhibit to you so fully the progress of the negotiation . . . that few additional remarks from us will be necessary. . . .

From the time when the project of the treaty presented by us was returned with the proposed alterations, it was apparent that, unless new pretensions on the part of Great Britain should be advanced, the only important differences remaining to be discussed were those relating to the mutual restoration of territory taken during the war, to the navigation of the Mississippi by British subjects, and to the right of the people of the

United States to the fisheries within the British jurisdiction. Instead of a general restitution of captured territory, which we had proposed, the British Government, at first, wished to confine it to the territory taken by either party belonging to the other. On our objecting that this would make each party the judge whether territory taken did or did not belong to the other, and thereby occasion new disputes, they acknowledged it to be their object that each party should, until a decision had taken place with respect to the title, retain possession of all the territory claimed by both parties, which might have been taken by such party during the war. They proposed, however, to limit the exception from mutual restitution to the islands in the bay of Passamaquoddy. As it had been on both sides admitted that the title to these islands was disputed, and as the method of settling amicably those disputes was provided for in the treaty . . . we finally consented, as an alternative preferable to the continuance of the war, to this exception, upon condition that it not be understood as impairing, in any manner, the right of the United States to these islands. . . .

At the first conference on the 8th of August, the British plenipotentiaries had notified to us that the British Government did not intend, henceforth, to allow to the people of the United States, without an equivalent, the liberty to fish, and to dry and cure fish, within the exclusive British jurisdiction. . . . And, in their note of the 19th of August, the British plenipotentiaries had demanded a new stipulation to secure to British subjects the right of navigating the Mississippi. . . . Our instructions had forbidden us to suffer our right to the fisheries to be brought into discussion, and . . . no new stipulation was necessary to secure to the subjects of Great Britain the right of navigating the Mississippi. . . . On the other hand, no stipulation was necessary to secure to the people of the United states the liberty to fish, and to dry and cure fish, within the exclusive jurisdiction of Great Britain. . . . To place both points beyond all future controversy, a majority of us determined to offer to admit an article confirming both rights; or, we offered at the same time to be silent in the treaty upon both, and to leave out altogether the article defining the boundary from the Lake of the Woods, westward. They finally agreed to this last proposal, but not until they had proposed an article stipulating for a future negotiation for an equivalent to be given by Great Britain for the navigation of the Mississippi, and by the United States for the liberty as to the fisheries within British jurisdiction. This article was unnecessary, with respect to its professed object, since both Governments had it in their power, without it, to negotiate upon these subjects if they pleased. We rejected it, although its adoption would have secured the boundary of the forty-ninth degree of latitude west of the Lake of the Woods, because it would have been a formal abandonment, on our part, of our claim to the liberty as to the fisheries, recognized by the treaty of 1783. . . .

To guard against any accident which might happen in the transmission of a single copy of the treaty to the United States, the British plenipotentiaries have consented to execute it in triplicate. . . .

We have the honor to be, very respectfully, sir, your most humble and obedient servants,

> John Quincy Adams,
> J. A. Bayard,
> H. Clay,
> Jona. Russell,
> Albert Gallatin

1815 Waterloo

Dispatch from U.S. Secretary of Legation in France Henry Jackson to Secretary of State James Monroe

As John Quincy Adams had predicted, the fortunes of French emperor Napoleon Bonaparte declined rapidly after his retreat from Moscow (see "Napoleon's Retreat from Moscow," p. 71). Within eighteen months, Paris fell to European forces allied against Napoleon and the emperor abdicated and went into exile on the Mediterranean island of Elba. In 1815, after less than a year in exile, Napoleon staged a comeback. He landed with a small force in the south of France, quickly gathered thousands of adherents, and soon was back in power in Paris. His restored rule lasted a hundred days, until his defeat at the Battle of Waterloo on June 18, 1815. No U.S. minister was accredited to France at the time, but the secretary of the U.S. legation in Paris filed a brief dispatch reporting the great event. After the battle Napoleon was exiled to the island of St. Helena in the South Atlantic, where he died six years later.

> Paris, 24 June 1815

Sir:

A severe attack of disease has kept me to my room & in a great measure to my bed during the past week. I am to day certain that its effect will be temporary and that my recovery will be immediate.

The Emperor commenced the campaign with some prospects of success. These, however, were followed by a dreadful reverse—and the army under him was, it may be said, annihilated near Brussels in an attack of the English under [Sir Arthur Wellesley, the Duke of] Wellington. No estimate of the loss has been yet made. Conjecture rates it from 50 to a hundred thousand men. The Moniteurs sent you will give you the official account and the events to the present day.

The Commissioners to treat with the powers are set out this morning. Among them are General La Fayette, La Foret, and Benjamin Constant. The three others I have not heard the names of. They are empowered to make peace, I understand, should this issue rest on the total exclusion of the Napoleon Dynasty. Paris which manifested some days since some symptoms of uneasiness appears now perfectly tranquil.

Have the goodness for to excuse this short note & believe me with sincere respect

Your most obedient servant,
Henry Jackson

PART II

Years of U.S. Expansion: 1816–1860

The Treaty of Guadalupe Hidalgo, signed in February 1848, extended American sovereignty from Texas to California. The treaty was negotiated by U.S. Executive Agent in Mexico Nicholas Trist, who in undertaking the negotiation defied instructions recalling him to Washington.

1818 Description of Oregon and California
Dispatch from Special Diplomatic Agent for the Columbia River and Agent for Commerce and Seamen in Lima John B. Prevost to Secretary of State John Quincy Adams

The American flag was first planted at the mouth of the Columbia River by explorers Meriwether Lewis and William Clark in 1805. Several years later an American trading company controlled by John Jacob Astor established a trading post called Astoria—later Ft. George—near the site. The post was captured by the British during the War of 1812 but returned, somewhat belatedly, under the terms of the Treaty of Ghent (see "Treaty of Ghent Signed," p. 73). The selection of the U.S. agent in Peru to travel north and retake possession is an indication of how remote Oregon was at the time. In this unusual dispatch Special Diplomatic Agent Prevost provides a rare account of the Pacific coast and argues that the United States, under the leadership of President James Monroe (1817–1825), should move to forestall Russian activity in the area.

Monte Rey, New California,
November 11, 1818

Sir:

In conformity with mine of the 27th July, which I had the honor to address to your Department from Lima, I proceeded in His Britannic Majesty's sloop of war Blossom to the mouth of the Columbia, and entered the river on the 1st of October following. A few days thereafter, to wit, on the 6th, as you will perceive by referring to a copy of the act of surrender, . . . I received in the name and on the part of the United States the possession of the establishment at Fort George, made under the first article of the treaty of Ghent, by Captain Hickey, of the royal navy, in compliance with the orders of the Prince Regent for that purpose. . . . The British flag was thereupon lowered, and that of the United States hoisted in its stead, where it now waves in token both of possession and of sovereignty.

The establishment . . . has been considerably extended and improved by the agents of the Northwest Company of Canada, who will continue to occupy and protect it under our flag, until it shall please the President to give orders for their removal. . . .

The bay is spacious, contains several anchoring places in a sufficient depth of water, and is by no means so difficult of ingress as has been represented. . . . It is true that there is a bar extending across the mouth of the river, at either extremity of which are, at times, appalling breakers; but it is equally true that it offers, at the lowest tides, a depth of twenty-one feet of water throughout a passage exempt from them of nearly a league in width.

The ocean teems with the otter, (mustela,) the seal, and the whale; while the main land affords, in innumerable quantities, the common otter, (musk,) the bear, the buffalo, and the whole variety of deer.

It has been observed by those exploring this coast that the climate to the southward of 53° assumes a mildness unknown in the same latitude on the eastern side of the continent. . . . The mercury during the winter seldom descends below the freezing point; when it does so, it is rarely stationary for any number of days, and the severity of the season is more determined by the quantity of water than by its congelation. The rains usually commence with November, and continue to fall partially until the latter end of March or beginning of April. A benign spring succeeds; and when the summer heats obtain, they are so tempered by showers as seldom to suspend vegetation. I found it luxuriant on my arrival, and during a fortnight's stay experienced no change of weather to retard its course. The soil is good; all the cereal, gramina, and tuberous plants may be cultivated with advantage, and the waters abound in salmon, sturgeon, and other varieties of fish.

The natives, in appearance as well as in character, differ essentially from those with us. They are less in stature, more delicately formed, and singular in the shape of the head, which, in infancy, is compressed between two small plates of wood or metal, so as in its growth to obtain the semblance of a wedge. They are inquisitive, cheerful, sagacious, possess fewer of the vices attributed to the savage, and are less addicted to cruelties in war; scalping is unknown to them, and a prisoner suffers the infliction of no other punishment than that of becoming a slave to the captor; but as they neither sow nor reap, an observer cannot easily discern in what the servitude consists. The wants of the one are supplied by his own address in the use of the bow and the spear, while those of the other require the same efforts and equal skill for their gratification.

. . . I met with several of the natives who had heretofore volunteered on board of some one of our vessels in their fur excursions, two of whom had acquired a sufficient knowledge of our language to speak it with some ease, and were extremely solicitous to embark with us.

I regret that I could not collect sufficient data upon which to ground an estimate of the furs gathered on the Columbia; it was impossible, for reasons that are obvious. . . .

Perhaps I have gone too much into detail; but it appeared to me that, by exhibiting the importance of the position only, I should not have fulfilled the object of the President; that it was equally incumbent upon me to present a view of the country, of its inhabitants, of its resources, of its approach, and of its means of defence. . . .

The speculations of [German naturalist Alexander von] Humboldt, his glowing descriptions of the soil and climate of this province, have probably given a new direction to the ambition of Russia, and determined its Emperor to the acquisition of empire in America. Until 1816 the settlements of the Power did not reach to the southward of 55°, and were of no consideration, although dignified by them with the title of Russian America. In the commencement of that year two distinct establishments were made, of a different and of a more imposing character: the first at Atooi, one of the Sandwich islands; the other in this vicinity, within a few leagues of San Francisco, the most northerly possession of Spain, in 37° 5'. . . . Two Russian ships left this on their way thither a few days anterior to our arrival; the one having on board mechanics of every description, together with implements of husbandry. We passed sufficiently near the spot assigned to it to distinguish the coast with some precision, and ascertained that it was an open road—a circumstance that renders the position liable to many objections, if intended to be permanent; in other respects, the choice is judicious for an infant colony. It enjoys a climate still milder than that of Columbia, is environed by a beautiful country, and its proximity to an old settlement enables the Russian to partake of the numerous herds of black cattle and horses that have been there multiplying for the last fifty years. The port of St. Francis is one of the most convenient, extensive, and safe in the world, wholly without defence, and in the neighborhood of a feeble, diffused, and disaffected population. Under all these circumstances, may we not infer views to the early possession of this harbor, and ultimately to the sovereignty of entire California? Surely the growth of a race on these shores, scarcely emerged from the savage state, guided by a chief who seeks not to emancipate but to enthral, is an event to be deprecated—an event, the mere apprehension of which ought to excite the jealousies of the United States, so far, at least, as to induce the cautionary measure of preserving a station which may serve as a barrier to a northern aggrandizement.

I have not been able to gather other information respecting the settlement at Atooi than that of an assurance of its existence. . . .

These islands yield the sandal wood, so much esteemed in China, and have been resorted to by our vessels for years past, not only in search of this valuable article, but of the necessary stock of fresh provisions to supply the crew during their cruise on the northwest coast. How far this intercourse may be affected hereafter by this encroachment, is also a subject for the consideration of the President. . . .

I have the honor to be, with great consideration, your very humble servant,

J. B. Prevost

1819   Assisting an American Seaman Stranded in Bermuda

Dispatch from U.S. Agent for Commerce and Seamen in Bermuda W. R. Higinbothom to Secretary of State John Quincy Adams

A continuing responsibility of American representatives in foreign ports was to see to the needs of stranded or destitute seamen. The standing consular instructions issued in 1815 enjoined U.S. agents and consuls to "be careful to return the seamen to the United States as soon as possible, that their health and morals may be preserved by employment." Consuls were authorized to expend public monies for the relief of seamen, using "economy and discernment in distinguishing . . . the profligate and idle from the meritorious in distress." An expenditure of up to ten dollars was allowed to pay a stranded seaman's passage home.

St. Georges, Bermuda
25th May, 1819

Sir:

I have the honor to report to you that Stephen Snow, Master of the American Schooner Minerva, left in this Island Ezra Sweet, one of his crew, a citizen of the United States, in consequence of his being unable to do duty, a fall from the mast-head rendering him incapable. He was put on shore at the west end of the Island, without my knowledge, the Captain taking away all his clothes and leaving him perfectly destitute. The vessel never having been reported, by which means he becomes a charge on the Government of the United States, as I must find him clothes and a passage home. The vessel, as he states, at the time of departure owed him one half month's pay, say eight dollars. I have reported this to the collector of the Custom at Boston, and have the honor to be,

Sir,
Your most obedient
Servant

W. R. Higinbothom

1820–1821   The Acquisition of Florida

Dispatches from U.S. Representatives in Spain and Florida

The United States and Spain signed the Transcontinental Treaty in 1819. The treaty delineated the border between United States and Spanish possessions throughout North America. A key provision was the cession of

Florida from Spain to the United States. In the first of these two dispatches the U.S. minister in Madrid reports secret intelligence that Spain's King Ferdinand VII ratified the treaty and annulled earlier Spanish land grants in Florida. In the second dispatch Maj. Gen. Andrew Jackson, appointed U.S. commissioner to receive West Florida, reports to the secretary of state the successful transfer of the territory.

News from Madrid

*From U.S. Minister to Spain John Forsyth to
Secretary of State John Quincy Adams*

Madrid, October 5, 1820

Dear Sir:

Three days since the political commission made a report to the Cortes, and this day in secret session, that body advised the King to cede the Floridas to the United States. They have also declared null and void the cessions of land to Alagon, &c., although the treaty of February, 1819, should not be ratified. I presume I shall receive from the Minister of State early information of the King's ratification of the treaty.

I am, dear sir, sincerely and respectfully, your obedient servant,

John Forsyth

Taking Possession

*From U.S. Commissioner Andrew Jackson to
Secretary of State John Quincy Adams*

Pensacola, July 17, 1821

Sir:

. . . I have now to inform you that, at 10 o'clock of this day, the province of West Florida, with its dependencies, &c., was delivered to me in due form by Don José Callava, the commissioner on the part of the King of Spain.

I shall take the earliest opportunity to communicate the circumstances preceding and attending the surrender. Suffice it to say, for the present, that it was accomplished in the most friendly and harmonious manner, although at one moment, from a misapprehension on both sides, I did not flatter myself with so happy an issue.

Some ordinances for the better government of the town and province, and in fact which are absolutely necessary, have been prepared; copies of these, as well as a report of my whole proceedings as commissioner for receiving possession of Florida, will be forwarded to you as soon as possible, and I am satisfied they will be found strictly within the powers with which I am clothed by the President.

None of the officers appointed by the President for this province have yet joined me; whether any of those appointed for East Florida have arrived, I am not certainly informed.

With great consideration, &c.

Andrew Jackson

1821 Surrender of Lima to San Martín: "South America . . . Forever Free"

Dispatch from U.S. Agent for Commerce and Seamen in Valparaiso Michael Hogan to Secretary of State John Quincy Adams

The turmoil caused by the Napoleonic Wars (1804–1815) in Europe had direct repercussions in Latin America. When French emperor Napoleon Bonaparte's forces occupied Spain, revolts erupted in many of Spain's American provinces. After the fall of Napoleon, Spain regained control of its former colonies but could not stamp out the spirit of independence. Revolutions swept South America, from Venezuela to Chile. One of the great figures of the independence period was José de San Martín. San Martín helped to liberate the Rio de la Plata (now Argentina), then crossed the mountains to liberate Chile. From Chile he moved north to Peru, seat of Spain's viceroy and center of Spanish administration in South America. The Spanish withdrawal from Lima before the army of San Martín marked the end of Spanish rule on the continent. The independence of Peru was proclaimed on July 28, 1821. In this dispatch the U.S. representative in Chile provides the first fragmentary report on the unfolding of events in Peru.

August 18, 1821

Sir:

I have now the honor to inform you that, on the 13th instant, a despatch vessel arrived here from Callao . . . with advices to this Government of the surrender of Lima to General San Martin, and of the inhabitants having sworn to the independence of the place. On the 12th July the Spanish troops proceeded to the mountains with their general, who first placed a garrison of two thousand men in Callao, which place had not surrendered when the despatch came away, but could not be expected to hold out, as there was not more than a week's provision in the fortress, which was to be attacked by land and by sea from the squadron. The sufferings of the people in Lima for want of bread-stuffs and other food had been great; but there is no public gazette issued explanatory of the proceedings, and private letters are short and unsatisfactory. It is impossible to say to what extent they had carried their attachment to royalty, or rather their opposition to being conquered by the forces of Chili, whom they had even treated and considered as an inferior people, not entitled to the enjoyment of equal rights with themselves. To expect them to submit tamely to the dictation of this slip of country is, I believe, more than will be realized, although there can never be any doubt of the country of South America facing the Pacific ocean being forever free from the Government of Old Spain.

. . . I send this letter in duplicate by two ships bound this day to London, in the hope that either may be put on board of some vessel bound to the United States.

M. Hogan

1821 Independence of Mexico

Dispatch from U.S. Commercial Agent in Mexico James Smith Wilcocks to Secretary of State John Quincy Adams

The pattern of events leading to independence in Mexico, or New Spain, was much the same as in the rest of Spanish America. Following a revolt in Mexico in 1808 in response to French emperor Napoleon Bonaparte's occupation of Spain, the Spanish reasserted control, only to be faced with a new and successful revolution in 1821. The U.S. commercial agent in Mexico presents a colorful account of that country's struggle for independence. He attributes the revolution's success to Gen. Agustin de Iturbide, one of "the greatest heroes that ever existed." Unknown to the U.S. agent, however, Iturbide soon would arrange to have himself crowned Emperor Augustin I, only to be overthrown less than a year later by one of his co-revolutionists, Antonio Lopez de Santa Ana.

Mexico, October 25, 1821

Sir:

The love of my country, the spring of every noble and generous action, induces me to communicate to you, for the information of the President, and for the benefit that may result to the Government and citizens of the United States, the following circumstantial and exact account of the happy revolution that has lately occurred in this kingdom of New Spain, which, by the blessing of God, the intrepidity, talents, and exertions of its patriotic chief, General Don Augustin Iturbide, the enlightened policy of its mother country, and the liberal and philanthropic ideas of its late captain general, Don Juan O'Donoju, has ended in its complete and entire emancipation.

That you may have a clear and distinct view of the subject, be fully impressed with the justice of the cause of this hitherto afflicted and oppressed people, and have also a general idea of the face of the country, its inhabitants, production, &c., it may not be improper to state that, since its conquest, (which if my memory serves me, was in the year 1521,) it has been governed by sixty-two viceroys, and innumerable commandant generals, governors, and superintendents of provinces, who, according to general tradition, have been, with very few exceptions, as many merciless and mercenary tyrants, the rapacity and unfeeling barbarity of whom nothing could have withstood for such a length of time but a land enriched by the beautiful hand of nature to a most extraordinary degree, and a people born and brought up, until of late, in all the intolerance of superstition and ignorance, and accustomed from their earliest infancy to the innumerable, and I may say almost incredible impositions of both church and state.

Few foreigners have, perhaps, had an opportunity of seeing as much of the kingdom as myself, having travelled on horseback from the port of Guaymas, on the Gulf of California, to almost every part of Sonora, and afterwards through the provinces and superintendencies of New Biscay, New Galicia, San Luis Potosi, Queretaro, and Mexico, to this city, a distance at least of seven hundred leagues, passing through all the principal cities, visiting the most celebrated mines, and conversing familiarly with all classes of people. . . .

Before the insurrection of the year 1810, the kingdom contained six millions of inhabitants; and it is worthy of remark, that Providence has been no less lavish in the distribution of her gifts as respects mankind, than in the fertility and production of the earth; the natives of this country, not excepting even the Indians, being endowed with a quickness of perception and ability to acquire and make themselves masters of the arts and sciences that is very notable, and far exceeds that of the inhabitants of Old Spain, and perhaps many other countries. At the above-mentioned period, the kingdom may be said to have been at its acme of prosperity; the royal revenue exceeding $20,000,000, and the money coined at the mint of this city upwards of $28,000,000 annually; it has, however, ever since been on the decline, in consequence of the devastations committed by both parties in the long and cruel war carried on between the Europeans and Americans, so that the population cannot now be computed at more than four millions, the revenue at more than half of what it was. . . .

I have been informed that a very correct history of this insurrection . . . has been written . . . and published; it is useless, therefore, to say more on the subject than that its commencement was undoubtedly caused by the abuses daily committed in all branches of the Government in this kingdom, by the disorder in which Spain was thrown in consequence of the invasion of the French, and by the imprudent measures adopted in this city. . . .

Among those that contributed most to quell the insurrection was the before-mentioned General Don Augustin Iturbide, then colonel of the regiment of Celaya, and native of the city of Valladolid, in the province of Mechoacan. Born of European parents, and animated by a mistaken zeal, he was induced to embrace the royal cause, and, with a fervor and impetuosity peculiar to his character, committed many arbitrary and violent acts, that in a great degree tarnished what would otherwise have been deemed brilliant achievements, and over which it is necessary to draw a veil, his subsequent conduct having entirely effaced them from the memory even of those most aggrieved. Indeed, it would appear that a sense of the injustice he had committed, and innate conviction of the impropriety of adhering to the party he had espoused, and a remorse of conscience, were the principal causes of the change in his political sentiments; for we see him all at once assuming a different character, and at a moment when his sovereign had heaped upon him innumerable honors.

The impossibility of re-establishing peace and quietness in the kingdom by the force of arms was fully ascertained, . . . the country being in a complete state of revolt, and full of chieftains that commanded from three to six hundred, and even a thousand men each, and bands of robbers that infested the highways in September, 1816. . . .

The crisis was too important and obvious to escape the penetration of our hero, Iturbide, who was also instigated to an immediate execution of the plan he had, in consequence, formed, of liberating his country forever from its thraldom, by the mutiny of several of the officers . . . and by the departure of a convoy for Acapulco with near a million of dollars, that was intended to be embarked in a ship bound to Manilla, that he resolved on detaining. He immediately, therefore, concerted his measures with the clergy and friars, and, with the specious pretext of upholding them in their privileges and immunities, secured their favor and protection. He also communicated his design to such of the governors of the provinces as he thought likely to aid him in the execution of it, and, on his arrival in Iguala, persuaded a great part of the troops under his command to join him in the undertaking. . . . [T]hus prepared, he openly declared the independence of the kingdom, swearing it in the most solemn manner at the head of his army, in the said town of Iguala, on the 24th day of February last, seizing, at the same time, and appropriating to the use of the nation, the treasure destined for the Manilla ship. . . .

The cry of independence was no sooner raised in Iguala than it spread in all parts, and an army was formed in the provinces of Puebla and Vera Cruz, by the Colonels Herrera, Bravo, and Santa Ana, that took possession of the cities of Orizaba, Cordova, and Xalapa. . . .

At Guanajuato, where is one of the richest minerals in the kingdom, a mint was established, that proved afterwards very serviceable to the Independents, and injurious to the royal party; the silver from all the neighboring mines taking the direction of that city instead of Mexico. . . .

While these scenes of glory were achieving in the provinces of Puebla and Vera Cruz, the siege of the city of Queretaro, one of the most beautiful in the kingdom, and the third in rank as respects size, opulence, and commerce, was pushed with much vigor by Iturbide in person. . . . This happy occurrence for the Independents was a deathblow to the Government. . . .

The city of Puebla de los Angeles, the largest in the kingdom except Mexico, next attracted the attention of General Iturbide. . . . Puebla was all-important to the Government in the critical situation in which it found itself, being one of the chain of fortified towns that connect Mexico with Vera Cruz, to which port it had resolved to retire with the European part of the army and inhabitants, in the event of not being able to sustain itself in the capital. Puebla was, therefore, well garrisoned, served with an excellent park of artillery, and defended with many cannon of a large calibre. . . . Iturbide, however, . . . surrounded the city with so many troops that resistance would have been nothing short of an act of madness; it therefore capitulated.

On the surrender of Puebla, the army of Iturbide, which had now augmented to the number of about eighteen thousand, and which was composed entirely of veteran troops that had been disciplined in the King's service, and had gone over to him clandestinely, or joined him on the fall of the various cities he had conquered, received orders to march in separate columns to different towns in the neighborhood of Mexico, with the intention of manifesting to the Government of that city the folly of any further resistance. . . .

To complete the independence of the kingdom, there . . . followed almost immediately the surrender of Acapulco, the castle of Perote, and Vera Cruz; the two former of which capitulated soon after, and the latter has, without doubt, ere this followed their example, advice having been received yesterday by the Government that it was on the eve of surrendering. The province of Guatemala, which has always been a separate viceroyalty from that of Mexico, was also sensible of the general impulse, and, desirous of becoming an integral part of the Mexican empire, has likewise sworn independence, which, without doubt, will extend to its neighboring provinces, Honduras, Nicaragua, Costa Rica, and Veragua, so that we may from this instant consider North America, with the exception of Canada, as divided into two grand and important commonwealths, that may, with the aid of those that are forming in South America be able, in the course of time, to give the law to the opposite continent.

. . . I shall, now that I have finished my narrative, take the liberty to add a few remarks, and to say, in the first place, that the revolution which I have attempted to describe is not one of those that have been accomplished by means of unbridled passions, cruelty, rancor, or revenge, but, on the contrary, has, from its commencement, been accompanied with brotherly love, patriotism, disinterestedness, truth, and good faith; so that the more I reflect on its origin and progress, the more is my admiration excited, and the more am I tempted to exclaim that America has produced two of the greatest heroes that ever existed—Washington and Iturbide. Secondly, that the new Government is established on a sure and solid foundation, the people being highly delighted with it, . . . the empire is . . . governed by a regency of five of its most distinguished and enlightened statesmen, who have elected General Iturbide President, and appointed him commander-in-chief of the land and sea forces, and by a convention of thirty-six of the principal personages in the empire, as respects talents, rank, and riches. The independence is to be sworn in this city on the 27th instant, and the Cortes are to meet on the 24th of February next, the anniversary of the declaration in Iguala. In the mean time, the convention will be employed in enacting the most salutary decrees; and among those already passed is one declaring the commerce of this empire free to all nations; another, doing away [with] all the arbitrary taxes, impositions, and excises imposed by the former Government; a third, reducing the duties from sixteen to six per cent.; a fourth, for the encouragement of the miners, relinquishing to them the quota of silver formerly paid to the King, with other imposts that amounted to seventeen per cent.; so that many poor minerals that could not be worked before, can now be used to advantage; and a fifth, recognising and making the new Government responsible for the debt contracted by the old one, of thirty-six millions of dollars.

That there is a strong bias in the minds of the people of this country in favor of the Government and citizens of the United States in preference to all other nations, is beyond a doubt. . . . On this subject I have had various conferences with the leading members of the administration, whose sentiments will be fully explained to you shortly by Don Juan Manuel de Elizalda, the minister plenipotentiary that is already named, and now preparing to go to Washington, where I have no doubt he will be received and acknowledged as the representative of a free and independent nation; the Mexican empire being so at this time to all intents and purposes. . . .

Your most obedient,
humble servant,

James Smith Wilcocks

1824 Suppression of the Slave Trade
Dispatch from U.S. Minister to Great Britain Richard Rush to Secretary of State John Quincy Adams

Slavery was abolished in British dominions in 1807 and throughout the British Empire in 1833. The United States outlawed the slave trade in 1808 and in 1820 declared it to be piracy, with offenders subject to the death penalty. Shortly thereafter the United States and Britain negotiated a formal convention for cooperation in suppressing the slave trade. Unfortunately, U.S. enforcement efforts over the next several decades were lax. In this dispatch U.S. Minister Richard Rush describes part of his successful negotiation with the British.

London, March 15, 1824

Sir:

I have the honor to inform you that I concluded and signed, on behalf of the United States, the day before yesterday, a convention with this Government for the suppression of the slave trade, which instrument I herewith transmit to your hands, to be laid before the President. . . .

The essential principles of our plan, as gathered from my best attention to it, in connexion with your instructions, I considered to be: 1st. That this nation was to declare the slave trade piracy by act of Parliament. 2d. That [any] captured vessel was to be sent to her own country for trial before its own tribunals, and never before those of the capturing power. 3d. That no individual belonging to the crew was ever to be taken out of the accused vessel. 4th. That the capturing officer should be laid under the most effective responsibility for his conduct, in all respects. 5th. That no merchant vessel under the protection or in the presence of a ship-of-war of her own nation was ever to be visited by a ship-of-war of the other nation. I informed the British plenipotentiaries, unreservedly, that I could consent to nothing that did not give full security to each and all of the above principles. I knew that some of them bespoke a great change in pre-existing principles and usages under the maritime code of the world; but the change was not for light but high objects, and was believed by my Government to be the only means by which they could be adequately and permanently secured.

. . . [T]heir counter-projet . . . acceded to all the principles that are above recapitulated, adopting, too, and largely, the language in which our own articles had been framed. . . .

The British plenipotentiaries, moreover, remarked that the whole convention exhibited a preponderance of concession on the side of Great Britain in accommodation to the principles and views of the United States. At our instance she was about, by a new statute of her realm, to make the slave trade piracy; at our instance she agreed that the captured vessel and crew should be sent to their own country for trial, a course also new to all her past maritime doctrines. . . . They said, too, that the preponderance of burden under the convention would lie with Great Britain, both in the greater number of public ships that she would employ in the suppression of the traffic, and in the fact of the United States not having colonial dependencies, as Britain had, to serve as ready depots for those detected in it. I was far from lending my concurrence to these sentiments, which were to be taken with their just qualifications. The occasion, I remarked, was one where, instead of each nation pushing adverse rights, or striving for superior advantages, it ought rather to be considered that each was equally and spontaneously surrendering up a portion of its anterior system; each moving under one and the same impulse, towards one and the same object; each proposing to itself no other interests than those of benevolence and justice; no other gain (yet how great the gain!) than that of protecting the innocent, and laying prostrate the guilty. It was a negotiation with this distinguishing feature, that it looked exclusively to the benefit of a third party, assuming reciprocal duties and burdens for its sake, and flinging aside, as alien to the benign spirit in which it was conceived and undertaken, every selfish end or feeling. To the obligations, no less elevated than interesting, that sprung from such a negotiation, it was believed that neither party was insensible, and that both stood alike anxious to hail its favorable results. In mentioning the sentiments which the British plenipotentiaries expressed it must not be understood that I report them as having been uttered in complaint; and it would be an omission inexcusable in me were I not to add that they cordially and zealously responded to the enlarged and animating objects of the international compact which we were endeavoring to adjust. . . .

I write . . . with a desire to secure for the convention as early an arrival at Washington as possible. . . . [S]hould the convention . . . meet acceptance in the eyes of my Government, and become, happily, the era of a new and saving spirit introduced into the laws of nations for the relief of Africa, her redeemed and grateful children will have cause to pour out the fervent thanksgiving of their hearts towards those Christian powers that have at length been enabled, and rejoice that they have been enabled, to arrest the portentous desolation that for long ages has swept over their land, filling it with the concentration of every human woe. Then, at last may we all hope, and not in vain, to see their tears dried up, their sufferings turned to joy, their groans to songs of benediction. . . .

I have the honor to remain, with very great respect, your obedient servant,

Richard Rush

1824   Pirates of the Caribbean
Dispatch from U.S. Agent of Commerce and Seamen in Porto Rico and Cuba Thomas Randall to Secretary of State John Quincy Adams

For at least the first fifty years of U.S. independence pirates continued to prey on American shipping along what was once known as the Spanish Main. American representatives in the Caribbean reported frequently on the depredations of pirates and just as frequently requested U.S. naval action to deal with the problem. This dispatch is typical of many from the period.

Havana, July 5, 1824

Sir:

The last letter which I had the honor to address to you was dated the 1st instant, and despatched via Charleston, by the brig Trader, which sailed the ensuing day. In that letter I advised you that information had been received at this place of the re-appearance of the pirates off the port of Matanzas, by which the sailing of a number of merchant vessels had been prevented. Recent captures made by those pirates off that port confirm the truth of the above report.

   Two American vessels are certainly known to have been captured and plundered, and there are reports of the capture of three others. Of the former, the brig Castor, of Portland, Capt. Hood, has arrived at this port. This vessel was captured entering the bay of Matanzas by seven men in an open boat[,] was taken thence to port "Escondido," in the neighborhood, where the pirates were joined by a large party from the shore with boats and horses, with the assistance of which the brig was plundered of everything portable or valuable, including all the clothes of the captain and his crew. The cargo being principally lumber, the amount taken from the brig was by no means considerable. The captain and his men were, as usual, most severely and cruelly beaten. This boat had previously captured, on the same morning, the brig Betsy, Done, of Newport; and after plundering the vessel and casting off her boats they set her on fire in several places and abandoned her. The crew succeeded in extinguishing the fire, and thus preserved themselves from the horrid death designed for them by their merciless captors. I thought it my duty to give you the earliest intelligence of those depredations, however imperfect in its details.

   The temporary absence of the United States cruisers from their usual station has emboldened those men to renew their piracies. The necessity which has caused this very short and casual absence of the whole American squadron from the neighborhood of Matanzas and this port is much to be regretted. Very great alarm prevails in this place among the masters of vessels, several of whom are fearful of putting to sea without convoy. A British cutter, the Grecian, has just arrived at this port. Mr. Mountain, our vice consul, solicited her commander to make a short cruise to Matanzas in pursuit of those pirates. He promised to sail this evening with that object.

This letter will be sent by the steamship Robert Fulton, which will sail for New York early to-morrow morning. I regret that the short stay of this vessel prevents me from enlarging my letter on this very interesting topic, as I had designed. I have been endeavoring to collect all the facts I could arrive at in relation to the piracies committed from this island, and shall take occasion to write more fully upon the subject by the earliest safe conveyance.

I have the honor to be, with the greatest consideration and respect, sir, your obedient servant,

Thomas Randall

1827 Consular Service on the Western Frontier: "The Indians Stole My Horses"

Dispatch from U.S. Consul in Texas David Dickson to Secretary of State Henry Clay

The United States appointed consuls at various towns in the Mexican province of Texas beginning in 1827. American ministers were accredited to the Republic of Texas from 1836 until Texas statehood in 1845. This dispatch, the first from an American representative in Texas, is unique in American diplomatic annals, offering a colorful description of conditions in Texas and some of the difficulties of life on the early frontier.

San Antonio de Bexar (Texas),
25 Ap. 1827

Sir:

I sailed from New Orleans on the 24th of February last for the mouth of the Brasos River and arrived at San Filipe de Austin on the 13th of the month following. Col. Austin and the Political Chief had gone to the eastward to settle the affairs of the Fredonian Republic. I remained eighteen days for their return and departed without an interview with either. On my way from San Filipe here the Indians stole my horses and I was twelve days confined at Gaudeloupe de Victoria with a severe inflammatory rheumatism. I arrived here on the 22nd instant, in bad health, with an escort of twenty men from La Bahia Espiritu Santo. At the latter place I saw Gen. Bustamante and his staff. He offered me every civility and eagerly enquired after the manners, customs, habits &tc. of our countrymen. He is endeavouring to assemble an army to operate against the Comanche Indians. This tribe are every week or two committing murder and theft upon the inhabitants, and I regret to say, with impunity. The soldiers are very unlike our countrymen. The name of a Comanche strikes terror to their souls. It is no less a fact that five or six Americans travel where they please with their long rifles.

This is but a small village very meanly built and the public works are all in a state of dilapidation. The commerce is nothing, comparatively speaking.

There will be some trade carried on between New Orleans and Matagorda, Brasos and Trinity. The Consular appointment should have been made for Texas and a discretion given the Consul to reside at one of the above places. The Government of this province is administered at Saltillo. The Political Chief who resides here is a mere organ through whom communications are made to the authorities of Saltillo. I will remain here until October, and hope by that time to hear from you. The office, if confined to this interior spot is not worth the farthing.

The Schooner Ring Sons was cast away on the Cat Fish bar on this coast on the 15th of March (I think). She was commanded by Collins and owned by Byrnes of New Orleans. She was in ballast, bound homeward. Crew saved.

So soon as my health is restored I will be more explicit.

I have the honour Sir, to be your obt., humble servant,

Respectfully,

David Dickson

1828–1829   The Demise of Greater Colombia
Dispatches from U.S. Minister to Greater Colombia
William Henry Harrison

William Henry Harrison, ninth president of the United States, had a brief career as a diplomat. He served for seven months as U.S. minister to La Gran Colombia, *or Greater Colombia, a short-lived union of the former Spanish territories of New Granada, Venezuela, and Ecuador. Greater Colombia, proclaimed in 1819 with Simon Bolívar as its president, was unstable from the start; by the time of Harrison's arrival separatist movements in Ecuador and Venezuela were on the verge of success. In his first dispatch to Washington, Harrison describes a nation in disarray and has harsh words for Bolívar, the preeminent liberator of South America. In a later dispatch Harrison reports the first indication of serious differences between Bolívar and his erstwhile ally José Paez, who went on to become president of separatist Venezuela. Harrison's diplomatic career was cut short after the Colombians perceived him to be meddling in local politics.*

Revolt in Greater Colombia
To Secretary of State Henry Clay

Maracaybo, December 23, 1828

Sir,

I have the honor to inform you, that, after a most boisterous and protracted voyage, I reached this place the day before yesterday in a small Dutch vessel, having left the *Erie* at the entrance of the Bay of Venezuela.

It is with great regret that I inform you, that the affairs of this country are not only in a most unsettled state, but that the prospect in advance is still more gloomy and ominous of future distress. You will have seen before this reaches you an account of the measures taken by General Bolivar in consequence of the attempted insurrection of the 25th of September. The severity exercised towards those who were concerned or suspected of being concerned in that affair, far from stifling the disposition to overthrow the existing government, has produced an open appeal to arms, sooner, perhaps, than it would otherwise have taken place, the standard of rebellion having been actually raised and the first effort of the insurgents successful.

The information received here is that a Colonel Obando (brother of a General of that name lately banished) had, with a force of four or five hundred men, attacked Popayan, the capital of the district of Cauca, and being joined by three hundred of the garrison, consisting of only six or seven hundred men, had compelled the Governor of that city to abandon it and the surrounding district, of which Obando now had complete possession; that he possessed himself of all the passes leading to Peru, and completely cut off the communication with that country and the district of Guayaquel, leaving the Government of Colombia in utter ignorance of the movements of the Peruvian troops, which, from the latest accounts, were expected to be on the point of commencing hostilities. On receiving information of the taking of Popayan, General Bolivar detached General Cordova with one thousand men in the direction of that city, and was to follow on the 30th ult. with an additional force. Obando had seized on all the property of the rich whom he supposed to be attached to the party of Bolivar, and distributed it amongst his followers and the poorer class of citizens.

The regular troops from the Atlantic districts had, previously to the insurrection of Obando, been ordered to Bogota, and are now in every direction marching on that city. Whether this measure was produced by an apprehension of the revolt which has taken place, or that the troops were destined to be employed against Peru, is not known. I think it most probable, however, that the latter was the object in view, as from the tenor of a late manifesto published by General Lamar, the President of Peru, there appears to be but little hope of an accommodation of the dispute between the two governments. All the towns and forts in the quarter are now garrisoned by militia, who have been called out in considerable numbers to replace the regular troops which have marched to the South. . . .

From the short time that I have been in this country, I am not able to form an opinion of the measures adopted by Bolivar since his assumption of the Supreme Authority or the necessity which existed for his taking that step. I have found it extremely difficult to obtain a knowledge of facts, different persons relating recent events in a different manner. I am fearful, however, that I run no risk of finding myself deceived when I say, that the Government appears to be a complete military despotism, and the agriculture and commerce appear to be in a most wretched and still declining state.

I have been received with great politeness by General Carreno, the Intendent of the district. I shall leave here on the 28th instant, and proceeding to the head of the lake of Maracaybo, strike the road from Caracas to Bogota between Fruxillo and Merida, having, by taking this route, made my journey by land 400 miles less than it would have been. . . .

I have the honor to be very respectfully your Excellency's hum. serv't.

William H. Harrison

Prelude to Venezuela
To Secretary of State Martin Van Buren

Bogota, March 28, 1829

Sir:

. . . General Paez has lately issued a Proclamation to the people of Venezuela, in which he informs them, that he knows "that Bolivar has never entertained any other wish than to place the liberties of his country upon the surest foundation, but should he depart from those principles, he (Paez) will be the first to plunge a dagger in his bosom." This unlooked for declaration has astounded the Ministers, who are endeavoring to suppress it. Some account for this procedure by supposing, that the nephews of Paez (his adopted sons), who have been educated in the United States and lately returned to Colombia, have infused into his mind the principles which they have imbibed in our country.

My own opinion is, that Paez has heard of the idea of making a Foreign Prince successor to Bolivar—an inheritance to which he probably supposes he has a better claim.

I have the honor to be, Sir, Your Dedicated Serv't,

W. H. Harrison

1830 The French in Algeria: "Fear and Blood"
Dispatch from U.S. Consul General in Algiers Henry Lee to Secretary of State Martin Van Buren

In April 1827 the dey of Algiers struck the French consul in the face with a fly whisk, setting off a chain of events that would lead to the French occupation of Algeria. The French demanded reparations to atone for the insult to their consul; the dey refused. France then blockaded the dey's ports, drawing fire from the Algerian shore batteries. By 1830 France, its honor still not suitably avenged, sent an expeditionary force under Marshal Bourmont to humble the Algerians. The force left France in June; by July 5 the dey had capitulated and gone into exile, leaving the French in command of his capital. French authority, however, did not extend beyond the gates of Algiers.

In this dispatch U.S. Consul General Henry Lee describes Marshal Bourmont's problems in trying to venture even a short distance from the city. Lee assessed that the French would face enormous difficulties in trying to exercise control in North Africa. Lee's comments proved prophetic. Within a week of this dispatch King Charles X of France abdicated under domestic pressure unrelated to Algeria, and Bourmont went into exile in Spain. It would take France twenty-seven years of bitter military conflict to complete the conquest of Algeria. Despite Henry Lee's early insights, the U.S. Senate refused to confirm his appointment as consul general; he returned home after serving only ten months.

Algiers 28th July 1830

Sir:

... No further development of the designs of France in regard to the government of this country has exhibited itself since the 15th. Their expedition against Bona, of which being meditated I formally gave you advice, departed yesterday, and the day before Marshall Bourmont returned from a military visit he paid on the 23rd to Blida a town inhabited by Moors, Jews and Arabs about 15 miles off. He was received by these without any signs of hostility, but a party of Kabyles had stationed themselves in the night behind the walls of such houses as had been overthrown by an earthquake some years ago, and attacked the French Commander in the morning while he was at breakfast. His first aide de camp and several other officers of rank and merit were among the slain, which amounted to 13, his wounded are stated at 30. The superiority of discipline over natural courage enabled him to effect his retreat which was attended with great hazard. This event shews the narrow and uncertain limits to which his conquest is confined and marks in characters of fear and blood the insecurity of any other than a Turkish administration over this region.

&c., &c., &c.,

H. Lee

1830 France's July Revolution: "One of the Most Wonderful . . . in the History of the World"

Dispatch from U.S. Minister to France William G. Rives to Secretary of State Martin Van Buren

After the defeat of Napoleon Bonaparte in 1815, the Bourbons were restored to the throne of France. Charles X, a brother of the executed Louis XVI, ascended the throne in 1824. Charles was a reactionary who tried to return France to the kind of absolute monarchy that existed before the revolution. When a party favoring restrictions on the king won a majority of seats in the Chamber of Deputies, Charles responded by issuing the "July ordinances." These restrictive measures dissolved the Chamber of Deputies, clamped down on the press, and revised voting requirements in a way that guaranteed a royalist victory in the next election. Charles imagined that the recently completed conquest of Algiers (see "The French in Algeria," p. 97) assured him sufficient popularity to extinguish domestic opposition. But he badly misjudged public sentiment. The ordinances sparked a general revolt that forced Charles to flee the country and abdicate. Louis-Phillipe, duc d'Orléans, was brought to the throne as a constitutional monarch. The dramatic events of the final week of July 1830 are reported here by U.S. Minister William Rives. The July Revolution was the catalyst for several other revolutionary outbreaks in Europe, including those in Germany and Italy and the successful revolution leading to Belgian independence.

Paris, July 30, 1830

Sir:

I enclose the copy of a letter which I addressed to Prince Polignac on the 23rd instant. Believing that a disposition was really felt, from whatever cause, to cultivate friendly relations with the U.S., I thought it important to intimate to him as intelligibly as I could that the preservation of those relations must depend on a prompt adjustment of the reclamations which had been so long pending. . . .

But these prospects have for the present, ceased, by consequence of one of the most wonderful revolutions which have ever occurred in the history of the world. At this moment, the tri-coloured flag waves over the Palace of the Tuileries, and the city of Paris, after passing thro' three days of . . . bloodshed, is now as tranquil under its provisional government, as I have ever seen it under the royal authority of the King, who, with all his Ministers, remained at St. Cloud during the troubles here, has, it is said, abandoned St. Cloud and taken the route of the Netherlands. The whole of his troops stationed at Paris amounting to thirty thousand, have after sustaining severe losses from the heroic and enthusiastic . . . people, either been driven out of the city or joined the standard of their fellow citizens.

The cause of this sudden and wonderful revolution is to be found in certain ordinances of the King which . . . announced the dissolution of the new Chamber of Deputies, made . . . changes in the system of elections established by law (depriving three-fourths of the electors of the right of suffrage, abolishing the secret vote, and reducing the number of deputies from 430 to 258), and, at the same time, suspended the liberty of the press, and suppressed all the Journals of the opposition. . . .

The ordinances were promulgated on Monday the 23rd instant and immediately produced a profound sensation through the whole population of Paris. No public disorder, however, occurred on that day. . . . On Tuesday the assemblage of people in the streets were increased by . . . the laboring classes, who had been thrown out of employment by the suppression of the journals, or other effects, direct or indirect, of the ordinances. The military, in attempting to disperse them, encountered a very spirited resistance, and several engagements took place between them and the multitude in different parts of Paris.

On Wednesday morning, a proclamation of the King appeared declaring Paris to be in a state of siege, and placing Marshall Marussot, the Duke of Reguson, at the head of the troops. In the meantime, the people also had extended their preparations and increased their force. Many members of the National guard, which had been suppressed in 1827, reappeared in uniform and with their arms, and the young men belonging to the Polytechnic School, the School of Medicine, and the School of Law united themselves, with enthusiasm, to the mass of the people. They took possession of one or two public depots of arms, and adding to that supply, the arms of the detachments of the Royal Guard whom they subdued in various posts throughout the city, they soon found themselves well furnished with the means of attack as well as defense. To prevent the advance . . . or retreat of the troops, they barricaded the streets and boulevards with carriages, or by tearing up the stones of the pavement, or cutting down the trees on the margin of the public walks.

Thus prepared on both sides, the contest on Wednesday assumed a more serious . . . character. There were . . . prolonged engagements at various points in the city. . . . The discharge of cannon and musketry was heard at intervals through the whole course of the night.

On Thursday, the people made vigorous assaults on the Louvre and the Tuileries, to which the military, having been beaten and driven back in all the previous engagements, had retired. Both were finally carried, and the remnants of the military force, thus driven from their last hold on the city, retired beyond the walls. At 2 o'clock, the whole contest was ended, and the tri-coloured flag floated peacefully from the domes of the palaces. Since then, not again has [there] been fire in the city, but in token of public joy. . . .

I have not heard of a single outrage perpetrated by the people, in this agitating crisis. Their conduct has been marked throughout by the . . . enthusiastic devotion of men, contesting for their rights . . . in the spirit of freedom. Indeed, nothing could more strikingly mark the wonderful advances made by this people in the knowledge and practice of their institutions, than their noble conduct, on the present occasion, contrasted with the masses of the first revolutionary convulsion. . . .

I have the honor to be, with great respect, your most obd. svt.

W. G. Rives

1831 Preserving the Peace

Dispatch from U.S. Minister to Great Britain Martin Van Buren to Secretary of State Edward Livingston

Known as "The Red Fox of Kinderhook" for his wily stratagems as head of New York's "Albany Machine," Martin Van Buren served as U.S. senator, then as governor of New York before resigning in 1829 to become secretary of state under President Andrew Jackson (1829–1837). In 1831 Jackson named Van Buren in a recess appointment as minister to Great Britain. Van Buren was at his post for only a few months when Congress reconvened and failed by one vote to confirm his appointment. Jackson, seeing this as a personal slight by Congress, retaliated by choosing Van

Buren as his vice president in 1832. In 1836, with Jackson's further support, Van Buren—by that time known as "Old Kinderhook" or "O.K." (regarded by some as the origin of the expression)—was elected the eighth president of the United States.

This dispatch, Van Buren's first report from London, recounts his presentation of credentials to King William IV. William was a son of George III, who was king when the United States won its independence. In this conversation with Van Buren, King William tries to reassure America that he—unlike his father who had fought two wars against the United States—desires friendly relations. William IV died in 1837 and was succeeded by Queen Victoria.

London, 21st September, 1831

Sir:

Agreeably to an arrangement made previously with Lord Palmerston, I had this day . . . an audience of His Majesty, to whom I delivered my letter of credence. . . . In reply to the assurances I gave him of the respect entertained by the President for his character . . . he said: That he had succeeded to the throne in a period when the political condition of Europe was most critical and when its peace could only be preserved by the exercise of the utmost prudence on the part of those entrusted with the Government of the principal Powers. That, for himself, if he had been ambitious, or willing to involve the country in a war, there had not been wanting occasions when he might have done so without subjecting himself even to the imputation of seeking to disturb the public tranquility; but he was not ambitious, and, believing as he did that the best interests of his own country, as well as the happiness of the world could only be promoted by the preservation of general peace, he had exerted all the power with which he was invested to accomplish that great end. He said the task had been a difficult one: That Great Britain had endeavored to exercise, and, he trusted, had succeeded in exercising an important influence on the side of peace; that the issue was in the hands of Providence, but that he entertained very flattering expectations of a favorable result. That, as to the country from which I came, he had always been anxious for the preservation of the very best relations between it and Great Britain; that not only did their common interests point to that course, but their common origin and the kindred relations subsisting between them should stimulate both Nations to practice forbearance toward each other, and to cultivate, in their intercourse, feelings of mutual kindness and good neighborhood. That, for himself, always mindful that his first duty lay at home, he should not fail to do all in his power to preserve the relations of friendship now so happily existing between the two countries. . . . He then referred to the President by name; said that he had observed the course followed by him since the affairs of the United States had been committed to his hands, with much attention and great interest, and, he took pleasure in adding, with great satisfaction; . . . from all he had seen of his public course, he had formed the highest estimate of his character . . . and that he did not doubt that the intercourse which it might be my duty to hold with his Government would amply convince me of the earnest desire to do us justice on all occasions, and to keep upon the most friendly terms with the United States. . . .

Martin Van Buren

1835 War in South Africa
Dispatch from U.S. Consul in Cape Town Isaac Chase to
Secretary of State John Forsyth

In many ways 1835 was a landmark year in the history of South Africa. The Afrikaners, or settlers of Dutch descent, had been chafing under British rule since the turn of the century (see "The British Move into Africa," p. 68). *Upset by the abolition of slavery the previous year, thousands of Afrikaners began the "Great Trek" inland to escape from British administration. Meanwhile, settlers of British origin were slowly expanding eastward from the Cape of Good Hope into an area known as Kaffraria. The European expansion brought the settlers into conflict with native groups (known at the time as Kaffirs or Caffres) who were themselves expanding southward from the interior. The result was a major "Kaffir War," reported almost nonchalantly in this dispatch by Isaac Chase, who served as U.S. consul in Cape Town from 1834 to 1851.*

Cape Town, 23d, March 1835

Sir:

It becomes my duty to inform the Department that a war is now in progress between the Colonists of this Country and a Tribe of Caffres inhabiting an extensive territory at the South East about 800 miles from Cape Town. The Caffres invaded the Colony with a force of 20,000 carrying destruction and devastation before them, killing the inhabitants, firing their houses and carrying off their cattle and effects to an immense amount. The Government have at present 10,000 men in the field which is supposed will be sufficient to subdue or effectively drive back the invaders at once.

I beg to say that I feel the want of some standard work on International Law and should be very glad to receive the Diplomatic and International Law as published by Jonathan Elliott Esq.

Any communication to this consulate if directed to the care of
Hezekiah Chase & Co.
Boston
Mass.
will be duly forwarded.

> I have the honor to be
> Sir
> Your obedient servant
>
> Isaac Chase

1838 Savagery in Tahiti: "Twelf Wounds, Five upon My Head"

Dispatch from U.S. Consul in Otaheite Jacob Antoine Moerenhaut to Secretary of State John Forsyth

Jacob Antoine Moerenhaut, a Belgian who previously had served as Dutch commercial agent in Chile, was appointed in 1835 as U.S. consul to the government of Otaheite (now Tahiti), making him the first person accredited by any Western power to a Pacific island government. It was not unusual at the time for foreigners to represent the United States. Moerenhaut recovered from the injuries he received in the attack reported in this dispatch and went on to become French consul on the island, eventually playing a pivotal role in the French takeover of the Society Islands. His wife died from her wounds.

> Otaheite, June 28, 1838

Sir:

Since my letter of January 1st no opportunity has offered of writing to America or, with the exception of [a] terrible occurrence which has taken place in my own house, has anything happened worthy communicating to Your Excellency. This Island has not been so much visited by whaling ships in the present year, as the two preceding ones, owing perhaps to a change in the best whaling ground.

On the morning Sunday June the 9th about 2 o'clock, hearing a noise by my bedroom, I got up, lighted a candle and had the imprudence to open my room door to see what had occasioned the noise, thinking that if there were robbers in the house they would run away when they saw that I had a light. I was deceived for I had hardly opened my room door, when I perceived a man close to the wainscot by the side of the door, at the same instant I received a blow upon the head, which made me stagger and drop the light from my hand. I received quickly a second and third blow that left me sometime insensible. On reviving a little I cried out for help, upon which the assassin returned to me and give me nine additional wounds with an axe, it being ascertained afterwards that it was with an axe he struck me, during the time Mrs. Moerenhaut awoke and threw herself between me and the assassin which act of courage and devotedness that saved my life cost her dear; she received five severe wounds, one on her head that has fractured her skull, leaving me but little hope of her recovery. Our cries having awakened the domestics and the robbers hearing the voices of natives approaching, the[y] left the house in the same way that they enter'd it, by an opening which they made in one of the windows. The state in which we were found was horrible. I had twelf wounds, five upon my head, two of which caused much alarm, my unfortunate wife had five, one so dreadful from an axe on her head as to cause me almost to despair of her surviving. The surgeon give me but faint hope of her, myself he considers out of danger.

One of the murderers is found out, a mexican Sambo or halfblack, a deserter from an American whaler. Another, an Englishman, also a deserter from an American whale ship, is in custody with strong reason to believe him guilty. This misfortune which has struck myself and family is, I must respectfully take the liberty to inform Your Excellency, owing in a great degree to the abandon and unprotected state that I have been left in for two years and a half, without receiving any support from the American flag, in a country not sufficiently advanced to afford the protection that consuls find in other places, both for their persons and property. Alone as I am in a place where there is neither police nor prison, judge nor any authority to whom I can address myself or who have any inclination to assist in any matter not of self interest, I have alone in all circumstances to act against mutineers, deserters and other culprits, so numerous at the present time on board of the whale ships in these seas, that there is hardly a day that I am not exposed to the vengeance of this refuse of society which frequently I have to correct; and witness as they are to the little support that I have to expect from the pretended government of the Island. It is even astonishing, sir, that I have escaped the knife of an assassin so long. The Island is full of deserters and other white persons of lawless and dishonest habits, almost all of which have come here in American whale ships. It is in vain that I have urged the natives to put in force one of their laws which sentences deserters to labor on the roads. They will not do anything, and desertion is rather encouraged than punished by them. . . . In a few words, Sir, the natives are perfectly indifferent about the affairs of white people whenever they are not led to anticipate some pecuniary benefit. Such is the country where I have to exercise the duties of my office. Your Excellency may judge of the difficulty and how little is the security for my person and property.

Another effect of the residence here of so many depraved characters is the example given to the natives. Their manners are infamous and their language encourages every thing that is bad and going on board vessels, communicating with the crews, they cause mutinies and desertions. It is the same, Sir, in all the Islands frequented in these Seas, which, if some measures are not taken promptly, to remove indistinctly all bad characters living on them, without any object or means of honest existence the [Islands] will soon all become so many nests of pirates and places where ships will not be able to frequent without the greatest danger.

The United States having ten times the number of ships, ten times more commerce than any other nation in these Seas, Your Excellency will conceive how it is in the interest of their commerce that these evils may be stopped in time and how necessary it is for ships of war to visit regularly the ports most frequented. Myself, in order to fulfill the duties of my office in a port that from 60 to 70 large ships with crews of 30 or 40 men each visit annually, it is absolutely necessary that I should have that support, without which it will become impossible to do the good which I desire although I devote my time and my whole attention to the object. . . .

I am, respectfully of Your Excellency the most humble and obedient servant

J. A. Moerenhaut

1840   Prelude to the Opium War

Dispatch from U.S. Consul in Canton Peter W. Snow to
Secretary of State John Forsyth

As Western trade with China increased, so did tensions and mutual grievances between the small Western colony in Canton and its reluctant Chinese hosts. By the 1830s the traditional Chinese system of trading with foreigners, as described by U.S. Consul Samuel Shaw in 1786 (see "Trade with China," p. 39), was breaking down. British impatience with being treated as a subservient nation and Chinese efforts to keep the British in line resulted in short-lived hostilities in 1834. The next five years were relatively calm. Then new hostilities erupted, sparked by Chinese efforts to stamp out the lucrative trade in opium between British India and China. In an effort to make British traders give up their stocks of opium, Chinese authorities first blockaded the foreign community in Canton and later forced the British to retreat to the Portuguese island of Macao. British officials called for military reinforcements from Europe. This dispatch reports the arrival in Macao of a British fleet. Open hostilities began shortly thereafter.

The first Anglo-Chinese War, or Opium War, ended in a complete victory for the British. By the Treaty of Nanking (1842) the Chinese ceded Hong Kong to Britain, opened additional Chinese ports to foreign trade, and paid a large indemnity to the British.

Macao, June 10, 1840

Sir:

I have the honor to inform you that by the arrival of the Frigate *Alligator* yesterday from Singapore, we learn that . . . seventy four . . . vessels of war with several transports would leave that place for China on the 20th of May. We are therefore hourly expecting their arrival. The forces come on by divisions, each stopping a few days at Singapore. We are of course looking for events of interest and importance. The American merchants, it is thought, will all be out of Canton by the first of May. Two American ships are on their way out, five at Whampoa, three of those will be out in a week or ten days, leaving two uncertain.

Nothing as yet has transpired as to the first operations of the British forces. The Chinese have a number of large junks prepared to stop up the channel to Whampoa, above the Bogue, by sinking them as soon as an attack is made on the forts at the Bogue.

The overland mail by the *Alligator* brings us London accounts up to the 5th of March—96 days.

Lord John Spencer Churchill, Senior Officer of H.B.M. Naval Forces in China, died on the 3d inst. after a short illness.

With great Respect
Your Obt. serv't,

P. W. Snow

June 22

P.S. Since writing the forgoing, the fleet has arrived, two steamers form a part of the force. Hostilities will not commence, it is said, until the Admiral's arrival, who is shortly expected from the Cape of Good Hope bringing with him an additional force.

1840 Napoleon's Remains Go Home
Dispatch from U.S. Consular and Commercial Agent in St. Helena
William Carrol to Secretary of State John Forsyth

Great events occur occasionally even in the remotest consular posts. This was the case in 1840 on the tiny South Atlantic island of St. Helena. French emperor Napoleon Bonaparte had been exiled to the island after his defeat at Waterloo in 1815 (see "Waterloo," p. 75). He died there six years later. On the twenty-fifth anniversary of Napoleon's arrival in St. Helena, his remains were returned to France with royal honors. The event is reported in this dispatch by William Carrol, who spent fifteen years (1831–1846) as U.S. representative on St. Helena.

> Island of St. Helena,
> 26th Oct. 1840

Honorable Sir:

I have the honor to report that on the 15th instant, the Mortal Remains of the late Napoleon Buonaparte (being that day 25 years on which he arrived here) were embarked with Royal honors, on board H.M.C.M. Ship "Belle Poule" commanded by His Royal Highness the Prince de Joinville: and on the 18th in company with H.M.C.M. Sloop "Favorite" departed for France.

His Royal Highness and the French Commissioner Comte de Chabot are charged by His Majesty the King of the French, with the execution of this special mission, accompanied by Generals Bertrand & Gourgoud, Mons. Las Casas and Mons. Marchand with four of Napoleon's former domestics. . . .

> I have the honor to be
> Honorable Sir
> Your most obed't. Servant,
>
> W. Carrol

1842 "Texians" to Arms as Mexicans Invade
Dispatch from U.S. Chargé d'Affaires to the Republic of Texas
Joseph Eve to Secretary of State Daniel Webster

In 1836 Texas declared its independence from Mexico, sparking a war that came to a quick conclusion with Mexico's defeat at the battle of San Jacinto. Although most of the American settlers in Texas wished to join the United States, U.S. domestic politics prevented annexation for almost a decade. In the meantime, Texas led a sometimes precarious existence as a republic, struggling against financial insolvency, Indian raids, and incursions by Mexican forces seeking to reoccupy their lost territory. The onset of one such Mexican attack is reported in this dispatch by Joseph Eve, one of six Americans to serve as chargé d'affaires to the Republic of Texas. Eve comments—in this somewhat disjointed dispatch—on the disorganized state of the government at "Galvaston" and describes the "Texian" reaction to the unsuccessful Mexican incursion.

Galvaston, March 10, 1842

Sir,

. . . The President and Secretary of State [of Texas] are in Galvaston and are now engaged in issuing Orders to have the militia equipt and ready to march to any point and at any moment. News has reached here to day by express that Sanantonia, about three hundred miles South West from Galvaston has been taken by the Mexican Army supposed to be twenty thousand strong. It is believed here that Corpus Christi seventy miles below here has fallen into the hands of the Mexicans, and great fears are entertained that they are in Austin before this time.

It has been rumored here for the last ten days, that the Mexicans were coming in great force, But the President did not believe the report, I however on yesterday addressed a letter to him, requesting to be informed whither he intended to remove the Archives of this Government from Austin a copy of which I herewith enclose for your inspection; I have received no written answer from the President as he has been much engaged but in a conversation with him this evening he informed me that he had given orders to have all the Archives removed forthwith. I have therefore considered it to be my duty to have the Archives of the United States belonging to this Legation removed; As the people here believe that the Mexicans will not respect the flag of the United States in Texas; I cannot myself entertain the least fears either for the Archives or for myself, or family.

I consider this Government in a most deplorable condition without a dollar in the Treasury and without credit to borrow money here or abroad with not a regular Soldier belonging to the Army, and a very great excitement against the President for not having ordered out the militia previous to this time. . . . The people in almost every county have organized, armed and equipt themselves by voluntarily contribution and about two thousand are on their march to Sanantonia. At least two hundred Volunteers will leave this city tomorrow at their own expense it is said that the President has issued orders that no citizen is to leave this Island as he anticipates great danger of an attack upon Galvaston; but the Volunteers will disregard the order. The district court was in session here but has adjourned this evening and the Judge with every member of the bar except one has volunteered and will leave here for the Army tomorrow. I have never seen so much enthusiasm among any people. All seem to be anxious to meet the foe, and all seem to think that if they can embody five thousand Texians they can defeat twenty thousand Mexicans....

Since my arrival at this place from Austin, the Merchants and traders, from the United States, have expressed great dissatisfaction at the advantages given by this Government to the commerce of France over that of the United States. On the 27th of February I addressed a note to Doctor Jones Secretary of State for Texas; on that subject....

> I have the honor to be
> Your Obt. Servt.,
>
> Joseph Eve

1842 The French Seize Tahiti
Dispatch from U.S. Consul in Tahiti Samuel Blackler to Secretary of State Daniel Webster

After describing the wreck of an American vessel on an uncharted Pacific island, the U.S. consul reports, almost nonchalantly, the establishment of a French protectorate over Tahiti. In later dispatches Consul Samuel Blackler reported that he could have easily prevented the French action by offering a modest financial guarantee to France on behalf of the Tahitian queen. He reasoned, however, that since the United States would not take control of Tahiti, a French takeover was preferable to continuance of the inefficient native government or to the likely alternative of the British taking control.

Blackler served as American consul in Tahiti for five years beginning in 1839. During that time, he gained a reputation as an unscrupulous scoundrel. The Tahitians twice officially requested his recall, accusing him of bootlegging liquor, offering consular immunity to other lawbreakers, drawing a sword against local officials, and willfully violating quarantine regulations resulting in an outbreak of smallpox. According to the Tahitian complaint, Blackler also was an adulterer and a fornicator, crimes that, they alleged, he committed "before our eyes, without shame, and in defiance of us." The U.S. government, however, took no action on the Tahitian complaints. Blackler remained U.S. consul in Tahiti until his death in 1844.

Society Islands,
September 10, 1842

Sir:

I have the honour to advise the Department of the total loss of the American Ship Cadmus of Fairhaven on a low Lagoon (island) supposed to lie in the latitude of 23° 14′ to 26°S, & Longitude of 138°W, or thereabouts.

The disaster took place at night, of the 4th of August 1842, at about half an hour before midnight. The ship became a total wreck in a short time after she struck.

The crew succeeding in saving one boat only out of six, with which the Captain, mate and four seamen embarked on the 7th inst. following for this place, leaving eighteen remaining officers & crew on the Island, scantily supplied with water & and damaged bread, to await the result of the voyage. . . .

They . . . arrived at this port on the 21st inst. following.

On the 22d at noon after having previously advertised for proposals, I effected a charter of the Am. Schooner Emerald, C. I. Hall Master, well provided with boats & a chronometer, for one thousand dollars, & five dollars for provisions for each of the seamen recovered, to proceed to their rescue, giving him official instructions to determine as nearly as possible the true position of the Island. . . .

I have the honour to enclose to the Department a copy of the Declaration of the Admiral A. Du Petit Thouars, commanding the Naval Station of France, against Pomare V. Queen of Tahiti, also copies of my correspondence with the Admiral relating thereto.

The object of this Declaration and demand, as will be perceived by your Excellency, is to obtain possession of the Island and its dependencies.

This object has been assiduously pursued by other secret means previous and subsequent to the arrival of the Admiral. A document asking protection of the French, was drawn up by the French Consul . . . to which he obtained the signatures of some of the chiefs. The Queen subsequently, on her arrival at Tahiti, issued a Circular, disclaiming any knowledge of or participation in the act. A document of similar import, but more explicit in character previously signed by four high chiefs, has this day received the signature of the Queen. I have been fortunate before closing my despatches to obtain a copy of the same together with the Admiral's reply, which I have the honor to enclose, and which will supersede the necessity of further detail.

The French flag has not yet been hoisted. All manifestations of hostility has ceased. I am however able from good authority to state that troops will be landed, a governor hereafter appointed, & that the Queen & high chiefs will receive a yearly allowance sufficient to maintain the dignity of their rank.

> I have the honour to be
> &c&c&c
> Your Excell'cy's obedient Servant
>
> S. Blackler

1843 Insurgents Take Madrid

Dispatch from U.S. Minister to Spain Washington Irving to Secretary of State Ad Interim Hugh L. Legaré

In the decades that followed the Napoleonic Wars (1804–1815), Spain was wracked by instability, civil war, and revolution. American author Washington Irving was U.S. minister to Spain for several years of this tumultuous period. This dispatch describes the siege and capture of Madrid by Gen. Ramón María Narváez, who overthrew then-regent Baldomero Espartero. Narváez remained in power for eight years, holding sway over Queen Isabella II, who was just thirteen years old when Irving penned this report.

Madrid, July 22, 1843

Sir:

Since the date of my last despatch Madrid has been in a state of siege. The insurgent troops from Leon and old Castile under General Aspiros took a position on one side while a superior force under General Narvaez, who had managed to out maneuver or out march the regent's generals, invested it on the other. They had brought no artillery and evidently calculated on a cooperation from within expecting that a pronunciamento would take place and the gates be thrown open to them: or at least that the city being defended mainly by the national guard would soon surrender. In this expectation they were disappointed. The militia behaved admirably. Martial law was proclaimed on the 10th inst. On the 12th the whole population seemed under arms, and twenty thousand men well equipped were at the orders of the Captain General of Madrid. The gates were barricaded, batteries planted commanding the approaches to the city, trenches digged and breastworks thrown up in the principal streets, troops stationed in the houses on each side to fire from the upper windows and every preparation made to defend the city street by street and step by step; and to make the last stand at the palace.

For three days and nights the siege continued with much skirmishing about the gates; the city holding out in the hope of relief from troops . . . which were known to be on the march for the capital. Aware of their approach the besiegers repeated their demands to surrender, with threats of a general attack and of rigorous terms in case the place were carried by storm. . . .

Apprehension that should the city be carried by storm the lives of the youthful queen and her sister might be endangered by the defense being pushed to an extremity, and the palace used as a citadel; the Diplomatic Corps addressed a note to the government, urging the utmost caution with respect to the safety of the royal children, and offering to repair in person to the palace and be near the queen at any moment their presence might be deemed useful. This offer was respectfully declined.

Two days since the besieging troops finding the advancing forces of the regency were near at hand, drew off to a distance of two or three leagues, where they took up a position. . . . Tidings are incessantly expected of a battle decisive of the fate of the capital.

July 23. The question is decided. The armies met yesterday morning; a few shots were exchanged when a general embracing took place between the soldiery, and the troops of the regency joined the insurgents. . . . The city was overwhelmed with astonishment. The members of the cabinet resigned their positions, . . . the municipal authorities have taken the management of affairs and have sent out deputations last evening and this morning to treat for terms. The last deputation has not yet returned. The main point difficulty is the demand of Narvaez that the whole national guard be disarmed. This may occasion some trouble; and some scenes of violence. Narvaez, however, has the power at present to impose his own terms, but will doubtless be influenced by leading men of his party within the city, who will be cautious not to exasperate the populace.

I consider this blow as decisive of the political fortunes of the Regent. Other troops from various points are marching upon the capital; where the insurgents will soon concentrate a force of between thirty and forty thousand men. The insurrection is too wide and general to be quelled by any troops the regent can collect. He is at present in Andalusia; seeking it is said to bring that rich province into obedience. Others think he is desirous of making his way to Cadiz; from whence, in case of extremity, he may embark and save himself by sea. On hearing of the single defection of the army and the capture of the capital it is thought he will either resign or endeavor to leave the kingdom.

I shall keep this despatch open until the last moment, to give any further tidings that may arise. . . .

> I am Sir,
> Very respectfully
> Your obedient
>
> Washington Irving

1843 Arabian Horses for President Tyler
Dispatch from U.S. Consul in Zanzibar Richard P. Waters to Secretary of State Daniel Webster

American representatives abroad regularly have had to contend with gifts from foreign dignitaries—a significant challenge when the gifts are alive. In this unusual instance the horses made it safely from East Africa to Washington, a journey of five months.

Zanzibar, December 30, 1843

Sir:

About two months since, his Majesty the Sultan of Muscat sent one of his secretaries to my house with two Arabian horses, as a present to the President of the United States, with the request that I would send them to America by the first of our vessels. I now ship them, under the care of his Majesty's groom, by the barque Eliza, bound to Salem, Massachusetts; and have requested David Pingree, esq., of Salem, to receive and hold them, subject to the President's orders.

I am, sir, very respectfully, your obedient servant,

Richard P. Waters

1846 The Acquisition of New Mexico: "Our Country Has Acquired without Bloodshed a Province"
Dispatch from U.S. Consul in Santa Fe Manuel Alvarez to Secretary of State James Buchanan

In 1845 the United States admitted Texas to the Union, bringing to an end the nine-year life of the Republic of Texas. Mexico, still not resigned to the loss of its former province, immediately broke relations with the United States. With the borders of Texas in dispute, the United States moved troops south to enforce its claim to all land above the Rio Grande. American and Mexican patrols clashed in the contested area, and President James K. Polk, asserting that the Mexicans had invaded American territory and taken American lives, sent a war message to Congress in May 1846. Mexican and American troops fought for over a year, until Gen. Winfield Scott captured Mexico City on September 14, 1847. Meanwhile, an American column moved west to capture New Mexico.

Manuel Alvarez was the longest-serving American consul in Santa Fe, Mexico, holding office until the U.S. takeover. In this, one of his final dispatches, Alvarez reports learning belatedly of the onset of the Mexican War and describes his efforts to encourage a peaceful transition to American rule.

Santa Fe, New Mexico,
September 4th, 1846

Sir:

Since my communication of the 26th May last to the Department over which you preside, things highly important to this remote province have taken place.

Though we had vague reports of the commencement of the war between the two countries near Matamoros, no intelligence was received of the invasion of this province until the 17th June. This was confirmed on the 26th by the arrival of the first caravan of traders from Independence Missouri.

I sought an immediate interview with Governor Armijo, the civil & military commandant of this Territory, who was also appraised of the intended operations of the Army of the West under the orders of Genl. Kearny, and used my best endeavours to convince him that it would be better for himself and the people under his government to capitulate, and far preferable to become an inconsiderable portion of a powerful Republic, than a considerable one of a nation, continually engaged in revolutions, with no stability in the public administration of their affairs and powerless to defend the citizens of this province from the thousands of hostile Indians who surround them and who have since the time of the Monarchy preyed almost continually upon all parts of the country and have by a long course of murder, rapine and plunder almost become the lords of the soil.

I succeeded badly at first but with the other Officers and his confidential advisers I had far better success. They not holding such high places, nor so responsible commissions and yet exposed to the same dangers were rather easily won over . . . whereas the Governor could never calculate on being invested with the same amount of Authority under the new order of things, he was vaccillating to the last, and though a great man in small matters I found to be a small one in great affairs.

However I succeeded in one most important point and which came more particularly under my duties as Consul of the United States, at least acting as such in this City, to have all of our citizens well treated even to the very entry of General Kearny.

. . . It will be indispensable that a strong military force of at least 2000 men should garrison the country, for some time to come, as well to guard against the machinations of intriguing clergy, as to meet any armed force from the interior, that the hostile Indians should be conquered, or forced to live on friendly terms, that the industry of the people should be encouraged with all fostering care, that the laws should be ably and faithfully administered, & that a good portion of the public offices should be filled by native citizens, all this will contradict the thousand reports that are in constant circulation . . . that we intend to make slaves of them; or at least grind them into the dust. This policy pursued for a year or two until they become acquainted with our liberal institutions & convinced that we are consulting their real interest may make them in time most valuable citizens, and this Territory a respectable State of the Union. . . .

I must also beg leave to likewise call the attention of the Department over which you preside to the memorial presented by me on the 2nd of February 1842, with my claim for indemnity, from wounds and sufferings caused by the attempt to assinate me in September 1841 during the excitement caused by the first Texan expedition & which bears date the 2nd of March 1842 & is appended to said memorial or is on file in the Department. The grievancy endured & the losses sustained by me were severe and though the Hon. Mr. [Daniel] Webster the then Secretary of State seemed not disposed to investigate the claim I flatter myself that a more equitable disposition, at present prevails in the Councils of our nation.

. . . [O]ur Country has acquired without bloodshed a province most rich in the precious metals, invaluable for stock growing, especially for the production of the finest wool on the continent, of a salubrity unparalleled on the globe, with medical springs unsurpassed any where, of immense extent, capable under our fair and liberal institutions of supporting a large population being the connecting link between the Valley of the Mississippi and the Bay of San Francisco through which only a good and almost a direct road can be made to the Pacific Ocean. . . .

I am, Sir, Respectfully
Your Obedient Servant

Manl Alvarez

1847 The Treaty of Guadalupe Hidalgo: Expanding the Country without Instructions
Dispatch from U.S. Executive Agent in Mexico Nicholas P. Trist to Secretary of State James Buchanan

During the Mexican War, President James K. Polk adopted an unusual procedure when he appointed Nicholas Trist, chief clerk and second-ranking official of the Department of State, as executive agent in Mexico and asked him to accompany Gen. Winfield Scott to that country to negotiate a peace treaty at the most propitious moment. As the months passed, Polk had second thoughts about his actions and issued orders recalling Trist. By the time the instructions reached Mexico City, however, Trist already was involved in talks with a fragile new Mexican government, and he decided to ignore his instructions and conclude the negotiations. In this dispatch Trist explains to Secretary of State James Buchanan why he decided to violate his instructions.

The Treaty of Guadalupe Hidalgo, signed in February 1848, acknowledged American sovereignty as far south as the Rio Grande and gave the United States title to western lands from Texas to California. President Polk was outraged that the "impudent and unqualified scoundrel" Trist had violated his instructions. Nevertheless, the draft treaty fulfilled America's war aims. Polk, faced with growing antiwar sentiment in Congress, submitted the document for Senate approval, but not before dismissing Trist from government employment. More than twenty years would pass before Congress vindicated Trist by voting to pay his longstanding claims for salary and personal expenses during the negotiations.

Mexico, December 6, 1847

... I place my determination on the ground of my conviction, "*first*, that peace is still the desire of my government; *secondly*, that if the present opportunity be not seized *at once*, all chance for making a treaty at all will be lost for an indefinite period—probably forever; *thirdly*, that this (the boundary proposed by me) is the utmost point to which the Mexican government can, by any possibility, venture." ... These points constitute the heads under which the development of the subject naturally arranges itself.

1. "*First*, that peace is still the desire of my government." Upon this point the words of the President, as I took leave of him, are still fresh in my memory: "Mr. Trist, if you succeed in making a treaty, you will render a great service to your country." ...

I have carefully examined the despatches last received by me, (those by which I am recalled). ... I have found ... the President is still of the same mind as when I left Washington; that now, as then, he considers the protraction of the war a great evil; that now, as then, he believes that to restore peace would be to render a great service to our country; in a word, *"that peace is still the desire of my government."* . . .

2. *Secondly,* that if the present opportunity be not seized *at once,* all chance for making a treaty *at all* will be lost for an indefinite period—probably forever. . . .

The friends of peace . . . have succeeded in bringing together at the seat of government the governors of the respective States; and, after full conference, in obtaining their concurrence (with one single exception—the governor of Potosi) in the peace policy, and the pledge of their support. . . .

But this party cannot possibly stand, *unless the object for which alone it has formed itself be speedily accomplished.* Without this its destitution of pecuniary resources must become aggravated every day; and this cannot continue much longer without sealing its fate: a catastrophe which would involve a total dissolution of the federal government and of the Union. . . .

3. "*Thirdly,* that this (the boundary proposed by me) is the utmost point to which the Mexican government can, by any possibility venture."

Under this head, I can do but little else than state my perfect conviction, resulting from the best use I am capable of making of the opportunities afforded by my position, that such is the fact. The nature of the subject scarcely admits of my doing more. I will, however, call attention to the fact, that, independently of Texas, this boundary takes from Mexico about *one half of her whole territory;* and upon this fact remark, that, however helpless a nation may feel, there is necessarily a point beyond which she cannot be expected to go, under any circumstances, in surrendering her territory as the price of peace. . . .

Nicholas Trist

1848 Recognizing the Republic of Venice

Dispatch from U.S. Consul in Venice William A. Sparks to Secretary of State James Buchanan

The year 1848 was one of revolutionary upheavals in Europe. Across the continent popular discontent with authoritarian rule combined with ethnic and nationalist sentiments to sweep monarchies from power in favor of liberal republican governments. The states composing the Austrian Empire were among those most affected. After an uprising in Vienna, Austria's Italian provinces revolted. In this dispatch the U.S. consul in Venice, William Sparks, describes the establishment of a Venetian republic and informs Washington that he has (without instructions) accorded recognition to the new government.

Although the consul welcomed the establishment of a republic, American leaders were preoccupied with events closer to home (such as the discovery of gold in California and the 1848 presidential election) and displayed little interest in the European revolutions. Moreover, the initially successful revolutionary movements tended to be of short duration. Austrian armies crushed the fledgling Italian independence movements. Venice, besieged and bombarded, held out for a month before succumbing to the combined ravages of war, starvation, and a cholera epidemic. Among the victims of cholera during the siege was U.S. Consul Sparks, who died ten days before Austrian forces recaptured the city. Another two decades would pass before Austria, defeated in a war with Prussia, would cede Venice to the newly established Kingdom of Italy.

Venice, 30th April 1848

Sir,

On the 5th of the present month I had the honor of transmitting to the Department of State a dispatch containing the announcement that by a capitulation signed by the military Commander of this city & fortress on the 22nd ult., that civil and military government of Austria had ceased to exist in Venice, and that in its stead, a Republic had been proclaimed, & received with acclamations of joy by the people.

As at that period, on account of the internal commotions of the country, the general communications on the route to England were for a time suspended, & in some instances letters and papers did not reach their destinations, and fearing less a similar fate might have attended the above mentioned communication to the Dept. of State, I deemed it my duty on this occasion to repeat some of the important particulars contained there, transmitting at the same time a second copy of the letter addressed by the Venetian Republic to the U.S. of America.

I informed the Department in that paper of the part I felt myself called upon to act, upon the occasion of the proclamation of the Republic and gave the details of my official visit to the Provisional Government. I presented myself before them as the representative of the U.S. charged with the protection of the commercial interests of my country for the port of Venice, to offer them my congratulations upon the new order of things, & expressing the conviction that the step I had taken, though without instructions, would meet with the approbation with my government. . . .

The Republic has been in existence six weeks and numerous ameliorations which have been introduced during that period in the internal affairs of the city & provinces, such as in the reduction of the price of salt, the abolition of the "personal tax" & the revision of the tariff, have established confidence, elicited the good wishes of the people, & produced a strong party who will employ all their energies to sustain it in preference to any other form of government. At present, however, few occupy themselves about the affairs of the future. The whole energies of the nation are directed toward the one great object of expelling the Austrians from Italian soil, and the Governments of Milan & Venice have announced that when that great end is accomplished, it is their intention to call together two assemblies, one for Lombardy & one for the Venetian provinces. If the two thus separately called shall deem a junction possible, they are to constitute one General Assembly for the purpose of deliberating upon the choice of some form Government which may appear them best adapted to promote the course of liberty and above all to consolidate the union of all Italian States.

I have the honor to be &c., &c., yours respectfully

W. A. Sparks

1851 Gold and Opportunity in Australia
Dispatch from U.S. Consul General in Sydney James H. Williams to Secretary of State Daniel Webster

Australia, although discovered by the Dutch in the early seventeenth century, was not populated by Europeans until more than 150 years later. In 1788 Captain Arthur Phillip led a convoy of eleven ships carrying 717 convicts to establish a settlement near what is now the city of Sydney. Over the next half century tens of thousands of convicts and an even greater number of free settlers established themselves in the new colony, making Sydney the commercial hub of the South Pacific. By the early 1850s Australia had become a thriving British colonial outpost. The discovery of gold in 1851 sparked a further influx of population and a commercial boom. Finally, Australia eclipsed its history as a penal colony and seemed to many a land of riches and opportunity.

Among those who foresaw a bright future for Australia was James Williams, the first U.S. consul in Sydney. In this dispatch Williams announces the discovery of gold in the interior. He also takes the opportunity to report on Australia's other resources and riches, comparing it favorably to California, where gold had been discovered just three years earlier.

Sydney, New South Wales,
31st May, 1851

Sir:

I have the honor to communicate for your information the important fact of the discovery in this colony of gold in quantity. . . .

That this event will exercise a vast and accumulating influence upon the destinies of this colony and also upon the social and commercial interests of mankind is not, I think, open to doubt. Nor can I doubt either that the ever ready and active enterprise of our countrymen will eagerly seize upon this new field of profitable adventure and that we shall consequently witness a large and increasing intercourse between the United States and New South Wales.

It therefore appears to me as not being out of place to draw your attention to the general condition and circumstances of this country at the present.

Rich copper and iron ores have for sometime past been known to abound in the district of the country in which gold has now been found. . . . Since the discovery of gold it has been announced that diamonds and other stones have been found. I believe the report to be correct.

The same district and its neighborhood are among the most fertile . . . to be found in the country and fitted to produce grains. . . .

There are very extensive and rich agricultural districts both south of Port Jackson consisting of rich alluvial deposits along the rivers and which but await the introduction of a sufficient population to abound in plantations of cotton and in various semi-tropical products which may be cultivated by European labor. The vine is already cultivated in the earlier settled portions of the colony. . . .

The country abounds in extensive coal fields. . . .

A railway to the interior has been commenced which undoubtedly is the first of a series that will ere long intersect the country in every direction. . . .

The native timber is so nearly incombustible that an extensive fire has never occurred in Sydney, the principal city, not withstanding the reckless character of its earlier inhabitants.

The city of Sydney already contains upwards of 40,000 people and abounds with commodious stone and brick dwelling houses, workhouses and manufactories, wharves, marine railways, and all the conveniences and appliances of a large commercial depot equal at least to those of any city of its size either in Great Britain or the United States. Its harbor is unsurpassed for commodiousness and security and a thousand ships might safely reside at anchor in its waters. . . .

Thus I have endeavored to place before you some of those natural resources and acquired advantages which are in my opinion calculated to raise this country to an important position in the commercial world. I trust that an extensive intercourse with our own countrymen may result in benefit to both. . . . To those who bring either their property or their persons to this distant portion of the world are assurances of greater security and comfort than existed in California at the time gold was discovered there, in as much as the country already abounds with comfortable dwellings . . . whilst to those whose sole capital is their power to labor and who are disappointed in their search for gold, there is the security of ample remunerative employment from the existing interests of a country 60 years established. . . .

In connexion with the subject of this communication I may mention that I have noticed both in California and New York newspapers charges against the Government of New South Wales and Van Diaman's Island for furnishing convicts with the means of emigrating to California. So far as this colony is concerned, I unhesitatingly find the charge to be unfounded. . . .

> I have the honor to be
> Sir
> Your most obedient servant,
>
> J. H. Williams

1853 Guerrilla Warfare in Southeast Asia: The British in Burma

Dispatch from U.S. Consul in Calcutta Charles Huffnagle to Secretary of State William L. Marcy

British expansion in India brought the British Empire into conflict with the Kingdom of Burma, leading to three wars between 1824 and 1886. The Second Burmese War (1852–1853) is reported in this dispatch from U.S. Consul in Calcutta Charles Huffnagle. The war began over insults to British subjects by Burma's rulers. British forces captured Rangoon in April 1852 but then faced a difficult guerrilla campaign in the jungles of Southeast Asia. A combined force of infantry and steam-powered gunboats eventually subdued the Burmese. In the wake of the British victory the king of Burma was deposed, the British annexed Lower Burma, and the new king moved his capital to Mandalay.

> Calcutta, April 18th, 1853

Sir:

My last despatches being under the date of January 3rd, sending the usual Consular documents as required, announcing the annexation of the southern portion of the Burmese Empire by public proclamation, and transmitting a Govt. map of the provinces thus subjected to British rule & subjoined to their vast Empire.

I have now the honour to beg reference to former communications and in continuation to report that the war against Burmah still continues with varied success, always however resulting in the triumph of the British army, which, supported by the steam fleet (upon the rivers everywhere intersecting the invaded district) appears notwithstanding most annoying opposition to be steadily advancing towards the Capitol. The rumour of the dethronement of the King, & the investiture of a new sovereign consequent on a new revolution at Ava, led to the belief that the war would be speedily terminated, and the annexed provinces ceded by treaty as the price of peace.

This however has as yet not been the result and fresh outbreaks in localities where disturbances were not anticipated lead to the opinion that the struggle will be prolonged.

The season is already from the great heat very adverse to hostile operations, where Europeans are concerned; and the approaching rains will still further add to the distress of the British troops, it is therefore very probable that the invading forces will be compelled to prosecute their march upon Ava the Burmese capitol.

We have seventeen (17) American vessels now lying off Calcutta. . . .

> I have the honor Sir
> to remain
> Yr. faithful servant
>
> Charles Huffnagle

1853 First Visit to the Interior of China
Dispatch from U.S. Commissioner in China Humphrey Marshall to Secretary of State William L. Marcy

The mid-nineteenth century was a period of tremendous turmoil in China. In the 1840s China was compelled by the British, under force of arms, to open several cities to foreign commerce and to grant trade concessions to Western countries. This led to further foreign encroachments, including an increase in the opium trade, establishment of consular courts to try foreigners accused of crimes, and tolerance of Christianity. The Ching dynasty had not recovered from these capitulations when the most significant domestic revolt of the century, the Taiping Rebellion (1850–1864), swept across China. By 1853 the Taipings had captured Nanking, China's second largest city, and controlled a huge area of central China.

The U.S. commissioner in China during part of this period of upheaval was Humphrey Marshall. Based in Canton like his predecessors, Marshall became the first American to travel in an official capacity to the more northern port of Shanghai and to penetrate even a few miles into the interior of China. In this dispatch Marshall describes in detail his brief but historic trip inland from Shanghai.

Shanghai, 6th July, 1853

Sir:

I informed . . . the Provincial Judge, who is also called *Taoutai*, . . . of my wish to send a letter to the Emperor from the President of the United States, and that a personal interview [with the viceroy] would be necessary for that purpose. . . . On the 28 of June I learned that His Excellency . . . had directed the Provincial Judge to arrange the meeting for Kwoonsan, a walled city ninety le from Suchow (thirty miles/200 le) from Shanghai and accessible from both places by water. . . .

As occasions like this cannot frequently occur, it may be useful to my successors in office to record minutely the arrangements for this official interview, and the manner in which it was conducted. My escort being small, seven boats were employed to transport us to Kwoonsan, one for myself and one for each of the citizens of the United States accompanying me, one for the Chinese writer and teachers, one for the chairbearers and servants, and one for the culinary department and mess stores. Sedan chairs were employed for each of the persons attached to the commissions. To mine were assigned eight bearers, to the Consular Clerk (acting on this occasion as Consul) four, to the Capital Secretary and each of the others two bearers. As belonging to my rank, my chair was attended by two personal servants (like outriders to a gentleman's carriage) and to the Consul one.

The flag of the United States floated at the masthead of my boat, and I kept it flying during the voyage and until my return to this port.

I congratulate myself that I have been the first to display the National Ensign in the interior of China, and I am gratified to report that, unassisted by force of any description, it was treated everywhere with the most perfect respect. To exhibit my reliance on the flag, it was festooned also around my chair. I arrived at the Pagoda, three miles from Kwoonsan, after midnight on the 3d of July. . . . The excitement of the populace was manifested by the hurrying to and fro of the men, women and children, of whom there were thousands upon the shores of the Sankanku, to behold the strange flag and people now, for the first time, entering the "flowery land." At the landing I was received by salutes from the mandarin vessels attached to the Custom House, and from the boats of Mandarins who had come to Kwoonsan for this occasion. Lines of Chinese soldiery were drawn up on the shore. As I passed to my chair on the landing, bands of Chinese music struck up airs—which my musical attainments are altogether inadequate to describe. There were thousands of persons, known to me as gentlemen by their silk and crepe robes, and the fans which they held over their heads, who thronged the open space in front of the landing. The Chinese women, contrary to what I had supposed was the national custom, in their holiday attire were in the doors and windows, and on all the sidewalks in front of all the houses. I have never in my life seen a whole population as well dressed as this at Kwoonsan—never a more healthy and good looking people, or one more gentle and well-behaved. The chairs were escorted by a core soldiery, and I remarked that policemen were stationed on either side of the streets at intervals of some thirty or forty paces, but I saw nothing in the demeanor of the people to call for any such precautionary measure. Both of the streets, from the landing to the temple (about three quarters of a mile) were literally lined by masses of human beings, animated by the most intense curiosity. This I gratified so far as I was able. I have never seen more perfect order preserved in such an assemblage of people. There was no noise or confusion—no crowding and rushing upon each other with exclamations and cries, as I have sometimes witnessed elsewhere. The curious feature in this scene was *the entire population, habited in their best attire,* and engaged in the duty of "accepting" the guests of the Viceroy. I did not see one single man who was not cleanly dressed. The women wore flowers in their hair, and the children were neatly clad as for a gala. There was no such thing as mistaking the intent of the people to give me a welcome, as well as the public authorities.

Arriving at the Temple, I was introduced into a large court, where the departmental authorities were drawn up in order to pay their respects. I made my bow in acknowledgement of the courtesy. I now saw a very venerable man, of near seventy years of age, advancing to meet me. It was the Viceroy, I Liang, a kinsmen of the Emperor and now holding a rank—as Governor General of *three* Capital Provinces—second only to that of His Imperial Majesty. . . . Though evidently he is a well-bred gentleman, the occasion of meeting a foreigner was so perfectly new to him, that his manner was perceptibly constrained. He advanced to salute me at first in Chinese fashion, inclining the body forward and holding his hands closed and clasped in front, at the same time moving them up and down as if shaking hands. I offered him, in Western fashion, the open right hand, which he then clasped in both his palms and shook right heartily. . . . I was now invited to a seat, and was placed on the left hand of the Viceroy. . . . Tea and other refreshments were now handed to the company. His Excellency welcomed me to China. . . .

The Viceroy then said very solemnly that he would guarantee, if delivered to him, that the President's letter should go without unnecessary delay direct to His Imperial Majesty, and that it should be acknowledged in becoming terms—he thought the reply could be received in forty days. It would require sixteen days to reach Peking, and sixteen to return by the circuitous route at present travelled from this province to the capital. I then remarked that I would deliver the President's letter to him under these assurances. . . . The letter of the President accrediting me as

Commissioner, was then delivered to I Liang to be transmitted to Peking and he accepted the same with evident satisfaction. . . .

The conversation was for sometime confined to such inquires as our ages and my voyage to China &c., &c., and then His Excellency delicately alluded to the disturbed condition of China, offering that as an apology for what he was pleased to say was a failure to receive me on a scale equal to his own desire and proportional to my high rank.

I begged to assure him of the great satisfaction I experienced from the cordial welcome that had been extended to me, and especially for the kind consideration of my convenience which had induced him to leave the theatre of his official duties and to come so far to receive me. Then I remarked that I had learned with profound regret that China is afflicted by civil war and that Nanking is held by the rebel forces, that I trusted to the good sense of her rulers and to the patriotism of the people to restore China to peace and prosperity. I asked how large a force now holds Nanking. His Excellency replied that, there were "many tens of thousands" in force at Nanking . . . and that their presence imposed on him the most onerous duties—that the city of Nanking was his own proper official residence, but he regrets that he was unable to see me there on account of the rebels. I said that I hoped to have the pleasure yet of seeing him peaceably enjoying at his capital the honors due to his exalted station, and services to the Empire. I expressed my pleasure at the appearance of the country through which I had passed, at the friendly demeanor of the people and my astonishment at the quiet which seems to prevail in the country so near to the revolutionary forces. . . . I then remarked that if I resided at Shanghai, and could improve my acquaintance with him by seeing him at Suchow or Nanking, and occasionally at my own residence, I thought my public duties besides being rendered pleasant might serve to efface prejudices . . . which retarded that intimate friendly intercourse which ought to exist between the United States and China. The *Taoutai* interposed with a remark that he could see no occasion for my going to Canton to live, that Shanghai was a much better place, and the people were very friendly, and if I lived at Shanghai there would be many pleasant excursions I could make into the interior . . . when peace was restored. . . . The conversation was turned again to the matter of the rebellion, and I think that great anxiety sat on the countenance of the Viceroy. Among other things, he desired to know if I would permit him to consult with me occasionally on points of interest to China. I said it would afford me infinite pleasure to serve his country and himself, whenever I could do so with propriety. I took the liberty to repeat that the Emperor . . . would appeal strongly to Western Nations by reversing his policy at once, liberalizing the regulations of commerce, giving absolute freedom of conscience, and opening his country at large to foreigners. I said that I understood all these points to be promised by the rebels at Nanking, as the first fruits of their success. The Viceroy said he could not say all he desired, lest his conversations might be overheard and reported. It was arranged that we should write directly to each other as occasions seemed to required. . . .

I venture to express the hope that the President will see in the results of this visit enough to justify my remaining at Shanghai. . . . The flag of the United States under my guidance is the first that has ever gone independently yet amicably into the interior of China. . . .

The simplicity and the timidity of some of the country people may be imagined, when I inform you a crowd of women and children who were gazing at me saw my servant hand me a bunch of cigars, and they took to their heels as if I was about to open a battery upon them. They thought the cigars were implements of war. I was careful to collect them again to assure them of their safety, and to smoke the pipes of peace with the men of the vicinity. I was very particular to land frequently on my voyage, and to communicate with the people whenever I could do so, to assure them that the flag they now saw belonged to a Great Power and a good friend of the Chinese. We returned to Shanghai after midnight on the 5th of July without having met any incident to mar the pleasures of the excursion. . . .

Were steam introduced upon the Yangtsze and its affluents, I have no doubt that Shanghai would instantly appear the natural port for eight of the richest provinces of the Empire. . . . Nor would her rising grandeur necessarily destroy Canton. . . . This despatch is already of such length that I forebear entering upon this great subject at present.

There is no ship of the U.S. on the coast of China. I send you a copy of a letter I received a few days since from citizens of the United States at Fuhchaufoo. The rebellion has extended inland from Amoy; another city in that quarter has fallen into the hands of the rebels. . . .

                          I am Sir, most respectfully
                          Your very obedient Servant

                          Humphrey Marshall

1854   First Attempt to Annex Hawaii
Dispatch from U.S. Minister to Hawaii David L. Gregg to Secretary of State William L. Marcy

The United States was the predominant trading and whaling nation in the South Pacific as early as the 1820s, but unlike its maritime rivals, Great Britain and France, the United States initially refrained from territorial acquisitions. American representatives on the Hawaiian islands frequently urged a U.S. takeover, in this instance going as far as negotiating a treaty providing for Hawaiian statehood. Despite the optimistic tone of this dispatch, a treaty of cession was not signed for almost another fifty years.

Honolulu, August 7, 1854

Sir:

I am only able to write briefly by the mail which goes this afternoon, being much debilitated by an attack of sickness from which I am just convalescent.

The Government here rests on a volcano. Its subversion is within the power of the foreign residents, and I am prepared to witness an outbreak at any moment. The dissatisfaction with the present state of things is daily increasing, and a crisis of some sort is inevitable.

On Tuesday evening last there was an intense alarm among the native population on account of the supposed presence of "filibusters." The troops were called out and remained under arms all night. The apprehension seems to have been excited by the discovery of a box of pistols among some goods landed at the custom-house.

I have succeeded in arranging the terms of a treaty of annexation with the minister of foreign relations, which meets the approval of the Crown Prince and cabinet. But it is not yet signed, and I am unable to give you any assurance that it will be immediately completed. The pretense of delay is the supposed necessity of consulting the King, which for sometime has been impossible on account of His Majesty's illness.

The great difficulty I had to encounter was the inveterate prejudice of the Hawaiian authorities against a territorial form of government, which could not be overcome. Finding it impossible to provide otherwise, I finally consented to agree to the admission of the islands as a State, as soon as it could be done in conformity with the principles and requirements of the Federal Constitution, leaving the existing laws, so far as they are republican and consistent with such Constitution, in full force and effect in the meantime.

There was also much controversy as to the extent of consideration. The Government absolutely refused to listen to anything short of annuities to the extent of $300,000, and I finally listened to the *sine qua non* which they presented, with the understanding that it was solely *ad referendum*.

I had intended to send you a copy of the treaty as agreed on, for information, but I have been altogether unequal to the task of making it in time for the present mail.

I have, etc.,

David L. Gregg

1854 The Ostend Manifesto
Dispatch from U.S. Ministers to Spain, Great Britain, and France
Pierre Soulé, James Buchanan, and John Mason to
Secretary of State William L. Marcy

The enormous U.S. territorial acquisition resulting from the Mexican War did not put an end to the American desire for more land. President Franklin Pierce owed his election in 1852 in part to the support of expansionists who wanted to extend U.S. rule over the Caribbean, Mexico, and Canada. Pierce appointed advocates of expansion to several European diplomatic posts. Most notable was Pierre Soulé, an impetuous former senator from Louisiana who was appointed minister to Spain with secret instructions to purchase Cuba or to "detach" it from Spanish rule. Soulé's initial efforts, however, were rebuffed by the Spanish.

In 1854 Soulé arranged to meet in Ostend, Belgium, with the American ministers to France and Great Britain to coordinate an approach to acquiring Cuba. The three ministers produced this dispatch which came to be known as the "Ostend Manifesto." It supported the purchase of Cuba or, if necessary, the seizure of the island from Spain. The confidential dispatch quickly leaked to the press and caused a furor not only in Europe but also among Northerners in the United States who were opposed to acquiring more slave territory. Pierce and his secretary of state, William Marcy, were forced to back down and disclaim their ministers' suggestion. Soulé resigned in disgust. Coauthor James Buchanan became the next president of the United States, partly on the strength of the southern support he won through his association with the Ostend Manifesto.

> Aix la Chapelle,
> October 18, 1854

The undersigned . . . have met in conference, first at Ostend, in Belgium, on the 9th, 10th, and 11th instant, and then at Aix la Chapelle, in Prussia, on the days next following, up to the date hereof.

There has been a full and unreserved interchange of views and sentiments between us, which we are most happy to inform you has resulted in a cordial coincidence of opinion on the grave and important subjects submitted to our consideration.

We have arrived at the conclusion, and are thoroughly convinced, that an immediate and earnest effort ought to be made by the government of the United States to purchase Cuba from Spain. . . .

It can scarcely be apprehended that foreign powers, in violation of international law, would interpose their influence with Spain to prevent our acquisition of the island. Its inhabitants are now suffering under the worst of all possible governments, that of absolute despotism, delegated by a distant power to irresponsible agents, who are changed at short intervals, and who are tempted to improve the brief opportunity thus afforded to accumulate fortunes by the basest means.

As long as this system shall endure, humanity may in vain demand the suppression of the African slave trade in the island. This is rendered impossible whilst that infamous traffic remains an irresistible temptation and a source of immense profit to needy and avaricious officials, who, to attain their ends, scruple not to trample the most sacred principles under foot. . . .

Under no probable circumstances can Cuba ever yield to Spain one per cent on the large amount which the United States are willing to pay for its acquisition. But Spain is in imminent danger of losing Cuba, without remuneration.

Extreme oppression, it is now universally admitted, justifies any people in endeavoring to relieve themselves from the yoke of their oppressors. The sufferings which the corrupt, arbitrary, and unrelenting local administration necessarily entails upon the inhabitants of Cuba, cannot fail to stimulate and keep alive that spirit of resistance and revolution against Spain, which has, of late years, been so often manifested. . . .

After we shall have offered Spain a price for Cuba far beyond its present value, and this shall have been refused, it will then be time to consider the question, does Cuba, in the possession of Spain, seriously endanger our internal peace and the existence of our cherished Union?

Should this question be answered in the affirmative, then, by every law, human and divine, we shall be justified in wresting it from Spain if we possess the power. . . .

We should . . . be recreant to our duty, be unworthy of our gallant forefathers, and commit base treason against our posterity, should we permit Cuba to be Africanized and become a second St. Domingo, with all its attendant horrors to the white race, and suffer the flames to extend to our own neighboring shores, seriously to endanger or actually to consume the fair fabric of our Union. . . .

Pierre Soulé
James Buchanan
John Mason

1855 British Ignorance of U.S. Politics

Dispatch from U.S. Minister to Great Britain James Buchanan to Secretary of State William L. Marcy

James Buchanan, fifteenth president of the United States (1857–1861), served for three years as minister in London (1853–1856). Earlier, Buchanan had served briefly as minister to Russia and as President James K. Polk's secretary of state. While in London, Buchanan expressed frustration at the British lack of interest in American politics, a situation that would change only with the onset of the American Civil War.

London, 5 April, 1855

Sir:

... There is one circumstance calculated to exercise an unfavorable influence on the relations between the two countries to which I desire to call your special attention: and this is, the profound ignorance which prevails among the mass of otherwise well informed people here concerning the government policy and institutions of our country. All Americans who have travelled in England can testify to the fact. The cause is apparent. The London Journals never republish even a sketch of the debates or proceedings in Congress, and the same may be said, with rare exceptions, of which the President's message is always an instance, in regard to our most important official documents.

A discussion in the legislative assemblies of Prussia, Sardinia, Belgium, or any other European State, on any important subject, is always noticed in these journals, and the character of their leading statesmen and debaters is brought before the British people. American statesmen and Parliamentarians who would do honor to any country are here entirely unknown even by name.

... According to my best recollection, no political article from the Washington Union, or any other Press of a similar character, has ever been republished in London since my arrival in this country.

When other nations are assailed or misrepresented for some reason or other, one or more London Journals are always ready and willing to defend them; but against such assaults the United States have no means of self-protection. In this respect, no reciprocity exists between the two countries; because the British Government is always defended in our country, and British editorials, as well as news, constitute a principal staple of the whole American Press. . . .

It might be inferred from what has been said, that as the Public Press is generally a fair reflection of public opinion; the British people must necessarily be unfriendly or indifferent in their feelings toward the people of the United States. Judging both from my social intercourse in this country, which has been pretty extensive, and from manifestations which I have observed on public occasions such an inference would not, in the main, be correct. . . .

Having a leisure hour morning, before going to the Foreign Office by appointment at 4 o'clock, I thought it might not be either uninteresting or useless to you to have your attention directed to the facts stated in this Dispatch.

Yours very respectfully,
James Buchanan

1855 A Consular Case: "Assault with Intent to Commit Murder"

Dispatch from U.S. Consul in Liverpool Nathaniel Hawthorne to U.S. Minister to Great Britain James Buchanan

American consuls in foreign ports had to deal with all manner of seamen's problems: mutiny, desertion, disabled or destitute sailors, and crimes committed at sea. In the 1850s much of the commerce between Britain and the United States was carried on through the bustling port of Liverpool, which saw more than its share of such maritime problems. The U.S. consul in Liverpool from 1853 to 1857 was eminent author Nathaniel Hawthorne. In this dispatch Hawthorne relates the evidence in a case of attempted murder and asks the U.S. minister in London, James Buchanan, to arrange for the arrest of the suspect. Hawthorne describes the incident through affidavits of generally illiterate seamen; the resulting narrative would be worthy of a novel.

Liverpool, 30th July, 1855

Sir:

I beg to enclose herewith affidavits of the master and three of the crew of the American Ship "Cultivator," charging Henry Morris Johnson with the crime of assault with intent to commit murder, on board the said vessel, while within the jurisdiction of the United States, in order that you may make requisition for the surrender and extradition of the accused, under the tenth section of the treaty with Great Britain of 1842.

Johnson is now in confinement on board the vessel in the dock at this Port, and must be kept there until the magistrate can issue a warrant for his apprehension, which he cannot do until he is notified by the Secretary of State of your having made the requisition.

With high respect I have the honor to be Your Obed. Servant

Nath'l Hawthorne

ENCLOSURE

Be it known that on this twenty-eighth day of July, year of our Lord one thousand eight hundred and fifty-five before me Nathaniel Hawthorne, Consul of the United States of America for the Port of Liverpool and its dependencies, personally came and appeared Charles Ryan and being by me duly sworn upon the Holy Gospels says, "I am a seaman on board the American ship Cultivator of New York, now lying in the river Mersey; I shipped in her at New York about the third day of July, present; about seven days after sailing, I cannot recollect the day of the month, it was on a Tuesday morning, between two and three o'clock, a man we call Tom, whose other name I don't know, was at the wheel, the second mate went to brace the yards in, myself, Stephen Brogan (a boy) and William Green were on deck; I and the boy were on the port side. The second mate sung out to the man Tom at the wheel, 'Where was he going with the vessel,' twice. The man made no answer. The second mate then sung out, 'Whose wheel is it?,' and the man William answered it was his. The second mate said, 'Well you had better go and take it,' and he went, and Tom left the wheel, and came towards where I was, near the main hatch, and I said to him, 'You are a pretty bugger, couldn't steer the vessel,'—with that he drew off saying 'You son of a bitch you are one of them,' and struck me, and I immediately began to tremble and feel as if the breath was going from me and felt at my side. The boy sung out 'Oh! He has stabbed you,' and I then saw he had a knife in his hand. I then ran across the hatch and called to the second mate 'I am stabbed.' I then fell and remember nothing more. When I came to, the Captain was sewing the wound. I have been laid out ever since and am now able to move about a little but feel a great deal of pain in my side. I never had the least difficulty or quarrel with the man before. I never saw him before seeing him on board the Cultivator. When I said to him 'You are a pretty bugger couldn't steer the vessel,' he stabbed me immediately."

          Charles Ryan
          X (mark)

          Sworn before me this
          28 day of July, 1855
          Nathaniel Hawthorne

At the same time came and appeared before me the said Consul, Stephen Brogan, the boy referred to by the last witness, and being sworn (first being questioned respecting his knowledge of the nature of an oath) says, "I am twelve years old and have been about a year to sea, all the time on board the Cultivator. I saw the man Tom stab the last witness. I was close to them—near the main hatch—and as soon as I saw him do it I jumped across the hatch and ran away, I thought he was going to stab me. I was standing alongside of the man Ryan, the last witness, when Tom came from the wheel towards us. I did not see anything in his hand then—I did not hear him say anything. I heard Ryan say to him when he got to us, 'You are a hell of a bugger not to steer the ship, the ship's easy to steer.' Those were the words as near as I recollect and Tom then stabbed him—he did it at once. I did not hear anything else pass between them. I didn't see the knife only when he was pulling it out of him, Ryan,—I never knew them to have any quarrel before. I did not hear what passed between the second mate and Tom. It happened between two and three in the morning, on a Tuesday morning."

> Stephen Brogan
> X (mark)
>
> Sworn before me at Liverpool,
> this 28th day of July 1855
> Nath'l Hawthorne

At the same time before me the said Consul personally appeared and came William Green, and being by me duly sworn said, "I am a seaman on board the Cultivator. I shipped in her at New York. About a quarter before three in the morning of the tenth of July, seven days after we left New York on the passage to Liverpool, I was one of the watch on deck and I was walking forward then I heard the second mate sing out, 'Whose watch is it?' and I told him it was mine, and he told me to go and take it. I went aft to take the wheel from the man Tom. When I got to the wheel I asked him what was the matter he couldn't steer. He made answer it was the first time he was ever sent away from a ship's wheel and it would be the last. To take the wheel I had to go round behind him and when I was taking the wheel from him I saw him take the knife out of his sheath and look at it and turn it round in his hand and put it in the sheath again.

He stood there about two minutes and then took it—the knife—out again, looked at it and put it in the sheath again and then went away forward. I saw no more of him until I was relieved at the wheel, when I saw him made fast by a rope on deck. I don't know the man's name—he went by the name of Tom. I never heard of any quarrel between him and Ryan."

> William Green
>
> Sworn before me at Liverpool,
> this 28th July 1855
> Nat'l Hawthorne

Be it known that on this thirtieth day of July in the year of our Lord one thousand eight hundred and fifty-five before me the said Consul, personally appeared and came George Blackstone Austin, master of the American ship Cultivator of New York, and being duly sworn, said that he sailed with said vessel from New York on the third day of July, instant; that on the tenth of said month about two in the morning, said vessel being then in about 40° North latitude, he was called on deck by the second mate and informed that a man had been stabbed and he immediately went to his assistance—found him dangerously wounded on the left side near the fourth or fifth rib— that his name is Charles Ryan—that he then had the perpetrator put in irons—that his name is Henry Morris Johnson—that he has kept him in irons since.

> G. B. Austin
>
> Sworn to before me
> this 30th July 1855
> Nath'l Hawthorne

1857 The Indian Mutiny: "India Is Held by the Sword"
Dispatch from U.S. Consul in Calcutta Charles Huffnagle to Secretary of State Lewis Cass

By the mid-nineteenth century, India had become the most important of Great Britain's colonies. British control over the subcontinent expanded steadily each year as British governors assumed direct rule over additional territories. The problems accompanying modernization and colonial administration, however, led to frequent tensions and occasional revolts. The British maintained control by recruiting an enormous army of Indian soldiers, "sepoys," commanded and led by British officers. In the army of Bengal, sepoys outnumbered Europeans by seven to one.

The Indian Mutiny of 1857 was different in scope and ferocity from any other conflict the British faced in India. Tens of thousands of sepoys revolted. To regain control, the British were forced to deploy more troops than had fought in the recently concluded Crimean War. The trouble came about in an astounding manner. The sepoys were issued new Enfield rifles whose cartridges were greased with pork and beef fat. The standard loading drill required that the cartridges be held in the soldiers' mouths. This procedure offended both Hindus and Moslems, uniting them against the British. The cartridge problem eventually was corrected but too late to stem the discontent. The mutiny began in Meerut; within days the mutineers controlled much of northern and eastern India.

The outbreak of the mutiny is reported in this dispatch by U.S. Consul Charles Huffnagle, written seven weeks after the revolt began. Huffnagle reports optimistically that British troops are on the verge of recapturing Delhi. In fact, Delhi would hold out for another three months and the mutiny would not be entirely quelled for another year.

Steamer "Ava," Red Sea
June 29, 1857

Sir:

It is with extreme regret that I have to inform the Department that a recurrence of the fever from which I last year suffered has compelled me to leave my duties & seek for health (under the advice of the medical man who has attended me) by a sea voyage away from the shores of India. . . .

With reference to the . . . very peculiar state of political affairs in the East . . . I have deemed it more prudent to return home in the anticipation of the honor of a personal interview with His Excellency the President & yourself, than to pass the time required for my recovery in expensive & tedious voyages across these Eastern Seas.

I cannot in closing this despatch avoid averting to the political condition in which I have just left the great Indian Empire. The Department are aware that India is held by the sword & that thro' the instrumentality of mercenaries enlisted from among the people, the country is chiefly kept in subjection by the sword of the native soldier. These "Sepoys" are selected in Bengal from the higher castes of the Hindoo population & each of these seventy-four regiments of native infantry &c. contains also a large population of Mohammedans. Early in April serious dissatisfaction became apparent, chiefly from objections being made to a new description of cartridge, prepared in England of glazed paper & sent out to Calcutta for the use of the Indian army. The native soldiers declared that these cartridges were made up with the fat of beef & pork & as it was necessary to bite the cartridge the Hindoo would be defiled with the beef & the Mohammedan by the pork & that consequently their caste would be lost forever. They further declared that this was a scheme devised by the Government to destroy their religion & force them to become Christians!

Many believe that disaffection had been spreading for months far & wide throughout the native army, excited by mysterious influences, fostered by religious prejudices & encouraged everywhere by the Brahmins who are looked up to with awe and reverence by the whole of this weak, ignorant & preeminently superstitious population, & who are notoriously & for obvious reasons are hostile to the advance of Christianity. The cartridge question therefore was considered as only a pretext for revolt. . . .

On Sunday the 10th of May between 5 & 6 o'clock in the evening the open revolt commenced at Meerut; the native troops at that important station rebelled, shot their officers, fired the buildings in the lines & after the most horrible & revolting excesses, murdered all the Europeans they could find including women & children & then with yells of triumph marched on towards the city of Delhi. At Delhi they were received with open arms by the troops there, who instantly fraternizing with the mutineers carried on another frightful butchery, every European being ruthlessly slaughtered who had not time or opportunity to fly for life. From station to station this disloyal spirit is now steadily travelling & fears were at one time reasonably entertained for the safety of Calcutta itself. Day by day the British (European) troops are being collected at the capital, by means of steamers despatched to the different parts of the Empire & at date of this departure (6th June) a strong force has already arrived & detachments are being hastened up the country to reinforce the European army.... Major General Anson the Cdr. in Chief has hastened at the head of all the European troops he could collect towards Delhi (now the head qrts. of the mutineers who have declared a king) but Genl. Anson from exposure to the sun was attacked by Cholera & died after a couple of hours on the 27th of May. The command was then assumed by Major General Sir H. Barnard & while this vessel was lying at Madras on the llth of June a despatch was rec'd from Govt. stating that "the European troops had reached Delhi, killed & routed a force sent out of the city to oppose them & that they had seized all the heights & outer wall & captured 26 guns." I have thus given you the latest intelligence & such is the state of affairs in India! Confidence in a Sepoy army is gone forever. India must be reconquered by an army of Europeans & when reconquered must be held by a large European force.

> I have the honor to be Sir,
> Yr. obt. Servant,
>
> Charles Huffnagle

1858   Emancipation of the Russian Serfs
Dispatch from U.S. Consul in Moscow Francis S. Claxton to Secretary of State Lewis Cass

The reign of Czar Alexander II (1855–1881) was a period of liberalization in Russia. He is best known for emancipating Russia's serfs, who lived in conditions of near slavery. Russian nobles "owned" the serfs in their domains—that is, serfs could be purchased and sold, or pressed into occupations other than agriculture. One of Alexander's early acts was the establishment of a special committee to study the problem of serfdom and recommend how the system could be ended without harm to the national economy or to the gentry. The process stirred a tremendous national debate. In 1858, as reported in this dispatch, Alexander issued a decree freeing the slaves of three provinces. This was followed in 1861 by an edict emancipating all of Russia's serfs.

Americans at that time—on the eve of the Civil War—were preoccupied with domestic issues and generally showed little concern about developments in Europe. The question of emancipation, however, was relevant enough to developments at home that it generated substantial interest.

Moscow, Jany. 1st, 1858

Sir,

... I have the honour to report that the whole of the central and southern portions of this Empire are now being agitated by the momentous question of the rumoured contemplated emancipation of the serfs.

Opinions are divided even amongst the proprietors as to the results of such a measure, some few contending that the country will be benefited and the fortunes of the nobles unimpaired; whilst by far the greater portion fear that anarchy & confusion will result, and that the peasantry should be educated & prepared for the change in this political & social condition.

By an Imperial decree to take effect 1st Jany . . . the serfs of [some] . . . provinces . . . are declared free. . . . The Imperial Govert. may . . . receive the benefit of . . . suggestions as to the best mode of carrying out the avowed wishes of the Emperor for the amelioration of the condition of this vast majority of his subjects.

In a country where there are so few public journals, & their circulation so limited, the transmission of intelligence is dependant upon the memory, & subject to the imagination & invention of the passing traveller or trader, hence it is not surprising that this action & movement of the govert in their regard, is deemed by the peasants as the final & conclusive declaration of their efranchisement & that the idea prevails, that the nobles retain them in bondage unlawfully & this has engendered ill feeling & disagreements so that to use the words of an extensive proprietor "all white (central) Russia is in a blaze", and the fear is freely expressed and appears to be generally entertained that serious troubles may arise & blood may be shed; as an indication of this feeling, remonstrances have been made that a translation into Russ of "Uncle Tom's Cabin" now in press, . . . is . . . purposely incendiary and calculated "to mislead the peasantry into the idea that they are no better circumstanced and treated than the slaves in America." . . .

> I have the honour to remain
> very respectfully
> Yr obet. servt.
>
> F. S. Claxton

1858 Nicaragua: An Incident en Route to the Capital
Dispatch from U.S. Minister to Nicaragua Mirabeau B. Lamar to Secretary of State Lewis Cass

Mirabeau Lamar was president of the Republic of Texas from 1838 to 1841. A decade after the admission of Texas to the Union, Lamar served briefly as an American diplomat. He was appointed minister to Argentina, but before his departure for Buenos Aires, his assignment was changed to Central America. In February 1858 Lamar arrived in Managua to take up his duties as U.S. minister to Nicaragua and Costa Rica. Traveling by river from the coast to capital, Lamar was involved in an incident that he perceived as a clear case of harassment—or even extortion—of an American. While the type of incident he describes in this dispatch is familiar to many Americans abroad, Lamar thought the case sufficiently significant to report it to Washington as an indication of the difficulties he faced in Central America. Lamar remained in Nicaragua for only a year; he died shortly after his return home in 1859.

Managua, February 26th, 1858

Sir:

Captain Sands of the Susquehanna, fitted up the Steamer Morgan for my conveyance up this river. I left San Juan Del Norte on the 23rd of January and arrived at Castillo Viejo on the 26th of the same. The Commander of the fort had been apprised of my coming by the Consul at San Juan; yet on my arriving within cannon shot of the Castle, a blank cartridge was discharged as signal for us to stop. We came to anchor accordingly, and Lieutenant Hamilton and others went on shore to learn the reason of this detention. The Commandant admitted that he was apprised of my being on board and of the purpose of my ascending the river; but gave no explanation as to his motive for interrupting our passage. We were permitted without further trouble to approach the Castle; on reaching which most of the passengers went on shore to lighten the boat that she might be able to pass over the rapids. She passed without difficulty and immediately made the shore for the purpose of taking in the passengers and also for putting out some freight. This was executed with rapidity and despatch; and the boat was just getting under way again when I heard the screams of a woman and of a boy about 13 or 14 years old, perhaps mother and son, and at the same time the cry of the soldiers, "Stop the boat—stop the boat." On looking out I found the soldiers under arms marsheld by the side of the boat and ready to fire upon us. Not knowing the cause of this uproar and violence I landed immediately and went to the Commandant to inquire into the affair. I was told that an American had attempted the life of a boy and had injured him very seriously. I called for the boy, who was brought forward bellowing vociferously that he was almost killed. I was astonished and indignant to find that the lad was scarcely hurt in the slightest degree. It appeared that Mr. Dunn, a worthy and good man, citizen of the United States but then residing on the San Juan, had in the hurry and confusion of landing the freight, accidentally struck the boy with a barrel while pitching it either into or out of boat. The barrel had slightly touched the boy's upper lip without breaking the skin or drawing one drop of blood. And for this trivial accident the military was brought into requisition, the steamer stopped and Mr. Dunn arrested amidst the loud clamor of the natives. After much excitement and confusion the matter was settled mainly through the interposition of Col. Canty, an Englishman in the Costa Rican Service who was a fellow passenger on the Steamer. The commandant of the Castle agreed to let Dunn go, on his paying something to the boy; and turning to the lad, asked him if he would be satisfied with two dollars. The boy said he would; the money was paid; Dunn released; and the lad went his way contented and cheerful. In the mean time the military was withdrawn and the boat permitted to proceed. Thus ended the affair. I have no comments to offer; but have the honor to be very respectfully.

Your obt. servt.
Mirabeau B. Lamar

PART III

The Civil War Era: 1861–1867

President Lincoln, shown here with his Union generals, led the nation through the turbulent Civil War years. U.S. envoys in Europe found that most governments there were greatly surprised by the secession of the Southern states and the onset of the war.

1861 Reactions to the American Civil War
Dispatches from U.S. Ministers Abroad

The secession of the Southern states and the onset of the American Civil War were viewed with tremendous surprise in many of the courts of Europe, where American domestic politics was little known or understood. The U.S. minister to France characterized the mood on much of the Continent when he reported that "a revolution was as little anticipated in the United States as an earthquake in Paris." In their first reactions, reported in these dispatches, most governments express their support for the Union, but a few remain noncommittal.

The French Reaction
From U.S. Minister to France Charles J. Faulkner to Secretary of State Jeremiah S. Black

Paris, March 19, 1861

Sir:

... I need hardly say to you that the events which have signalized the history of the United States for the last few months have occupied the attention of a very large share of the statesmen and people of Europe. In all my intercourse, public and private, from the Emperor to the peasant, embracing all grades of ministerial and diplomatic agents, it has been the engrossing, I might almost say the only topic of conversation. A revolution was as little anticipated in the United States as an earthquake in Paris.

That large communities should be casting off the protection of a government to which thousands on this continent were looking for the realization of all their dreams of happiness on earth; that a system should be pronounced a failure which has produced, within a few years, the most extraordinary developments of national prosperity and power of which history has left any record; that a flag should be trampled in the dust which has never been stained by oppression, and which is hailed as the emblem of civil and religious freedom in every corner of the globe, were problems well calculated to rouse the inquisitive and to puzzle the uninformed. The consequence was, that there has been, within the last four months, throughout Europe a more thorough and general discussion, by the press and by individuals, of American institutions than had occurred for the previous twenty years. ...

You have not in your despatch informed me what line of policy it is the purpose of the federal government to adopt towards the seceding

States. . . . If I correctly construe the intentions of the government, it looks to a pacific solution of the difficulties which now disturb its relations with the seceding States. In other words, it does not propose to resort to the strong arm of military power to coerce those States into submission to the federal authority. If this be a correct view of its proposed action, and all who understand the genius of our institutions and the character of our people must hope that it shall be such, the only difficulty will be in making European governments appreciate the spirit of such wise and conciliatory policy. . . .

I have no hesitation in expressing it as my opinion, founded upon frequent general interviews with the Emperor [Napoleon III], . . . that France will be the last of the great states of Europe to give a hasty encouragement to the dismemberment of the Union. . . . The unhappy divisions which have afflicted our country have attracted the Emperor's earnest attention. . . . He looks upon the dismemberment of the American confederacy with no pleasure, but as a calamity to be deplored by every enlightened friend of human progress. . . .

I have not, so far, heard that any commissioners have been sent by the seceding States to France. Should they, as you anticipate, arrive shortly, I think I am not mistaken in saying that they will find that the imperial government is not yet prepared to look favorably upon the object of this mission.

I have made this despatch longer, perhaps, than was necessary, for I have not had time to elaborate and digest my ideas very carefully, and submit them as suggestions to elicit more fully the views and instructions of the government.

I am, sir, very respectfully, your obedient servant,

Chas. J. Faulkner

The Portuguese Reaction

From U.S. Minister to Portugal George W. Morgan to Secretary of State William H. Seward

Lisbon, April 6, 1861

Sir:

. . . During the evening his Majesty inquired with interest as to the condition of affairs in the United States, but when I assured him, as I had before done on a similar occasion, that the Union would be preserved, his manner was more expressive of doubt than belief, though he replied that he hoped I was not mistaken, as it would be a great pity to see so fine a country ruined, and I regret to say that my colleagues, and European politicians generally, regard the disruption of the States as an established fact. . . .

With high respect, I have the honor to be your obedient servant,

George W. Morgan

The Russian Reaction
From U.S. Minister to Russia John Appleton to
Secretary of State William H. Seward

St. Petersburg, April 8–20, 1861

Sir:

The despatch of the department No. 10 and your circular of March 9th have been received, and I have had several interviews with Prince Gortchacow on the subject of them. . . . No agent was here from the Confederate States, and none was immediately expected. . . . I . . . expressed the hope that our government might receive from Russia, at this crisis, a renewed manifestation of that friendly disposition which had always marked the intercourse between the United States and that empire. Prince Gortchacow replied that the question of recognizing the Confederate States was not now before the Emperor, and for the present he did not think it would be. I might assure you, he said, that his Majesty was not unmindful of the friendly relations which had so long subsisted between the two countries, and that he sincerely desired the harmony and prosperity of the Union. . . . It was only frank, however, to say, that while things continued as they were, the commerce between the Confederate States and Russia would not be interrupted. . . .

The policy, he said, involved no recognition of nationality, but was only a concession in aid of commerce. I replied that my only interest was to prevent this recognition. . . .

This is the substance of our conversations, and I need hardly trouble you with any comments. . . .

I am, very respectfully, yours,

John Appleton

The British Reaction

From U.S. Minister to Great Britain George M. Dallas to Secretary of State William H. Seward

London, April 9, 1861

Sir:

... I have now the honor to state that [Foreign Minister] Lord John Russell accorded me an interview at the foreign office yesterday....

We conversed for some time on the question of recognizing the alleged southern confederacy, of which no representative has yet appeared, and may not appear until the end of the month.

His lordship assured me with great earnestness that there was not the slightest disposition in the British government to grasp at any advantage which might be supposed to arise from the unpleasant domestic differences in the United States, but, on the contrary, that they would be highly gratified if those differences were adjusted and the Union restored to its former unbroken position....

He seemed to think the matter not ripe for decision one way or the other, and remarked that what he had said was all that at present it was in his power to say. The coming of my successor, Mr. [Charles Francis] Adams, looked for from week to week, would doubtless be regarded as the appropriate and natural occasion for finally discussing and determining the question....

English opinion tends rather, I apprehend, to the theory that a peaceful separation may work beneficially for both groups of States and not injuriously affect the rest of the world....

I have the honor to be, sir, your most obedient servant,

G. M. Dallas

The Spanish Reaction

From U.S. Minister to Spain William Preston to Secretary of State William H. Seward

Aranjuez, April 22, 1861

Sir:

An interview has taken place between the minister of foreign affairs and myself in reference to the subject embraced in your circular.

In conformity with your instructions, I presented the inaugural address of the President as expressive of his policy towards the seceding States....

The minister replied with courtesy, expressing pain at the posture of affairs in the United States, but said that her Majesty's government was informed that extensive military and naval preparations were making in the north to enforce the federal supremacy in the south, and that the consequences were to be dreaded. I replied that I felt assured his information was erroneous.

No commissioners from the Confederated States have yet applied for the recognition of the Southern confederacy. . . .

I have the honor to remain your obedient servant,

W. Preston

The Prussian Reaction

From U.S. Minister to Prussia Joseph A. Wright to
Secretary of State William H. Seward

Berlin, May 8, 1861

Sir:

I have, since my return, had a long interview with Baron Von Schleinitz, the minister for foreign affairs, who . . . gave me the most positive assurance that his government, from the principle of unrelenting opposition to all revolutionary movements, would be one of the last to recognize any *de facto* government of the disaffected States of the American Union. . . .

I have the honor to be, most respectfully, your very obedient servant,

Joseph A. Wright

The Mexican Reaction

From U.S. Minister to Mexico Thomas Corwin to
Secretary of State William H. Seward

City of Mexico, May 29, 1861

Sir:

. . . The present government of Mexico is well affected towards us in our present difficulties, but, for obvious reasons, will be unwilling to enter into any engagement which might produce war with the south, unless protected by promise of aid from the United States.

I am, &c.,

Thomas Corwin

The Turkish Reaction
*From U.S. Minister to Turkey John P. Brown to
Secretary of State William H. Seward*

Constantinople, June 11, 1861

Sir:

... I do not believe that any agents of the "Confederate States" have, as yet, visited this place, and should any come here that the Porte would admit or recognize them. I receive from H. H. Aali Pacha, minister of foreign affairs, and H. H. Mehemed Kibrish Pacha, grand vizier, repeated assurances of the most friendly sentiments towards the government of the United States, and expressions of warm sympathy for the present unhappy state of popular excitement in the slave States of the Union.

I have the honor to be, sir, respectfully, your obedient servant,

John P. Brown

1861 The Death of Cavour, Hero of Italian Unification
Dispatch from U.S. Chargé d'Affaires in Italy Romaine Dillon to
Secretary of State William H. Seward

Camillo di Cavour was the principal architect of Italian unification, orchestrating the great events of 1860–1861 in which the Kingdom of Sicily incorporated most of the Italian peninsula into the Kingdom of Italy. But Cavour, who became the chief minister of the new state, died at age fifty-one less than three months after the new kingdom was established. At the time of this dispatch U.S. envoys were still accredited to the Italian government in Turin; Rome would not be annexed to the kingdom for another decade.

Turin, June 10, 1861

Sir:

It is my painful duty to communicate . . . the sudden death, on the 6th instant, of his excellency the Count Camillo Benso de Cavour, late president of his Majesty's council and minister of foreign affairs. The count was taken ill on the evening of the 29th of May last at his residence, the hotel of his elder brother, the Marquis de Cavour, of what proved to be typhus fever. Injudicious and repeated bleedings at the commencement of the fever, though, I am told, at his own instance, hastened the sad event.

The count was never married.
Europe still echoes with eulogies to his memory....
I am, sir, your obedient servant,

Romaine Dillon

1862 Confederates Chained in the Consulate
Dispatches from U.S. Consul in Tangier James de Long to Secretary of State William H. Seward

In one of the most bizarre diplomatic episodes of the Civil War, the American consul in Tangier, Morocco, discovered the presence of two Confederate agents in the city. Then, in an amazing and questionable display of extraterritoriality, he had them arrested and kept them chained in the consulate. Over the initial objections of local authorities, and in the face of a hostile mob, the consul arranged for U.S. Marines to land and take the prisoners aboard a U.S. warship, which conveyed them to the United States.

Arrested and Put in Irons

Tangier, February 20, 1862

Sir:

I have the honor to inform you that two secessionists . . . were landed here yesterday from a merchant French steamer . . . to purchase coal to supply the *Sumter*, which is still in the port of Gibraltar, uncoaled.

One of these men, I am informed, is a lieutenant of the *Sumter*; the other, Mr. Tunstall, who has been acting as United States consul at Cadiz, up to some time last summer, and was intending to return to the southern States on board of the *Sumter*.

Having received this information from what I considered reliable authority, I made application to the Moorish authorities for soldiers, and had them arrested at the beach, at about 4 o'clock in the afternoon of yesterday, as they were about to return to the steamer to proceed to Cadiz.

They are now confined in one of the rooms of the United States consulate, awaiting the arrival of the *Tuscarora*, which is expected to morrow, as I wish to place them in the charge of the commander, to be conveyed by him to the United States on his return. . . .

I had no way to confine them safely without putting them in irons, and even then I have to keep four soldiers guarding them day and night. . . .

I must add that the Moorish authorities are entitled to great credit for their prompt assistance in aiding the arrest of these men. . . .

American citizens may talk and plot treason and rebellion at home, if they can, but they shall not do so where I am, if I have the power to prevent it.

Hoping the government will approve of what I have done in this matter, I have the honor to be, sir, your obedient servant,

James de Long

A Protesting Mob

Tangier, February 27, 1862

Sir:

I have the honor to inform you that I was disappointed in my expectation in regard to the arrival of the *Tuscarora* on the 26th instant. . . . On the evening of the 25th, about 6 o'clock, I received a despatch from the Moorish minister, a copy of which, with my reply thereto, is herewith enclosed, in which he demanded a surrender of the prisoners.

My reply was conveyed to the minister at 8 o'clock of the 26th, which was read and explained to him by my interpreter, who was informed by the minister that there would be no impediment offered to my removing the prisoners. By the time my interpreter had arrived at the consulate, the United States ship-of-war *Ino* had anchored in the bay. Leaving off all formalities, her commander with three of his junior officers came on shore, and thence proceeded to the American consulate. The commander, accompanied by my interpreter and myself, proceeded to the residence of the Moorish minister to pay our respects to him, and to make arrangements for firing a salute, and about the embarcation of the prisoners. Our interview took place at 11 o'clock a.m., and in which it was repeated that there would be no objections made to their removal on board of the *Ino*.

After exchanging a salute of 21 guns, which took place at 1 o'clock p.m., I consulted with the commander of the *Ino* about the manner of conveying the prisoners on board, and we came to the conclusion, to prevent any demonstration that might be made on the conveyance of the prisoners to the beach, that it would be advisable to order thirty marines to come on shore, fully armed, to accompany the prisoners. Prior to the arrival of our men on shore I discovered that there was a plot going on, formed out of European subjects residing in Tangier, to prevent the embarcation of the prisoners, and to take them out of our hands at the time of conveying them to the beach. Although I had not at first much confidence in the report, bearing in mind the strict neutrality of European nations in relation to our civil war, nevertheless, by the time the marines had landed on the beach, the gates of the port were closed, and an armed mob of between three and four hundred Europeans, residing here under the protection of foreign representatives at this place, had assembled at the American consulate. On hearing a noise in the street leading to the consulate, the commander of the *Ino,* his purser, surgeon, and Mr. Train, master's mate, and myself, went into the street. I enquired of one of the mob, who would speak English, what they wanted. He replied that they were determined to have the prisoners in my custody released. We immediately made a rush at them and drove them out of the street. We then returned into the consulate and closed the doors. The mob then returned and tried to break into the consulate. I immediately sent a note to my interpreter to inform the Moorish minister of what was going on, and to demand of him soldiers to suppress the mob. Fortunately, before my interpreter got my note, he had gone to the minister and informed him in relation to the mob; then the minister sent a message to the foreign representatives to withdraw their subjects, and he also sent troops to protect the United States consulate and to disperse the mob; all of which was attended to promptly.

The commander of the *Ino,* accompanied by three of his junior officers, my interpreter and myself, then proceeded to the residence of the minister at about 3 o'clock p.m., and after a few preliminary remarks I gave the minister to understand the ultimatum of what I required, and nothing short of which would I accept, which was in the following words:

1st. That the gates of the port should be opened.
2d. That the marines be permitted to march uninterrupted to the American consulate.
3d. That he furnish a sufficient number of troops to keep down the mob and to accompany the prisoners to the beach.
4th. All of which must be complied with, within one hour, or I would strike the American flag and quit the country.

The minister replied, no, no, your request shall be acceded to, but I desire you to hold over until to-morrow, when all will be quiet; I replied that I would consent to no delay, for the reason that it would only give the mob an opportunity to make further preparations.

This closed the interview and we returned to the consulate, and in less than one hour the gates of the port were opened, the marines marched to the consulate, the Moorish troops were on hand, and the prisoners were then brought out, and we marched down to the beach in the presence of at least three thousand spectators, without the least interruption, and they were placed on board of the *Ino,* which sailed last night. I must add that the commander of the *Ino,* his junior officers and marines, all acted their part bravely to sustain the honor of the American flag.

I have the honor to be, sir, your most obedient servant,

James de Long

1862 The *Monitor* and the *Merrimac:* A Swedish Victory?
Dispatch from U.S. Minister to Sweden J. S. Haldeman to Secretary of State William H. Seward

The Union's Monitor *and Confederacy's* Merrimac *(rechristened the C.S.S.* Virginia*) fought to a draw off Hampton Roads, Virginia, on March 9, 1862, in the first clash between ironclad warships. The battle forever changed the face of naval warfare. The* Monitor *was constructed from designs by Swede John Ericsson, while another Swede, John Dahlgren, designed its guns. News of the battle drew a curious reaction from Stockholm.*

Stockholm, April 24, 1862

Sir:

It is impossible to convey to you the excitement and joy created in this city by the news of the naval battle between the Monitor and Merrimack. Captain Ericsson is a Swede; born, and educated in this city; his brother Colonel Ericsson, whose acquaintance I have made, is engineer-in-chief of all the railways in Sweden and Norway. Captain Dahlgren's parents were Swedes who emigrated to America; hence they say, with that pride peculiar to a brave and spirited though numerically weak nation, that a Swede invented the Monitor, a Swede invented the guns with which she was armed: "Ergo," how great is the obligation—the debt of the United States to the genius of Sweden. We have also received a telegram of the great victory [Battle of Shiloh] near Corinth. No one *now* doubts of a speedy termination of the rebellion and triumph of the government. The result of my diplomatic experience is that in all international affairs respect and sympathy are the natural parasites of success.

I remain your obedient servant,

J. S. Haldeman

1862 Bureaucratic Mysteries in Japan
Dispatch from U.S. Minister to Japan Robert H. Pruyn to
Secretary of State William H. Seward

Robert Pruyn was the second American minister to Japan, serving at Yedo (now Tokyo) from 1862 to 1865. In this dispatch he comments on the difficulty of obtaining accurate information on changes within the bureaucracy of Imperial Japan.

Yedo, May 26, 1862

Sir:

I have the honor to inform you that on the 11th instant I received a letter . . . informing me that . . . Audo Tsusima No Kami had been promoted to the rank of Tamari Dsumi Kakee. . . .

There are now, therefore, three ministers for foreign affairs.

. . . I feel gratified to be able to say that thus far I can perceive no change in the conduct of the governor for foreign affairs or any of the officials.

It would be impossible for them to be more friendly. . . .

It is worthy of notice, also, that this is the first instance which has occurred of any such change having been communicated to the ministers of foreign powers at the time of its occurrence. The process heretofore has been, when one of the ministers absented himself from the meeting of the Gorogio, to attribute his absence to sickness, to give the same excuse at subsequent interviews, and finally to announce, after the expiration of months, the appointment of a successor, the continued sickness of the minister having compelled him to ask to be relieved. . . .

Everything is so enveloped in mystery here that it is extremely difficult, and in some cases impossible, to arrive at the truth. An amusing instance of this is associated with the assassination of the Gotairo, (the regent,) whose head was cut off in a public street. The British minister was led to believe that he was in a fair way to recover from his wound, and his proffer of his surgical services was courteously declined.

I ride almost daily through the streets of Yedo . . . and never carry arms. I have never been molested, nor seen any evidence of hostility on the part of its population.

The ministers of Great Britain and France have, respectively, a guard of soldiers and marines. . . . All were armed with sabres and revolvers.

It has appeared to me that any such exhibition of arms will only provoke hostility.

The British and French ministers continue their residence at Yokohama. The consul general of Holland resides at Nagasaki, and the consul general of Russia at Hakodadi.

I am the only minister who resides in Yedo.

I have the honor to be, sir, very respectfully, your most obedient servant,

Robert H. Pruyn

1862–1864 The Confederate Raider *Alabama*
Dispatches from U.S. Ministers and Consuls

The steam/sail cruiser Alabama, *the most celebrated and successful vessel in the small Confederate navy, captured sixty-four American ships in the course of her short career. For two years after the* Alabama's *surreptitious launching in Liverpool, England, the raider's movements and depredations were the subject of innumerable diplomatic dispatches from the far corners of the globe. Finally, in 1864, the* Alabama, *commanded by Capt. Raphael Semmes, was sunk by the U.S.S.* Kearsarge, *under Capt. John Winslow, off the coast of France. As young officers years before, Semmes and Winslow had been friends who shared a cabin aboard a U.S. naval vessel during the Mexican War. These dispatches report the* Alabama's *construction and launching, its activities as described by U.S. consuls at far-flung ports, and its final battle.*

Great Britain: The Launching of a "Formidable Gunboat"
From U.S. Minister to Great Britain Charles Francis Adams to Secretary of State William H. Seward

London, July 9, 1862

Sir:

... I ... forward copies of the correspondence, so far as it has gone, touching the preparation of the formidable gunboat at Liverpool for the use of the rebels. ... I have directed the vice-consul at Liverpool ... to prepare and send to the collector of customs there such further evidence as he may obtain of the true destination of that vessel. ... As a last resource, I have taken the responsibility of sending for the Tuscarora. Captain Craven has arrived at Southampton, and has been here to see me. I regard the case as so important that if the evidence shall prove in any way sufficient to justify the step, I shall authorize him to try to intercept her on her way out. ...

I have the honor to be, sir, your obedient servant,

Charles Francis Adams

London, July 31, 1862

Sir:

You must long before this have received all the information respecting the Laird gunboat, No. 290, for which you ask in your despatch No. 299, of the 12th of July. It only remains for me to continue the narrative of that transaction down to this date. In spite of all my efforts and remonstrances, which as yet wait the opinion of the law officers of the crown, I received on the 29th instant from Mr. Dudley, the consul at Liverpool, the news that she sailed without register or clearance from that port on that day. I immediately communicated the intelligence by telegraph to Captain Craven, at Southampton. I learn from the consul at that place that the Tuscarora sailed from thence at 8 p.m. on the 29th instant. Should the captain be so fortunate as to encounter the vessel on the high seas, I have every reason to believe that he will attempt her capture. But I have given him no instructions how far to pursue her, or what to do in case of failure. In these respects he is left entirely to his own discretion.

    I have the honor to be, sir, your obedient servant,

Charles Francis Adams

London, October 3, 1862

Sir:

I regret to be obliged to state that accounts are coming in of the ravages committed by the gunboat 290, now called the Alabama, which has been cruising off the Azores. So long ago as the 5th of last month I felt it my duty to apprise the consul at Gibraltar of the position of that vessel, and to warn him, and through him the vessels on that station, to be on the alert. . . . The probability is that the Alabama will next turn up somewhere in the West Indies, or on the coast of South America.

    There are rumors from Liverpool of the preparation of several steamers to sail as privateers. . . . There is no doubt that the presence of one or two fast United States steamers, commanded by efficient officers, would be of use in the European waters.

    I transmit the copy of another note which I have addressed to [Foreign Minister] Lord Russell . . . to add to those already accumulated in the case of the gunboat 290. It will be a little difficult for this government to justify its want of energy in enforcing the provisions of the law in regard to that vessel.

    I have the honor to be, sir, your obedient servant,

Charles Francis Adams

Portugal: News of the "Piratical Cruiser"
*From U.S. Minister to Portugal James E. Harvey to
Secretary of State William H. Seward*

Lisbon, November 5, 1862

Sir:

... It appears from news just received here that the piratical cruiser Alabama, after destroying a large number of whaling ships near the Azores, steered westward towards the banks of Newfoundland, so as to be in the track of regular trade on the Atlantic, where several other vessels, one of them freighted with flour and grain for this port, were destroyed. I take it for granted that as soon as that intelligence reached Washington prompt measures were adopted to protect our outgoing commerce.

The commander of the Alabama is too shrewd, however, to expose himself voluntarily to capture, and too active in the enemy's service to remain long in one locality....

I am, sir, very respectfully, your obedient servant,

James E. Harvey

Brazil: Six American Vessels Destroyed by the *Alabama*
*From U.S. Consul in Pernambuco, Brazil, Thomas Adamson Jr. to
U.S. Minister to Brazil J. Watson Webb*

Pernambuco, April 27, 1863

Sir:

I am under the very painful necessity of announcing to you the destruction, by the pirate Alabama, of six American vessels.

The very short time between this and the sailing of the English mail packet will prevent me from giving you the full particulars. I can only say now, that the Brazilian schooner Sergipano arrived here yesterday from the island of Fernando de Noronha, with sixty-one persons on board as passengers, being the officers and crews of the schooner Kingfisher, of Fairhaven, ship Nora, of Boston, ship Charles Hill, of Boston, and ship Louisa Hatch, of Rockland, Maine. The crews of these vessels are under my protection....

The pirate stripped the vessels of their small stores, chronometers, &c., took all the money from the captain, about 280 tons of coal from the Louisa Hatch, and then burned the vessels.

From the 10th to the 16th of April the Alabama was in the port of the island of Fernando de Noronha; during this time, viz., on the 15th of

April, the Alabama captured in Brazilian waters two other American vessels. . . . These vessels were touching for supplies. The Alabama went out and seized them within two miles of the shore. The pirate set fire to and . . . burned both. . . .

Comment is quite unnecessary. It is impossible to say what complications may arise from these circumstances, and I would, therefore, be happy to receive any advice you may have to offer.

I remain, with the highest regard, your obedient servant,

Thomas Adamson, Jr.

Cape Town: "Alabama Arrived on This Coast"
From U.S. Consul in Cape Town Walter Graham to U.S. Minister to Great Britain Charles Francis Adams

Cape Town, Cape of Good Hope, August 17, 1863

Sir:

The confederate steamer Alabama arrived on this coast on the 27th day of July, having captured six American vessels from the time she left Bahia, Brazil, viz: The Amazonian, Conrad, Gildersleve, Talisman, Anna F. Schmidt, and Express.

. . . No intelligence was received here that she had entered any of the ports or bays of this colony until Tuesday, August 4, when the British schooner Atlas reported that she had entered Saldanha bay on the 28th, and was still there, her crew being engaged in painting her. Captain Boyce, of the Atlas, said he was requested by Captain Semmes to take some prisoners to me at Cape Town, but he declined to do so.

On hearing this intelligence I wrote . . . the governor . . . to . . . protest against the vessel remaining in any port of the colony another day. . . .

Next morning, August 5, . . . it was reported from the signal station of the harbor that the steamer Alabama was standing in, and also an American bark, and shortly after it was signalled that the steamer was standing towards the bark. On hearing this I at once took a cab and proceeded in the direction of Green Point, about two miles from my office, where I witnessed the capture of the bark Sea Bride by the Alabama. I immediately proceeded to the governor's house and told him what I had seen, protesting at the same time against the capture, because it was permitted in British waters. . . .

About 5 o'clock his excellency sent for me to the custom-house, and informed me that Captain Semmes desired to land some prisoners, and that he, the governor, would grant permission, provided I would agree to support them. This I consented to do. . . .

All the prisoners were landed, fifteen of whom were the crew of the Anna F. Schmidt, fifteen of the Express, and twelve of the Sea Bride. . . .

I have little else to communicate beyond what is embraced in my correspondence. . . .

No American war ships have yet appeared here, but they are anxiously looked for.

Two merchants from this place have gone to Saldanha bay to buy prize cargoes. When they return I will watch their proceedings closely.

A company of speculators offered Captain Semmes £4,000 for the Sea Bride and cargo, and he would have taken it, but he wanted a bond that they would not revert to the enemy. They offered me a large bribe if I would give my authority to have them sold here for the benefit of the underwriters, they asking £7,000 for the ransom, but I refused to give them my authority to sell. This was before Captain Semmes spoke of the bond.

Should anything else occur in connexion with this affair, I will let you know as soon as any mail leaves here.

I have the honor to be, sir, your most obedient servant,

Walter Graham

France: "The Kearsarge Sunk the Alabama This Morning"
From U.S. Consul in Paris William L. Dayton to
Secretary of State William H. Seward

Paris, June 20, 1864

Sir:

By a despatch sent you by the last steamer, I informed you that a fight was anticipated between the United States ship Kearsarge and the Alabama, and that I had . . . sent my son to Cherbourg with a communication for Captain Winslow. . . . The next information I received was at about half past 2 p.m. on Sunday, by telegram from my son, in these words: "Cherbourg, 19th June, 1864, 1 o'clock 22'.—The Kearsarge sunk the Alabama this morning, after a fight of one hour and a half. The Alabama sunk five miles from the shore." This was confirmed by a second telegram, somewhat later in the day, with the additional information that he had been on board the Kearsarge since the fight; that but three of her seamen were wounded; no officers were injured; that there was no important damage to the Kearsarge; that they had taken sixty-five prisoners, but that Captain Semmes and his first lieutenant had made their escape on board an English yacht. . . . I subsequently received from him a hastily written letter, dated Sunday, 1/4 before 2 p.m., in which he tells me that from an elevated position near Cherbourg he saw the entire fight—that it lasted an hour and a half, at the end of which the Alabama tried to run away, but could not escape. The Kearsarge pursued, apparently, he says. She then surrendered, for the firing ceased. A few minutes after two boats were seen to put off from the Kearsarge, but before they could reach the Alabama she went down in a second, apparently without anything on board.

. . . The destruction of this vessel off the French coast has excited a great sensation here, and will help to redeem our naval prestige, much diminished abroad of late years. . . . The whole affair was clearly visible to all those well placed on the shore. Many boats went off towards its close, and helped to pick up the swimming and drowning men. Some were brought by our own boats to the Kearsarge, some were carried on shore, and some got off in an English vessel, and were landed, I am informed by telegram, at Southampton. I have written you a rambling despatch, because in this way only could I send to you the facts which I thought it might be of interest for you to know.

I am, sir, your obedient servant,

Wm. L. Dayton

1862 Foreign Recruits
Dispatch from U.S. Vice Consul in the Hanseatic and Free Cities Charles Boernstein to Secretary of State William H. Seward

After the outbreak of the Civil War, American legations and consulates in Europe were crowded with prospective foreign volunteers for military service. Dispatches such as this one from a U.S. consulate in Germany led to a circular instruction that no foreigners were to be recruited for the Union Army.

Bremen, September 13, 1862

Sir:

This consulate is daily crowded with men wishing to enlist in our army.

Having received no orders to this effect from the department, I am bound to send them off again.

Could no arrangement be made to send those men to the States free of charge, as emigrants? Some of them are even willing to have the travelling expenses deducted from the bounty or wages. Had I authority I could have sent a few brigades to the States already.

I am, sir, very respectfully, your most obedient servant,

Charles Boernstein

1862 A Diplomatic Blunder: Garibaldi and the Civil War
Dispatches between U.S. Consul in Vienna Theodore Canisius and Secretary of State William H. Seward

In what may have been the most unusual recruiting effort of the Civil War, the American consul in Vienna took it upon himself to seek military support for the United States from Gen. Giuseppe Garibaldi, one of the heroes of Italian unification. Curiously, the consul approached Garibaldi while the general was in prison after his abortive attempt to make Papal Rome part of the newly formed Kingdom of Italy. For his unauthorized effort to recruit the Italian general, who earlier had lived briefly in the United States, the consul was reprimanded and removed from office. The story, however, had a happy ending when the Italian government intervened in behalf of the dismissed consul and President Abraham Lincoln acceded to the request that the consul's "imprudence" be overlooked.

Consul Canisius Approaches Garibaldi

September 17, 1862

Sir:

After the capture of Garibaldi I addressed the following letter to the great leader of the Union party of Italy:

Vienna, September 1, 1862

GENERAL: As you have failed for the present to accomplish the great and patriotic work you lately undertook in the interest of your beloved fatherland, I take the liberty to address myself to you to ascertain whether it would not be against your present plans to lend us a helping hand in our present struggle to preserve the liberty and unity of our great republic. The battle we fight is one which not only interests ourselves, but also the whole civilized world.

The welcome and enthusiasm with which you will be received in our land, where you once lived, will be boundless, and your position to lead our brave soldiers into battle, to strike for the same principle for which you have fought so nobly during your whole life, will be such as you may desire.

I would be happy, general, to receive a reply from you if possible. I have the honor to be, very respectfully, &c.,

Theodore Canisius,
United States Consul

General Garibaldi
Spezia, Italy

To this General Garibaldi replied as follows:

> Varignana, September 14, 1862
>
> Sir:
>
> I am a prisoner and dangerously wounded; therefore it is impossible for me to dispose of myself.
>
> I believe, however, that when my imprisonment shall cease, and my wound heal, the favorable opportunity shall have come in which I will be able to satisfy my desire to serve the great American republic, of which I am a citizen, and which to-day fights for the universal freedom.
>
> I have the honor to be, very respectfully,
>
> G. Garibaldi
>
> Theodore Canisius,
> United States Consul at Vienna

I received the above letter on the morning of the 18th of September, and hasten to report the above to you without delay.

I have the honor to be, very respectfully, &c.,

T. Canisius

October 4, 1862

Sir:

The letter addressed to me by General Garibaldi has, as I expected, created a great commotion throughout Europe, and has produced the very best effect for the north. When, in consequence of the unfavorable news brought by every steamer, the sympathy in Europe for us grew less and less, I thought the time had come to let the world know what the great hero at the castle of Varignana thinks of us and our cause. I deemed this the more important while the great Garibaldi demonstrations in England were taking place. The correspondence was therefore published by me at once. Subsequent events have shown that my calculation was a correct one, because, since the publication of this correspondence, our cause has undoubtedly gained ground in Europe. . . .

I have the honor to be, very respectfully, &c.,

T. Canisius

Secretary of State Seward Replies

Washington, October 10, 1862

Sir:

Your despatch of the 17th ultimo brings a letter which was written by you to General Garibaldi on the first of September last.

I am directed by the President to inform you that your proceeding in writing that letter is disapproved.

First. It is, in its nature, not a consular but a diplomatic act, transcending your proper functions, which is considered the more unpardonable, when it is remembered that the United States are represented, not only at Turin, but at Vienna, where you reside, by a minister invested with the most ample diplomatic authority. . . .

Secondly. Although the proceeding of inviting General Garibaldi to join the armies of the United States may have seemed to you to have been warranted by the fact that this government, a year ago, tendered a command in our armies to that distinguished soldier, yet your proceedings are not at all parallel to those which attended that case. . . .

Thirdly. . . . General Garibaldi was taken in arms against that government. The policy of the United States, in regard to Italy, is absolute abstinence from all intervention in its domestic affairs. . . .

At the present conjuncture, when every care is necessarily taken to avoid injurious complications in foreign affairs, and especially in Europe, proceedings on your part, so entirely divergent from this judicious policy, cannot be overlooked. Upon these grounds your commission as consul at Vienna is withdrawn.

I am, sir, your obedient servant,

William H. Seward

Washington, December 8, 1862

Sir:

The government of his Majesty the King of Italy having been informed of the revocation of your commission, and the grounds for that proceeding, has generously acknowledged the consideration thus manifested for that kingdom by the United States, and has reciprocated it by requesting that the imprudence on your part, which rendered the revocation necessary, may be overlooked.

The President has had great pleasure in acceding to this request, and you will, therefore, resume your official functions as consul at Vienna.

I am, sir, your obedient servant,

William H. Seward

1862 The Ottoman Empire: A Public Execution
Dispatch from U.S. Minister to Turkey Edward Joy Morris to Secretary of State William H. Seward

During the Civil War many American envoys had to devote all their energies to supporting the war effort. U.S. representatives in remoter capitals, however, continued to deal primarily with local affairs. In Turkey, for example, U.S. ministers and consuls expended enormous efforts in trying to protect Christian missionaries. The missionaries, who often lived in remote areas, frequently were targets of bandits and of antiforeign elements. The execution reported in this dispatch prompted a message of thanks from President Abraham Lincoln to Turkish sultan Abdul Aziz.

Constantinople,
October 16, 1862

Sir:

I have the honor to inform you that Ahmet, one of the assassins of the American missionary, Rev. J. G. Coffing, who was murdered some months since in the vicinity of Alexandrette, was executed by decapitation at Adana on the 25th of September last.

The proceedings, according to the report of the United States consular agent at Adana, were conducted with unusual solemnity, in order to make a lasting impression on the public mind. The firman ordering the immediate execution was presented and publicly read, after which the sound of a trumpet was heard, and the prisoner appeared in chains, followed by one hundred regular troops. Khoorshid Pasha, the governor of Adana, the consular agents of the United States of America, France, Russia, and Italy, followed in procession to the place of execution.

After the criminal had been surrounded by the armed soldiers, the chains were taken from his neck and feet, a jug of water was given him to drink, and he was allowed to perform his prayers and ablutions, (being a Mussulman,) which lasted for about half an hour. Afterwards he was made to kneel in the centre, his eyes being bound with a white handkerchief; and in the presence of the above-named persons, and at least 5,000 spectators, he underwent the punishment of his crime. Not a single word was uttered by any spectator against the execution, and many, in sign of their approbation of it, exclaimed aloud, *"Padishad sagh olsoun!"*—"May the Sultan live!"

... The persevering pursuit of the executed assassin through the mountains and wilds of Syria, and the summary manner in which he was brought to justice, will do much to enforce respect for the lives and property of American citizens residing in or travelling through the Turkish empire. It is the more striking because of the impunity which criminals have too often enjoyed who have murdered the subjects of other Christian powers.

With great respect, your obedient servant,

E. Joy Morris

1862 China's First Flag
Dispatch from U.S. Minister to China Anson Burlingame to Secretary of State William H. Seward

China traditionally considered itself the center of the world; other peoples were either tributaries or barbarians. Not until the 1860s did China's world view change enough that Chinese officials thought it necessary to adopt a flag as a national symbol. By this time the major European powers had forcibly established themselves at the court in Peking. Anson Burlingame was American minister to China from 1862 to 1867. This dispatch was written just one week after he took office.

Peking, October 27, 1862

Sir:

I have the pleasure to inform you that the Chinese government has adopted a national flag. It is a dragon flag, to be triangular in shape, and ten feet broad for the largest vessels, or between seven and eight feet for smaller craft. The length is immaterial. The ground color is yellow, and a dragon is painted on it, the head pointing upwards. . . .

Hitherto there have been individual and local flags, but until now no national flag. Surely the words "immovable civilization of China" have lost their significance. By this act the imperial government, casting down the last shred of its exclusiveness, confronts us with a symbol of its power, and demands a place among the nations. Permit me to suggest that it might be well to bring [this] . . . to the attention of our naval officers and captains of our commercial marine as soon as possible.

I have the honor to be your obedient servant,

Anson Burlingame

1862 The Emancipation Proclamation: Turning the Tide in Europe

Dispatch from U.S. Minister to the Netherlands James S. Pike to Secretary of State William H. Seward

American diplomats in Europe during the Civil War frequently faced local populations sympathetic to the South. According to U.S. Minister James Pike, they perceived that the South's rebellion was in response to Northern oppression. The Emancipation Proclamation, issued in September 1862 by President Abraham Lincoln, did a great deal to change popular attitudes in Europe by aligning the South with slavery and the North with emancipation of the slaves. This dispatch from the Netherlands is representative of American diplomatic reporting on the subject.

The Hague, December 31, 1862

Sir:

I have to acknowledge the receipt of your despatch of December 6, No. 70.

The President's message [has] . . . given a great fillip to the discussions of the American question.

The anti-slavery position of the government is at length giving us a substantial foothold in European circles. And the seceding States are at the same time feeling the heavy weight of the slavery load.

If we could have begun where we now stand, our position in Europe would at this moment be well nigh impregnable in the field of discussion. The American question has now become a dangerous one for the ruling classes, in every deliberative body in Europe.

So long as it was a question between a government and a revolt, the instincts of even the liberal masses had a tendency to side with the rebellion; revolts being instinctively regarded as merely protests against some form of oppression. But everybody can understand the significance of a war where emancipation is written on one banner and slavery on the other. And thus, though we have no strength with any political organization in Europe, we are now strong in the public assembly and in the press, constraining, at least, the respect of even the paid advocates of dynastic rule; while the solid weight of debate, private and public, goes wholly in our favor. We need not now fear, but rather welcome the parliamentary discussions which it is to be supposed will come in England and elsewhere during the winter.

The main drawback to these considerations is to be found in our repeated misfortunes before Richmond. The repulse of [Union] General [Ambrose] Burnside at Fredericksburg is a heavy blow to the remaining belief in Europe of our ability to conquer the rebellion in the field. If the emancipation scheme fails, there is danger that we shall soon be regarded everywhere on this side as being destined to fail altogether. . . .

I have not yet received any reply from this government in relation to the proposed emigration of colored persons to its colonial possessions from the United States.

I have the honor to be, with great respect, your most obedient servant,

James S. Pike

1863   Turmoil in the Balkans
Dispatch from U.S. Minister to Austria John Lothrop Motley to Secretary of State William H. Seward

The United States was not the only part of the world in turmoil in the early 1860s, as is clear in this dispatch from Vienna. The Turkish Empire was decaying, the Austrian Empire was being torn by internal strife, and Greece was teetering between governments. Serbia, an autonomous principality of the Turkish Empire, had a ruler intent on uniting the Balkans against the Turks.

The author of this dispatch, John Lothrop Motley, was an eminent historian at the time of his appointment to Vienna; he went on to serve as U.S. minister to Great Britain. Motley, a cantankerous gentleman of the old school who sometimes sported a monocle, ran into difficulty in each of his ministerial positions. He left Vienna under a cloud for alleged public criticism of President Andrew Johnson (1865–1869) and later was removed from his post in London after a policy disagreement with President Ulysses S. Grant (1869–1877).

Vienna, January 27, 1863

Sir:

. . . A few general observations upon the condition of this part of the world may be useful.

There is tranquillity in this empire, while in many directions, and in its immediate neighborhood, are indications of approaching storm.

Here the sincere, and thus far prosperous, effort to convert the despotic empire of Austria into a constitutional monarchy continues. . . .

The provincial diets, or landtage, (having a certain analogy to our State legislatures,) are now in session. One of their principal functions is to choose members to the lower house of the national Reichsrath. The seventeen diets "on this side of the Leitha" are now in full operation. But Hungary, Transylvania, and Croatia maintain their attitude of quiet defiance. There is no meeting of the diets of those provinces, and they will send no representatives at present to the Reichsrath. Meanwhile great complaints are heard from those districts of highway robbery on an extensive scale, by which the inhabitants are suffering much loss and general inconvenience. The imperial taxes are now collected, however, without the necessity of military force, and the government cherishes hopes that the passive resistance will, in due time, come to the same end which active opposition to central authority seems to have reached.

The late revolution in Greece, of which the quiet exclusion of King Otho was the singular catastrophe, has left that country, according to the accounts which reach us here, in a very unsettled and anomalous condition. Correspondents from Athens describe the outlying districts as entirely given over to brigands, who exercise an organized system of plunder, ransom, and black-mail; and even in the capital itself, if the same authorities may be relied upon, the highway robbers give the law, in broad daylight, to the passengers in public places, robbing and ransoming at their pleasure.

I am far from giving you this account as implicitly to be relied upon. The dethronement of a sovereign so nearly allied to this imperial house as King Otho has, of necessity, inspired great indignation here against his late subjects, and the accounts concerning the country are doubtless darkly colored. In the apparent impossibility of finding any prince willing to accept the throne there seems a chance that the republican form of government may be adopted, and that, according to the views prevalent in Europe, would be the most fitting and most severe punishment for their sins which could be inflicted on the Greeks. It must be confessed that with its geographical position, overshadowed by the great monarchies of Russia, Austria, and Turkey, a small confederation of Greece and the Ionian islands, under the protection of England, would be the merest shadow of a republic. All the virtues which it might display would be attributed to its powerful protection; all its vices would be ascribed to the inherent evil of the republican form. . . .

The oriental question, however, is rapidly assuming its old prominence in the affairs of the world. The maintenance of the integrity of the Turkish empire is considered by England as vital to the perpetuity of its own empire. Russia, by the results of the Crimean war, and by that vast, noble, but somewhat perilous and exhausting measure, the emancipation of its serfs, has been supposed to be no longer so dangerous.

Nevertheless, there is great commotion in the Danubian principalities. The transportation of arms into Servia, with many movements throughout those semi-Turkish, semi-independent countries, seems, to European politicians, to reveal the hidden but ever-suspected presence of the subtle and restless Russian diplomacy, and it is believed that Servia is to be made the arsenal out of which an armed attack is to be made, under Russian guidance, by the Slavonic populations of Turkey against the

Porte. I do not undertake to give you these matters as facts, but as current suspicions, rumors, hopes, and fears.

The natural, or at least historical, antagonism between Austria and Prussia is at this moment more pronounced than ever. . . .

You may well suppose that with so many topics of nearer moment agitating the public mind, there is less of absorbing interest in our own affairs here. . . .

I have the honor to be your obedient servant,

J. Lothrop Motley

1863   Japan: Legation Destroyed, No Fire Insurance
Dispatch from U.S. Minister to Japan Robert H. Pruyn to
Secretary of State William H. Seward

In addition to contending with antiforeign sentiment and the mysteries of Japan's bureaucracy (see "Bureaucratic Mysteries in Japan," p. 153), *U.S. Minister Robert Pruyn had to face personal losses and possible arson. Pruyn was the only foreign representative based at the shogun's seat in Yedo (now Tokyo); the other ministers and most private citizens were located in Yokohama. Pruyn's presence in Yedo was opposed by many Japanese, prompting suspicion of possible foul play when the legation burned down.*

Yedo, May 26, 1863

Sir:

I regret to have to announce to you the total destruction by fire of the buildings occupied by this legation in this city at two o'clock in the morning of the 24th instant.

The books and archives of the legation, with the exception of some printed volumes, I am happy to say are saved, though mostly in a more or less damaged condition. A heavy rain was falling at the time, and it is difficult to say which had the mastery in the work of destruction, rain or fire.

Although the buildings were about two hundred feet long, and the fire commenced at the end farthest from the office, when I attempted to save some of my clothing and furniture, after attending to the public property, I was borne off by the Yakunius in charge, who remonstrated on account of the danger.

In fifteen minutes the entire building was in flames. You will find it difficult to understand this unless you bear in mind that all the partitions are of exceedingly light wood and paper, with thicker paper where privacy is to be secured.

All my furniture, with a few trifling exceptions, is destroyed, but I think myself and each of my family can boast a change of clothing. . . .

I desire to believe, for the sake of this government as well as our own, that this fire was purely accidental. Still, for weeks, and even for months past, repeated attempts have been made to induce me to leave Yedo. . . .

While desiring to avoid the charge of being foolhardy, and not disguising the fact that all our citizens at Yokohama advise and desire me to leave Yedo, I have determined not to do so at least till other quarters have been assigned me, and my right of residence here be thus acknowledged. . . .

The number of guards around the premises on the night of the fire was over 500. As the flames spread I was obliged to go from building to building on the premises, and it was a singular spectacle, as I passed the different guard-houses, to witness the men seated quietly at their posts, while the air was filled with huge sparks which were flying over them.

If the building was purposely fired, no better night could have been selected to prevent the spread of the conflagration.

The adjoining temple was not destroyed, only the legation buildings, three dwellings occupied by priests, the building occupied by the officers of the guard, and a few of the guard-houses. . . .

While believing that my remaining at Yedo thus far will meet the approval of the President, I hope that, should I find it advisable to leave for a season, it will not receive his censure, but that he will kindly consider that I have stood fire long enough in the absence both of life and fire insurance companies in this city.

I have the honor to be, sir, very respectfully, your most obedient servant,

Robert H. Pruyn

1863 Discovery of the Source of the Nile
Dispatch from U.S. Consul General in Alexandria William S. Thayer to Secretary of State William H. Seward

The source of the Nile was one of the great geographical mysteries of all time. In the mid-eighteenth century British adventurers and explorers (prominent among them Sir Richard Burton, missionary David Livingstone, and Samuel Baker) determined to find the great river's source, launching a series of dangerous and controversial travels into the unknown African interior. The laurels finally went to John Speke, whose arrival at Alexandria, Egypt, after his successful expedition to the interior of Africa, accompanied by James Grant, is reported here by the American consul general. William Thayer was the principal American representative in Egypt through most of the U.S. Civil War; he died at post in April 1864.

Alexandria, June 9, 1863

Sir:

Messrs Speke and Grant arrived at Alexandria last week. . . . The report of their discovery of the sources of the Nile is confirmed. . . . Nyanza (called by the explorers *Victoria Nyanza*) is the principal source of the Nile, and . . . the name of the other lake which they have lately discovered is Nzige, through which body of water the Nile in its course from Nyanza passes. Nyanza had been discovered by Speke on his former expedition, but it was not until the present voyage that it was fully ascertained to be the origin of the White Nile. Lake Nyanza may be found on the map of Africa contained in the atlas of Alexander Keith Johnson, the edition of 1861.

The Viceroy, immediately on hearing by telegraph of the arrival of the travellers at Assonan, sent up the river a government steamer which brought them here. On reaching Alexandria they were presented to his Highness, who treated them with special honor.

Messieurs Speke and Grant left Zanzibar, on the east coast of Africa, on the 1st of October, 1860, and for about two years and a half, until reaching Khartoom, were deprived of all news from the civilized world. During that time they had not heard even a word of the American war. In consequence of hardships they have become old and much worn in appearance, especially Mr. Grant. Mr. Speke, however, contemplates organizing another expedition in England to revisit the region about the Lakes Nyanza and Nzige. The latter is the lake (and not Nyanza) which Mr. Baker has gone to explore.

The report of the resources of the upper country has stimulated the formation of a company here with a capital of ten million dollars for the purpose of carrying our trade there, as well as in Egypt. Among other objects, it is proposed to . . . import ivory, ostrich feathers, gums and cattle. . . .

I have the honor to be, sir, your obedient servant,

William S. Thayer

1864 Tunisia's Tax Revolt
Dispatch from U.S. Consul in Tunis Amos Perry to
Secretary of State William H. Seward

Some of the earliest American consulates were those established in the Barbary States of North Africa. The United States opened its first consulate in Tunis in 1795, largely to deal with the problem of piracy and captive American seamen in the Mediterranean (see "Jefferson Urges War against the Barbary States," p. 38). These problems were long solved by the time Amos Perry, a native of Rhode Island, was appointed consul in Tunis in 1862. This dispatch focuses on internal affairs in Tunis.

Tunis, April 23, 1864

Sir:

I have the honor to report that a rebellion of considerable magnitude has recently broken out in this regency threatening serious consequences unless soon checked. Since the adoption of the constitution in 1860 a personal tax of four and a half dollars has been levied on all male Tunisian subjects above 15 years of age. . . . The tax had encountered some opposition; but this year, in consequence in part of the tax being doubled, the opposition has become violent, and several mountain tribes, occupying a part of the regency towards the line of Algeria, have revolted and are now in open rebellion.

Another complaint brought against the government by disaffected parties is, that the constitutional tribunals are corrupt, causing great expense to litigants by reason of delay and bribery. Formerly the Bey [ruler of Tunis] administered justice in person, daily hearing and deciding cases in the grand hall; and the . . . promptitude with which judgments were pronounced and executed, united to the honor of appearing before the sovereign, seemed to accord with the ideas of this people. . . .

I believe the Bey to be well disposed towards all progressive measures; but, as he has assured me, he can give constitutional liberty and privileges only as his people are prepared to receive them.

The Tunisian government is now actively occupied in raising and bringing together troops (10,000 is the complement) with which to overcome the rebels. . . .

One of the Bey's generals and a few of his soldiers have been slain while attempting to quell a mutiny in the rebellious country. Kairwan, the holy city, has been taken, the governor of it fleeing at the approach of an army of Bedouins. Considerable depredations have been made within ten miles of this city. There is much restlessness and agitation here arising from disaffection, fear, or the hope of plunder, and some families have suddenly left the country. . . .

But I have now to report, receiving my information direct from the minister of foreign affairs, that "the Bey has so far yielded to the pressure upon him as to abolish *provisionally* the constitution and its tribunals, and to allow the personal tax to remain at four and a half dollars." This action, together with the appearance of the Bey this morning in the hall of justice, has awakened a strong feeling in his favor, and hopes begin to be entertained of a reconciliation between him and his rebellious subjects. . . .

To give an air of friendliness . . . the presence of the (U.S. warship) Constellation is, I think, at this time desired; and I have, after confidential consultation, sent word to Commander Stellwagen that an early visit from him would be especially acceptable.

                              Very respectfully, &c., &c.,

                              Amos Perry

1864   Progress in Russia

Dispatch from U.S. Minister to Russia Cassius M. Clay to Secretary of State William H. Seward

The reign of Czar Alexander II in Russia was characterized by sweeping reforms, progress, and the advance of the Russian Empire into central Asia. The most fundamental of the reforms was the emancipation of serfs, which was proclaimed in 1861 (see "Emancipation of the Russian Serfs," p. 136). Three years after the great event, the U.S. minister in St. Petersburg, Cassius Clay, comments on its success and, more generally, on progress throughout the empire. Clay was a fiery Kentuckian who gained a reputation in Russia for amorous exploits and who once challenged a Russian nobleman to a duel with Bowie knives.

                              St. Petersburg, Russia,
                              June 27, 1864

Sir:

The emancipation of the Russian serfs has so far proved a success. Turbulence on the part of the liberated, and revolutionary attempts on the side of their late masters, are no longer thought of. Society moves steadily on in its new career. The Emperor has ordered the soldiers of all the regiments to be instructed by regimental officers, and old and young have made great progress. The village priests are also allowed pay for teaching the peasants, and independent schools are rapidly increasing. The aristocracy who exhausted the empire by "absenteeism," now return to their estates. Russia reaps the double advantage of interested labor and more intelligent direction. Rapid advances are made in the introduction of new processes and machinery in farming; ship-building and general manufactures are increased, monopolies abolished, telegraphs and railroads extended; the American system of street railroad is introduced into St. Petersburg, even into the most fashionable streets; the bonds of caste are being broken down, and the rank of the nobles and the wealth of the laboring class begin to mingle in marriage; the liberal policy of the Emperor, I know by personal observation, has infused new life into Finland; the same policy begins to bear fruit in Poland; the whole empire has entered on a new career of more liberal institutions and fixed forms. I doubt not that the imperial policy now looks to an ultimate constitutional empire. . . .

The world should not regard [Russia's] progress into Asia with distrust, but gratification. The new life must come from the west, and Russia is the only nation which can give it. No people are making more advances comparatively than the Russians in the fine and useful arts, in science and letters, and in general intelligence. A great destiny lies before her; let us be careful for our own sakes, and the cause of humanity, to reciprocate her friendly sentiments towards us.

The renomination of Mr. Lincoln inspires new confidence in national success.

There is a moral fitness in the continuation of Abraham Lincoln in office, till the rebellion is suppressed. It was the revolt of conservative error against progressive right, of the few against the many, of the aristocracy against the people. Jefferson Davis represents the one idea, Abraham Lincoln the other; personally and politically half the fruits of our hard struggle would be lost under any other leader. I rejoice in his nomination, and have confidence in his triumph in the elections and in the war.

Your obedient servant,

C. M. Clay

1864 Karl Marx Congratulates Abraham Lincoln
Dispatch from U.S. Minister to Great Britain Charles Francis Adams to Secretary of State William H. Seward

The U.S. diplomatic archives are replete with letters of congratulations from foreign governments, individuals, and groups, sent on virtually any occasion of note. A particularly unusual example of such a note was delivered to the American minister to Great Britain in 1864 by the International Workingmen's Association, also known as the First International, which was founded in London earlier that year. The letter, which congratulated President Abraham Lincoln on his reelection, was signed by members and officers of the organization, including Karl Marx. Although Marx was only one of many signatories of the letter, his influence in the association already was substantial and soon would be dominant; the International Workingmen's Association came to be the leading proponent of Marxian socialism. By the time this letter was sent, Marx already had published Manifest der Kommunistichen Partei (The Communist Manifesto), *but his major work,* Das Kapital (Capital), *did not appear until 1867. The low-key manner in which the U.S. minister transmitted the letter to Washington indicates that it was not regarded as being of particular importance.*

London, December 23, 1864

Sir:

I now have the honor to transmit the address of the Central Council of the International Workingmen's Association. . . .

    I have the honor to be, sir, your obedient servant,

Charles Francis Adams

Sir:

    We congratulate the American people upon your re-election by a large majority. . . . The triumphant war-cry of your re-election is death to slavery.

    From the commencement of the titanic American strife the workingmen of Europe felt instinctively that the star-spangled banner carried the destinies of their class.

    . . . The working classes of Europe understood at once, even before the fanatic partisanship of the upper classes for the confederate gentry had given its dismal warning, that the slaveholders' rebellion was . . . a general holy crusade of property against labor. . . .

    The workingmen of Europe feel sure that as the American war of independence initiated a new era of ascendency for the middle class, so the American anti-slavery war will do for the working classes. . . .

    Signed on behalf of the International Workingmen's Association.

> Le Luber, (French,) corresponding secretary
>
> Carl Marx, corresponding secretary for Germany
>
> G. R. Toutana, corresponding secretary for Italy
>
> George Adger, President of Council
>
> [and 53 other signees]

1865 Lincoln Assassinated
Dispatches from U.S. Ministers

Diplomatic letters of congratulations are commonplace on occasions of celebration, and letters of condolence are standard fare in the wake of disasters. President Abraham Lincoln's assassination on April 14, 1865, sparked a worldwide outpouring of grief and sympathy. These dispatches report the belated reception of the tragic news in two of America's remoter outposts. They are typical of hundreds of similar letters that flooded into Washington after the sad event. The first of the two dispatches also refers to the simultaneous but unsuccessful attempt on the life of Secretary of State William Seward, during which Seward's son Frederick, assistant secretary of state at the time, also was injured.

Monrovia: "Very Melancholy Tidings"
From U.S. Minister to Liberia Abraham Hanson to Secretary of State William H. Seward

Monrovia, July 5, 1865

Sir:

On the 30th ultimo the very melancholy tidings reached us of the sad loss which our nation has sustained by the death of our honored President, and also of the murderous attempt made upon your valuable life and that of your beloved son.

I assure you my grief at this great national calamity is profound, and my sympathy with you, in your sore affliction, deep and sincere. . . .

The universal sympathy of the people of Liberia is accorded to us in our deep distress. Flags at half-mast have been floating daily from all the principal residences, &c., and expressions of condolence come to me from every quarter.

It is gratifying to my feelings to forward to you, herein, a proof of the interest felt in our affairs by the President of Liberia and his cabinet. At 12 p.m. yesterday a deputation, comprising all the members of the cabinet, called upon me at the legation for the purpose of presenting a preamble and certain resolutions adopted at a full meeting of the President and his cabinet, with a request that I would forward them to their proper destination. I left my bed of sickness to entertain them. . . .

I have the honor to remain, sir, with deep sympathy and profound respect, your very obedient servant,

Abraham Hanson

Peking: The News Reached Us in Forty Days
From U.S. Minister to China S. Wells Williams to
Secretary of State William H. Seward

Peking, July 11, 1865

Sir:

. . . The mail has brought full accounts of the lamentable assassination of our beloved President, and I have . . . notified the Chinese government of this sad event. Prince Kung responded in a friendly spirit. . . .

The telegraph brought the first notice to Peking via Russia in forty days, but nearly a fortnight elapsed before further news arrived to induce us to believe that such a horrid deed could have been committed in the United States.

The contentment and joy caused by the previous news of the fall of Richmond and the surrender of Lee's army, foretokening the cessation of arms and final suppression of the rebellion and restoration of the Union, were turned into grief and indignation at learning that the President had been thus removed. All the Americans in Peking alike mourned his death. . . .

The limits of a despatch will hardly allow me more than to add my tribute of admiration to the character of Mr. Lincoln. . . . His name is hereafter identified with the cause of emancipation, while his patriotism, integrity, and other virtues, and his untimely death, render him not unworthy of mention with William of Orange and Washington.

I have the honor to be, sir, your obedient servant,

S. Wells Williams

1865 Pestilence and Conflagration in Constantinople
Dispatch from U.S. Minister to Turkey Edward Joy Morris to
Secretary of State William H. Seward

Throughout history great cities of the Near East frequently have fallen victim to natural disasters. In this dispatch the American minister in Turkey reports how the ancient capital of Constantinople (now Istanbul), while recovering from pestilence, was consumed by fire.

Constantinople,
September 11, 1865

Sir:

The last bulletin of the medical commission reports but nine deaths by cholera. This . . . is not reliable . . . as a large proportion is unreported. It would be fair to estimate the daily mortality by cholera in Constantinople at from eighty to a hundred even now, including, of course, the immediate environs. At no time has the official report been correct. The deaths, which at the maximum, according to this authority, reached four hundred in one day, are known to have been over two thousand. . . . [F]or several days the mortality was considerably over two thousand, and I find, from inquiry among official sources, that the total deaths cannot be less than fifty thousand. Indeed the desolation has been frightful; in a single night, certain quarters of the city have been bereft of two-thirds of their inhabitants. . . . Although the poorer classes chiefly suffered, the greatest care in dietary regimen was required by all, the least excess being dangerous, and in many cases conducing to fatal results. The epidemic seems to be of a more malignant and contagious nature than its predecessors, to judge by the great mortality here and in Egypt, and Arabia, and its fatally rapid termination. It is to be hoped it will not remain with us for another year. . . .

I regret to report another terrible calamity to this already sorely afflicted capital. At about midnight, on the 5th of September, a fire broke out in Stambol, (Constantinople proper). . . . Under the influence of a violent north wind it soon spread with great fury, carrying everything before it. It reached the enclosure within which stand the government buildings known as the Porte, having levelled every intervening obstacle, but at this moment the wind changed, deflected the flames and they took a course around the wall, on the north of this enclosure, and rushed like a sea of fire on to the Hippodrome and the neighborhood of the mosque of Sultan Ahmet. Nothing could arrest the flames, not even the solid walls of the Khans and mosques, and the pulling down of squares of houses. The fire raged until 6 p. m., on September 6, having, in this time, destroyed about eight thousand houses, ten mosques, twelve baths, twenty khans, two Greek churches, and one Armenian church. The length of the track of the fire is one and a half mile, and its breadth half a mile. Many palaces were destroyed, and among the rest one occupied by the Persian embassy. No such fire has occurred in Constantinople since the memorable one which happened in the time of the Crusaders, and which consumed one-third of the city. The present fire is the cause of immense distress; thousands of families are without homes and are reduced to helpless poverty, and many of them after having already lost valuable members from cholera. The losses from the destruction of property are immense, and at present beyond estimate. Generous as the government is disposed to be, it is almost beyond its power to afford relief to a population which is suffering so fearfully under the scourge of fire and pestilence. . . .

    I have the honor to be, very respectfully, your obedient servant,

E. Joy Morris

1865 Pope Pius IX Comments on World Affairs: "Anything but Satisfactory"

Dispatch from U.S. Minister to the Holy See Rufus King to Secretary of State William H. Seward

The reign of Pope Pius IX saw the end of the papacy's temporal power. The unification of Italy (1859–1860) included the incorporation of the Papal States into a new Kingdom of Italy under Victor Emanuel II, former king of Sardinia. With the help of French troops the pope retained control of the city of Rome until 1870, but when French forces were withdrawn, Rome too was incorporated into the Italian kingdom.

Pope Pius became an outspoken adversary of the liberalism and progress that was sweeping the Europe of his day. One particularly notable development of his tenure was the proclamation of the dogma of papal infallibility.

Representatives of the United States were accredited to the Papal States and the Holy See from 1848 until 1867, when Congress refused to appropriate any more funds for a mission there. Formal diplomatic relations between the United States and the Vatican were not reestablished until 1984. Rufus King was the last of the early U.S. representatives to the Holy See. In this dispatch he captures the pontiff's despondency over political developments in Europe.

November 18, 1865

Sir:

I had the honor, yesterday, of an interview with the Holy Father, and enjoyed a long and interesting conversation with him about American affairs, as well as the condition of things in Italy and Europe. The Pope . . . expressed great satisfaction at the return of peace and the reconstruction of the Union. . . . He warmly approved the clemency which had been shown the rebel leaders, and hoped, he said, that Jefferson Davis would also receive the executive pardon. The most difficult problem he thought for the United States to solve was the proper disposition of the negroes; and he seemed to apprehend that we should find the question a troublesome one. Passing to European affairs, his Holiness remarked that there was great political agitation all over the continent; not in Italy only, but in Germany, Spain, France, and England, there seemed to be trouble brewing. Ireland was restless and discontented, and Fenianism uttered ominous threats. He had no idea, he said, that this movement would affect British rule in Ireland. . . . His Holiness spoke, I thought, despondingly of the aspect of affairs in Italy. Within another fortnight, he said, Saxony and Bavaria would reorganize the kingdom of Victor Emanuel. The Emperor of France was about to withdraw from Italy, and "the poor Pope would be left all alone in his little boat in the midst of the tempestuous ocean." What would happen God alone knew, and to His will and protection the Holy Father committed himself. . . . His Holiness adverted to the concessions which the different governments of Europe seemed to be making "to the revolutionary spirit of the age." They would not, he said, satisfy those who were clamoring for change, but only encourage them to make further demands until they would finish by telling governments themselves that they could dispense with their further services. Evidently the Holy Father looked upon the condition of affairs in Europe as anything but satisfactory, and it was with deep and manifest emotion that he referred to the Supreme Ruler of the universe as his only guide and refuge in the apprehended troubles. . . .

The cholera still prevails with great severity at Naples, but, as yet, there has not been a case in Rome, and the authorities here hope to escape the visitation of the pestilence, at least during the present season. . . .

The French troops continue to leave Rome by detachments. . . .

I have the honor to be, very respectfully, your obedient servant,

Rufus King

1866 The Fenian Invasion of Canada
Dispatch from U.S. Consul in Ft. Erie Freeman N. Blake to Secretary of State William H. Seward

One of the more bizarre episodes of American foreign policy was a privately organized invasion of Canada in 1866. The perpetrators were the Fenians, an Irish-American brotherhood dedicated to ending British rule in Ireland. The Fenians judged that defeating British forces in Canada would further the cause of Irish independence. The more ambitious among them even thought of establishing a territorial foothold in North America on behalf of a new Irish Republic. The Fenians hoped the United States might back their invasion, either through lingering support for "manifest destiny" or out of pique at British actions seen as favoring the South during the Civil War. Official American support, however, was not forthcoming. After an initial Fenian success in capturing Ft. Erie, Ontario, the invasion collapsed in just three days. In this dispatch the American consul in the captured Canadian town relates the major events of the brief conflict. The Fenians organized a number of other raids into Canada over the next five years but none on the scale of the 1866 invasion.

Fort Erie, June 20, 1866

Sir:

In several telegrams I informed you of the progress of the invasion of Canada, at this point, by an armed force called "Fenians."

Its duration was so brief and my time so occupied with the new duties occasioned by it, I had delayed making a formal mention of it to the present time.

On the 1st June instant, in the morning, between the hours of two & three, a body of Fenians about (800) eight hundred, under the command of Col. O'Neil, crossed the Niagara River from Lower Black Rock, or North Buffalo, and effected a successful landing on the Canada shore, and immediately occupied this village.

When apprised at an early hour of the movement I raised the American flag to indicate the perogative of the United States over the premises occupied by me, and set apart for the transaction of official duties.

Its appearance elicted loud applause from the invaders who halted for a moment in a square nearby.

Their first act was to require rations of the authorities of the town, sufficient to breakfast one thousand men. The supplies were speedily gathered for them.

I was called upon by Col. Bailey, Capt. Canty, and another officer of the Fenian army to assure me of their respect to the United States authority accredited here.

During the time there was considerable excitement and alarm among the residents, many of whom crowded my premises imploring protection and security.

I acceded to the request of several prominent persons to call upon the Fenian commanders in company with Mr. Graham, Her Majesty's Collector of Customs at this port, for the purpose of gaining assurances of safety to the people and allaying their fears.

Col. O'Neil very frankly stated in my interview with him that the object of the expedition under his command was an attempt to liberate Ireland & to establish a foothold for the Irish Republic in these provinces by over-throwing the British authorities here, that all persons who made no resistance to him should be respected and in no ways molested.

So far as I can learn these assurances of security as to noncombatants were very nearly carried out.

During the night of the 2d inst. the Fenians broke camp and moved down the river a short distance towards Chippawa, but finding a strong column of British regulars under the command of Col. Peacock, the Fenian forces turned back. . . .

In the morning of the 3d inst. the Fenian pickets fell in with the Provincial Volunteers "Queens Own," under Col. Brookes, despatched from Toronto via railway. . . .

This brought on a severe engagement at a place called "Limestone Ridge" not far from Ridgeway, causing the troops under Col. Brookes to fall back for support to Port Colburn.

The Fenians gave up further pursuit, and made a forced march down the Garrison Road leading to the village of Fort Erie.

On their approach to this place another fight occurred between their advance and the Canadian force which had been sent from Port Colburn by the steam tug "W. J. Robb," fitted up as a gunboat.

The Canadians were disbursed, several taken prisoner, and a few killed and wounded on both sides. The boat with all on board at the time was saved by moving out into the river.

To avoid capture by the heavy columns of Canadian troops concentrating from below & above, a large portion of the invaders hastily reembarked for the United States, between the hours of 2 & 3 on the morning of the 3d inst. on board the scow "A. B. Wait."

On reaching the American waters the whole party was captured by W. G. Morris commanding propeller tug "J. C. Harrison" detailed for that purpose by Capt. Bryson of the U.S. ship "Michigan."

Here they were held as prisoners until the terms of their release were made known by the government.

During these proceedings I went aboard the "Michigan," and witnessed the promptitude of the officers in the discharge of that duty.

Through the alacrity and the decisive action of Commander Bryson and the officers & men under him, and through the vigilance of the military and the civil authorities of the United States stationed at Buffalo, a formidable invasion of upper Canada by the discontents of English supremacy in Ireland has been prevented, while the honor of our government in efforts to maintain its laws and good faith towards a foreign power has been nobly vindicated. . . .

It is believed that a better and more friendly feeling towards the United States government will be the result of these late disturbances so effectually & humanely terminated by it. . . .

      I am, Sir
      Your Obedient Servant,

      Freeman H. Blake

1866 Insurrection in Spain: "My House Was Hit by One Cannon Ball"

Dispatch from U.S. Minister to Spain John P. Hale to
Secretary of State William H. Seward

Unstable governments were the rule throughout much of Europe in the mid-nineteenth century, and Spain was no exception to this trend. In his 1843 dispatch U.S. Minister to Spain Washington Irving described the capture of Madrid by insurgent forces (see "Insurgents Take Madrid," p. 111). In this dispatch, written twenty-three years later, John Hale reports the second major insurrection since his arrival in Madrid nine months earlier. While this insurrection was unsuccessful, its guiding spirit, Gen. Juan Prim, would succeed in taking power two years later.

Madrid, June 24, 1866

Sir:

It is my duty to inform you that Madrid has been the scene of a fearful insurrection, which has been completely quelled by the government. The first manifestation of the insurgents was early Friday morning, (22d instant,) when two regiments of artillery, stationed at the barracks of San Gil, not more than a quarter of a mile north of the royal palace, raised the standard of a revolt. It began by some of the men shooting their officers, who were supposed to be loyal to the government....

The insurrection was not confined to the military, but extended over a great part of the city, and barricades were formed in numerous places—it is difficult now to say how many, but they were formed in many streets of the city. The house where I live and keep the legation is in Culle de Barquillo, No. 26. The Prussian legation is under the same roof, and the Brazilian is in the same street, on the opposite or northern side, No. 13, and the Belgian legation at No. 14, on the same side with mine. At the very corner of my house the insurgents erected a barricade, three or four feet high, in the course of the afternoon, across the street, women and children assisting in doing the work, unmolested. The insurgents, for some hours, appeared to have undisturbed possession of this street, or that part of it where these several legations are situated. No violence or injury of any kind was done or threatened to any of them, and I had no apprehension of any, not either for myself or family, save what might occur from the effects of some random shot. These apprehensions were not altogether unfounded, as you may infer from the fact that the corner of my house was hit by one cannon ball, the marks of which very palpably remain, and also by one musket or rifle ball. These I suppose to have been fired by some government troops in clearing the streets, and that the hitting of my house was purely and entirely accidental. I learn that a somewhat similar casualty happened to the Brazilian legation. The shield of the arms of Brazil over the door was carried away by a cannon shot.

Marks of cannon and musket balls are to be seen in various parts of the city and frequently pools of blood were seen standing in the streets on the morning of the 23d instant. The insurrection was not quelled without a great sacrifice of human life. By the morning of the 23d the government were in complete possession of the whole city, and had taken, it is said, between one and two thousand prisoners. As this is the second attempt at revolution made within the short time I have been in Spain, in each of which the government has triumphed, I am apprehensive that they will feel it to be necessary to deal severely with such of the rebels as they have in their power. Indeed, I hear that many executions have already taken place. . . .

I have the honor to remain, with the highest respect, sir, your obedient servant,

John P. Hale

1866 The Austro-Prussian War: Moving toward a German Empire

Dispatch from U.S. Minister to Austria John Lothrop Motley to Secretary of State William H. Seward

From 1815 to 1866 Germany was a very loose confederation of thirty-nine independent states. Among these, only Prussia was a significant power. When Otto von Bismarck was named chief minister of Prussia in 1862, he began to work for Prussian expansion, provoking war first with Denmark, then with Austria. Prussia won a sweeping victory over Austria, attributable to superior generalship and to the use of the new needle gun, with which an infantryman could shoot five rounds a minute. During the war Prussia also overran and annexed several of the larger German states; within five years it had incorporated the rest into the new German Empire. After the war Bismarck was able—with difficulty—to restrain the victorious Prussian generals from marching into Vienna itself. This Prussian restraint allowed Austria to save some face and laid the first building block of what would become the German-Austrian alliance of World War I. In this dispatch American minister John Lothrop Motley reports, from the perspective of his post in Vienna, news of the crushing defeat of the Austrian army (also see "Turmoil in the Balkans," p. 166).

Vienna, July 11, 1866

Sir:

When I was writing my last despatch, No. 192, of July 4, no one in Vienna was aware of the extent of the military disaster which had befallen this empire. It was known only that there had been a decided repulse near Koniggratz; yet, before my despatch had left the post office, on its way to the United States, the startling news of the utter overthrow and flight of the great army of the north was spread over Europe.

. . . Even now, the amount of the loss to the imperial army can only be guessed at approximately. . . .

The Prussians claim to have taken 120 cannon and 20,000 prisoners. . . .

The active campaigning in the north lasted hardly longer than ten or twelve days, and it is very probable that the war is already finished. . . .

Austria went into this tremendous war with nothing but muzzle-loaders against Prussian needle-guns.

I suppose the day is not far distant when muskets with ramrods will be as obsolete as bows and arrows.

Certainly the advantage in weapons has seemed to make the Prussian army comparatively superhuman; yet I suppose it to be certain that the Prussian gun is inferior in rapidity of firing and simplicity of mechanism to the last rifle used in the United States.

It would be difficult to describe the gloom, almost amounting to despair, which has held possession of this city and the whole empire ever since the fatal 4th of July, when the disaster was first revealed in its full extent. . . .

No soldiers have ever fought with more reckless bravery than the imperial troops. The instances of individual heroism and self-devotion have been manifold, but the army was outgeneraled, outweaponed, and outflanked, and for the last seven days a sickening expectation has been almost universally prevalent of seeing the victorious enemy enter Vienna. . . .

The war at this moment still continues, but the news of an armistice is daily expected. . . .

Prussia . . . has gained in her rapid and startling campaign, besides Schleswig-Holstein, Hanover, Electoral Hesse, Saxony, the sovereigns of which countries are either in prison or in exile, and Bohemia, in which kingdom her united armies are established, while in its capital, the imperial city of Prague, a Prussian garrison is quartered. . . .

I have the honor to remain, sir, your obedient servant,

J. Lothrop Motley

1866 The Continents United: The Transatlantic Cable
Dispatch from U.S. Minister to France John Bigelow to
Secretary of State William H. Seward

The first telegraph message was transmitted in 1844 between Washington and Baltimore under the direction of Samuel Morse. Within five years the first submarine cable was laid, connecting Great Britain and France under the English Channel. In 1866, after two unsuccessful attempts spanning more than a decade, American businessman Cyrus W. Field completed a cable from Europe to Newfoundland, providing instantaneous communication between the Eastern and Western Hemispheres.

The advent of long-distance telegraph transformed the practice of diplomacy. Rapid communications allowed leaders in Washington and other capitals to maintain greater control over the actions of their diplomats and to react more quickly to fast-breaking events. The telegraph also gradually transformed the nature of diplomatic reporting; telegrams eventually superseded almost entirely the traditional handwritten dispatch. One of the first messages transmitted over the new transatlantic cable was sent by Field to the U.S. minister to France, who reports receipt of the message in this dispatch.

Paris, August 3, 1866

Sir:

The news of the successful union of the eastern and western hemispheres by electric telegraph reached this legation on the 28th of July last, at twenty-eight minutes past five in the morning, in the following despatch from Mr. Cyrus W. Field:

Friday—11 p. m.

His Excellency the American Minister, Paris:

The Atlantic cable is successfully laid. May it prove a blessing to all mankind.

Cyrus Field, Newfoundland

On the first day of August the Paris papers contained despatches from New York of that date. . . .

I am, sir, with great respect, your obedient servant,

John Bigelow

1866   Arresting a Lincoln Conspirator
Dispatch from U.S. Consul General in Egypt Charles Hale to Secretary of State William H. Seward

The assassination of President Abraham Lincoln in April 1865 led to a massive manhunt for the conspirators. Assassin John Wilkes Booth was shot while trying to make his escape. Several other participants in the plot were convicted by a military tribunal; four were hanged. One alleged conspirator escaped—John Surratt, son of Mary Surratt, the lone woman among those executed. Surratt made his way to Canada, then England, and then Rome, where he enlisted in the Zouaves, the pope's guards. After being recognized in Rome, Surratt escaped to Egypt where the U.S. consul, who had been warned of his arrival, arrested him and arranged for his return to the United States to stand trial. Surratt was acquitted in 1867.

> Alexandria, Egypt,
> November 27, 1866

Sir:

I have the honor to report that, in consequence of a telegram received via Constantinople from Mr. King, United States minister at Rome, and of several letters received from Mr. Winthrop, United States consul at Malta, . . . I have this day arrested a man calling himself Walters, dressed in the uniform of a zouave, who arrived at Alexandria on the 23d instant in the steamship Tripoli from Naples, and who is believed to be John Harrison Surratt, one of the conspirators for the assassination of President Lincoln.

The telegram and some of the letters having been delayed in transmission, I was fortunate in finding the man still in quarantine among the third-class passengers, of whom there is no list whatever. It was easy to distinguish him among seventy-eight of these by his zouave uniform, and scarcely less easy by his almost unmistakable American type of countenance. I said at once to him, "You are the man I want; you are an American." He said, "Yes, sir; I am." I said, "You doubtless know why I want you. What is your name?" He replied promptly, "Walters." I said, "I believe your true name is Surratt," and in arresting him mentioned my official position as United States consul general. The director of quarantine speedily arranged a sufficient escort of soldiers, by whom the prisoner was conducted to a safe place within the quarantine walls. Although the walk occupied several minutes, the prisoner, close at my side, made no remark whatever, displaying neither surprise nor irritation. Arrived at the place prepared, I gave him the usual magisterial caution that he was not obliged to say anything, and that anything he said would be at once taken down in writing. He said, "I have nothing to say. I want nothing but what is right." He declared he had neither passport, nor baggage, nor money except six francs.

His companions confirm his statements in this respect. They say he came to Naples a deserter from the Papal army at Rome. I find that he has no papers, and no clothes but those he is wearing.

The appearance of the prisoner answers very well the description given of Surratt . . . officially sent to me by the government. . . .

The prisoner's quarantine will expire on the 29th; he will then be received into the prison of the local government, which cordially gives me every assistance.

It will readily occur to you that the only convenient way of transferring the prisoner to the United States will be by an American man-of-war, and I earnestly hope that one may soon come here to receive him. . . .

I have the honor to be, sir, very respectfully, your most obedient servant,

Charles Hale

1867 The Purchase of Alaska: "Seward's Folly"
Dispatch from U.S. Minister to Russia Cassius M. Clay to Secretary of State William H. Seward

The purchase of Alaska from Russia for $7 million was widely criticized at the time as a waste of government funds. Opponents of the purchase dubbed it "Seward's folly" and "Seward's ice box" in honor of the secretary of state, William H. Seward, who negotiated the agreement. Opposition in Congress was sufficiently outspoken that the Russian minister in Washington is said to have liberally distributed bribes to members of Congress to gain their support. One person who foresaw the benefits of acquiring Alaska and who worked hard to arrange the purchase was the U.S. minister to Russia, Cassius M. Clay (see "Progress in Russia," p. 172). In this dispatch Clay describes the European reactions to the purchase.

St. Petersburg, Russia,
May 10, 1867

Sir:

Your despatch No. 241, April 1st, 1867, enclosing me the treaty between Russia and America, ceding us all Russian America, was duly received. . . . I congratulate you upon this brilliant achievement, which adds so vast a territory to our Union, whose ports, whose mines, whose timber, whose furs, whose fisheries are of untold value, and whose fields will produce many grains, even wheat, and become hereafter in time the seat of hardy white population. I regard it as worth at least $50,000,000, and hereafter the wonder will be that we ever got it at all. . . . I trust I have aided indirectly in this final cession. . . .

The Russians are very jealous of foreigners, and traditionally opposed to ceding territory; yet in consequence of the good feeling everywhere prevailing in our favor, I regard the *rôle* as popular. I have heard it said, "Well, we have sold to you too cheaply, but 'tis all in the family;" and others look upon it with favor, because we are to be near their eastern possessions, and us they regard as perpetual friends. . . . It went very hard with the English, and also with the French; and if you had given time and publicity to your movements I have no doubt you would have had most energetic protests, if not positive armed intervention to prevent it. . . . But the strange and unexpected good alliance between Russia and America has taken them by surprise, and disables all their projects. The truth is, England and France are no match now for the United States and Russia, and the weight of power with the coming years will be still more on our side. I have done all I could here to bring about this most desirable result. . . .

Believe me truly, my dear sir, your obedient servant,

Cassius M. Clay

1867 The Saga of Maximilian
Dispatches from U.S. Representatives in Mexico to Secretary of State William H. Seward

Political turmoil in Mexico after 1855 and American preoccupation with its own domestic strife during the Civil War provided an opening for European powers, which had never accepted the Monroe Doctrine, to intervene in Mexican affairs. Citing Mexican nonpayment of debts and other pretexts, French emperor Napoleon III sent troops to occupy the country and arranged to have Archduke Maximilian of Austria proclaimed emperor of Mexico. By 1866, however, Napoleon III had abandoned Maximilian to his fate. In doing so, Napoleon was bowing to pressure from the United States (which, after the Civil War, was once again considering developments abroad), the civil war raging in Mexico, and the need for his troops at home. With the departure of the French, republican forces in Mexico loyal to Benito Juárez gained ascendency. Maximilian was captured at Querétaro and executed by firing squad on June 19. The next day Mexico City, having endured a long siege, fell to the republicans under a young general, Porfirio Diaz, who a decade later became president of Mexico.

The U.S. minister to Mexico was on leave during these dramatic developments and resigned rather than return to post. The United States, however, was represented in major Mexican cities by consuls who reported on events. In some instances they relayed their dispatches to Washington through a newly designated American chargé d'affaires, who was in New Orleans en route to Mexico when Maximilian's short-lived empire came to an end.

The Siege of Mexico

From U.S. Consul in Mexico City Marcus Otterbourg to Secretary of State William H. Seward

City of Mexico, June 21, 1867

Sir:

The capital of Mexico was surrendered yesterday, the 20th, at 7 1/2 p. m. to General Porfirio Diaz, in command of the liberal army, after a rigorous blockade of more than 70 days. . . .

Referring to the diary, enclosure No. 1, for details connected with the siege, I have the honor to submit to the department a report of my proceedings during the delicate and perilous crisis through which this consulate has passed without compromitting, I trust, the neutrality or dignity of the United States government. . . .

I have the honor to be, very respectfully, your obedient servant,

Marcus Otterbourg

ENCLOSURE: OTTERBOURG'S DIARY ENTRY—JUNE 21, 1867

My last despatch, dated May 26, left matters in such a state that an early solution seemed almost certain. The situation, however, has gone on dragging beyond all expectations until yesterday, when at last the so-called imperial authorities gave up the city of Mexico to General Porfirio Diaz. The liberal troops have entered this morning in the most orderly manner, and the republican government remains, consequently, established anew in the capital of Mexico.

After announcing this happy and long-expected event, I must recur briefly to the facts which have marked the three last weeks of the siege. . . .

Flour and corn were almost exhausted and began to reach prices never known before. Bread ceased to be found at the bakers' since the 11th; corn continued to be sold irregularly until the 5th, but the crowd which accumulated at those points was such that the majority could not get even a handful of grain. Deaths by starvation began to be announced in the suburbs, and matters reached soon such a point that every kind of food had to be resorted to by people of every class. Bean cakes, barley bread, horse meat became gradually the almost regular diet of even the richest families, the most lucky of those who, by foresight, had kept in store a small provision of biscuit. What was meantime the condition of the crowd can be more easily conceived than depicted. Dog and cat meat have been of no uncommon use during these three weeks. But even so famine was daily on the increase, until at last the authorities felt the necessity of leaving free scope to the emigration of the perishing multitude. Thousands of men and women left the city every day, and it is calculated that almost a third of the whole population had gone out, though this diminution of consumers relieved in no way the condition of those who remained. . . .

On the 7th and 8th there were some symptoms of riot among the populace, on account of the increasing scarcity of every kind of food. The Iturbide theatre, where corn was said to be stored, was attacked and partly sacked; but General O'Horan soon appeared and quieted the crowd by offering to direct in person the investigations. He effectively began to go from one house to another, taking possession of every provisions he found and distributing them promiscuously to the people. This kind of organized pillage continued the whole day. . . . Almost every kind of eatable was exhausted in the city. Flour had reached the fabulous price of one dollar and seventy-five cents to two dollars per pound. Corn was worth thirty to thirty-five dollars per hundred weight. What meat could be had must be paid one dollar a pound for, and horse flesh, after selling at six cents, had already gone up to eighteen or even twenty-five cents. The impossibility to confront for a long time such a way of living was becoming more and more apparent. . . .

On the fourteenth there came suddenly a new levy of horses, while forced contributions were exacted from almost anybody on whom the government agents could lay their hands. Some of the most respectable foreign merchants were arrested, imprisoned at Fort Santiago, and kept there for hours, even for days, without food, without a mattress, and even without a chair. Among them was Mr. Bennecke, an old and most honored gentleman, who could not even be protected by his title of Prussian consul. He had to pay $6,000 in order to recover his liberty. So general was the money hunt that almost everybody who had anything to lose was obliged to conceal himself to escape prison. . . .

Neither the men nor the horses were now able to confront the besiegers, in consequence of their utter exhaustion; they could scarcely stand up, and it was not an uncommon thing to see either man or beast fainting in the streets from want of food. . . .

The Execution of Maximilian

From U.S. Chargé d'Affaires Designate E. L. Plumb in New Orleans to Secretary of State William H. Seward

New Orleans, July 3, 1867

Sir:

By the mail at hand to-day from Matamoros, I have received a copy of the official paper of San Luis Potosi of the 19th ultimo, which contains the telegrams and orders relating to the trial and execution of the Archduke Maximilian, and the efforts made to save his life, and which are of exceeding importance and interest. I would translate the same, but it is not possible to do so in time for this mail, and I would respectfully suggest that they be read to you by the translator of the department, as they throw much light upon the different steps that have been taken and the motives that have actuated the Mexican government. For that purpose I beg to enclose the paper herewith.

I have also a letter from Mr. Marshall at Matamoros, dated the 27th ultimo, in which he says:

> I have just sent you despatch by telegram announcing the untimely death of the Archduke Maximilian.
>
> This event has cast a gloom over all the foreign residents of the city.
>
> His self-sacrificing determination to share the fate of his followers challenged the admiration even of his enemies.
>
> There were no demonstrations of joy exhibited at the news, which, like a shudder, passed from lip to lip.

I am, sir, very respectfully, your most obedient servant,

E. L. Plumb

PART IV

A Period of U.S. Isolation: 1868–1882

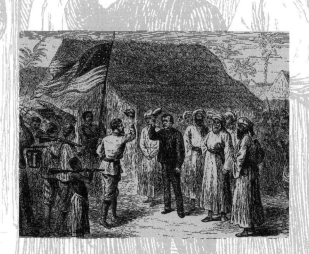

"Dr. Livingstone, I presume?" American journalist and explorer Henry Morton Stanley, left, arrived in Africa in early 1871 in search of the celebrated African explorer and missionary David Livingstone. Stanley's departure for central Africa and Livingstone's death some years later were reported by the U.S. consul in Zanzibar, Francis Webb.

1868 Eyewitness to a Hara-Kiri
Dispatch from U.S. Minister to Japan Robert B. Van Valkenburgh to Secretary of State William H. Seward

The year 1868 saw the beginning of a fundamental transformation in Japan. On January 1 Hiogo (now Kobe) and Osaka were opened to foreign trade. Two days later a new mikado (emperor) assumed nominal control of the government, ushering in the Meiji period of rapid modernization. One immediate change was a greater acceptance of Westerners. When an anti-Western official in Hiogo ordered an attack on foreigners in the newly opened city, he was promptly tried and sentenced to death. After the trial, the American minister was among the foreign diplomats who reviewed and upheld the Japanese court's verdict. On the minister's instructions, an American naval officer attended the execution, as reported in this dispatch. Under Japanese custom, the official was permitted to commit hara-kiri, suicide by disembowelment.

Hiogo, March 4, 1868

Sir:

In my No. 14, under date of March 1st, I had the honor to inform you that Taki Tensaboro, the officer who ordered the fire upon the foreigners at Hiogo on the 4th February, had been found guilty, and his execution was directed to take place on the next day (March 2) at Hiogo. The culprit was an officer of rank, and in accordance with the laws of Japan was permitted to commit hara-kiri.

On that day two Japanese officers, in accordance with what is understood to be the custom in this country, called upon the representatives unofficially to ask if the man's life could not be spared, and whether we would not request the Mikado to reprieve him. In all cases of sentence of death I am informed this custom prevails throughout the land. We held a conference at once, lasting about four hours, desiring, if possible, to comply with the request of these gentlemen, and ask for a reprieve; but the conclusion arrived at was, that the safety of foreigners in the future would prevent the exercise of such clemency, and we declined to accede to the request. . . .

We were then informed that the execution of the sentence would take place that evening at a temple in Hiogo, and were asked to designate each representative a witness. I accordingly appointed commander J. Blakely Creighton, of the United States steamship Oneida, the senior naval officer at this port, as such witness from this legation. The execution took place about half past 10 o'clock in the evening, witnessed only by seven foreigners and about an equal number of Japanese officials. It is said to have been a very solemn and impressive scene. I enclose . . . [a] copy of Commander Creighton's official report to me of the execution.

We entertain the belief that the punishment of this man will have a salutary effect in preventing similar acts in the future, to some extent at all events, while it satisfies us of the good intentions and power of the Mikado....

Trusting that my action in this matter will be approved, I have the honor to be, sir, very respectfully, your most obedient servant,

R. B. Van Valkenburgh

ENCLOSURE

Hiogo, Japan, March 3, 1868

Sir:

In compliance with your request, I witnessed the execution of the Japanese official who ordered his troops to fire on the foreigners at this place, on the 4th ultimo. The particulars are as follows:

I left the legation at about 9 p.m. last evening, in company with the officers attached to the foreign legations, and proceeded to Hiogo, where we were met by a guard who escorted us to the temple where the execution was to take place. There was a large number of people on each side of the street leading to the temple, and quite a number of soldiers drawn up inside and about the temple. We were shown into a room adjoining the Japanese officials, where we were asked if we wished to question the person about to be executed, (to which we answered in the negative,) and also the names of the officials present.

After waiting about a half hour, we were conducted by the Japanese officials into what appeared to be the principal room of the temple, which was lighted with candles, and in front of the altar was a raised platform of about a foot in height, which extended across the room, and we were placed on the right of the altar, within a few feet of where the execution was to take place, with the Japanese officials on the left. In front of the altar there was a green cloth, and in front of that a red one. We were informed that the execution would take place on the red cloth. Seating ourselves upon the mats on the platform, we awaited the execution.

In a few minutes the prisoner came in, dressed in the usual Japanese dress of a person of rank, accompanied by the executioner. He walked, with a steady, firm step, in front of the altar, where he knelt in prayer. He then arose and went to the red cloth, where he knelt and made the confession that "he was the officer that ordered the troops to fire upon the foreigners, and also to fire upon them when they were trying to escape." He then disrobed himself to his waist, and reached out for a knife that was near him, which he thrust into his bowels, and leaning forward at the same time, the executioner, with one blow from his sword, severed his head from his body. This occurred about 10:30 p.m. The Japanese then bowed to the floor, on which we all did the same.

We were then asked if we were satisfied with what we had witnessed, when we replied in the affirmative. After a lapse of a few moments we were informed that all was over, when we arose and took our departure. The whole scene was one of great solemnity, and very impressive.

Very respectfully, your obedient servant,

J. Blakely Creighton,
Commander

1868 A Grave Robber in Korea
Dispatch from U.S. Consul in Shanghai George F. Seward to
U.S. Chargé d'Affaires in Peking S. Wells Williams

Korea was the last of the major kingdoms of East Asia opened to contact with the West. By the late 1860s, however, Western missionaries, mariners in distress, and even occasional small military expeditions were disturbing the enforced isolation of the "Hermit Kingdom." In what may have been the most remarkable intrusion into Korea during this period, a private expedition of adventurers—including an American, F. H. B. Jenkins—landed on the coast and attempted unsuccessfully to plunder the royal tombs. Jenkins later was tried in the consular court in Shanghai, which had jurisdiction over Americans accused of crimes in China. He was acquitted for lack of evidence. The case is described in this dispatch from U.S. Consul George Seward, who later was appointed as U.S. minister to China.

Shanghai, July 13, 1868

Sir:

I inclose the supreme court and consular Gazette's report of the trial in the consulate of F. H. B. Jenkins, for setting on foot an expedition to Corea, having for its object to exhume the remains of a dead sovereign, or other person or persons of that country, and to hold the bones for profit.

This expedition left Shanghai in April last. There were apparently three leaders: a French priest named Farout, a citizen of Hamburg named Oppert, and our countryman above named.

A steamer under the North German flag, named the China, of 648 tons, was chartered for it, and steam tender of 60 tons, about, also provided. About eight Europeans, 20 Manilas, and 100 Chinese sailors, beyond the complement of the ship, were engaged and embarked. At Nagasaki muskets enough were taken to arm all these. Arrived on the coast of Corea, two small boats were seized, and within a few hours the tender towing them steamed up a river about 40 miles. Here the crowd of armed men landed and made their way across the country to a graveyard, where the surrounding hills were covered with Coreans; they went to work to exhume the bones for which they had come. These were contained in a stone or mason work sarcophagus, and having penetrated through the earth to it, they found themselves unable to do more, and returned to the large steamer, having met no opposition which they had not overcome by the simple display of their arms, or by firing them in the air. . . .

Before the departure of the expedition, Mr. Jenkins had told me that he was about making a visit to Corea with a French priest and Mr. Oppert, to open negotiations which he said were invited by the Corean government, looking to the sending of an embassy to Europe and America. . . . After his return he told me of the real object of the expedition—to exhume the bones of a former king, and to hold them, to force a large payment of money. He at the same time declared that he was innocent of any knowledge of the purpose until after sailing from Nagasaki, when it was too late to leave the vessel.

I was not at all satisfied with this statement, and set to work to sift it. The result of my inquiries was a conviction that Mr. Jenkins ought to be put on trial.

I accordingly instituted legal procedure against him, as seen in the above-mentioned report of the Gazette, resulting in his acquittal.

The indictment as noticed charged him with setting on foot an expedition, &c. I did not feel authorized to take jurisdiction of anything done outside of my consular district, but had I been authorized to do so, the result on the evidence gleaned must have been the same.

You will notice that the verdict is a simple acquittal. This is equivalent, under our rules, to the Scotch verdict not proven. For while the evidence would not at all justify a conviction, it left an unfavorable impression on my mind, and with the associates. The presence of the accused with the expedition, his furnishing a large amount of money, although ostensibly this was a loan, and a large quantity of arms; his failure to indicate that he remonstrated when told of the real purpose of the expedition, and his reliance on the weakness of the prosecution rather than on the strength of his own case, all conspired to prevent us from giving him a verdict of honorable acquittal. But it was completely evident that not he, but the French priest and the Hamburgher Oppert were the persons most concerned.

I presume that no future steps will be taken. The evidence given is not sufficient to enable the consul general for Prussia to institute proceedings against the master and crew of the steamer. The French priest has wisely gone off from Shanghai. The Hamburgh consul has not sufficient judicial powers. So the persons who set on foot this disgraceful expedition will all go clear, and an offense which must be ranked in the opinions of the Chinese and of Coreans, who have, I believe, common ideas of the sacredness of burial places, one which might have resulted in severe loss of life, and which cannot but grievously interfere with efforts to open relations with Corea, will remain unredressed. . . .

I have the honor to be your obedient servant,

George F. Seward

1868 Earthquake: "Ecuador Is in Ruins"
Dispatch from U.S. Minister to Peru Alvin P. Hovey to Secretary of State William H. Seward

The Pacific Rim of the Americas has throughout history seen some of the world's worst natural disasters. In September 1868 a particularly severe earthquake devastated large areas of Ecuador and Peru.

Lima, Peru, September 14, 1868

Sir:

In my dispatches Nos. 144 and 145, dated the 22d and 28th of August, respectively, I gave you a slight account of the terrible earthquake which on the 13th ultimo laid desolate a large part of Peru, and now, again, it is my painful duty to inform you that a large and the most prolific part of the republic of Ecuador is in ruins, caused by a similar shock at 1:30 on the morning of the 16th of the same month. This earthquake seems to have had its center in the province of Imbabura, near the volcano of Ocampo, about sixty miles north of the city of Quito. Eight towns, with the adjoining haciendas and populations, are said to have been entirely destroyed, numbering from forty to fifty-four thousand inhabitants. The cities of Otovalo and Cotacachi, containing respectively about twelve and eight thousand inhabitants, and both situated on the shores of the Lake Mojanda, are said to have been swallowed up with their entire populations, and their sites have become a part of the lake. The city of Ibarra, with a population of thirteen thousand, is totally destroyed. . . . Nor is the injury confined to the cities and towns, but all of the haciendas of the province, the richest in Ecuador, growing sugar and grain, and producing large numbers of cattle and sheep, have, as it were, been swept out of existence.

Quito did not suffer in the same ratio in the loss of life, but its walls and houses are destroyed. The most of its inhabitants, including the

English chargé d'affaires, Mr. Hamilton, with his large family, were driven to the open plaza or square in the center of the city; and he, more fortunate than the others, is now enjoying the great luxury of a tent, while thousands of the best citizens are without shelter. To heighten the gloom, despondency, and misery of all, the terrific thunder-storms of the tropics seem to have redoubled their forces, and have literally deluged the whole country.

The losses in Imbabura will cause great suffering in Quito, as nearly all the necessaries of life for that city were drawn from that province. . . . If relief in some form is not speedily given, many of the sufferers will be compelled to reach the sea-shore or perish. . . . [T]hese shocks have almost ruined the republic of Ecuador. . . . In Peru, also, as I have heretofore informed you, proud and rebellious Arequipa is levelled with the dust; Arica swept from the sea-shore, with but one solitary house remaining; while the district and city of Moquegua, with its rich villages, vineyards, and haciendas, are but the wrecks of things that were. Had the earthquake in Peru taken place at night-time, as it did in Ecuador, the loss of life would have exceeded one hundred thousand souls. As it was, that loss in Peru is less, but the loss of property far greater.

Want, hunger, and famine, in these now unhappy countries, are striding through all classes in the midst of the unburied dead, and a general paralyzation of thought and action seems to pervade the land. This is, no doubt, caused by the continuous shocks since, and the great fear of other calamities; and, to add to the consternation of the weak, fearful, and helpless, robbers, in some localities, are said to be sacking and pillaging everything within their reach. . . .

The generosity of our country, in days gone by, has left a record that will never be forgotten—Greece, Poland, Hungary, and Ireland, with no greater, if not far less claims for aid or charity, have found that in the United States there were feeling hearts and open hands for those who deeply suffer. Will not our generous-hearted countrymen add Peru and Ecuador to their noble list?

. . . I most earnestly urge and entreat that you appeal to the good men of our country to aid by charity the suffering people of Peru and Ecuador. . . .

I have the honor to be your obedient servant,

Alvin P. Hovey

1871, 1874 Stanley and Livingstone
Dispatches from U.S. Consul in Zanzibar Francis R. Webb to Secretary of State Hamilton Fish

In 1870 James Gordon Bennett Jr., publisher of the New York Herald, *commissioned journalist Henry Morton Stanley to find the celebrated African explorer and missionary David Livingstone, who had not been heard from for several years. Stanley organized a successful relief expedition but found that Livingstone did not wish to leave central Africa. These dispatches from the U.S. consul in Zanzibar report Stanley's departure for the interior and Livingstone's death some years later.*

Stanley's First Expedition

Zanzibar, Feb. 6, 1871

Sir:

I have the honor to inform you that on the 6th ulto there arrived here from Seychelles Mr. H. Stanley the travelling correspondent of the "New York Herald" who has organized an expedition & started yesterday for the coast with a large party of followers including two white men.

His intention is to carefully explore the lake regions of Central Africa and either return to this point or return to Europe down the Nile, and will probably be absent about a year. He may possibly meet with Dr. Livingstone.

I have the honor to be Sir
Your Obedient Servant

Francis R. Webb

The Death of Dr. Livingstone

Zanzibar, January 3, 1874

Sir:

I have the honor to inform you that I have this day received a communication from Capt. W. F. Prideaux, H.B.M.'s Acting Political Agent and Consul General, from which I learn that he has just received intelligence of the death of Dr. David Livingstone, H.M.'s Consul for Central Africa, and that on the 5th inst. the British Flag will be displayed at half mast over the residency from sunrise until sunset as a mark of respect to the memory of the great explorer.

A private note accompanying the dispatch informed me that the sad event occurred sometime in June 1873 in about Lat. 10S. and Long. 28E. near lake Bemba and that Lieut. Cameron R.N. who commands the "Livingstone Search and Relief Expedition" writing from Unyanyembe under the date of October 20th, 1873 expected to receive the remains at that place shortly after. "Dr. Livingstone had been obliged to wade through marshes up to his waist for two or three weeks and an attack of dysentery at last carried him off."

I shall join the British representative here in the tribute of respect shown to the memory of the great traveller and good man who has gone.

I have the honor to be, Sir,
Your Most Obedient Servant

Francis R. Webb

1871   A Prussian Victory: "Paris Seems . . . to Have Died"
Dispatch from U.S. Minister to France Elihu B. Washburne to Secretary of State Hamilton Fish

In 1870 France and Prussia went to war, ostensibly as a result of a disagreement over whether a German prince could become king of Spain. The war easily could have been avoided, especially since the question of Spanish succession was resolved before hostilities began. Prince Otto von Bismarck—the guiding force in Prussia—believed, rightly, that war with France would assist him in his goal of incorporating the still independent southern German states into the new German Empire. In France, Emperor Napoleon III hoped a quick victory would both restore flagging public support for his regime and humble an increasingly powerful eastern neighbor.

France declared war on July 15. Within six weeks its armies were devastated, Napoleon III was taken prisoner, and the Prussians were at the gates of Paris. The French capital held out under a bitter siege for four months before capitulating to the invaders.

The American minister to France during the war was Elihu Washburne, a one-time member of Congress from Illinois who had been appointed secretary of state in 1869. Washburne served just eleven days as secretary— the shortest period on record—before resigning to leave for France. He remained in Paris throughout the siege, even when the French government and most other diplomats evacuated. When German diplomats left the city, Washburne inherited the unenviable task of protecting Germans in wartime Paris, in addition to the already difficult problems of meeting the needs of Americans in the beleaguered city. In this dispatch Washburne describes the climactic entry of German troops into Paris.

Paris, March 1, 1871

Sir:

They have come in. At 9 o'clock this a.m. three blue hussars entered the Port Maillot, proceeded up the avenue of the Grand Army, and walked their horses slowly down the magnificent avenue of the Champs Elysées, with carbines cocked and fingers upon the trigger. These hussars looked carefully into the side streets and proceeded slowly down the avenue. But few people were out at that early hour in the morning. Soon after, six more made their appearance by the same route, and every few minutes thereafter the number increased. Then came in the main body of the advance guard, numbering about one thousand men, consisting of cavalry and infantry, Bavarian and Prussian, forming part of the eleventh corps, under the command of General Kamichi. By this time the crowd on the Champs Elysées had increased and met the advancing Germans with hisses and insult. A portion of the German troops then halted and with great deliberation loaded their pieces, whereat the crowd, composed of boys and "roughs," incontinently took to their heels. According to a previous understanding among the French, all the shops and restaurants along the route had been closed. . . . It was not until about half past one o'clock in the afternoon that the royal guard of Prussia, in four solid bodies, surrounded the Arc of Triumph. Then a company of Uhlans, with their spears stuck in their saddles and ornamented by the little flags of blue and white, headed the advancing column. They were followed by the Saxons, with their light blue coats, who were succeeded by the Bavarian riflemen, with their heavy uniform and martial tread. Afterward followed more of the Uhlans, and occasionally a squad of the Bismarck cuirassiers, with their white jackets, square hats and waving plumes. . . . Now come the artillery, with its pieces of six, which must have extorted the admiration of all military men by its splendid appearance and wonderful precision of movement. Next fell into line the royal guard of Prussia, with their shining casques and glittering bayonets, which had been massed around the world-renowned Arc of Triumph, erected (and with what bitter sarcasm it may now be said!) to the glory of the grand army. . . . At first the troops were met with hisses, cat-calls, and all sorts of insulting cries, but as they poured in thicker and faster, and forming by companies, as they swept down the avenue to the strains of martial music, the crowd seemed to be awed into silence, and no other sound was heard but the tramp of the soldiery and the occasional word of command. . . . The entry of the main body of the troops occupied about two hours, and, after that, they began to disperse into the various quarters of the city. . . . We were busily engaged at the legation almost the entire day, endeavoring to secure protection for American apartments and property. . . .

As I now write it is eleven o'clock at night. The day opened cloudy and somber, with a raw and chilly atmosphere. A little after noon the sun came out bright and warm, and the close of the day was magnificent. . . . From the Boulevard du Temple to the Arc of Triumph not a store or a restaurant is open, with the exception of two of the latter on the Champs Elysées, which the Germans have ordered to be kept open. There are no excited crowds on the boulevards, and, what is very remarkable and without precedent in the memory of the "oldest inhabitant," not an omnibus is running in the whole city and every omnibus office is closed. Neither is there a private or a public carriage to be seen, unless a hearse shall be deemed and taken as a "public carriage;" unfortunately, too many of which are to be seen now every hour of the day. Paris seems literally to have died out. There is neither song nor shout in all her streets. The whole population is marching around as if under a cloud of oppression. The gas is not yet lighted, and the streets present a sinister and somber aspect. . . . I have, this evening, sent you a telegraphic dispatch stating that the entry of the German troops has been quiet and peaceful, and that all is calm in Paris. I do not know that it will reach you. . . .

I have, &c.,

E. B. Washburne

1871   The Paris Commune
Dispatches from U.S. Minister to France Elihu B. Washburne to Secretary of State Hamilton Fish

After the Franco-Prussian War (1870–1871), the people of Paris, who had endured four months of suffering during the German siege of the city, could not reconcile themselves to the peace terms accepted by the French National Assembly (see "A Prussian Victory," p. 202). In March 1871 disgruntled citizens and national guardsmen threw up barricades and seized the city, forcing the government to flee to nearby Versailles. Once established, the government of the Commune held sway over the city for two months. In late May loyalist troops from Versailles stormed Paris and put an end to the Commune amid an orgy of bloodshed and destruction. Supporters of the Commune executed innocent hostages and set fire to huge sections of the city. The victorious government forces retaliated by putting twenty thousand "Communards" to death. In these dispatches U.S. Minister Elihu Washburne reports first his surprise at the initial rapid success of the insurgents and then the conflagration with which the Commune came to an end.

The Commune Begins

Paris, March 19, 1871

Sir:

In my No. 390, of day before yesterday, I alluded to the insurrectionary movements in Paris, and expressing the opinion that they would not amount to much, and that no great degree of violence was probable. It was not then possible for me to conceive that in a little more than twenty-four hours from that time Mr. [Adolphe] Thiers ["chief of the executive power"] and all the members of his government would be obliged to flee from Paris, and that an insurrectionary committee of the national guard would, at the moment I am writing, be complete masters of the city. Yet such is the fact. The attempt of the government to dislodge the insurgents at Montmartre, and to get possession of the cannon there installed before daybreak yesterday morning, proved a complete failure, the troops of the line fraternizing with the national guard and refusing to fire upon them. All was lost from that moment, though the government did not appear to realize it, and various feeble demonstrations were made during the day to vindicate the public authority. All day long, whenever the troops of the line and the national guard came within reach of each other, they reversed their muskets in token of peace. Without knowing the full gravity of the situation, I started about noon yesterday to make a trip into the country. On my return at six o'clock in the evening, by the way of the Bastile, I found the circulation for carriages interdicted on the principal streets. Being turned into the by-streets, I soon found my way impeded by barricades which had been improvised, and everywhere the insurrectionary national guard. After making various turns, however, I was enabled to get through the obstructed quarter. While I saw so many evidences of great public commotion, I had no idea how serious matters were until this morning, when, in coming down to my legation, I found the city full of the most fearful rumors. I at once went to the Foreign Office, and found that Mr. Jules Favre [minister of foreign affairs] and the whole government had left for Versailles at half past nine o'clock last night. . . . The ministry of the interior and the ministry of justice, as well as the prefecture of police and the Hotel de Ville, are occupied by the insurgents. The central committee of the insurrectionary national guard has issued a proclamation, which is placarded on the walls this afternoon, stating that they have taken the power of the government, driven out the members thereof who betrayed it; that their mission so far is ended, and they call upon the people of Paris to elect a government to-morrow. The regular government of France, constituted by the will of the people, as expressed through the National Assembly at Bordeaux, having been driven from Paris, by the insurrectionary movement, and established itself at

Versailles, I deem it my duty to follow that government, and shall, therefore, on to-morrow or the next day, remove thither with the legation, leaving one of the secretaries in charge here. Every member of the diplomatic corps will also leave. If the seat of government shall remain at Versailles, which is now very doubtful, my removal will be more nominal than real, for while I shall have my official residence at Versailles, I shall come into Paris every day.

I have, &c.,

E. B. Washburne

Paris in Flames

Paris, May 24, 1871

Sir:

. . . Prodigious events . . . have been transpiring in Paris. . . . At half past 5 or 6 o'clock of yesterday it was evident that an immense fire had broken out at the chancellerie of the legion of honor. Soon we saw the smoke arising in other parts of the city, showing but too plainly that the terrible threats of the commune of a general conflagration had commenced to be carried out. . . . At 1 o'clock this morning I was awakened by a friend, who told me that the palace [of the Tuileries] was all in flames. I hurried to a position from which I had a full and complete view of the fire. It was a starlight night, calm and beautiful. An insurgent battery, which had been for twenty-four hours shelling our part of the town, was still sending its bombs into the immediate neighborhood of the legation every fifteen minutes. The roar of other cannon . . . fell upon the still of the night. The lurid flames rising from the burning palace lighted up half the heavens, and the whole scene was the most terrible I had ever witnessed. To the fire of the Tuileries were added other conflagrations, the ministry of finance, the buildings of the Rue Royal, and other fires which seemed just started. . . . Coming to the legation at 9 o'clock, I heard that the Versailles troops had captured the strong positions at the Place de la Concorde and the Place Vendome. . . . Here the most desperate fighting took place for a period of nearly thirty-six hours. The neighborhood presented a most dreadful appearance this morning. The sidewalks of the splendid Boulevard Malesherbe were filled with horses, baggage-wagons, and artillery carriages. The houses had been more or less torn with shot and shell; the trees were all cut to pieces by the fire of the artillery and musketry, and their branches filled the street. A dead national guard was lying in an excavation for a cellar near by. In a small open space in the next street was the blood of two soldiers of the line, who had been summarily shot as deserters. Proceeding further, I reached the front of the church of the Madeline, at the head of the Rue Royale, and many of the buildings of that great thoroughfare were in flames, and others seemed literally to have been torn in pieces by the fire of the cannon and musketry. Going further up the Boulevard Capucines, I found many of the buildings completely riddled, and upon the sidewalk was a dead national guard, and in a side street, a short distance from there, yet another dead body of the insurgent guard, people passing by and looking on them with apparent satisfaction. I went to the Place Vendome, which had been evacuated during the night, and there for the first time saw the great column lying in the position in which it had fallen. . . . The Tuileries building was still burning, and the flames were bursting out in a part of the building where they had not before reached. It seemed that it would be impossible to save the Louvre, but I hear, as I write, that its preservation is secured, with all its treasures of art and its historic interest. During the entire afternoon the fires have been raging in many directions, and from the legation the sound of battle can be distinctly heard, but it is almost impossible to procure any reliable intelligence in regard to what is taking place. Most certainly something more definite can be ascertained in the morning.

Thursday, May 25.—When I closed my dispatch last night it was fire and battle. It is the same this morning. There were frightful burnings all the night. The great Hotel de Ville, with all its traditions and souvenirs of history, exists no longer. . . . All has been the work of organized incendiarism, and the insurrectionists have done everything in their power to destroy Paris. If the entry of the troops had been delayed much longer, they would certainly have succeeded. . . . Bands of men, women, and children were organized to do this diabolical work. During the past two days immense numbers of these persons have been detected in distributing these boxes [of petroleum], and in every case the most summary vengeance has been inflicted upon them, without regard to age, sex, or condition. An employé of this legation counted, this afternoon, on the Avenue de Autin, the dead bodies of eight children, the eldest not more than fourteen years of age, who had been seized while distributing their incendiary boxes, and shot on the spot. The state of feeling now existing in Paris is fearful beyond description. Passing events have filled the whole population opposed to the commune with horror and rage. Arrests are made by the wholesale, of the innocent as well as the guilty. . . . The fire was still raging in the Rue Royale. The ministry of finance is completely consumed, with every record and paper—a loss that is utterly incalculable. The insurgents having been driven beyond the Place Bastile, I was able to go much farther than I went yesterday. I passed up the Rue de Rivoli by the smoking ruins of the Tuileries, and had the inexpressible pleasure of seeing for myself that the Louvre, with all its untold and incalculable treasures, had been preserved. As I continued up the street it seemed as if I were following in the track of an army. Reaching the Hotel de Ville, I found the neighborhood had all the appearance of an intrenched camp. Immense barricades were on every street leading into the square. But I am told that the insurgents abandoned it without a fight, finding themselves upon the point of being hemmed in. But before leaving, they applied the torch to that pile so interwoven with the history of Paris and of France, and the pride of all Frenchmen for centuries gone by. Now there was nothing but a mass of smoldering ruins. . . . At the Place de l'Opera, I saw some five hundred prisoners, men, women, and children, who were being driven to Versailles. There was a squad of cavalry marching in the front and in the rear of them, and foot soldiers marching on either side. I must say they were the most hideous and sinister-looking persons I ever saw in the whole course of my life. . . . An officer told me this afternoon that the order was to shoot every man taken in arms against the government. I do not vouch for the truth of what he told me, but I do know that large numbers of the national guard and many others, caught in some criminal act, have been summarily executed. . . . It is with no small degree of satisfaction that I am able to inform you that during all these horrible excesses in Paris for the past ten weeks no material damage has been done to the property of Americans, neither to the property of the Germans, with whose interests I still continue to be charged. Some few Americans have been arrested, but all were immediately released on my application. As I have written you before, the number of Germans and Alsatians whose release from prison I have obtained is quite large. Among the last persons to be released were eleven German nuns who had been seized at the convent of Picpus. . . .

I have not time now to speak more fully of the scenes of carnage, fire, and blood, of which Paris has been the theater for the last four days. They are without parallel in all its history. . . .

I have, &c.,

E. B. Washburne

1871 Indian Depredations: "Murdering and Marauding Savages" on the Mexican Border

Dispatch from U.S. Commercial Agent in Piedras Negras William Schuchardt to U.S. Vice Consul in Matamoros B. J. Gautier

In addition to normal commercial and consular business, U.S. representatives in northern Mexico had to deal with Indian problems and banditry along the frontier. Commercial Agent William Schuchardt spent a great deal of his time on such matters. In this dispatch Schuchardt vents his

exasperation at Indian depredations, while providing a broad overview of the problem. One of Schuchardt's unenviable tasks was to ransom captured American women and children from the Indian camps on the Mexican side of the border; he had mixed success. Schuchardt also reports on the widespread occurrence of cross-border cattle rustling by Mexican bandits. He is, however, even-handed enough to acknowledge that raids into Mexico by Texas outlaws also are a frequent problem.

Piedras Negras, Mexico,
May 6, 1871

Sir:

I have the honor to acknowledge the receipt of your letter, dated March 23, 1871, asking for information in regard to depredations on this frontier, committed by Indians from Mexico, and in reply I have to state as follows:

A great many of these depredations on the Texas frontier, there is no doubt, are committed by Kickapoo, Lipan, and Mescalero Indians, living off a short distance from the Rio Grande, and, so to speak, under the protection of the Mexican authorities, they sanctioning the sale of stolen animals by these Indians, and allowing the citizens to trade with and supply the murdering and marauding savages with ammunition and other things they need for making new raids into the settlements of a friendly country. Some time in December last a band of Mescaleros crossed the Rio Grande, at some place above here, into Texas; stole down the country for about thirty-five miles, where they at once commenced their depredations, killing a Mr. Adams, together with two vaqueros [cowboys]; stole all the horses in the vicinity; from there went up the country, attacked a Mexican cart train on the main road from Eagle Pass to San Antonio, took everything belonging to the train, and captured a little boy who had hidden himself near the said train. Thence they went to Mr. Spear's rancho, situated on the San Antonio road, crossing the Turkey Creek, where they took, in bright daylight, out of Mr. Spear's pen, all the horses they could find. The Indians wearing hats and other apparel of civilized people, the inhabitants of the rancho for some time took them for cattle-drivers, and when they became aware of their mistake had hardly time enough to escape into the bushes which surround the rancho.

The Kickapoo Indians, who, since the year 1863 or 1864, live near Santa Rosa, Mexico, about one hundred miles from here, also make their raids into Texas, leaving the ranchos of Western Texas for the distance of one hundred and twenty miles from the Rio Grande bare of good horses. Several times the owners have gone to Santa Rosa to claim their property, knowing it to be there and already sold to citizens of that place, and in some instances they succeeded in obtaining their property, but in others, where the horses or mules were found in the possessions of influential men of the village, the delivery of them was refused. . . .

I am informed that in Saltillo, Parras, and Alamo de Parras there is an immense number of valuable American horses obtained through the raids into Texas by the Kickapoos, the Indians knowing very well that, once across the Rio Grande into Mexican territory, they are out of the reach of their pursuers, and so always escape punishment. . . .

Here can be seen the unfriendly feelings of the Mexicans toward their American neighbors, manifesting joy at the misfortunes caused by raids of a cruel savage enemy from Mexico. . . .

Besides the raids of the Indians at peace in Mexico, are those of the Mexicans, who are doing a wholesale cattle-stealing in Texas, and after once reaching the Mexican side with their plunder, offer openly and undisturbed, at very low prices, the stolen cattle, and there is no authority who interferes in this traffic. . . .

A Mexican criminal is here considered as entitled to more consideration than an honest Texan, who is nearly driven to desperation through the continual suffering from Mexican outlaws, and they are excusable in some measure when they take justice into their own hands. . . .

Yours, &c.,

William Schuchardt

1873 Earthquake in San Salvador: "A Terrific Reverberation, which Baffles Description"

Dispatch from U.S. Minister to Salvador Thomas Biddle to Secretary of State Hamilton Fish

In an unusual and moving dispatch U.S. Minister Thomas Biddle describes his personal experience and near-miraculous escape from harm in the great earthquake that leveled San Salvador in 1873. Biddle would not be so lucky at his next post; he fell victim to an epidemic and died in Guayaquil, Ecuador, shortly after his arrival there as U.S. minister in 1875. Biddle previously had served as an American diplomat in Brazil and Cuba.

San Salvador, March 22, 1873

Sir:

. . . At two o'clock a.m. of the 19th, a fearful earthquake overwhelmed the whole city of San Salvador and its vicinity.

The dreadful catastrophe, with its startling phenomena, may pardon a digression from the formality of official correspondence to a narrative of personal experience. My family, who had found refuge in the mountains from the alarm of the 4th instant, had returned to the city with the subsiding anxiety. All had continued tranquil, when at about two o'clock on the morning of the 19th I was aroused by a violent earthquake. I hastily dressed and hurried my family to the open air. Although in the dry season, heavy clouds obscured the moon, and the atmosphere was oppressive. These meteorological indications have been frequently noticed at such times. For some fifteen minutes all was still. We were on the eve of returning to rest when a terrific reverberation, which baffles description, proceeded from subterranean depths, as if the very globe was being rent in twain; the earth swelled and heaved, and split in chasms, and within less time than I can write it the whole city was a chaotic ruin. It came crashing down with dreadful din, and above all arose a maddened yell from the frantic populace, and then there was a dreadful silence, with clouds of stifling dust; then another loud concussion under foot, and another terrible convulsion of the earth, with the crash of buildings and the wild outcry from men and animals.

We were saved as by a special interposition of Providence. In the center of the "patio" or court-yard of my residence is a little orange tree. In the black night this indicated the spot farthest from any falling wall or roof. Here we collected, and clung to its branches, as the surging ground yawned, and closed, and quivered, and shock succeeded shock; thunderings under foot growing louder and yet more awful, and a dreadful concussion distinguishable above all from the simultaneous crash of a falling city. Not only our whole house, furniture, &c., was completely demolished, but the ground had opened and one-half of our garden had slid into the valley below!

This experience was that of all. It seemed as though daylight would never dawn; and at last it disclosed a dreadful scene of devastation—palace, churches, court-houses, warerooms, dwellings of the poor and rich, all suffering one common fate, whilst the avenues to the ruined chapels were thronged with tearful multitudes who knelt in the open air to supplicate Heaven for safety.

Our own preservation seemed almost miraculous; our house a shapeless ruin, and heavy beams and fragments of masonry surrounding us and within two feet of the little tree round which we had rallied as our only sanctuary from inevitable death. I breathed a prayer, silent but fervent, to the Great Being who had preserved us from the dangers of the past night. . . .

Daylight disclosed the most appalling spectacle—a prosperous mountain city reduced by one mighty blow to shapeless ruin. . . .

The thoroughfares were filled four feet deep with the debris of buildings, and any there must have hopelessly perished. The terrified population poured in swarms to encampments in the open fields.

I promptly visited President Gonzalez, whom I found in a tent pitched in the public plaza. He was calm and energetic, devising means for the general safety and tranquillity. I offered deepest sympathy and any services within my power. He answered with a tear and a pressure of the hand. . . .

> I have, &c.,
>
> Thomas Biddle

1873 The Shah of Persia: "Studded All Over with Diamonds, Rubies"

Dispatch from U.S. Minister to the German Empire George Bancroft to Secretary of State Hamilton Fish

The first visit to Europe of Nasir ud-Din, shah of Persia, created a substantial stir in European royal courts. The glittering presentation of the shah to the diplomatic corps in Berlin provides an example of a classic ceremonial occasion that would have been familiar to any American minister in Europe at the time. The reception is described in this dispatch by George Bancroft, the eminent historian, who was the American minister in Berlin during the shah's visit. Bancroft also had served a tour twenty-five years earlier as U.S. minister to Great Britain.

Despite his description of the pomp and riches surrounding the shah's arrival, Bancroft was not much taken with the Persian monarch as an individual. In a dispatch written after the shah's departure, Bancroft commented that he "did not make a very favorable impression on the people. . . . He himself had rather the air of a semi-civilized chieftain."

Berlin, June 2, 1873

Sir:

To-day the diplomatic corps at Berlin was presented to the Shah of Persia. The visit of the sovereign of that kingdom in Europe takes place, I believe, for the first time since Xerxes crossed the Bosphorus. But that rich country, with a fertile and unexhausted soil, now becomes of importance, and, whether it will or no, is forced into near relations with the European powers. Bounded by Russia on the one side and by a country under the protection of Great Britain on the other, it has no choice, at a time when Asia is falling under the influence of the dominion of those two European powers, but to become familiar with European politics and European culture.

Soon after 12 the Shah entered the saloon of the Royal Castle, in which the corps was assembled, studded all over with diamonds, rubies, and precious stones, in rows on his breast, as buttons to his epaulettes, ornaments to his sword-belt in front and rear, on the hilt of his sword and all the length of the scabbard, and an aigrette of diamonds on his tiara. I have heard some, who professed to be good judges, estimate the value of the stones at twenty millions of francs. The most moderate say more than ten millions of francs. He had on the one side of him an interpreter, on the other his Persian secretary of state, who spoke French very well. Of Persians there were besides in the room the brother of the Shah and about twenty others of the great dignitaries of his kingdom. In these I thought I could plainly see the distinctive marks of two different races. The features of some of them were of the Aryan type, of others, as it seemed to me, clearly Semitic. The Shah passed rapidly along the diplomatic circle, speaking a few words to each chief. His gait was singular and far from graceful or easy; his speech short and deep in its tones, abrupt, thrown forth rather than uttered, very unlike the manner of speech of the rest of them. Of me he inquired after the health of the President, and after my reply he bade me send to the President a message of the interest he took in his welfare. Two reasons, he said, stood in the way of his visiting the United States: first, he was obliged to make haste and return to his own dominions, and then he could not bear the thought of so long a journey by sea as the passage across the Atlantic.

The whole interview lasted less than an hour. The result of the Shah's visit to the European powers may be to direct their attention to his dominions more than heretofore, and in this way to add something to his security.

I remain, &c.,

Geo. Bancroft

1873   Slaves for the Harem: Helpless Women and Eunuchs

Dispatch from U.S. Minister to Turkey George H. Boker to
Secretary of State Hamilton Fish

The United States outlawed the slave trade in 1808 and freed its own slaves with the adoption of the Thirteenth Amendment to the Constitution in 1865. In the intervening years the country undertook some naval operations to stop the trade in African slaves, but the efforts were generally lackluster and had very limited results. The British fleet was far more active and effective in its efforts to suppress the trade.

Once slavery was abolished at home, Americans became more outspoken in their opposition to slavery elsewhere. Just eight years after the Civil War, American diplomats around the Mediterranean were asked to report on the slave trade from Africa to Turkey and how it might be ended. Although the Turks had outlawed the trade, heavy clandestine traffic was still under way between Turkey and the Levant, the countries bordering on the eastern Mediterranean. In this dispatch the U.S. minister to Turkey reports on some aspects of the slave trade and gives his recommendations on how to curb it.

Constantinople,
August 25, 1873

Sir:

... In my previous dispatch I also mentioned the real or feigned activity of the Ottoman authorities in searching for slaves in vessels arriving at this port from Africa, and of the zeal with which papers of manumission are thrust into the hands of every negro suspected of the slightest taint of slavehood. I have some doubts of the genuineness of this ostentatious display of virtue. It is performed with too much noise, too much parade, and too much is said to the simple public about the matter. I do not observe that the number of slaves is diminishing in Constantinople, not even of eunuchs, which latter sexless things should be on the decline were there not a regular source of supply and a way of importation, which are kept carefully hidden from all but the faithful.

Perhaps the clamor made by the Turks over the introduction of African slaves is for the purpose of leading our eyes away from the much greater and more nefarious traffic in female slaves for the harem which is carried on from the north by way of the Black Sea. Abhorring, as all Christians must, this latter infernal trade in helpless women, whose very charms and lovely sensibilities—gifts which to a higher degree give them a natural right to freedom—are used but to increase their price to the chaffering sensualist, I am astonished that such representations have not been made to the Russian government as would induce that power, in the name of our common humanity, to put down this business with the strong hand, if need be. Holding the key of the Caucasus and dominating the Black Sea, it would cost Russia no great effort so to set her face against the commerce in women that its extinction must soon follow. ...

While on the general subject of slavery in Turkey, permit me to call the attention of the Department to that branch of it which relates to trade in eunuchs, carried on between Egypt and the Levant, and which, I believe, might be suppressed by a joint action of the powers. ...

These unfortunate creatures are manufactured in Upper Egypt, not one in ten surviving the barbarous operation. At an early age they are brought through the whole length of Egypt, and those that are not sold for the harems of Cairo and Alexandria are exported from the latter city to stock the harems of the Levant. In the various conversations which I have had with the Khedive [viceroy] and his minister of foreign affairs on this subject, they have invariably replied to me with complacent irony: "The eunuchs are made by Christians in a region beyond our jurisdiction, and in purchasing them we greatly better their condition." These unqualified facts, facts though they are, involve a fundamental lie when unexplained. Without the encouragement of the harem system of the Turkish Empire, eunuchs would not be made at all. The producers of them, the Copts of Upper Egypt, Christians in name, would disgrace any religion that was ever contrived by pagandom. Over the region which the Egyptian government affects to have no jurisdiction it has nevertheless perfect control; or, granting the official assertion to be true, it is equally true that the trade in eunuchs could not exist for a day after the Khedive prohibited their transportation through Egypt. I beg the Department to consider the above suggestions; for, leaving religion out of the question, the horrible practice of eunuch making and selling, which exists only because of the Turkish market for these maimed beings, is a reproach to any organized government, whether living under the law of the Bible or the Koran. . . .

In accordance with the instructions of the Department, I shall continue my investigations of the matter in hand, and report any new information as soon as it may be obtained. . . .

> I have, &c.,
>
> Geo. H. Boker

1875 Anti-Jesuit Riots in Argentina
Dispatch from U.S. Minister to Argentina Thomas O. Osborn to Secretary of State Hamilton Fish

Argentina suffered from chronic instability through much of the nineteenth century. Many of the internal tensions grew from disputes over the position of Buenos Aires within the Argentine Confederation; others resulted from military conflicts with neighboring states and with Great Britain and France. An additional source of occasional tension was the role of the Catholic Church in Argentina. In this dispatch Thomas Osborn, who represented the United States in Argentina for more than a decade, reports on a major riot against the Jesuit influence.

Buenos Ayres, March 1, 1875

Sir:

Yesterday, Sunday, February 28, the palace of the archbishop was sacked, and the magnificent Jesuit College San Salvador, of this city, was burned to the ground by a mob variously estimated at twenty to thirty thousand, incensed and exasperated against the order of Jesuits by a recent pastoral letter of the archbishop, and his demand on the provincial government to return to the Jesuits the property taken from them by Rosas.

To-day the national government declared this province to be in a state of siege for thirty days, and called out two regiments of guardia nationales; and, while rumors are afloat of the burning of churches, the destroying of property, and the killing of the Jesuit priests, yet all is now quiet, and I believe the government is master of the situation.

The order of the Jesuits has in the last past ten years been tolerated but not recognized by this government. The first settlement in this portion of South America was made by the Jesuits in 1557. They were expelled by Charles the Third, King of Spain, in 1767. General Rosas, dictator of the Argentine Confederation, recalled them in 1836, putting them in possession of St. Ignatius Church and the university, (originally built by the Jesuits;) but, upon their refusal to comply with his order to place the picture of himself, Rosas, on the altars of all their churches, he expelled them again, in 1842. . . . In 1863, two batches of Jesuits made their appearance in the Rio de la Plata, one settling in Rosario, province of Santa Fe, the other in this city, and established two important colleges, without, however, demanding the recognition of the order by the government, which doubtless would have been refused. But they went to work quietly, and in the past ten years they have filled Buenos Ayres with converts and schools, having now under their control thirteen or fourteen establishments of great importance, and certainly monopolizing education to a very great extent.

It is generally believed that the present troubles are the results of the warm zeal of the archbishop in behalf of the Jesuits.

During the last session of congress, the archbishop, who is a member of the lower house, claimed, on behalf of the Jesuits, St. Ignatius church, the adjoining buildings of the National College, and the university. As soon as the fact became known, the press, echoing public sentiment, raised a clamor against it. The archbishop, in defense, published a pastoral letter, couched in harsh language, calling his opponents impious unbelievers and wicked. . . .

After speeches by the president of the National College and others, and issuing a protest, in the shape of an address to congress, against the claims of the archbishop and Jesuits, the cry was raised, "Down with the Jesuits;" "Free church and state;" "To the palace of the archbishop and

Salvador College;" and the crowd rushed out of the theater, being joined by thousands of people by the time it reached the palace and college. Eight are reported killed and many wounded, but it is hardly possible to obtain the facts.

I have, &c.,

Thomas O. Osborn

1875 A Court Occasion in Athens: Dancing with the Queen
Dispatch from U.S. Minister to Greece John Meredith Read to Secretary of State Hamilton Fish

The royal court of Greece was a curious invention. When Greece won its independence from Turkey in 1829, the Western powers arranged that a European prince would be offered the throne. Thus Otto, prince of Bavaria, became king of Greece in 1832 at age seventeen. He reigned unhappily for thirty years before being ousted in a coup. The Greek assembly then offered the throne to a British prince, who declined, and finally to Prince George of Denmark, another seventeen-year-old. George I reigned over Greece for fifty years (1863–1913). His queen, Olga, was a member of the Russian royal family.

This dispatch from the U.S. minister to Greece provides a glimpse of a court occasion in Athens. Clearly, the minister was quite taken by the opportunity to lead a dance with the queen.

Athens, March 8, 1875

Sir:

A magnificent ball took place at the palace on the 3rd instant. On that occasion the American minister had the honor to be selected to lead a contra-dance with the Queen.

The spacious salons were filled at half past nine, and the festivities continued until half past five in the morning. The arrangements throughout were of the most admirable character. An elaborate supper for eight hundred guests was laid in the royal *salle à manger* and in the two large adjoining rooms, while the ministers of state and the diplomatic corps were entertained by the King and Queen in the beautiful private apartments of their majesties.

The palace is well adapted for social assemblages upon a grand scale. The ample entrances and stately corridors are adorned with rare plants and flowers. The crimson carpets bring into brilliant relief the white marble floors. On either hand a double row of attendants display the splendors of the national costume. The two principal ball-rooms are of vast size. Their highly decorated walls and lofty ceilings stand revealed in the soft rays of two thousand wax candles. . . .

> I have, &c.,
>
> John Meredith Read

1875 Eyewitness to an Attempted Revolution in Bolivia: "A Memorable Day"

Dispatch from U.S. Minister to Bolivia Robert M. Reynolds to Secretary of State Hamilton Fish

U.S. diplomatic archives are replete with reports of revolts, revolutions, and civil unrest in Bolivia, one of South America's least-stable republics. In 1875, while President Tomas Frias was away from the capital overseeing military operations against a revolt in the provinces, a group of disaffected citizens attempted to seize power in La Paz. The U.S. minister witnessed eight hours of intense combat between the insurgents and a small force of loyalist soldiers. Although Frias's regime survived this attempt at revolution, he was overthrown in a coup d'état the next year.

La Paz, Bolivia, March 20, 1875

Sir:

This will long remain a memorable day for La Paz as the scene of another attempt at revolution. . . . At 11 o'clock, the cry ran through the streets, "Revolution!" "Revolution!" . . .

About 200 men, taking advantage of the absence of the army and President Frias, had plotted the taking of the palace and then pillaging this city.

The palace building was defended by thirty-seven young men of the city, belonging to what is known as "the national guard," while there were in the palace also some twelve or thirteen civilians without effective arms, among whom were the minister of justice and the minister for foreign affairs, who were at their desks dispatching business as usual. The attack was entirely unexpected at that hour, yet the volleys of musketry following the yells in the street admonished all that the struggle had begun.

Within thirty minutes the revolutionists found they had much mistaken the mettle of the citizen soldiery in the palace, and their dead lying in the plaza and on the corners of the square admonished them that their task was a bloody one, if not desperate.

I was situated so as to witness the whole combat, which lasted without cessation from 11 o'clock a.m. till 7 1/2 o'clock p.m. No interval of over half a minute transpired, so steady was the musketry, with occasional firing of artillery.

The revolutionists being beaten back with loss at every attempt at assault on the palace building, they next attempted to fire the palace with balls of turpentine thrown on the roof, and at 3 o'clock p.m. they succeeded in igniting the wooden partitions of the roof in such a manner that the inmates could not extinguish it.

From that time the struggle was exciting indeed. The yells of the assaulting party, the steady fire of the guards, with the rapid burning of the palace, which was now covered with black smoke, with an occasional wild leap of the flames, made a scene not readily forgotten nor often witnessed.

As the fire advanced and consumed the roof the guard abandoned the upper floors and steadily fired from the lower stories, and when at last the rolling smoke and terrible heat compelled them to abandon the palace building, they boldly sallied out on the plaza in front of the palace with two pieces of artillery, and delivered a rapid fire upon their assailants. This was about 7 o'clock p.m., and it was fortunate indeed for them that success came at that moment, as they were reduced to 18 effective men. . . . It was clear moonlight, and a few volleys closed the battle for the day.

It is 8 o'clock, and all firing has ceased except an occasional volley tells that some prisoners just captured are "biting the dust of death."

The loss in the palace force is stated at 22 in killed and wounded which is a very heavy percentage of loss. The loss on the part of the revolutionists is not known. . . .

You will pardon me for so long a dispatch, which you may well say is fitted for the Department of War rather than that of State, yet I deem this important. . . .

This legation has not been disturbed except in receiving three random shots; two shots from muskets through the windows and one shot through the flag flying from the flag-staff. . . .

Your, &c.,

R. M. Reynolds

1877 Unearthing the Arms of Venus de Milo
Dispatch from U.S. Minister to Greece John Meredith Read to Secretary of State William M. Evarts

John Meredith Read of New York, the third American minister to Greece, was the longest-serving envoy to Athens in the nineteenth century. During his tenure from 1873 to 1879, he took an active interest in archaeological discoveries. In this dispatch he concludes—prematurely—that some recently discovered marble arms are those of the famous Venus de Milo.

Athens, May 10, 1877

Sir:

I have the honor to acquaint you with the remarkable fact that the arms of the celebrated Venus of Milo have been discovered within a few days in the island of Melos, at a distance of less than thirty feet from the place where the statue itself was found in 1820. The arms are exquisitely modeled. One hand holds a kind of disk or shield. The workmanship and the locality compel even the skeptical to acknowledge the authenticity of these wonderful relics. I have applied to the Greek Government for permission to take a plaster cast, and if I am successful I shall pray the Department to accept the same with the Alcibiadean treaty, which I have nearly ready also to present to it.

It is not a little singular that the news of the death of the finder of the famous Venus Victrix of Milo, now in the Louvre, has just reached Greece, at the moment when the other portions of that great work of art are being brought to light.

I have, &c.,

John Meredith Read

1877 Freeing a Slave in Egypt
Dispatch from U.S. Agent and Consul General in Egypt Elbert E. Farman to Secretary of State William M. Evarts

Elbert Eli Farman served for five years as U.S. representative in Cairo (1876–1881) and later as a judge in the Egyptian mixed court system, which at the time had jurisdiction over legal issues relating to foreigners in Egypt. In 1879 he arranged for the transfer of the obelisk "Cleopatra's Needle" from Alexandria to New York as a gift of the khedive, or viceroy (see "Cleopatra's Needle: An Obelisk for New York," p. 228). This unusual dispatch, describing the emancipation of a twelve-year-old slave, was written in the first year of his tenure as consul general.

Cairo, June 27, 1877

Sir:

I have the honor to inform you that I yesterday obtained the freedom of a negro boy, about twelve years of age, under the following circumstances: He was found in a street in Cairo by an American lady, who speaks Arabic, and of whom he asked food, saying he had had nothing to eat during the day. After hearing his story she took him to the dwelling of an American citizen residing in Cairo, who, the next day, came with him to the consulate-general and asked that measures be taken to procure his freedom, promising to see that he was properly provided for.

According to the story of the boy, he was born in Soudan, and was brought to Tanta when he was very small by a slave dealer and sold to a man who lived at Saccara, a small village near the pyramids. During the Abyssinian war his master went as an Egyptian soldier to that country and was killed, leaving a widow at Saccara. Afterward his master's brother forcibly took him away from the widow and treated him badly, often beating him without cause. Desiring to escape, he watched his opportunity and came to Cairo, where he met the lady who had kindly taken him to the house of the gentleman who had accompanied him to the consulate.

I sent my janizary (guard) with the boy, and a letter asking his manumission, to the chief of police, and in a short time both returned with a paper in Arabic, of which I inclose a translation.

You will see that this paper is given him "to show that he is free and can go where he will," for the reason that he "complains of not being satisfied with the treatment he receives at his master's and because slavery is prohibited, in pursuance of the orders and regulations decreed by the government of the Khedive."

I have narrated very briefly the principal facts in this case, to show with how little difficulty slaves are freed.

It would appear that, according to law, there are no slaves in Egypt. Practically this is not so, but any slave can procure his freedom by applying at a consulate.

Such applications are rare, but when one is made the consul-general promptly asks the liberation of the slave, and the authorities immediately grant the request. I have acted in the case according to the usual custom. The boy will be sent to the American Mission School at Assiout and properly educated.

I have, &c.

E. E. Farman

1877 Shooting at the Moon in Constantinople: "A Curious Custom"

Dispatch from U.S. Minister to Turkey Horace Maynard to Secretary of State William M. Evarts

The most colorful diplomatic dispatches often are those that deal not with political developments but with local customs. In this instance, an American minister reports without regret the demise of an unusual local practice. The Turkish government abolished the custom by decree and ensured compliance by levying a fine of one Turkish pound against offenders.

Constantinople,
August 24, 1877

Sir:

A curious custom has prevailed time out of mind, it seems, of discharging fire-arms during an eclipse, to deter the monster which, according to the popular belief, had fatal designs upon the heavenly orb. So effective, apparently, have been the means employed, that in every remembered instance the danger has been averted and the luminary, after more or less delay, has reappeared in all its wonted brilliancy. This custom, originating in superstition, had become, like similar displays elsewhere, little more than a piece of juvenile sport, amusing to the young and the thoughtless, but annoying and even dangerous to others.

Late last evening I received from the Sublime Porte a note, of which I inclose a copy and a translation, announcing that the custom has been abolished. It reached me too late to give the notice [to American citizens] . . . in time for the eclipse of the moon last night, but it may be gratifying to learn that none of our countrymen appear to have incurred the penalty for violating the new regulation. Indeed, the ordinance was so generally observed, that I heard not a single report, whereas heretofore an eclipse was like the 4th of July in one of our noisiest towns.

I have, &c.,
Horace Maynard

1878 The Royal Court of Spain: Pageantry and Tragedy
Dispatches from U.S. Minister to Spain James Russell Lowell to Secretary of State William M. Evarts

In some instances, American diplomatic reports are so eloquent, insightful, and entertaining that they are well worth reading even though the subject matter may not otherwise be particularly noteworthy. This is the case for many of the dispatches of James Russell Lowell. Lowell has been described as America's foremost man of his letters of his time. His list of achievements is enormous: he excelled as an author, poet, satirist, critic, editor, abolitionist, and educator, as well as in his diplomatic endeavors. Lowell was appointed minister to Spain in 1877, where he served for three years, then as minister to Great Britain for another five years. These dispatches report the marriage of Spain's young king Alfonso XII to his cousin Mercedes and her death just five months later at the age of seventeen.

The Marriage of the King: "Comically like a Scene from Cinderella"

Madrid, February 6, 1878

Sir:

In these days of newspaper enterprise, when everything that happens, ought to happen, or might have happened is reported by telegraph to all quarters of the world, the slow-going dispatch-bag can hardly be expected to bring anything very fresh or interesting in regard to a public ceremonial which, though intended for political effect, had little political significance. The next morning, frames of fire-works are not inspiring, unless to the moralist; and Madrid is already quarreling over the cost and mismanagement of a show, for the tickets to which it was quarreling a week ago.

Yet a few words will not be out of place upon a royal holiday which but yesterday divided the attention of the world. . . . Nowhere in the world could a spectacle have been presented which recalled so various, so far-reaching, and in some respects so sublime associations, yet rendered depressing by a sense of anachronism, of decay, and of that unreality which is all the sadder for being gorgeous. . . . There was everything to remind one of the past; there was nothing to suggest the future.

And yet I am unjust. There were the young King and his bride, radiant with spirit and hope, rehearsing the idyll which is charming alike to youth and age, and giving pledges, as I hope and believe, of more peaceful and prosperous years to come for a country which has had too much glory and too little good housekeeping. . . .

I was struck also with the look of genuine happiness in the faces of the royal bride and bridegroom, which strongly confirmed the opinion of those who believe that the match is one of love and not of convenience.

The ceremony over, the King and Queen, preceded by the cabinet ministers, the special ambassadors, and the grandees of Spain, and followed by other personages, all in coaches of state, drove at a foot-pace to the palace, where their Majesties received the congratulations of the court, and afterwards passed in review the garrison of Madrid. By invitation of the president of the council, the foreign legations witnessed the royal procession from the balconies of the presidency. It was a very picturesque spectacle, and yet so comically like a scene from Cinderella as to have a strong flavor of unreality. It was the Past coming back again, and thus typified one of the chronic maladies of Spain. There was no enthusiasm, nothing more than the curiosity of idleness which would have drawn as great a crowd to gape at the entry of a Japanese ambassador. . . .

On Thursday there was a grand public reception at the palace, at which 5,000 persons are said to have filed before their Majesties in witness of their loyalty. All the palaces since the *grand siècle* have been more or less tawdry, but that of Madrid has a certain massive dignity, and the throne-room especially has space and height enough to give proper effect to ceremonies of this kind. The young Queen wore her crown for the first time, and performed her new functions with the grace of entire self-possession. The ceremony, naturally somewhat tedious in itself, acquired more interest from the fact that the presence or absence of certain personages was an event of more or less political importance.

In the evening there was a dinner to the special ambassadors and the diplomatic corps, followed by a very crowded reception at the palace of the presidency, at which all of Madrid that has a name seemed to be present. The fine apartments were crowded until half past two in the morning. The street on which the palace stands (the Alcala) was so crammed for its whole length with people that the carriages of ministers on their way to the dinner were unable to pass. The mob (and a Madrid mob is no joke) became so threatening that foreign representatives were forced to renounce their privilege of free passage and to reach their dinners in a more roundabout and diplomatic fashion. It is to the credit of their professional ability that all arrived in season. I have seen nothing so characteristic since my arrival as the wild faces, threatening gestures, and frightful imprecations of this jam of human beings, which, reasonably enough, refused to be driven over.

On Friday took place the first bull-fight, at which every inhabitant of Madrid, and all foreigners commorant therein, deemed it a natural right to be present. The latter, indeed, asserted that the logical reason for the existence of legations was to supply their countrymen with tickets to this particular spectacle for nothing. Though I do not share in the belief that the sole use of a foreign minister is to save the cost of a *valet de place* to people who can perfectly well afford to pay for one, I did all I could to have my countrymen fare as well as the rest of the world. And so they did, if they were willing to buy the tickets, which were for sale at every corner. The distribution of them had been performed on some principle unheard of out of Spain, and apparently not understood even there, so that everybody was dissatisfied, most of all those who got them.

The day was as disagreeable as the prince of the powers of the air could make it, even with special reference to a festival. A furious and bitterly cold wind discharged volleys of coarse dust, which stung like sleet, in every direction at once, and seemed always to threaten rain or snow, but, unable to make up its mind as to which would be most unpleasant decided on neither. Yet the broad avenue to the amphitheater was continually blocked by the swarm of vehicles of every shape, size, color and discomfort that the nightmare of a bankrupt livery-stabler could have invented. All the hospitals and prisons for decayed or condemned carriages seemed to have discharged their inmates for the day, and all found willing victims. And yet all Madrid seemed flocking toward the common magnet on foot also.

I attended officially, as a matter of duty, and escaped early. It was my first bull-fight, and will be my last. To me it was a shocking and brutalizing spectacle, in which all my sympathies were on the side of the bull. As I came out I was nearly ridden down by a mounted guard owing to my want of any official badge. For the moment I almost wished myself the representative of Liberia. Since this dreadful day the 16,000 spectators who were so happy as to be present have done nothing but blow their noses and cough.

By far the prettiest and most interesting feature of the week of the festival was the dancing in the *plaza de armas*, before the palace, of deputations from all the provinces of Spain in their picturesque costumes. The dances were rather curious than graceful. . . . One was struck by the general want of beauty, whether of face or form, in both sexes, and by the lowness of stature. But there was great vigor of body, and the hard features had an expression of shrewdness and honesty. By far the prettiest among the women were those from Andalusia.

The same evening (Sunday) the King entertained the special ambassadors and diplomatic body at dinner, and this was followed by a reception. A dinner, where one is planted between two entire strangers, and expected to be entertaining in an alien tongue, will, one may hope, be reckoned to our credit in another world. The reception had one striking and novel feature, and this was the marching past of the Madrid garrison with colored lanterns and torches. It was a spectacle of vivid picturesqueness. Besides these hospitalities there were two performances at the opera, which I did not attend. During the whole week the city was gay with colored hangings by day, and bright with illuminations (some of them very pretty) by night.

At last the natural order of things began again. As on all such occasions, there had been long and constantly heightening expectation, short fruition, and general relief when all was over. Everybody grumbled, everybody could have managed things better, and yet, on the whole, I think everything went off almost better than could have been expected.

I have, &c.,

J. R. Lowell

Death of the Queen: "A National Calamity"

Madrid, July 3, 1878

Sir:

At my first interview with Mr. Silvela after my return from my furlough, he told me that the Queen was ill. Driving too late, he said, by the side of the lake in the Casa del Campo, she had taken cold; some symptoms of fever had shown themselves; there were fears lest these should assume a typhoidal character; the symptoms were complicated and the diagnosis made less easy by her being with child; as she had already miscarried once, the doctors might order her to keep her bed or a reclining-chair for months to come; naturally there was some anxiety but her youth and strong constitution were greatly in her favor. Mr. Silvela spoke with a great deal of feeling, but certainly did not give me the impression that the case was so very serious, much less that it was hopeless. It seemed rather to be only a question whether the Queen would be able to hold the reception which had been announced for her birthday (the 24th).

This was on the 19th of June. Two days afterward I read in the morning paper that the case was putting on a grave look, and that the physicians hitherto in attendance (all of them accoucheurs) began to fear that the real disease was gastric fever, all the more to be dreaded in the Queen's case, as one of her sisters had died of it, and one of her brothers, after lingering a year, of the weakness consequent upon an attack of it. I at once went over to the palace to make inquiries and to inscribe my name in the book placed for the purpose in the Mayordomia Mayor. I did not see Mr. Silvela, but Señor Ferraz, the under secretary, told me that the Queen's condition was alarming.

Next day the crowd of inquirers (a crowd embracing all classes) became so great that a separate register for the diplomatic corps was placed in the department of state, and regular bulletins began to be issued three times a day. . . .

From this time forward I went several times every day to ask for news at the palace. Even so late as Tuesday the 25th the case was not thought desperate. On that day I was assured that it was the opinion of the physicians that if the internal hemorrhage (which had been one of the worst features of the case) did not recur during the night, recovery was certain. It did not recur, but nevertheless the weakness of the sufferer became so excessive that extreme unction was administered early on the morning of Wednesday. After this there was a slight rally, followed by a rapid loss of strength and consciousness, ending in death at a quarter past twelve.

During the last few days of the Queen's illness, the aspect of the city had been strikingly impressive. It was, I think, sensibly less noisy than usual, as if it were all a chamber of death, in which the voice must be bated. Groups gathered and talked in undertone. About the palace there was a silent crowd day and night, and there could be no question that the sorrow was universal and profound. On the last day I was at the palace just when the poor girl was dying. As I crossed the great interior courtyard, which was perfectly empty, I was startled by a dull roar not unlike that of the vehicles in a great city. It was reverberated and multiplied by the huge cavern of the palace court. At first I could see nothing that accounted for it, but presently found that the arched corridors all around the square were filled, both on the ground floor and the first story, with an anxious crowd, whose eager questions and answers, though subdued to the utmost, produced the strange thunder I had heard. It almost seemed for a moment as it the palace itself had become vocal. . . .

Sorrow and sympathy were in every heart and on every face. By her good temper, good sense, and womanly virtues, the girl of seventeen had not only endeared herself to those immediately about her, but had become an important factor in the destiny of Spain. I know very well what divinity doth hedge royal personages, and how truly legendary they become even during their lives, but it is no exaggeration to say that she had made herself an element of the public welfare, and that her death is a national calamity. Had she lived she would have given stability to the throne of her husband, over whom her influence was wholly for good. She was not beautiful, but the cordial simplicity of her manner, the grace of her bearing, her fine eyes, and the youth and purity of her face gave her a charm that mere beauty never attains.

Seldom has an event combined more impressive circumstances. Youth, station, love, happiness, promise, every element of hope and confidence, were present to give pathos to the sudden catastrophe. It seemed but yesterday that she had passed through the city in bridal triumph. . . .

I have, &c.,

James Russell Lowell

1879 Cleopatra's Needle: An Obelisk for New York
Dispatch from U.S. Agent and Consul General in Egypt Elbert E. Farman to Secretary of State William M. Evarts

American agent Elbert Farman was able to convince Khedive Ismail, ruler of Egypt, to present an ancient obelisk as a gift to the city of New York, where it still stands. The obelisk chosen was known as "Cleopatra's Needle." According to Farman, it was one of only two ancient monuments of interest in Alexandria, Egypt's second largest city.

Cairo, May 22, 1879

Sir:

I have the honor to inform you that the negotiations entered into to procure an Egyptian obelisk for the city of New York have been successful.

The government of His Highness the Khedive has generously given to that city the obelisk at Alexandria, known as "Cleopatra's Needle."

. . . The gift of this ancient and well-known monument cannot be regarded as other than a very great mark of favor on the part of the Government of Egypt towards that of the United States, and a proof of its high appreciation of the friendship that has ever existed between these countries.

The two obelisks that have been removed to Europe in modern times were obtained under circumstances entirely different from those now existing, and they were themselves objects which, in consequence of their situation and condition, were much less appreciated than Cleopatra's Needle. They were both presented many years ago by Mohammed Ali, one to the English, and the other to the French Government. The latter, now at Paris, was taken nearly a half a century since from Luxor, in the vicinity of which are three other obelisks and many colossal ruins, which were at that time seldom visited by Europeans. The one lately taken to London had long been lying on the shore of the sea at Alexandria, nearly or wholly buried in the sand. That, however, which is given to the city of New York is still standing, and is the veritable Cleopatra's Needle, and the only obelisk properly known by that name. It constitutes, with Pompey's Pillar, the only relics of the ancient city of Alexandria that are of any interest. It is known by every school-boy in the United States, and its removal to New York will long remain one of the marked events of history.

From the inscriptions upon it it is supposed to have been erected at Heliopolis . . . in the reign of Thothmes III, about 1,590 years before the commencement of the Christian era. . . .

Cleopatra's Needle was taken to Alexandria previous to or during the reign of Tiberias (A.D. 14–37), and was placed, with its companion now in London, on the shore of the sea in front of the temple of Caesar.

Why it bears the name of Cleopatra's Needle is not known. She died about sixty years before the completion of this temple, but it may have been commenced by her....

I hope to be able to send you hereafter a full translation of all its hieroglyphics.

I have, &c.,

Elbert E. Farman

1879 A Plague of Grasshoppers in the Caucasus
Dispatch from U.S. Chargé d'Affaires in Russia Wickham Hoffman to Secretary of State William M. Evarts

American representatives abroad have witnessed and reported on many of the great disasters of the past two centuries: fire, pestilence, earthquake, volcano, and famine. In this dispatch from St. Petersburg the U.S. minister reports on the reappearance of another ancient affliction—locusts—in the Caucasus region of Russia. Russian experts visiting the scene of the disaster estimated concentrations of as many as two million locusts per acre in the most heavily infested areas.

St. Petersburg, May 26, 1879

Sir:

... The plague of grasshoppers has appeared in the Caucasus. In the village of Elizabethpol the streets were so blocked up with them that circulation was seriously impeded. They have destroyed the vines and the fruit trees, and infested the houses. The wells and springs are so infected by them that the water is offensive and unhealthy.

The police have ordered that each inhabitant should kill two poods (36 pounds to a pood) of them, but such is the superstition of the people that it is with the greatest difficulty that the order is enforced. In some neighborhoods the people regard the grasshopper as powerful and malignant spirits, and, instead of destroying, seek to propitiate them by crossing themselves and burning tapers before them, as they do before the sacred pictures of the Saviour and the virgin....

I have, &c.,

Wickham Hoffman

1879   Morocco: Inspiring Terror among the Rebels
Dispatch from U.S. Consul in Tangier Felix A. Mathews to Secretary of State William M. Evarts

The sultan of Morocco, faced with a continuing rebellion among a group of his nomadic Berber subjects, resorted to a very ancient method of inspiring obedience. The incident is reported here by the American consul in northern Morocco.

Tangier, June 5, 1879

Sir:

I have the honer to inform you that the Sultan of Morocco has encamped with his army near Rabat, where he is expected this week.

He has brought under subjection during his progress the Berber tribes in the province of Fedla, who have been in a state of insurrection during the last twenty years. Thirty-four heads of rebels have been sent to be exposed on the walls of Rabat to inspire terror among the rebel tribes of Zayr, who have been committing numerous robberies and murders this year in the neighborhood of that town.

It is reported that the Sultan will not remain more than ten days at Rabat. . . .

I have, &c.,

Felix A. Mathews

1879   The German-Austrian Alliance
Dispatch from U.S. Minister to Germany Andrew D. White to Secretary of State William M. Evarts

In this dispatch from Berlin the U.S. minister reports a fundamental shift in alliances among the major powers of Europe. Russia and Prussia had been on close terms since the Napoleonic Wars of the early nineteenth century. Prussia and Austria, in contrast, had fought a short but bitter war in 1866, in which Prussian forces crushed the Austrian army within only seven weeks (see "The Austro-Prussian War," p. 183). The Prussian victory paved the way for the unification of Germany, which followed shortly thereafter.

The guiding force in German politics at the time was Otto von Bismarck, who determined that the vital interests of the newly formed German Empire lay more with its German-speaking neighbor to the south, Austria-Hungary, than with Slavic Russia, which was actively pur-

suing expansionist aims in eastern Europe. Russia's expansionism led it to war with Turkey in 1877. After that conflict, Bismarck organized a general congress in Berlin to sort out the spoils of the essentially inconclusive Russo-Turkish war. In the guise of an "honest broker," Bismarck managed to win European approval for a substantial increase in Austrian influence in the Balkans at the expense of both Russia and Turkey. This laid the groundwork for a secret German-Austrian alliance, in which each pledged to aid the other in the event of war with Russia. The alliance increased Germany's short-term security, but at the same time contributed to the tensions in Europe that eventually would result in World War I. The American minister in Berlin correctly assessed the significance of the new alliance and foresaw the likelihood of a general war in Europe. He predicted wrongly, however, that England would join the German-Austrian alliance. This dispatch was written one month after the secret German-Austrian pact was concluded.

Berlin, November 18, 1879

Sir:

You have doubtless been cognizant of the many reports which have found their way into the public prints regarding a recent remarkable change in European international relations; a change by which alliances, binding together two of the great European powers for more than sixty years, have apparently been suddenly shattered, and intimate relations established between powers which, during one hundred and forty years, have regarded each other always with distrust and sometimes with hatred. The reports of this change have not only awakened deep and general interest in this capital, but in all countries in any way related to Europe.

Now, that the lapse of time has in some measure cleared the air of mere rumor, I send you the following account of the events in which these reports originated, with such conclusions as, from my intercourse with official and diplomatic persons, I judge to be warrantable.

Close as may have been the understanding between the Prussian and Russian Governments since 1812, a feeling of distrust has long been growing between the two peoples. I became aware of this as long ago as 1855–'56, when I was attached to the United States legation at St. Petersburg. . . .

Toward the close of September last, Prince Bismarck went to Vienna. The cordiality with which he was received by the Emperor . . . and the enthusiasm with which the populace greeted him, were eagerly commented upon in every political circle. It soon became understood that an alliance between Germany and Austria-Hungary had been completed. As regards internal affairs, it was hailed with joy by liberals of every shade in Germany as putting an end to that Russian influence which, in their opinion, had been so injurious for many generations. As regards external affairs, it was received by all parties as another great step toward the consolidation of German-speaking peoples against Panslavism, and, therefore, as giving strength to German ideas and a more peaceable development to German civilization. That such an alliance had been concluded, seems to me beyond doubt; and, from very high sources in this capital, I have obtained the following information regarding its general character. The document signed by the German chancellor and the Austro-Hungarian minister insures . . . a mutual defensive alliance against attacks from any side. . . . In response, the Russian Government declare, in general terms, that, so far as they are concerned, the alliance is purposeless. . . .

The first result was a cloud of rumors of war. An acknowledged authority assured me at that time that, in his belief, a general European war would begin early next spring. The argument was, war must come sooner or later, and every one feels that, relatively, Germany is stronger now than she may be a few years hence. But opinion rapidly changed, and there now seems a general impression that the new alliance has done much to strengthen the prospects of a continuance of peace. Russia, it is believed, will never attack Germany and Austria, with whom England would then be leagued, without powerful alliances; and to secure these further diplomatic action and the lapse of considerable time are indispensable. . . .

While no one can doubt that the logical result of this German-Austrian alliance is a league which shall embrace England, the best opinion here just now seems to be that great care is taken by the German Government to avoid any appearances of any such league at present. . . . There seems to be a strong desire on the part of those in power here to have it understood that the alliance made at Vienna is strictly what it claims to be, that is, one between the two German speaking nations with reference to dangers which may beset them, and that it shall not be developed into anything more offensive to Russia than it now is. . . .

The essential nature of the new alliance . . . if persisted in, it cannot fail to draw England eventually within its scope.

I have, &c.,

And. D. White

1880–1886   French Conquests in Africa
Dispatches from U.S. Representatives in Liberia and France

The 1880s saw the beginning in earnest of the "Scramble for Africa," during which European powers vied for control of the still largely unknown interior of the "dark continent." The Berlin Conference of 1885 went so far as to establish internationally recognized guidelines for taking control of new African domains. The French, British, Germans, Portuguese, and Italians moved inland from coastal trading stations they had in some instances held for centuries, transforming interior regions into protectorates and colonies. In a separate but similar venture, King Leopold II of Belgium and American explorer Henry Morton Stanley formed the International Congo Association, which took control of a huge section of central Africa. By the end of the century only Ethiopia and Liberia remained independent of European control. These dispatches provide an overview of the evolution of French efforts to take control of portions of West Africa, central Africa, and Madagascar.

French Expansion in West Africa
*From U.S. Minister to Liberia John Smyth to
Secretary of State William M. Evarts*

Monrovia, February 12, 1880

Sir:

I have the honor to send by this mail, as book-postage, a copy of the Bulletin de la Societe de Geographie de Marseille, for November, 1879, containing an account of the discovery of the source of the Niger . . . which discovery was made the latter part of the year last past by two Frenchmen, Messrs. Zweifel and Moustier, who started from Sierra Leone. . . .

The French are making the most vigorous efforts throughout Senegambia for the command of the trade of Soudan and even for political influence.

I learned a few days ago from a friend of the late French commandant of Mellicouria, a French station about forty miles northwest of Sierra Leone, that 500 French troops are now stationed at Sego, the capital of the most powerful kingdom of Nigritia, and that a portion of these troops will soon be transferred to Barnillo, the head of navigation of the Niger, visited by Mungo Park in 1797. . . .

I regard the recent movement of the French, and it is regarded by experienced men in Western Africa, as one of the most important in the history of this particular portion of Negroland. They seem determined to work their way down along the interior of the western coast and to establish an invincible prestige among the tribes.

The appointment of a French consul at Monrovia . . . is a part of their commercial plan.

The Liberians are trying to push their settlements to the interior, and to make treaties with the powerful tribes within three or four hundred miles of the coast, but in their feebleness it is very little that they can do. They deserve all the assistance and encouragement which it may be in the power of the government to render, in view of the intimate relations which a portion of the Negro race bears to the United States, and which has been borne by their immediate ancestors for upward of two hundred years.

The newly appointed secretary of the interior of Liberia, Hon. E. W. Blyden, is now on his way to the United States. I hope that he may have an opportunity of giving some information bearing on the subject of his country and of Africa in general to the Department.

I have, &c.,

Jno. H. Smyth

The French Move into Central Africa

From U.S. Minister to France Levi P. Morton to Secretary of State Frederick T. Frelinghuysen

Paris, December 6, 1882

Sir:

I have the honor to send you herewith the text and translation of a convention concluded in the name of France by M. de Brazza with an African King who answers to the name of Makoko.

The convention was signed—if such expression is applicable here for His Majesty could only make his mark—on the 10th of September and the 3d of October 1880. . . . It assures to Makoko the protection of France over his Kingdom, and secures to France the possession of a portion of that Kingdom. The text of the instrument conveys little more, for it states distinctly that Makoko cedes his territory to France, together with all his hereditary rights. The treaty, however, is drawn up in such language that it is not easy to understand exactly its meaning. . . .

The geographical data conveyed by the convention are so meager and the French orthography of the local names is often so different from the ones used in English, that the exact location of the Kingdom of Makoko remains somewhat uncertain. It seems, however, that it is situated near the Stanley Pool, on the right bank of the Congo River and extends over all the country inhabited by the native tribes called Batekes.

The territory specially transferred to France, where a station called Brazzaville is established, with a guard of three men, has been described . . . as being located . . . just above the last cataract of the Congo; that is to say, at the precise point where that great stream is navigable and where it will be easy to command its whole course.

. . . Senator Zavier Blanc . . . insisted on the peaceful character of this establishment, and on the fact that it could not conflict with the rights of any one, particularly with those of the International Association (Stanley), whose seat was on the other side of the river, and whose promoter, the King of Belgium, was the chief of a friendly power.

Speaking of the Portuguese, he said the French establishments on the Congo could not give them umbrage. . . .

It is proper to add here that the existence of this Brazza convention is flatly denied by Mr. Stanley. In a public speech which he made here about six weeks ago he said that the most influential of the Makoko chiefs, represented by de Brazza as having agreed to his treaty, declared to him (Stanley) in the most emphatic terms that he had never seen the treaty and had not even heard of it; that the only thing he had granted to the French envoy was a lease of a piece of land.

I have dwelt rather at length on this affair because it is a good illustration of the policy of colonial extension which is now evidently favored by the French Government.

I have, &c.,

Levi P. Morton

A French Protectorate in Madagascar

Dispatch from U.S. Minister to France Robert M. McLane to Secretary of State Thomas F. Bayard

Paris, February 3, 1886

Sir:

I send herewith a copy and a translation of the treaty between France and Madagascar of the 17 December, 1885, which has just been made public.

France assumes by this treaty a full and unqualified protectorate over the whole of the island of Madagascar; formerly she only claimed to protect the Sakalavas and the Antankares, of the northwest coast. The governmental powers are now divided between France and Madagascar. A French resident at Antananarivo will take charge of all the foreign relations, and will try according to French law all litigation between Frenchmen or between Frenchmen and foreigners. He will also try, with the assistance of a native judge, all litigation between Frenchmen and natives. Frenchmen will have the same right to reside, travel, and trade on the island as the natives enjoy.

The right to hold real estate . . . is conceded in fact, if not in express terms, to Frenchmen. . . .

Authority over local matters is left to the queen, who shall continue, says the treaty, to direct the interior administration of the island. France, however, binds herself to assist the Queen in defending her state and to protect her subjects abroad. She undertakes, besides, to provide such military instructors, engineers, professors, and artisans and overseers as may be asked for, a clause which in due course of time will, if skillfully availed of, place the whole island under the control of France. . . .

The queen is to pay 10,000,000 francs, not as war indemnity, but in settlement of all French private claims and damages sustained by foreigners during the war.

I have, &c.,

Robert M. McLane

1880–1881   Czar Assassinated

Dispatches from U.S. Representatives in Russia to Secretary of State William M. Evarts

Czar Alexander II ruled Russia for twenty-six years. While essentially an autocrat, Alexander instituted a number of sweeping reforms. The most significant of these was the emancipation of the serfs in 1861, but Alexander also liberalized the judicial system and took the first halting and limited steps toward representative government (see "Emancipation of the Russian Serfs," p. 136). *On the very day of his assassination, Alexander had signed an edict providing for nationally elected commissions to help govern Russia. The pace of reform in Imperial Russia, however, was not keeping pace with popular sentiment. Discontent mounted and secret revolutionary societies were formed. Several attempts were made on Alexander's life. The first of these dispatches is a brief telegraphic report of the unsuccessful attempt of 1880, in which the czar's life was saved only because a dinner guest was late in arriving at the palace. The second dispatch reports in more detail the circumstances of the czar's death a year later. The assassination was carried out by a secret society known as the People's Will.*

"Dinner Fortunately Delayed"
From U.S. Chargé d'Affaires in Russia Wickham Hoffman

St. Petersburg,
February 18, 1880

Explosion in winter palace, in cellar under Emperor's dining-room, at dinner time last evening. Dinner fortunately delayed. Floor broken up. At least eight soldiers killed, fifty wounded.

"Emperor Dead"
From U.S. Minister to Russia John W. Foster

St. Petersburg, March 14, 1881

Sir:

On yesterday afternoon, at three o'clock, I sent you the following telegram:

Emperor wounded in carriage to-day by bomb. Extent injury not yet known.

And at 4.15 p.m. I sent second telegram, as follows:

Emperor dead.

The circumstances of this terrible event are briefly these:

Following his frequent practice, His Majesty the Emperor went on yesterday to the Sunday morning review in the riding-school of the Palace of Engineers. He left the review about one o'clock, and drove to the Michel Palace, where he made a short call upon his niece, the Grand Duchess Catherine, and then continued on his return to the Winter Palace. Just before crossing the stable bridge of the Catharine Canal, at 1.45 p.m., a hand-bomb was thrown by a young man, dressed in the garb of a street-cleaner, directly under the Emperor's carriage, shattering in its explosion the rear of the vehicle, but without injuring the Emperor. His Majesty jumped from the carriage, and while the guards were arresting the assailant a second bomb, thrown by another person, was exploded at the feet of the Emperor, shattering both his legs below the knees and inflicting other serious wounds on his person. He was placed in the sleigh of the military officer who accompanied him and driven immediately to the Winter Palace. The loss of blood was so great and the wounds so severe that he expired at 3.35 p.m., within less than two hours after the explosion. The holy communion was administered just before his death, but it is not certainly known that he recovered his consciousness after the assault.

It is understood that one cossack of the Emperor's guard was killed, and one officer and a number of soldiers and civilians (variously estimated) were wounded by the explosion. The two authors of the assassination are believed to have been arrested.

At a late hour last night the Czarevitch, the heir apparent, assumed the supreme power of the empire as Alexander III, and his proclamation of ascension of the throne, of which I inclose herewith a translation, was published this morning. I have also advised you of this latter event by telegram at eleven o'clock to day in these words: "Czarevitch ascended throne as Alexander Third."

I am, &c.,

John W. Foster

1880 The Consulate in Bangkok: In a "Disgraceful Condition"

Dispatch from U.S. Consul in Hong Kong John Singleton Mosby to Assistant Secretary of State John Hay

In the years after the Civil War the spoils system guided the appointment of consuls. Corruption was widespread, with many appointees proving to be an embarrassment to the government. Some consuls, however, remained impeccably honest and campaigned actively against wrong-doers. One such consul was John Singleton Mosby, who had gained a reputation during the Civil War as a fearless and skillful guerrilla fighter, leading the Confederate band that came to be known as Mosby's Raiders. Mosby was appointed consul in Hong Kong in 1878 and served there for seven years. In this dispatch he rails against corruption at the American consulate in nearby Bangkok. Mosby notes that he received complaints about the Bangkok consulate from a visiting American admiral, describes the consul and vice consul there in unflattering terms, and laments that an official inspector was in league with one of the culprits.

Hong Kong, March 17, 1880

Sir:

Referring to my former communications on the subject of the Bangkok Consulate, I will add that yesterday Rear Admiral Patterson called at the Consulate to see me, and urged upon me to represent to the Department the disgraceful condition of affairs at Bangkok. Sickles [the consul] is an imbecile and a mere figure-head and the consulate is entirely controlled and conducted by Torrey, the Vice Consul, who lived a great many years in Hong Kong and is a notorious scoundrel; the Admiral is thoroughly acquainted with his character. Torrey has written to a friend here that Mr. Studer [the inspector] had investigated the charges against him, and "had given him a clean bill of health," which everybody expected, who knew the intimate relations between them. When Studer went to Bangkok to make the investigation, I am informed that Miss Studer was at that time a guest in Torrey's house. Studer and Torrey have, I believe, been jointly engaged in a Borneo speculation, and claim the titles of Rajahs.

> I have the honor to be, Sir
> Your obedient Servant
>
> Jno S. Mosby

1881   Lima Surrenders to Chilean Forces
Dispatch from U.S. Minister to Peru Isaac P. Christiancy to Secretary of State William M. Evarts

The War of the Pacific was sparked by disputes between Chile and Bolivia over rights to rich nitrate deposits along South America's Pacific coast. Peru was drawn into the conflict through its alliance with Bolivia. Chile emerged victorious on all fronts, seizing mineral-rich areas in both Bolivia and Peru and occupying the Peruvian capital of Lima.

Isaac Christiancy was American minister to Peru when the War of the Pacific broke out in 1879. This dispatch recounts the capture of Lima by Chilean forces. Chilean forces still occupied Lima when Christiancy departed post in mid-1881. A peace treaty was not signed until 1883.

Lima, January 22, 1881

Sir:

Lima was quietly surrendered to the Chilian forces on the 17th instant. I wished and intended to have given you a detailed account of the events and causes which have led to this result. But on the 15th instant, at 2 o'clock p.m., I went with the whole diplomatic corps to Miraflores, some 5 miles (in a direct line) from Lima, to receive from President Pierola his answer to the terms offered by the Chilian general, Baquedano, through the committee of our diplomatic corps. . . . We found Pierola and his staff at breakfast in a large house at Miraflores, and were waiting for him to come out, and some of his officers were just coming out from the table, when a single heavy gun was heard, and in less than a minute the battle opened along the whole lines, and at a distance of but about 80 rods south of us, the shot, even from the small arms, pattering thick and fast upon the buildings around us, and the air being filled with flying shells exploding all around us. It is not yet fully known who fired the first gun, but it is, I think, quite evident that both the Chilian commander and Pierola were equally taken by surprise, and the probability is that it was the unauthorized act of some subaltern officer.

The diplomatic corps fled to the rear towards Lima for their lives and got somewhat scattered, some of them reaching the railroad train (which had taken us out) . . . and some, like myself, endeavoring to strike the railroad ahead of the train, but being cut off by walls and ditches, were compelled to walk a devious course back to Lima. I was one of the latter unfortunate class, was under the shells of the Chilian fleet and army, falling thick around me, for two hours before I could get out of range, climbing smooth perpendicular walls between fields and around chacras and old buildings, wading water-courses, and traveling some 8 miles to get 4 miles ahead, until my muscular powers were thoroughly exhausted; finding on my return some 600 to 700 refugees, women and children, in the legation, who had sought asylum there, and before 9 o'clock at night over 1,200, which increased next day and night to over 1,500 of all nationalities, and all this while more than half the time I was unable to stand upon my feet from the fatigue.

I have just got rid of the refugees, but the strain upon my muscular powers has been such that even yet I cannot walk or stand for half the time, and yet I am constantly besieged with complaints from Americans, Swiss, and Colombians against depredations upon their persons or property from the Chilian soldiery, which I endeavor to get redressed as well as I can.

I will only say here that, from all the reports I hear from every quarter, the Chilians killed all the Peruvian wounded they found upon the field. They deliberately burned Chorillos, after all necessity for such outrages had ended. They did the same with Barranca and Miraflores; and since all the fighting has been over they have burned sugar plantations with standing cane upon them. They have robbed, as I am informed, some haciendas belonging to Colombian citizens, under the protection of this legation, and I fear, also, some belonging to Americans. . . .

The Chilians have, as yet, behaved remarkably well in Lima, and thus far respected their promise to protect life and property; and I must do their officers the justice to say, I think they intend to enforce order in the city and to treat the inhabitants kindly.

Pierola, who constitutes the only recognized government of Peru, was last heard of at Canta, some fifty miles northeast of Lima. He is at present supposed to intend to arouse the interior to arms. But he has no money or arms, and, I think, would have acted more wisely if he had remained here. The Chilians, I feel quite sure, would have treated him kindly, and recognized him as the only government with which they could treat for peace. I think they would be glad to have him return for that purpose. I am quite unable to write you further to-day, as I am scarcely able to be out of bed.

> I have, &c.,
>
> I. P. Christiancy

1881 Immigration and Epidemic in Hawaii
Dispatch from U.S. Minister to Hawaii James M. Comly to Secretary of State William M. Evarts

The United States had an official agent in Hawaii as early as 1820, but did not accredit a minister to the Hawaiian government until 1863. American diplomats served in Hawaii from that date until the islands were annexed to the United States in 1898. U.S. diplomatic and consular dispatches from Hawaii provide a colorful picture of developments in the islands over most of the nineteenth century. This dispatch from Minister James Comly touches on two phenomena that permanently altered Hawaii: immigration and epidemic.

> Honolulu, February 14, 1881

Sir:

During the past three weeks about 1,700 adult male Chinese immigrants have been added to the population of these islands and 1,500 more are said, on good authority, to be on their way here. A majority of the adult male population of the islands, is now Chinese.

So long as the chief demand of the islands shall continue to be more laborers, they will continue to come; and it is a question not necessary for me to discuss whether their coming is in the nature of an unmixed blessing.

It is an evil not necessarily chargeable to the Chinese immigration that the Chinese steamer Meifoo, which arrived last week, and the Quinta, which arrived a fortnight earlier, both had cases of small-pox on board. The captain of the Quinta misrepresented the facts to the authorities, and infected passengers were landed, from whom an epidemic has broken out in Honolulu. . . .

The result has been that there has been something of a panic. . . .

The ministry and the board of health, determi ned not to be criticised for further inactivity, have adopted the most stringent measures for confining the plague and stamping it out.

No vessel is allowed to leave the harbor for any of the other islands, and every road out of Honolulu is strictly guarded, so that communication is absolutely severed between Honolulu and the rest of the island of Oahu, as well as between the other islands.

. . . All infected persons are sent at once "to the reef," a barren island in the harbor, where quarantine quarters have been built. . . . It would be difficult for any person away from here to conceive the horror of being sent "to the reef" with this disease, in company with a thousand or more Chinamen and natives, with squalid wretchedness for one's only companionship.

There are nearly 1,000 Chinese alone who may be seen from the wharves of Honolulu swarming down to the shore of the barren island, in helpless misery, waiting for their term of quarantine to expire. A call was issued several days ago for clothing donations for the poor wretches, many of whom have gone through the recent "Koua" storm with insufficient clothing. Such calls are promptly responded to in Honolulu. In fact the government and the people are doing their best, with the means at hand, to properly care for the quarantine, as well as for the actual cases of small-pox, and to end the epidemic with the first crop of cases, if possible.

I have, &c.,

James M. Comly

1881 Pogroms in Russia: "More Worthy of the Dark Ages than of the Present Century"

Dispatch from U.S. Minister to Russia John W. Foster to Secretary of State James G. Blaine

Alexander III became czar of Russia in 1881 after the assassination of his father (see "Czar Assassinated," p. 236). Given the circumstances of his father's death, Alexander III moved vigorously to crush revolutionary movements. His reign was autocratic, many of the reforms instituted by his predecessor were undone, and the regime took a hard line against both religious and ethnic minorities. Within weeks of Alexander III's accession to power, anti-Jewish riots, or pogroms, broke out first in the Ukraine and then elsewhere on a scale unprecedented in modern history. The U.S. minister reports the pogroms with a sense of horror and indignation.

St. Petersburg, May 24, 1881

Sir:

A disgraceful series of disorders have occurred during the past month in the southwestern provinces of Russia, directed against the Jewish residents, resulting in the loss of a number of lives and the destruction of an enormous amount of property. The scenes of these riots have been at and in the vicinity of Elizabethgrad and Kief, with less serious demonstrations at Odessa and other places. The participants have been almost exclusively of the lowest and most ignorant classes in the towns and cities, joined by the peasants, and the demonstrations in the two localities first named appear to have been so powerful that for days the authorities were paralyzed, and the rioters were able to give full sway to their work of bigotry and destruction. In Kief, a city of over one hundred thousand inhabitants, with a large Jewish population, the work was so thorough, it is stated, that not a single Jewish house escaped, the inmates being driven out, beaten, and stoned, and some of them killed, and the contents plundered or thrown into the streets. The damage there is estimated at several millions of roubles, and business has been seriously affected thereby; many commercial houses have suspended payments, other bankruptcies are feared, and the prices of provisions and articles of prime necessity have temporarily risen greatly in price. Massacre and destruction of property have become so threatening in other localities, where no actual outbreaks have taken place, that the Jews in large numbers have fled from their homes and taken refuge across the frontier in Austria or in Moscow, where the military force is sufficient to guarantee safety. In some instances the railroad officials have refused to run the trains by which the Jews were seeking to escape, for fear of attack from the infuriated mobs debauched with liquor and plunder.

Indiscriminate pillage became so much feared that Christians chalked their houses with crosses or exhibited holy images with lighted lamps before them to save themselves from the fury of the rabble. The acts which have been committed are more worthy of the Dark Ages than of the present century.

The authorities were slow to realize the extent of the danger, but when once awakened to its wide-spread and deeply-seated character they have manifested a commendable zeal in suppressing the riots and in arresting and punishing the offenders. National troops have been freely used, sending them to the most threatened districts, and in some places, as at Odessa, they have promptly intervened with force to put down the riots.

Various causes have been assigned for these outbreaks additional to the prevailing bigotry and religious hatred of the lower classes towards the Jews. The country has not been prosperous for some time past; taxes have been heavy and exacted with severity; the depreciated paper currency has increased the cost of all commodities; the winter has been one of privation and suffering, and with many families indebtedness has been the rule annually. The Jews being the money changers, traders, and speculators, have profited by this state of affairs, and the poorer classes have felt that undue advantage has been taken of their misfortunes. Following the long fast so faithfully observed in the Russian national church, which was broken by Holy Week and its usual excesses in drinking, it has been easy to work upon the passions and prejudices of the hungry and ignorant. . . . It is believed that the Emperor has no sympathy with the spirit manifested against the Jews, and, in addition to the active use of the imperial army to put down the riots, he has given orders to have an investigation made of the causes which have occasioned the disturbances. I have in previous dispatches referred to the proscriptive laws and disabilities imposed upon the Jews in Russia. If these events lead to a serious consideration of the wisdom of abolishing all the Jewish disabilities, and of placing Russian legislation on this subject alongside of that of the other enlightened nations, the loss of life and property will not have been in vain. . . .

I am, &c.,

John W. Foster

1881 A Memorial for President Garfield
Dispatch from U.S. Minister to Turkey Lew Wallace to Secretary of State James G. Blaine

On July 2, 1881, four months after taking office, President James Garfield was shot while boarding a railroad car. The assassin was Charles J. Guiteau, a disgruntled applicant for a federal position. Garfield was in a coma for almost three months before he died on September 19. His murder prompted expressions of condolence and memorial services around the world. The memorial in Constantinople is reported here by Lew Wallace, the U.S. minister. Wallace first made a name for himself as a Union general during the Civil War. He is best known as the author of Ben Hur.

Constantinople,
October 3, 1881

Sir:

On the 26th ultimo the Americans . . . resident in Constantinople, and the localities nearby, assembled at the Legation to render fitting memorial honors to President Garfield. The day, it will be observed, was that of his burial. The hour of meeting—one o'clock—was chosen because it was supposed the funeral cortege in Cleveland would be in movement about that time.

Nearly one hundred persons were present. With very few exceptions, they were Americans. Had there been space to accommodate a larger assembly, it could, by notice and invitations given, have been swollen to several hundred; for this is probably the most cosmopolitan city in the world, and everybody in it was sympathetic with us, and would have been pleased with an opportunity to make his feelings known. . . .

I acknowledge, with gratification, the courtesies received from my colleagues of the Corps Diplomatique. The English were exceedingly kind and considerate. . . . A ball in honor of the officers of the *Antelope*, the British *Shalionaine*, had long been fixed for Monday the 26th of September. Finding that this was the day of the President's funeral, the social event was changed to a day later. . . .

> I have the honor to be,
> very respectfully,
> your friend and servant
>
> Lew Wallace

PART V

The Late Nineteenth Century: 1883–1897

The Statue of Liberty, a gift in celebration of a century of friendship between France and the United States, was presented to U.S. Minister to France Levi Morton in Paris on July 4, 1884. The monument was dedicated in New York harbor by President Grover Cleveland in October 1886.

1883 The Steamship *Aurania*: "The Most Remarkable Ship that Has Ever Been Built"

Dispatch from U.S. Consul in Glasgow Bret Harte to
Assistant Secretary of State John Davis

Born in 1836, American author Bret Harte published his first book of verse at age eleven. In 1854 Harte journeyed to the mining camps of California. His experience in the American West helped to mold a writing style that catapulted him to success with stories such as "The Luck of Roaring Camp" and "The Outcasts of Poker Flat." In 1878 Harte accepted an appointment as consul in Crefeld, Germany; he moved on to become consul in Glasgow, Scotland. In this dispatch Harte describes the launching in Glasgow of a revolutionary new type of steamship by the Cunard Company, Great Britain's most prominent shipping line.

Glasgow, February 16, 1883

Sir:

In submitting the accompanying description of the Cunard Steamship "Aurania" lately launched at Glasgow, I venture to call the attention of the Department to two points, viz:

First, the departure from previous models of construction in the vessels of this line as shewn in the increased breadth of beam.

Second, the now admitted fact that an essential feature in their general construction is their ability for self defense in time of war and the probability of their being used and utilized by the Admiralty in such an emergency.

I have the honor to remain
Very respectfully
Your obedient Servant,

Bret Harte

ENCLOSURE

DESCRIPTION OF S.S. "AURANIA"

The new Cunarder Aurania . . . is a vessel of 7500 tons gross register. . . . [S]he is in some respects the most remarkable ship that has ever been built on the Clyde. . . . [T]hey decided to build a vessel of the following dimensions:—Length between perpendiculars, 479 feet, breadth extreme, 57 feet, depth moulded, 39 feet. . . . [T]he great beam of the Aurania . . . gives her very great stability, so that even with nothing in her holds she is quite capable of being easily handled, a quality which probably, no other merchant ship possesses. Such stability will be of great service to her should this country ever be engaged in maritime war, as the Aurania will be enabled to carry many heavy guns on all her decks, and therefore be practically self-protecting. Every merchant ship which is not able to do this will require in such an emergency protection from war ships, and therefore must be of considerably less value to the country than one which is able to a certain extent to protect itself. The Cunard Company's ships have often been placed at the service of the country, and that company has therefore given especial attention to the requirements of merchant vessels in time of war. Consequently the decks of the Aurania have been made more than ordinarily strong, in order that they might carry heavy armaments without danger to the structure. The other parts of the hull have been made proportionally strong, the outside plating being made upon what is known as the "edge and edge" system. The internal arrangements of the ship have been subordinated to considerations of strength and safety, for she has no less then eleven water tight bulkheads, all of which are carried up to the upper deck. She will therefore not only fulfil the Admiralty condition of being able to float with one compartment filled, but she would be quite safe with any two completely flooded. The Aurania has an enormous spread of sail, and she looks more like a large sailing ship than a steamer. She could, therefore, make a very rapid passage under sail alone, and would probably beat any sailing ship afloat. Should the Admiralty at any time take up merchant ships for use as cruisers they would naturally have to rely very much upon the sailing power of these ships, so that it is exceedingly probable that this vessel would be one of the first to be taken up. She could, however, carry coal sufficient to enable her to go round the world at 15 knots an hour without calling at any port to replenish. The Cunard Company . . . certainly deserve credit for their foresight in providing this ship with qualities which will make her so valuable in time of war, although it is principally by her merits as a passenger steamer carrying cargo that her success must be judged. She has accommodation on two decks for 500 first class passengers in 158 state-rooms. These rooms are of exceedingly spacious dimensions, being 11 ft. by 6 ft. She has a very handsome saloon, 54 ft. by 52 ft., with the necessary pantries, galleys, receiving rooms, hoists, &c, &c. The public rooms, such as the ladies room, smoking room, bar, &c.,&c., will be very handsomely decorated and fitted with all the latest improvements—both for heating and ventilation. Amidships for the length of 250 ft. she has a promenade deck, which forms an admirable shelter for the upper deck. The great beam of this vessel causes the deck to be a magnificent promenade, and in fact it is more like a street than a ship. She has accommodation on her lower decks for a few emigrants, but as the fittings are all portable, and as she is supplied with spare cabin fittings for these places, there is no doubt that very few emigrants will ever travel in this ship.

The facilities for rapid discharge and shipment of cargo have received great attention, for she is fitted with five of Muir & Caldwell's most powerful winches. . . . She will have 12 boats, all carried well above the promenade deck so that they will be practically free from chance of damage.

. . . The ship will be lighted throughout with the Swan electric light, having about 600 lights in all. The lamps for these fittings will be very elegant. . . .

The new vessel is now in dock getting her machinery fitted in and is expected to be ready for her station in April.

1883   The Siamese Royal Elephant Hunt
Dispatch from U.S. Minister to Siam John A. Halderman to Secretary of State Frederick T. Frelinghuysen

The United States sent a series of diplomatic agents and consuls to Siam (now Thailand) beginning as early as 1834 but did not assign a minister resident until 1882. John Halderman of Missouri was the first to hold this post, serving until 1886. Halderman delighted in reporting on affairs at the royal court and on unusual aspects of life in his country of assignment.

Bangkok, Siam, June 1, 1883

Sir:

The Royal Elephant Hunt is to Siam what the Derby Day is to England or the Grand Prix to France.

I know of nothing like it in the United States, unless it be the Great Fair at Saint Louis.

Everybody in holiday attire is supposed to go, leaving dull care behind, and dedicating the day to the pleasures of the present. In years gone by, these hunts were annual, but now they are more rare. The last, prior to the one just closed, came off in May 1878.

This has been discussed many months and was duly notified by Royal order; and as the popular appetite therefor had been whetted by a long hunger, the occasion was seized with avidity by this pleasure loving people.

As a consequence, there was a general rush to Ayuthia, the old capital 60 miles north, at the time described in Siamese computation as the "fifth day of the waning moon of the sixth month of the year of the Goat, fifth of the decade of the Siamese astronomical era 1245, and 16th of His Majesty's reign," corresponding to Saturday, May 26, 1883.

State barge, steamboat and launch, show-boat, dugout and catamaran were brought into requisition, at just such prices as one pays at Epsom Downs, Long Champ or Saint Louis.

The Elephant herds of Siam are the property of the King. They find pasturage upon the alluvial plains of the peninsula bounded by the mountains and the sea, where ward and watch are kept of them by guards to prevent dispersion or seizure. There they live in security and multiply.

At the Royal command, the keepers collect these scattered and roaming herds and drive them to Ayuthia, where, the court is assembled to witness the interesting exhibition of Hunt and Capture.

The rectangular stockade, as it has appeared for many years past, has narrowing approaches, and encloses an area of not more than one acre. It is formed by stout posts securely planted in the ground, just far enough apart to admit through the interstices the passage of a man, but not of a larger animal.

Into this corral, I saw 245 wild elephants decoyed and driven, by well trained female and male pachyderms, the former leading and the latter driving the wild herd.

In this spectacle alone, the Siamese proverb "it takes an elephant to catch an elephant," found ample verification.

Within the pen, experienced hunters from the backs of trusty male elephants, adroitly noosed the hind leg of each choice "tusker" or young male elephant and made fast the long rope attached to posts hard by, for that purpose.

In this perilous undertaking two days were employed, meanwhile light and darkness were made hideous by the bellowings of these infuriated beasts, which are here kept without food or water. In the corral, one young elephant was crushed to death, and others were left hors de combat.

The lassoing of each animal was greeted with exclamations of satisfaction from the assembled multitude, as was the discomfiture or failure of each hunter visited with words and signs of disapprobation.

The captured pachyderms detained in the stockade are starved into submission, tamed, trained and either kept at Ayuthia that they in turn may become captors, or they are transported to Bangkok where, in the King's stables, they find shelter, food, good treatment, and no work.

The herd just liberated was represented to be smaller than that of the last hunt. The keepers were engaged two months or more in collecting them, and some of the animals were driven from Karat, a twelve days' journey north.

The sport is exciting, though somewhat hazardous. It is no rare occurrence to see men killed or maimed for life. In the late hunt I heard of but one serious casualty—a mahout [elephant driver] killed by a blow from the trunk of an enraged elephant.

The Grand Stand, overlooking the stockade, was occupied by the King, Queen Consort, Crown Prince, several of His Majesty's wives, twenty or more of his children; and by Princes, Nobles and dignitaries of the realm surrounded by their harems. The Duke of Mecklenburg was present, as were also the Diplomatic and Consular Corps.

The Hunt occupied three days, and was witnessed by many thousands of delighted spectators.

> I have the honor to be, Sir,
> Your obedient servant,
>
> John A. Halderman

1883   Eruption of Krakatau

Dispatch from U.S. Consul in Batavia Stewart Hatfield Jr. to Assistant Secretary of State John Davis

The eruption of the island volcano Krakatau on August 26, 1883, was one of the most violent and celebrated volcanic eruptions in history. The island of Krakatau, located in the Dutch East Indies (present-day Indonesia), disappeared completely in the massive explosion, and the resultant tidal wave killed 36,000 people in West Java. The sound of the explosion was said to have been heard in Istanbul, Australia, Japan, and the Philippines. Volcanic dust from the eruption lingered in the atmosphere for almost a year and was considered responsible for the globally cool summer of 1884. In this dispatch the U.S. consul in Batavia, Dutch East Indies (now Jakarta, Indonesia), reports on his experience during the eruption and on its devastating results.

> Batavia, 1st September, 1883

Sir,

... On Saturday afternoon the 26th ... loud reports similar to the discharge of heavy artillery in our immediate vicinity astonished Batavia; it was soon understood that these sounds issued from the volcano on Krakatau island, situated in Sunda Straits between Java and Sumatra. ...

All throughout the night of the 26th these reports which were tremendous continued, gradually lessening however as day drew near, but when I state that the gas street lamps, and those in private houses were extinguished and that doors, windows and even houses were shaken by the concussions caused by a volcano situated 90 miles away as the crow flies, the force of the explosions can be better appreciated.

Morning at last arrived but as the day passed it grew gradually darker; at about 9 o'clock a.m. it commenced to rain ashes slightly, in an hour this had increased to such an extent that it resembled a heavy snow storm and by 11:30 a.m. Batavia was in utter darkness as night, which continued until about 1:30 p.m. when the atmosphere slowly cleared. The fall of ashes is stated to have amounted to 5 centimeters, or say 2 inches.

Business was of course entirely suspended—at about noon a tidal wave reached this city, the water rising between 8 and 10 feet and flooding the lower town, sending . . . small river craft generally into confusion, and landing many of them in the streets and on the roadways.

. . . Several steamers were in danger and increased the confusion by firing distress guns.

The dry dock . . . has been carried away, the last seen of it was . . . 4 miles off the coast. . . . Ashes fell at Sourabaya in Java, and Penang, in the Malacca Peninsula, and in Singapore the reports were heard.

The section which felt the full force of the eruption was the Java coast bordering on the Straits of Sunda; . . . it has been completely altered in appearance and entirely not one stone remains on another. . . . [M]ost of the inhabitants have perished, the entire coast facing the Straits has been swept clean and where last week there were villages, buildings, fields, etc., there is at present a veritable dismal swamp of mud and water. . . . [S]maller places situated on the coast . . . actually no longer exist.

. . . The island of Krakatau has disappeared and the sea covers that place now, but between Krakatau and Sebessie Island 16 new formations have appeared and a sort of reef bearing five active craters.

The Western part of the province of Bantam (Java) is quite a desert being covered with ashes and mud. Trees and all vegetation have perished, in fact everything has been carried away, cattle are deprived of food and the outlook is certainly disheartening for that district. Full details have so far not been received as everything is naturally in confusion but navigation of the Straits is certainly dangerous on account of the changes and the fact that the lighthouses have been destroyed. . . .

I have the honor to be, very respectfully, your obedient servant,

S. Hatfield

1883 Antiforeign Riots in Canton: "An Interesting Day"
Dispatch from U.S. Consul in Canton Charles Seymour to
U.S. Minister to China John Russell Young

Throughout the nineteenth century, and especially after the Opium War of 1839–1842 (see "Prelude to the Opium War," p. 105), the European presence and influence in China expanded rapidly. Many Chinese resented European encroachments and the special privileges won by Europeans through force of arms. As a result, antiforeign incidents were common and became a staple of consular reporting from China during the period. This dispatch reports a serious, though not unusual, antiforeign disturbance in Canton.

> Canton, September 10, 1883—
> 10 p.m.

Sir:

I have the honor to inform you that the Europeans and Americans residing in Canton and on the Shameen have had an interesting day during which some lives were lost and considerable property has been destroyed, amounting in value to about $200,000, with incidental damages to business of steamers and ships to enough more to make a total loss of about a quarter of a million of dollars.

The immediate cause of the outbreak of the mob was the death of a Chinaman this morning on board the British steamer Hankow, caused by the kicks of a Portuguese employee (watchman), who killed the Chinaman, or caused him to roll insensible into the water, where (it is commonly alleged) he was drowned, although it is probable the man died of the kicks.

Immediately thereafter the Chinese mob fired the wharf and sheds where the steamer Hankow was moored, and would have set the steamer on fire if she had not promptly cast off lines and steamed up the river in front of the Shameen or European settlement.

The mob, gathering strength with the excitement of the occasion, forced their way quickly upon the European reservation (Shameen), and, commencing with the new ice factory of Mr. Raven, which was soon destroyed, looted or pillaged nearly all of the dwellings and business places, to the number of a dozen valuable buildings, east of the British consulate and east of Messrs. Russell & Co.'s establishments, which were entered by the leaders of the mob, five of whom were captured while attempting to fire the main building, from which they were ejected in time to save it from destruction.

Four of the five captured persons escaped. From 8 o'clock a.m. until after 1 o'clock p.m. the mob encountered no resistance worth mentioning; but after five hours of pillage and incendiarism the mob were interrupted by the viceroy's soldiers, who are now in possession of the Shameen and its approaches.

The steamer Hankow, instead of proceeding from Canton to Hong-Kong, has remained in port, as all concerned regarded it extremely hazardous for the steamer to carry away the body of the recovered Chinaman or the person of the Portuguese who caused his death, no one feeling authorized to act for the Portuguese.

This afternoon the body of the murdered Chinaman was removed from the steamer, which is still here, awaiting action in regard to the Portuguese.

In the mean time the ladies and children of nearly all of the foreigners who could reach steamers in port took refuge, and still remain thereon, while the citizens of western nations, to the number of about sixty persons, are patrolling the Shameen, agreeably with an organization effected at a public meeting in the Canton Club House at 5 o'clock this evening.

The consular corps, representing the United States, Great Britain, Germany, France, Denmark, and Sweden and Norway, met in the United States consulate at 3 p.m. and acted unitedly in reference to the emergency. A copy of the dispatch adopted by all the consular officers is appended.

At present matters have apparently quieted down; but with over three millions of Chinese within a radius of six miles, and over six millions within a radius of twelve or fifteen miles, the materials are abundant for a continuance or renewal of the deplorable scenes that have been enacted this day in Canton.

I just came off my evening patrol, and return to it at 4 p.m.

I can only assure you that, whatever may be the result of the present disturbed condition of the Chinese in regard to foreigners, it will be my endeavor to maintain fidelity to American interests and honor, while performing my duties toward all concerned.

Telegraphic communication is broken and mail facilities are somewhat disturbed, but I will try to get this dispatch to you through the hands of the United States consul at Hong-Kong.

I am, &c.,

Charles Seymour

1884 Early Vladivostok: "Caviar and Vodka"

Dispatch from U.S. Minister to Siam John A. Halderman to Secretary of State Frederick T. Frelinghuysen

Imperial Russia longed for a warm water port that would guarantee its access to the open seas when its own northern ports froze for the winter. When the Russian drive for a Mediterranean port was thwarted by the Crimean War (1853–1856), the czar turned his attention to the Pacific Ocean. In 1860 China ceded disputed territory to Russia, which founded the town of Vladivostok. Russia's attempts to expand farther south were blocked by the other great powers, leaving the Russian dream of a warm water port unfulfilled. Vladivostok, although frozen over in the winter, became the major Russian commercial center in the Far East.

John Halderman, who served as the first U.S. minister to Siam (now Thailand) from 1882 to 1885, was forced by illness to leave Bangkok for cooler climates in the summer of 1884. As he traveled north, he found time to file an interesting description of early Vladivostok.

Vladivostock, Siberia
June 14, 1884

Sir:

This port is Russia's principal military and naval station on the Pacific. It has a population of 10,000 and a prospect of healthy growth. It is connected with Nagasaki, Japan, 800 miles distant, via the Corean ports Fusan and Yuen-San, by monthly steam service. During four months of the year navigation is suspended by the rigors of winter. On the west it has uninterrupted connection with St. Petersburg by post-route and telegraph.

The situation is pleasing, and the harbor safe and capacious. It would seem easy of defense.

An iron floating dry-dock, with capacity for the largest vessels, is under contract and will soon be completed.

On the adjacent lands cereals and vegetables thrive. It is not at all improbable that Siberia may yet supply Asia with bread. . . .

Here, as elsewhere in the East, Chinamen are the workers, the day laborers, brick-makers, butchers, bakers, shopkeepers, &c. A few Coreans are employed in the brick-yards. Russians, Siberians, and Cossacks are the soldiers, sailors, and drosky drivers.

Meat is the staple article of food. Good beef is abundant. People of all conditions affect *caviar* and *vodka*. Ladies smoke cigarettes at the dinner table, and dress with the elegance of their sisters in Washington or Paris.

Though the trees are in leaf, and the hillsides are carpeted with green, the mercury marks 40° Fahrenheit, while men and women wear winter clothing, wraps, and furs. Later in the season 80° of heat may be reached.

The Western powers are not represented by consuls; Japan alone having a commercial agent. I was told that such representation was not desired, inasmuch as this is a Government station, and not an open free port soliciting trade with the outside world. No one may venture hither without a passport. . . .

En route to Vladivostock I visited Fusan and Yuensan (Gensan) on the east coast of Corea. From what I saw and learned of the "hermit kingdom" I could hardly recommend Americans to quit their own country and go thither.

I have, &c.,

John A. Halderman

1884 Accepting the Statue of Liberty
Dispatch from U.S. Minister to France Levi P. Morton to Secretary of State Frederick T. Frelinghuysen

The Statue of Liberty was a gift in celebration of a century of friendship between France and the United States. First suggested by the French historian Edouard de Laboulaye as a way of commemorating the common pursuit of liberty by the two nations, the statue was presented to American minister Levi Morton in Paris on July 4, 1884. This dispatch reports the ceremonies surrounding the transfer of the statue. It was later disassembled and shipped to New York, where U.S. citizens contributed funds to erect a base on which to place it.

The statue was designed by French artist Frédéric-Auguste Bartholdi, with a supporting framework by Alexandre Eiffel, of Eiffel Tower fame. The Statue of Liberty was dedicated in New York harbor by President Grover Cleveland in October 1886. Two years later Minister Levi Morton was elected vice president of the United States.

Paris, July 5, 1884

Sir:

Mr. Bartholdi, the eminent French sculptor, author of the statue of "Liberty Enlightening the World," called upon me some weeks ago to say that the statue was now complete, and that, as the labor of taking it down for shipment to America would require at least three months, it was the intention of the committee of the Franco-American Union to present it at once to me, as the representative of the Government and people of the United States. Mr. Bartholdi added that Mr. Jules Ferry would seize this occasion to associate the French Government with the undertaking of the Franco-American Union, and that he (Mr. Ferry) and other members of the Government would officially take part in the ceremony of presentation.

A few days later Mr. Ferry himself confirmed this statement at my house. He said that the statue of Liberty was not only wonderful as a work of art, but as a work entirely due to the individual initiative of Frenchmen friendly to America, and that it was the first time such an undertaking had been successfully carried out without Government aid. The government, however, did not wish to stand aloof from this great manifestation. It wanted to show publicly that it shared the sentiments which had inspired Mr. Bartholdi, and with this view the minister of the navy, Admiral Peyron, would place a state vessel at the disposition of the committee for the transportation of the statue to New York. . . .

The statue was formally presented to me on the morning of the 4th of July, and I accepted it in the name of the President of the United States and the American people.

The ceremony was an interesting and imposing one. It took place in the foundry yard of Messrs. Gaget & Gauthier where the monument has been made, and in presence of a large audience of distinguished guests. Upon a tribune erected in front of the colossal bronze sat the Franco-American Union Committee with its president, M. F. de Lesseps, with the author of the monument, Mr. Bartholdi, and members of the Government. . . .

The yard, which was appropriately decorated with French and American flags, was filled by a large number of citizens of both countries. A band of music played alternately the French and American national airs. . . .

M. de Lesseps then, speaking in the name of the Union, presented to me the great statue—the eighth wonder of the world, as he called it. His remarks, partly foreign to the object, were, nevertheless, greeted with cheers; for they expressed in warm terms the generous feeling which had inspired this spontaneous manifestation of friendship on the part of the French people. I responded by reading your telegram directing me to accept the statue and by explaining the action of the President and of Congress in the matter. . . .

I enclose herewith, with the original deed of presentation and a translation of the same. . . .

I have, &c.,

Levi P. Morton

1885 Korea: Execution of Revolutionists
Dispatch from U.S. Chargé d'Affaires in Korea George C. Foulk to Secretary of State Frederick T. Frelinghuysen

Korean reformers who wished to follow Japan's example of modernization attempted an unsuccessful coup d'état in Seoul late in 1884. At the time Japan was seeking to increase its influence over Korea, but China remained the predominant foreign power in the country. The would-be modernizers were executed in a very traditional manner.

Seoul, Corea, January 31, 1885

Sir:

I have the honor to submit the following relative to the situation in Corea:

His Majesty the King is authoritatively stated to have yielded the administration of the Government exclusively to the Oi-jong-pu (or ministerial body) upon the demand of the conservative faction of the Government. This faction has also demanded the execution of Kim-Ok-Kiun and four other of the late conspirators, all of whom are now in Japan, to which country they escaped immediately after the late revolutionary attempt.

His Majesty, exhausted with care and business consequent upon the recent difficulties, and augmented by exposure, has been quite ill, but is now recovering.

The torture and trial of twelve persons implicated in the conspiracy were concluded on the 27th instant, and they were sentenced to death. Six were executed a few hundred yards from this legation and five on the main street of the city on the 28th and 29th instant.

These persons were placed face down in the streets and decapitated by from six to ten blows of a dull instrument, while a rope secured to the ques served to open the wounds. The bodies were all dismembered and distributed about the streets for exposure for three or four days. The twelfth victim died in prison from voluntary starvation and the effects of his torture. Of these twelve persons one was a student of high birth, the others underlings and headmen of the houses of the conspirators.

A great number of other persons had been hunted down and tortured. . . . [T]housands of citizens fled from the city; these are now returning and the populace in general is quieting down.

The two Chinese ambassadors yet remain in the city with a considerable body of troops. The Japanese legation, temporarily outside the west gate of the city, is in charge of a chargé d'affaires, and is the headquarters of six hundred Japanese soldiers under the command of a colonel.

Japanese civilians come into the city, but through distrust on the part of the Coreans, may not rent quarters within the walls. . . .

>I am, &c.,
>
>George C. Foulk

1885 The Central American Union: A Month of Turmoil
Dispatches from U.S. Ministers to Central America to Secretary of State Thomas F. Bayard

Justo Rufino Barrios, longtime ruler of Guatemala (1873–1885), proclaimed a Central American Union in 1885, with himself at its head. Barrios then promptly went to war with his neighbors in a futile effort to bring his plan to fruition. He assumed the support of El Salvador and Honduras whose leaders he had helped install, but he found that only Honduras supported his unification bid. The "Union" lasted less than a month, collapsing when Barrios died in battle against El Salvador. Its beginning and end are described in these dispatches from two successive U.S. ministers to Central America. From 1873 to 1891 U.S. diplomatic representation in Central America consisted of a single minister commissioned to the Central American states and resident in Guatemala.

The Union Proclaimed
From U.S. Minister to Central America H. Remsen Whitehouse

>Guatemala, March 6, 1885

Sir:

. . . I have the honor to inclose herewith a . . . decree issued by President Barrios, proclaiming the union of the central American States into one republic under one military chief, which supreme command he himself assumes.

I cabled you to-day the following in regard to this action:

Central American Union proclaimed by decree of President Barrios.

The publication of the decree was unexpected and is causing considerable excitement. The crowd invaded the opera where the performance was in progress, and the decree was read from the stage amidst great applause.

Resistance on the part of Nicaragua, and especially Costa Rica, is anticipated, and due preparation for such a contingency is made.

The decree, of which I will send a copy by next mail, states that any person declaring against the Union shall be held a traitor to the great national cause, and shall be subject to the consequences and responsibility of the acts he may have executed.

Officers and officials who declare for the Union shall be advanced one grade in the army of the Central American Republic.

No treaties, foreign loans, or analogous stipulations arranged by the other States after the date of this decree (February 28th) shall be recognized.

I have just learned that the Presidents of Salvador and Honduras have declared for the Union.

As the mail leaves very shortly, I have no time for more details.

I am, &c.,

H. Remsen Whitehouse

The Union Ended

From U.S. Minister to Central America Henry C. Hall

Guatemala, April 11, 1885

Sir:

I have time by this mail only to make a cursory report of the principal events which have transpired here during past fortnight.

The advanced forces of Guatemala and Salvador met at a place called El Coco on the 31st ultimo. The Salvadorians, according to the Guatemalan reports, were routed, with the loss of one field-piece, one mitrailleuse [early machine gun], and a considerable quantity of ammunition. The Guatemalans followed up their success by invading Salvador. ... General Barrios was killed, while leading a charge against the Salvadorian intrenchments. His death caused a panic among his troops, which at once commenced a retreat. The Salvadorians, however, were in no condition to improve the advantages they had gained by Barrios' death. From that moment there appears to have been a complete cessation of hostilities, which have not been resumed.

There is now a greater feeling of confidence among the people, and tranquillity seems in a fair way to be restored.

Many families have left the country, among them the widow and family of General Barrios.

Since writing the foregoing, a telegram from President Zaldivar announces that peace has been made between Honduras on the one part and Salvador, Nicaragua, and Costa Rica on the other. It only remains for Salvador and Guatemala to come to an arrangement, of which there is a probability.

I have, &c.,

Henry C. Hall

1885 Conditions in Central Africa
Dispatch from U.S. Agent to the States of the Congo Association W. P. Tisdel to Secretary of State Thomas F. Bayard

In 1878 King Leopold II of Belgium and American explorer and adventurer Henry Morton Stanley founded the International Congo Association, a private organization aimed at developing the Congo basin. In subsequent travels through Africa, Stanley signed treaties with hundreds of tribal chiefs, bringing them under the umbrella of the association. In 1885 the United States became the first country to grant official recognition to the International Congo Association—later the Congo Free State and then the Belgian Congo—as a friendly state. The American recognition stemmed in part from the reports filed by U.S. Agent W. P. Tisdel, the first American official to travel through portions of central Africa. This dispatch is Tisdel's first report home describing conditions and trade opportunities in central and western Africa.

Lisbon, Portugal,
April 25, 1885

Sir:

I have the honor to report my return to the coast at Banana, the 20th ultimo, having traveled by special caravan to the interior of Africa as far as Stanley Pool, around and to the north and east of which I made several explorations, calling at Kinchassa, De Brazzaville, and other points, and visiting the native villages bordering the Pool. I regret to inform you that I was unable to proceed farther into the interior, as was my intention, but the want of river transportation prevented, and I was reluctantly compelled to turn back.

. . . I recommend most earnestly that Americans who contemplate establishing themselves on the Lower Congo, or anywhere on the west coast of Africa, should not do so unless supplied with a large capital, which will enable them to compete with the long-established Dutch, English, and German houses which control almost the entire trade of the west coast. . . . They must locate "factories" or stations in different parts, engage help acclimated and familiar with the country and the natives, and with a knowledge of both the Portuguese and Fiote languages, make presents to chiefs of tribes, and in this manner induce the natives to come in to the newly-established "factories." All this takes time and money, and little or no return can be expected for at least a year. . . .

The most valuable productions of the country, and for which there is an ever-increasing demand, are rubber, palm kernels and palm oil, gum copal, ground-nuts, and wax. The rubber and palm trees are of spontaneous growth and to be found everywhere in the lowlands. The supply is not equal to the demand, yet there is no limit to the quantity of these rich products which might be taken from the country if the natives could be induced to work. Here again arises the question of labor, and to me it seem feasible to create wants amongst the tribes of the low and coast lands which will after a time induce them to gather and bring to the traders in large quantities the products which they can so readily exchange for anything which they may require. . . .

In no sense of the word can this be called an agricultural country. Nothing is cultivated. . . .

The country is densely populated, yet . . . with the exception of the Loaugo and Kabinda tribes, they are a wild, savage, and cruel people. They do not like the white man; and while they are glad to have his cloth and gin, they would much prefer never to see a white man within their domain. . . .

I may remark here that a few bottles of trade gin will go much farther in trade with the natives than ten times its value in cloth; and it often happens that traders are compelled to return to the coast without having accomplished a trade, because the natives insist upon having gin, while the trader was supplied with cloth alone. A native man can be induced to work at a "factory" for one or two days at a time upon the assurance that he can at the expiration of that time have a bottle or two of gin, while if you offer him a piece of cloth it is doubtful whether he would work at all.

The coast women are fond of cloth, having a preference for the gaudy colors. They are the work-people of the country, and if it were not for their industry little or nothing would be gathered for foreign markets. The men lounge about, drinking, gossiping, fighting, or hunting, as it may suit their tastes.

. . . Very great precaution must be exercised during the first year's stay in the country, in order that the system may be kept free from the poisonous influences of the malaria which overhangs the entire country. . . . Good shelter, with an abundance of good wholesome food and a fair allowance of pure Bordeaux or Portuguese wine, with indoor occupation or amusement after nightfall, would, I am sure, go very far towards a guarantee of fairly good health on the coast and in the lower river countries. . . .

Common cotton and woolen goods, rum, gin, glass beads, guns, powder, tobacco, and common cutlery make up the principal imports. . . . It is the only currency known. . . . The gin comes from Holland, and is manufactured expressly for the trade, the quantity being about 40 per cent of all the imports. . . .

The Congo River is navigable for the largest ocean steamers to Boma, a distance of 70 miles from the sea. Steamers drawing 17 to 18 feet can go safely to Noki, 30 miles above Boma. . . .

I send you herewith a sample of each kind of cloth in use for native trade on the Congo and in the surrounding country, with cost price per piece, and number of yards in each piece. I send also a sample of blue and white beads, which are in general use for trading purposes throughout the entire country, and are greatly appreciated by the natives. . . .

Whether or not the cotton goods of American manufacture can be laid down on the Congo and along the coast as cheaply as those from England, I cannot say (certainly we cannot produce them of a *poorer* quality than sample!), but I am well satisfied that . . . "Yankee notions" generally can be delivered to the traders along the coast at lower prices than they are now being invoiced from Europe. . . .

There are no hotels or even stopping places, and several cases of extreme hardship and suffering have come to my notice, where agents have been sent to the coast without knowing where they were going or what they were going for. . . .

As to government on the Lower Congo or on the coast north of Angola there is none, nor even a semblance of government, until we arrive at Gaboon or Fernando Po, where we first come upon the military rule of the French and Spanish.

At Banana, at points along the Lower Congo, on the coast, and in the lowland interior, at each station or "factory," the traders have a small armory, and not infrequently are they required to resort to arms for defense from attacks by the natives, or to punish the natives for some offense committed. Upon the slightest provocation or even without provocation, the natives often attack the "factories," burn the buildings, and plunder the stores. . . . Every employee in the service of the trading companies must act as an armed policeman, not only for self-protection but for the protection of the property intrusted to his care.

The natives are all armed with old flint-lock muskets which have been sold to them by the traders, and it is an exceptional case to meet a native man without one unless he be a slave, and even slaves are oftentimes armed. They do not well understand the use of fire-arms, and, notwithstanding they carry guns, they prefer the poisoned arrow or spear, with which they do much better execution. I may add, however, that they are informing themselves in the matter of improved fire-arms, and chiefs of tribes are now demanding repeating or magazine rifles with prepared metallic cartridges, where until recently they were well satisfied with old flint-locks.

South of the Congo, in St. Paul de Loando, Benguela, and Mossamedes, there is, in my opinion, an opportunity to place American goods of all kinds. The climate is not at all unlike that of our Southern States, and the requirements of the people are much the same as our own. . . .

There are no manufactories in the country, excepting for rum; consequently everything but the commonest articles of food is required from abroad. . . .

Proceeding north from the Congo, I found at St. Thome a possible market for American goods of all kinds. This is one of the richest islands in the world, densely populated. . . . I saw in one shop a case of American sheeting and "blue jeans," which the proprietor informed me he had ordered especially through an English house. . . .

In Cameroon, the Germans, by reason of recent conquests, control the trade, and, though the country is very rich, I do not think it possible for an American to get a foothold there. The same may be said of Fernando Po, under Spanish rule, and of the lower Niger country, Dahomey, the Gold Coast, and Ashantee, all English possessions.

Of Liberia I cannot write . . . but I visited Bolama and Bissao, seventy-five miles in the interior, and I have never seen a country which offers such extraordinary inducements to the trader as this. . . . I learned that a Boston house had arranged for an agency in Bissao, to which place they propose running a sailing vessel monthly, in connection with an already established line to the Cape de Verd islands, between which and Boston a good paying trade is well inaugurated.

Goree, Daker, and San Luis, in the French African possessions of Senegal, are thriving business places, but the French look so well after their trades-people that I could hardly recommend an American merchant to venture in these parts. Yankee enterprise, has, however, shown itself in Goree, where an American house, against great odds, is doing a fair business. . . .

I have, &c.,

W. P. Tisdel

1886 End of Arab Power in East Africa
Dispatch from Acting U.S. Consul in Zanzibar E. D. Ropes Jr. to Secretary of State Thomas F. Bayard

The Berlin Conference of 1885 established internationally accepted ground rules for African colonization, giving priority to countries with settlements on the coast but requiring real occupation of the interior before a colony could be declared. The conference touched off the "Scramble for Africa." Within fifteen years virtually the entire continent was under European rule. This dispatch reports the German occupation of a portion of the coast of East Africa, at the expense of the sultanate of Zanzibar and, according to the American consul, to the detriment of long-established U.S. trading interests.

Zanzibar, December 20, 1886

Sir:

I have the honor to inform you that the 14th inst a fleet of six German men-of-war under Admiral Knorr arrived at this port followed on the 15th by two French, and one English is now lying in the harbor.

The object of their movement has not yet been made public but it is understood that the Sultan has been compelled to cede a large portion of his coast territory to Germany and one seaport to England.

This, of course, is the end of Arab power on this coast forever.

In my opinion American interests and all foreign interests but Germany will suffer greatly by these changes and it is greatly to be regretted that some government would not assist the Sultan's government against this German robbery.

Considering that the Sultan's power to control the various wild and lawless tribes which are under his suzerainty, will be materially weakened and that our large American interests are absolutely without protection in case of riot or bombardment, and that as the first treaty power with the Sultan we should be in some way represented in the important changes and transfers soon to take place—I recommend that an American man-of-war of good size be sent to remain here at Zanzibar until this trouble is definitely settled.

As representative of the two largest houses in Zanzibar I feel very anxious about the large amount of property belonging to me lying exposed to fire or any incendiary acts, also the future of the American trade seems very uncertain and I fear will be much injured by the precedence which this affair will give Germany.

I have the honor to be, Sir,
Your obedient Servant

E. D. Ropes, Jr.

1887 The Trans-Siberian Railroad
Dispatch from U.S. Minister to China Charles Denby Jr. to
Secretary of State Thomas F. Bayard

The first transcontinental railroad in America was inaugurated in 1869, with a golden spike driven into the ground at Promontory Point, Utah, connecting the lines of the Central Pacific and Union Pacific Railroads. Twenty years later the Russian dream of a similar line across Asia was still five thousand miles short of its goal. Already, however, the U.S. minister to China foresaw the fundamental changes such a railroad would bring to the Far East. The trans-Siberian line was not completed until 1903.

Peking, September 9, 1887

Sir:

What effect the railway schemes of Russia may have on the policy of the Chinese Government it is impossible to prognosticate but the effect of the completed lines on China is not difficult to forecast.

The scheme of a trans-Uralian railway which will connect St. Petersburg, on the Baltic Sea, with Wladiwostock, on the Pacific Ocean, is vast but feasible. The construction of our own transcontinental railways, and particularly the completion of the Canadian Pacific, have at the same time demonstrated the feasibility of building railways of great length, and their usefulness when completed.

England finds, over the Canadian Pacific, a new route to India, partly on her own soil, and the balance on the sea which her navy dominates. Russia is keenly alive to the advantages which would thus accrue to her great rival in the event of a war for India, which has so often been imminent, and, some day, as the world believes, must transpire. But the country which is most threatened by the proposed Russian line is China.

The trans-Siberian railway is now completed from St. Petersburg to Tiumen, a trans-Uralian city. As the new line is laid, it depends somewhat on steam navigation. But, as the waters in Siberia are closed by ice from the 10th of November to the 10th of April, the railway line to serve the required purposes must be continuous. The line must rely largely on governmental aid. A railway can not compete with the Amur river steamers in carrying tea, nor probably with the caravan route across the desert to Irkoutsk. Grain and cattle are cheap in Siberia, but so they are in Russia. It will take many years to develop the immense mining interests in Siberia. The road will be very costly to build, and can not rely on its own revenues. Military exigencies for such a road are pressing. In 1878 and 1879 war nearly resulted between Russia and China over the rejection by China of the treaty made by Chung How. The immense labor and expense of accumulating men and munitions of war at Wladiwostock, the insufficiency of the fleet in the Pacific, the want of a base of operations, the absence of arsenals, all taught Russia a lesson.

She abandoned the treaty as made and gave back to China the largest part of Ili, retaining, however, some strategic positions.

Russia now recognizes that by existing means of communication she can not move troops and stores in requisite quantities. She realizes that, by building a road to the Pacific, she may become the greatest power on that ocean. It is true that her Pacific port, Wladiwostock, is closed by ice during the winter, but when once she has grasped the Pacific, she will not be slow in seizing a more southern port, perhaps Port Lazaref.

The necessities of the Chinese Empire thus become clear. She must build railways to preserve her lines of communication, and to enable her to mass troops. She must build a line to Moukden, with a branch thence to the Amur, and another to Possiet; so as to give strategic communication with Corea. She must defend her frontier with forts and men, and there must be communication to them by rail. . . .

I have, etc.,

Charles Denby

1888 The Rothschilds at the Court of Vienna: "A Great Sensation"

Dispatch from U.S. Minister to Austria-Hungary Alexander R. Lawton to Secretary of State Thomas F. Bayard

In 1885 the Austro-Hungarian government refused to accept the appointment of Anthony Keiley as U.S. minister because his wife was Jewish. The State Department protested vigorously but unsuccessfully and then left the position vacant for two years to demonstrate its continuing displeasure. It was thus a surprising development when the Baron and Baroness Albert Rothschild were admitted to the court three years later.

Vienna, January 6, 1888

Sir:

In view of the anti-Semitic imbroglio which somewhat excited the Governments of Austria-Hungary and the United States, not long since, it is interesting to note that during the recent "holidays" the Baron and Baroness Albert Rothschild were declared by imperial decree *hoffähig*, that is to say, they will for the future be admitted to court balls. This is the first time that such a privilege has ever been conceded to persons of Jewish origin or faith, and it is causing a great sensation in the highest society of Vienna. Very many quarterings of nobility (sixteen, I believe) are the usual requisites of *Hoffähigkeit*; and it was not until last year that the wives of cabinet ministers, not being members of noble families, were admitted to court by reason of their husbands' offices.

This exclusion from court circles has long been sorely felt by the Rothschild family, and it has been rumored during the past year that Baron Albert intended to dispose of his palace residence and other property in Vienna, and retire altogether from Austria with his colossal fortune.

I have, etc.,

Alexander R. Lawton

1888 Slavery: Down but Not Out
Dispatches from U.S. Ministers to Brazil and China

By the late nineteenth century the world had made tremendous progress toward the abolition of slavery, but its remnants survived in disparate parts of the globe. Slavery continued to be an issue of note in U.S. diplomatic reporting, as evidenced by these dispatches from distant legations.

China: Slavery Still Exists
From U.S. Minister to China Charles Denby Jr. to Secretary of State Thomas F. Bayard

Peking, February 24, 1888

Sir:

As some discussion has lately taken place in the United States touching slavery in China I submit the following observations thereon:

The origin of slavery in China is given in an ancient writing. . . . The first slaves were felons who lost their liberty by reason of their crimes. . . . Prisoners and captives taken in war introduced a second species of slavery. Finally, in the troubles and misfortunes of the third dynasty, the poor who were without resources gave themselves with their families to the great and rich who were willing to support them. These last two forms of slavery caused the condition to be regarded rather as a misfortune than a shame. . . .

All modern writers agree that slavery still exists. Every native may purchase slaves, and the condition is hereditary. Freedom is forfeited by crimes or mortgaged for debt. Slaves are so few that they attract little attention. At Peking girls bring higher prices than boys, varying, according to age up to eighteen years, from 30 to 300 taels. Needy parents sell their children, and orphans are sold in times of famine for a few taels in cash. . . .

That slavery is tolerated by Chinese law will sufficiently appear from the statutes which, although fallen somewhat in disuse, still exist. I quote a few of these laws.

By section 115 of the penal code a master soliciting and obtaining in marriage for his slave the daughter of a freeman suffers eighty blows. . . .

Under the head of "slaves striking their masters," section 314, the punishments are very severe. For striking the master the punishment is beheading; for killing him, death by the slow process; for accidental killing, death by strangling; for accidental wounding, one hundred blows and banishment. . . .

If the master beats the slave to death for having committed a crime he suffers one hundred blows. . . .

The Chinese have a great horror of this condition, and the law has done much to put a stop to this abuse, and in certain districts has succeeded. Mr. Crossette [a missionary] personally knows that large numbers of girls were carried off and sold into slavery during times of famine in the province of Shantung. A Chinese convert at Tsi-nan-fu sold his little daughter for $16 to serve as a maid of all work in a rich man's family. Boys were not marketable. Another Christian sold his wife for $2.50 to pay a debt of that amount.

Mr. Crossette says that there exists in some parts of China a peasant servitude, such as formerly existed in Russia.

I have, etc.,

Charles Denby

Brazil: Emancipation

From U.S. Minister to Brazil Thomas J. Jarvis to Secretary of State Thomas F. Bayard

Petropolis, May 14, 1888

Sir:

. . . I have the honor to inform you that yesterday the general assembly of Brazil finally passed, and the Princess Imperial Regent approved, a law abolishing slavery in Brazil. . . .

While I expected the speedy enactment of such a law, I did not anticipate such unanimity in its passage. Every indication of public sentiment is in hearty accord with this action of the general assembly, and I may add that this sentiment has been well prepared for the changes to take place in the labor of the country. I therefore do not share in the fears expressed by some as to its immediate effect on the various industries.

The maturing coffee crop is exceptionally large, and some, either honestly or for purposes of speculation, have expressed the apprehension that the immediate effect of emancipation would be so to disorganize labor as to render it difficult, if not impossible, to save the crop. In my view, the country has been so well prepared for this action that its present effect will not be deleterious, and its future results will be most advantageous, as we all know it has proved in our own land, to the general prosperity of the country.

I have, etc.,

Thomas J. Jarvis

1889 The Birth of International Organizations
Dispatch from U.S. Minister to Switzerland Boyd Winchester to Secretary of State Thomas F. Bayard

The second half of the nineteenth century witnessed the development of multilateral diplomacy and the birth of international organizations as they are known today. Much of this activity was located in Switzerland, an ideal venue because of its central location and its neutrality. In this dispatch the U.S. minister chronicles Switzerland's emergence as a headquarters for international conferences and organizations, a role still played by that nation today.

Berne, February 1, 1889

Sir:

... Several international unions have their seat in Berne; the number is gradually increasing, and it is conferring upon Switzerland, in the eyes of the world, a peculiar position of honor, distinction, and usefulness. It may not be uninteresting to give a short summary of the history of the rise and progress of these international unions.

The neutrality of Switzerland was guaranteed by the powers represented at the Congress of Vienna. . . . She was thus mapped out to be a neutral state, and the neutrality then acquired, and her central position in Europe, were in themselves sufficient to recommend her, when occasion offered, to be selected as the seat of an international union of any kind. . . .

Again, besides their neutral position, the Swiss possess perhaps the most marked genius of any people for the administration of an office. . . .

In 1863 the first step was taken which has since resulted in a general consensus as to the superior inducements presented by Switzerland for international bureaus. In that year a private committee, the members of which belonged to different nationalities, assembled at Geneva and drew up a plan for the protection of the wounded in battle. . . . It will always redound to the honor of Switzerland that upon her soil the first international conference was held with a view to the mitigation of some of the horrors of war. . . . A conference which was held in Geneva the following year . . . was brought to a successful conclusion by the signing of the memorable "Geneva Convention of the 22d August, 1864. . . ." The treaty embraces a wide field of practical philanthropy, being designed to remove soldiers, when sick or wounded, from the category of combatants, and to afford them relief and protection without regard to nationality. . . . The distinctive mark of hospitals and ambulances is the Swiss flag with its colors reversed, a red cross on a white ground, and individuals wear a white armlet with a red cross, and every red-cross flag must be accompanied in time of war by the national flag of those using it. It is one of the wisest and best systems of philanthropic work. . . . Certainly it is no mean distinction for the Swiss Confederation that the national emblem has been so intimately and exclusively associated with a most conspicuous work of charity and humanity. The United States Government gave its adherence to the treaty in July, 1882, and in the international conventions held since that date . . . no one commanded more attention and wielded a greater influence than a lone American woman who was accredited as a delegate from her country. Clara Barton, whose name is known the world over in connection with the burning cross on a white ground, the only feminine delegate in the assemblage, carried resolutions and amendments that materially enlarged the scope of red-cross activities. . . .

In 1865, one year after the signing the treaty of the Red Cross, the birth was witnessed of the International Telegraph Union through the signature of the convention of Paris. . . . It was then agreed that there should be a permanent seat of administration, and the Swiss Confederation was requested to give it shelter. . . .

Next came the Postal Union, in 1874, and immediately upon the exchange of ratifications of the convention, a year later, the central office of this Union was likewise constituted at Berne. . . .

The next important event was the union for the protection of industrial property, which after ten years' negotiation was concluded at Paris in 1883. . . . Under the terms of the convention, Switzerland became liable for the management of the central administration, and the bureau joins the others at Berne. . . .

The last international union and one very properly following the protection of industrial property, was the union for the protection of literary and artistic property, concluded at Berne in 1886.... The failure of the United States to join this union was regarded as depriving the convention of much of its value. Let us hope that so just a cause as that of international copyright may be within measurable distance of triumph in our country and that it will not be long before the reproach will be removed by the request that a place be made for us in the union....

It will not do to close this summary of international organizations and movements in Switzerland without a reference to the first great international court of arbitration which had its seat in Geneva under the treaty of Washington in 1872 to settle the Alabama claims. Over this most memorable court a Swiss was called to preside. Since that time the Swiss high federal council has been frequently addressed and its aid solicited in promoting a permanent international high court of arbitration, a court permanently established for the settlement of international disputes, to take its place beside the other highly useful and successful international courts established at Berne. That the realization of this aspiration and hope would be of almost incalculable benefit must be allowed on all hands....

Whilst it would be vain to look for the political millennium; for the day...

When the war-drum throbs no longer, and the battle-flags are furled
In the parliament of man, the federation of the world,—

we must be content if a stronger organization of international law and a better regulation of international differences makes war rarer.

I am, etc.,

Boyd Winchester

1889 New Constitution for Japan: "The Most Important Political Event in the History of the Empire"

Dispatch from U.S. Minister to Japan Richard B. Hubbard to Secretary of State Thomas F. Bayard

An important aspect of Japan's rapid modernization in the second half of the nineteenth century was the transformation of its political system into one more closely approximating the Western systems of the time. Under Mutsuhito, the Meiji emperor (1867–1912), constitutional government was initiated in 1889 after several years of careful preparation. Suffrage was confined to about 1 percent of the population, basic individual freedoms were proclaimed but limited, and the powers of the new Diet, or parliament, were balanced against those of traditional power centers.

Given these constraints, the American minister's comments on the new constitution seem somewhat exaggerated. Nevertheless, the establishment of constitutional government and a representative Diet were to have an increasingly important impact on Japan's future development.

Tokio, February 14, 1889

Sir:

I have the honor to transmit official copies of the constitution of Japan. . . .

On the 11th February, at 10 o'clock a.m., the constitution was promulgated by his majesty the Emperor in the throne-room of the new palace with suitable and most imposing ceremonies. . . .

The occasion was a most impressive one.

If I may be allowed to express my views, I am convinced . . . that the substance of this most important instrument, its declaration of rights to be held sacred alike by the Crown and its subjects, and to be hereafter inviolate, not only should have made the day memorable forever in the annals of the Empire, but should be a cause of sincere congratulation from all Western nations.

My observation and experience—personal and official—at this court and among this people since 1885, convinces me that all their progress, of which so much has been written and spoken—a progress in wise and freer government, of which this constitution is the highest and noblest testimonial—is not a short-lived or experimental thing, nor a thin veneering of Western civilization, so to speak, on the still vigorous body of oriental political systems, but rather proof of a solid and permanent triumph over the past of her history which ushers in a new era for Japan among the nations.

. . . The event, having been for years eagerly awaited, was celebrated with rejoicing by all Japanese subjects from the homes of fishermen and peasants to the palace of the Emperor.

The day was observed as the most important political event in the history of the Empire throughout the entire country with illuminations, bonfires, military and naval salutes, ringing of bells, processions, and decorations of houses and the streets of towns and cities with bunting and evergreens; and to the inspiring sounds of music the people literally "danced for joy."

In an interview with his majesty in the evening of the day of the promulgation of the constitution, he having invited a large company of guests to dine at the palace, I took occasion to tender to him the earnest congratulations of my Government and of its representative on the completion of this glorious day's work.

The Emperor, with evident gratification, replied, expressing his thanks for my words of congratulation, and expressed the hope that the occasion of the promulgation of the constitution which guaranteed in a liberal sense political and religious liberty to his subjects might be an event which would increase the sympathy and friendship which the Government and people of the United States had so long cherished for Japan.

. . . This . . . greatest political event in the history of the Empire . . . henceforth places the Empire among enlightened constitutional monarchies.

I have, etc.,

Richard B. Hubbard

1889 Revolution in Brazil: "The Most Remarkable . . . in History"

Dispatch from U.S. Minister to Brazil Robert Adams Jr. to Secretary of State James G. Blaine

The Portuguese monarchy fled Europe and established itself in Brazil during the Napoleonic Wars (1804–1815). When Portuguese king John VI returned to Lisbon in 1821, he left his son Pedro I as prince regent of Brazil. The next year Pedro declared Brazilian independence and was named emperor. His son, Pedro II, was the second and last emperor of Brazil, reigning for half a century before he was deposed in a largely peaceful revolution in 1889. The revolution was brought on by the growth of republican sentiment among the middle classes and royal friction with powerful interests in the clergy and the army. Major landowners were disaffected from the regime by the emancipation of the slaves a year earlier (see "Slavery: Down but Not Out," p. 270). Despite these signals of discontent, U.S. Minister Robert Adams, reporting the revolution in this dispatch, was clearly astounded by the turn of events. Adams left Brazil shortly after the fall of the empire, declining an appointment as U.S. minister to the provisional government of the new United States of Brazil. Emperor Pedro II died in exile.

Rio de Janeiro,
November 19, 1889

Sir:

I have the honor to report on the revolution which has just taken place in this country, the most remarkable ever reported in history. Entirely unexpected by the Government or people, the overthrow of the empire has been accomplished without bloodshed, without riotous proceedings, or interruption to the usual avocations of life.

I will endeavor to give a succinct account of the events which led to this result.

In . . . the elections of August 31, . . . the liberal candidates were elected almost universally. With the liberal ministry so strongly intrenched, the Emperor began to take measures to secure the succession to the Princess Isabel, as his health is much impaired. Being distrustful of the army, a national guard was formed, and the regular troops were being gradually transferred to the interior. The idea was to rely on the national guard to maintain order in Rio and protect the succession against any opposition from the people. On Friday, November 15, a . . . battalion was ordered from Rio, but on that morning all the garrison marched to the great square called "Campo da Acclamacao," joined also by the officers and sailors of the navy, the city police, and firemen, all of whom are armed, where they declared for a republic, arrested and deposed the ministry. Baron Ladario, minister of marine, resisted arrest, drew a pistol on the officers which missed fire, when he was immediately shot down, wounded in four places. He served in the United States Navy during the rebellion, and was the only one in the city who made any resistance.

I am happy to state he will probably recover. Marechal Deodoro formed a provisional government. . . .

The Emperor was summoned from Petropolis, and naturally could hardly realize the situation. The ministry having resigned, at midnight he attempted to form a new one, whereupon he was made a prisoner in the palace, all communication denied, and the Imperial family ordered to leave Brazil in twenty-four hours.

The steam-ship *Alagoas* was placed at their service, with the iron frigate *Riachuelo* to escort them. . . .

On Sunday a constitution was promulgated and a complete ministry formed.

The Imperial family sailed at 3 o'clock that afternoon, at which time I telegraphed the Department of that fact, also of the existence of a *de facto* government, and urged the recognition of the "United States of Brazil."

In my opinion the republican form of Government is securely established, even though the present ministry should fall. Our constitution and flag have been copied, and, looking to future relations, I desire our country to be first to acknowledge the Republic.

I mail copies of "Diario Official" of November 16, 17, and 18, containing all official decrees. . . . Decree No. 2 confers a settlement in money on the late Emperor, his acceptance of which is considered an abdication.

                I am, etc.,

                Robert Adams, Jr.

1890 A Sacred and Curious Gift from Japan: A Rope of Human Hair

Dispatch from U.S. Minister to Japan John F. Swift to Secretary of State James G. Blaine

American representatives abroad frequently are entrusted with gifts for American dignitaries or for the American people (see "Arabian Horses for President Tyler," p. 113). *This dispatch reports a very different sort of gift that a group of Japanese monks made to the Smithsonian Institution. The relic in question was transmitted safely to Washington and deposited with the Smithsonian. Secretary of State James Blaine penned a note of thanks for the "greatly prized gift."*

Tokio, March 18, 1890

Sir:

Some time since Mr. V. Marshall Law, a citizen of the United States residing in Tokio, informed me that he had in his possession a section of rope made of human hair which had been used as an ordinary cable in lifting building material in the construction of a Buddhist temple at Kioto, in Japan, which he desired to transmit as a free gift to the Smithsonian Institution for final deposit as an object of general public interest. . . . As I understood Mr. Law to say, the priests of the temple only consented to part with the piece of rope upon the positive assurance from him that the rope was not for Mr. Law, but for the American nation, and that it would be placed in the Smithsonian Institution as a public deposit, and, in fact, that they intended it as a gift to the people of the United States, positively declining to allow any private person to have what they regarded as a sacred thing.

Under these circumstances, I have thought it proper to assist in its conveyance and delivery . . . in the belief that you will consider this curious relic worthy of being so officially forwarded and approve my action.

I have the honor, therefore, to request that you will cause the section of human hair rope, with the accompanying photograph of the entire rolls of cable still remaining at the new Buddhist temple at Kioto, as well as the papers and documents, including a copy of the letter from Mr. Law, to be delivered to the Smithsonian Institution in such manner as you may deem suitable and proper.

I have, etc.,

John F. Swift

1890 Revolution and War in Central America
Dispatches from U.S. Minister to Central America Lansing B. Mizner to Secretary of State James G. Blaine

When war broke out in Central America in 1890, U.S. Minister Lansing Mizner found himself accredited to both belligerents, Guatemala and El Salvador, as well as to neighboring states. As a result, he was well positioned to help mediate a settlement. This series of succinct dispatches describes the brief hostilities and their resolution.

The curt nature of the dispatches illustrates how the advent of the telegraph transformed the nature of diplomatic reporting on fast-breaking events. Some of the dispatches were hand-carried to El Paso, Texas, from where they were transmitted telegraphically to Washington; others were transmitted through the U.S. legation in Mexico City. Their brevity provides readers with only the scantiest outline of the breaking news. Mizner supplemented his telegraphic dispatches with the traditional longer ones, but they were so slow in reaching Washington that they had little impact on U.S. policy. The curious third-person reporting style used by Mizner in his telegrams was standard at the time.

Revolution

Guatemala, June 23, 1890

Mr. Mizner informs Mr. Blaine . . . of a successful revolution in Salvador on the night of the 22d instant, during which the President and others were assassinated.

War

Via El Paso, Tex., July 8, 1890

Mr. Mizner reports that serious troubles between the Government of Guatemala and Salvadorian provisional leaders exist; that armies of 10,000 are prepared for battle in either state, and that the presence of a United States naval vessel on the Pacific coast of Central America is necessary for the protection of our interests in those states.

Request for Assistance

Guatemala, July 22, 1890

Mr. Mizner reports the great apprehension and danger existing in the city of Guatemala, the rumored defeat of the Guatemalan army and of the nonarrival of any answer to his communications for two weeks. He adds that Guatemala, Nicaragua, and Costa Rica—Honduras consenting by telegraph—have signed a treaty securing constitutional government in Salvador, and that they request the good offices and moral support of the United States. He asks that instructions be sent him by way of El Paso, Tex., and suggests the necessity for a United States naval vessel in Central American waters.

Armies at Rest

Guatemala, July 29, 1890

Through the United States legation in Mexico Mr. Mizner reports the interruption of diplomatic correspondence by the Provisional Government of Salvador, and says that he will press his demand for an explanation thereof. He advises Mr. Blaine that the armies are resting after many engagements, and that it has been announced by the President of Guatemala that all the expenses of the war shall be paid by Salvador.

Good Offices

Guatemala, August 18, 1890

Mr. Mizner informs Mr. Blaine that . . . when in Salvador on the 12th instant he offered the good offices and mediation of the United States to the Provisional Government there and they were accepted. Returning to Guatemala City on the 14th instant and finding that our good offices had been accepted there also, he reports that he convened the diplomatic body that evening and bases of peace were suggested by the meeting, of which the ministers of both belligerent powers signified their acceptance. . . . The terms of the agreement, he goes on to say, were that the Provisional President of Salvador should retire from the exercise of all civil functions, and that the First Vice President should assume power in his stead for three weeks, and call an election for President; . . . that both Governments should withdraw their armies . . . and that they should be reduced to a peace footing; that no demand should be made for reclamation or for any indemnity. . . .

Armies Withdraw

Via El Paso, Tex.,
September 3, 1890

Mr. Mizner reports the withdrawal of both armies from the frontiers and their rapid disbandment, the success of the officious mediation of the diplomatic corps, and the approval with which the country regards the course of that body. He adds that the intention is to declare peace the coming week.

Armies Disband

Guatemala, September 11, 1890

Mr. Mizner telegraphs through Mr. Ryan [U.S. minister to Mexico], announcing the complete compliance with the bases of peace and the disbandment of the armies, and stating that the presence of the vessels of war are no longer required.

Peace and Order

Guatemala, September 21, 1890

Mr. Ryan states that a telegram from Minister Mizner asks him to telegraph the Department that peace and order reign in Guatemala. . . .

1890 Conditions in Haiti: "Full of Promise"
Dispatch from U.S. Minister and Consul General to Haiti
Frederick Douglass to Secretary of State James G. Blaine

Frederick Douglass already had completed a long and distinguished career as an abolitionist and crusader for freedom when at the age of seventy-two President Benjamin Harrison appointed him as minister to Haiti. Although Douglass was the best-known African American to represent his country abroad, he was not the first—Ebenezer Bassett had preceded him as minister to Haiti (1869–1877) and William Liedesdorff had served as vice consul in Mexican San Francisco (1846–1847).

Much of Douglass's time in Haiti was spent in an ultimately unsuccessful attempt to obtain a naval base for the United States. In this dispatch Douglass describes a rare peaceful period in Haiti, a country plagued with instability through most of the nineteenth century.

Douglass served in Haiti from 1889 to 1891. His tenure there took a toll on his health; he died four years after his return to the United States.

Port-au-Prince, June 27, 1890

Sir:

The political situation in Haiti, which exhibited a momentary perturbation a few weeks ago . . . speedily assumed, after that affair, even more than its usual tranquil aspect. At no time since the election of General Hyppolite has the country afforded stronger assurance of the stability of its Government than at present. If there is not perfect concord between its executive and legislative departments, which may be true, the alleged differences are not such as to cause any doubt that they will be easily composed in the spirit of patriotism and with the settled determination manifested on the part of both branches of the Government to heal as speedily as possible all the wounds left by the late revolution.

The augmentation of public confidence is seen on every hand—in the appreciation of the national currency, in the manifold projects for improving streets, roads, and wharves, and in the increasing number of private dwellings in process of erection both within and without the limits of Port-au-Prince. The sound of the hammer and the trowel is heard late and early. Soon an electric cable from Port-au-Prince will connect with the cable at the Mole St. Nicolas, and thus bring Port-au-Prince *en rapport* with the outside would.

But, perhaps, one of the best guaranties of peace, as it certainly is one of the best guaranties of prosperity, is providential, and that is a large harvest of coffee. In this respect the outlook at this writing is full of promise. The coffee plantations of Haiti have never looked better than now, and on this much hope is predicated for the country. It is not, however, to be presumed from this favorable aspect of the political and material situation that there is no language of complaint to be heard in the voices of the citizens or to be read in the columns of the newspapers.

I am, etc.,
Frederick Douglass

1891 Civil War in Chile
Dispatch from U.S. Minister to Chile Patrick Egan to
Secretary of State James G. Blaine

Although Chile won a decisive victory over Peru and Bolivia in the 1883 War of the Pacific (see "Lima Surrenders to Chilean Forces," p. 239), all was not well at home. Tensions over the role of the Church, differences between liberals and conservatives, and disputes between Congress and the president led to civil war in 1891. Congressional forces took the city of Valparaiso in August, leading to the resignation of President José Manuel Balmaceda. The dramatic events in the capital of Santiago are reported here by the U.S. minister to Chile, who dwells at length on the issue of refugees and asylum-seekers at the legation—a problem frequently encountered by U.S. missions during times of trouble abroad.

The victorious Chilean congressional forces perceived that the United States and other countries giving refuge to leaders of the former regime were hostile to the new government. This led to an extended period of strained relations between the United States and Chile. The legation of Argentina, which gave refuge to President Balmaceda, found itself in an even more awkward position. Balmaceda remained a virtual prisoner in that legation for three weeks and then, in despair, took his own life.

Santiago, August 31, 1891

Sir:

. . . On the 28th was fought at Placillas, near Valparaiso and Viña del Mar, another sanguinary battle, in which the Government forces, amounting to about 9,000 men, were again completely routed, with the loss of about 2,000 in killed and wounded. . . .

The true result of the battle only became known outside of the President and some two others at close to midnight on the 28th, and then the excitement was intense. I immediately went to the Moneda at midnight, saw Señor Manuel A. Zañartu, minister of foreign relations, and from him received the confirmation of the news and the assurance . . . that President Balmaceda was at that moment writing his . . . resignation. At about 3 o'clock on same night the wife of the President, his three daughters and two sons, came to this legation for asylum, and are still here, but will leave to-night. All that night and next day numbers of prominent Government supporters, including ministers of state, senators, deputies, judges, and others, sought asylum with their families in this and other legations; and I have now in my house about eighty refugees. The only legation which closed its doors and denied asylum was that of England, which refused to admit a single person. The Spanish legation has about the same number of persons that are here, and the French, the

German, the Argentine, and the Brazilian legations have each more or less people.

In the morning of 29th, at 8 o'clock, was publicly read the resignation of President Balmaceda and the temporary transfer of authority to Gen. Baquedano. . . .

As soon as the news got out through the city the military and police became greatly demoralized; the latter, about 1,000 men, dissolved and absolutely disappeared with their horses and arms, and most of the military officers abandoned their posts, leaving their men without direction.

By 10 o'clock in the morning mobs began to collect, and very soon began the most desperate attacks on the houses and property of all the prominent supporters of the late Government. This sack was not a spontaneous outburst, but the result of a carefully organized plan, carried out under regular gangs, commanded by recognized leaders, each gang having a regular list of houses to be sacked. It was originated by the more extreme sections of the revolutionary element, but I am quite sure without the knowledge of the responsible leaders of the movement. The sacking continued nearly all the day. The palatial residences . . . were completely gutted, all the furniture and valuables destroyed or carried away, and in most cases even the doors and windows of the houses carried off. The loss inflicted by this wanton destruction can not be less than some $5,000,000, and the lives of the proprietors would also have paid the sacrifice had they not sought asylum in the legations and other places of safety. . . .

Having so many prominent refugees, and especially the family of the ex-President, I considered it prudent to ask for special protection, and I have now a guard of 10 soldiers at the legation supplied to me by the authorities.

I have, etc.,

Patrick Egan

1891 A Chinese Emperor's Daily Routine: "More Work than Any Other Sovereign"

Dispatch from U.S. Minister to China Charles Denby Jr. to Secretary of State James G. Blaine

The Kuang Hsu emperor (1875–1908) was the last significant monarch of imperial China; the Manchu dynasty ended just three years after his death. For China the years of his reign were characterized by domestic upheaval, foreign wars, and Western encroachment. But the emperor, in fact, had little more than nominal power; the Chinese court was dominated by his aunt, Dowager Empress Tz'u-hsi. In this dispatch the U.S. minister describes a typical day in the life of the then twenty-one-year-old emperor, who apparently rose at midnight and slept in the afternoon.

Peking, December 28, 1891

Sir:

It may be of some interest to you as indicative of progress in China to know that the Emperor has commenced the study of the English language. Two students of the Tung-wen college are his teachers. They attend him every morning at 1 o'clock. For several days they were required to kneel in his presence, but latterly they have been permitted to stand while giving him his lesson. It is said that he has a remarkable memory and is learning fast. This addition to his ordinary labors shows that he is possessed of considerable firmness and determination. I suppose that he does more work than any other sovereign in the world. His day commences at 12 [midnight]. He first sees the members of his privy council; then he devotes an hour to the study of the Manchurian language; then he studies English; then receives one or more members of the various boards, and then the governors, viceroys, and other officials who have come to Peking to be presented and for instructions.

Whenever any of the numerous boards has anything to communicate to the Emperor, two of their number go to the palace at 2 a.m. They wait sometimes two hours before one of them is ordered to the imperial presence. The Emperor receives them alone. He is seated on a raised platform; they are on their knees. It is said that the ministers who thus attend the Emperor take some pains to pad their knees with cushions. . . . After the receptions are over the Emperor rides on horseback and practices shooting with the bow and arrow. These exercises are *de rigueur*; they are prescribed and can not be avoided. A given period of time is allotted to them by ancient custom which amounts to law. The Emperor retires about 2 p.m. The diet of the Emperor is rigorously prescribed. It is supposed that he takes his meals alone. Should he desire to partake of any article not on the menu, the board having charge of the imperial table must be consulted before he is supplied. A son of Prince Ching is also studying English under a competent teacher. It is a matter of regret to foreigners that the Emperor is not physically strong, and that there is danger that he will not be long-lived. It is believed that he favors progress.

I trust that these details will not be considered as too undignified for transmission.

I have etc.,
Charles Denby

1892 Famine in Russia: "The Distress . . . Can Hardly Be Overstated"
Dispatch from U.S. Minister to Russia Charles Emory Smith to Secretary of State James G. Blaine

Russia modernized rapidly in the second half of the nineteenth century. The serfs were emancipated in 1861 (see "Emancipation of the Russian Serfs," p. 136) *and by the 1880s Russia was rapidly becoming industrialized. The movement toward modernization, however, did not translate into prosperity for the peasantry and the working class, which continued to live in conditions of deprivation. Their plight was heightened by the great famine of 1891–1892, which dealt a devastating blow to millions of Russians.*

St. Petersburg, January 11, 1892

Sir:

. . . There are thirteen provinces of European Russia where the drought was well-nigh unbroken and where the famine may be said to be general. . . . There are five others where it prevails in part. . . . Some conception of the magnitude of the calamity may be gathered from a few comparisons. The thirteen provinces where the destitution is general are a third larger than all Germany. They cover an area equal to that of the States of Maine, New Hampshire, Vermont, Massachusetts, Rhode Island, Connecticut, New York, New Jersey, Pennsylvania, Delaware, Maryland, Virginia, West Virginia, North Carolina, South Carolina, Georgia, and Kentucky, all put together. They have about the same population, that is, about 27,000,000. . . .

The distress through most of this vast agricultural section, embracing much of the richest and ordinarily most fruitful soil of Russia, can hardly be overstated. The destitution, it is true, is not universal. There are those whose accumulations save them from want. There are spots blessed with irrigation where, surrounded by the fatal blight, the harvests were good, but at the best the proportion of sufferers is enormous. An official estimate made some time ago placed the number of persons who were without food or means of support and who require assistance through the winter at nearly 14,000,000. In reality, appalling as this figure is, it is probably below the truth. It must be borne in mind that it is not the failure of the harvest for a single year alone which has produced this disaster. For three successive years the crops have fallen short of the average. There was thus little reserve of grain in the desolated provinces, and the great deficiency of the past season finds the storehouses already well-nigh empty. . . .

It is important, first of all, to understand that the great proportion of the peasants make no savings and are wholly dependent on the yearly crop. If widespread and long-continued drought makes the earth unfruitful, their only hope is outside relief. But the general scarcity of provisions is far from being the only misery. The loss of the harvest inevitably draws a long train of various evils. The crops are the foundation of the whole economic structure. When they fail the Government misses revenue and the peasants lack the necessaries of life; clothing, firewood, taxes, farming requirements, sustenance of horses and cattle, all depend on this one resource. At present in some sections it is almost as difficult to get fuel as food. The suffering is nearly as great from cold as from hunger. Neighborhoods huddle together in the most available house to keep warm. In some quarters, away from the forests the barns have found their way, board by board, to the fire place. In extreme cases the thatched roofs of the peasants' homes are torn up that the straw may feed the dying embers. Under the stress of overmastering necessity, clothing is almost given away for bread. Horses and cattle are sacrificed at a tithe of their value. Fodder is as scarce as human food, and the support of the farm animals becomes a burden. . . .

During the winter days there is little or no work to be had, and the only recourse is to wait for relief. Not infrequently fathers of families have left their wives and children to fight the battle of want alone and have gone away because they could do nothing, and their absence would leave fewer mouths to feed at home. . . .

These terrible conditions inevitably produce disease. . . .

Both the Government and people of Russia are deeply sensible of the spontaneous offerings in various parts of the United States, and the Emperor's ministers, as well as others, have spoken of them to me with expressions of the deepest appreciation and gratitude.

I have, etc.,

Chas. Emory Smith

1893 Punishment in Persia: Eighteen Lashes for Insulting an American

Dispatch from U.S. Minister to Persia Watson R. Sperry to Secretary of State John W. Foster

This unusual dispatch gives special meaning to the diplomat's duty of protecting Americans abroad and illustrates vividly the deference accorded to Westerners in much of the world throughout the Victorian era. Watson Sperry's career as a diplomat was brief, consisting of just six months' service as U.S. envoy in Persia.

Teheran, Persia,
January 16, 1893

Sir:

I have the honor to report that on the 10th January instant, a complaint was received at this legation from the Rev. Lewis F. Esselstyn, in regard to an insult received the day before, the 9th of January, in the streets of Teheran by Mrs. Lewis F. Esselstyn, his wife, and a request made that the offender be arrested and punished. . . .

Mrs. Esselstyn's case was promptly brought to the attention of the police, and arrest was made, but not of the right person; this error was promptly rectified by arresting the real offender, who was brought to this legation, identified, and his guilt proven, and adequate punishment administered, under such circumstances and conditions as are fully set forth in the report of the matter which I made to Mr. Esselstyn on the 14th January. I take pleasure in stating that the public authorities of Teheran supported and cooperated with the legation in every respect.

The munshi of this legation was sent as an official witness of the punishment. A copy of his report in Persian and English accompanies this dispatch.

. . . The necessity for the punishment of the boy was as frankly admitted by the public authorities of Teheran as it was evident to me, although heretofore the duty of whipping men or boys has never been laid upon me.

I have, etc.,

Watson R. Sperry

DECLARATION BY THE MUNSHI OF THE LEGATION

I, Mirza Abul Kassan Khan, the chief munshi of the United States legation in compliance with the orders of his excellency the minister of the United States, on the evening of Friday the 23 of Jamadi the second, A.H., corresponding to the 13th of January, 1893, went to the chief police office of this city for the purpose of being a witness to the punishment of Ali Akbar Khan, who had insulted Mrs. Esselstyn, a native of the United States of America, in the public streets, hereby testify that eighteen stripes with a cat of five tails (over a thin coat and shirt) were given on the back and shoulders of Ali Akbar Khan, and so severely was the punishment inflicted that the culprit was overcome by it, and he cried, and begged for mercy. Thereupon I, on the part of the legation and the lady insulted, ordered the boy to be released and be let go.

Then, in my presence, a bond was taken from the culprit, his brother, and uncle, binding him over to keep the peace toward Mrs. Esselstyn for the remainder of his life.

Mirza Abul Kassan

1893 Hawaii: A U.S. Protectorate
Dispatch from U.S. Minister to Hawaii John L. Stevens to Secretary of State John W. Foster

As early as the 1820s the United States emerged as the dominant commercial power in Hawaii. In the 1850s American representatives in Hawaii sought unsuccessfully to annex the islands (see "First Attempt to Annex Hawaii," p. 126). By 1890 American settlers were dominating trade, business, agriculture, and even the national legislature. When independent-minded Queen Liliuokalani ascended to the throne in 1891, the stage was set for a confrontation. In 1893 her policy of "Hawaii for the Hawaiians" sparked a revolt by American settlers intent on provoking American annexation. U.S. Minister John Stevens, an ardent annexationist, seized the moment by ordering U.S. Marines to come ashore to keep order. He then hoisted the Stars and Stripes over Honolulu and declared a "temporary" U.S. protectorate until the new provisional government could establish itself more firmly. In this dispatch Stevens explains his reasons for establishing a U.S. protectorate over Hawaii. Just two weeks later a treaty of annexation was signed.

This was not the end of the story, however. The United States was in the midst of a presidential transition and the treaty was not ratified. When Grover Cleveland became president in March 1893, he withdrew the treaty, sent a new anti-imperialist minister to replace Stevens, and recognized the new Hawaiian republic as an independent country. Not until 1898, when Cleveland had left office and the Spanish-American War had altered American views on expansion into the Pacific, did the United States formally annex the Hawaiian Islands.

Honolulu, February 1, 1893

Sir:

To-day the undersigned and Capt. Wiltse of the *Boston* are compelled to assume a grave responsibility. The inclosed copies of official notes will explain the reasons which have led to this action on our part.

I have time before the departure of the mail steamer only to state briefly the additional reasons which caused us to assume temporary protectorate of these islands. The Provisional Government must have time to organize a new police and to discipline a small military force. When the monarchy died by its own hand there was no military force in the islands but the royal guard of about 75 natives, not in effective force equal to 20 American soldiers. These were promptly discarded by the Provisional Government, except 16 left as the guard of the fallen Queen at her house.

The white men here, as well as the natives, have not been much accustomed to the use of arms. There are scarcely any men familiar with military discipline. Companies are now being organized and drilled. They must have a few weeks for drill. Only a small force of a few hundred will be required, but these must be disciplined men. So far the Provisional Government has been sustained by the uprising and union of the business men and best citizens. Bankers, merchants, clerks, professional men, respectable mechanics have stood manfully by the new Government and kept guard by night. This kind of defense must give place to a small, reliable military force. Time is the necessity of the new Government. There are 40,000 Chinese and Japanese on the islands, and evil-disposed persons might stir some of them to disorder. But the chief elements of evil are in Honolulu, where are the renegade whites at the head of the lottery and opium rings, and a considerable number of hoodlum foreigners and the more vicious of the natives.

Another important reason for our action is the possibility of the arrival here of a British war vessel, and that the English minister here, thus aided, might try to press unduly the Provisional Government. With the islands under our protection we think the English minister will not attempt to insist that his Government has the right to interfere while our flag is over the Government building. This is all I have time to write before the departure of the mail. We shall continue to maintain our present position with great caution and firmness until we hear from the President through the Secretary of State. As a necessary precaution against all contingencies, I advise that Admiral Skerrett be promptly sent here with one or two ships in addition to the *Boston*.

I am, sir, etc.,

John L. Stevens

1893 Riots in Peru: Bullet in Leg but Archives Saved
Dispatch from U.S. Minister to Peru John Hicks to
Secretary of State Walter Q. Gresham

While anti-American riots and the deliberate destruction of American embassies abroad have become somwhat commonplace over the past century, on occasion U.S. offices—and officers—also have been the accidental victims of civil disturbances.

Lima, April 3, 1893

Sir:

Late on the evening of Monday, March 27, a report reached Lima that a serious riot had occurred at Mollendo, a small village about 400 miles from Lima, in the south of Peru, in which the American consular agency was sacked and the acting consular agent wounded by a bullet. I at once telegraphed Mr. A. J. Daugherty, consul at Callao, to ask if he had received any report from the consular agent. He had not, and then, at my suggestion, after the arrival of the steamer, he telegraphed the consular agent as follows:

> Henry Meier:
> Acting Consular Agent, Mollendo:
> Are you wounded? Was consulate invaded? Nothing received from you by mail.
>
> Daugherty

Two holidays intervened when no business was done, and on April 1, Mr. Meier replied:

> Bullet in the left leg. Office partly destroyed. Archives saved. Wrote today. Feel better.
>
> Meier

. . . The unfortunate affair is explained in this way: Senor de Cazorla, a prominent Peruvian and member of the Peruvian Senate . . . died at La Paz, Bolivia, a short time before, and his remains were brought home and buried. The Masonic lodge at Mollendo, of which Senor de Cazorla had been a member . . . made arrangements to pay their respects. . . . About 8:30 p.m. the lodge room was attacked by a mob, which threw stones and clubs at the doors and windows, broke up the meeting, drove the audience into the street, and created a period of terror and consternation. . . .

The office of Henry Meier, the acting consular agent of the United States, was near the lodge room and suffered from the attack. Several persons were reported seriously wounded by stones and Mr. Meier is said to be suffering from the effects of a bullet in his leg. One person is said to have been killed.

It is said that the action of the mob grew out of a bitterness felt by the people against the Masonic fraternity, and it is also further alleged that one or more priests were present at the time of the attack and urged the rioters to their work. . . .

Without having the official report of the acting consular agent at hand, I am of the impression that the attack was a domestic affair growing out of religious differences, and that the damage or injury to the consular agency was incidental to the attack upon the Masonic meeting.

As soon as the official report is received from Mr. Meier, I shall give it prompt attention.

I am, etc.,

John Hicks

1894 The Mosquito Reservation: "American to the Core"
Dispatch from U.S. Minister to Nicaragua, Costa Rica, and El Salvador Lewis Baker to Secretary of State Walter Q. Gresham

The "Mosquito Reservation," or Mosquitia, comprised what is now eastern Nicaragua. The British established settlements there in the mid-1700s as a consequence of their rivalry with Spain in the Caribbean and in the hope of exploiting the precious woods of the indigenous forests. By the 1820s the British had declared a formal protectorate over the Mosquito Indians or the "Kingdom of the Mosquitoes." In midcentury the area gained greater international significance as a possible route for a transoceanic canal. The United States, not wanting a canal to be controlled by a European power, pressured the British to withdraw. In 1850 Great Britain and the United States agreed by means of the Clayton-Bulwar Treaty that neither would colonize any portion of Central America. The British recognized Nicaraguan sovereignty over the area in 1860, but did not yield political control until 1894. By that time, however, American commercial interests had eclipsed those of Great Britain in the territory, and the transfer of power to Nicaragua was not without controversy. The U.S. minister, who was residing in Managua, visited Bluefields, the major town of the "Reservation," shortly before its return to Nicaragua and filed this dispatch on conditions there.

Bluefields, May 2, 1894

Sir:

In obedience to your cable . . . I lost no time in procuring . . . information . . . as to the . . . present condition of affairs in the Mosquito Reservation. . . .

This is a prosperous community from Bluefields to Rama, a distance of 60 miles, a remarkably thrifty community for Central America—the most prosperous, I think, within the five Central American States. The trade is considerable already, has been rapidly growing . . . and is substantially all with the United States.

The most enterprising business men are chiefly Americans. The town is American to the core. There is no semblance of the slothful, indolent and filthy habits so conspicuous in the interior towns. The houses are clean and handsomely painted; the women dress neatly, and are not made beasts of burden; the men are busy at useful occupations and do not devote their time to petty politics, cockfighting, and parading with muskets. The community has been peaceable throughout. No soldiers existed, for none were required. The civil power has always had full sway, and justice has generally been secured through the courts. . . .

There is a distinctively antagonistic feeling among the Spanish Nicaraguans toward Americans. The former are jealous of the enterprise and prosperity of the latter. . . . The Nicaraguans say that Americans come here, get rich in a few years, and then carry their wealth to the States. The fact is to the contrary; the Americans spend money liberally in improvements which add to the prosperity of the country.

There are a large number of Americans in business—agriculture, mining, lumbering, and in commercial enterprises—who have acquired titles to lands. Many have expended large sums of money in improving and developing their lands.

Substantially everybody—business men and laborers—in this reserve use the English language and they know no other. The Nicaraguans insist that the Spanish language must be used in all business and public affairs, in the courts, etc. . . .

No American here has denied to Nicaragua the sovereign power over this territory, but they do believe they have a right to appeal to the Government of the United States with confidence that the Government will use its best offices with the Government of Nicaragua for the protection of their vested rights in this territory, and for securing to them a local government which shall protect them and their families in their persons and property. . . .

It will be necessary for a United States man-of-war to remain as close to this harbor as possible, until the two Governments come to an amicable understanding by which American residents will be protected.

The natives of every shade are in full accord with the Americans. The Nicaraguans, being of different blood, speaking a strange language, possessing radically different ideas of methods of government, can not assimilate with the English-speaking people here. . . .

I will remain here probably two weeks yet, leaving for Grey Town about the 13th of May. . . .

Awaiting your instructions at Managua, I am, etc.,

Lewis Baker

1894 Troubles in Baghdad

Dispatches from U.S. Consul in Baghdad John C. Sundberg to Assistant Secretary of State Edwin F. Uhl

The United States opened its first consulate in Baghdad in January 1889. Consul John Henry Haynes traveled overland by caravan from Constantinople to Alexandretta to reach his post, a journey of over three months. Haynes was captivated by the ancient splendors of Mesopotamia; after a little over a year as consul he resigned to join the University of Pennsylvania's archaeological excavations in the region.

Haynes was replaced by John Sundberg, a physician who had migrated to San Francisco from his native Norway. Sundberg chose the ocean route to Baghdad, traveling by steamer to Hong Kong then to India. From Calcutta, he reported that he would be delayed several weeks because his wife had contracted pneumonia, leading to premature childbirth, while sailing around Singapore and through the Straits. From Calcutta the Sundbergs traversed India by train and then took passage on a boat to Basra. Sundberg had his first run-in with local authorities when he stepped off the boat. A lazy and officious customs inspector left him and his still weak wife standing in the desert sun for two hours for no apparent reason. To get action, Sundberg reported, he had not only to pull the man's beard but also to twist it! Sundberg's official dispatches provide glimpses of some of the problems and issues facing early consuls in Baghdad.

Epidemic

Bagdad, June 20, 1894

Sir:

I beg to report that since the flood of which I wrote in dispatch No. 26, dated May 10, began to subside, a malignant and very fatal fever has prevailed in the city and suburbs, more especially among the Fellahs (tillers of the soil) down along the river; and these poor people are left to die without the aid of doctor or medicine. Having lost all their crops, I also fear the survivors of the fever will soon be starving. I learned only yesterday of this sad state of affairs, and this morning, before sun rise, I embarked in a kuffah (a circular boat made of wicker work and coated with bitumen) armed with two ounces of quinine, some calomel, Dovers powder and Epson salts, for a reconnoitering tour among the huts of the Fellahs with which the banks of both sides of the river, for thirty or forty miles down, are thickly dotted. About four miles down I landed; and in the first court yard I looked into, I saw scattered all over and mixed up with donkeys, buffaloes, dogs and chickens, heaps of filthy rags, around which millions of flies held carnival, and which when stirred, disclosed, each a human being. I salamed and enquired about their health, and was told they were nearly all sick. I then said that I was a physician and had come to give them medicine, upon which they set up a cry of lamentation, saying they had no money with which to pay. Evidently the word physician was to them synonymous with highway robber or tax collector. On being told that I would treat them, not for money, but for Allah's sake, the sound of their voices changed to shouts of jubilation. Alas that their momentary hopes and rejoicings should be so groundless! The fever, of paludal [marshy] origin, as the surroundings fully showed, was mostly of a continued type, though in some cases intermittent. As soon as the purpose of my visit was known, crowds began to gather from neighboring huts begging me to come and see their sick, and I continued my visits, giving each adult 20 grains of quinine with other remedies according to needs, as long as my stock of drugs held out. From what I could gather the mortality during the past week had been very high, many dying after only one day's illness, others holding out from three to five days. The misery I saw no one who has not practised medicine in the Orient, and among the poor during epidemics, can have any conception of; and I was told that it was the same as far as the river bank was settled.

I walked home again, and everywhere were stagnant pools of green slimy water, emitting a stench which even I, who have been toughened in such matters, could hardly stand. A caravan of Persian pilgrims bound for Kerbelah and Nedjef, holy shrines venerated by the Shiah sect of Mohammedans, was just arriving, and many of the mules were loaded with coffins containing corpses that had been dead for months, some perhaps for years. The immigration of defunct Persians having just been reopened, many thousand corpses will pass through Bagdad this summer for their final resting place. It is a source of both revenue and pestilence.

During the recent inundation most of the cemeteries which completely surround Bagdad, were under water, and the dead had to be buried, wherever a spot of elevated ground could be found outside the walls; and I am told that the graves were again opened at night by robbers for the sake of the clothes the corpses had on. The graves of the poor are always thus plundered. That this is a means of spreading contagion will be readily understood. But the fear of having the graves plundered led, more than at other times, to surreptitious interments in the cellars of the dwelling houses—a common practice during epidemics.

During the feast of the sacrifice which began in the evening of the 13th inst. (the 9th of the month Zil-Hyjah the last month of the Mohammedan year, which is eleven days shorter than ours) and ended on the 17th (13th Zil-Hyjah) probably not less than 20,000 sheep were sacrificed, besides buffaloes and camels. This wholesale slaughter which is done with barbarous cruelty, will not improve the sanitary condition. Last year it was followed by an epidemic of homicides which preceded the outbreak of cholera.

Great floods, such as we have witnessed this year, are usually, so the health inspector as well as other old citizens inform me, followed by the plague, and a visitation of this dreaded scourge is expected next winter, if not sooner.

If I had a large supply of quinine and other remedies, I might be able to save the lives of some of the fever sufferers; but with no salary and but a trifling income from fees, what can I do? I have given two ounces of quinine today to about fifty patients; but who will give tomorrow or the day after, and who will help the many hundreds that I cannot reach? Shall we shut our eyes and ears and hearts, and let our fellow beings perish without an effort to save?

> I have the Honor to be, Sir,
> Your obedient servant
>
> John C. Sundberg

Slavery

> Bagdad, July 9, 1894

Sir:

Although slavery has theoretically been abolished in Turkey, and slave trade is now forbidden, practically they continue to flourish, and will probably so continue, as long as the Mohammedan religion prevails. Slaves, it is true, are no longer bought and sold openly in the market places, but nearly all prominent men, both in Bagdad and Bassorah own domestic slaves and black eunuchs still guard the harems and profit by love intrigues. The greater number of slaves are carried from Africa across the Red Sea to Jeddah, where they are sold to pilgrims and brought by them overland through Central Arabia, which is yet the favorite route for pilgrims to Mecca, though many go now by sea, several steamers leaving Bassorah every year. Some slave dhows [ships] land their cargo at Muscat, whence the slaves are carried either by land or coasting craft to Bassorah, care being taken to avoid British cruisers and also the Persian war ship, the

"Persipolis." If a slaver is boarded, however, the cargo will nearly always claim to be the crew and their wives, and the vessel is allowed to proceed unmolested. Many of the Arab slavers fly the French flag. Circassian slaves for the harems are brought from Constantinople, Trebizoud or Erzroou.

> I have the Honor to be Sir,
> Your obedient servant
>
> John C. Sundberg

Persian Rugs: A Health Hazard

> Bagdad, October 25, 1894

Sir:

With regard to invoice No. 181 of 15 bales of old and new Persian rugs, shipped to New York by Keropi Konyourndjian of Bagdad, it was found impossible to particularize contents of each bale as required according to dispatch No. 6, dated April 6, 1893. As the goods, however, were packed in the custom house, it is not probable that other and more valuable goods could be secreted in the bales—at least not without bribing the custom house officers who, by the way, are not incorruptible in this city.

I desire to point out—nay, I consider it my duty to do so—that Persian rugs, whether old or new—and in this shipment are both—are a menace to public health.

Even "new" rugs may have lain years in dwellings so filthy that no American who has not resided in the Orient and associated intimately with the natives, can form any idea thereof. There they receive bacteria-laden dust (tubercle bacilli, diphtheria bacilli, possibly plague bacilli, and other numerous hordes of pathogenic microbes), many of which—tubercle bacilli for instance—possess great vitality. On the journey from Persia to Bagdad they have also in all probability, nay, certainty, been exposed to the exhalations of putrid corpses, as all caravans from Persia bring defunct immigrants for interment at the sacred shrines of Kerbela and Nejef.

I would not have a Persian carpet in my house except after the most thorough disinfection by hot steam and SO_2, or chlorine gas which no doubt would destroy the color.

I regard them as very dangerous and I doubt not but the Surgeon-General of the Marine Hospital Service as well as Surgeon-General Sternberg or Surgeons J. S. Billings, or A. L. Gilion, or anyone else who has devoted his life to sanitary science, will agree with me.

I have sounded the warning note and with that done my duty.

> I have the Honor to be, Sir,
> Your obedient servant
>
> John C. Sundberg

1894 The Sino-Japanese War
Dispatch from U.S. Minister to China Charles Denby Jr. to Secretary of State Walter Q. Gresham

Rivalry for dominance over Korea led Japan and China to war in 1894. Japan's rapid and decisive victories in land and sea battles demonstrated the power it had developed in less than twenty-five years of the Meiji period of modernization. The war resulted in Korea's formal independence—with Japan as the predominant outside power—and the cession of Formosa and other territory from China to Japan. In addition, Japan won new international respect and was granted the same treaty rights in China as the Western powers. China, in contrast, was pushed further into decline as foreign powers scrambled for additional concessions in the war's aftermath. This dispatch from the U.S. minister to China reports the defeat of the Chinese forces.

Peking, September 22, 1894

Sir:

I have the honor to state that the vague news which reached Peking some days ago of a battle at Ping-yang, in Korea, on the 15th instant, has now been confirmed.

It is reported that 16,000 out of 20,000 Chinese troops engaged were killed or captured and the remainder dispersed. The strength of the Japanese forces engaged is unknown, but they are supposed to have numbered about 40,000. The Viceroy Li is said to take a most despondent view of the outlook.

Some details of the naval engagement reported in my telegram of the 19th instant are also at hand. . . . Every ship of the Chinese squadron is reported badly damaged, so much so that the protection of the gulf of Pechili is supposed to be no longer possible.

Mr. von Hanneken, a German military officer attached to the staff of the Chinese Admiral Ting, reports that in evolution, tactics, and discipline the Japanese showed themselves superior, but that the bravery of the Chinese was unquestionable. . . .

No newspaper reports of these battles are as yet at hand.

I have, etc.,

Chas. Denby, Jr.

1894 An Arrest on the Mexican Border
Dispatch from U.S. Vice Consul in Nogales Reuben D. George to U.S. Minister to Mexico Isaac P. Gray

U.S. consulates along the border with Mexico frequently became embroiled in unusual problems. In this dispatch an American vice consul reports that a Mexican suspected of violating U.S. laws was pushed across the border and arrested in the United States. The episode caused a minor furor. A subsequent American investigation concluded that at the time of the Mexican's arrest "it is possible that his head and a small portion of his body were on the Mexican side" of the border. The American government expressed its regret for the incident.

> Nogales, Mexico,
> December 4, 1894

Sir:

I have the honor to inform you that on the 23d of July, 1893, Jesus Garcia, a Mexican citizen, was arrested by the local authorities at Nogales, Ariz., for disturbing the peace. He broke away from the officers and ran across the line into Mexico, but was pushed back again into the territory of the United States by Mr. A. Bachelier, an American citizen, and as he fell was rearrested by the American authorities, was tried, convicted, and sentenced to serve a term of sixty days' imprisonment.

The Mexican local authorities took the matter up, claiming that the rearrest occurred upon Mexican territory, and examined quite a number of witnesses to establish that fact, and bad blood apparently existed on both sides of the line and it was only a question of time before the quarrel would become violent unless peace could be restored. I investigated the matter and came to the conclusion that Mr. A. Bachelier had done wrong in pushing the man back after he had crossed into Mexican territory, and that the Mexican authorities had just cause for complaint; and in order to prevent the matter from being referred to the respective State Departments and burden them with useless correspondence, I called upon the Mexican local authorities and asked them if they would drop the matter if I turned their man over to them the next day. They agreed to this, whereupon I held a consultation with the justice of the peace before whom the man had been tried; and upon additional evidence being introduced, the justice concluded to remit the fine and turn the prisoner over to the Mexican authorities, which was done at 10 o'clock the next day, and peace and good will was apparently again restored. It appears now, however, that the Mexican local authorities here have not kept faith with their agreement, and have referred the matter to their General Government, and the Mexican Federal Government has issued an order to arrest Deputy Sheriff Roberts and A. Bachelier should they cross into Mexican territory.

Mr. A. Bachelier conducts a bakery and delivers bread on both sides of the international boundary line, and so long as the order of arrest remains in force his business will be handicapped.

I am convinced that the Federal Government at the City of Mexico is not aware that any compromise had been agreed upon, and that the man over which all this trouble occurred was not of good standing, but one of those individuals who are more or less of a disturbing element on the frontier. I trust that you will use your good endeavors to bring this matter before the proper Mexican authorities and have the order of arrest rescinded.

I am, etc.,

Reuben D. George

1896   Shah of Persia Assassinated

Dispatch from U.S. Minister to Persia Alexander McDonald to Secretary of State Richard Olney

Shah Nasir ud-Din, who ruled Persia for almost fifty years (1848–1896), is generally regarded as the most capable ruler of his dynasty (see "The Shah of Persia: 'Studded All Over with Diamonds, Rubies,'" p. 212). *His death, reported in this dispatch, was followed by decades of instability in Persia, coupled with intensified British-Russian rivalry for predominant influence in the country.*

Teheran, Persia, May 4, 1896

Sir:

It is my melancholy duty to report for your information the facts, as far as they can be ascertained, in connection with the assassination of His Majesty the Shah. . . .

Historically considered, the facts of the crime may be briefly stated as follows:

On Thursday, the 30th of April, it was announced that the Shah would pay a visit to the shrine of Shahzadeh-Abdul-Azim, situated about 6 miles south of Teheran, on the site of the ancient city of Rhey, or Rhages. This previous notice gave the assassin time to mature his plans. Friday being the Mohammedan day of rest, generally large numbers avail themselves of the opportunity to pay their devotions at the tomb of the saint. It has always been customary when the Shah entered the court of the shrine to turn out the ordinary visitors and make it quite private. On this occasion, however, the Shah refused his sanction to this precaution, and said he would go in with the people, and gave orders to have his prayer carpet taken into the inner sanctuary containing the shrine. This was about midday. On the Shah entering the sanctuary, a man standing behind some women (not disguised, as at first reported) pushed forward, and, under the pretense of presenting a petition, fired a revolver at his heart. One of his attendants rushed forward and took hold of His Majesty, who, after walking a few paces, sat down and expired.

The body was immediately brought back to Teheran and . . . temporarily deposited in a tomb in the large religious theater adjoining the palace, where it will remain until the arrival of the present Shah, when it will be removed to the royal mausoleum at the holy city of Koom, 100 miles south from Teheran on the direct highway to Ispahan and Bushiri.

It is not yet certain when the Shah will arrive in Teheran, but it is generally supposed within a very few days, if his health is sufficiently strong to bear the fatigue of a rapid journey from Tabriz, 400 miles distant.

This abominable and detestable crime, for which no justification whatever can be admitted, has sent a thrill of horror into every heart, and cast a gloom over the whole country which will not be either easily or quickly removed. The late Shah was a man of most generous sentiments and active sympathies, and had won for himself the love and veneration of his people and the highest respect and esteem from all other nationalities. He was the fourth ruler of this dynasty and the second to meet his death at the hands of an assassin.

The criminal, who was seized immediately after firing the fatal shot, is now lodged in a room near the palace. His name is Mohammad Riza, a native of Kerman, in the southeast of Persia. He is about middle age, of slight build, and for some years followed the trade of a small broker or dealer in second-hand goods. Some years ago he imbibed socialistic and revolutionary principles, and for his connection with a number of persons holding subversive doctrines he was arrested and imprisoned. He was kept in confinement for about two years and liberated a little more than three years ago. . . . He is no doubt a fanatic, and it is reported that his mind is deranged as well.

Up to the present he denies having any accomplices and that both in the inception and execution of the crime he had no confederates.

. . . The Valiahd, or Crown Prince, governor of Tabriz, and also of the Province of Azerbaijan, has succeeded to the throne, and was proclaimed on the night of the 1st of May, as Muzaffar-ed-din Shah, Kajar, the latter being the name of the tribe from which this dynasty is descended.

The new Shah is about 43 years of age, rather shorter in stature than his father, of an amiable and conciliatory disposition, of considerable experience in the conduct of affairs, and favorably inclined toward the development of the resources of the country, and close relationship with foreign countries. . . .

I have, etc.,

Alex. McDonald

PART VI

Emergence of the United States as a World Power: 1898–1919

In 1905 President Theodore Roosevelt, middle, was instrumental in mediating the end of the Russo-Japanese War; the peace treaty was signed at Portsmouth, New Hampshire, on September 5. For his efforts Roosevelt earned a Nobel Peace Prize. The award was accepted on his behalf by U.S. Minister to Norway Herbert Pierce.

1898 The *Maine*

Dispatches from U.S. Consul General in Havana Fitzhugh Lee to Secretary of State William R. Day

An ongoing revolt in the Spanish colony of Cuba prompted U.S. officials to send the battleship Maine *to Havana in late January 1898. The U.S. consul general in Havana had warned in mid-January that if riots in the city got out of hand a visit by the ship might be warranted, but he urged that any such visit be delayed as long as possible to avoid inflaming local tensions. Nevertheless, he was overruled and the* Maine *arrived on January 25. A week later the Navy Department sought to withdraw the ship from Havana, citing "sanitary reasons"—the danger of tropical fevers endemic in Cuba. With the ship's visit going well, however, the consul general urged strongly that the* Maine *be ordered to stay.*

On February 16 a mysterious explosion sank the battleship; over 250 American seamen were lost. Although clear blame for the disaster was never affixed, the incident inflamed public sentiments in the United States and helped to propel the country to war with Spain two months later. This series of brief telegraphic dispatches from Consul General Fitzhugh Lee relates part of the saga of the sinking of the Maine.

Rioting and Rumors

Havana, January 12, 1898

Mobs, led by Spanish officers, attacked to-day the offices of the four newspapers here advocating autonomy. Rioting at this hour, 1 p.m., continues.

Havana, January 12, 1898

Much excitement, which may develop into serious disturbances. The trouble commenced by those who oppose autonomy, and so far is directed against those who advocate it. No rioting at present, but rumors of it are abundant. Palace heavily guarded. Consulate also protected by armed men.

Havana, January 13, 1898

After a day and night of excitement, all business suspended, and rioting, everything quiet at this hour. City heavily guarded. Soldiers protect public squares and threatened points. . . . Contest between Spanish factions. Attention has not yet been directed to other issues. Heard once yesterday of a few rioters shouting a proposal to march to our consulate. Presence of ships may be necessary later, but not now.

Excitement and Uncertainty

Havana, January 13, 1898

Three newspaper offices, not four, as previously cabled, were attacked yesterday by Spanish officers and mob. Saw mob assault two; saw soldiers sent to protect them fraternizing with mob; two attacks were attempted to-day. . . . Uncertainty exists whether [Governor General] Blanco can control the situation. If demonstrated he can not maintain order, preserve life, and keep the peace, or if Americans and their interests are in danger, ships must be sent, and to that end should be prepared to move promptly. Excitement and uncertainty predominates everywhere.

Quiet

Havana, January 14, 1898

Noon. All quiet.

Havana, January 15, 1898

Quiet prevails.

Postpone Ship's Visit

Havana, January 24, 1898

Advise visit [of battleship *Maine*] be postponed six or seven days, to give last excitement more time to disappear. Will see authorities and let you know result. Governor-General away for two weeks. I should know day and hour visit.

Havana, January 25, 1898

At an interview authorities profess to think United States has ulterior purpose in sending ship. Say it will obstruct autonomy, produce excitement, and most probably a demonstration. Ask that it is not done until they can get instructions from Madrid. . . .

The *Maine* Arrives

Havana, January 25, 1898

Ship quietly arrived 11 a.m. to-day. No demonstration so far.

Havana, January 25, 1898

Have just received visit of commander of *Maine* and will return it tomorrow. He had already returned official visits of Spanish and other naval officers. No disorders of any sort.

Havana, January 26, 1898

Have just had pleasant visit on *Maine*.

Havana, January 28, 1898

Acting Governor-General Parrado and staff went with me this morning to . . . the *Maine,* were entertained and given the appropriate salute. Expressed pleasure at their reception and admiration for the splendid battle ship.

No Sanitary Danger

Havana, February 4, 1898

Do not think slightest sanitary danger to officers or crew until April or even May. Ship or ships should be kept here all the time now. We should not relinquish position of peaceful control of situation, or conditions would be worse than if vessel had never been sent. Americans would depart with their families in haste if no vessel in harbor, on account of distrust of preservation of order by authorities. If another riot occurs . . . might include anti-American demonstration also. First-class battle ship should replace present one if relieved, as object lesson and to counter-act Spanish opinion of our Navy, and should have torpedo boat with it to preserve communication with admiral.

The *Maine* Destroyed

Havana, February 16, 1898

Maine blown up and destroyed to-night at 9:40 p.m. Explosion occurred well forward under quarters of crew; consequence many were lost. It is believed all officers saved, but Jenkins and Merritt not yet accounted for. Cause of explosion yet to be investigated. Captain-General and Spanish army and navy officers have rendered every assistance. Sigsbee and most of his officers on Ward steamer *City of Washington.* Others on Spanish man-of-war and in city. Am with Sigsbee now, who has telegraphed Navy Department.

1898 Anti-American Riots in Spain
Dispatch from U.S. Consul in Malaga R. M. Bartleman to
U.S. Minister to Spain Stuart Woodford

Demonstrations and riots against American establishments abroad have become relatively commonplace in the second half of the twentieth century. They were substantially less common in the nineteenth century, in part because America's generally isolationist outlook tended to keep the country out of international controversies. The dawning of America's imperial age at the turn of century saw U.S. consulates and embassies come under attack more frequently. Since some of the first U.S. imperial acquisitions came at the expense of Spain, it was not surprising that American consulates in that country found themselves under attack. In mid-April 1898, with the United States and Spain on the verge of war over developments in Cuba (see "The Maine," p. 305), the American consulate in the Spanish city of Malaga was attacked by angry mobs. Although by this time President William McKinley (1897–1901) had asked Congress to declare war, the consulate remained open and the Spanish authorities did their best to protect it. The riots are described in this dispatch by U.S. Consul R. M. Bartleman. A week later war was declared and the consulate was closed.

Malaga, April 18, 1898

Mr. Minister:

On the evening of the 15th instant, about 8 p.m., a group of students, bent upon showing their patriotism, started from the neighborhood of the institute toward the central part of the city, shouting praises to the army and navy; en route . . . to the consulate. . . . The consulate was demolished, the coat-of-arms removed, and in its place was hanging the Spanish colors. Meantime, the house occupied by the vice-consul and myself came in to a share of this patriotic display. Thinking we were not at home, our visitors soon left us to visit the house of an American citizen. . . . Before reaching his residence, however, they were met and turned back by the civil guard, now arriving on the scene of action, and finding it impossible to again attack the consulate, they proceeded toward the opera house, stopping the performance. The rioting continued until 1 or 1:30 a.m.

Early the following morning I requested my colleagues of Great Britain and Colombia, the latter residing with me, to do me the favor of calling upon his excellency the civil governor, as I had no desire to see him before receiving an apology for what had transpired; to protest against what had taken place, and to know if his excellency was able to give proper protection to the consulate, my residence and self; if not, I desired to be informed of the fact. On their return they stated what the governor had said—that the consulate, my house, and myself were now well protected, both by the civil guards and police; that he had received a telegram from Madrid directing him to restore the coat of arms in its place, using the military forces, if necessary, to accomplish this act, and wishing to know if I had another. I informed him that I had an old one. The chief of police, who accompanied my colleagues to take back my reply, then stated that as soon as the cavalry and infantry were in line and ready he would send for it. At 1 o'clock all was ready, the pieces were loaded before the crowd, and the arms of the United States was in view once more. This act brought forth a storm of protests from the assembled multitude. Their fury knew no bounds, and they promised themselves that it would again be removed that evening. . . .

Throughout the day the demonstrations continued; windows and lamps were broken by hundreds; shopkeepers were obliged to close their places of business; the riot and confusion that took place is indescribable.

During the evening it finally became necessary for the cavalry to make several charges at a full gallop, using their sabers right and left, inflicting and receiving wounds and making many arrests.

All entrances to the streets near to the consulate were now closed and guarded by the cavalry. These precautions continued over Sunday, when more trouble was anticipated, but the wounds received by the people cooled their desires, and up to the hour of writing this dispatch (11 p.m.) nothing more has taken place, and I trust the city will soon regain its normal condition. . . .

I have for days past been expecting this trouble and took the precaution to have the archives in a safe place. That I could not remove them elsewhere was owing to the exposed position of the building, which is located in front of the Military and Liceo Club from whence all my actions for days past have probably been observed. Knowing this, I have used the utmost caution in all my movements; I have avoided public places where an insult could possibly have been offered to me; moreover, my daily life for a long time past has been to go to my office and return home again at the end of the day. . . .

I improve this occasion, etc.,

R. M. Bartleman

1898 The Battle of Manila Bay
Dispatch from U.S. Consul in Manila Oscar F. Williams to Secretary of State William R. Day

A general insurrection broke out in 1895 in Cuba, then still a colonial possession of Spain. The harsh treatment inflicted by the Spanish on the rebels sparked anti-Spanish sentiment in the United States. The irresponsible American press of the day—known as the "yellow journal" press—ran sensational stories aimed at building circulation by inflaming American opinion. The mysterious sinking of the U.S. battleship Maine *in Havana's harbor in February 1898 helped to push the United States to declare war on Spain two months later (see "The Maine," p. 305).*

One of the most spectacular engagements of the Spanish-American War was the Battle of Manila Bay, in which an American fleet under Commodore George Dewey destroyed the Spanish fleet in the Philippines. The U.S. consul in Manila at the outbreak of the war, Oscar Williams, quietly gathered information on Spanish defenses in the Philippines and on the eve of the war made his way to Hong Kong to pass the intelligence to the U.S. Asiatic Squadron under Dewey. Williams accompanied the American fleet back to Manila Bay and observed the decisive battle from the bridge of the American flagship. This dispatch provides his eyewitness account of the destruction of the Spanish fleet.

> "U.S.S. Baltimore," Bay of Manila, Philippine Yslands, May 4, 1898

Sir:

I have the honor to briefly report to you concerning the battle of "Manila Bay"—fought on May 1, 1898.

Heeding your mandate, and by repeated request of Commodore George Dewey of the U.S. Asiatic Squadron, I left Manila on Sat. Apr. 23 and on Wed. Apr. 27—at about 1 o'clock p.m. boarded the Flag ship "Olympia" in Mint Bay near Hong Kong. After meeting the Commodore and his Captains and Commanders in Council, the Commodore at once ordered his fleet to start at 2 p.m. for Manila Bay. . . .

At about 5:30 a.m. Sun. May 1—the Spanish guns opened fire at both the Manila break-water battery and at Cavilt, from fleet and forts.

With magnificent coolness and order but with greatest promptness our fleet, in battle array, headed by the flagship answered the Spanish attack and for about two and a half hours a most terrific fire ensued.

The method of our operations could not have shown greater system or guns greater effectiveness or our officers and crews greater bravery. And while Spanish resistance was stubborn and the bravery of Spanish forces such as to challenge admiration, yet they were out classed . . . and after less than three hours perilous and intense combat one of Spain's war ships was sinking, two others were burning and all other with land defenses had severely suffered when our squadron with no harm done its ships retired for breakfast.

At about 10 o'clock a.m. Commodore Dewey renewed the battle and with effects most fatal with each evolution.

No better evidence of Spanish bravery need be sought than that after the castigation of our first engagement her ships and forts should again answer our fire. But Spanish efforts were futile. Ship after ship and battery after battery went to destruction before the onslaught of American energy and training, and an hour and a half of our second engagement wrought the annihilation of the Spanish fleet and forts with several hundred Spaniards killed and wounded and millions in value of their Government's property destroyed. While, amazing, almost unbelievable as it seems not a ship or gun of our fleet had been disabled and, except on the "Baltimore" not a man had been hurt.

One of the crew of the "Baltimore" had a leg fractured by slipping and another hurt in the ankle in a similar manner while four rec'd slight flesh wounds from splinters thrown by a six inch projectile which pierced the starboard side of the Cruiser.

But in the battle of "Manila Bay" the U.S. Squadron of six war ships totally destroyed the Spanish fleet of eight war ships, many forts and batteries and accomplished this work without the loss of a man.

History has only contrasts—there is no couplet to form a comparison. The only finish fight between the modern warships of civilized nations has proven the prowess of American naval men and methods and the glory is a legend for the whole people. Our crews are all hoarse from cheering and while we suffer for cough drops and throat doctors we have no use for liniment or surgeons. . . .

It was my lot to stand on the bridge of the "Baltimore" by the side of Capt. Deyer during the first engagement and to be called to the flagship "Olympia" by the Commodore at whose side on the bridge, I stood during the second engagement. And when the clouds roll by and I have again a settled habitation it will be my honor and pleasure to transmit a report showing service somewhat in detail and for which commanders promise data.

Meanwhile our Commodore will officially inform you of events which will rival in American history the exploits of Paul Jones.

> I have the honor to be, sir,
> your most obedient servant,
>
> Oscar F. Williams

1898–1900 The Great Gold Rush
Dispatches from U.S. Consul in the Yukon Territory James C. McCook

One of the more unusual episodes in U.S. diplomatic history was the establishment of a consulate in Dawson City which remained open through the Yukon and Alaska gold rushes (1898–1906). So many Americans went north to Alaska and Canada's Yukon Territory in search of riches that Dawson for a short time ranked just behind the major cities of Europe in consular business. Some consular officials themselves neglected their official duties to stake their claims. U.S. Consul James McCook reports on desperate hardships, fantastic riches, and the spirit of gold fever that seized the northwest frontier.

Gold in the Yukon
To Assistant Secretary of State J. B. Moore

Dawson City, August 2nd, 1898

Sir:

I am waited on daily by persons who have spent their all in the wild stampede for gold and been unsuccessful, some who have contracted scurvy and are really in a pitiable condition. There is no provision I know—to help such people out of the country. Some few have been aided who belong to Masonic or similar organizations. Those who call on me think it very hard when I tell them that I have no authority to send them to the States. This is of course outside of the hundreds of complaints of seemingly unjust treatment of which I will later on write when I get to know as near the facts as I can in the cases. Now as to stranded people of which I have no doubt a great many will be who cannot get away before navigation closes and afterwards not at all and as provisions naturally will be out of reach on a/c of higher prices this winter. I don't anticipate any scarcity as hundreds of people are daily going away down the river and over the trail, down the river to prospect in U.S. Territory.

I wish to know in view of the aforesaid circumstances if it wouldn't be advisable to obtain a certain amount of provisions here, store them away before winter sets in and when destitute citizens apply for relief portion some out to them. This state of affairs may never occur again in a Foreign country. Awaiting your instruction I have the honor to be your obedient servant.

J. C. McCook

The Rush to Nome
To Assistant Secretary of State David J. Hill

Dawson Y., June, 20th 1899

Sir:

I have the honor to state that my reports . . . of the finding of gold in the vicinity of Cape Nome Alaska, have been fully confirmed by recent advices sent here, and also by the news having been sent to the States. This also bears out my predictions, that, from Alaska's Territory more gold will be taken out than will ever come from this Territory. . . . Alaska is rich in placer mining but requires, as I have frequently written, developing. In the various mining camps, along the Yukon in Alaska last winter very little prospecting work has been done. The would be miners simply sat in their cabins and gossiped, did nothing but eat up their grub, waiting for some body else to do the prospecting and if they find something then they would go and try to work themselves. They go on a stampede, dig a hole or two, and because they cannot find pay dirt at once, say the creek is no good. Alaska is a hard country and requires indomitable pluck and nerve. Taking good care of one self is the most important essential, the continual living on canned goods is the worst feature, that with bad cooking, the stomach finally rebels and gets knocked out, and if one cannot get on the outside for a few months to give his system a change of diet, it is generally a long good bye to every one. The cost of fresh vegetables here is too high, but if we want to live we must have them. A few days ago at a restaurant I paid 50¢ for one small boiled potatoe, and at another one I went into, the waiter said an order of fresh potatoes was but 25¢ extra, and when I said bring me an order on the side, I was served with 1/2 a potatoe for my quarter of a dollar. Green goods, such as a small portion of lettuce is $1.00. I hope that at the Cape Nome Mining District some parties will send in a supply of vegetables, it would pay immensely. Re, Cape Nome, it has been the means of diverting the most of the Passenger trade from here. . . . One has to be very careful in reading accounts put in the papers on the outside, purporting to come from here. There has been enough false statements sent from here since this has been a camp to more than keep a corps of typesetters busy on any newspaper. Some one sent word to a certain town in the States, that four of their citizens, giving their names, were sentenced to be hung in Dawson for murder. . . . The whole thing was as usual false.

. . . A great number of people are stampeding to the new gold fields at Cape Nome, all the boats sailing from here taking away all they can carry. . . .

Typhoid fever has already broken out in Dawson, six weeks earlier than last year and there are several cases in the hospitals and some under private treatment. Dawson is overcrowded at present, most of the work on the mines, having ceased for the season, and the gambling fraternity and saloons are raking in the shekels.

. . . The unexpected has happened; instead of about $20,000,000.00 reported as the probable output for this district for the past twelve months, I am creditably informed about one half or $10,000,000.00 will fully cover all that will be taken out. The miners overestimated their dumps in this way, they usually panned out last winter from parts of the diggings that showed up good, or picked ground, as it were, and they overestimated the balance of the dirt gotten out. The first instalment of gold goes out today . . . about half a million.

> I am Sir,
> Your Obedient Servant,
>
> J. C. McCook

The Vice Consul's Claim

To Third Assistant Secretary of State Thomas W. Cridler

> Dawson Y.T., Canada
> April 17, 1900

Sir:

Replying to your No. 137, dated March 15, 1900 in which you call attention to the absence of the Vice Consul from the office, while I was away on leave, and to Mr. Adams signing Acting U.S. Consul, I beg to state that we are particularly situated here in Dawson. Mr. Morrison the Vice Consul, is a responsible man and very careful, but he found the claim he was working, some thirty miles from Dawson, required his almost constant attention, and he was obliged to remain on his property coming into Dawson but once or twice a month to see how things were getting on at the Consulate. There were no documents of particular importance passing through the office, excepting those powers of attorney for Cape Nome, which had to be made out, expeditions leaving daily, and the people could not wait for the Vice Consul to come into town, so Mr. Adams felt compelled to act and accordingly signed Acting U.S. Consul. He thus kept the office open for business, other wise citizens would have gone to Mr. Everette, for the service, who as you know was illegally appointed a Commissioner of Deeds, which would have looked bad for the Consulate. I am not writing this to excuse Mr. Adams, but under the circumstances there appears to be some justification for his action which was in good faith and under an emergency such as probably never occurred before, and possibly may never happen again.

> I am Sir,
> Your obedient Servant.
>
> J. McCook

1900 The Boer War: "The Afrikander... Is to Be the Ruling Race of South Africa"
Dispatch from U.S. Consul in Pretoria W. Stanley Hollis to Assistant Secretary of State David J. Hill

The origins of the Boer War can be traced back to 1795, when the British first seized the Cape of Good Hope from the Dutch settlers who had established themselves there in 1652 (see "The British Move into Africa," p. 68). Over the next century tensions repeatedly flared between the British and Dutch, who were known as Afrikaners or Boers. The Boers trekked inland to escape British rule, setting up independent states in the African interior in the 1850s. Troubles continued, however, including numerous armed conflicts between the British and the Boers. By the end of the century, British expansionism and Boer restrictions on the thousands of settlers—"uitlanders"—who swarmed to the Transvaal gold fields had led to the outbreak of the Boer War.

For the British the conflict developed into the largest military operation since the Napoleonic Wars almost a century before. The Boers initially won a series of victories, reaching their height at the close of 1899, about the time this dispatch was written. Within six months, however, British armies had routed the Boers and occupied Pretoria, capital of the South African Republic. The American consul in Pretoria at the time, Stanley Hollis, worked to ameliorate the plight of British prisoners of war and to educate his own government on conditions in the Transvaal. As is evident from this dispatch, Hollis's sympathies lay with the Boers.

> Pretoria, January 5, 1900

Sir:

... The world at large has been made to believe that [President of the South African Republic Paul] Kruger and his supporters were little better than a band of pirates; that the average Boer was worse than a Kafir, and that the whole nation was a mass of corruption and wickedness.

Horrible tales have been printed of the indignities that women and children have had to suffer at the hands of the Boers.

Now I want to state that I have been a close observer of South African affairs for more than ten years and . . . there has been nothing connected with my whole career in this country that would cause me to favor the cause of one antagonist more than that of another, or to cause me to depart from the absolutely neutral attitude that I constantly maintain.

But, as a matter of simple justice; as a matter of official duty to the Government that I have the honor to represent, I must warn the Department and the American people that the newspaper reports referred to, and concerning these people, are not only misleading but are, in 99 cases out of 100, utterly devoid of any foundation whatever.

The respect that the Boers have for home life and family ties, and their reverence for womanhood, is as deep as is that of our own people. In the Boer commandoes the religious idea predominates, and morning and evening hymns and prayers are the order of the day. When in darkness or in doubt they go to the Bible for inspiration and for comfort.

When one considers the lives that these people have led: of dangers and hardships during the many Kafir wars the country has passed through, and of Puritanical simplicity during times of peace, one must realize that such people are Nature's own noblemen.

It is true that many of the common Boers are rough in their dress and in their manners, and that the educated ones are suspicious and reserved; but approach these people honestly and openly and you will find that, although the exterior may be rough—and in some cases forbidding—underneath are kind hearts that are as true as steel, and you will also find that careful consideration for the feelings of others that is the distinguishing characteristic of the true gentleman.

The Boers are carrying on this war in an honorable and civilized manner and, I have seen in the Natal papers, the British commanders in South Africa are already beginning to recognize the honorable and chivalrous conduct of the Boers.

Officially this Government recognizes me only as the representative of the United States. They have taken particular pains to impress this fact upon me.

But, unofficially, I have been allowed to do many little things for the British prisoners here, and for their friends.

I have a little commission on hand now to supply every British soldier in prison here with a pipe and a handfull of tobacco.

This Consulate is being turned into a post office for prisoners' letters.

Everything outside of my purely professional duties as United States Consul is done with the full knowledge and consent of this government.

Now what I have written will, I trust, give you an insight into the Boer character.

In addition to this I find that these people have always respected and looked up to the American people, and have regarded us with the simple faith and admiration with which a little child would regard an honest, upright, and powerful man. . . .

Whatever happens the Afrikander race can neither be crushed nor exterminated. It is like a rich field that has been allowed to lie fallow for years but which afterwards can produce rich and abundant crops.

What are the facts?

Their simple pastoral lives have given them sound bodies, keen senses, and healthy minds. In this country where practically every male inhabitant big enough to carry a gun is liable to military service not more than two or three per cent are physically unfit for such service.

Intellectually the Afrikander children are much brighter and quicker to learn than are English or European children.

This is not a random statement. Mrs. Hollis has verified it by careful research and enquiry. . . .

Boiled down and condensed the official British reason for this war is that "Great Britain is bound to protect its subjects and to uphold their rights in this country."

Now I know for a fact that all foreigners in this country who have behaved themselves and who have not been concerned in schemes to upset and overthrow this Government have enjoyed fully the rights accorded to all citizens, or subjects, of the most favored nation.

I have not yet met one respectable American who found the conditions of life in this country unbearable, or even onerous. But I have met hundreds of good honest Americans and a goodly number of people of other nationalities who have all praised this country as the ideal country for the working man and for the mining man.

The bare fact that hundreds of non-British uitlanders are to-day fighting in the Republican ranks, and that many more are remaining here at work in the mines and elsewhere, proves that these non-British uitlanders are satisfied with the conditions of life in this country.

Thus it will be seen that the true cause of this war is that Britain sees that another of her children—or, to be more correct in this instance, one of her step-children—has grown to man's estate and wishes to run his house to suit himself and not to suit his step-relatives who wish to deprive him of the keys of his cash box; and, such being the case, Britain endeavors to prevent this by force of arms.

I would not presume to expect that the American Government or people would take one side or the other in this contest.

I simply wish to present the facts as they appear to me after more than ten years of careful study of South African questions, and to let the American people judge for themselves. But we must look into the future.

I am firmly convinced that the Afrikander, Dutch-Huguenot race is to be the ruling race of South Africa, and that it will absorb the other races possessing less individuality, as the United States has already done. . . .

Our people should endeavor to keep the friendship, or at least the friendly regard of these people. . . .

Let us hope that the good feeling between the two peoples will be maintained and that it will lead, in the coming years, to a close and friendly understanding between the two countries. . . .

> I have the honor to be,
> Sir,
> Your obedient servant,
>
> W. Stanley Hollis

1900   The Boxer Rebellion: The Siege at Peking
Dispatch from U.S. Minister to China Edwin H. Conger to Secretary of State John Hay

Antiforeign sentiment in China reached crisis proportions at the turn of the century. A secret society, dubbed the "Boxers" by Westerners, gained popularity throughout much of northern China. The movement initially was opposed both to Chinese authorities and to foreign influence, but the ruling Ch'ing dynasty was able to co-opt the movement by endorsing and joining in its goal of expelling foreigners from China. By early 1900 bands of Boxers were openly murdering European missionaries and their Chinese converts. When European forces attempted to take action against them, Chinese imperial troops joined with the Boxers.

On June 20, 1900, the German minister in Peking was murdered and the foreign legations in the city were cut off and besieged. About nine hundred foreigners and thousands of Chinese Christians endured a harrowing siege for fifty-five days in a small diplomatic quarter within the walls of the Chinese capital. They finally were relieved on August 14 by a combined force from eight nations.

In this dispatch, sent shortly after the siege was lifted, American minister Edwin Conger describes the eight-week ordeal. He correctly accuses the Chinese government of complicity in the siege. Conger served seven years as U.S. minister to China. He previously had served as minister to Brazil and would go on to a short stint as ambassador to Mexico.

Pekin, China, August 17, 1900

Sir:

. . . The morning of [June] . . . 20th, . . . the German minister, Baron von Ketteler, . . . was brutally murdered, shot through the head by a man (so says his interpreter, whose chair immediately followed) wearing the insignia of a Chinese official. The interpreter, Mr. Cordes, was at the same time seriously wounded, but succeeded in escaping to the American Methodist Mission compound, which was guarded by American marines. . . . The body was found yesterday, buried in a rough coffin near where he fell, and to-day was decently interred in the German legation. . . .

The Chinese army . . . turned out against us; the whole quarter of the city in which the legations are situated was surrounded by its soldiers, firing began on all sides and the battle against the representatives of all foreign governments in China was begun.

The Methodist compound where all our missionaries had gathered was abandoned; all coming to the legation at 12 noon. By 4 o'clock the situation had become so acute that all foreigners, except the guards and a few men in each legation, repaired to the British legation, and the refugee native Christians, about 2,000, were placed in the grounds of Prince Su, near by.

Our lines of defence were quickly shortened and strengthened, trenches and barricades built, and the siege was on.

Four hundred foreigners, 200 of them women and children, with over 100 soldiers, were crowded into the British legation. In the house given to our legation 30 people were for two months crowded into six small rooms; but all were thankful that there existed so convenient and safe a place to go.

The first attempts of the enemy were to burn us out by firing buildings adjoining us, but by means of heroically fighting those inflamed by the enemy, burning and tearing down others ourselves, we soon had the British legation pretty safe from this danger. However, from this date until July 17 there was scarcely an hour during which there was not firing upon some part of our lines and into some of the legations, varying from a single shot to a general and continuous attack along the whole line.

Artillery was planted on all sides of us, two large guns mounted on the walls surrounding the palace, and thousands of 3-inch shells and solid shot hurled at us. There is scarcely a building in any of the legations that was not struck, and some of them practically destroyed. Four shells struck our gatehouse, tearing away our flagstaff; four exploded in the servants' quarters; three struck my residence, two of them exploding inside; two struck the office building, and two the house of Mr. Cheshire, while the roofs of nearly all the buildings in the compound were sadly damaged by innumerable bullets. To show in what storms they came, five quarts of them were picked up to be remolded into new ammunition in one hour in our small compound.

Our lines were at first made as short as possible and inclosed all the legations except the Belgian, and were still further shortened after the burning of the Austrian, Italian, and Dutch legations and the imperial customs. Trenches were dug, streets barricaded along these lines as fast as possible, but nearly all the work on these had to be done under cover of darkness.

A veritable fortress was made of the British legation, walls were strengthened and raised, openings filled, bombproof cellars constructed, counter tunnels to prevent mining made, and everything possible with our poor tools and materials was effectively done. In our first barricades carts and furniture were employed and thousands upon thousands of sand bags made in which every obtainable material was used—satin portières, silk curtains, carpets, oriental rugs, table linen, towels, bedding, embroideries, cloths, silks, etc.

Fortunately for us we had the missionaries and their converts with us. The former, being familiar with the Chinese language and character, ably organized, superintended, and directed the Chinese, who were invaluable help in constructing fortifications, and without which it could not have been done. . . .

Sir Claude MacDonald, the British minister, was chosen for the general command, and gave every satisfaction. He selected Mr. H.G. Squiers, first secretary of this legation, as his chief of staff, whose military training and experience had not been forgotten, but which, thrown with energy and determination into the work, were invaluable to the end.

Necessary committees were created, and the camp was thoroughly organized. Stores of wheat, rice, and coal found within our lines were quickly gathered into a general commissariat, which, with such canned goods as we had in store, together with all our riding horses and cart mules, have furnished us a substantial if not a very palatable subsistence since.

The Chinese seem to have an innumerable soldiery and an inexhaustible supply of ammunition. We began with only 400 marines, sailors, and soldiers altogether, and some 50 miscellaneously armed civilians. For the most part, therefore, we simply sat and watched, firing only when necessary; but occasionally a severe attack had to be resisted or a sortie made, which invariably, on our side, was successful. But these frequently cost lives of brave men. Altogether we have lost—killed, 65; wounded, 135; died of disease, all children, 7. Of the United States marines, Sergeant Fanning and Privates King, Kennedy, Turner, Tutcher, Fisher, and Thomas were killed; Captain Myers, Dr. Lippett, and 14 others wounded. The loss of the Chinese is known to be ten times as great as ours.

To our marines fell the most difficult and dangerous portion of the defense, by reason of our proximity to the great city wall and the main city gates, over which large guns were planted.

Our legation, with the position which we held on the wall, was the key to the whole situation. This given up, all, including many Chinese Christians, would at once be drawn into the British legation and the congestion there increased by several hundred. The United States marines acquitted themselves nobly. Twice were they driven from the wall and once forced to abandon the legation, but each time, reenforced, immediately retook it, and with only a handful of men, aided by 10 Russian sailors and for a few days a few British marines, held it to the last against several hundred Chinese with at least three pieces of artillery.

The bravest and most successful event of the whole siege was an attack led by Captain Myers, of our marines, and 55 men—Americans, British, and Russians—which resulted in the capture of a formidable barricade on the wall defended by several hundred Chinese soldiers, over 50 of whom were killed. Two United States marines were killed and Captain Myers and 1 British marine wounded. This made our position on the wall secure, and it was held to the last with the loss of only one other man.

This position gave us command of a water gate under the wall, through which the entrance of the relief column was made into this, the Tartar city. The English arrived first, and General Chaffee, with the Fourteenth Infantry and Captain Riley's battery, a few moments thereafter. . . .

During the siege the Belgian, Austrian, Italian, Dutch, and most of the French legations were burned, and the post-office, three foreign banks, residences and offices of all the customs officials, and all the missionary compounds, except the Peitang, have been totally destroyed. . . .

It was reasonable supposition that the Chinese Government had fled, abandoning the city to the fury of the fiendish soldiers. But we have since found proof abundant and absolute that the Empress Dowager and council remained in the city until just before the arrival of the relief and that the attacks were organized and directed by them. . . .

Their barricades were everywhere mounted with flags bearing the name and designations of regular officers and their commands, and whenever men or guns fell into our hands they were those of the Chinese army.

It is very likely the Boxers joined them in the attacks, but if so, they donned the army uniform and carried the imperial arm. . . .

Another convincing proof that it was soldiers who were besieging us is the fact that whenever the Chinese Government wanted to communicate with us, they could stop the firing and come through their lines whenever they pleased.

The Chinese Government was pretending to us and proclaiming to the world that they were "protecting" us, when in fact if a thousandth part of the shots fired at us by their soldiers had taken effect we would all have been killed long ago. . . .

On the 14th, as I have already written, we were relieved. . . .

So the movement began, first upon the native Christians, thousands of whom have been most brutally butchered, then against the missionaries, many of whom have been murdered and their property destroyed. The most harrowing details are coming in of horrible atrocities perpetrated in the country districts while we have been besieged; then against the foreign merchants and all foreign business interests, and finally against all the official representatives of foreign powers in Pekin.

The Government has fled, and up to the present no one to speak for it has put in an appearance. . . . Further developments will be reported in my next despatch. . . .

I have the honor to be, etc.,

E. H. Conger

1901 End of an Era: The Death of Queen Victoria
Dispatch from U.S. Ambassador to Great Britain Joseph H. Choate to Secretary of State John Hay

The last British monarch of the House of Hanover, Victoria was, according to a popular story, unaware of her possible succession to the throne until the age of twelve. When told of her likely future, her reputed response was, "I will be good."

Victoria became queen in 1837 at the age of eighteen, beginning the longest reign in English history. Her sixty-four years on the throne marked the height of Great Britain's supremacy in commerce, industry, and force of arms, the period during which the sun never set on the British Empire. Victoria came to symbolize Britain of the nineteenth century and ultimately gave her name to the entire era. She was succeeded to the throne by her eldest son, Edward VII.

Joseph Choate was American ambassador to Great Britain from 1899 to 1905 during the final years of Victoria's reign. A respected and wealthy New York lawyer, Choate won enormous popularity in England, where he was extremely active on the lecture circuit.

London, January 23, 1901

Sir:

Her Illustrious Majesty the Queen closed her long and splendid career at half past 6 o'clock yesterday afternoon at Osborne, in the Isle of Wight. Although she had been in declining health for some months, it was not generally known until she was seized with a fatal illness a few days ago. She died surrounded by her children and grandchildren, including the Emperor of Germany, whose coming on this pious pilgrimage has made a deep impression here. She commanded, as no other personage of modern times has done, the affectionate homage of mankind, and I am glad to see that the people of the United States are foremost among her admirers outside the British Empire.

Near midnight I received your instructions to express to Lord Lansdowne the sympathy of the Government and people of the United States, with which I have already complied by addressing to his Lordship a note.

The new King enters upon his reign with the good will not of his own subjects only, but of all the world. He is at this moment (2 p.m.) holding his first council, and to-morrow at 10 o'clock he will be proclaimed.

The President's tender message of sympathy to the King has been highly appreciated here.

I have, etc.,

Joseph H. Choate

1901 Greece: Rioting against a Vulgar Bible
Dispatch from U.S. Minister to Greece Charles S. Francis to Secretary of State John Hay

Rioting over religious issues has been as common in the twentieth century as it was in earlier years. In 1901 the citizens of Greece rose up in protest against a new edition of the Bible in modern vernacular—the Bible in general use in Greece at the time dated from the Byzantine period (A.D. 395–1453). In the end, the protesters had their way: within days the Greek Holy Synod issued a decree prohibiting, on pain of excommunication, the sale or reading of any translation of the Bible. The disturbances are reported in this dispatch from U.S. Minister to Greece Charles Francis.

Athens, November 22, 1901

Sir:

I have the honor to report that during the last few days Athens has been the scene of mob demonstrations which yesterday almost assumed the proportions of a revolution. Briefly, the reason for this disturbance was the recent translation and publication in Athens of the Bible in vulgar Greek. Expressions were employed by the translators, which the Hellenes regard as unfit to be printed in the Holy Scriptures. The work was inaugurated and completed with the approval of the Metropolitan, the head of the synod of the Greek Church in Greece.

The students of the university at Athens and the Greeks generally are bitterly opposed to any change in the text of their Bible, which, while of ancient origin and dating back to the Byzantine period, is understood by all and is written in the purest Greek.

Mass meetings were held in front of the university buildings on the afternoons of November 19 and 20, at which violent speeches were made in denunciation of the objectionable biblical translation and of all those identified with it. Large crowds of excited citizens paraded the streets, and the signs were ominous of a serious public demonstration.

Yesterday, November 21, was a fête day. The shops and factories were closed and the streets were thronged with all classes of people. A public demonstration was announced to take place in the afternoon, in which it was advertised that the different labor unions would participate. Fearing the result, the Government ordered out all the military troops in the city, and 800 marines were brought to Athens from the Greek men-of-war at Piraesus. Infantry, cavalry, and large bodies of gendarmes were posted at different points in the city and a cordon of marines was thrown about the palace.

This show of military force had the effect of aggravating the situation, and late in the afternoon the expected collision took place between the authorities and the aroused Athenians. The mob, now numbering over 25,000, proceeded to the ministry of finance and demolished the windows of the building. Thereupon, shots were fired upon the crowd by police officers and employees of the ministry. The rioters responded with pistols and stones, and were only dispersed after a cavalry charge and several carbine volleys. A few minutes later another mob demonstration was made in front of the residence of the premier, Mr. Theotaky, and again the troops and gendarmes made use of their rifles to clear the streets.

The casualties were as follows: Eight killed and upward of 60 wounded. The dead bodies and 32 of the wounded were carried to the municipal hospital. Probably as many more were wounded, but escaped identification, as they were conveyed by friends to their respective homes. That the casualties were not greater may be explained by the fact that the soldiers were unquestionably in sympathy with the sentiments of the rioters, and did not direct their fire upon the crowds, the effective shooting being done by the police or gendarmes.

After a conference had been held during the night between King George and the members of the ministry and prominent citizens, the resignation of the Metropolitan, the titular head of the church in Greece, was accepted at 4 o'clock this morning (November 22). By royal decree, signed at the same hour, the director of police and the prefect of police were both removed and their positions filled by new appointees. The Government printing office issued an edition of the Official Gazette at 6 o'clock a.m. containing the above announcements.

The burial of the victims of yesterday's conflict took place this afternoon. Many thousands of people followed the single funeral procession to the cemetery, every shop in Athens was closed, and on all sides profound regret and grief were expressed at the outcome of yesterday's tragedy.

> I have, etc.,
>
> Charles S. Francis

1901   First Nobel Prizes
Dispatch from U.S. Minister to Sweden and Norway
William W. Thomas Jr. to Secretary of State John Hay

Alfred Nobel, born in 1833, was a Swedish chemist who worked to develop a stabler form of the volatile explosive nitroglycerin. Regarded as a "Mad Scientist" after his laboratory blew up, killing his brother Emil and four others, Nobel moved his research to a moored barge, where he perfected and patented dynamite and blasting caps. Although Nobel's invention made him one of the world's richest men, he was chagrined when dynamite—intended to make blasting safer for industry, mining, and construction—also was used to make deadlier and more powerful weapons. A committed pacifist, Nobel used his fortune to endow prizes for individual contributions to the "good of humanity." As described in this dispatch, the first of what were to become annual Nobel Prizes were handed out by the crown prince of Sweden in an impressive ceremony on the fifth anniversary of Nobel's death.

> Stockholm, December 11, 1901

Sir:

I have the honor to inform you that events of exceptional import and interest took place yesterday at Stockholm and Christiania.

December 10, 1901, was the fifth anniversary of the death of Alfred Bernhard Nobel, the great Swedish engineer and inventor, and on yesterday were awarded for the first time the prizes instituted by him in his testament to those persons who have contributed most materially to benefit mankind in the domains of physics, chemistry, medicine, literature, and in the works of peace.

The prizes were awarded as follows: In physics, to Wilhelm Conrad Röntgen, professor at the University at Munich, the discoverer of the Röntgen rays; in chemistry, to Jacobus Henricus van't Hoff, professor at the University of Berlin; in medicine, to Emil von Behring, professor at

Halle, the discoverer of the diphtheria serums; in literature, to Sully-Prudhomme, member of the French Academy; in the works of peace, this prize was divided in two, and awarded in equal parts to Henri Dunant, of Switzerland, the leading spirit in bringing about the Geneva convention and in instituting the Societies of the Red Cross, and to Frederick Passy, national economist, of France.

The first four prizes were given out at Stockholm with impressive ceremonies. The place was the grand hall of the Royal Academy of Music, which was tastefully decorated. This spacious hall was filled with a brilliant gathering of gentlemen and ladies, the leaders in Swedish science, literature, art, and public life, and the occasion was especially honored by the presence of the Crown Prince and other members of the royal family.

The exercises were enlivened by addresses appropriate to the event, and by music and song. The prize diplomas were given out by the Crown Prince in person and were received in person by Professors Röntgen, van't Hoff, and Behring.

As M. Sully-Prudhomme was unable to be present on account of sickness, the diploma in literature was delivered to the minister for France at Stockholm, to be forwarded by him to M. Sully-Prudhomme.

On the same day the prize in the works of peace, divided in two parts, as above mentioned, was awarded to M. Dunant and M. Passy at Christiania by the Norwegian Storting convened in solemn session.

Each of the five prizes is for the sum of over 150,000 crowns (150,782.23 crowns exactly), or more than $40,000—an amount sufficient of itself to place each recipient in independent circumstances, and to permit him untrammeled to pursue his investigations and life work, which have already been of so great benefit.

Furthermore, five prizes of like, or perhaps greater, amount will be awarded every year on December 10 hereafter forever.

I think it may be said that these prizes, in kind as well as in amount, are unparalleled in the history of science, literature, and humanity, and that the day these prizes were for the first time awarded marks an epoch in the advance of the human race.

Alfred Nobel directed that substantially the whole of his vast fortune be used for the benefit of mankind. Though the discoverer of dynamite, he instituted one of his grand prizes for the works of peace. His beneficence is as broad as humanity. He was more than patriot; he was the friend of the human race. In his last will he directs that in awarding the prizes no consideration whatever be paid to nationality, but that the worthiest be awarded the prize, whether he is Scandinavian or not.

Peace to his ashes. His great and enduring work reflects honor upon himself and upon the race from which he sprung.

I have, etc.,

W. W. Thomas, Jr.

1902 Universal Suffrage Riots in Belgium
Dispatch from U.S. Minister to Belgium Lawrence Townsend to Secretary of State John Hay

By the late nineteenth century, rich coal mines and rapid industrialization had transformed tiny Belgium into Europe's fourth largest manufacturing power. The rapid growth of the working class led to demands for political reforms. In 1893 suffrage was extended to all males—but under a system that gave disproportionate representation to landholders and to more educated and older men. The workers, however, were not satisfied and continued to agitate over the next twenty years for "one man, one vote." In this dispatch U.S. Minister Lawrence Townsend reports a series of sometime violent demonstrations. The Belgian government agreed in 1913 to revise the electoral system, but the reforms were further delayed by the onset of World War I.

Brussels, April 19, 1902

Sir:

The struggle between labor and capital in Belgium has become extremely acute in the past few years. A large industrial population, confined to a small superficial area, with long hours of labor and small wages, have combined to produce a feeling of discontent among the working classes, who, perhaps unjustly, blame the existing Government for a condition of affairs which may be due to economic conditions rather than political.

This is a factor which may be largely responsible for the rapid growth of Socialism in Belgium during the past few years. Liberals and Socialists have combined to fight for universal suffrage, and have raised the cry "one man one vote" as a panacea for the existing ills.

The Clericals maintain that the existing system of plural voting meets the present requirements of the country; that it places a premium on education, and acts as a check to the power of the ignorant, who are prone to resort to violence and disorder.

During the past fortnight, while the debates on the subject of revision were being held in the House of Representatives, the socialists and workingmen have held nightly meetings at the Maison du Peuple, and have frequently paraded the streets shouting for universal suffrage and "one man one vote." But the ranks of the paraders have been swelled by the addition of the very lowest and criminal classes of the population, the result being a conflict with the police followed by the breaking of windows and other damages to property. Shots were exchanged between the gendarmes and rioters, several of the latter being killed and wounded. Similar scenes were at the same time enacted in other towns in Belgium consequently the Government called out the troops.

Order has been restored, but the streets of Brussels, as well as the large towns, are lined with soldiers. A general strike has taken place in all the industrial centers of Belgium, with the avowed object of forcing the Government to grant universal suffrage, but without success. The feeling of unrest is very general all over the country. . . .

I have, etc.,

Lawrence Townsend

1902 Establishing the Rhodes Scholarship
Dispatch from U.S. Ambassador to Great Britain Joseph H. Choate to Secretary of State John Hay

Cecil Rhodes was prime minister of Cape Colony in South Africa from 1890 to 1896. Ever the empire builder, he secured British control over much of southern Africa and even dreamed of bringing the "American Colonies" back under the influence of Great Britain. As one of the founders of DeBeers Consolidated Mines, Rhodes amassed a fortune through control of most of the world's diamond production. In 1902 Rhodes died of tuberculosis at the age of forty-nine. He bequeathed his fortune to strengthen the British Empire. A portion went to Oxford University where it was used to establish the Rhodes Scholarship Program, designed to foster unity among English-speaking peoples. The program remains highly regarded almost a century later, with about ninety scholarships awarded annually, thirty-two in the United States.

In this dispatch the American ambassador in London reports the establishment of the scholarship program and the effort to set up a procedure for American applicants.

London, June 19, 1902

Sir:

I have the honor to report that I have received from the trustees, under the will of the right honorable Cecil John Rhodes, and herewith transmit a printed extract from his will relating to the scholarships to be established from the States and Territories of the United States. . . .

By this it appears that the trustees are desirous of making regulations with regard to the method by which qualifications of candidates are to be ascertained, and as to the examinations, and have asked me to bring the matter to the notice of the Government of the United States. . . . As it is a matter of first-rate importance to the whole country, I think you may find a way to communicate with the governors of the several States and ascertain and transmit to the trustees their views and those of the chief officials having control of education. . . .

You will observe that it is the hope of the trustees that the students can be elected in time to go into residence in Oxford in 1903. . . . I shall be obliged if you will promptly advise me.

> I have, etc.,
>
> Joseph H. Choate

1903 Lawlessness in Lebanon: "Beirut Is Unsafe"

Dispatch from U.S. Consul in Beirut G. Bie Ravndal to
Acting Consul General in Constantinople William Smith-Lyte

Throughout the late nineteenth and early twentieth centuries Beirut was an intellectual and cultural hub of the Middle East. In many ways, however, it also was a dangerous place, with local authorities unable to keep brigands, thieves, and other lawbreakers under control. U.S. Consul Bie Ravndal's 1903 description of conditions in Beirut brings to mind the unsettled circumstances in today's Beirut.

> Beirut, August 28, 1903

Sir:

I have the honor to report that Vice-Consul Magelssen last Sunday evening was attacked by an unknown person standing under a street gas light near the consulate, who fired at the carriage in which Mr. Magelssen was riding, at such close range that it seemed to Mr. Magelssen as if the whole carriage were ablaze. Nobody was injured, however. Frightened, the horses dashed forward, and before they could be controlled and the carriage stopped the assailant had disappeared. Mr. Magelssen reported the incident at once to the nearest police station, and the next day a complaint was filed with the local authorities. . . .

In my five and one-half years' experience in Beirut, though there have been times when murders and robberies and the like seemed to be the order of the day, the city never before approached the present standard, because foreigners are now affected as well as natives. My Italian colleague the other night was robbed in his own bedroom. No foreigners have been murdered so far this season, but an unusual number of murders have recently occurred among the natives. Beirut is unsafe, and the local government, being implicated with law breakers (smugglers, brigands, etc.), as most people believe, Moslems as well as Christians being compelled to obtain money somehow to satisfy demands from above, is powerless to correct abuses, if not indifferent. If I am correctly informed the German, Austrian, Italian, and British consuls-general here, and most likely other consuls, have reported on these conditions to their embassies very recently. The attack on Mr. Magelssen has stirred the city from center to circumference. It is considered more or less as the climax.

Last year as Mr. Magelssen returned from his lunch to the office, between two cactus hedges behind the consulate, he was set upon by two natives, who evidently thought they could hold him up. Instead of submitting to this kind of treatment, Mr. Magelssen hit one of the aggressors in the eye and kicked the other one. We complained to the vilayet [district office] and a dozen natives, more or less, were arrested. It is said that one of them was imprisoned, perhaps wrongfully, for the assault and that he was only recently released. Some people think that he was the assailant of last Sunday evening. I improved the opportunity last year and got a police station established near our consulate.

We, however, do not know where to put the blame except on the local government, which is so utterly lax as to allow almost any miscreant to pose as the cock of the walk. . . .

I am, etc.,

G. Bie Ravndal

1904   Kurdish Outlaws: "Love of Blood and Pillage"
Dispatch from U.S. Minister to Persia Richmond Pearson to Secretary of State John Hay

For centuries the Kurdish people have occupied the territory that today lies at the juncture of Iran, Iraq, and Turkey. Traditionally a herding society, the Kurds became known in the Middle Ages for their military ability. The famous Saladin, who established the Ayyubid dynasty of Egypt and held back Richard the Lion-Hearted during the attempt of the Third Crusade (1189–1192) to recapture Jerusalem, was a Kurd.

Over the centuries Kurdistan was overrun by the Persians, Turks, and other invaders, but the Kurds never lost their sense of identity or their independent spirit. After World War I the Treaty of Sèvres (1920) provided for an autonomous Kurdistan, but its terms—and Kurdish hopes for independence—were superseded by the Treaty of Lausanne in 1923, which reapportioned lands held by Turkey before World War I.

This dispatch reflects the difficulties faced in dealing with Kurdish outlaws in the early years of the twentieth century. At the time, Ottoman influence in the region was in decline and Persia was ruled by a partic-

ularly weak monarch. The dispatch was written by Richmond Pearson, who served for five years as U.S. minister to Persia and then moved on to become minister to Greece and Montenegro.

Teheran, April 18, 1904

Sir:

It is now forty-one days since the Rev. Benjamin W. Larabee, the American missionary, was murdered near Khoi, almost under the shadow of Mount Ararat. I had hoped before this to cable you that one or more of the murderers had been arrested, but I can only report at present that a large expedition, under command of an energetic general who is highly respected and commended by missionaries, is actively scouring the mountains in search of any and all of the gang who are all known and identified.

It will be seen that while only four men actually participated in the killing of Mr. Larabee and his servant, ten other Kurds of the same gang were accomplices. They had simply taken another road for the purpose of entrapping their prey and must be held guilty as accessories before the fact.

The brutality and atrocity of the murder remove any doubt as to its motive, and eliminate entirely the suggestion in my first cable that the motive was apparently robbery. The stealing of the horses and other property was a mere incident. The inspiration of the deed was religious and race hatred, without the slightest personal animosity. The fact that the chief and leader of the criminals is a "Seyid," an alleged lineal descendant of Mahomet, adds greatly to the difficulty of the arrest. These Kurds are all Mohammedans of the Sunni sect, and their fanaticism, which is both ardent and sincere, added to their heredity and instinctive love of blood and pillage make them a dangerous and difficult population to deal with.

The home of the Kurds or "Kurdistan" is an indefinite geographical expression, but may be roughly understood as beginning at Mount Ararat on the north and stretching south to where the mountains fade away into the plains of Mesopotamia above Bagdad, say, 300 miles; the width of the region may be measured by the distance between Lake Urumia in Persia and Lake Van in Turkey—something like 100 miles; the area of this region is as large as the State of South Carolina. It disregards imperial boundaries, as its inhabitants disregard imperial laws and orders; it extends into Persia or Turkey according to the pleasure and habits and wanderings of these wild people. . . .

Notwithstanding the strict laws that require passports to enter Turkey or Persia, the Kurd relies with confidence and success upon his rifle and scimitar rather than upon papers and seals and visas, and so crosses indifferently into either territory to commit crimes, or to escape the consequences of his crimes. This is the Kurd, the creature we have to deal with in this case. . . .

I am, etc.,

R. Pearson

1906 Unrest in Moscow
Dispatch from U.S. Consul in Moscow Samuel Smith to
U.S. Ambassador to Russia G. von L. Meyer

Despite some movement toward modernization, Russia at the onset of the twentieth century remained far behind most other nations of Europe in democratic reforms. A number of political groups opposing the regime were formed but were forced into exile. After Russia's defeat at the hands of Japan in the Russo-Japanese War (1904–1905), active agitation erupted in major Russian cities. Dozens of peaceful demonstrators were killed by security forces on "Bloody Sunday," January 22, 1905, leading to a year of protests, strikes, and internal disorder. The turmoil induced Czar Nicholas II to grant a constitution and form a Duma, or parliament, but these reforms did not succeed in ending the unrest. In October, workers in St. Petersburg formed the first Soviet, or council. The government's arrest of almost two hundred Soviet members two months later ignited a workers' insurrection in Moscow, described in this dispatch by U.S. Consul Samuel Smith. The army and police, however, remained loyal to the regime and the revolt was put down within ten days.

Moscow, January 2, 1906

Sir:

I have the honor to report to you regarding the riots which took place in Moscow, commencing the 20th and continuing until the 31st of December, giving each day separately:

December 20th—At 12 o'clock noon a general political strike was ordered by the deputies of the workmen and it was resolved to turn the strike into an armed revolution to upset the present existing government, to attack and arrest the officials and proclaim a temporary government, and to call an assembly to elect representatives. It was recommended at the meeting of the workmen that no demonstration should be made until all were armed and to withhold from attacking the military forces.

At 12 o'clock the strike commenced and all works, mills, and factories stopped work and the strikers congregated at different parts of the city and marched around to every manufacturing establishment and made the workmen join the strikers. All workmen in the employ of the Moscow municipality joined the strikers, excepting the workmen of the city water and gas works, who were allowed to continue work. . . .

Revolutionary militia forces were formed in large numbers and ordered to parade the streets, carrying red flags and singing the Marseillaise anthem. The chief of police ordered out at once the dragoons and cossacks to disperse the mob, but as soon as one mob would be dispersed another would gather in another part of the city. In these charges of the cavalry several were wounded and killed. Toward evening the policemen were ordered off their posts and replaced by soldiers armed with guns and bayonets.

All the railways stopped operations with the exception of the Nicolai Railway, and the workmen joined the strikers. All restaurants, club houses, theaters, and amusement places were closed for an indefinite time.

The same evening a mass meeting was held at the theater in the city, called the "Aquarium," where nearly 10,000 men congregated and while the meeting was in progress a cordon of cavalry and infantry were ordered to the place and surrounded the same. The strikers were, however, informed in time of this movement and made good their escape by climbing over the fences of the adjoining houses and only 70 men were arrested. At this meeting it was resolved to capture the governor-general at any cost.

December 21—Life in the city seemed to be extinct, as all business offices, stores, and banks were closed, no newspapers came out, the schools were closed. . . .

December 22—A meeting of the revolutionary party, consisting of about 500 men, took place in Mr. Fielder's house, located on Lebkevsky Pereoulok. The police ordered the revolutionists to leave the building and to surrender, but they refused, and the military force, consisting of cavalry and artillery, were ordered to the place. The revolutionists were given two hours to do so, but they refused, fired at the military forces and threw several bombs into the street. Then the artillery opened fire on the house and bombarded same by shells. The casualties were, two officers and several soldiers killed and a number wounded, several of the revolutionary party were killed and a great many wounded, and 120 of them arrested. The police confiscated a large quantity of rifles, revolvers, knives, and 13 bombs.

During the night the revolutionists commenced to construct barricades in different parts of the city, from all sorts of rubbish, using wooden and iron gates, bricks, and cutting down telegraph and lamp posts and using the telegraph and electric light wires for making all kinds of entanglements to stop the quick movement of the cavalry.

December 23—During the night of this date two bombs were thrown into the detective department, a tremendous explosion took place, and the building was almost demolished. A sergeant of the police, one policeman, and one soldier were killed. Barricades were again constructed in several parts of the city, but soon destroyed by the soldiers. . . .

December 24— . . . Late at night the Nicolai Railway station was attacked by a large number of revolutionists, but the military forces dispersed them by using Maxim quick firing guns, field guns, and making cavalry charges.

By order of the police authorities all local telephone communication was stopped. My telephone was kept intact, but was only to be used for official business.

December 25—One of the largest printing establishments was taken possession of by the revolutionists for the purpose of holding meetings, and to issue from there orders to their detachments for further attacks on the authorities. The soldiers were ordered to surround the building, which was accomplished, but the strikers set the house on fire, by which means the larger number of the strikers made their escape during the commotion and conflagration. The balance was either killed or wounded. Fighting between troops and strikers was kept up continually in different parts of the city.

December 26—The revolutionists had posters put up on prominent places with instructions for the strikers to go around in small squads and to fire on the troops whenever they had a chance, also to disarm all policemen, officers, and soldiers and to arrest them when that could be done. To conceal themselves around corners of streets and take refuge in yards and houses, and to fire from there on the troops at every opportunity. An attack was made by a large number of strikers on an incoming military train with troops returning from Manchuria, and all the officers and soldiers were disarmed. Fighting was kept up all day in different parts of the city and many were wounded and killed. The troops used cannon in destroying the barricades and firing on several houses which were occupied by the revolutionists. Many policemen were killed while standing in their posts.

December 27—At 6 o'clock p.m. the house where the chief of the secret police, Mr. Vollocheinkoff, resides, was surrounded by a revolutionary party and by their insistent demands the front door was opened. Six men rushed into his apartments and arrested the chief, and read the death sentence of the revolutionary party to him. His wife and three children pleaded to the revolutionists for mercy, but the revolutionists would not listen to their pleading, and allowed Mr. Vollocheinkoff a short time to prepare for death and then took him out into a side street where he was shot to death, and his body left in the street.

Disturbances and shooting were carried on in the different parts of the city, and new barricades erected.

December 28— . . . The Semenoff Guard Regiment and artillery arrived from St. Petersburg and were temporarily put under command of General Michenko, who had just arrived from Manchuria. The general at once gave severe orders to the military garrison, and the soldiers did excellent service and put terror amongst the revolutionists and mobs. All the policemen were given rifles, which had a good effect on the mobs. Barricades commenced to disappear in the central streets of Moscow.

December 29—Shooting was going on as usual in all parts of the city, but not so much as before. The city is overrun with tramps and peasants, who are mostly begging and holding up people for the purpose of robbing them. Houses in places where people have deserted their homes and where disturbances took place are being robbed.

The revolutionists removed their headquarters to the outskirts of the city and commenced to build new barricades and to take possession of houses from where they could do damage to the troops when attacked. . . .

December 31—The troops bombarded the large Procharoff spinning mills, where a large number of revolutionists made their last stand. Many houses in the vicinity of the mill were either burnt down or wrecked by cannon balls. Many of the revolutionists and strikers were killed, wounded, or captured and the weapons confiscated. The general strike has been called off.

The governor-general issued several proclamations to the people asking all peaceable citizens to assist him in subduing the disturbances.

Moscow is under a strict state of siege. . . .

At the present moment it is quite impossible to state correctly how many were killed and wounded during the riots, but there should be approximately 1,000 killed and 3,000 wounded from both sides.

The city telegraph system is completely wrecked, as all the poles were cut down and the wires used in barricading the streets. Many of the electric tram cars and horse cars were also used for barricades, and it will take several months to put everything in proper order.

All periodicals stopped printing from the 20th to the 31st of December.

I am, etc.,

Samuel Smith

1906 A Nobel Prize for President Roosevelt
Dispatch from U.S. Minister to Norway Herbert H. D. Pierce to Secretary of State Elihu Root

Theodore Roosevelt became the twenty-sixth president of the United States in 1901 after the assassination of President William McKinley (1897–1901). Recognized abroad for his policy of "walk softly and carry a big stick," Roosevelt was far more interested in foreign affairs than were his predecessors. He worked hard to enhance American power abroad. In 1905 Roosevelt was instrumental in mediating the end of the Russo-Japanese War; the peace treaty was signed at Portsmouth, New Hampshire, on September 5. Roosevelt earned a Nobel Peace Prize for his efforts. The award was accepted on his behalf by U.S. Minister to Norway Herbert Pierce, who filed this dispatch on the ceremonies, which were held in the Norwegian Storting, or Parliament. The only other American president to be awarded the Nobel Peace Prize was Woodrow Wilson in 1919, for his contribution to the peace treaty ending the First World War.

Christiania, December 12, 1906

Sir:

... An extraordinary session of the Storthing was called for 1.30 o'clock, on Monday, December 10, which the members of the diplomatic corps and the officials of the Government were invited to attend. A row of chairs had been placed in front of the seats of the deputies, facing the president, for the Nobel committee, and an additional chair for the representative of the recipient of the prize. So quietly had the matter been kept that no member of the Storthing, even, was aware of the decision of the committee, and there was much speculation as to who would receive the award. In the diplomatic loge intense interest was manifest, and while President Roosevelt's name was frequently spoken as being the most fitting choice, the absence of any intimation of the fact was regarded as an indication that this had not been decided upon.

The session was called to order by President Knutsen at 1.45 o'clock, and immediately Mr. Lovland, as chairman of the Nobel committee, announced the decision of the committee in a few brief and formal words.

The president then said the following, which I translate:

... The cause of peace, gentlemen, presented quite a different aspect twelve to fifteen years ago to what it does today. The cause of peace was then considered to be utopianism and the champions of the cause were considered as well-intentioned but enthusiastic idealists, with whom one could not count in practical politics and who had no comprehension of the realities of life.

Since then a complete change has taken place in this respect. . . . And it is, in the first place, the United States of America which have taken the lead in this work tending to the introduction of the cause of peace into the domain of practical politics. Treaties of peace and arbitration have been concluded by the United States with the governments of several countries, and a circumstance which more than anything else has directed the attention of the friends of peace as well as of the whole civilized world toward the United States is President Roosevelt's philanthropic efforts tending toward bringing about the termination of the bloody war which recently raged between two of the world's great powers, Japan and Russia. . . .

He then handed me the diploma, medal, and order upon the Nobel trustees for the amount of the prize, and upon receiving them I spoke as follows, ending by reading the President's telegraphed words of thanks and statement as to the disposition he has determined upon for the sum of money which constitutes the prize:

> Mr. President, gentlemen of the Norwegian Storthing: I deeply regret that my residence in your capital has been as yet too brief to enable me to address you in your own vigorous language. But "had I a thousand several tongues" they would be inadequate to express to you the deep emotion with which I appear before you to receive on behalf of the President of the United States, the distinguished testimonial of your recognition of those acts which stamp him as preeminent in devotion to the cause of peace and good will on earth. . . .
>
> The President has directed me to read to you, Mr. President, the following message which he has telegraphed to me for this purpose:
>
> "I am profoundly moved and touched by the signal honor shown me through your body in conferring upon me the Nobel peace prize. There is no gift I could appreciate more, and I wish it were in my power to fully express my gratitude. I thank you for and thank you on behalf of the United States; for what I did was I was able to accomplish only as the representative of the nation of which, for the time being, I am President.
>
> "After much thought I have concluded that the best and most fitting way to apply the amount of the prize is by using it as a foundation to establish at Washington a permanent industrial peace committee. The object will be to strive for better and more equitable relations among my countrymen who are engaged, whether as capitalists or as wage-workers, in industrial and agricultural pursuits. This will carry out the purpose of the founder of the prize; for, in modern life, it is as important to work for the cause of just and righteous peace in the industrial world as in the world of nations.
>
> "I again express to you the assurance of my deep and lasting gratitude and appreciation.
>
> "Theodore Roosevelt"

The President's telegram has given great satisfaction here, and is everywhere most favorably commented on, as is the award of the prize to him. I am informed that the King of Sweden has expressed himself as much gratified. The King of Norway is absent, but I have no doubt he will be greatly pleased both with the award and the President's noble application of the fund.

I may perhaps be permitted to say that this has been one of the most gratifying occasions of my life, and that it was with unspeakable pride that I had the honor of receiving on his behalf this token of a nation's recognition of the President's high purpose toward mankind, and that I continue to hear the words of encomium and congratulation which everywhere comes to me.

I have, etc.,

Herbert H. D. Pierce

1908 Atrocities in the Congo
Dispatch from U.S. Consul General in Boma James A. Smith to Secretary of State Elihu Root

The exploration of the Congo basin by explorers such as American Henry Morton Stanley hastened the European scramble for control of Africa. Stanley's efforts helped to establish in 1878 the International Congo Association, a curious organization that effectively put much of central Africa under the personal control of King Leopold II of Belgium (see "Conditions in Central Africa," p. 263). The Congo Association became the Congo Free State in 1885.

King Leopold administered the region for personal profit. Natives were forcibly enlisted to mine gold and copper, gather rubber, and act as porters. Abuses were horrific, with many natives killed, maimed, or reduced to virtual slavery. An international scandal erupted in 1903 when a British consul reported the nature of conditions in the interior. Despite a number of efforts to bring the situation under control, abuses and atrocities continued.

In 1908 the U.S. consul general in the Congo Free State, James Smith, submitted this report on conditions in the Ituri district of northeastern Congo. A year later King Leopold was forced to relinquish his personal control of the Congo. He ceded the huge territory to the Belgian nation; today the former Congo Free State is the Republic of Zaire.

Boma, March 21, 1908

Sir:

I have the honor to inclose herewith a report on the political conditions of the upper Ituri district. . . .

I have the honor to call your particular attention to the conditions brought about by the excessive rubber tax imposed on the unfortunate natives in this district. . . . It is no uncommon thing for the rubber gatherers to be eaten by leopards, which abound in many regions of the State, and I well recall the case of a native who had been thus eaten and whose remains—what was left of them—were brought to the State post at Yambata while I was there. The so-called police expeditions mentioned in the report are nothing more than armed raids for nonpayment of rubber taxes and for the purpose of securing laborers to work on the railroad from Kindu south to Portes d'Enfer.

I would further call your attention to that part of the report regarding the working of the Kilo mines by forced labor. This system is plainly contrary to the law. . . . I fail to see how the development of a gold mine for the personal benefit of the King can properly be called a work of public utility. . . .

I have, etc.,

Jas. A. Smith

ENCLOSURE

INFORMATION ON POLITICAL CONDITIONS IN THE UPPER ITURI DISTRICT

. . . Police expeditions are constantly being made into the district by the authorities. These expeditions . . . are conducted with the greatest energy; entire villages are burned and the few prisoners taken are chained together by the neck and sent to forced labor on the railroad now building south from Kindu to Portes d'Enfer.

The rest of the region comprised in the upper Ituri district, and which formerly paid taxes in rubber to the State, has revolted, the natives refusing to gather any more rubber. The tax on rubber has been a collective one, the villages furnishing a given quantity monthly, based upon the number of inhabitants. . . .

To furnish the monthly rubber tax imposed by the State the natives in this district are obliged to work the entire month. They are frequently obliged to go a distance of 15 days' march from their villages to find it. No time remains for the native to attend to the cultivation of his garden.

The revolt is a pacific one, being limited to a refusal on the part of the natives to gather rubber. Some of the natives interrogated . . . as to their reason for refusing to pay their taxes replied as follows:

"To pay the monthly impost we must go into the forest and work almost the entire month. Leaving for the forest with 50 men, we return with only 25 or 30; the others die of hunger or are eaten by leopards. Our women must bring us our food; no one remains to work our gardens. Upon our return we are at once obliged to leave again for the forest. Therefore, to die of hunger working or die from a shot from an Albini is the same. Let the soldiers come and kill us, but we will no longer gather rubber."

. . . The Mambuti (pygmies), a most warlike people, patrol the region seeking to create an armed uprising of the other natives, but with little or no success. Besides being most impressive, . . . this peaceful revolt is truly pitiful. It is a people living continually in a state of slavery, not daring to rise in arms, but, tired of suffering, preferring death rather than life without hope. . . .

Porterage . . . is forced on the people by requisitioning the necessary men from the villages. During the march, arriving at the end of the day's journey, the porters are imprisoned within a stockade with a sentinel at the gate to prevent flight. . . .

The gold mines of Kilo are worked by forced labor. The State, profiting by small revolts, secures the laborers in the Manyema district to the south, and transports them chained together by the neck to Kilo. They are paid, it is true, one "doti" (2 fathoms) of cloth per month, besides food, but every liberty is denied them and they can not abandon their work. . . .

1908 Constitutional Government in Turkey
Dispatch from U.S. Ambassador to Turkey John G. A. Leishman to Secretary of State Elihu Root

By the late nineteenth century the Ottoman Empire was decaying; its possessions in the Balkans and elsewhere were breaking away one by one from the centuries-old grip of the sultanate. Turkey's archaic administration, its capitulations to Western encroachments, and its slow pace of modernization won it the epithet "the sick man of Europe." Western-educated Turks began to agitate for reforms, initially with little success. The year 1876, however, saw the accession of a new sultan, Abdülhamid II, and the promulgation of a constitution limiting the power of the monarchy. The reform, however, was short-lived and within a year the sultan suspended the new constitution and returned to the repressive system of his predecessors.

The remainder of Abdülhamid's tenure saw the growth of the "Young Turk" movement, which sought to revitalize the empire on a more liberal and national basis. In 1908, as criticism of the sultan's rule spread—and amid fears that Turkey was about to relinquish control of some of its Balkan territories—a Young Turk, Maj. Ahmed Niyazi, and two hundred of his followers began a revolt that forced the reestablishment of constitutional government. Abdülhamid was deposed the next year. In this dispatch the U.S. ambassador comments in glowing terms on the revolution and the positive impact he expects it to have on Turkey's future.

Constantinople,
September 28, 1908

Sir:

Although it could scarcely be said that the new constitutional Government in Turkey is as yet thoroughly established, the administration, which is simply a provisional government pending the assembly of Parliament, being largely directed by the chiefs of the so-called Young Turk Party—I am quite convinced that the new constitutional regime has come to stay, and that the reign of the absolute monarchy in Turkey is a thing of the past.

In making this statement I am not blind to the fact that Turkey is liable to undergo many of the troubles experienced by other countries which have gone through the throes of a revolution, and I fully realize that she is exposed to more than the usual dangers, owing to her heterogeneous population and the jealousies and ambitions of her neighbors; but I am strongly of the opinion that she will surmount all difficulties that can ordinarily be foreseen and finally emerge from all her troubles—perhaps somewhat battered and scarred, but thoroughly purified and ready to take her place among the progressive nations.

It is quite apparent that the decline of the Empire has been arrested; and if one may judge the future by the reforms that have already been instituted, it will not be many years before Turkey will become a highly civilized and progressive nation, and, with her great natural resources, one of the richest, as existing conditions warrant the opinion that the march of progress will be even more rapid than it has been in Japan.

What European diplomacy failed to accomplish Turkey has done for herself, and, as if by magic, the reforms which combined Europe sought for years to impose have been accomplished over night, and, wonderful as it may seem, revolutionary bands, brigands, and grafters of all grades have suddenly disappeared, let us hope for good, leaving the country for the moment in the most peaceful condition it has enjoyed for centuries, which is all the more remarkable when one stops to think that the country is temporarily being controlled by sheer moral force, as many of the districts are without organized government, the old officials having either been dismissed or chased away by the inhabitants and having not as yet been replaced.

Of course much remains to be done, as it is not an easy task to replace the machinery of the Government that has so suddenly been destroyed. . . . It would indeed be a miracle if trouble of a more or less serious character did not break forth from time to time . . . but even admitting the realization of the very natural fear of disturbances of one kind or another, I am quite of the opinion that Turkey has taken on a new lease on life and will continue on its progressive march despite all the difficulties that may be encountered, both from without and from within. . . .

> I am, etc.,
>
> John G. A. Leishman

1914–1917 Crisis with Mexico
Dispatches from U.S. Representatives in Mexico

In 1911 a revolution overthrew Mexican president Porfirio Diaz, who had ruled the country for almost thirty years. Gen. Victoriano Huerta seized power in 1913, sending the country into a period of civil war. The United States refused to recognize Huerta and funneled support to Constitutionalist forces under Venustiano Carranza.

In April 1914 an American force occupied the Mexican port of Veracruz after a number of American seamen were arrested in nearby Tampico. The U.S. intervention sparked further anti-American actions in other parts of Mexico.

In July, Carranza unseated Huerta, but disaffected revolutionary commanders, including Francisco "Pancho" Villa and Emiliano Zapata, continued to fight for control of the nation. The struggle continued for several years. In an attempt to bring the United States into conflict with the Carranza government, Pancho Villa crossed the American border in 1916 to stage raids on Columbus, New Mexico, and Glen Springs, Texas. The U.S. government responded by sending Gen. John Pershing at the head of twelve thousand troops to Mexico on a punitive expedition to seize Villa and put an end to his brigandage. The American action was taken over the objections of erstwhile U.S. ally Carranza, who was sufficiently embittered by the experience that his government leaned toward Germany in World War I. In the end, the expedition failed in its goal of capturing Villa, and, with U.S. entry into the war in Europe looming, American forces were withdrawn from Mexico in early 1917. Carranza remained president of Mexico until he was overthrown by another revolutionary movement in 1920. In 1923 Villa was ambushed and killed.

These dispatches report various phases of the crisis with Mexico: the occupation of Veracruz, a retaliatory outrage by Huerta forces on the U.S. consulate in Monterey, Pancho Villa's raid on Glen Springs, and depredations and atrocities in Mexico by Villa's forces.

Occupation of Veracruz

From U.S. Consul in Veracruz William W. Canada to Secretary of State William Jennings Bryan

Vera Cruz, April 21, 1914

Marines and bluejackets landed at 11.30 this morning. . . . Notwithstanding firing from housetops we are masters situation so far without use heavy guns. Firing all around consulate several shots having struck building. . . . Our men now simply defending themselves but may have to use big guns from ships if Mexican troops do not cease firing soon. . . . At this time reported four our men killed, twenty wounded. . . . Several Americans including some women who refused to go aboard refugee ship now marooned in hotels within firing line. . . . Am now making efforts to reach General Maas, Commandant of Port, requesting him in name of humanity cease firing to prevent necessity our ships bombarding city. . . .

Canada

Prisoner of the Mexicans

From U.S. Consul in Monterey Philip C. Hanna to Secretary of State William Jennings Bryan

Monterey, April 24, 1914

On the 21st of April a federal military officer . . . evidently instructed by the federal military commander to tear down all American flags, arrived at this Consulate General with a street mob which he had gathered . . . and pounded in the door and demanded that the American flag over this Consulate General be immediately lowered or he would shoot it down, and the other federals proceeded to tear down all American flags, standing on them . . . burning some of them, and tearing them up and leaving them piled in the middle of the streets. It was the most insulting act that I or any of the people of Monterey have ever witnessed. They then placed a police guard in front of this Consulate General, and all the inmates in this building were considered prisoners. The next morning, the 22nd of April, about 10 o'clock, a police lieutenant arrived with a force of men and advised me that he had been instructed to search the building. The insulting search was completed about noon, when your Consul General was taken prisoner through the streets with the mob, and carried first to the penitentiary, and afterwards to the state government palace. . . . While I was placed under heavy guard in the grand reception room of the state palace I fully realized that I was constantly being considerably insulted and greatly humiliated . . . on account of my official position as representative of the United States Government in northern Mexico. At about 8 o'clock in the evening of April 22nd I was taken before the military court and notified that I was charged of being in sympathy with the Constitutionalist chiefs and as being friendly to certain Constitutionalist generals, and especially General Pablo Gonzales and General Antonio Villareal. I was kept a prisoner incommunicado until the evacuation of the city by the federal troops and arrival of the Constitutionalist forces early this morning. . . . The officers of the Constitutionalist army inform me that they heard that I was taken prisoner and the American flag ordered down from over this Consulate General. A Constitutionalist officer . . . with a company of men hurried to the state palace . . . and broke into the locked door early this morning, furnishing me with a saddled horse and accompanied me to the suburbs of the city, where I met General Antonio Villareal. . . . In company with General Villareal and some of the foreign consular representatives in Monterey, we proceeded to the state palace, where speeches were made to the people . . . giving assurances of full protection to all foreign and non-combatants, and the fullest degree of freedom and protection of law-abiding people. . . .

Hanna

Mexican Raid on Texas

From U.S. Vice Consul in Piedras Negras William P. Blocker to Secretary of State Robert Lansing

Piedras Negras, May 8, 1916

Sir:

I have the honor to report to the Department that on Friday night May 5, the Columbus raid was repeated at Glen Springs, and Boquillas, Texas.

. . . Mexican bandits estimated to number 200 men entered Glen Springs, Texas, some 200 miles from the border. Only 9 American soldiers were in the town, which were routed after a fight lasting two hours, resulting in the killing of 3 soldiers, a nine year old boy, wounding two soldiers and carrying away 2 Americans by the name of M. J. Deemer and L. Coy.

After the raid they then returned toward the border and attempted to raid Boquillas, Texas, on the next night (Saturday), but were driven off by the armed employees of the mining company at that place. . . .

A recent report states that Deemer and Coy have been found dead with their throats cut from ear to ear near the boundary line.

Army trucks have been despatched to the scene to carry away the women and children, and two troops of cavalry, one machine gun platoon left yesterday from Fort Clark, Texas, commanded by F. W. Sibley. . . .

A report is current that Rosalio Hernandez, ex-Villa commander is in command of the band, that he left Sierra Mojada several days [ago] at the head of five hundred men in the direction of the border. The Vice Consul does not place any faith in this rumour and neither do the military. It is believed that the small band reported to be using the Sierra Del Burro as a rendezvous and are commanded by ex-Villa officers or Diaz supporters, who had rather see intervention than submit to Carranza as head of the Mexican Republic; and making such raids with that end in view. . . .

William P. Blocker

Pancho Villa's Depredations: "Bodies Left like Carrion"

From U.S. Vice Consul in Piedras Negras William P. Blocker to Secretary of State Robert Lansing

Eagle Pass, January 12, 1917

. . . Villistas personally commanded by Villa, healthy and strong, entered Torreon December 24 after Government forces in demoralized condition evacuated city unknowingly leaving five hundred Yaqui Indians there who turned in favor Villistas joining their column. Sixty Chinese, five Arabs and approximately eighty Carranza sympathizers were murdered, the bodies left like carrion in the street, and had not been buried on 8th when messenger left. All printing establishments were destroyed, several dwellings, stores looted . . . one hundred fifty cars merchandise loaded on trains and carried north which bandits abandoned near Jiminez on account lack of coal. . . . Villistas strength estimated after being joined by bands operating around Torreon at four thousand men. Stirring speeches were made by Villa at Casino in Torreon saying next move would be defeat of General Murguia then drive Pershing from Mexican soil. Torreon in worse condition than ever before. . . .

Blocker

1914 Assassination of Archduke Franz Ferdinand

Dispatch from U.S. Ambassador to Austria-Hungary Frederic Courtland Penfield to Secretary of State William Jennings Bryan

Throughout the late nineteenth and early twentieth centuries the Balkans were a region of tremendous turmoil, beset by a multiplicity of nationalist movements and by great-power rivalries. Several wars broke out, most of which remained localized. Serbia, which became a nation in 1878, had designs on the territories of Bosnia and Herzegovina, which were controlled by Austria-Hungary but populated by a large number of Serbs. Several terrorist actions were undertaken by Serbs against the Austro-Hungarians, most of them committed by secret societies such as "Union or Death" or "The Black Hand."

In June 1914 the heir-apparent to the Austro-Hungarian throne, Archduke Franz Ferdinand, was assassinated in Sarajevo, Bosnia, by a Bosnian revolutionary acting with the knowledge of the Serbian government. Austria demanded retribution from Serbia, threatening war. The crisis triggered World War I, which began about a month later. The assassination was reported in a matter-of-fact manner, with no comment on its possible importance, in a telegram from the American ambassador to Austria-Hungary.

Vienna, June 28, 1914

I regret to report assassination today at Sarajevo, Bosnia, of Archduke Franz Ferdinand, heir apparent to the thrones of Austria-Hungary, and his wife, the Duchess of Hohenberg, by pistol shots fired by a student. The Archduke and wife were attending an official function. The Austrian Emperor returns to Vienna Monday from Ischl.

Penfield

1914 Europe on the Brink of War

Dispatches from U.S. Representatives in Germany, Austria-Hungary, France, Great Britain, and Russia to Secretary of State William Jennings Bryan

The conflict between Austria-Hungary and Serbia over the assassination of Archduke Franz Ferdinand (see "Assassination of Archduke Franz Ferdinand," above) would have had every chance of remaining a regional dispute had it not been for the complex series of alliances among the European states. Russia, hoping to win favor in Balkan politics, assured the Serbs of aid in the event of Austro-Hungarian aggression. Austria-

Hungary took the precaution of confirming that its ally Germany would support it in any conflict. Russia likewise obtained assurances of support from its ally France.

When Austria-Hungary declared war on Serbia on July 28, 1914, the announcement set off a series of military mobilizations and declarations of war. In a preemptive strike against France, Germany moved through neutral Belgium after being refused permission from King Albert I to travel across the country as a nonhostile force. The king reportedly told the Germans that Belgium was "a nation, not a road" and called on the British to honor a treaty to defend Belgian neutrality. By early August 1914 all the major European powers were embroiled in what would come to be known as "The Great War," World War I.

American diplomatic dispatches sent during the week of prewar crisis show that much of Europe was unaware of the disaster toward which it was hurtling. Those who did perceive the danger could do no more than express a sense of helplessness that events were spiraling out of control.

No War

From U.S. Ambassador to Germany James W. Gerard

Berlin, July 27, 1914

I have reason to believe matter will be arranged without general European war. . . .

Gerard

Localized War

From U.S. Ambassador to Austria-Hungary Frederic Courtland Penfield

Vienna, July 27, 1914

War certain and probably localized Balkans. . . .

Penfield

Civilization Threatened

From U.S. Ambassador to France Myron Timothy Herrick

Paris, July 28, 1914

Situation in Europe is regarded here as the gravest in history. . . . Civilization is threatened. . . .

Herrick

"Great Gloom"
From U.S. Ambassador to Great Britain Walter Hines Page

London, July 31, 1914

... There is great gloom here this afternoon. As [Foreign Secretary Sir Edward] Grey expressed it, "It looks as if Europe were in the clutch of blind forces."

Page

Country Unanimous for War
From U.S. Chargé d'Affaires in Russia Huntington Wilson

St. Petersburg, July 31, 1914

Situation becoming steadily more hopeless. Complete mobilization now in progress. Whole country, all classes, unanimous for war. ...

Wilson

Tears and Heartbreak
From U.S. Ambassador to Great Britain Walter Hines Page

London, August 4, 1914

Sir Edward Grey has just informed me that his Government has this afternoon sent an ultimatum to the German Government expiring at midnight to-night. The ultimatum is that Germany must withdraw her demands made of Belgium and respect the treaty insuring the integrity of Belgium. ...

Sir Edward explained at length the designs of Germany. If Belgium were acquired, then of course Holland would be, then Denmark. ... The Germans had made proposals to England to secure English neutrality which England regarded impossible. Sir Edward said: "All governments must rest on mutual agreements and the sacredness of treaties is all that separates us from unorganized society. England's position becomes impossible if we accede to the violation of the treaty insuring Belgium's neutrality."

During his long explanation made in the most impressive way tears came into his eyes as he declared that he was heart-broken to think that what he had so long and earnestly striven for had now failed. "It gives one the feeling of a life [of] wasted effort.". ..

American Ambassador

1914 Germany Victorious

Dispatches from U.S. Representatives to Belgium, Great Britain, and Germany to Secretary of State William Jennings Bryan

As would be the case in 1939 at the outset of World War II, at the commencement of hostilities in 1914 the German military was the strongest and best equipped in Europe. The French, who provided the bulk of the military opposition to Germany until 1915, were reliant on a strategy known as Plan XVII for their defense. But Plan XVII, the creation of Gen. J. J. C. Joffre, underestimated both German strength and the direction of the main German attack. In the early weeks of the war the Germans were victorious on every front, sweeping through Belgium and advancing to within twelve miles of Paris. These dispatches report reactions in Brussels, London, and Berlin.

Occupation of Brussels

From U.S. Minister to Belgium Brand Whitlock

Brussels, August 20, 1914

Twenty thousand Germans under command of General von Jarotzky occupied Brussels this afternoon. Headquarters established in the Hotel de Ville. Civil authorities carry on administration under the supervision of military authorities. Except for a small force to guard Grand Place, Hotel de Ville, and railway stations, all the troops are encamped outside the city. I omitted to state in my telegram of yesterday evening that the Spanish Minister and I represented to the military governor that the resistance which he expected to offer would entail the loss of innocent human life and the destruction of artistic treasure which are of the greatest value to civilization. In view of these and other considerations he abandoned his plan and at a late hour last night disbanded the Garde Civique. The occupation of the city was effected quietly and perfect order prevails.

Whitlock

A Long War

From U.S. Ambassador to Great Britain Walter Hines Page

London, September 3, 1914

To the President: The idea is becoming common here that if the Germans take Paris, the German Emperor (William II) will make a proposal for peace and call on you to witness his unwillingness to shed another drop of blood. His proposal will, of course, be essentially the proposal of a conqueror. He will seek to save himself, his throne, and his bureaucracy. The dominant English opinion is that if he be let off, then the war will have been in vain. The resolve is to give a deathblow to the Germans at any cost in time, men and money. The English are preparing for a long war and, as I read their mood and character, they will not stop till they have succeeded. Many men freely express the hope to me that neither our Government nor American public opinion will regard any proposed peace as worth while that stops short of a final blow to bureaucracy.

So far as I can make out, the opinion of Europe outside of Germany is fast solidifying into severe condemnation of German methods, and the Germans are arousing the strongest moral condemnation. The burning of Louvain and other towns, the murder of non-combatants, the crimes against women and children, which are not printed but which are repeated everywhere, are producing in this kingdom a mood of grim determination.

[British foreign secretary] Sir Edward Grey told me today that the Germans are preparing for a regular Zeppelin campaign to drop bombs on London. It is impossible to form an independent judgment about such a rumour, but Grey is the last man to indulge in gossip or to entertain groundless fears. The censorship here is so severe and effective that we hear nothing about the war till days after the events have occurred.

I am doing all I can without producing a degree of alarm that would offend the British Government to induce all Americans to go home. There are a good many here who remain merely to enjoy the excitement and the English are beginning severely to criticize them privately. They are in the way. They are in the wrong mood for such a time. Perhaps a proper expression of such an opinion by our Government would have an effect on them.

American Ambassador

Germany Walking through the Opposing Forces
From U.S. Ambassador to Germany James W. Gerard

Berlin, September 2, 1914

Sir:

Very little news is given out here, but please be sure of one thing, and that is that Germany is walking through the French, English, and Russian armies as if they were paper hoops. The Germans will soon have a position near the seacoast in the neighborhood of Ostend, and then they can send Zepplins to England. . . . The war spirit here is extraordinary; Berlin is as calm as in time of peace. There is no confusion. . . .

One million, two hundred thousand volunteers enrolled in a few days, this of course in addition to the millions already on the army lists; this will give you an idea of the spirit of the people. The people are far more incensed against England than France or Russia. . . .

I am writing this under constant interruptions from Americans asking me to prophesy about the war, which accounts for the disjointed style. . . .

James W. Gerard

1915 The Political Process in Haiti
Dispatches from U.S. Representatives in Haiti

Haiti, one of the first independent republics in the Western Hemisphere, also has been one of the least stable, with its political system often in the hands of brutal dictators. In 1915 a particularly ugly revolution, accompanied by the danger of European intervention, led to the American occupation of Haiti. U.S. forces arrived during a moment of crisis, but they would remain in Haiti for almost twenty years before withdrawing in 1934.

The first of these brief dispatches was written in response to an inquiry from the secretary of state about the nature of Haiti's electoral system. The second reports the gruesome death of Haitian president Vilburn Guillame Sam; it also notes the arrival of U.S. forces in the Haitian capital of Port au Prince. Sam had seized power by force of arms just five months earlier. His attempt to seek refuge in the French legation from a new group of revolutionaries was not successful.

Elections
From U.S. Minister to Haiti Arthur Bailly-Blanchard to Secretary of State William Jennings Bryan

Port au Prince,
February 27, 1915

. . . Elections as understood in America do not exist in Haiti. Elections being simply a continuation of military system under which the country is governed. The population generally takes no part in elections, the voting being done by soldiers acting under instructions. Few voters who vote many times. . . .

Blanchard

Death of a President

From U.S. Chargé d'Affaires in Haiti Robert Beale Davis Jr. to Secretary of State Robert Lansing

Port au Prince, July 28, 1915

At 10.30 mob invaded French Legation, took out President, killed and dismembered him before Legation gates. Hysterical crowds parading streets with portions of his body on poles.
   U.S.S. *Washington* entering harbor.

Davis

1915   Human Shields at Gallipoli

Dispatch from U.S. Ambassador to Turkey Henry Morgenthau to Secretary of State William Jennings Bryan

Ottoman Turkey maintained a precarious neutrality for the first three months of the Great War, then entered the conflict on the side of Germany and Austria. With the war deadlocked on the western front, some British leaders, notably Winston Churchill, conceived the idea of an attack on Turkey. The campaign began in April 1915, with its main thrust aimed at the Dardanelles, the narrow straits dividing European and Asian Turkey. The attack, which came to be known as the Gallipoli Campaign, was a military disaster for the British, who withdrew after several months of heavy fighting. In this dispatch U.S. Ambassador Henry Morgenthau reports his partially successful effort to prevent the Turks from sending hundreds of British and French civilians as human shields against the British bombardment of Gallipoli.

Constantinople, May 11, 1915

Sir:

Confirming the Embassy's various telegraphic despatches I have the honor to inform you of the deportation of certain English and French to Gallipoli. Since the beginning of the war a great deal of indignation has been caused among the Turks by bombardments on the part of the Allied fleets to which they were powerless to respond, and which they declared aimed at non-combatants. The theory of utilizing the English and French here resident as hostages . . . was therefore invoked and . . . it was proposed to expose the subjects of the belligerents to the fire of their own ships. . . . Now that the action at the Dardanelles is in full swing and has, it is said, caused some loss of life to non-combatants, it was announced that the English and French here resident would be sent to Gallipoli . . . in order that they be exposed to the effects of the bombardment. When news of the measure became generally known it caused very considerable consternation here. The Embassy was besieged by the local English and French subjects who begged for my intercession. In the Diplomatic Body as well the measure was very severely judged. At the same time the only weapon in my power to prevent it lay in moral persuasion. I solicited the assistance of those of my colleagues who I thought could assist me, but apart from the German Ambassador, the efficacy of the aid of the others was very questionable. . . . While the Grand Vizier whom I had seen on the subject gave me hopes of a two days' delay, the real decision lay entirely with the Minister of War, Enver Pasha. . . .

Enver Pasha has always proved himself extremely friendly to me and on this occasion I had the impression that my personal relations stood me in good stead, for he could easily have avoided the interview until after the departure of the hostages which had been fixed for the following morning. . . . As he was absolutely determined to enforce the principle, I endeavored at least to modify the practice and succeeded in his reducing the number from the entire foreign belligerent male population which would have amounted to several hundreds, as first intended, to fifty selected from the English and French of between twenty and forty years of age. He also allowed Mr. Philip, the First secretary of the Embassy who very generously volunteered for this purpose, to accompany them provided he should do so in an unofficial capacity, also two American correspondents. . . .

By further conference with the Prefect of Police, Bedri Bey, I succeeded further in having the number of hostages, instead of being selected from the notables of the colonies as desired by him, chosen from the youngest upward. . . .

I have [etc.]

H. Morgenthau

1915 Armenian Genocide

Dispatch from the U.S. Ambassador to Turkey Henry Morgenthau to Secretary of State Robert Lansing

The largely Christian Armenian population of the Ottoman Empire suffered periodic repression during the nineteenth century. With the outbreak of World War I, Turkish rulers considered the loyalty of their Armenian population suspect and began a concerted campaign against them. When Russian troops invaded Turkish-held areas of the Caucasus, some

Armenians welcomed and joined the invaders. Armenians in the city of Van rose in revolt against their Ottoman rulers. The Turkish response was swift and savage. In 1915 most of Turkey's Armenian population was forcibly uprooted and dispersed to distant parts of the empire, amid terrible conditions in which hundreds of thousands perished. According to U.S. Ambassador Henry Morgenthau, the Turks were attempting to "exterminate a race." In this dispatch from the Turkish capital, Morgenthau reports the disaster befalling the Armenians and recounts his efforts to intervene on their behalf.

Constantinople, July 10, 1915

Persecution of Armenians assuming unprecedented proportions. Reports from widely scattered districts indicate systematic attempt to uproot peaceful Armenian populations and through arbitrary arrests, terrible tortures, wholesale expulsions and deportation from one end of the Empire to the other accompanied by frequent instances of rape, pillage, and murder, turning into massacre, to bring destruction and destitution on them. These measures are not in response to popular or fanatical demand, but are purely arbitrary and directed from Constantinople in the name of military necessity, often in districts where no military operations are likely to take place. The Moslem and Armenian populations have been living in harmony, but because Armenian volunteers, may of them Russian subjects, have joined Russian Army in the Caucasus and because some have been implicated in armed revolutionary movements and others have been helpful to Russians in their invasion of Van district, terrible vengeance is being taken. Most of the sufferers are innocent and have been loyal to Ottoman Government. Nearly all are old men [and] women. All the men from 20 to 45 are in Turkish army. The victims find themselves dispossessed of their homes and sent on foot to be dispersed in districts where they are unknown, and no provisions have been made to lodge or to feed them. We have in several places been refused permission to relieve their misery or to have access to them. In some few instances where they opposed these measures and took refuge in the mountains and some arms or bombs were found, it provoked the authorities to further cruelties which they attempt to justify by the opposition. Untold misery, disease, starvation, and loss of life will go on unchecked. Consul David of Harput reports:

> Professors American College have been tortured. Some others have died under torture or lost mind. Many hundred young Armenian men originally taken as soldiers, some of whom were students American College, have been sent away without food, clothing, or money. Night of June 23 several hundred other Armenians, recently arrested, includ-

ing professors American College, were sent away in the middle of the night without food, clothing, or money. Many deaths are reported en route in both lots of prisoners. Preparations are being made apparently to send away many more. I was informed confidentially today that an enormous sum of money is now being demanded of the local Armenians. There seems to be a systematic plan to crush the Armenian race. All things make us apprehend permanent closing of American schools.

That only refers to one place. Many Armenians are becoming Moslems to avoid persecution. In addition to humanitarian considerations we have real interest through the fact that certain objectionable Armenians involved in these forced dispossessions and deportations are naturalized citizens of the United States and that the charitable and education work of the American Board will suffer considerably and in many places will cease altogether.

The only embassy here which might assist in lessening these atrocities is the German, but I believe it will simply content itself with giving advice and a formal protest probably intended for record and to cover itself from future responsibility. German Ambassador is about to leave on a six weeks' vacation. Have impressed on him that he and his Government will have considerable share in the odium. Immediately upon arrival of his substitute I shall make Herculean efforts to enlist his sympathies. Austrian Ambassador has promised me to try to influence Minister of the Interior. . . .

I have repeatedly spoken to the Grand Vizier and pleaded earnestly with Minister of the Interior and Minister of War to stop this persecution. My arguments were unavailing. . . . Turkish authorities desire to avail themselves of present conditions when three of the great powers are at war with them, Italy in strained relations, and the two others are their allies and therefore will not interfere when they are successfully defending the formidable attack at the Dardanelles. . . .

Turkish authorities have definitely informed me that I have no right to interfere with their internal affairs. Still I desire to ask whether you have any suggestions.

American Ambassador

1915 An Ambassador's Observation: "The Whole German People Is Dangerously Mad"

Dispatch from U.S. Ambassador to Germany James W. Gerard to Secretary of State Robert Lansing

In view of the early victories of the German army and the expanses of territory taken, the German people had little reason not to be enthusiastic about the war. The hardships of war—the rationing and shortages and the death and maiming of an entire generation of young men—had yet to arrive. This dispatch from the American ambassador in Berlin describes German determination and confidence one year into the war. The dispatch also notes domestic support for Germany's controversial war methods, including submarine warfare against civilian ships such as the Lusitania. *Continued use of submarines was one of the principal issues that led to America's entry into the war against Germany in 1917.*

Berlin, July 13, 1915

Sir:

... The spirit of the people is absolutely unbroken; they believe in ultimate victory and certainly have had no defeats. The wonderful organization takes care of everyone; money is plentiful, in fact there is a period of inflation. Wives of soldiers get a war allowance and so much per child and are better off than in peace times.

Public works, such as extending the underground railroad in Berlin, are being carried on. Small towns and villages feel the war more than Berlin; but there are no signs of failure of war spirit. Perhaps if the war means another winter campaign there may be a different spirit. I have heard many hints to that effect.

As to Germany's war methods, they have the full approval of the people; the sinking of the *Lusitania* was universally approved, and even men like Von Gwinner, head of the German Bank, says they will treat the *Mauretania* in the same way if she comes out.

The general public want to keep Belgium. They say the sacrifices of the war demand a compensation. They are led by the official opinion. Only the Socialists want no new territory and there is a dissenting party even among them. People in Government circles say that to give up Belgium would be to invite a revolution and the expulsion of the Hohenzollerns. The whole German people is dangerously mad. I cannot give you in detail the sources of my information, most of it is confidential, but I have personal relations with all classes.

I have [etc.]

Gerard

1917 The Zimmermann Telegram
Dispatch from U.S. Ambassador to Great Britain Walter Hines Page to Secretary of State Robert Lansing

In 1916 the United States volunteered to act as a mediator among the warring nations of Europe. Responding to a complaint by the Germans that they were unable to communicate with their ambassadors abroad, the American government allowed Germany access to U.S. government telegraphic channels. The German foreign ministry then began to communicate with its embassies in Washington and Mexico City, in code, through the American embassy in Berlin and the Department of State. One of the messages sent over this wire came to be known as the "Zimmermann telegram," after German foreign minister Albert Zimmermann. The cable contained an astounding proposal to Mexico that if it were to enter the war on the side of Germany, it might reconquer territory lost to the United States in earlier wars. This communication in American diplomatic channels was intercepted and deciphered by the British, who turned it over to the American ambassador in London. When the telegram was made public several days later, it inflamed American opinion against Germany and helped to solidify American sentiment to enter the war five weeks later.

London, February 24, 1917

[British foreign secretary Arthur] Balfour has handed me the text of a cipher telegram from Zimmermann, German Secretary of State for Foreign Affairs, to the German Minister in Mexico, which was sent via Washington. . . . I shall send you by mail a copy of the cipher text and of the decode into German and meanwhile I give you the English translation as follows:

> We intend to begin on the 1st of February unrestricted submarine warfare. We shall endeavor in spite of this to keep the United States of America neutral. In the event of this not succeeding, we make Mexico a proposal of alliance on the following basis: make war together, make peace together, generous financial support and an understanding on our part that Mexico is to reconquer the lost territory in Texas, New Mexico, and Arizona. The settlement in detail is left to you. You will inform the President of the above most secretly as soon as the outbreak of war with the United States of America is certain and add the suggestion that he should, on his own initiative, invite Japan to immediate adherence and at the same time mediate between Japan and ourselves. Please call the President's attention to the fact that the ruthless employment of our submarines now offers the prospect of compelling England in a few months to make peace. Signed, Zimmermann.

The receipt of this information has so greatly exercised the British Government that they have lost no time in communicating it to me to transmit to you, in order that our Government may be able without delay to make such disposition as may be necessary in view of the threatened invasion of our territory.

Early in the war, the British Government obtained possession of a copy of the German cipher code used in the above message and have made it their business to obtain copies of [German ambassador to the United States Johann von] Bernstorff's cipher telegrams to Mexico, amongst others, which are sent back to London and deciphered here. . . . This system has hitherto been a jealously guarded secret and is only divulged now to you by the British Government in view of the extraordinary circumstances and their friendly feeling towards the United States. They earnestly request that you will keep the source of your information and the British Government's method of obtaining it profoundly secret, but they put no prohibition on the publication of Zimmermann's telegram itself. . . .

I have thanked Balfour for the service his Government has rendered us and suggest that a private official message of thanks from our Government to him would be beneficial. . . .

Page

1917   The Russian Revolution
Dispatch from U.S. Consul in Petrograd North Winship to Secretary of State Robert Lansing

By 1917 the Great War had taken a heavy toll on Russia. At least two million Russian soldiers were casualties, and the major cities, including the capital of Petrograd, were facing serious shortages of food and fuel. On March 8 food riots broke out in Petrograd. Troops sent to put down the disturbances clashed instead with police loyal to the czar. Within days revolutionaries were in full control of the city, Czar Nicholas II had abdicated, and Russia had become a republic. These dramatic events are reported in this dispatch by the American consul in Petrograd, North Winship.

The United States lost no time in recognizing the new government. Indeed, the fall of the Russian monarchy removed the last obstacle to America's entry into the war by lending credence to the U.S. goal of championing democracy in Europe. America declared war on Germany just two weeks after the czar's abdication. The Russian provisional government lasted just eight months before it was overthrown by the Bolsheviks, the Marxist party led by V. I. Lenin, in November.

Petrograd, March 20, 1917

Sir:

I have the honor to report that as a result of serious economic, political, and military disturbances, the government of this city and district has been completely assumed by an Executive Committee of the Imperial Duma, at least for the time being.

On the beginning of the week of March 4, a shortage of black bread was noticeable. This at once caused unrest among the laboring classes. All other prime necessities within the means of the working classes had already gradually disappeared as the winter advanced: meat, sugar, white flour, buckwheat, potatoes. Fish, fowls, eggs, milk, cheese and butter had for a long time been so expensive that they were only within the means of the very well-to-do classes. The unrest first took visible form in the outskirts and factory districts of the city Wednesday, March 7, when the workmen struck after the dinner hour and met in groups to discuss the situation.

The next day, Thursday, March 8, there were spontaneous and isolated demonstrations. In many places, a few of the working class, mostly women, tired of waiting in bread lines in the severe cold, began to cry "give us bread." These groups were immediately dispersed by large detachments of mounted police and cossacks.

March 9, large crowds of women marched to Kazan Cathedral (opposite the Consulate) with bared heads, still crying for bread and shouting to the police "Give us bread and we will go to work." This crowd was peaceable and was dispersed.

Saturday morning the crowds, composed of working men and students, visibly with a serious purpose, came from all districts to the center of the city. Besides calling for bread, these crowds shouted "Down with the Government," "Down with the Romanoffs," and occasionally "Down with the War." The mounted police endeavored to drive the mobs from the Nevsky, the main street, but resistance was made and barricades built on side streets. The police withdrew after firing on and charging the crowds with whips without success. Their place was taken by infantry who fraternized with the people. Announcement was made by the police that after 6 o'clock that day, all groups of persons would be fired upon. The crowds did not disperse, and street battles took place, especially on the Nevsky, resulting in great loss of life.

At this time the infantry and cossacks refused to fire on the crowds or to charge them. Towards evening a detachment of cossacks actually charged and dispersed a body of mounted police.

Sunday, when the it became known that the Emperor had prorogued the Duma and that it had refused to recognize this order, there was disorganized and sporadic fighting all over the city, with heavy loss of life. The unmounted police were withdrawn from the streets. Many regiments which had been locked in their barracks mutinied during the night, killed some of their officers, and marched to defend the Duma, which was still sitting.

By Monday the disorganized riots developed into a systematic revolutionary movement on the part of the working men and the constantly growing numbers of mutinied troops, to capture the city of Petrograd. The fighting moved rapidly across the city from the Duma as a center, so that by Monday night, only isolated houses and public buildings, upon which machine guns were mounted, were held by the police and the few remaining loyal troops. At midnight the Duma had announced that it had taken the Government into its own hands and had formed an Executive Committee to be the head of the temporary Government.

Tuesday and Wednesday the fighting was confined to volleys from machine guns fired by the police from the isolated housetops, public buildings and churches, and the return fire by the soldiers, such fighting continued until all police were taken. Violence necessary in arresting Government, army and police officials, took place at this time. . . .

On the 2nd of March the Emperor abdicated for himself and his son in favor of his brother, the Grand Duke Michael. On the 3rd the Grand Duke Michael declined the throne unless it should by offered him by the Constitutional Government. This again averted further civil war as it put all parties in agreement to await the Constitutional Convention. . . .

A new Mayor has been chosen by the Aldermen. He is attempting to control and improve the local food supply which is again at the danger point as at the beginning of the revolution. All necessities have to be brought to Petrograd from the provinces and a serious food shortage now exists. If it is not relieved at once it will cause further serious disorders capable of developing into new revolutionary movements with greater socialistic tendencies than heretofore.

Today, March 20, for the first time in ten days, a very few electric street cars are running but not enough to constitute a resumption of the service. The workmen have not returned to the factories as hoped.

                                        I have [etc.]

                                        North Winship

PART VII

The World in Upheaval: 1920–1945

This political cartoonist was among those urging the United States to stay out of World War II. U.S. Ambassador to Great Britain Joseph Kennedy also repeatedly beseeched President Franklin Roosevelt not to get involved.

1921 Sun Yat-sen Elected President of China
Dispatch from U.S. Vice Consul in Canton Ernest B. Price to Secretary of State Charles Evans Hughes

With the end of the Manchu dynasty in 1912, China's internal strife erupted into a civil war that would rage until the establishment of the Chinese Communist government in 1949. Throughout this period various regions of China came under the rule of warlords, each with a private army and an eye on ruling all of China. Dr. Sun Yat-sen, however, was another kind of leader, who became known as the father of modern China. Educated in the West, Sun founded the Koumintang, or National Party, and was a strong believer in parliamentary government. Sun was elected president of China in 1911, but he stepped down the next year to promote national unity when a rival national assembly elected Yüan Shih-k'ai, commander of the army, as provisional president. Dissatisfied with Yüan's almost dictatorial government, Sun Yat-sen declared a second revolution in 1913. This revolution, however, was put down, and Sun was forced into exile. With the death of Yüan in 1916, the way was opened again for the warlords. In 1921, with the support of the southern warlords around Canton, Sun reattempted to establish a central government founded on democratic and nationalist ideals. In this he succeeded, and he was elected president. The 1921 election is described in this dispatch from the U.S. vice consul in Canton.

In 1925 Sun Yat-sen died of cancer. His disciple Chiang Kai-shek assumed leadership of the Koumintang and became the dominant figure in China.

Canton, April 20, 1921

Sir:

I have the honor to report on political conditions in this consular district. . . .

Probably not for some time has the political situation in South China been more interesting or more fraught with serious possibilities affecting not only the South but all of China. In my telegram of April 8, 1921, 10.00 a.m., to the Department and to the Legation I reported what I had prophesied in my telegram No. 248 of two days previous, the election by remnants of the so-called "Old Parliament" sitting in extraordinary session in Canton of Dr. Sun Yat-sen as President of the Republic of China. While anticipated, the actual consummation of this act came, I believe, as a general surprise and is commonly believed to have been premature. My understanding of the election is that the Parliamentarians met informally to decide whether they should convene as an extraordinary session of the old parliament and, agreeing that they should so convene, they decided to do so at once; and finding on their agenda the one piece of business of paramount importance, namely, the election of a president, they proceeded to the election then and there. I understand that there were 225 members present and that 222 votes were cast for Dr. Sun Yat-sen. . . .

Regarding the legality and propriety of a group of 222 men out of nearly one thousand who composed the old parliament electing a president for the whole of the country, the representative consensus of opinion among Southern leaders seems to be this: Whether or not 222 out of 1,000 members of parliament could be said properly to represent the country, they were, after all, members of the only legally elected parliament in China; and therefore Dr. Sun's claim to the Presidency is the best approximation of Constitutionality that can be obtained in China.

In conclusion, the general consensus of opinion among persons friendly to the present political leaders in South China, both Chinese and foreign, would seem to be that if the Government, as reconstituted in South China, can devote its energies primarily to building up an efficient and upright administration and to promoting the economic development of the people of Kwangtung, it has a very good chance to become heir to the power over a much larger portion of China when the forces of disintegration elsewhere in China have accomplished their work.

I have [etc.]

Ernest B. Price

1922 Nicaragua: The U.S. Minister Quells a Revolution
Dispatch from U.S. Minister to Nicaragua John Edward Ramer to Secretary of State Charles Evans Hughes

President Theodore Roosevelt initiated a policy of active intervention in the Caribbean and Central America that would persist for decades. Spelled out in 1904, the "Roosevelt Corollary" to the Monroe Doctrine stated that since no European country could intervene in the Western Hemisphere, the United States would have to exercise international police power in the area. The policy was used to justify intervention in the Dominican Republic, Haiti, Nicaragua, and elsewhere. In several instances, the United States took control of local customs houses to ensure that foreign debts were paid. Such was the case in Nicaragua in 1911. When popular disturbances broke out there the next year, U.S. Marines landed. They remained in the country for thirteen years.

The United States had a strong stake in Nicaraguan stability during this period. In 1922, when a military faction revolted and seized strong points around the capital, U.S. Minister John Ramer was able to put down the revolt by warning the rebels that they faced additional U.S. military intervention unless they desisted. The incident is described in this dispatch.

Managua, May 21, 1922

About one hundred revolutionists representing dissatisfied faction of the conservative party under Generals Arsenio Cruz and Salvador Castrillo quietly seized Loma fortress about noon today. . . .

Major Marston warned Cruz that any firing upon the American camp or the city of Managua would result in immediate intervention of American forces to preserve order and protect American interests (situation makes it impossible to fire upon Managua without jeopardizing American life and property). Cruz replied that he had no intention of firing upon city or camp.

Legation repeating the warning of possible military intervention proposed and secured the agreement of both sides to a conference which was held in the Legation during the afternoon under the auspices of Major Marston, Mr. [Benjamin] Muse [third secretary of the U.S. legation] and myself. Representatives of President Chamorro, Adolfo Cardenas, Acting for Foreign Minister, and Fernando Solorzano; [of] General Cruz, Adan Canton and Ramon Molina. Following is abbreviated text of agreement signed.

> Loma Fortress evacuated before ten oclock this evening. All arms and ammunition to be left in fortress as found. Fortress surrendered to American marine officer who will see that terms of agreement regarding arms is carried out. General amnesty extended to all civilian participants and maximum punishment of 30 days detention to all military participants in revolution.

Marston, Muse and I signed arrangement as witnesses. Seal of the Legation affixed.

Loma Fortress surrendered to Captain Gregory of Marine Corps at eight o'clock according to agreement and Government forces took over half an hour later.

Most of the American residents gathered in the marine camp during the afternoon as well as Nicaraguan officials with their families including President Chamorro and his Cabinet to all of whom protection was extended. Two insurgents and five regulars were wounded in desultory fighting before and during conference. No killed, no Americans or American property touched.

Admiral Cole with squadron due here on 25th for courtesy visit was telegraphed to proceed immediately to Corinto.

The Legation acted drastically in this crisis and I am eager to secure the Department's approval. As only hope of averting imminent bloody civil war I informed both parties that my Government would not permit this revolution in Nicaragua. In reply to repeated promise of the insurgents to respect the inviolability of Managua and of the American camp I indicated to them that they could not carry out their revolutionary plans without eventually pressing it and preserving order. I informed them of Admiral Cole's approaching visit and added that 10,000 additional Marines were within a few days call.

Populace still agitated but Government has situation well in hand.

Ramer

1923 Earthquake in Japan
Dispatch from U.S. Consul in Kobe Erle R. Dickover to Secretary of State Charles Evans Hughes

The Japanese islands were formed as the result of violent geologic activity, much of which continues today in the form of earthquakes and erupting volcanoes. The worst natural disaster in Japan's modern history was the great earthquake of 1923, which leveled Tokyo and Yokohama and sparked fires and tidal waves that compounded the destruction. An estimated 200,000 people were killed in the quake, including American consul general Max Kirjassoff and vice consul Paul Jenks. With communications from Tokyo disrupted, news of the disaster was cabled to Washington by the consul in Kobe.

Kobe, September 5, 1923

... Yokohama completely destroyed by earthquake and fire, no business houses nor homes remaining standing. Consulate General collapsed and burned killing Kirjassoff and wife, Vice Consul Jenks, Kuribara, and Russian clerk. Kirjassoff's two children, Vice Consuls Sturgeon, Nason, and Wardell and Miss Martin safe. Naval Hospital destroyed, Commander Webb badly injured, pharmacist Zembsch and wife killed, and two enlisted men reported killed. Owing to complete destruction of city, lack of food and water, and danger from hunger-driven and uncontrolled Japanese, all foreign residents are proceeding to Kobe. Four refugee vessels have arrived already. Miss Martin with Kirjassoff children has arrived, and Nason, Sturgeon, and Wardell expected today. Ambassador Woods and entire staff of Embassy Tokyo reported safe and well. Approximately half Tokyo destroyed by fire, and some foreign residents proceeding to Kobe. Kobe residents have raised funds and are working day and night to assist refugees but funds insufficient for lengthy period and aid desired. Tokyo and Yokohama banks not functioning and funds should be sent to me through International Banking Corporation.

Suggest send $50,000 for relief destitute foreigners. No estimate can be made of aid required by Japanese in Yokohama and Tokyo as communications still out but shall communicate with Tokyo as soon as possible regarding most necessary requirements. . . . Owing complete disorganization Tokyo district, necessary use Kobe as center consular activities in Japan for some time to come.

Dickover

1925   Revolt in Damascus
Dispatch from U.S. Consul in Damascus James Hugh Keeley to the U.S. Consul in Beirut

After World War I the Ottoman Empire was dismembered. In the empire's former Arab territories, sentiment for independence ran high, but British and French occupation forces held sway on the ground. In Syria a national congress declared independence and named a king, but the European powers refused to recognize the move. Instead the League of Nations approved a mandate for France to govern Syria, and French troops forcibly occupied Damascus and the countryside. Both Syrian nationalists and traditional ethnic leaders opposed the French regime. In 1925, after the arrest of some Druze leaders in Damascus, the Druze population rose in revolt. The people of Damascus joined the insurrection, driving the French from the city. The French responded by bombarding Damascus from the air. French forces retook the city within days, but the revolt was not entirely quelled for almost two years. This dispatch from U.S. Consul James Keeley describes the critical situation in Damascus in November 1925. Keeley sent the dispatch through the U.S. consulate in nearby Beirut.

Damascus, November 3

Despite official French communiqué to the effect that, except southeast of Damascus where a small band has been dispersed by French cavalry, complete calm reigns in all other parts of Syria, I consider that the situation generally in this district becomes more serious daily. Rebel forces reliably estimated at 3,000 reported to be advancing on Damascus. Bombs dropping from aeroplanes plainly visible from the consulate roof and gunfire distinctly heard for some time during battle this afternoon between the rebels and a French detachment about 5 miles east of Damascus. French forces insufficient to subdue rebels, who easily elude small detachment set after them. French are destroying all villages the inhabitants of which do not themselves drive off bandits, which tactics steadily increase number of the enemy. . . .

It is reported reliably that all territory in this district except principal town on the railroad now in hands of the rebels. It is impossible to communicate with naturalized American citizens residing in troubled areas and I fear that some of them may be in danger and in distress.

Inhabitants of Damascus panic stricken, thousands trying to leave daily, food becoming scarce, cost of living rising, business dead.

Keeley

1927 Besieged by a Chinese Mob
Dispatch from U.S. Minister to China John Van A. MacMurray to Secretary of State Frank B. Kellogg

After the death of Dr. Sun Yat-sen, the situation in China worsened to the point that warring among factions became common even in the major cities (see "Sun Yat-sen Elected President of China," p. 363). *In this dispatch the U.S. minister to China relays a report from his consul in Nanking. The consul reports that after severe fighting in Nanking, he and a party of Americans were forced to abandon the consulate and seek shelter with other foreign nationals in a more defensible location.*

Peking, March 25, 1927

Following just received by Navy radio from Consul Davis, Nanking:

March 24th, about noon. After both British and Japanese consulates had been attacked and the consuls reported killed and after the known cold-blooded murder of one American missionary and attempted murder of many others, all by Nationalist soldiers, Chinese police informed me that we would be destroyed unless we could escape. Accordingly our party of 1 officer, 11 sailors, 9 civilians and 2 children escaped under constant fire across country to Standard Oil Company's house on Standard Oil Hill just above city walls which are visible from river and where many Americans and British already were. Although repeatedly robbed and threatened by Nationalist soldiers, vice consul and Standard Oil Company manager managed to keep them out of house for 2 hours but finally they broke in and, seeing our numbers, retired and commenced firing upon us in ever increasing numbers. American and British naval vessels then dropped shells around house and we escaped over hill. Consulate forced by Nationalist soldiers and reported by Chinese as thoroughly looted. Not ascertained whether safe forced and code lost. . . .

MacMurray

1927 The Kellogg-Briand Pact: A Protocol to Outlaw War
Dispatch from U.S. Chargé d'Affaires in France Sheldon Whitehouse to Secretary of State Frank B. Kellogg

In the wake of World War I, the 1920s were a period of peace building in Europe. The major powers entered into a series of treaties guaranteeing each other's borders. The "spirit of Locarno," so-called after the Swiss town where several treaties were signed, reflected a new international confidence that countries could resolve their differences by peaceful means. The process advanced a step further in 1927 when French foreign minister Aristide Briand proposed to Secretary of State Frank Kellogg a pact outlawing war between France and the United States. Kellogg, however, feared such an agreement would tie the United States too closely to a European power; he suggested instead a treaty outlawing all war. The Pact of Paris, ultimately signed by almost every country in the world, renounced war as an instrument of national policy. For his efforts, Kellogg won the Nobel Peace Prize in 1929 (Briand had won the prize in 1926 for his earlier peace efforts).

Despite his successful conclusion of the peace pact, Briand was deeply disappointed to have failed in his goal of linking the United States and France more closely. This dispatch reports his unhappy acceptance of Kellogg's proposal. The treaty itself—which had no enforcement provisions—proved ephemeral (see "Views on Japan's Invasion of Manchuria," p. 372).

Paris, December 31, 1927

I saw Briand and explained to him your views. He replied that he quite understood. . . . The following is a statement of Briand's views:

On several occasions the League of Nations had publicly indicated its belief that all disputes should be settled by pacific means and its opposition to any recourse to war. As far as it went this was good, but such a manifestation would be greatly strengthened by the adhesion of the United States. Briand had believed, therefore, that if America and France should solemnly declare their condemnation of recourse to war . . . it would promote the cause of peace. He believed that such a declaration should be made in a solemn form in view of the ancient friendship between the American and French peoples. . . . His attitude would be entirely sympathetic if you wished at the same time to draft a protocol outlawing war and to invite the leading states of the world to sign it. Briand stated that he thought from the last telegram sent to him by Ambassador Claudel that we were in agreement as to points of view and that all that remained to be settled were minor details. He said he hoped that you would not make public your note to Ambassador Claudel of

December 28 without an understanding between the American and French governments as to what should be given to the press.

A friend at the Foreign Office privately said to me something that led me to think that Briand is much disappointed at the nature of my reply as he had hoped it was possible to have a bilateral convention. The terms of such a convention obviously could be more explicit than would be the case in a multilateral one. I think Briand now understands our situation and is ready to accept what you can offer him.

Whitehouse

1930 An Early Nazi Victory: Banning a Movie
Dispatch from U.S. Ambassador to Germany Frederic Mosley Sackett to Secretary of State Henry L. Stimson

The 1930s saw the dawning of Hollywood's Golden Age, with film maturing into an art form as well as a medium of entertainment. With its ability to reach a mass audience and manipulate their emotions, film also became a powerful political tool. The members of Germany's National Socialist German Workers' Party—the Nazis— were among the first to realize the political impact of film, using productions such as "Triumph of the Will" to further their propaganda. Hollywood's release in 1930 of "All Quiet on the Western Front," with its depiction of German defeat and its antiwar theme, was seen by the Nazis as insulting to German patriotism and injurious to the country's prestige. Although the Nazis were still a minority party at the time, their daily agitation against the film created a cause célèbre that resulted in its withdrawal from German theaters. As reported by the U.S. ambassador in Berlin, the Nazi success in banning the movie was both a serious blow to the German government and a taste of Nazi policies and tactics still to come.

Berlin, December 17, 1930

Sir:

With reference to my despatch No. 646 . . . and to my telegram No. 140, . . . reporting respectively, the disturbances resulting from the showing in Berlin of the American-produced Universal Film company's version of Eric Remarque's "All Quiet on the Western Front," and the decision of the Appellate Board of Film Censors, on December 11th, to prohibit its further production in Germany, I have the honor to report further as follows:

As stated in my telegram aforementioned, the film had been approved by the primary Board of Film Censors, but, on complaint of five German

States . . . the Appellate Board of Film Censors ruled that it was calculated to injure Germany's prestige abroad and therefore should be withdrawn. The chairman of the board declared that, as a whole, the film did not do justice to the frame of mind of those who participated in the war, if the film were continued to be shown, other countries would feel that Germany had approved the representation. . . .

It is interesting to report, in this relation, that "West Front, 1918," a talking film, produced in Germany, of a distinctly anti-war character, is now being shown in smaller theaters and no disturbances in connection therewith have occurred.

The immediate cause for the suppression of the film was undoubtedly the pressure of the mob, which made demonstrations every evening under the leadership of members of the National Socialist Party. However, after the first disorders in the theater, reported in my despatch above-mentioned, the management of the theater was able to continue the performance for six days, before crowded houses, without further disturbance. Later disorders took place in the square outside the theater, where hundreds of youths assembled every evening, but were held back at a safe distance by a cordon of police. As a result of the strong guard outside of the theater, the Nazi leaders also conducted demonstrations in nearby public squares.

It is strongly indicated that the showing of the film was only a pretext for demonstrations by the National Socialist Party. Most of the youthful participants in the disorders never saw it at all, and even some of the Nazi leaders who agitated against the film, admit that they had not seen it. On the evening of the first public showing in Berlin several Nazi leaders, it will be recalled, were in the audience, but as the performance was interrupted after the first few scenes they, therefore, did not see the whole picture. . . .

The grounds on which the film was suppressed are not convincing and cannot be accepted by an impartial observer. . . .

The widespread editorial comment on the suppression of the film was influenced principally by the political affiliations of the respective journals. The Nazi press, of course, acclaimed the decision of the Board as a signal victory over the hated Republic by the "patriotic" elements under their leadership. The *Völkische Beobachter* of December 14th declared that the Appellate Board of Film Censors had no intention of prohibiting the "Jewish film" and that it was finally forced to take this step as a result of organized resistance by the Nazis. Other Nazi journals, notably Dr. Goebbels' *Der Angriff,* boastfully declared that the Nazis would likewise proceed in future against all films and theatrical productions with anti-national tendencies. . . . [T]he moderate Right journals greeted the decision because it put an end to an incident which was rapidly assuming an importance out of all proportion to the many real political and economical difficulties with which Germany is confronted. . . .

The suppression of the film version of "All Quiet on the Western Front" has undoubtedly assumed great importance. The National-Socialist Party has succeeded in giving a blow to the prestige of the Government of the Reich, in that it yielded to Nazi compulsion on a clean-cut political issue. . . .

>Respectfully yours,
>
>Frederic M. Sackett

1931 Views on Japan's Invasion of Manchuria
Dispatch from U.S. Minister to China Nelson T. Johnson to Secretary of State Henry L. Stimson

In 1928 the major nations of the world signed the Kellogg-Briand Pact, outlawing the use of war as an instrument of national policy (see "The Kellogg-Briand Pact," p. 369). The pact, however, was little more than symbolic because it contained no enforcement mechanism.

The first major violation of the pact was Japan's invasion of Manchuria. On the night of September 20, 1931, Japanese troops in Manchuria staged an explosion along a stretch of the Japanese-controlled South Manchuria Railway, and then used the incident as a pretext to occupy the rest of Manchuria. When the League of Nations criticized the action, Japan responded by withdrawing from the League. Japanese troops would remain in Manchuria until the end of World War II.

In this dispatch Nelson Johnson, who served for fifteen years as American minister and ambassador to China, vents his anger over the Japanese action in Manchuria. Nelson sees the invasion as a clear violation of Japan's obligations under the Kellogg-Briand Pact. The lack of a concerted international response to Japan's aggression set the tone for the policy of appeasement that would characterize foreign affairs in the 1930s.

>Peiping, September 22, 1931

. . . According to all information available to me here, I am driven to the conclusion that the forceful occupation of all strategic points in South Manchuria, including the taking over and operation of public utilities, banks, and in Mukden at least the functions of civil government, is an aggressive act by Japan apparently long planned and when decided upon most carefully and systematically put into effect. I find no evidence that these events were the result of accident nor were they the acts of minor and irresponsible officials.

By article 1 of the Kellogg Treaty the high contracting parties, among which is Japan, renounce war "as an instrument of national policy in their relations with one another." By article 2 they agree "that the settlement or solution of all disputes [or] all conflicts of whatever nature or of whatever origin they may be, which may arise among them, shall never be sought except by pacific means."

It is my conviction that the steps taken by Japan in Manchuria must fall within any definition of war. . . .

It seems to me that the powers signatory to the Kellogg Treaty owe it to themselves and to the world to pronounce themselves in regard to this Japanese act of aggression which I consider to have been deliberately accomplished in utter and cynical disregard of obligations which Japan as a nation shares with the other signatories of that pact.

Johnson

1932 Communist Uprising in El Salvador
Dispatch from U.S. Chargé d'Affaires in El Salvador William J. McCafferty to Secretary of State Henry L. Stimson

El Salvador entered the twentieth century under an authoritarian political system. For fourteen years the presidency was in the hands of three different members of the same family. Beginning in 1927, however, more enlightened rulers held sway for several prosperous years, instituting reforms and allowing the development of an active labor movement. When Gen. Maximiliano Hernández Martínez seized power in December 1931, a general insurrection broke out. Hernández Martínez took vigorous measures to put down the revolt, including arresting and executing Farabundo Martí, leader of El Salvador's five-year-old Communist Party. In this dispatch, which seems to preview events half a century later, the U.S. chargé d'affaires describes the unrest and attributes it to the growth of communism in El Salvador.

San Salvador, January 20, 1932

During the past 3 years . . . communism has been permitted to be spread throughout Salvador. It is now very well organized and has been actively carrying on radical propaganda. . . . The leaders have taken advantage of the unsettled condition of the government to intensify their activities and have succeeded in inciting the farm laborers to take over control of several large coffee plantations and the government has been obliged to use force to expel them. About 10 days ago in the city of Ahuachapán the Communists attacked the government offices and were driven off by the police and the National Guard and it is estimated that at least 30 people were killed. An active radical campaign has been carried on in Santa Anna. The night before last communistic activities were discovered among the soldiers of the infantry barracks here. A number of sergeants were under arrest last night. A crowd of several hundred Communists including students well armed and with dynamite bombs attempted to attack the cavalry barracks here but were repulsed. It is said that a number were captured including the notorious agitator Augustin Marti.

It is difficult to obtain absolutely accurate information and while the details of the above may not be exact I believe that they are fundamentally true. The de facto government claims that it has the situation well in hand. It is difficult however to ascertain to what extent the loyalty of the Army has been undermined by radical propaganda. Even the most soberminded Salvadoreans and foreigners are becoming deeply concerned regarding the situation and fear that the authorities may not be able to continue to suppress these communistic outbreaks. While I do not wish to be an alarmist I am inclined to feel that the present situation is serious.

McCafferty

1933 The Reichstag Fire: The Nazi Ascent to Power
Dispatch from U.S. Ambassador to Germany Frederic Mosley Sackett to Secretary of State Henry L. Stimson

By 1933 the National Socialist German Workers' Party, the Nazis, had made considerable political gains and had won a plurality in the Reichstag, the German parliament. Nazi leader Adolf Hitler was appointed chancellor in January but under such a divided government that he was forced to call for new elections within weeks. The crucial event of the brief and violent election campaign was a mysterious fire that destroyed the Reichstag. Under the pretext of "protecting the state," Hitler used the incident as a rationale to launch a campaign of terror and intimidation against his political opponents. In this dispatch from Berlin the American ambassador reports and analyzes the results of the Reichstag fire.

With other parties restricted or banned, the Nazis emerged victorious from the March 5 elections. The new government moved promptly to suspend the constitution and begin the Nazi dictatorship that would rule Germany until the end of the Second World War.

Berlin, March 3, 1933

... The burning of the Reichstag gave the Nazis the pretext they needed for further repressive measures against political opponents. In addition to the planned decree sharpening the penalties for treason, sedition and subversive activities which now provides the death penalty for the betrayal of military secrets, the Government promptly issued a presidential decree putting into effect a state of exceptional emergency, suspending those articles of the Constitution which practically constitute the German Bill of Rights.

According to semi-official statement, "it had been proved beyond doubt that Communist leaders were directly connected with the incendiarism and that Communists had planned other acts of terrorism. . . ."

On these grounds and by virtue of the unlimited powers granted him by the Emergency Decree, Minister [Hermann] Goering immediately ordered a wholesale arrest of Communist deputies in the Reichstag and Prussian Diet, as well as prominent pacifists, journalists, authors, educators and lawyers who defended Communists in political trials, and a number of Social Democrats. Several thousand persons, many of whom are intellectuals and not registered members of a political party, are now being detained in custody for an unlimited time, without being informed of the reason. At a meeting of his party last night, Minister Goering boasted that alone in the Rhineland and Westphalia 2000 persons have been put behind bars.

All Communist newspapers have been prohibited in Prussia for four weeks, Social-Democrat newspapers for two weeks. A similar prohibition has been imposed on all periodicals, handbills and placards of the two parties. . . .

In Prussia and other parts of Germany, the Auxiliary Police—composed of members of the Nazi Storm Detachments and the Stahlhelm—are being mobilized in large numbers, and cases are reported where uniformed Nazis acting as police have searched the homes of individuals and organizations opposed to the present regime. To demonstrate that the Communists have been definitely downed, a Nazi Storm Detachment paraded before the Karl Liebknecht house, Communist headquarters in Berlin recently closed by the police, and, with appropriate ceremonies, hoisted the Nazi flag over the building.

Of the opposition parties, aside from the very small Staatspartei, only the Center Party is still able to conduct its campaign in Prussia and other states dominated by the Nazis, despite the drastic restrictions imposed by the decrees. The centrist party can still hold political meetings and appeal to the voters by means of placards and election literature; its press has not been suppressed. As far as the Left parties are concerned, however, the campaign was definitely over immediately after the fire in the Reichstag. For these parties the election on March 5 is a farce, as they have been completely deprived during the last and most important week of the campaign of the constitutional right to appeal to their following. In most parts of Germany, the Social Democrats have been so completely muzzled and repressed that, outwardly at least, they have ceased to exist.

On the other hand, the Nazis are winding up the campaign in impressive style. The numerous brown uniforms, the huge Nazi placards with which the cities and countryside are dotted, the frequent parades of the

Brown Army, the mass meetings and the daily broadcasting of election speeches by Nazi leaders, tend to create the impression that even now there is only one large party in Germany. . . .

Hitler and Goering are very indignant that certain foreign journals refuse to believe that the German Communist Party had anything to do with the arrested incendiary, some even attributing the crime to the Nazis themselves. While there is no reason to doubt the official statement on this point, one can readily understand why some foreign correspondents in Berlin take such an attitude. Deliberate acts of terrorism have up to now seldom been attributed to the Communist party as such. In recent years their crimes consisted for the most part of so-called literary treason or sedition, of subversive acts such as attempts to disintegrate the Reichswehr and the police, and frequent instigation to a general strike. The German Communists have not, to my knowledge, resorted to anarchist methods with which Bolshevists in the United States and other countries are usually identified. . . .

It is a fact that many people in Germany really believe—though they are afraid to say so openly—that the Dutchman arrested is an *agent provocateur,* or that he acted on his own initiative, without the knowledge of the Communist Party. They contend that the Communists had little to gain from such an act of terrorism and that the Communist leaders must have known that the Nazis would not fail to exploit it in order to hasten the advent of a purely Fascist regime in Germany. It is pointed out that the circumstances under which the incendiary was arrested, and the readiness with which he allegedly associated the Social Democrats with the crime, without, however, divulging the identity of his accomplices, has led many to view the Government's assertion with skepticism. According to the official investigation, inflammable material had been set on fire at more than twenty different points and the arrested Dutchman must therefore have had at least from seven to ten accomplices. . . .

The Nazis have exploited the incident to the utmost, in their press and political meetings, as well as in broadcasts of strongly colored reports from the scene of the fire. Past masters of propaganda that they are, they have managed to stir up the country to a pitch comparable only to wartime hysteria. The enthusiasm of the growing Nazi following knows no bounds, while the rest of the population—intimidated and nervous—is awaiting the week-end with anxiety and misgivings.

Conscious of their growing strength, the Nazis will stage, on the eve of the elections, impressive demonstrations throughout Germany, with torchlight processions and, what Dr. [Joseph] Goebbels calls, "liberation bonfires" along the German frontiers. Hitler will speak in Konigsberg, the capital of East Prussia, on the night before the election. The speech will be broadcast over a national hook-up and Dr. Goebbels, as chief propagandist of the party, has ordered that loud-speakers be set up in all public squares throughout the country, and that people with radios in their homes open the windows "in order that every man in the street may hear the words of the Fuhrer."

The fire has caused the heaviest damage to the assembly hall of the Reichstag, completely destroying that chamber, while the main structure of the massive building, which outwardly resembles the Library of Congress in Washington, has suffered comparatively little damage. It has been estimated that it will take at least a year to restore the building. . . .

Sackett

1933, 1934 The National Socialist German Workers' Party: Seeking to Dominate the Globe

Dispatches from U.S. Representatives in Germany to
Under Secretary of State William Phillips

By 1933, when Adolf Hitler became chancellor of Germany, Nazi methods and policies already were clear to American representatives in Berlin. As for the ultimate Nazi goals, these also were evident to those who listened closely to Nazi rhetoric and who took the time to read Hitler's Mein Kampf *published several years earlier. Among those who raised their voices in early warning were American diplomats George Messersmith and Douglas Miller. These dispatches are illustrative of their early understanding and their attempts to warn others of the Nazis' aggressive and expansionist aims. Messersmith, a career Foreign Service officer, was consul general in Berlin until 1934, when he moved on to become minister to Austria. Douglas Miller was commercial attaché in Berlin.*

Germany: "A Very Dangerous Situation"
From U.S. Consul General in Berlin George S. Messersmith

Berlin, June 26, 1933

Dear Mr. Phillips:

I think the Department must be exceedingly careful in its dealings with Germany as long as the present Government is in power as it has no spokesmen who can really be depended upon, and those who hold the highest positions are capable of actions which really outlaw them from ordinary intercourse.

I think we must recognize that while the Germany of to-day wants peace, it is by no means a peaceful country or one looking forward to a long period of peace. The present German Government and its adherents desire . . . to make Germany the most capable instrument of war that there has ever existed. . . . Wherever one goes in Germany one sees people drilling, from children of five and six on, up to those well into middle age. A psychology is being developed that the whole world is against Germany . . . and the idea of war and danger from one's neighbors is constantly harped upon. I wish it were really possible to make our people at home understand, for I feel that they should understand it, how definitely this martial spirit is being developed in Germany. . . .

This country is headed in directions which can only carry ruin to it and will create a situation here dangerous to world peace. With few exceptions, the men who are running this Government are of a mentality that you and I cannot understand. Some of them are psychopathic cases and would ordinarily be receiving treatment somewhere. Others are exalted and in a frame of mind that knows no reason. The majority are woefully ignorant and unprepared for the tasks which they have to carry through every day. Those men in the party and in responsible positions who are really worth-while, and there are quite a number of these, are powerless because they have to follow the orders of superiors who are suffering from the abnormal psychology prevailing in the country. . . . There is a real revolution here and a very dangerous situation.

Very sincerely yours,

George S. Messersmith

An Assessment of the Nazi Leadership: "Unscrupulous Adventurers . . . Touched with Madness"

From Minister-Designate to Austria George S. Messersmith and Acting Commercial Attaché Douglas Miller

Berlin, April 21, 1934

Dear Mr. Phillips:

In my last letter I mentioned that Miller, the Acting Commercial Attaché, was preparing a resume. . . . As I anticipated, it is a very excellent review of certain aspects of the situation here and I am sending a copy to you now as I feel sure it will be of interest to you and to others in the Department. . . .

Miller's conclusions have been entirely independently arrived at and in no way influenced by my own, and yet it will be apparent that we are very much in accord in our appraisal of the situation. . . .

Cordially and faithfully yours,

George S. Messersmith

ENCLOSURE

April 17, 1934

MAIN PURPOSE OF NAZIS

The fundamental purpose is to secure a greater share of the world's future for Germans, the expansion of German territory and growth of the German race until it constitutes the largest and most powerful nation in the world, and ultimately, according to some Nazi leaders, until it dominates the entire globe.

The German people, suffering from a traditional inferiority complex, smarting from their defeat in the war and the indignities of the post-war period, disillusioned in their hopes of a speedy return to prosperity along traditional lines, inflamed by irresponsible demagogic slogans and flattered by the statement that their German racial inheritance gives them superior rights over other peoples, have to a large measure adopted the National Socialist point of view for the time being.

ECONOMIC AIMS

There are two other purposes subsidiary to the main purpose. Germany is to be made the economic center of a self-sustaining territorial block whose dependent nations in Central and Eastern Europe will look to Berlin for leadership. . . .

SOCIAL AIMS

The second subsidiary purpose is the welding of all individuals in the present and future Greater Germany into a homogeneous racial family, gladly obedient to the will of its leader, with class and cultural differences inside the country eliminated, but a sharp line drawn between Germans and the foreign world outside. In carrying out this purpose, the Jews are to be entirely eliminated, the Slavic or eastern elements in the population to be minimized and eventually bred out of the race. A national religion is in process of organization; trade unions, political parties and all social, political, cultural, trade or other organizations not affiliated with the National Socialist party, have been abolished, the individual's rights have been largely taken away. In the future the nation is to count for everything, the individual for nothing. Germany is to engage in a gigantic struggle with the rest of the world to grow at the expense of its neighbors. . . .

DANGER OF WAR

The Nazis are not satisfied with the existing map of Europe. They are at heart belligerent and aggressive. True, they desire nothing more than a period of peace for several years in which they can gradually re-arm and discipline their people. This period may be 5 years, 10 years, or longer, but the more completely their experiments succeed the more certain is a large-scale war in Europe some day.

NAZIS WANT TO WIPE OUT 1918

... The real emotional drive behind the Nazi program is not so much love of their own country as dislike for other countries. The Nazis will never be content in merely promoting the welfare of the German people. They desire to be feared and envied by foreigners and to wipe out the memory of 1918 by inflicting humiliations in particular upon the French, the Poles, the Czechs and anybody else they can get their hands on.

A careful examination of Hitler's book and his public speeches reveals the fact that he cannot be considered as absolutely sane and normal on this subject. The same is true of many other Nazi leaders. They have capitalized [on] the wounded inferiority complex of the German people, and magnified their own bitter feelings into a cult of dislike against the foreign world which is past the bounds of ordinary good sense and reason. Let us repeat this fact and let it sink in, the National Socialist movement is building a tremendous military machine, physically very poorly armed, but morally aggressive and belligerent. The control of this machine lies in the hands of the narrow, ignorant and unscrupulous adventurers who have been slightly touched with madness from brooding over Germany's real or imagined wrongs, as well as the slights and indignities thrown in their own individual way as they attempted to organize the movement. Power of this kind concentrated in the hands like these is dangerous. The Nazis are determined to secure more power and more territory in Europe. If this is voluntarily given to them by peaceful means, well and good, but if not, they will certainly use force. That is the only meaning behind the manifold activities of the movement in Germany today.

1933 Batista Seizes Power in Cuba

Dispatch from U.S. Ambassador to Cuba Benjamin Sumner Welles to Secretary of State Cordell Hull

Sgt. Fulgencio Batista was an army stenographer when he took part in the "Sergeant's Revolution" that ousted the Cuban government in 1933. Although Batista at first declined a formal office, he was the principal power in the new government and served as president from 1940 to 1944. Batista's government instituted major reforms in education, public works, and the general economy, but it also took strong measures against its opponents. Batista retired in 1944 but sought reelection eight years later. With defeat at the polls imminent, the former sergeant staged a coup and seized power, thereby setting the tone for the rest of his political career, in which he wielded dictatorial powers.

The 1933 coup is described in this dispatch by U.S. Ambassador Sumner Welles, who had a long career with the State Department. Welles was serving as assistant secretary of state when President Franklin D. Roosevelt appointed him as ambassador to Cuba in 1933, shortly before Batista's first coup. The new Cuban government was hostile to the United States, which did not recognize it. Welles returned to the United States within weeks of writing this dispatch, where he served again as assistant secretary and then as under secretary of state. Contrary to Welles's intimation that the new regime would not last, Batista remained the dominant political figure in Cuba for the next twenty-five years. He was overthrown by Fidel Castro in 1959.

Habana, September 5, 1933

All of the officers in the Habana Government have been forced to leave their posts by the non-commissioned officers and enlisted men. Some of the officers have been permitted to leave freely; some are detained in the barracks; and a few have been sent to the Army prison. Sergeant Batista has either named himself or been selected by the enlisted men at Camp Columbia as Chief of Staff of the Cuban Army.

The troops in Habana have announced that the mutiny in which they are engaged is receiving the support of the troops throughout the Republic. . . .

At 5 o'clock this morning a so-called revolutionary government was proclaimed. . . .

This proclamation is signed by Sergeant Batista who adds the title of "Sergeant and Revolutionary Chief of all the Armed Forces of the Republic" and is likewise signed by a group of the most extreme radicals of the student organization and three university professors whose theories are frankly communistic. Five of the signatories of this proclamation have constituted themselves an executive committee to govern the Republic and have announced their intention of taking possession of the Palace during the course of the morning. . . .

The situation in the city this morning appears to be quiet. I repeat that it is urgently necessary in my judgment, however, that two destroyers arrive here at the earliest moment possible and that a battleship likewise be sent. As stated in my previous telegram, a warship should be sent to Santiago without delay. It is very likely on account of the serious labor agitation which had existed already that additional vessels should be sent to other ports to guarantee the safety of American lives. I shall so recommend if I later believe it necessary.

I wish to make it emphatically plain that I shall do my utmost to prevent in every possible way the necessity of any armed intervention by the United States. Since such a step, however, may have later to be taken by our Government I strongly urge the desirability now of explaining the Cuban situation fully to the representatives of all the Latin American Republics. It appears hardly likely that a so-called revolutionary government composed of enlisted men of the Army and radical students who have occupied themselves almost exclusively during the last 10 days with the assassination of members of the Machado Government can form a government "adequate for the protection of life, property, and individual liberty." All of the important leaders of the existing political parties in the Republic . . . are definitely hostile to this movement and it is highly problematical how many hours or days will elapse before violence and open dissensions take place throughout the Republic.

Welles

1934 Establishing Relations with the Soviet Union
Dispatch from U.S. Ambassador to the Soviet Union William C. Bullitt to Secretary of State Cordell Hull

Although the United States quickly recognized the provisional government of Russia after the overthrow of the czar in March 1917 (see "The Russian Revolution," p. 358), the United States did not grant recognition to the Bolshevik government that seized power eight months later. In fact, official American ties with the Soviet Union were withheld for sixteen years. In 1933 Franklin D. Roosevelt, newly elected president, did not feel bound by more than a decade of Republican Party precedent. He thought it odd that the United States should not have relations with a major European power and hoped that reestablishing ties might boost trade and help to counter the growing strength of Germany and Japan. The Soviets, for their part, welcomed U.S. recognition and hoped for an infusion of American capital (but they were to be disappointed). At the time the Soviets also were preoccupied with the fear of a Japanese attack in the Far East, and thus they welcomed relations with another Pacific power.

Roosevelt's choice as ambassador to the Soviet Union was William Bullitt, a prominent Philadelphia liberal who had tried to negotiate the establishment of relations with Bolshevik leader V. I. Lenin in 1918. Bullitt later would serve as American ambassador to France during the Nazi invasion. This dispatch reports Bullitt's first visit to Moscow as ambassador and describes the warm welcome he received from the Soviet leadership.

On Board Steamship
"Washington," January 4, 1934

Sir:

I have the honor to report to you the details of my visit to the Soviet Union December 10–22, 1933.

We reached Moscow on Monday, December 11. . . . We were taken to the Hotel National, where the American flag was suspended over the entrance. The apartment reserved for me was, curiously enough, the same which I was occupying when Austria sent her ultimatum to Serbia. It had been beautifully refurnished and was most comfortable. The hotel was adequately heated and the food and service were good.

I was received at once by [Foreign Minister Maksim] Litvinov at the Commissariat for Foreign affairs and had a brief, friendly conversation. . . .

December 13, at noon, I presented my credentials to [President Mikhail] Kalinin in the reception room of the large palace of the Kremlin. Mr. [Joseph] Flack [first secretary of the U.S. embassy in Germany] and Mr. [George] Kennan [third secretary of the U.S. legation in Latvia] accompanied me. . . .

After I had presented my letters, Kalinin invited me to accompany him to an adjoining room and we had a delightful conversation of a half hour. I had never met Kalinin and had thought from what I had read and heard of him that he was a simple-minded old peasant. I was surprised to find that he is far from simple-minded. He has a delightful shrewdness and sense of humor and had evidently followed with considerable attention the development of the President's program in America. He requested me to say to the President that he and everyone else in Russia considered the President completely out of the class of the leaders of capitalist states; that it was clear to them all that the President really cared about the welfare of the laboring men and the farmers and that he was not engaged in protecting the vested rights of property.

Kalinin said that he hoped that I would travel in every part of the Union of Soviet Socialist Republics, and I told him that I should be delighted to do so. . . .

Kalinin was very agreeable to me personally, saying that Lenin had talked to him about me on several occasions, and that he felt as if he were welcoming someone he had known for a long time. . . .

The entire press of the Soviet Union published articles on my arrival and . . . were not only enthusiastic but undeservedly complimentary. . . .

I had a long talk with [Premier Vyacheslav] Molotov and found that I had underrated him as I had underrated Kalinin. He has a magnificent forehead and the general aspect of a first-rate French scientist, great poise, kindliness and intelligence. He talked freely about the difficulties of the Soviet Union in the Far East, saying that the primary desire of the entire Soviet Government was to avoid war and to obtain time to work out the domestic reconstruction which had scarcely been begun. He said that he feared greatly that Japan would attack this spring; that he considered an eventual attack inevitable and 1935 as the probable limit of peace.

That evening, December 15, Litvinov gave a formal dinner in my honor at which Molotov and nearly all the Commissars were present. It was a superb banquet and many toasts were drunk to President Roosevelt, to myself and to the United States. . . .

I had a long talk with [Communist Party Secretary General Joseph] Stalin. He regards an attack by Japan this spring as certain and on introducing Egorov, the Chief of Staff, to me said, "This is the man who will lead our Army victoriously against Japan when Japan attacks." Stalin then [said] . . . "There is one thing I want to ask of you. The second line of our railroad to Vladivostock is not completed. To complete it quickly we need 250,000 tons of steel rails at once. They need not be new rails. Your rails are so much heavier than ours that the rails you discard are good enough for us. . . ." I replied that I should be glad to do anything I could in the matter. . . .

Stalin had evidently followed the development of the President's program with close attention and expressed an admiration for the President which seemed to be genuine, saying finally, "President Roosevelt is today, in spite of being the leader of a capitalist nation, one of the most popular men in the Soviet Union."

Before I left Stalin said to me, "I want you to understand that if you want to see me at any time, day or night, you have only to let me know and I will see you at once." This was a somewhat extraordinary gesture on his part, as he has hitherto refused to see any Ambassador at any time.

In order to avoid the jealousy of my colleagues, I said to Litvinov that it seemed to me desirable that it should be made known to the press merely that I . . . had had a talk with him. It was so arranged. It is valuable to have the inside track, but it seems to me not desirable to emphasize the fact to the world. . . .

Stalin went to the door of the apartment with me and said, "Is there anything at all in the Soviet Union that you want?" I told him that I should be glad to know that the property on the bluff overlooking the Moscow River might be given to the American Government as a site for an Embassy. Stalin replied, "You shall have it." The next day Litvinov told me that Stalin had given order to the Moscow Soviet that the property in the park should be ours if we wished to have it.

I had a long and important conversation with Litvinov. . . .

Litvinov began by saying that he wanted to have a serious talk with me and asked me whether the Government of the United States would have any objection to the Soviet Government joining the League of Nations. I replied that as I had no codes I could not communicate with my Government, but speaking for myself I could say without hesitation that the Government of the United States would have no objection. . . .

Litvinov . . . said that . . . the Soviet Government considered an attack by Japan in the spring so probable that everything possible must be done to secure the western frontier of the Soviet Union from attack; that he did not fear an immediate attack by Germany or Poland or both combined, but that he knew that conversations had taken place between Germany and Poland looking toward an eventual attack on the Soviet Union if the Soviet Union should become embroiled in a long war with Japan; that he feared that a war with Japan might drag on for years and that after a couple of years Germany and Poland combined might attack the Soviet Union. . . .

We had a long discussion of the situation in the Far East and he expressed the opinion that no one could say, not even in Japan, whether or not an attack by Japan would be made this spring. . . .

He then said that he felt that anything that could be done to make the Japanese believe that the United States was ready to cooperate with Russia, even though there might be no basis for the belief, would be valuable. He asked whether it might not be possible for an American squadron or an individual warship to pay a visit during the spring to Vladivostock or to Leningrad. I said that I could not answer that question, but would submit it to my Government. . . .

Litvinov gave a tremendous reception for me on the next afternoon, December 21, and that evening we left for Paris, crossing the Russian border at noon, December 22.

> Respectfully yours,
>
> William C. Bullitt

1934 Nazis Assassinate the Austrian Chancellor

Dispatch from U.S. Minister to Austria George S. Messersmith to Secretary of State Cordell Hull

After World War I the Austro-Hungarian Empire was broken up into a number of smaller nation-states, among them Austria, which struggled with reconstruction and democracy throughout the postwar period. Austrian chancellor Englebert Dollfuss was vehemently opposed to the Nazis. He turned to fascist Italy as a guardian of Austrian independence and began to reform Austria on the Italian fascist model.

In mid-1934 the Nazis made their first bold step toward territorial aggrandizement. A group of Nazi storm troopers seized Vienna's radio sta-

tion and government offices, fatally wounding Chancellor Dollfuss and taking most remaining cabinet members hostage. Austrian police stormed the building and freed the hostages. This dispatch reports the 1934 hostage incident, which was still under way when the dispatch was written.

Although Germany disassociated itself from the culprits, Nazi influence continued to grow in Austria, culminating in the Nazi takeover and annexation of Austria in 1938.

Vienna, July 25, 1934

About 1 o'clock small group Nazis took possession Vienna radio and at same time about 100 men in police and army uniforms took possession Foreign Office where Cabinet had been in session. The Chancellor, Fey and Karwinski were made prisoner the Chancellor being shot in breast and gravity of wound not yet definitely determined.

Remainder Cabinet met under [Minister of Justice and Education Kurt von] Schuschnigg and endeavored open communication with Nazis in the Foreign Office. . . . President [Wilhelm Miklas] . . . stated he could not recognize any communication from imprisoned members of Cabinet acting under duress. Minsters were informed by Nazis that unless entire Cabinet resigned imprisoned members would be shot.

Although Ministers hesitated to order police surrounding building to clear it fearing besieged would carry out threat necessity for action became evident and ultimatum was issued to besieged to surrender and they would be given safe conduct to border. No definite answer being received police were ordered to clear building using first gas which action in progress. . . .

The whole country is quiet as is Vienna where action has been localized at radio station and the Foreign Office.

While all circumstances not yet clear . . . factors would indicate today's events an abortive attempt of Nazis to secure control of the Government through terrorizing Cabinet.

Messersmith

1936 The Italian Invasion of Ethiopia

Dispatch from U.S. Minister to Ethiopia Cornelius Van H. Engert to Secretary of State Cordell Hull

Benito Mussolini, head of Italy's fascist movement, became premier of Italy by constitutional means in 1922. Once in power, he dismantled the political opposition and entrenched himself at the head of a nationalistic, fascist government.

By the 1930s Mussolini was intent on building Italian glory through the acquisition of a colonial empire. Part of Mussolini's aspirations centered on East Africa, where Italy had had territorial ambitions since the nineteenth century. When Italian troops in Somaliland clashed with Ethiopian troops along the poorly defined border, it provided the pretext for the Italians to launch a full-scale invasion of Ethiopia, which began in October 1935. The Italian forces made slow progress, but, with the use of modern armaments and poison gas, advanced within six months to the capital, Addis Ababa. The League of Nations imposed sanctions on Italy in response to its aggression but lacked the will to take actions that might have compelled an end to the invasion. After Italy's conquest was complete, the League further demonstrated its impotence by voting to end the sanctions, thereby destroying whatever influence the League had as a keeper of international peace.

Cornelius Engert was appointed U.S. minister to Ethiopia early in 1936. This dispatch, dated May 1, reports his moving encounter with Emperor Haile Selassie just days before Italian forces entered the Ethiopian capital. By May 9 Haile Selassie was in exile and Mussolini had proclaimed the Italian annexation of Ethiopia. Engert remained in Addis Ababa for a year. He showed his disdain for the new administration by refusing to comply with regulations that all foreigners give the fascist salute to the governor general and the Italian flag. Haile Selassie was restored to power in 1942 and remained emperor of Ethiopia until 1974.

May 1, 1936

My private audience of the Emperor was a unique experience which confirmed the high opinion I had formed of him. Considering the tragic hour in his country's history he showed remarkable sangfroid and conducted the interview with the same gracious unhurried suavity which had always impressed me on previous occasions. His frail body seemed perhaps a trifle frailer and his thoughtful deepset eyes showed a profoundly perturbed soul. But his handshake had its usual firmness and his inscrutable features were lit up by the same winsome smile.

After receiving my letter of credence he said that United States had always been conspicuous by their devotion to certain fundamental ideals and that the President's recent vigorous denunciation of dictatorships as a menace to individual liberty and international peace proved that American public opinion shared the desire of the world to see a restraining influence exercised over those who disregard their solemn agreements.

The Emperor said he was perplexed by the strange maneuvers of European diplomacy and the half measures of the League. He realized of course that the stage was set for another European war and that in the present confusion arising from Germany's defiance of Locarno, Ethiopia's fate is relegated to a secondary place. But he found it difficult to understand British inconsistencies and France's inability to see that if Italy had been checked in time Germany would never have dared follow in her footsteps.

Ethiopia could easily have been saved by the application of oil sanctions which would have forced Italy to abandon the war. He now saw clearly that his faith in the League of Nations was not justified and that though his advisors who had urged him to attack Italy before she could complete her preparations had probably been right, in this country the powers had permitted everything to drift to such lengths that a catastrophe was inevitable.

Referring to the possibility of a cessation of hostilities he said that the thought of peace at any price was intolerable to him. He had no intention of capitulating in the face of a premeditated murderous assault and the rumors of his imminent departure from the country were entirely baseless. He would remain and go on fighting so long as one Abyssinian soldier was left to help him. But of course he had always been and was now ready to submit to any peace proposals within the framework of the League and the spirit of the Covenant.

As I took leave the Emperor held my hand in his while he said, "Convey my greetings to your President and tell him the fate of my country may serve as a warning that words are of no avail against a determined aggressor who will tear up any peace pacts whose terms no longer serve his purpose."

I was deeply moved by the whole interview and in submitting this report I cannot help expressing the hope that when the proper time comes it may be possible for us to exert such moral influence as we possess in favor of an equitable settlement that upholds as far as may be feasible international morality rather than international crime. Having seen this nation and its ruler in their dire extremity I cannot believe Italy will be permitted to dictate terms based solely on her recent victories. Surely the time has come for plain speaking for if unilateral denunciation of treaties are tolerated not only collective security but collective civilization will receive a blow from which they may never recover.

Engert

1936, 1938   The Spanish Civil War
Dispatches from the U.S. Embassy in Spain to
Secretary of State Cordell Hull

In 1931 Spanish king Alfonso XIII, bowing to the growing pressure from the populace for a Spanish republic, left Spain. During the period of restructuring that followed, tension increased between the republicans who controlled the government and their opponents in the clergy, nobility, and military. In 1936 the army, led in part by Gen. Franciso Franco, revolted against the government. The Spanish Civil War that followed would last three years and cost more than half a million lives.

The conflict became a magnet for international intervention, with Italian and German troops joining Franco, and Soviet Russia providing arms and supplies to the republicans. One of the most deplorable military innovations of the war was the indiscriminate aerial bombardment of civilians, a practice to be repeated by all sides in World War II. These dispatches report the outbreak of the civil war in 1936 and the 1938 bombing of a town by Franco's forces.

The Revolt Begins
From Counselor of Embassy Herschel V. Johnson

San Sebastian, July 20, 1936

Revolutionary movement apparently led by Generals Franco, Queipo de Llano, and Mola and supported by Fascists and other Rights has assumed large proportions but definite information is hard to obtain. Chief of Foreign Office Section here states he has no information as to progress or suppression of movement. Wires are cut between here and Madrid and impossible to communicate by telephone with any of our Consulates. Have telegraphed every Consulate in Spain to inquire as to situation and welfare of Americans but have no security that telegrams will be delivered. General strike probably exists all over Spain and train service is largely stopped. Government asserted yesterday over radio that movement in Madrid and Barcelona has been put down. There are, however, rumours that revolutionary troops are in control of these cities. Radio stations in Seville and Burgos in hands of insurgents report movement in many cities successful.

Impossible to verify attitude of Navy or whether Navy has transported insurgent regiments from Spanish Morocco to Spain. Government has requested all loyal supporters to arm themselves and has distributed arms to Socialist youth and other Republican organizations.

In San Sebastian and neighboring towns proletariat has certainly obtained arms, and barricades have been erected and bridges blown up on roads leading to Vitoria and Pamplona, from which places it is alleged that revolutionary forces are now advancing on this city. Attitude of regiment here doubtful. Sporadic shooting in streets and roads probably thus far the result of arms in inexperienced hands. Civil Governor states frontier is closed to all except diplomats.

Have read over telephone greater part of this cable to Ambassador Bowers who is, at the moment, at his house 5 miles from here at Fuenterrabia but telephone connection no longer obtainable. Civil Governor has just advised over radio that public other than defenders of the city keep indoors and close all shutters. Apparently immediate attack is expected.

Johnson

Bombing Civilians
From U.S. Ambassador to Spain Claude G. Bowers

St. Jean De Luz, June 2, 1938

I have the honor to report that in continuance of their criminal policy of bombing civilian peoples in the hope of breaking the morale of the republicans, the Fascist Powers, allied with General Franco, reached the climax thus far in bombing the little town of Granollers, thirty kilometers from Barcelona, and killing between 350—according to some reports—and 500—according to most—women and children. The London *Times* rather tamely offers an apologetic explanation to the effect that the bombs were intended for Barcelona but since the anti-aircraft guns there drove the Italian and German planes away they "had to drop their bombs before landing," the presumption being that it was impossible to drop them in the open fields or any place else except a market town.

The town of Granollers ordinarily has a population of but 10,000, but because of refugees from Barcelona it is now said to contain 20,000 people.

The attempt of the Fascists to make it appear that this village has military objectives will not wash, in view of the fact that the two or three small factories were not touched and the bombs were aimed at the center of the town by the City Hall and the market place. It was market day and fifty peasant women at the stalls were mangled. . . .

After talking with most rabid Spanish supporters of Franco from across the border I am convinced that this bombing wholesale of villages and civilians is exceedingly distasteful to a large part of the Spaniards. They frankly expressed abhorrence of this practice and ascribe it to the insistence of the Italians and particularly of the Germans. There is no doubt that the Germans have insisted on this policy of extermination regardless of women and children from the early days of the war. A portion of the German press has recently been bitterly denouncing the Loyalists for not surrendering, and I am personally convinced that in their anxiety to end the war—and the expense—as quickly as possible, an intensive policy of terrorism may be expected in the hope of breaking the spirit of the people behind the lines. The general effect of these bestial acts, however, has been to stiffen the resistance and to convert the indifferent into militants.

Respectfully yours,
Claude G. Bowers

1940 Great Britain on the Verge of Defeat
Dispatches from U.S. Ambassador to Great Britain Joseph P. Kennedy to Secretary of State Cordell Hull

In the spring of 1940 German forces swept north and west, occupying first Denmark and Norway, then the Netherlands, Belgium, and Luxemburg. Soon, German forces also were racing through France. The British expeditionary force in Belgium and northern France was quickly evacuated from Dunkirk, leaving most of its equipment and many dead behind. The effectiveness of the German blitzkrieg—lightning war—*was so overwhelming that the fall of France seemed imminent and Great Britain's defeat was regarded as a strong possibility. During the critical days of late May, U.S. Ambassador Joseph Kennedy reported Britain's appeals for American assistance and his assessment that Great Britain could well lose the war. By late September, with Germany bombing London and other British cities daily, Kennedy was reporting that Britain's prospects were continuing to decline. In fact, Kennedy's dispatches were consistently pessimistic, and he urged that the United States stay out of the war.*

Joseph Kennedy, father of President John F. Kennedy (1961–1963), was the first Irish-American to represent the United States as ambassador in London. He was appointed early in 1938 by President Franklin D. Roosevelt and left post in October 1940, shortly after submitting the last of these dispatches.

Churchill: England Will Never Give Up

London, May 15, 1940

I just left [Prime Minister Winston] Churchill at 1.00 o'clock. He is sending you a message tomorrow morning saying he considers with the entrance of Italy, the chances of the Allies winning is slight. He said the German push is showing great power and although the French are holding tonight they are definitely worried. They are asking for more British troops at once, but Churchill is unwilling to send more from England at this time because he convinced within a month England will be vigorously attacked. The reason for the message to you is that he needs help badly. I asked him what the United States could do to help that would not leave the United States holding the bag for a war in which the Allies expected to be beaten. It seems to me that if we had to fight to protect our lives we would do better fighting in our own backyard. I said you know our strength. What could we do if we wanted to help you all we can. You do not need money or credit now. The bulk of our Navy is in the Pacific and we have not enough airplanes for our own use and our

Army is not up to requirements. So if this is going to be a quick war over in a few months what could we do. He said it was his intention to ask for the loan of 30 or 40 of our old destroyers and also whatever airplanes we could spare right now.

He said regardless of what Germany does to England and France, England will never give up as long as he remains a power in public life even if England is burnt to the ground. Why, said he, the Government will move to Canada and take the fleet and fight on. I think this is something I should follow up. If the Germans carry on there will be some conversation on what England will eventually do. Churchill called in the First Lord of the Admiralty [Archibald] Sinclair and [War Secretary Sir Anthony] Eden and although they are tough and mean to fight they are very low tonight.

Kennedy

Kennedy: "The Situation . . . Could Not Be Worse"

London, May 27, 1940

Personal for the Secretary. My impression of the situation here now is that it could not be worse. Only a miracle can save the British expeditionary force from being wiped out or as I said yesterday, surrender. . . . I think the possibility of the French considering a peace move is not beyond the realm of reason and I suspect that the Germans would be willing to make peace with both the French and British now—of course on their own terms, but on terms that would be a great deal better than they would be if the war continues. The method to be used to force the French to consider peace is probably annihilation from the air of one city after another. I talked with an airman this afternoon who has been in charge of one of the air squadrons and he said Calais is practically razed to the ground, that the fighters cannot locate the bombers any longer because of the terrific amount of smoke. The people here whose judgment I respect feel that if they start doing this to Lille and other French cities the French will not take it very long.

I realize this is a terrific telegram, but there is no question that it's in the air here. The result of that will be a row amongst certain elements in the Cabinet here; Churchill, [Clement] Attlee, and others will want to fight to the death, but there will be other numbers who realize that physical destruction of men and property in England will not be a proper offset to a loss of pride. In addition to that, the English people, while they suspect a terrible situation, really do not realize how bad it is. When they do, I don't know which group they will follow—the do or die, or the group that want a settlement. It is critical no matter which way you look at it.

Kennedy

An Ambassador's Plea: Stay Out of the War

London, September 27, 1940

... The night raids are continuing to do, I think, substantial damage and the day raids of the last three days have dealt most serious blows to Bristol, Southampton and Liverpool. Production is definitely falling, regardless of what reports you may be getting, and with transportation being smashed up the way it is, the present production output will continue to fall. ...

They are hoping and praying every minute that something will happen that will bring the United States in. ...

My own feeling is that they are in a bad way. Bombers have got through in the day time on the last 3 days and on four occasions today substantial numbers of German planes have flown over London and have done some daylight bombing. ... Without being an expert, I cannot help feeling that the evidence in Norway, Dakar and Dunkirk and the fate of the destroyers traveling in the English Channel indicate that naval units are in a bad way when they are within a couple of hundred miles of the enemy's aerodromes.

I cannot impress upon you strongly enough my complete lack of confidence in the entire conduct of this war. I was delighted to see that the President said he was not going to enter the war, because to enter this war, imagining for a minute that the English have anything to offer in the line of leadership or productive capacity in industry that could be of the slightest value to us, would be a complete misapprehension. ... If by any chance we should ever come to the point of getting into this war we can make up our minds that it will be the United States against Germany, Italy and Japan, aided by a badly shot to pieces country which in the last analysis can give little, if any assistance to cause. It breaks my heart to draw these conclusions about a people that I sincerely hoped might be victorious but I cannot get myself to the point where I believe they can be of any assistance to the cause in which they are involved.

Kennedy

1940 The Fall of France

Dispatches from U.S. Ambassador to France William C. Bullitt to Secretary of State Cordell Hull

As German forces swept through northern France in the spring of 1940 the French army crumbled before them. By late May and early June the fall of France seemed inevitable. French political leaders were divided on the course of action to follow. Former prime minister Edouard Daladier

was pessimistic but determined to resist. Others, such as aging World War I marshal Henri-Philippe Pétain, were convinced of British perfidy and preferred to come to the best available terms with the German invaders. On June 16 Pétain became head of government and sued for an armistice, which was signed in the same railroad car in which Germany had signed the armistice ending World War I. Pétain served as head of the "Vichy" government of France, which cooperated with the Germans until the liberation of France in 1945.

Throughout the critical period of May–June 1940, developments in France were reported in urgent dispatches from U.S. ambassador to France William Bullitt. In the first of these dispatches Bullitt reports some early French losses, attributing them to a communist "fifth column" in the French army. The two other dispatches report a plea by Daladier for American help and a conversation with Pétain previewing the French capitulation.

Communists in the French Army

Paris, May 17, 1940

Personal for the President. I regret to be obliged to send information of the sort in this telegram by cable but I felt that it may be important at a time when we are enlarging as rapidly as possible our Army, Navy, and Air Force.

The Belgian railway strike was organized by the Communists on orders from Moscow. It has now been broken by the shooting of the Communist ringleaders.

Two infinitely more serious "fifth column" operations have taken place in the French Army.

Nearly all the French heavy tanks were manned by Communist workmen from the Renault works in the outskirts of Paris. When they were given the order at a most critical moment to advance against the German tanks they did not move. In one case when 63 French heavy tanks were ordered to make an attack only 5 went forward and 58 remained where they were. Furthermore, the men in the tanks in a number of cases smashed vital parts of the machinery.

I am informed that these men will be shot tonight.

An even more serious "fifth column" action in cooperation with the Germans on orders of the Soviet Government are the Chasseurs. One regiment of Chasseurs which was composed of Communists from the Paris industrial suburbs revolted 3 days ago, seized the vital town of Compiegne on the German path to Paris and are still in possession of the town. They number 18,000 and I am informed that they will be attacked by the air force and tanks this evening.

Please keep this information for your most private ear. It is not known in France and in all sincerity I believe that it is not mortally serious. As soon as [Prime Minister Paul] Reynaud has the nerve to act on Napoleon's excellent principle "from time to time it is necessary to shoot a general in order to encourage the others" the "fifth column" will disappear.

Please for the sake of the future, nail every Communist or Communist sympathizer in our Army, Navy, and Air Force.

Bullitt

France Defenseless

Paris, May 28, 1940

For the President and Secretary. I had a long discussion on the present situation with Daladier today.

He said that . . . morale in France had never been higher than today and the determination to carry on the war whatever the cost had never been stronger (this is entirely true).

He went on to say that war nowadays unfortunately was no longer a question of the human spirit but a question of machines. An enormous proportion of French war material had been destroyed by the Germans or captured by them.

He was convinced that the French would fight on with a spirit which would command the admiration of the world but whether they could fight on successfully with the material that remained in their hands was another question.

He felt certain that if Italy should attack either in North Africa which was now virtually defenseless or with bombing planes on the Riviera and Marseille which were totally denuded of planes the destruction of France would be rapid.

He therefore appealed to me once more to attempt to obtain some action from the United States which would prevent Italy's entry into the war. Words and sympathy were all very well but at this moment acts were needed. The act which he felt could prevent action by Mussolini would be the sending of the Atlantic fleet to the Mediterranean. Short of that he saw nothing.

It was sad that civilization in the world should fall because a great nation with a great President could simply talk.

Bullitt

"The Greatest Attack in Human History"

Paris, June 4, 1940

Personal for the President. Marshal Pétain lunched with me alone today. After luncheon, talking in the garden, he said that he wondered if the French Government had ever given you a completely frank view of the present situation. . . . [H]e would like to let you know how he personally viewed the situation.

The threefold superiority of the Germans in man power was accompanied by a much greater superiority in aeroplanes and in tanks.

The airplane had proved to be the decisive weapon in this war. France was hopelessly outnumbered in the air.

Against the German attack which would be made before the end of this week on the Somme and in the region of Laon and the region of Reims the French had nothing to oppose but their courage. In all forms of material they were now desperately outclassed.

He did not wish me to conceal from you the fact that he himself envisaged very definitely the possibility that the Germans would be able to cross the Somme and the lower Seine and envelop Paris. Every inch added to the length of the French line would make the German superiority in numbers more effective.

As if the odds were not already enough two new elements had now entered into his calculations.

(1) It was certain that Italy would enter the war. There were no planes to combat the Italian planes and the destruction which the Italian planes might inflict on the southern portions of France would be terrible. Moreover the Italians might land troops from parachutes and take the entire French Alps region from the rear.

(2) Even more serious was the behavior of the British during the last few days. So long as the British Army had been in Flanders the British had engaged their Air Force fully. But they had insisted that their Army should be taken off first and that the French divisions should hold the lines fighting against the Germans while the British were embarked. Since all the British had been embarked the British had ceased to send their planes in anything like the numbers they had employed so long as the British Expeditionary Force was at Dunkirk.

Furthermore, at this moment when the French had almost no reserves and were facing the greatest attack in human history the British were pretending that they could send no reserves from England. . . .

Moreover, they had refused to send over the British aviation, which alone could combat the German Air Force, to support the French Army. . . .

Under the circumstances he was obliged to feel that the British intended to permit the French to fight without help until the last available drop of French blood should have been shed and that then with quantities of troops on British soil and plenty of planes and a dominant fleet the British after a very brief resistance or even without resistance would make a peace of compromise with Hitler, which might even involve a British Government under a British Fascist leader. . . .

He felt that unless the British Government should send to France, to engage in the battle which was imminent, both its air force and reserve divisions the French Government would do its utmost to come to terms immediately with Germany whatever might happen to England. He added that it was not fair for any French Government to permit the British to behave in a totally callous and selfish manner while demanding the sacrifice of every able-bodied Frenchman.

Bullitt

1941   Early Warning of Pearl Harbor
Dispatch from U.S. Ambassador to Japan Joseph C. Grew to Secretary of State Cordell Hull

While Germany was solidifying its hold on Europe from 1939 to 1941, Japan was expanding in eastern Asia. Japanese forces occupied much of China, moved into French Indochina, and threatened the Dutch East Indies. On December 7, 1941, Japan launched a surprise attack on Pearl Harbor in Hawaii, sinking several American battleships and destroying or damaging more than two hundred aircraft. In recent years much controversy has surrounded the question of whether the United States should have been more aware of the likelihood of an attack. This dispatch from the American ambassador in Tokyo, declassified and printed in its entirety for the first time in this collection, reveals that U.S. officials gave serious warnings of a possible attack on Pearl Harbor almost a year before the event.

Joseph Grew was one of the foremost American diplomats of the twentieth century. A career Foreign Service officer, he served successively as American chief of mission in Austria-Hungary, Denmark, Switzerland, and Turkey before beginning a decade of service as ambassador to Japan. Grew also served twice as an under secretary of state.

January 27, 1941

My Peruvian Colleague told a member of my staff that he had heard from many sources including a Japanese source that the Japanese military forces planned, in the event of trouble with the United States, to attempt a surprise mass attack on Pearl Harbor using all of their military facilities. He added that although the project seemed fantastic the fact that he had heard it from many sources prompted him to pass on the information.

Grew

1942 Gandhi and Civil Disobedience
Dispatch from U.S. Officer in Charge in New Delhi George R. Merrell to Secretary of State Cordell Hull

Hundreds of thousands of Indians took up arms in behalf of Great Britain during World War II. While fighting raged in both Europe and the Far East, however, Indian political leaders continued to focus on matters closer to home. From the early 1920s the preeminent figure in Indian politics was Mohandas Gandhi, who captured the popular imagination and developed a huge following through campaigns of satyagraha *(noncooperation) and civil disobedience against British colonial rule. By the outbreak of the war, Gandhi had led a series of such campaigns over a period of twenty years, and his efforts landed him in prison several times. As the war dragged on, Indian leaders, including Gandhi, grew impatient with Britain's decision to postpone political reforms in the colonies until after the war. They began to consider additional measures to bring an end to British rule in India.*

In this dispatch U.S. Representative in New Delhi George Merrell reports in unflattering terms Gandhi's reported intention to launch another civil disobedience campaign. Merrell judges that if such a campaign begins, India's contribution to the war effort will disappear. In fact, Gandhi's Congress Party did decide to continue its noncooperation with colonial authorities, landing the entire leadership in prison within weeks of this dispatch.

New Delhi, May 25, 1942

Information received from extremely reliable private sources in Bombay and Wardha is to the effect that Gandhi is planning to launch mass civil disobedience in near future in contrast to his Satyagraha Program instituted 2 years ago which was civil disobedience only by selected individuals. Gandhi went to Bombay last week to consult with his most trusted lieutenants and the latter (Patel, Prasad, and Gopich among others) are now touring the provinces to ascertain what measure of support mass civil disobedience would receive. Gandhi has been warned that such a program would result in civil war in this country, cause absolute chaos, and make India an easy prey for the Japanese. He is reliably reported to be unmoved by such warnings.

It is anticipated that the movement, aside from the usual disobedience of the law, will take the form of agitation against recruitment, war production and the general war effort. It is estimated that Gandhi will require from 4 to 6 weeks to organize the movement properly. I am firmly convinced that if this program is launched India is lost as far as being of any further use to the United Nations is concerned.

Recent developments indicate that the Gandhi element in the Congress is now in the saddle. . . .

As far as I can ascertain, Gandhi has not consulted [Congress Party leader Jawaharlal] Nehru and it is almost certain that he has not consulted [Nationalist leader Chakravarti] Rajagopalachari.

Nehru returns to Delhi from a brief holiday on Saturday morning and [Secretary of the U.S. Mission in Delhi James] Berry proposes to see him soon after his arrival. A report of the interview will be telegraphed to you.

Merrell

1945 Suing for Peace
Dispatches from U.S. Minister to Sweden Herschel V. Johnson to Secretary of State Cordell Hull

After more than five years of war in Europe, Allied forces, under the command of U.S. general Dwight D. Eisenhower, fought their way into Germany from the west. Russian forces, meanwhile, advanced from the east and were within thirty miles of Berlin by February 1945. At the end of April, with Germany's collapse imminent, German deputy leader Heinrich Himmler approached the neutral Swedes through Count Folke Bernadotte, president of the Swedish Red Cross, about possible surrender terms. Himmler, claiming to be acting for ailing German leader Adolf Hitler, proposed German capitulation to U.S. and British forces on the western front, but not to the Russians in the east. The Allies did not take up the proposal. Within ten days Germany surrendered unconditionally.

The war against Japan continued for three more months. In early August the United States dropped atomic bombs on Hiroshima and Nagasaki with devastating effects. Two days after the second explosion Japan approached the Swedes and the Swiss to convey its terms of surrender. The only condition proposed by Japan was that the emperor's sovereignty not be touched.

In both instances the peace proposals were communicated to Washington by Herschel Johnson, the American minister to Sweden. Johnson, a career Foreign Service officer, earlier had served in Spain (see "The Spanish Civil War," p. 388). *He later was appointed ambassador to Brazil.*

Himmler's Peace Proposal

Stockholm, April 25, 1945

Foreign Minister Günther sent for the British Minister and me at 11 o'clock this evening to meet with him . . . [and] Count Bernadotte who has just returned from Germany. . . . Bernadotte reports that Himmler although tired and admitting that Germany was finished, was calm and coherent. Himmler told him that Hitler was so ill that he might be already dead or could not be expected to live more than two days longer (General Schellenberg, Himmler's confidential staff officer, told Bernadotte that Hitler was suffering from brain hemorrhage). Himmler said that while Hitler was still active he would not have been able to take the step he now proposed to take but as Hitler was finished he, Himmler, is in a position of full authority to act. He asked Count Bernadotte to forward to the Swedish Government his request that the Swedish Government should intervene in order to arrange for him to meet General Eisenhower. The purpose of this meeting would be to capitulate on the whole western front (including the Netherlands). . . . He hoped to be able to continue to fight on the eastern front at least for a time. Bernadotte said that this would be scarcely possible to put in practice and would not be acceptable to the Allies. Bernadotte had the impression that Himmler hopes the Allies would be the first to enter into northern and western Germany into Mecklenburg for instance (which district was mentioned by Himmler) rather than the Russians for the sake of the civilian population.

General Schellenberg is in Flensburg near the Danish border eagerly waiting to hear anything which Bernadotte can convey to him. He is in hourly contact with Himmler and could ensure immediate delivery to him of any message it may be desired to send.

Mr. Günther thought this information was of such importance that it should be communicated at once to the American and British Governments. . . .

. . . I remarked that Himmler's refusal actually to order surrender on the eastern front looked like a last attempt to sow discord between the western Allies and Russia. . . . Mr. Günther . . . while admitting this motive could not be excluded pointed out that the fact that the Nazi chief would order capitulation of all troops on the whole Western Front and in

Norway and Denmark must be of great advantage to all the Allies including Russia and would in fact lead to early total capitulation. . . .

Count Bernadotte is of the opinion that if no reaction at all is forthcoming to this proposal of Himmler's it would probably result in a lot of unnecessary suffering and loss of human life.

Johnson

The Japanese Propose Surrender

Stockholm, August 10, 1945

The British Minister has just called to inform me that he and the Soviet Minister had been requested this morning to see Foreign Minister Unden with great urgency. Mr. Unden communicated to them a request from the Japanese Govt that the British and Soviet Ministers in Stockholm be informed of the Japanese Govt's acceptance of the declaration made at Potsdam regarding Japanese surrender. It was stipulated that Japanese Govt understood that declaration to mean that the sovereignty of the Emperor of Japan would not be touched. Subject to the Japanese Govt's understanding of this point, the unconditional surrender terms at Potsdam are accepted.

Foreign Minister Unden informed the British Minister that Japanese Minister in transmitting the foregoing had stated that the Japanese Minister at Bern had instructions to request the Swiss Govt to transmit the same offer of unconditional surrender to the US and China through their respective Ministers at Bern, and that he understood that this action was being taken simultaneously with the action at Stockholm.

The British and Soviet Ministers asked Mr. Unden's permission to inform me and the Chinese Minister unofficially of the foregoing, to which the Foreign Minister agreed. The Soviet Minister is informing the Chinese.

Mr. Unden requested the British and Soviet Ministers to regard this communication as of the highest order of secrecy.

Johnson

PART VIII

The Cold War: 1946–1964

After World War II the Allied powers divided Germany and its capital, Berlin, into four occupation zones. When the Soviets restricted Allied land access to Berlin in 1948, the Americans airlifted supplies to the three Western sectors of the city. Robert Murphy, U.S. political advisor to Germany, reported the historic operation.

1946 Progress in Honduras
Dispatch from U.S. Ambassador to Honduras John D. Erwin to Secretary of State James F. Byrnes

Political life in Honduras was characterized by its brevity until the assumption of power by Gen. Tiburcio Carías Andino in 1933. Carías remained in power for sixteen years before stepping down peacefully in 1949. He was able to survive so long in part because he was a master of what was known as continuismo, *or the indefinite continuance of office, usually achieved by rewriting the constitution to lengthen the term of office.*

Carías governed autocratically and took actions favorable to the U.S. fruit companies that dominated the export sector of the Honduran economy. His relations with the United States were excellent, as revealed in this laudatory dispatch. John Erwin served for thirteen years as U.S. representative in Honduras, from 1937 to 1947 and again from 1951 to 1954.

Tegucigalpa, February 1, 1946

General Tiburcio Carías Andino today completed 13 years of continuous service as President of Honduras. This is without precedent in Honduran history: with the exception of General Luis Bográn (1883–1891) no other Honduran President held power continuously for as long as 8 years, and the average tenure was scarcely two years. In the 112 years from the Declaration of Independence in 1821 to the accession of Carías in 1933, some 12 Presidents were overthrown by violence, several others were forced to resign under pressure, and one was murdered; various others were faced with rebellion (which is to say unsuccessful revolution) during their terms in office.

President Carías soon put an end to this chaos, although he never applied the death penalty to a political opponent. He has now been without effective internal opposition for several years and, aside from the possibility of death from assassination or natural causes, has a reasonably good chance of completing his tenure on December 31, 1948.

Honduras is one of the few countries on earth in a better position today than in 1933. President Carías has halved the national debt, stabilized the exchange value of the currency, and put the country on what is virtually a pay-as-you-go basis; even schoolteachers are paid promptly, and in cash rather than by means of Government warrants (I.O.U.'s) so often used during previous administrations. All this has been accomplished through the exercise of the old-fashioned orthodox values of hard work and frugality, without recourse to screwball economics. There is no income tax, nor are there any excessive taxes of any kind; only 22 percent of the national revenue is derived from import duties.

There is no unrest among the laboring classes. Monetary and real wages seem to be somewhat higher than in neighboring countries, and there is no unemployment. The well-to-do classes must have confidence in President Carías and in his ability to install an eventual successor without major disorders, since Tegucigalpa is enjoying an unprecedented building boom. There is scarcely a block in the city where new houses are not being constructed or old ones remodeled; adobe is being replaced by reinforced concrete and stucco. The central part of Tegucigalpa now has an adequate system of underground sewers and is well-paved (for the first time since its foundation in 1578), and such improvements are being continued towards the outskirts.

In the international field, President Carías has attended strictly to his own business; he has crossed no frontiers, rattled no sabers, nor interfered in any way with the affairs of his neighbors. His attitude towards the United States has been fully cooperative at all times, and he broke relations with Germany by expelling its Chargé d'Affaires (Zinsser) several months before the attack on Pearl Harbor! Several years previously he had been wise enough to refuse permission for the establishment of a Japanese colony of alleged cotton growers in an area along the Gulf of Fonseca!

Erwin

1946 Revolution in Bolivia: Chance for Democracy
Dispatch from U.S. Ambassador to Bolivia Joseph Flack to Secretary of State James F. Byrnes

Bolivia remained as politically unstable in the twentieth century as it was in the nineteenth. During World War II, a group of fascist-oriented military officers led by Maj. Gualberto Villarroel seized power. Relations with the United States then deteriorated rapidly. Villarroel's rule was short-lived, however; in 1946 an angry mob stormed his office and hanged him from a lamppost in a city square. The American ambassador was enthusiastic about the change in government, as reflected in this report of the revolution. Contrary to the ambassador's hopes, however, Bolivia's new government proved to be neither stable nor democratic.

La Paz, July 22, 1946

A popular revolution in every sense of the word has just occurred in Bolivia. Every indication is that this may prove first democratic government in Bolivian history. Immediate prospects are greatly improved relations with United States, moderately improved relations with Peru, Chile and Brazil. . . .

I . . . urge that we be prepared ship any food necessary on any terms to prevent this democratic movement falling victim to Fascist reaction because of people's hunger. Also that tin negotiations be brought to prompt satisfactory conclusion as soon as recognition is accorded.

Democracy's first steps are apt to be faltering and in Bolivia they should be supported in every reasonable and decent way by our country. The last days of Villarroel's tyranny were so frightful that no opportunity should be lost to avoid a repetition. . . .

Flack

1948 Churchill on the Soviets: "Raze Their Cities"
Dispatch from U.S. Ambassador to Great Britain
Lewis Williams Douglas to Under Secretary of State Robert Lovett

Victory over Germany was less than three months old and Japan had not yet surrendered when the British electorate swept wartime prime minister Winston Churchill out of office in 1945. Churchill, however, remained active politically. He championed the cause of Western strength and solidarity against what he regarded as the growing Soviet menace. On March 5, 1946, Churchill delivered his famous "iron curtain" address at Westminster College in Fulton, Missouri, where he told his listeners, "I am convinced there is nothing they [the Soviets] admire so much as strength, and there is nothing for which they have less respect than weakness, especially military weakness."

His views had not changed two years later when he suggested to American ambassador Lewis Douglas that the United States bring the Soviets into line by threatening the use of atomic weapons while the West still had a monopoly on the bomb. At the time, tensions between Western countries and the Soviet Union were growing, with occupied Berlin emerging as a central cause of tension. Douglas did not accept Churchill's line of reasoning, but he nevertheless reported it to the State Department in this dispatch.

London, April 17, 1948

Dear Bob:

I have had several visits with Churchill since my return, the last being on Thursday when he discussed the possibility of war with the Soviet.

You probably know his view, that when and if the Soviet develop the atomic bomb, war will become a certainty, even though by then Western Europe may have become again the seat of authority and a stable political part of the world. He believes that now is the time, promptly, to tell the Soviet that if they do not retire from Berlin and abandon Eastern Germany, withdrawing to the Polish frontier, we will raze their cities. It is further his view that we cannot appease, conciliate, or provoke the Soviet; that the only vocabulary they understand is the vocabulary of force; and that if, therefore, we took this position, they would yield.

You know better than I the practical infirmities in the suggestion. They cover a wide range, including the political.

Churchill believes also that if the Soviet try to inconvenience us in Berlin, we should retaliate by insisting upon a careful examination of the crews of every one of their ships putting into our ports, by annoying their shipping and their use of the Suez and Panama Canals, and by any other method which appears to be appropriate.

I, myself, doubt the wisdom of this policy, principally because it won't cause enough inconvenience. It seems to me to wave the strand of straw, disguised as a club, would have no effect. On every score the other measures about which we have been talking, if taken reasonably soon, may present to our friends to the east such a demonstration of solidarity and irresistible force that we may be able to deter the Soviet and to quash any ideas that they may have. I am inclined to think that such a demonstration, even though the Soviet may ultimately develop—if they have not already developed—the atomic bomb, may deter them.

I think there is much in what Churchill says; that we cannot appease, conciliate, or provoke the Soviet; that we can only arrest and deter them by a real show of resolution. Such a demonstration of determination, combined with the re-establishment of Western Europe as a center of power, may lead to a satisfactory settlement.

Kindest regards and best wishes.

Yours ever,

Lew

1948 The Birth of Israel
Dispatches from U.S. Representatives in Jerusalem to Secretary of State George C. Marshall

When the Ottoman Empire was dismantled after World War I, the administration of Palestine fell to Great Britain. The British had pledged to establish a national home for the Jewish people in Palestine, but on the understanding that nothing would be done to prejudice the civil and religious rights of non-Jews, who still formed the majority. This formula, however, proved unworkable. Throughout the 1920s and 1930s Arab-Jewish tension in Palestine mounted, much of it focused on the issue of increasing Jewish immigration. Rioting and terrorism by both sides were frequent. By the end of World War II, Palestine was in a state of virtual civil war.

The British, unable to bring the Arabs and the Jews to a peaceful settlement, turned the problem over to the United Nations and prepared to withdraw. On November 29, 1947, the United Nations voted to partition Palestine into an Arab state and a Jewish state, with Jerusalem to remain an international city. Jewish leaders reluctantly accepted the formula while Arab states rejected it and threatened war to prevent the partition. On May 14 the British withdrew, the State of Israel was proclaimed, and full-scale war erupted. Over the next several weeks Israeli forces won decisive victories which put them in control of territories well beyond those allocated by the UN partition.

These dispatches from Jerusalem describe the unfolding of events. The first, written on the eve of British withdrawal, reports Jewish forces already making advances into Arab areas. The next reports the assassination of U.S. Consul General Thomas Wasson by an unknown sniper as Wasson returned from a meeting of the UN peace commission. Two dispatches report the particularly severe fighting for the city of Jerusalem. Cease-fire lines eventually divided the city. The final dispatch transmits a report from American UN official Ralph Bunche describing the assassination by Jewish terrorists of Count Folke Bernadotte, the senior UN peace mediator in the region. Bernadotte, a Swede, had long been active in the cause of peace (see "Suing for Peace," p. 399).

Prelude to Independence

From U.S. Consul General Thomas C. Wasson

Jerusalem, May 13, 1948

Recent successes . . . have given Jews new hope and courage. Proclamation of Jewish state following termination of mandate is awaited by Yishuv [the Jewish community in Palestine] with greatest excitement and jubilation. Jewish national administration which is already functioning in wholly Jewish areas and partly in Jerusalem will become government of new Jewish state. So far . . . Jews have observed territorial limits imposed by UN resolution of 29 November. However speculation rife as to whether newfound strength may not encourage Jews to attempt to acquire new territory. . . . Most observers believe Jews are winning first round at least of their battle and will desire consolidate positions.

Arab opposition to Jews in towns has completely disintegrated. Haifa is under Jewish domination; Jaffa is deserted city and has been declared "open city". . . . It is not believed Jerusalem Arabs would be able to present much opposition to Jews if latter decided to occupy city. Most representative Arabs have fled to neighboring countries and Arabs of authority are found only after most diligent searching. Consequently truce and cease-fire talks are greatly hampered and slowed down. It is possible Arabs do not wish to be put in difficult position of having to make definite decisions which would be public admission of fact that Jews have upper hand. Perhaps they hope events will decide future course of policy. We believe Arab Legion and other Arab armies will march into Arab areas of Palestine after termination of January mandate but will not risk major operations with Jews. . . .

Wasson

American Consul General Shot by Sniper
From U.S. Vice Consul William C. Burdett

Jerusalem, May 22, 1948

Wasson left on foot from Consulate-General this morning about 12 noon local to attend meeting Truce Commission, which was held as usual at French Consulate-General. He left French Consulate-General, still on foot, shortly after 1300 hours local. As he crossed Wauchope Street to alley along west side Consulate-General, he was hit by sniper's bullet presumed to have come from direction junction Julian's Way and Wauchope Street. Identity of sniper cannot be established. He was carried by members of Consulate-General to first aid room Consulate-General, where he was immediately attended by public health surgeon. Armored ambulance came within ten minutes from Red Shield Society and Wasson was taken to Hadassah English Mission Hospital, where acting director Hadassah has assured us every facility, including private room and nurse will be placed at his disposal.

According to doctor's report, 30-calibre rifle bullet entered right upper arm, passed through chest, and exited at level left second costal cartilage. Wound in upper arm excised and exit wound excised, explored and closed. Is now out of shock and resting quietly. Condition good, and barring complications, has more than even chance recover.

Burdett

The Battle for Jerusalem
From U.S. Vice Consul William C. Burdett

Jerusalem, May 23, 1948

Following is situation report as of 0800 hours local May 23:
In greater part of Jerusalem last night was quietest since fighting began.

In southern outskirts of city heavy artillery bombardment commenced at about 0300 hours. Unconfirmed report states Egyptian Army now in Bethlehem and may have been shelling Jerusalem. Heavy explosions direction Old City started at 0600 hours and still continuing. Cease-fire in Hadassah Hospital and Hebrew University area maintained throughout night and believed still in effect. . . . Ramat Rahel Jewish settlement on Bethlehem road evacuated by Jews last night and Arabs reported advancing on Talpioth Jewish southern suburb of Jerusalem.

Consul General Wasson died of wounds at 0600 hours local. . . . Otherwise Consulate, Navy, UN staffs and American correspondents well.

Burdett

The Siege of Jerusalem
From U.S. Vice Consul William C. Burdett

Jerusalem, May 27, 1948

Battle of Jerusalem has now reached what may be described as near stalemate. Jews are in control of most areas of city while Arabs with sizeable garrison Arab Legion and irregulars still retain old city, except Jewish quarters, and all approaches to old city except Zion and Jaffa gates. Neither side has been able to break grip of other side on areas held by it. Arab Legion and Arab operation army artillery continue bombardment several times daily of Jewish quarters new city from northern outskirts Jerusalem and Arab armies have blocked all roads leading into Jerusalem. Mortar, automatic and sniper fire continues daily throughout city in varying intensity and it appears that major effort has, however, shifted on both sides to battle for roads leading to Jerusalem. . . .

Jews report they have sufficient food and water to last for long period in new Jerusalem and that they prepared turn city into "another Stalingrad." However American correspondents believe that food, fuel and water supply situation in new Jerusalem is grave. Conditions in Jewish quarters old city desperate and may only be question of time before inhabitants and Haganah [Israeli military forces] there capitulate. Arabs in old city probably have sufficient water for considerable period and are able receive food and fuel from Jericho area and Transjordan.

It, therefore, seems that Arabs are preparing for long siege of Jewish Jerusalem in hope starving inhabitants into submission while at same time Jews equally preparing withstand siege. Nobody cares hazard guess how long such siege could last.

Burdett

Assassination of a UN Envoy
From U.S. Consul General John J. Macdonald

Jerusalem, September 17, 1948

Please pass United Nations Paris for Secretary General from Bunche, Jerusalem, 17 September.

Following for information Security Council.

Count Folke Bernadotte, United Nations Mediator on Palestine, brutally assassinated by Jewish assailants of unknown identity, in planned, cold blooded attack in the new city of Jerusalem at 1405 GMT today, Friday, 17 September. Mediator, in Jerusalem on official tour, was en route from Government House to YMCA in a convoy of three cars, two of which were flying United Nations flags and one a Red Cross flag. Party accompanied by an official liaison officer of the Jewish forces. In the Katamon quarter of new city, well within Jewish lines, all three cars were stopped at a road block in which was parked an Israeli Army type jeep filled with men in Jewish Army uniforms all of whom got out but the driver. Two of these men, apparently recognizing the Mediator's car approached it, stood by the window and fired at point blank range. Count Bernadotte and Colonel Andre P. Serot, French Air Forces, United Nations Observer, sitting beside him in rear of car, were both hit several times, Colonel Serot being killed instantly, and Count Bernadotte having lost consciousness almost immediately, dying within a few minutes of his arrival at Hadassah Hospital, where he was driven by UN Secretariat Officer Frank Begley, who was driver of Mediator's car at time of attack and who suffered only powder burns. General Aage Lundstroem, Chief of Staff of Truce Supervision, also seated in rear of car, miraculously escaped injury. Commander William R. Cox, United States Navy, United Nations Observer, seated in front of car also uninjured. . . .

Situation in Jerusalem tense. Consulting with Truce Commission and senior observers concerning future arrangements affecting observer personnel in Jerusalem who are in constant danger. . . .

All members of Observer Corps and United Nations Secretariat staff deeply shocked at sudden loss of their leader in this work whose high integrity, tirelessness, devotion to his mission and great personal courage were inspiration to us all.

Signed Bunche.

Macdonald

1948 The Berlin Airlift
Dispatch from U.S. Political Adviser for Germany Robert Daniel Murphy to Secretary of State George C. Marshall

After World War II the Allied powers divided Germany into four occupation zones. The capital, Berlin, was entirely within the Russian zone, but it too was divided into four sectors, each occupied by one of the major Allies. By 1948 Great Britain, France, and the United States were seriously at odds with the Soviet Union over the future of Germany. The Western powers favored a reunified and prosperous Germany as a necessary element of reconstruction and long-term peace in Europe. The Soviets favored a weak and neutral Germany. In an effort to thwart Western moves to unify Germany and reform its currency, the Soviets began to restrict Allied land access to Berlin. This provoked one of the first major crises of the postwar era. American leaders seriously considered the possibility of war against the Soviet Union. Rather than give in to Soviet pressure or adopt a military option, however, the Allies decided to resupply West Berlin by air.

This dispatch, written two days after the Soviets suspended all road traffic to West Berlin, reports the modest beginning of the Berlin airlift. The resupply effort expanded rapidly, soon employing hundreds of planes ferrying thirteen thousand tons of supplies a day. In the meantime, American bombers were transferred to Europe in preparation for possible war. The airlift lasted for almost a year before the Soviets reversed their policy and lifted the blockade.

The American political adviser in Germany at the time was Robert Murphy. He had a long career with the State Department, beginning as a clerk at the embassy in Bern in 1917 and working his way up to under secretary of state by 1959.

Berlin, June 26, 1948

General Clay in cooperation with General Le May, Commanding General USAFE, gave orders this morning for the organization of air lifts between the Western Zones and Berlin on the basis of an estimated daily supply of 225 tons. 70 planes are immediately available which will make an estimated 100 trips daily. There is under consideration the question of adding an additional 30 planes which if brought into the service would enable the shipment eventually of up to 500 tons daily. For the supply of the UK and US forces only 50 tons daily are necessary. The balance will be devoted to the needs of the German population and Military Government is establishing a priority list of commodities. As a comparative figure, the daily food supply required for the population of the three western sectors of Berlin is 2,000 tons. General Clay also issued orders placing all US personnel on an austerity basis today with regard to supplies of food and the use of electric power, etc.

Murphy

1949 China Goes Communist
Dispatches from U.S. Representatives in China to
Secretary of State Dean Acheson

China emerged from World War II victorious over Japan but badly fragmented internally. With the common enemy defeated, China's major factions—the Communists and the Nationalists—fell upon each other. Although the Nationalists initially were stronger militarily, the regime's corruption and disorganization led to its slow collapse. By late 1948 Communist forces had taken over Manchuria; in January 1949 they took Peking. By late spring it was clear that a total Communist victory was imminent. The Nationalist government fled to the island of Formosa (Taiwan).

The United States lent its support in the civil war to the Nationalists. As the Communists extended their control southward, many American diplomatic and consular officials remained at their posts, sometimes to face mistreatment at the hands of the new rulers. The American ambassador left the mainland in August 1949 after reporting he was no longer in a position to protect Americans in China and could not even communicate freely with Washington. Other American officials remained in China until 1950 when they were withdrawn because it had become clear that the United States would not recognize the new Chinese government.

These dispatches from three different Chinese cities report on some of the dramatic events of 1949 in China: a violation of the American ambassador's residence, the physical abuse of an American consul, and the creation of the People's Republic of China.

A Call on the Ambassador
From U.S. Ambassador to China John Leighton Stuart

Nanking, April 25, 1949

The Ambassador's residence was violated this morning at 6:45 by 12 armed Communist soldiers. They persuaded the Chinese porter to open the front gate of the compound and then came in the back door of the residence where they asked the servants how many Chinese and how many foreigners lived in the residence and where the Ambassador was. On receiving reply to the last question, the soldiers all mounted the stairway promptly, went to the Ambassador's room and entered. The Ambassador was not quite awake at that hour and their appearance in his bedroom was something of a shock. While they did not threaten him, the first to enter room spoke in loud and angry tones. Those that followed were more civil and said that they had come to "look around." They wandered about the bedroom inspecting its contents and making remarks to the effect that all this would eventually go to people to whom it should belong anyway.

They . . . left the house and the compound without having removed anything. They told one of the servants that the Ambassador should not leave the compound but this was not conveyed to the Ambassador or any other member of his official staff. No other houses in the compound were visited. . . .

Stuart

Beaten in a Communist Jail: "No American Now Safe in China"
From U.S. Consul General in Shanghai John Moors Cabot

Shanghai, July 9, 1949

. . . [U.S. Vice Consul William] Olive released about noon today, allowed return home accompanied by wife whom police had summoned by phone. Consulate General will shortly submit his detailed story, salient points of which follow:

After leaving Consulate General about 1.30 pm of 6th, Olive had crossed Garden Bridge, was proceeding along Broadway . . . when police signalled him to turn off small side street. As way blocked by two carts he sounded horn, hallway cleared and was about to proceed when several heavily armed Communist soldiers apparently infuriated over coolies being forced make way for foreigners came up and compelled him back all way to Broadway. On reaching Broadway he started return to Consulate General and was nearing Garden Bridge when civilian police halted him in rough manner. Same group of soldiers then appeared, harangued him, forced him to wait about 2 hours, then took to Wayside police station. . . .

During ensuing talk with Sergeant, Olive, while appealing for sergeant's intercession to prevent detention, was gripping and leaning on table edge. Soldiers reappeared and forcibly jerked him away from table, causing him to lose balance, knock ink wells and cup from table and himself to floor, one arm inadvertently striking soldier as he fell. Soldiers, tempers inflamed, instantly surrounded him with gun barrels, etc., and terrifying him to point where he resisted in instinctive self-defense.

He was then put in handcuffs (which not removed for almost 24 hours), brutally beaten up about body and legs and then hauled to preliminary detention cell (housing three other prisoners). . . . Later was taken to another cell in which were already crowded 15 poor Chinese who treated him kindly, even offering tea.

Next morning he was compelled (with armed soldiers surrounding) to write "full confession" of guilt for various offenses including assault and original traffic "violation". . . . Drafted three statements none of which satisfied police who then made him write 4th statement with virtually every word dictated by them. During this and various other humiliating points of his experience he was repeatedly photographed. . . .

Following preparation of his confession he was given farcical "trial" charged with no less than 8 offenses, lectured lengthily (several times) on American Government's sins, manner in which foreigners should conduct themselves under people's regime, etc. Was then compelled write down summary of what had been told him.

Following trial he was taken solitary confinement cell in which, while lying, was not even allowed to turn over and while sitting forced maintain painful crouched position for hours—at point of guard's guns.

Only nourishment he received during entire stay police station was bread and water—not enough water.

His requests for doctor examine his injuries were refused. He was not even permitted wash till shortly before release.

Such was severity and brutality of his treatment he cannot even recall clearly sequence and character events during latter part his detention—is hazy for example as to number and differentiation of apologies he was forced to sign. He clearly recalls however that subsequent to trial he was twice forced make additions to his original confession: first, that he had been well treated and "suffered no injuries while under detention" . . . and second, that his confession was made voluntarily. . . .

In connection with his apologies he was forced to make 3 waist-deep bows while photographers took pictures. . . .

Olive . . . is naturally in highly exhausted, nerve-shaken state—dreading further arrest and torture; and psychological shock believed probably more serious than bodily wounds.

This grim affair impressively confirms my conviction that no American now safe in China. . . .

                Cabot

The People's Republic Established
From U.S. Consul General in Peiping Edmund Clubb

Peiping, October 3, 1949

Final session PCC [Political Consultative Conference] September 30 unanimously elected Mao Tze-tung chairman of Central People's Government of People's Republic of China. . . . Central organ of state authority is People's Government Council with 56 members. . . . September 30 session also elected 180 members of National Committee Chinese People's PCC of which 18 seats reserved for areas to be liberated. . . . Central People's Government of People's Republic of China established here October 1 with proclamation by Chairman Mao. . . .

Mao stated Central People's Government Council took office October 1. . . . Mao proclamation further stated Central People's Government Council decided to declare to governments all other countries that this government is sole legal government representing all peoples of People's Republic of China. . . . [S]econd sentence final paragraph of proclamation reads "this government is willing to establish diplomatic relations with any foreign Government which is willing observe the principles of equality, mutual benefit and mutual respect of territorial integrity and sovereignty."

Clubb

1949 Indonesian Independence
Dispatch from U.S. Ambassador to the Netherlands Stephen Chapin to Secretary of State Dean Acheson

Soon after the defeat of Japan in 1945 Indonesian nationalists declared their independence, but the former colonial power, the Netherlands, was not prepared to give in to the nationalists. In the fall of 1945 Dutch forces arrived to reclaim their prewar position in Indonesia, a step that led to a protracted and bitter conflict. The Dutch arrested nationalist leaders and used tanks and aircraft to capture and hold major cities. Guerrilla resistance continued, however, and in 1949 the Dutch agreed to withdraw. Indonesian independence was granted at a ceremony in The Hague in December 1949. In the years to come, the same pattern of indigenous resistance leading to the collapse of colonialism would be repeated elsewhere in Southeast Asia and throughout the world.

The Hague, December 27, 1949

Transfer of sovereignty ceremony took place 10 a.m. today, Royal Palace, Amsterdam, and was both solemn and moving. Queen's [Juliana's] address, which . . . was written by herself, very human in its appeal to two countries to forget past differences, accept solution and strive earnestly "to cooperate loyally in the new system." After stating readiness of Netherlands "to render assistance as soon as and when Indonesia should ask for it," address concluded with these extraordinary words: "It is a privilege to perform this act of transfer as it stands in history, or rather in the face of God, who knows why this march hand-in-hand in freedom was not achieved sooner nor later, and who knows the feelings of generations, but who also watches whether we can use this plan for the progress of mankind. May this now be so."

Following conclusion of ceremony I proceeded with Canadian and Indian ambassadors to informal reception at Groote Club, where my colleagues delivered formal written messages of congratulation to Prime Ministers of Netherlands and Indonesia, and the British Ambassador presented note . . . formally recognizing Indonesian Government. I, therefore, took occasion to present orally to both Prime Ministers the message contained in Department's 1171 of December 29, 5 p.m.

I presume formal recognition being extended Indonesia directly through our representative in Batavia.

Chapin

1950 Tito Comments on His Revolution
Dispatch from U.S. Ambassador to Yugoslavia George V. Allen to Secretary of State Dean Acheson

Marshal Joseph Broz Tito, leader of the Yugoslavian resistance to Nazi Germany, assumed power in Belgrade in 1945. He established a communist government and concluded a series of friendship and economic agreements with the Soviet Union and other East European countries. Tito, however, was a communist with a difference. His independent outlook and policies resulted in a clear break with the Soviet bloc and much improved relations with the West as early as 1949. This dispatch reports Tito's comments on the rough measures he used to consolidate his power, comparing them to actions taken by patriots during the American Revolution.

February 3, 1950

During my conversation with Tito January 26, 1950 he said he was aware of considerable discontent in Yugoslavia, particularly among peasants, and that this discontent was due not only to disruption of previous Yugoslav economic and social system but also to "rough" methods he had had to employ. He expressed regret at necessity for these methods and said he had been "as little rough" as possible and would relax to extent future permitted. (I quote words used by translator, Prica, Deputy Foreign Minister. Tito spoke in Serbian after few introductory words in English, which he speaks very slightly.)

Tito went on to point out that any revolutionary movement, and particularly a social revolution, must employ rough methods to establish itself. He said even in the American Revolution, which was largely political but somewhat social in character, the American patriots had handled the Tories and loyalists "somewhat roughly" in certain cities, "seized their villas, etc.". He hoped he could begin to relax his rough methods soon, and said the sooner he no longer needed them the better he would like it.

This gave me good opportunity to point out that one of outstanding things which created misunderstanding between Americans and Yugoslavs was considerable number of Yugoslav political prisoners who had relatives in U.S. or some American connection. I said many Americans found it difficult to understand how Yugoslav Government could in any logic express desire to develop friendly relations with U.S. while still retaining in prison at hard labor persons, including former employees this Embassy, who were charged with espionage on behalf of U.S. . . .

Tito smiled, said he was fully aware of American interest in subject and said he thought something could be done, although development might have to be gradual.

I did not consider it advisable to press the point further with Tito at the moment but plan to mention it to Prica again soon. Principal difficulty is that some prisoners on whose behalf I have been requested to intercede by members U.S. Congress were actually engaged, I have now learned, in subversive activity on behalf royalist Yugoslav refugees. I believe we should be most careful to avoid giving Tito any basis for believing we are concerned with restoration of Yugoslav monarchy.

George V. Allen

1950 The Perón Regime: "One of the Most Dramatic... Experiments in the History of the World"
Dispatch from U.S. Ambassador to Argentina Stanton Griffis to President Harry S. Truman

Before World War II Juan Perón was an Argentinian military attaché to Italy, where he was much impressed with the fascist model of government. In 1943 Perón joined with other military officers to overthrow the Argentine government. Within a few months, however, he eclipsed his military colleagues and became the real power in Argentina. Perón was elected president in 1946 and again in 1952. As president, he became immensely popular and powerful by virtue of his personal charisma, his policies favoring the working class, and the able efforts of his second wife, Eva. He entrenched himself in power by eliminating constitutional liberties and persecuting his opponents. In 1955 Perón was deposed in a military coup and exiled to Madrid. He returned to power in 1973, only to die a year later. This dispatch comments on the Perón regime at its height in 1950.

Buenos Aires, March 1, 1950

It hardly seems possible for me to realize that it is almost six months since you appointed me for this post, for the time has passed so rapidly and the complex problems of American business in Argentina have so completely filled my time. I have long intended to write you a brief note on the general situation, but, as you know, hell is paved with good intentions.

I have been witnessing one of the most dramatic and interesting social experiments in the history of the world—"Peronismo"—an effort to create changes in the economy of a country in four short years that should, under even a less ill-adroit government, take at least 20 years; a strange mixture of nationalism, dictatorship and paternalism which may produce a great social result—if the whole laboratory does not blow up.

Here is a dictatorship which does not dictate, for Perón's mind does not accurately function on economic matters, and after taking over the vast enterprises of railroads, merchant marine, public utilities, air transportation and public health, he has turned the operation over to unskilled and ill-trained ministers who seem to spend about half of their time in their operational jobs and the other half jockeying for position among their fellow ministers and against ambitious members of the party. I can readily believe the reports that the nationalized properties are running at a loss of some millions of pesos a day and that very little progress in efficient management is being made. When a government gives jobs for votes, efficiency flies out of the window.

From the point of view of external financial health, it is obvious that the situation is becoming daily worse. . . .

Here, too, is a country of two Presidents: one the duly elected President, General Perón, and the other his "esposa", Señora de Perón, whose voice, influence and finger are apparently in everything affecting labor and social welfare. So far this two-cylindered machine has functioned smoothly, but it would be an unconscionable situation if these two began to fail to function in harmony.

I am constantly asked by American travelers and others my opinion of the political situation in Argentina. As I see it, there is no political situation here. The Peróns are firmly in control. A free vote tomorrow would, I think, give them a large majority of the votes of the nation. They will continue in firm control of the nation just so long as the price of bread and meat and the elemental necessities of life can be held down to a price which makes them available to the working man within his true income. They are held down at the moment by every conceivable form of direct and indirect subsidy, but unless the productivity of the country can be greatly improved, this cannot last forever, and the spiral of increasing circulation, rising labor costs, and lowered productivity can already be clearly charted.

The press is in general thoroughly anti-American, and the ghosts of Braden, Wall Street and "Yanqui imperialism" rove through the newsprint. There is no freedom anywhere in press, radio or public speech, and in general the principles of civil liberties have disappeared in Argentina. The intensity of nationalism, the inability to convert pesos into dollars, and the practical shutting off of American products into this market has substantially discouraged large and small American companies here.

This is a pretty black picture. . . . I do not want to go into too many details for you to read in your crowded life, so I can say in summary that the situation vis-à-vis the United States is dark but I do not think hopeless.

I am leaving in three days for Rio de Janeiro to attend the South American ambassadors conference there. Of course this letter indicates no answer, and I merely wanted to give you a brief travelogue of the Argentine picture as I see it.

With warm personal regards to you and Mrs. Truman,

Sincerely yours,

Stanton Griffis

1950 Riots in South Africa
Dispatch from U.S. Chargé d'Affaires in South Africa
Bernard C. Connelly to Secretary of State Dean Acheson

In 1948 the Afrikaner-based National Party, led by Daniel F. Malan, came to power in South Africa, defeating the United Party in a general election. The National Party would hold power for almost fifty years, totally eclipsing the United Party and other white opposition groups. The Nationalists began immediately to formalize their segregationist and white supremacist policies into the doctrine of apartheid, which advocated separate development of the races, each "along its own lines in its own areas." Blacks were relegated to small areas of the country and were denied political and social rights. "Pass laws" placed severe restrictions on blacks' freedom of movement. Disturbances broke out almost immediately. The government response was to enact more restrictions to prevent dissent and to cement apartheid institutions. In this dispatch the American chargé comments on recent rioting and predicts—correctly—more disturbances and further repression to come.

Capetown, June 8, 1950

The clashes between Natives and police on May 1, 1950 at several locations in and around Johannesburg, despite the Government ban on demonstrations, were part of a pattern of racial tension which threatens the internal stability of the Union of South Africa. Overtly similar to previous riots, the May Day disturbances were uglier in mood than any in the recent past. Hostility between Natives and police reached a new high. Although elementary economic benefits, elimination of the pass system, and the right to present legitimate grievances constituted the immediate objectives of the Natives, there were signs of a new spirit of nationalism among the natives, which, despite its vagueness, is becoming the basis of a growing faith. But for a growing number of Natives this goal of nationalism is not enough and these despondent ones are turning to communism because it holds out the promise of equality—racial, economic and political.

Content to do no more about this riot than blame it on communist agitators and gird itself for the next one, the Malan government pretended to be unshaken. The United Party supported all the Government's precautionary measures, floundered briefly immediately after the riots, and then launched a political attack on the "apartheid-mad" Nationalists. A few liberals urged the initiation of a debate on the riots as an urgent matter of public importance, but received virtually no parliamentary support. And here the matter might have rested, if it were not for the fact that this was South Africa's most serious postwar racial clash. A surprisingly large and vocal minority . . . challenged the complacency of the majority of white South Africans who feel, as a simple expedient of self-preservation, that the Native must be "kept in his place". But they were not successful. South Africa is reluctant to face this issue, and yet it is unmistakably clear. The Union can continue to practice uncompromising "white-supremacy" risking large scale Native uprising . . . or recognition of the seriousness of the current racial tension can force all sides to sit down with the Natives and attempt to work out a compromise. The future of South Africa depends on the answer and only three answers are possible: Compromise, further riots, or a "police state". Malan's Government appears to be trending toward the latter. . . .

The May day riots are the most serious in recent South African history. They are an accurate clue to the tension between Natives and Whites. In this tension respect between the parties has virtually disappeared. The Government did not want any mass demonstrations, no matter how peaceful, and it did not want to see any inter-organizational unity on the part of the Natives. Most of those who took the trouble to examine the situation knew that trouble was coming and it came. The reason it was not worse is because the Native leaders restrained their people, and because they had no guns. What surprised the Government most was the number who stayed away from work. If further riots are to be avoided certain obvious steps must be taken such as securing higher wages, more housing, health benefits, lessening the stringency of the pass laws, and giving the Native a greater role in the Nation's life. None of these steps will be taken. The obvious answer is more riots. The present Government will seek to prevent such riots by rigid control over the Natives. It can only exercise effective control through the passage of such legislation as the Population Registration Bill, the Group Areas Bill, and similar anti-civil rights measures. Taken together these legislative acts and pending bills reflect all the traditional trappings of the police state. The South African police-state-in-the-making is not directed against other Whites, as yet, despite what the United Party says. Its aim is the legislation necessary to perpetuate White supremacy in an Afrikaans republic.

For the Chargé d'Affaires, a.i.:

Joseph Sweeney
Attaché

1950   The Korean War
Dispatches from U.S. Ambassador to Korea John J. Muccio to Secretary of State Dean Acheson

Korea became a Japanese protectorate in 1910. After Japan's defeat in World War II, Korea was artificially divided, with Japanese troops north of the thirty-eighth parallel surrendering to the Soviet Union and those in the south surrendering to American forces. Separate governments were established in each half of the country. In 1949 the United Nations recognized the southern Republic of Korea as the only legitimate Korean government. Tensions continued into 1950 with each of the Korean states intent on absorbing the other. North Korea was more aggressive in pursuing its designs, launching several large-scale raids across the border. On June 25 North Korean troops attacked in force across the thirty-eighth parallel, setting off the Korean War. South Korean president Syngman Rhee appealed for U.S. assistance. In response, President Harry S. Truman, deciding that vital U.S. interests were at stake, ordered U.S. forces into action under the command of Gen. Douglas MacArthur. These dispatches, both sent on the opening day of the conflict, recount the perspective from the South Korean capital.

"An All Out Offense against ROK"

Seoul, June 25, 1950

. . . North Korean forces invaded ROK [Republic of Korea] territory at several points this morning. Action was initiated about 4 a.m. Ongjin blasted by North Korean artillery fire. About 6 a.m. North Korean infantry commenced crossing parallel in Ongjin area, Kaesong area, Churchon area and amphibious landing was reportedly made south of Kangnung on east coast. Kaesong was reportedly captured at 9 a.m., with some 10 North Korean tanks participating in operation. North Korean forces, spearheaded by tanks, reportedly closing in on Churchon. Details of fighting in Kangnung area unclear, although it seems North Korean forces have cut highway. . . .

It would appear from nature of attack and manner in which it was launched that it constitutes all out offensive against ROK.

Muccio

Korean President: "The Situation Came as No Surprise"

Seoul, June 25, 1950

... I called on the President by appointment at 11:35 at his residence.

The President appeared under considerable emotional tension, but was nonetheless composed. I opened the conversation by saying that I had just visited Korean Army headquarters, where I had found both the Korean military establishment and the American advisors moving quickly and efficiently to cope with the emergency. . . . I had found that the city of Seoul appeared calm and normal.

The President said that Korea needed 'more rifles and ammunition'. He subsequently made specific mention of 'more rifles'. I told him that the Korean Army was far better trained than it had been last year (when the North Koreans had made several strong raids along the 38th parallel). I said that there was a sufficient supply of artillery ammunition to last for the time being. President Rhee, apparently implying he hoped for support in that quarter, said he had not notified General MacArthur because his government had no code.

The President mentioned the various points under attack. . . .

I informed the President the American advisors were on duty with all Korean divisions along the parallel. . . . I pointed out that he would be under pressure from various civilian groups along the parallel to despatch reinforcements but the Korean Army must act as a coordinated unit despite local situations and that there would be temptation to interfere with military decisions which should be avoided. I commented that it was important for everyone to maintain calm.

The President said that there would be a cabinet meeting at 2 p.m. to discuss the situation. He said that he was considering proclaiming martial law in Seoul and that the people must be told the facts. He remarked that the situation came as no surprise to anybody; that he had been warning the people about it a long time and calling upon every man, woman and child to come out and fight with sticks and stones if necessary. He seemed to feel that the people would support him in this way. He said that if it were certain that enough arms and ammunition would be available, this word would be passed from mouth to mouth and thus boost public morale. He stated that he had been trying to avoid making Korea a second Sarajevo; but perhaps the present crisis presented the best opportunity for settling the Korean problem once and for all. He commented that American public opinion seemed to be growing stronger day by day vis-à-vis Communist aggression. . . .

I concluded the conversation by assuring the President that I would be available all day and that I had confidence that the situation was being competently met.

Muccio

1951 Establishing a Mission in Kuwait
Dispatch from U.S. Consul in Kuwait Enoch S. Duncan to
Secretary of State Dean Acheson

Kuwait was able to break away from Ottoman rule in 1899 by seeking British protection. The discovery of oil forty years later transformed the country into the first of the wealthy Arab sheikhdoms of the Persian Gulf. The United States opened its first office in Kuwait—a consulate—in 1951 while Kuwait was still a British protectorate. Formal independence followed in 1961. Then, in a preview of the 1990 invasion, neighboring Iraq immediately claimed sovereignty over the newly independent country. In response, British and friendly Arab troops moved in to defend Kuwait. This 1951 dispatch describes the first meeting between a resident American representative and the Kuwaiti emir, Sheikh Abdullah es Sabah.

Kuwait, July 8, 1951

... I called on His Highness the Ruler of Kuwait, Sheikh Abdullah Salem es Sabah at 8:00 a.m. on Sunday, July 1, 1951. ...

His Highness greeted us at the second floor stair landing just outside the room devoted to his morning maglis. He extended his hand and spoke a word of welcome in precise English. We then entered his chamber and were seated.

The interview lasted thirty minutes. ... His Highness speaks in a low almost rumbling voice which I found in the initial interview difficult if not impossible to follow.

His Highness expressed the hope that I would find it possible to adjust myself to the heat and living conditions in Kuwait and enquired as to when my staff would arrive and where the consulate and residence would be established. I explained that I was engaged in looking at available buildings and that it had seemed better for me to come out alone to select accommodations and have the staff and furnishings follow in a month or so when there would be provision to receive them. I inquired if His Highness would care to make a suggestion about a suitable location, and he quoted in return an Arabic proverb to the effect that seeking would provide a suggestion.

His Highness then made a long statement to the effect that the American and the British people are friends, and that they are both his friends and that it would be this way in Kuwait; that all business and relations would be conducted in a spirit of cooperation. I thanked His Highness for the expression of this sentiment. ...

His Highness apologized for being unable to offer coffee or other refreshment because of its being the month of Ramadhan. I replied that rather I must thank him for being kind enough to receive me. ... His Highness accompanied us to the door of the car where he said goodbye in

English and shook hands holding my hand in the way of the Arab and applying a series of pressures, which act is difficult to interpret as to whether it means great pleasure at meeting, an effort to communicate more completely and express sincerity, or merely a reaction to custom. . . .

The Ruler is certainly impressive in his quiet dignity, and although he appeared somewhat tired, probably as a result of the rigors of fasting, he managed to convey by his looks and smiles a feeling of sincere friendliness.

Enoch S. Duncan

1953 The Mau Mau Revolt
Dispatch from U.S. Consul General in Nairobi Edmund J. Dorsz to the Department of State

Nationalist movements began to take root in earnest throughout sub-Saharan Africa in the years after the Second World War. In British Kenya, which had a large and prosperous settler community, one element of the movement turned violent. The revolt, known as Mau Mau, began among the Kikuyu people of Kenya's central highlands; they had seen much of their land overtaken by settler plantations. The insurgents attacked outlying farms, murdering their British owners and slaughtering cattle.

By late 1953 the situation was sufficiently severe that the colonial government declared a state of emergency. Jomo Kenyatta and other Kikuyu nationalist leaders were arrested, although they claimed to have nothing to do with Mau Mau. Moreover, tough counterinsurgency measures were taken. By the time the revolt was suppressed in late 1955, thousands of Kikuyu and about one hundred British had lost their lives.

Although Mau Mau was defeated as a military movement, it helped to entrench nationalism and hasten the transfer of power to the indigenous population. This dispatch recounts and analyzes the emergence of Mau Mau.

Nairobi, January 8, 1953

. . . In the last half of 1952, Kenya became one of the world's trouble spots. Formerly ignored by the world press and radio news services, the Colony now shares, from time to time, the news spotlight with Malaya and Indo-China. From an area covered by the occasional visiting correspondent, it has become the primary beat of twelve foreign correspondents and one BBC representative. The disturbances in Kenya have not and probably will not attain the magnitude of those in such trouble spots as Malaya and Indo-China because (1) the malcontents are not in as favored a position to receive arms and other forms of assistance from a neighboring or nearby communist state, (2) thus far, the unrest is confined to the Kikuyu who number about a fifth of Kenya's African population, and, (3) latent inter-tribal hostility may serve as a break in its spread throughout the area.

The essential nature of the change in the situation in Kenya is (1) the rejection by the Kikuyu of a multi-racial society as the goal which the colony seeks to attain, and (2) the resort to subversive tactics, particularly violence, in an effort to create a purely African state in Kenya.

This threat to the existing order is a two-prong challenge. The overt Kenya African Union (KAU) led by English-educated Jomo Kenyatta, is a political organization patterned along non-African lines and operating through such devices foreign to indigenous culture as schools and branch organizations with elected officers, charters and constitutions. From the secret society complex common to most African cultures has arisen the covert Mau Mau, the esoteric and "strong arm" phase of the opposition to duly constituted authority.

The convergence of these two streams of resistance to British rule is responsible for the serious nature of the disturbances in Kenya. Through the trial of Mr. Kenyatta and five other leaders of the KAU, the Colonial Administration seeks to prove that co-operation between Mau Mau and KAU has been deliberate and planned. It is, however, within the realm of possibility that congruent objectives furnished sufficient grounds for joint ad hoc action.

In its broadest context, the present disturbances in Kenya can be interpreted as an eruption of Kikuyu frustration produced by their failure to attain satisfaction (rewards) from participation in the complex European-Asian-African society being created in the Colony. The inability of the African to cope with the new situation is evidenced by the fact that he receives a smaller share of goods and services than members of other communities and is unable to command the means for improving his position. He is the most poorly housed, poorly clothed and poorly fed. He receives inferior educational facilities and medical attention. He is found most frequently occupying menial positions, is subject to wage and social discriminations and believes, with some justification, to discrimination in job opportunities. Lastly, he believes that he is herded into overcrowded reserves because European settlers have pre-empted all remaining land suitable for expanding native agriculture while on the other hand, his advancement in the skilled trades and commerce is blocked by superior Asian competition.

The appeal of Mau Mau lies in its simple and direct answer to African frustration. Like its predecessor *Dini ya Jesu Christo,* and its less successful contemporary *Dini ya Massabura,* Mau Mau would solve the problem by eliminating it. The clock would be turned back, Europeans and presumably Asians, would be driven out and pre-European contact conditions would be re-established.

In a more limited context, interest in the Kenya disturbances centers in their relation to world communism. At the outset it is necessary to distinguish between, (1) organized assistance by communist agents and provocateurs within and without the territory furnished on instructions from the Kremlin; (2) the encouragement of and sympathy for movements useful to communist objectives but unaccompanied by assistance in arms, funds or personnel.

The present unrest in Kenya is not receiving type one communist support. Kenya authorities are convinced that the subversive movement is entirely propelled from within.

... The unrest in Kenya which culminated in the proclamation of a State of Emergency on October 21st, has made significant changes in the life of the Colony. ... As the Emergency enters its third month, there is growing apprehension on the part of the Europeans that the government's efforts to deal with the situation will end in a stalemate and that, therefore, terrorism will become chronic rather than epidemic.

Considerable disruption in the normal routine of daily life has occurred for a period, virtually no public gatherings were held in Nairobi after dark. Attendance at the 9:00 p.m. cinema shows was cut by half and people still prefer to patronize matinee performances. European men have been called to serve with the Police Reserve and the Kenya Regiment which has created personnel problems for business firms and reduces audiences at public gatherings. Europeans, Asians and more recently Africans are participating in home guard duties which cover the hours from 8:00 p.m. to 5:00 a.m. Travel outside municipal areas is prohibited after 7:00 p.m. except by pass. Even with permission, no one travels outside city limits after dark except in an emergency. In most areas of Kikuyuland, the movement of Africans is forbidden by a 7:00 p.m. curfew. All Kikuyu are required to carry special identification.

The heaviest burden is borne by (a) loyal Africans, and (b) Europeans residing on isolated upcountry farms. While Mau Mau terrorism is directed against Europeans, it also seeks by terrorism to enforce African solidarity. Therefore, the number of murders and atrocities committed against Africans far exceeds those suffered by all other communities. The police have been signally unsuccessful in protecting headmen, chiefs, informers and government witnesses from Mau Mau vengeance. It is equally true that European farmers are, to a large measure, without police protection. Although the police have been fairly successful in apprehending offenders, it is necessary for Europeans and loyal Kikuyu to take positive measures to defend themselves against the commission of crimes. The possibility exists that the Kenya settler community, under the tension of ever lurking terror, may attempt to take matters into their own hands and defy constituted authority. With one lawless element pitted against another, the situation could rapidly get out of hand. Furthermore, resort to vigilante action holds unequalled possibilities for bringing tribes hitherto unaffected by Kikuyu nationalism into a common front against Europeans. . . .

It is too early and the possibility appears too remote to speculate on alterations in priorities which might follow a failure of the government to establish law and order in the colony. . . .

For the Consul General:

John A. Noon
Regional Public Affairs Officer

1954   Dien Bien Phu: The French Defeated in Vietnam
Dispatch from U.S. Chargé d'Affaires in Vietnam Robert McClintock to Secretary of State John Foster Dulles

French forces reoccupied their former colony of Indochina after the defeat of Japan in 1945. Almost immediately they found themselves embroiled in a bitter and losing war against Vietnamese nationalist guerrillas, the Viet Minh. Several years of fighting saw the French position steadily deteriorate. In an effort to lure the guerrillas into a conventional battle, the French established a remote but heavily armed fortress at Dien Bien Phu, near the northern border of Laos. The Viet Minh accepted the challenge, but to the surprise of the French the guerrillas were able to transport massive forces and heavy artillery to the hills surrounding Dien Bien Phu. They laid siege to the French garrison and pounded it for weeks while slowly tightening their noose around the fort. The French defenders beat back repeated attacks but finally were overrun on May 7, 1954. This dispatch describes the final hours of the battle, as recounted by the French commander in Indochina, Henri Navarre, to the American chargé d'affaires.

Shortly after the battle President Dwight D. Eisenhower wrote that "the heroism and stamina displayed by the gallant garrison at Dien Bien Phu . . . will forever stand as a symbol of the free world's determination to resist dictatorial aggression." Instead, Dien Bien Phu came to symbolize the end of almost a century of French control in Indochina. Within weeks the French and the Vietnamese reached a peace accord providing for French withdrawal.

Saigon, May 8, 1954

. . . I called on General Navarre this morning to present our official and personal homage to General De Castries and his heroic men at Dien Bien Phu.

Navarre gave us following account of end of battle.

Enemy commenced all-out attack at 9 p.m. May 6 and fighting was continuous thereafter for twenty hours. There was exceedingly heavy artillery barrage and for first time in Indochina war French Union forces were subjected to long-range rocket fire of type case from "Stalin organs". These were undoubtedly of Russian manufacture.

Last contact with De Castries was at 1700 hours yesterday when he reported that Viet Minh were within ten meters of his command post and that he was destroying his radio forthwith. Air reconnaissance yesterday afternoon revealed that sporadic fighting was continuing in and around central redoubt up to 1900 hours last night. . . .

At commencement of last assault evening of May 6 there were 1,200 wounded of whom 500 were litter cases. These figures do not, however, include large number, perhaps 1,500 in all, of walking wounded who were still in combat. Navarre estimates that following yesterday's carnage number of severely wounded must be not less than 2,000 and that out of a total garrison of 8,000 men probably forty percent were in some degree wounded. . . .

Navarre was icily calm but obviously a man who had gone through great strain. He said, although [Viet Minh military leader Vo Nguyen] Giap's losses had been terrific—latest assault waves of Viet Minh at Dien Bien Phu were made up 55 percent of raw recruits—he still has capability of bringing his divisions over to Tonkin delta. Navarre . . . did not think that rainy season would stop him since his troops were perfectly capable of going overland on any terrain. However, with rains it would be more difficult for enemy to move his artillery and heavy equipment. This gave opportunity to French Air Force "now that it had little else to do" to attempt interdiction bombing and strafing on route which Giap would be forced to use. Nevertheless, there was a distinct possibility that within one month Viet Minh would be in force in delta and decision might be taken to continue all-out war in delta despite difficulties of water and hot weather. If this happened Navarre said it would be beyond means of Franco-Vietnamese forces to prevent a defeat and that only other alternative would have to be internationalization of war.

McClintock

1955 Two Views of the Chinese Communists
Dispatches from London and Geneva

With the establishment of a Communist Chinese government in 1949 (see "China Goes Communist," p. 414), the United States closed its offices in mainland China and moved its embassy to Taipei, Formosa (Taiwan), where the Chinese Nationalist government led by Chiang Kai-shek had established itself. The new Chinese Communist government was regarded as a threat and menace and was considered a puppet of the Soviet Union. With no representation in Peking, the U.S. government sought information and opinions from a broad range of world leaders on the Chinese Communist government and its leader, Mao Tse-tung. These dispatches recount conversations on the subject with two of the most prominent non-aligned heads of government, Prime Minister Jawaharlal Nehru of India and President Joseph Tito of Yugoslavia. The second dispatch is of additional interest as it was sent by a secretary of state, John Foster Dulles, reporting on a conversation he had had while traveling abroad.

Nehru's Views
From U.S. Ambassador to Great Britain Winthrop W. Aldrich to Secretary of State John Foster Dulles

London, February 3, 1955

. . . I had half-hour conversation with Nehru this morning. . . .

. . . I told Nehru that I was sure Washington would be interested in his reaction to present situation in Far East. He smiled and then said very seriously that question was enormously complicated but that fundamental difficulty was that Chiang Kai-shek, who was a man about whom he did not wish to say anything derogatory because he had been his guest and had no personal feelings against him, had been passed by, by history and that his aspirations were no longer attainable but that Mao Tse-tung was nevertheless in constant fear that Chiang Kai-shek might attempt to invade the mainland with the help of the United States. Besides this the air raids on mainland and against shipping constituted continuous pinpricks. This situation he characterized as a running sore. He said that as far as Formosa was concerned Chinese Communists believed that it belonged to China which had held it for 1000 years before it had been taken from them by Japan, and all through the last war China had claimed that Formosa should be restored to them by Japan at end of war. These facts created a most difficult situation for Mao Tse-tung. Moreover India had recognized Mao Tse-tung's Government, which made it impossible for India to consider that Chiang Kai-shek had legitimate claim to occupy Formosa as part of Chinese territory.

At this point he reiterated statement that history had passed Chiang Kai-shek by and compared his position to Indian Princes who had been protected by Britain for so many years and who after the separation of India from empire, no longer had power to protect themselves. He said half facetiously, "we did not treat them badly. We have given them pensions and now, although they no longer have any power they are quite happy." I replied that it did not seem to me that there was any parallel at all between what happened to the Indian Princes and what might happen to Chiang Kai-shek, but that in any event it had already been made entirely clear that the United States was not prepared to throw Chiang Kai-shek to the Communist wolves. He replied that he of course understood that.

Nehru said that in his own interviews with Mao Tse-tung he had not found him unreasonable. He referred specifically to a conversation he had had with Mao Tse-tung at request of Pope for release of a Catholic Bishop which had resulted in release of Bishop after two days consideration by Mao Tse-tung in what Nehru described as a casual manner. He said he felt certain that the American airmen held by Mao Tse-tung would have already been released if the request from the United Nations had not been coupled with a resolution condemning the action of the Chinese Reds in holding them. . . .

I ended the interview by saying I appreciated what he had said and told him that if there was anything I could do to be helpful to him I was completely at his disposal.

Aldrich

Tito's Views
Dispatch from Secretary of State John Foster Dulles to the Department of State

Geneva, November 8, 1955

At Secretary's request Tito gave his views about Communist China saying that while Yugoslavia had not known too much about the country they were in a position to study it first-hand since the establishment of diplomatic relations.

Tito insisted Communist China was not a Soviet satellite. Although the Soviets had exercised great influence over Chinese Communists, Stalin had complained Mao was difficult to deal with during the partisan period. Soviets adopted a rather cautious attitude towards the Chinese. While they were helping China economically and technically, it was wrong to think the USSR was pushing China as its spearhead for Asian penetration.

Tito was sure Soviets exercised at times a restraining influence on Chinese, commenting that regime was young and in full flush of revolutionary fever which sometimes caused it to run a bit wild. He believed the Chinese have learned some lessons and were now wiser. Tito advocated Communist China's admission to UN on grounds it was important for it to have wider political and economic contacts and not to be forced into position whereby having relations [only] with USSR. China also could provide a wide market for many countries including the US. Tito commented that just as China had showed some elasticity in its international affairs so it might show similar elasticity in foreign policy which would not exclude difficulties with the USSR.

According to Tito the Chinese Communist Party while having relations with Soviet Communist Party was quite independent and certain pro-Russian elements had been largely eliminated. . . . At this point [Vice President] Kardelj said he knew from Stalin that latter was opposed to Mao taking over China by open revolution. It was paradox that Yugoslav and Chinese Communist revolutions which were completely successful were carried out against Stalin's wishes, because Stalin wanted all countries engaged in revolution to be dependent on Soviet Union.

Secretary explained US feeling against Chinese Communists deriving from their Korean intervention and efforts take over Indochina. Present situation in South Vietnam, Laos and Cambodia was such that these areas had good prospect of remaining free. Threats against Taiwan were another cause of American sentiment. . . .

In conclusion Secretary emphasized our loyalty to Chinese Nationalists who stood with us against Japanese. We have obtained Chiang agreement not act against Mainland except in agreement with us, thus giving us power of control over Chinese Nationalist action. Last January risk of war had been grave because of Chinese Communist attitude. Secretary referred to congressional resolution empowering President to use U.S. armed forces to assist in Taiwan defense; said situation had improved since then but Chinese Communists must realize American people still harbored strong feelings not because they were Communist regime, since we had good relations with Yugoslavia which was a Communist regime, but because of Chinese actions and threats in Far East.

                                                Dulles

1955 Military Tensions in China
Dispatch from U.S. Ambassador to China Karl L. Rankin to
Secretary of State John Foster Dulles

After the People's Republic of China was established on the Chinese mainland in 1949, and Chiang Kai-shek and his Nationalist followers fled to the island of Formosa (Taiwan), the United States continued to recognize Chiang's Nationalist government as the legitimate government of China (see "China Goes Communist," p. 414, and "Two Views of the Chinese Communists," p. 432). Military tensions between the two Chinas continued throughout the 1950s, with Chiang's supporters talking of a return to the mainland while Communist leaders called for the occupation of Taiwan. Military clashes were frequent and sometimes threatened to erupt into full-scale war. This dispatch reports the first air engagement between Nationalist and Communist forces over the Strait of Formosa and comments on the general military situation.

Taipei, October 20, 1955

... First engagement between GRC [Government of the Republic of China] and Communist jet aircraft along China coast October 15 presumably more or less accidental but provides useful occasion for assessment of probabilities. Obviously no one can predict future in detail and accidents can happen any time. But based upon what is known in Taipei of Red capabilities, activities and policies, following courses of action appear not improbable.

1. Communists will maintain varying degrees of tension in Formosa Strait by such means as occasional shelling of Kinmen and Matsu and by gradual increase of air activity. ...

2. While Reds are capable of assembling forces for larger scale assault on offshore islands in relatively short time, no evidence exists of active preparation for such attack. ...

3. Meanwhile Reds will continue systematic development of airfields and related facilities in South China until they are in position assume control of air over Formosa Strait. Some US military experts believe they could do this today with difficulty but at present relative rates of development on their side and ours they will be in much better position by next summer.

4. Assumption of air control over strait will be undertaken by Communists with due care to avoid clash with US forces such as to provoke atomic retaliation against Red airfields which probably alone could deal with ChiCom air power comprehensively and effectively under present conditions. ...

As seen from Taiwan, indispensible courses of action on part of US to meet above situation for immediate and foreseeable future include:

a. Maintenance of decisive atomic air superiority in China area without which success of US policy can not be expected even though this power may not be used.

b. Development of GRC defenses, both in air and on ground, with maximum rapidity and to maximum extent practicable.

c. Provision of adequate air base facilities at earliest possible date to accommodate USAF combat units when deployed on Taiwan. (Current plans call for 7 fighter squadrons in case of need but there are no adequate places to accommodate them. . . .) . . .

d. Maintenance of US position toward Red China which neither it nor others can regard as other than firm and devoid of any inclination toward appeasement.

Rankin

1956 The Suez Crisis
Dispatches from U.S. Ambassadors to Israel and Egypt to Secretary of State John Foster Dulles

The Suez Crisis had its origin in a combination of historical circumstances: the colonial legacy, the Arab-Israeli conflict, and the cold war. Egyptian leader Gamal Abdel Nasser, who had assumed power within a year of the overthrow of the monarchy in 1952, promptly negotiated the departure of British forces, which had occupied Egypt since the nineteenth century. Nasser subsequently contracted with communist governments for supplies of arms and recognized Communist China, leading the United States and Britain to withdraw aid offers for construction of the Aswan High Dam, Nasser's highest development priority. As an alternative source of revenue for the dam, Nasser nationalized the Suez Canal (connecting the Red Sea and the Mediterranean), which had been under British control. Britain and France saw this move as a threat to their strategic and economic interests. They therefore reached a secret agreement with Israel to invade Egypt, which would provide a pretext for British and French forces to seize control of the canal. The United States, still hoping to maintain an even relationship with Nasser and to avoid giving any cause for Soviet intervention, pressed its European allies and Israel to exercise restraint.

The crisis erupted into war on October 29, 1956, when Israeli troops invaded Egypt, followed within days by British and French forces. The first dispatch describes the final U.S. appeal from President Dwight D.

Eisenhower to Israeli prime minister David Ben-Gurion to step back from military mobilization. The second dispatch recounts a discussion with Nasser as Egyptian forces faced defeat. On November 6, under heavy U.S. pressure, Britain and France agreed to a cease-fire and then to the withdrawal of their forces from Egypt.

Ben-Gurion on Israeli Mobilization
From U.S. Ambassador to Israel Edward B. Lawson

Tel Aviv,
October 28/29, 1956—midnight

I delivered President's message to Ben Gurion at his home in Tel Aviv at 8 p.m. He appeared tired and voice weak. . . . [H]e said:

While Iraq's interest in penetration of Jordan remained threat, it was greatly over-shadowed by new military alliance of Egypt, Jordan and Syria which tightened noose around Israel's neck. Almost immediately after Jordan elections, [Jordan's king] Hussein announced his determination to fight Israel. Now there was unified tripartite military command which "even [a] child knows is not directed against US, Soviet or even Britain".

He continued: "We don't know from what point of ring around us we can expect attack if it is going to come. It may start from Syria where we have many settlements, or Jordan, or in south. We decided it was necessary to mobilize few battalions to face seven brigades which Syria has; put some on Jordan border; and few more in south. Mobilization is purely precautionary measure imposed on us by events. We shall be as happy as President if things remain quiet".

Against this encircling hostility, he repeated he had been obliged to call up "few more units." Such call up was conspicuous because unlike Arabs, who had large standing armies Israel had to rely on reserves. It had only tiny permanent establishment, maintained to manage military stores, camps and equipment and to receive and train new recruits. "We decided Friday and Saturday to mobilize few more units of our reserves. Then if we are attacked, they can hold line until rest are mobilized."

Developing his case of Israel being obliged to put itself in defensive posture from feeling of insecurity and frustration, he reviewed "disappointment" with SC [United Nations Security Council] decision on canal which he said had assured free transit to everyone but Israel. He declared Egyptian cabinet member after council meeting had specifically excluded Israel, and he said even "our good friend India" has declared that remedy for Israel lies in international court.

But even more important to Israel, he said, was Jordan and Egyptian blockade of Straits of Tiran which threatened Israel's very existence by choking flow of Israel manufactured goods to probably only real markets available to them in Asia and Africa.

In view of fact Ben Gurion spent so much time and effort in defense of his mobilization activity, I told him that my interpretation of President's letter was not that he objected so much to mobilization as such and for self defense but that he feared there might be elements and local developments not confined to self defense—that hostilities might come from such action.

He replied US would have no reason to worry if it succeeded in persuading other people to keep peace but "I am not sure you will succeed."

On question of safety US nationals, he avoided giving me unequivocal assurances, saying however, "I don't think there is any danger." We talked about air activity re my problem of women and children for whose safety as well as for all US nationals I had evacuation plan to invoke if necessary. He replied, "I cannot be certain but I think there is now sufficient means for aerial protection. We hope to intercept them before they come. We have good radar installations, but I cannot tell you with certainty that none would get through."

I raised question of Fedayeen [Arab guerrillas] as danger to US nationals. He admitted they were constant threat, although he said he did not think their activities would be directed against non-Jews.

Comment: Ben Gurion was in good spirits, despite degree or two of fever for which he had had medical attention today, and was very cordial to me. However, I felt he was deliberately minimizing extent of mobilization which still appears very large and is not to be dismissed in terms of "few battalions." He spoke, I felt, with considerable and deliberate caution and was not very effective in creating feeling of assurance there will be no hostilities.

Lawson

Nasser on Egypt's Military Reverses
From U.S. Ambassador to Egypt Raymond A. Hare

Cairo, November 2, 1956

Delivered President's message to Nasser this morning. He listened attentively and took notes. Then asked I convey his appreciation to President and also to say that, come what may, he and Egyptian people are resolved to fight to end in order maintain their honor. He asked that special mention be made of continuing heavy air attacks and report they are now to be extended to radio stations as well as military objectives.

Speaking then in a more personal vein he said he would adopt technique of frankness which I had used in our last conversation (Embtel 1240) and admit that Egyptians had never really believed us when we had indicated possibility that British and French might embark on an independent policy which did not have our approval. Now he recognized he had been wrong. Our action had been clear-cut and doubt had been removed.

Turning to the military situation Nasser said he had been very worried two days ago regarding Egyptian armor in Sinai which was fighting without air cover. Furthermore whole aspect of hostilities had been altered by Anglo-French intervention and it had therefore been decided withdraw armor from Sinai as well as Egyptian forces at Rafa, El Arish and El Agheila to west of canal in pursuance of new plan of not defending canal but rather using canal as line of defense. He had consequently been very relieved when large part of armor got safely back across canal yesterday and some scattered units arrived during night. However, small "suicide units" would remain east of canal.

Regarding type of campaign he would fight, Nasser indicated it would be a people's war; fighting town by town and house by house. There would be no evacuations. For instance his own family would remain in Cairo.

As to air activity, Nasser said his problem was shortage of pilots and he had decided would be wasteful to commit them against superior force. He preferred keep them in reserve for defense of Egypt proper, i.e. Delta. As consequence Egyptian planes have been kept on ground and heavy losses have been suffered.

. . . Nasser looked tired but he was calm, relaxed and friendly, and although I could well be mistaken, I for the first time gained impression of sincerity when he admitted he had been unduly suspicious our attitude.

Hare

1956 The Hungarian Uprising
Dispatch from U.S. Minister to Hungary Edward T. Wailes to Secretary of State John Foster Dulles

After the Second World War Hungary was occupied by the Soviet Union, which established a communist government there. Acting on growing dissatisfaction with Soviet influence, a group of students marched on October 23, 1956, to present a list of grievances to Prime Minister Erno Gero. They were joined by thousands of other protesters, but Gero dismissed the marchers with a curt, hostile speech. The peaceful march turned violent when police fired on the crowd, and within hours the Hungarian military joined the revolt.

Spurred on by American radio broadcasts they believed promised U.S. support, the Hungarians installed Imre Nagy as head of a coalition gov-

ernment. When Nagy declared Hungary was withdrawing from the Warsaw Pact (an alliance of the Soviet Union and its seven satellite states in Eastern Europe), the Soviets moved quickly to crush the uprising. Western reaction was muted, in part because war erupted in the Middle East on the eve of the Soviet crackdown (see "The Suez Crisis," p. 436). As Soviet tanks rumbled into Budapest, the overmatched Hungarians put up a short but valiant resistance. Within two weeks the Soviets had put down the revolt. Later, Nagy and several of his colleagues were executed by the Soviets. As reported in this dispatch, some of the nationalists sought asylum in the U.S. legation and complained bitterly that the United States had let them down in their moment of need.

Budapest, November 19, 1956

Bela Kovacs and two of his lieutenants sought asylum at US Legation on morning November 4. Asylum request denied but temporary shelter overnight granted due heavy bombardment. Legation officers who conversed with Kovacs impressed by his sincerity and honesty. Some hurt feelings involved on his part because he like Hungarians in general had presumed on greater American aid than was possible to grant. . . .

Kovacs expressed opinion that US radio misled Hungarian people into believing they could count on effective US aid in event of trouble with Soviets. Kovacs said official pronouncements from highest US Government levels had also lent toward creating this illusion. He vehemently stated his opinion that if US policy toward Soviet Communism was purely defensive one the US should have directed its anti-Communist propaganda activities at USSR and should have left the East European states alone. Kovacs left little doubt that in his opinion the US for attainment of its own selfish goals, had cynically and cold-bloodedly maneuvered the Hungarian people into action against the USSR.

Although in the opinion of the Legation the Hungarians would have acted the same way even though our radio media had pursued more moderate line vis-a-vis the Hungarian Communist Government, there is no question that our past radio propaganda is at present source of much embarrassment to us. Legation personnel who have lived through entire period here since October 23 are keenly aware of idealistic manner in which Hungarians have behaved and of the high moral plane on which revolution was conducted. This makes it all the more difficult to explain or attempt to justify our radio propaganda programs and political pronouncements—a fact which I feel most strongly should be borne in mind in formulating future programs and pronouncements both for Hungary and other curtain countries.

Information about Bela Kovacs temporary presence in Legation is not to be used by the media.

Wailes

1957 *Sputnik*
Dispatch from U.S. Ambassador to the Soviet Union
Llewellyn E. Thompson Jr. to Secretary of State John Foster Dulles

On October 4, 1957, the Soviet Union launched Sputnik, *the first manmade satellite, into orbit around the Earth, signaling the beginning of both the space age and the space race. The launch caught the American scientific community off guard and sparked an enormous furor in the United States. By a single act the Soviets had called into question America's scientific and technological superiority. Worse still, the launch had military implications and lent credence to the Soviet claim to have launched the first successful intercontinental ballistic missile (ICBM) two months earlier. Fear of a "missile gap" would haunt U.S. policy makers for years to come. American space researchers scrambled to catch up but faced several failures before* Explorer *was put into orbit early in 1958. By that time the Soviet Union had launched* Sputnik II, *with a dog aboard. This dispatch from Moscow outlines the Soviet reaction to* Sputnik *and analyzes some of its political consequences.*

Moscow, November 16, 1957

. . . Embassy believes Sputnik undoubtedly source pride to all elements Soviet society particularly intelligentsia. Regime attempt to equate communism and progress enhanced and its prestige probably raised, while disquiet certain professional and intellectual groups perhaps somewhat mollified. Although military angles not focus of principal stress, national sense of security also probably increased. However, Embassy contacts, though limited, indicate ordinary citizens remain more interested in bread and butter measures. . . .

Finally Sputnik not unalloyed gain for intelligentsia, since though already high status of science boosted further, there are indications regime may seek use Sputnik success to demand greater exertions for comparable triumphs in other fields. In bloc, Soviets are obviously using Sputnik as symbol of growth Soviet power which should be proof to peoples of bloc that communism is irreversible. Hopes for liberation which already dimmed by passage of time in general and by Hungary in particular presumably will be further reduced. Repeated demands by [Communist Party leader Nikita] Khrushchev (who will now seem to be leading from own "position of strength") that West recognize status quo in Europe will have some effect even if West maintains silence or gives verbal refusal.

On basis apparent Soviet analysis of new international opportunities now open to USSR, Embassy believes Dept estimate fails give sufficiently high rating to impact, especially in uncommitted areas, of present situation. This is one in which the USSR, after giving general impression of parity with US in nuclear field, has gone on dramatically to take stance of world leader in vitally important and imagination-catching field of future like rocketry, leaving US in position of catching up in science and technology which hitherto assumed US strong point. Embassy agrees that US launching satellite and ICBM might lessen impact, but there is no reason expect USSR rest on present laurels and meanwhile USSR has gone long way to establish picture of itself (which it is assiduously promoting) as world power on par with and conceivably superior to US. . . .

Immediate consequences appear to be Soviet effort to inflate pressure for big power talks, and possibly increased Soviet belief that US and West ready or can be forced discuss disarmament on Soviet terms, admit Soviet role in Near East, and accept postwar Communist conquests in Eastern Europe and Far East. Moreover, since USSR is combining its greatly increased prestige and enhanced political stature with continued foreign assistance program in key uncommitted areas, it can be expected that tendency to accept Soviet help and expanded trade (with all possibilities of penetration thus implied) will grow as target nations feel need accommodation with Soviets. . . . It is true that Sputnik-ICBM does not increase danger of devastation threatening US friends which is already huge, but its importance still great since for first time it brings into question US superiority or even certain parity vis-a-vis Soviet power on which these nations had been relying as shield.

Thompson

1959–1960 Castro and Communism in Cuba
Dispatches from U.S. Representatives in Cuba

Dictator Fulgencio Batista seized power in Cuba in 1933 and was the dominant power there for over a quarter of a century (see "Batista Seizes Power in Cuba," p. 380). *In 1956 a young lawyer-politician-guerrilla leader named Fidel Castro led a small band of revolutionaries home from exile in Mexico. They began a guerrilla campaign that won widening popular and military support. In January 1959 Batista fled, and the revolutionary forces marched into Havana, where Castro was given a hero's welcome.*

The United States, which dominated Cuba's economy and had maintained close relations with Batista, was uncomfortable with Cuba's new revolutionary leadership and wary of Castro himself. American representatives in Cuba at first judged the young leader to be irresponsible and erratic but not inherently anti-American. Relations worsened, however, when the new regime executed a large group of its opponents. A more substantial rift developed as the Cuban government embarked on agrarian reform and expropriated huge tracts of land from American sugar companies. The gap became unbridgeable when the United States cut off aid and Cuba turned to the Soviet Union for assistance.

These dispatches chronicle the changing American view of Castro and his policies during his first two years in power. At first, the embassy in Havana assessed that the United States could forge friendly ties with the new government, which it believed would need U.S. goodwill in view of Cuba's economic dependence on the United States. But by the end of Castro's first year in power official reports from Havana were questioning his mental balance and judging that his excesses would bring about the end of his regime within months. By early 1960 the embassy was reporting that there was no longer any prospect of good relations with a Castro government. By year's end it had concluded that Cuba had gone communist and was firmly entrenched in the Soviet camp.

The New Government: A "Friendly Relationship Can Be Established"
From U.S. Chargé d'Affaires in Havana Daniel M. Braddock to Secretary of State John Foster Dulles

Havana, February 18, 1959

Fidel Castro has set the general pattern for Cuba's current attitude toward the United States by his public speeches since January 1 and by his replies to questions put by press representatives. This attitude may be described as critical in specific respects but not generally unfriendly. It has long been clear that Castro felt that the United States gave moral support to the Batista Government when it should have been giving moral support to the revolutionary movement, and that it should have ceased arms shipments to Batista much sooner than it did and withdrawn at the same time its Military Missions.

Castro's feeling toward the United States became one of indignation after January 1 [when] the conduct of the revolutionary trials and executions of war criminals called forth some sharp criticism in the United States. At that time he made his much-publicized remark to an American reporter that if the United States tried to intervene by sending Marines to Cuba, there would be "200,000 dead gringos" in the streets—a remark he promptly regretted and attempted to soften by making another one almost equally unfortunate, that if the United States intervened in Cuba, it would have to kill six million Cubans first.

Castro is impetuous and emotional, and his worst enemy is his tongue, which he himself often acknowledges and then promptly forgets. There has not been a single public speech by Castro since the triumph of the revolution in which he has not shown some feeling against the United States, the American press or big American business concerns in Cuba, but he has also had a few kind words for the American public as a whole, for the United States Government, and for specific individuals. The Cuban press and people have for the most part followed blindly where Castro has led.

There is some reason to believe that Castro is not as anti-American as he sounds in his public pronouncements, and that he often resorts to this kind of nationalistic demagoguery because of its popular appeal. He has shown he is sensitive to criticism in the United States and wants a good press, and, busy and harried as he is, he can always find time to talk with an American reporter. Moreover, most responsible Cubans, including Castro himself, and probably the majority of the masses as well, recognize that good relations with the United States are a political and economic necessity for Cuba.

At the Ministerial and other working levels the Revolutionary Government shows signs of wanting good relations with the United States. . . .

The same spirit of cooperation has not been generally evident in the Cuban military organization. . . . Raul Castro, who since Fidel Castro's designation as Prime Minister is now the Commander-in-Chief of the Armed Forces, has at no time to the Embassy's knowledge shown any noticeable friendliness toward the United States. He is generally credited with more leftist sympathies than Fidel. It may prove possible in time to establish good relations with Raul Castro, but for the moment the prospect is not promising. It is still less promising as regards "Che" Guevara, commander of La Cabana fortress. Guevara is believed to be definitely anti-American and is acting like a Communist. It is not clear whether Guevara now follows directly after Raul Castro or after Camilo Cienfuegos in the military hierarchy of the revolution, but in either case he seems to have considerable freedom of action and to be growing in influence.

I believe that we can expect the resentment of Fidel Castro against the United States to take a while to cool off, but that in time a fully friendly relationship can be established between the United States and the new Cuba. The Revolutionary government may seek to develop closer ties with countries of Latin America. While unobjectionable in itself, this would tend to draw Cuba somewhat away from the United States. I believe we can even now count on continued good support from Cuba in issues between the free world and the Communist world, even though at home the Revolutionary Government will probably not take as strong action against the local Communists as we might like to see.

On the economic front, I see no reason why the American companies now in Cuba will not be able, with possibly one or two exceptions, to adjust themselves to the new situation, and I believe we can look forward to an increase in opportunities for business investment. United States exports to Cuba will in all probability be hurt in some respects by the higher protective tariffs which the Government means to adopt, but any growth of the Cuban economy should benefit United States trade in other respects. In the long run the United States should be far more comfortable in dealing with a government which advocates and is genuinely trying to carry out democratic procedure than it was the Batista dictatorship.

In view of the attitude and outlook as evaluated above, I recommend that the United States show a friendly and conciliatory disposition toward the Revolutionary government; that it be patient with the latter's mistakes and, to a reasonable degree, with its nationalistic gestures, even when these are directed at us; and that the United States respond promptly to any reasonable, specific request from Cuba for assistance.

Daniel M. Braddock

Reassessing Castro

From U.S. Ambassador to Cuba Philip W. Bonsal to Secretary of State Christian Herter

Havana, November 6, 1959

. . . [F]ollowing personal reactions to course of events since mid-October may be of interest.

1. Although the Castro magic still sways mobs and his political strength remains great, he has lost much "quality" support even in ranks own party and in government where enthusiasm of several important figures replaced by precarious fear-induced conformity. Doubts of his capacity as ruler becoming more insistent.

2. My previous view of Castro as highly emotional individual yet generally rational and often cold-bloodedly and cynically playing the demagogue replaced by opinion that evident cynicism goes hand in hand with definite mental unbalance at times. His performance of October 26 was not that of sane man.

3. Our efforts, direct and indirect, both here and in Washington to remove Castro's deep-seated hostility to USA and suspicion of our motives and actions have been unsuccessful. Malevolence and cynicism characterizing handling of so-called "bombing" incident on October 21 was revelation of tremendous perhaps insuperable obstacles in way of establishing relations of good faith and mutual respect with present leaders of GOC [Government of Cuba].

4. Contrary to our earlier hopes, moderating forces (National Bank group especially) have for present at least lost out in contest for influ-

ence over Castro. Our bitter enemies, Raul Castro and Che Guevara are very much in the saddle. They can be counted on to speed up radical agrarian reform as well as measures designed destroy or cripple US mining, petroleum and public utility interests.

5. As indicated above, there has been marked increase here in questioning of sanity and competence of Castro and of soundness of measures advocated by GOC and particularly by his principal followers. It is highly important, as long as our over-riding security interests permit, that this trend be not arrested by actions or attitudes of ours. I believe it can be counted on to grow as further developments occur which bring out characteristics of Castro and his principal aides as well as unsoundness their measures in terms achievement their stated objectives. We must, of course, defend our legitimate interests and those of our citizens in all ways open to us without appearing coerce Cuba's sovereignty or interposing punitive action or threats which will appear to involve such coercion or unnecessarily arousing easily exacerbated Cuban nationalism.

6. Restraint and patience must continue to characterize our policy. This regime—and I believe there is no doubt as to its nonviability due to its own excesses and deficiencies within a relatively short period (months rather than years)—must not be given "shot in the arm" of positive actions or threats by us (even assuming such actions were open to us). Our presentation of October 27 was right in tone and timing. We must, to extent possible, combat attempt to picture USG in general and Department of State in particular as having no policy other than defense of status quo (including that of all US corporations) in Cuba and we must continue demonstrate sympathy aims aspirations of Cuban people and realization many things can and should be changed here.

7. We have recognized and must continue to recognize that accusations of communism play into hands of communists and extremists here and help them to control and influence Castro. US press handling of this issue unhelpful. There is no real awareness here of the issues of the East-West struggle even on part Minister of State. Anti-communism considered merely a weapon of "US reactionaries" forged in time of McCarthy hysteria. At same time we should also recognize situation not working out entirely to communist satisfaction and that to some extent Washington and Moscow tarred with same brush in eyes of Castro and many of his followers. Although Fidel and Raul Castro and Guevara are playing game highly unpalatable to us and satisfying to Moscow to that extent, their indignant protest at being "smeared" as communists are symptomatic of underlying realities here. The

essentially individualistic "bourgeois" nature of aspirations cherished by most Cubans above the very lowest level is a factor of great importance and will, I am confident, exert increasing influence.

Bonsal

No Hope of Good Relations
From U.S. Chargé d'Affaires in Havana Daniel M. Braddock to Secretary of State Christian Herter

Havana, March 8, 1960

Country Team of unanimous opinion there is no hope that US will ever be able to establish a satisfactory relationship with Cuban Government as long as it is dominated by Fidel Castro, Raul Castro, Che Guevara and like-minded associates. . . .

Embassy believes . . . hostile acts of GOC and mounting anti-US frenzy [on the] part of government-controlled mass media indicate deliberate attempt to precipitate a crisis in Cuban-American relations and force US to take drastic measures re Cuba.

Country Team has considered following courses of action for US: (1) conciliation, (2) strong action including economic measures, (3) maintenance of firm, dignified, restrained attitude, reflecting disapproval of regime but doing nothing overtly to hasten its downfall or that would provide basis for charge of US intervention. Of these courses Country Team believe (3) is still most profitable for US to follow, but recognizes danger that (A) Cuban economy may not collapse under Castro and (B) 2 or 3 years of continued anti-US indoctrination of Cuban people, especially of youth, may do damage to Cuban-American relations that will take many years to repair. This attitude, while scrupulously non-interventionist, would provide tacit encouragement essential to development of an active political opposition to Castro.

Together with policy of restraint toward Cuba, Embassy believes US should continue discreet efforts to awaken other Latin American countries to dangers to continent from Castro's excesses and Communistic tendencies.

Braddock

Cuba Is Communist

From U.S. Chargé d'Affaires in Havana Daniel M. Braddock to Secretary of State Christian Herter

Havana, November 16, 1960

The communist position in Cuba has changed from April 1960 to November 1960 from one of influence and increasing infiltration to one of effective control. Cuban involvement in the international communist apparatus has reached the point of no return and is still increasing. The Castro regime is now believed to be so firmly committed to the communist camp that it could not extract itself even in the unlikely event that it might wish to do so.

Though Cuba is not a Soviet satellite in the traditional sense, it plays as active and as effective a role in Soviet plans for world conquest as any of the countries openly ruled by a communist party and directly controlled from the Kremlin (or from Peking). Though there is some question as to how completely and in what form the Castro regime falls within the Soviet discipline, the attitude, methods and objectives of Cuba's leaders are such that Cuba must now be regarded as an extension in the Western Hemisphere of the Sino-Soviet bloc.

It appears, then, that, far from indicating that the Castro regime is an independent, nationalist force, the fact that his movement and revolution are not at once ostensibly communist is simply in keeping with the united front tactics outlined by the communists for use in Latin America. Their Guatemalan experience would seem to have taught them that, chameleon-like, they must skirt around the communist label, changing colors at will. They can pass through the initial phases of a power seizure much more easily in a vehicle provided by an extremist, nationalist group such as Castro's then they can in a vehicle provided by the Communist Party itself. Yet they preserve their freedom of action.

Thus, the movement begins by advertising itself as nationalist. While playing on the theme of anti-Americanism and speaking much of economic progress, it gradually arrives at a virtual identification with the goals and ideology of the Communist Party. This step has now been reached in Cuba, as demonstrated at the recent Cuban Communist Party Congress where the Party almost totally identified itself with the Castro revolution. In the months ahead, ever closer cooperation and identification between the Castro regime and international communism are to be expected. . . .

Braddock

1961 The Berlin Wall
Dispatch from Principal Officer, U.S. Mission in Berlin
Edwin A. Lightner Jr. to Secretary of State Dean Rusk

Throughout the years of the cold war Berlin was a flash point for East-West tensions. One of the first major international crises after World War II occurred in 1948 when Soviet forces occupying East Germany (German Democratic Republic—GDR) restricted U.S., British, and French access to their zones of occupied Berlin. The Allied response was to launch the Berlin airlift, which continued for almost a year before the Soviets relented (see "The Berlin Airlift," p. 413). A decade later tensions flared again when Soviet premier Nikita Khrushchev demanded the end of the four-power occupation of Berlin. The United States, Britain, and France refused and reinforced their garrisons in the city. The highly charged situation contributed to a flood of refugees from East Germany to the West. To stem the tide of refugees, East Germany closed the border between East and West Berlin on August 13, 1961. Two days later it began construction of the Berlin Wall, which came to symbolize the division of Europe. This dispatch from the U.S. mission in Berlin assesses the situation at the height of the crisis.

August 16, 1961

Following is our estimate present situation.

As result increased refugee flow and related Communist prestige loss, SED regime with specific approval of Soviets and other Warsaw Pact countries has taken drastic control action to prevent entry their own people to West Berlin. Seal-off SovZone and East Berlin from West Berlin by military and police action has torn completely asunder residual web of one city fabric and of Four Power status Berlin. Such closure boundary around West Berlin was doubtless contemplated by East as one consequence of separate peace treaty with GDR. Timing of action was apparently altered by internal GDR pressures. Increased refugee flow forced Sov/GDR hand and action of direct brute force has created a fait accompli. Well planned and abundantly accoutered with a massive display of military and police power, action was initially unqualifiedly successful and continues thus far successful so far as population East Germany or Berlin reaction is concerned, not to mention overall Western reaction.

It appears to us that there are two alternative interpretations of significance of events past 4 days:

1) Since Sov/GDR have attained by direct action such important desiderata from their standpoint, it might be argued that it should be easier hence to negotiate with them an interim solution concerning West Berlin. Clear as it was before, it should now be crystal-clear that there

is no possibility whatsoever of effective negotiations now with the Sovs concerning a broad all-German settlement which would of itself take care of the Berlin problem. Having thus already obtained such important results by last Sunday's actions, Sovs/GDR may be more "reasonable" in negotiations on other aspects of a possible Berlin arrangement.

2) On other hand, it may be argued that if Sovs/GDR are able to "get away" with this fait accompli, other similar actions may be undertaken by them prior to any negotiations and they may be even more demanding in such negotiations. Having taken such a big slice of salami and successfully digested it, with no hindrance, they may be expected to snatch further pieces greedily. Sovs/GDR want to absorb West Berlin, drive out Western Allies, and break down German national resistance. They made a big step toward these objectives last Sunday on East-West Berlin sector line. Their apparent success will encourage them to take further steps.

We believe second alternative is proper interpretation of significance of past few days' events here.

Threatening and arrogant utterances of Sov/GDR leaders since Vienna meeting, as well as their actions, would tend to support second alternative. From local standpoint, we are impressed by how even within a few days one direct action is being followed by another. While the initial action Sunday was directed almost exclusively to control of the movement of SovZone and East Berlin residents, already the East Germans have been introducing regulations and practical measures having the effect of drastically controlling and restricting the movement of West Berliners into East Berlin (ref Berlin's 200 Dept). We anticipate renewal of last fall's effort to control entry of Allied personnel into East Berlin. Two Mission cars had difficulties today. We also note arrogant tone of Sov Commandant's reply to Western Commandant's protest of Aug 3 concerning border-crossers (Berlin's 212 Dept, 185 Bonn).

If our view as to proper interpretation is correct, it means we have now entered phase of actual practical confrontation with Sovs on Berlin, that we have moved out of phase of confrontation by words and threats and into phase of deeds. If so, it is highly doubtful whether it can possibly suffice to reply to deeds with words of protestation.

What actions should West then take to meet this situation? Suspension of issuance of TTDs we have already recommended (Berlin's 207 Dept, 180 Bonn); economic countermeasures likewise we believe should be instituted at once (Berlin 211 Dept, 184 Bonn); Western travel into SovZone should be discouraged so far as possible and Western participation in SovZone sports and cultural events should be prohibited, to match restrictions on East German participation in Western events which follows from TTD ban. There may be other countermeasures which should also be applied, but we here have not been privy to detailed discussions of possible countermeasures.

However, what is important is purpose of these measures. Is their purpose to slap Sov/GDR on the wrist for what they have done? Or is it our purpose by strong counteractions to endeavor to indicate to them by deeds the grave consequences of continuation on their part of their current aggressive policy with respect to Berlin? Briefly, our countermeasures should seek to have a deterrent effect. To have a deterrent effect, countermeasures must not be calculated to fit the violation, but must to a certain extent overshoot the mark. We recognize risk that countermeasures which seek to be deterrent may in turn bring on other Sov/GDR countermeasures. We believe this risk has to be borne. Abrogation of IZT by FedRep last Sept in response to GDR Sept 8 decree was a countermeasure which overshot the mark and hence had a deterrent effect, albeit for only a year. The Sovs/GDR have now resumed the encroachment program they interrupted last fall; it may be that our countermeasures will lead them to take other measures sooner than expected. However, that did not happen last fall and if we take totally ineffectual measures they will be encouraged to take further steps faster.

Seal-off of West Berlin has already changed status quo in Communist favor in a way that strengthens their bargaining position in negotiations. It has already weakened effect we hoped to derive from Western military preparations announced by President on July 25. Assuming as we do that negotiations on Berlin will still take place, it is important that our bargaining position be not further weakened by our failure to take impressive countermeasures that will be clearly and widely recognized as such.

Lightner

1961 Vietnam: A "Powder Keg"

Dispatch from U.S. Ambassador at Large W. Averell Harriman to Secretary of State Dean Rusk

The French withdrawal from Indochina in 1954 did not end the conflict in Vietnam (see "Dien Bien Phu," p. 430). The country remained divided between a communist North Vietnam and a southern Republic of Vietnam under President Ngo Dinh Diem. When President John F. Kennedy took office in 1961, the United States was providing financial assistance to Diem and had over six hundred military advisers in South Vietnam. As the communist insurgency in the south intensified rapidly in 1961, Kennedy sent his military adviser, Gen. Maxwell Taylor, and presidential aide Walt Rostow to investigate. Their report, which became the basis of U.S. policy, outlined the problem in Vietnam as a military one and recommended increased military assistance as the only way to rescue the tottering Diem government. Within a year the number of U.S. troops in Vietnam was almost ten thousand.

A few Americans sounded an early warning note about the escalation of American involvement and its military emphasis. Among them was Averell Harriman, at the time American ambassador at large but soon to become assistant secretary of state for East Asian and Pacific affairs. Harriman previously had served as American ambassador to the Soviet Union and to Great Britain. In this dispatch from Geneva, Harriman warns that the situation in Vietnam is explosive and will not lend itself to a strictly military solution.

Geneva, October 13, 1961

From Harriman. I am much gratified to learn of General Taylor's and Rostow's visit to Saigon. I trust that in addition to military appraisal, some analysis of political situation can be made. In my travels during past six months as well as here in Geneva, I find everywhere concern over Diem's dictatorial regime, Palace Guard, family and corruption. These comments come from friendly sources, both highest and lower levels, expressing view that after good early record Diem has become increasingly isolated, particularly since attempted coup last year. Various accounts indicate lack of confidence among military, provincial government officials, intellectuals, business, professional and university groups. There is general prophesy that another coup is apt to happen, in which case insurgents will not be as considerate of Diem as last year. The British come closer to recognizing our difficulties, since they see no alternative to Diem, but even they hope that increased pressures will be brought for major reforms, not alone in social and economic, but in political field, particularly elimination of undesirable family influence and broadening base of Diem Government.

I recognize extreme difficulties of the situation and have no recommendations to make from this distance, but believe we may well be sitting on powder keg that could blow up. . . . I only want to add my voice to those who believe more recognition must be given to political situation which no amount of military assistance or participation can cure.

1963 Fomenting a Coup d'État in Vietnam
Dispatches from U.S. Ambassador to Vietnam Henry Cabot Lodge to Secretary of State Dean Rusk

By 1963 the United States was deeply involved in Vietnam, with over fifteen thousand military advisers in the field attempting to help stem the growing threat of a communist takeover. Meanwhile, the luster of Republic of Vietnam president Ngo Dinh Diem, whom the United States had supported with economic and military aid since the French departure in 1955, had worn thin (see "Dien Bien Phu," p. 430, and "Vietnam: A "Powder Keg," p. 451). His initial support among the people had dissipated, his military forces had proved incapable against the communist insurgency, and he had begun to crack down heavy-handedly on his opponents. Buddhist riots and self-immolations in the summer of 1963 served to dramatize opposition to Diem's policies and underscore his lack of control.

Concluding that Diem had become a liability in the fight against communism, U.S. officials adopted a concerted policy of encouraging his generals to overthrow and replace his regime. The first of the three dispatches provides a startlingly blunt account of the U.S. plan to overthrow Diem. The second reports the onset, just over two months later, of the coup in which Diem and his closest followers were killed. The final dispatch portrays the coup as a popular success and urges prompt U.S. recognition of the new government.

Planning the Overthrow of Diem

Saigon, August 29, 1963

1. We are launched on a course from which there is no respectable turning back: The overthrow of the Diem government. There is no turning back in part because U.S. prestige is already publicly committed to this end in large measure and will become more so as facts leak out. In a more fundamental sense, there is no turning back because there is no possibility, in my view, that the war can be won under a Diem administration, still less that Diem or any member of the family can govern the country in a way to gain the support of the people who count, i.e., the educated class in and out of government service, civil and military—not to mention the American people. In the last few months (and especially days), they have in fact positively alienated these people to an incalculable degree. So that I am personally in full agreement with the policy which I was instructed to carry out by last Sunday's telegram.

2. The chance of bringing off a Generals' coup depends on them to some extent; but it depends at least as much on us.

3. We should proceed to make all-out effort to get Generals to move promptly. To do so we should have authority to do following:

   (a) That General [Paul] Harkins repeat to Generals personally messages previously transmitted by CAS officers. This should establish their authenticity. (General Harkins should have order from President [Kennedy] on this.)

   (b) If nevertheless Generals insist on public statement that all U.S. aid to Vietnam through Diem regime has been stopped, we would agree, on express understanding that Generals will have started at same time. (We would seek persuade Generals that it would be better to hold this card for use in event of stalemate. We hope it will not be necessary to do this at all.)

4. Vietnamese Generals doubt that we have the will power, courage, and determination to see this thing through. They are haunted by the idea that we will run out on them even though we have told them pursuant to instructions, that the game had started.

5. We must press on for many reasons. Some of these are:

   (a) explosiveness of the present situation which may well lead to riots and violence if issue of discontent with regime is not met. Out of this could come a pro-Communist or at best a neutralist set of politicians.

   (b) The fact that war cannot be won with the present regime.

   (c) Our own reputation for steadfastness and our unwillingness to stultify ourselves.

   (d) If proposed action is suspended, I believe a body blow will be dealt to respect for us by Vietnamese Generals. Also, all those who expect U.S. to straighten out this situation will feel let down. Our help to the regime in past years inescapably gives us a large responsibility which we cannot avoid.

6. I realize that this course involves a very substantial risk of losing Vietnam. It also involves some additional risk to American lives. I would never propose it if I felt there was a reasonable chance of holding Vietnam with Diem. . . .

Lodge

The Coup Under Way

November 1, 1963

As reported through separate channels, coup d'etat commenced at about 1345. Salient developments as of 1500 are as follows:

1. General Don has confirmed in two separate messages to us that coup underway.

2. Telecommunications center of Ministry of Interior taken by coup forces, believed to be Marines.

3. Little firing in streets.

4. Col. Tung Commander Vietnamese Special Forces reported captured and persuaded issue cease fire order to Special Forces.

5. Presidential Guard fully deployed around Palace but no firing this area.

6. Minister Thuan, Minister of Economy Thanh, Minister of Finance Luong are all at Italian Ambassador's apartment.

7. 103 truckloads of troops reported entering Saigon over bridge from Bien Hoa.

8. Col. Tung, Police Commissioner, Chief Air Force, Air Force Commander, Civil Guard Comdr, all captives at Joint General Staff Headquarters. Navy Commander reported killed in premature action by Navy this morning.

9. Coup Generals have attempted get through to Palace to issue ultimatum to Diem guaranteeing safe conduct out of country to Diem and Nhu if they capitulate within one hour. Unable get through. General Don says he will issue proclamation concerning coup by radio within the hour.

10. Condition Gray declared and Americans alerted over radio AFRS [Armed Forces Radio Service] to stay indoors.

Lodge

The Coup Succeeds:
"Every Vietnamese Has a Grin on His Face Today"

November 2, 1963

1. Agree we should move promptly to support and recognize. We should decide to resume commercial import payments but on a periodic and selective basis without public announcement so as to avoid appearance of blank check or of pay-off. We should not be first to recognize but should assure other friendly Embassies that this is our attitude that we will recognize as soon as a few others have done so. We should, of course, give unmistakable signs of our satisfaction to the new leadership.

2. Believe the very great popularity of this coup should be stressed. Every Vietnamese has a grin on his face today. Am told that the jubilation in the streets exceeds that which comes every new year. The Vietnamese employees at the Embassy residence, whom I know well, have an entirely different look on their face today. When I drove to the office with a very small US flag flying, there were bursts of applause from the side walk, people shaking hands and waving. The tanks which were standing at the street corners were being covered with garlands of flowers and the Army was evidently immensely popular with the people. At the big circle in which [stands] the statue of the Trung sisters which was modeled in the image of Madame [Ngo Dihn] Nhu [wife of President Diem's brother], young men were busy with acetylene torches cutting the statues off at the feet and putting cables around the necks so as to topple them to the ground.

3. Do not think the President should be identified with the story of the desire of the Diem regime to negotiate with the army. I know of no hard evidence of such a desire. . . .

Lodge

1964 The Gulf of Tonkin Incident

Dispatch from U.S. Ambassador to Vietnam Maxwell D. Taylor to Secretary of State Dean Rusk

An event that would have major repercussions on U.S. policy in Vietnam occurred on August 2, 1964, when three North Vietnamese patrol boats attacked the U.S. destroyer Maddox *in the Gulf of Tonkin. The destroyer, joined by planes from a nearby aircraft carrier, returned fire and damaged*

all three of its attackers; two, however, were able to escape. In response, President Lyndon B. Johnson, then in the midst of an election campaign, ordered the first U.S. bombing of North Vietnam. Within days the Congress overwhelmingly adopted the Gulf of Tonkin Resolution, which authorized the president to take all necessary measures to repel attacks against U.S. forces and to assist South Vietnam in defense of its freedom. Until its repeal in 1971, the resolution was used by Presidents Johnson and Richard Nixon as a legislative mandate for escalation of the Vietnam War. The day after the attack on the Maddox, *U.S. Ambassador Maxwell Taylor cabled this dispatch urging strong measures in response to the incident.*

August 3, 1964

... Unprovoked attack against U.S. destroyer in international waters by three illegal North Vietnamese torpedo boats will be received dramatically in current atmosphere Saigon. It is not adequate to local minds (nor indeed to ours) to state that attack was repelled and that patrol will continue.

This reaction if it constitutes totality of U.S. Govt intentions, will make it appear that we are prepared to accept regular Swatow harassment in international waters as normal concomitant our normal naval patrolling activities. Such an attitude would immediately be construed in Saigon as indication that U.S. flinches from direct confrontation with North Vietnamese, especially since we apparently did not press home total destruction those vessels which attacked Maddox.

To meet this situation, recommend prompt consideration of following actions:

a. Announce that Swatows will henceforth be attacked whenever found in international waters and maintain air and/or naval forces in readiness to do so.

b. Direct regular air surveillance of Swatows overflying DRV [Democratic Republic of Vietnam] air space as required.

c. Mine approaches to Swatow harbors.

d. Create a torpedo capability in GVN [Government of Vietnam] Navy for use against appropriate targets, such as Haiphong dredges.

These are quick thoughts without opportunity for consultation with experts. However, we are impressed with need for prompt reaction and timely private communication of intentions to GVN.

Request urgent consideration these matters and advice soonest re statements which we may make privately to GVN.

Taylor

Index

Adams, Charles Francis, 14
  on launching and ravages of *Alabama*, 154–155
Adams, John, 4, 30, 34–37, 52
  on Great Britain as a diplomatic challenge, 34–35
  on reception by King George III, 36–37
Adams, John Quincy, 4, 71
  on Napoleon's retreat from Moscow, 71–72
  on terms of Treaty of Ghent, 73–75
Adams, Robert, Jr., on revolution in Brazil, 276–277
Adamson, Thomas, Jr., on destruction of six American vessels by *Alabama*, 156–157
Africa. *See also* Belgium
  conditions in Central, 263–266
  European colonization of, 233, 267
  French colonization of West, 233–234
  French move into Central, 234–235
  North, 97–98
African American diplomats, 6–7
Alabama, Confederate raider, 154–159
Alaska, American purchase from Russia, 187–188
Aldrich, Winthrop W., on Jawaharlal Nehru's views regarding Communist China, 432–433
Alexander II (Czar of Russia), 137, 172, 236, 237–238
Algiers, 38–39, 69–70. *See also* Cathcart, James Leander
  attack of French commander in, 97–98
  release of American captives in, 51
Allen, George V., on Marshal Tito's comments on revolution in Yugoslavia, 419
Alvarez, Manuel, on acquisition of New Mexico, 114–115
ambassador, office of
  title and privileges, 10
Anderson, Eugenie, 6
apartheid. *See* South Africa
Appleton, John, on Russian reaction to American Civil War, 145

Argentina
  anti-Jesuit riots, 215–217
  Perón regime, 420–421
Astor, John Jacob, 79
Australia, 119–121
Austria, 47, 117–118, 167, 183
  anti-Semitism of government, 269
  assassination of Archduke Franz Ferdinand, 346
  assassination of Chancellor Dollfuss, 385–386
  defeat of Austrian army by Prussia, 184
  German-Austrian alliance under Otto von Bismarck, 231–232

Baghdad, Iraq, 294–298
Bailly-Blanchard, Arthur, on election system in Haiti, 351
Baker, Lewis, on the "Mosquito Reservation," Nicaragua, 293
Balfour, Arthur, 357–358
Balmaceda, Manuel José, 283–284
Bancroft, George, on shah of Persia's visit to Europe, 212–213
Barbary States, 51. *See also* Cathcart, James Leander; Jefferson, Thomas; Tunisia
Barlow, Joel, 7–8
Barrios, Justo Rufino, 261–262
Bartholdi, Frédéric Auguste, 258–259
Bartleman, R.M., on anti-American riots in Spain, 308–309
Barton, Clara, 273
Bassett, Ebenezer, 6
Bastille prison, storming of, 23, 44–46
Batista, Fulgencio, 380–381, 442
Belgium
  British ultimatum to Germany regarding, 348
  colonization of Africa, 233, 263, 338
  German occupation of Brussels (1914), 349
  universal suffrage and riots in, 327
Ben-Gourion, David, 437–438
Berlin airlift, 403, 414

Berlin Wall. *See* Germany
Bernadotte, Count Folke, 399–400
  assassination in Jerusalem, 412
Bible, translation of, 323–325
Biddle, Thomas, on earthquake in San Salvador, 210–212
Bigelow, John, on first telegraph message, 185
Bismarck, Otto von, 183, 202, 230–231
Blackler, Samuel, 5, 109
  on establishment of French protectorate over Tahiti, 110
Blake, Freeman N., on invasion of Canada by Fenians, 179–181
Blocker, William P.
  on atrocities in Mexico by Pancho Villa's forces, 345
  on Mexican raid on Texas, 344–345
Boernstein, Charles, on foreign recruits for the Union Army, 159
Boer War, 315–318
Bogota, Colombia, 96–97
Boker, George H., on slave trade between Turkey and the Levant, 213–215
Bolívar, Simon, 94–96
Bolivia
  attempted revolution (1875), 218–219
  assassination of Major Villaroel and hope for democracy in (1946), 406–407
  conflict with Chile (1881), 239
Bonaparte, Napoleon. *See* Napoleon
Bonsal, Philip W., on Fidel Castro, 445–447
Bosnia, 346
Bowers, Claude G., on bombing of civilians by Spanish Fascists, 390
Braddock, Daniel M.
  on effective communist control in Cuba, 448
  on new Cuban government and Castro's attitude toward United States, 443–445
  on United States relations with Castro's government, 443
Brazil
  abolition of slave trade, 270–271
  revolution (1889), 276–277
Briand, Aristide, 369–370
Brown, John P., 9
  on Turkish reaction to American Civil War, 148
Buchanan, James, 4, 129
  on British ignorance of U.S. politics, 130
  on Ostend Manifesto, 128–129

Bullitt, William C.
  on alleged communist presence in French army (1940), 394–395
  on French request for American military involvement in Europe (1940), 395
  on Marshal Pétain's assessment of France's situation with Germany (1940), 396–397
  presentation of credentials to Moscow by, 383–385
Burdett, William C.
  on American consul general shot in Jerusalem, 410
  on battle for Jerusalem after Israel's declaration of independence, 410–411
  on siege of Jerusalem by Arab armies, 411
Burlingame, Anson, on adoption of national flag by China, 164
Burma, Second Burmese War, 121–122
Bush, George, 4

Cabot, John Moors, on U.S. vice consul to Shanghai beaten by communist soldiers, 415–416
California, 81, 120
Canada, Fenian invasion of, 179–181
Canada, William W., on occupation of Veracruz by American troops, 343
Canisius, Theodore, on request for Giuseppe Garibaldi's support in American Civil War, 160–161
Canton, China, 40–42
  tension with China, 105
Carías, Tiburcio Andino, 405–406
Caribbean, 92–93
Carranza, Venusitano, 342–343
Carrol, William, on return of Napoleon's remains to France, 107
Castro, Fidel, 381, 442–448
Cathcart, James Leander, 5
  on onset of war between Tripoli and United States, 58
Cavour, Camillo di, death of, 148–149
Central American Union, 261–262
Chapin, Stephen, on independence of Indonesia from Holland, 418
Charles X (King of France), 97–98
Chase, Isaac, on Kaffir War, 102
Chiang Kai-shek, 363, 432–433, 435
Chile, 85
  civil war (1891), 283–284
  conflict with Peru and Bolivia (1881), 239–241

China, 176
    adoption of national flag, 164
    American commissioner's first visit to (1853), 123–126
    antiforeign riots in Canton (1883), 255–256
    Boxer rebellion, 318–322
    communist takeover, 414–416, 432
    effect of Trans-Siberian Railroad on, 268–269
    and Egypt. *See* Nasser, Gamal Abdel
    election of Sun Yat-sen as president, 363–364
    emigration of Chinese to Hawaii, 241
    establishment of People's Republic, 417
    foreign legations attacked in Peking (1927), 368
    Great Britain and, 105
    imperial life in, 285
    influence over Korea, 260
    military tensions in People's Republic, 435–436
    slave trade in, 270–271
    war between Japan and, 298
Choate, Joseph H.
    on death of Queen Victoria, 322–323
    on establishment of Rhodes Scholarship Program, 328
Christiancy, Isaac P., on capture of Lima by Chilean forces, 239–241
Churchill, Winston, 352, 391–392, 407
Civil War, American
    arrest of two Confederate agents in Morocco, 149–152
    European countries' reaction to, 143–149
    foreign recruits for Union Army, 159
    launching and ravages of *Alabama*, 154–159
    request for Giuseppe Garibaldi's support in, 160–161
Clark, Daniel, Jr., 54, 64
    appeal for U.S. assistance against pirates in New Orleans, 55–56
    on Spanish transfer of Louisiana to France, 65
Clark, William, 79
Claxton, Francis S., on emancipation of Russian serfs by Czar Alexander II, 137
Clay, Cassius M.
    on United States purchase of Alaska from Russia, 187–188
    on economic progress in Russia, 172–173

Clay, Henry, 73
Clayton-Bulwar Treaty, 292
Cleveland, Grover, 247, 289
Clubb, Edmund, on establishment of People's Republic of China, 417
Colombia. *See* Greater Colombia
Comly, James M., on immigration and epidemic in Hawaii, 241–242
commerce. *See* trade
Communist Party. *See also* Bullitt, William C.; China; Cuba; El Salvador
    in Germany, 375–376. *See also* Liebknecht, Karl
Conger, Edwin H., on foreign legations in Peking and Boxer rebellion, 318–322
Congo
    atrocities in, 339–340
    International Congo Association. *See* Belgium; Stanley, Henry Morton
Congress, U.S., foreign affairs and, 34–35
Connelly, Bernard C., on riots in South Africa, 422–423
consul, office of
    foreign trade and, 14, 17–18
    powers and functions of, 10–12, 50, 82, 131, 208–209, 287
    reporting by, 17–18
    Samuel Shaw's appointment to Canton as, 40
    spoils system and negative appraisal of, 15–16, 238
Corwin, Thomas, on Mexican reaction to American Civil War, 147
Costa Rica, 88
Crimean War, 257
Cuba, 308
    Fidel Castro and communists, 442–448
    intervention and sinking of battleship *Maine* in Havana, 305–308, 310
    proclamation of government by Fulgencio Batista after revolution (1933), 381–382
    United States attempt to purchase from Spain, 128–129

Daladier, Edouard, 393, 395
Dallas, George M., on British reaction to American Civil War, 146
Davis, Jefferson, 173, 178
Davis, Robert Beale, Jr., on death of Haitian president (1915), 352
Dayton, William L., on battle between *Alabama* and *Kearsarge*, 158–159

Deane, Silas, 3, 13, 17
  biographical background, 25
  negotiation for military supplies, 25–27
  presentation of Declaration of Independence to French court, 28
  recruiting of Marquis de Lafayette, 29
Declaration of Independence, 28
Denby, Charles, Jr.
  on daily routine of Chinese emperor, 285
  on effect of Trans-Siberian Railroad on China, 268–269
  on Sino-Japanese war over Korea, 298
  on slavery in China, 270–271
Department of State. *See* State Department
Diaz, Porfirio, 188–189, 342
Dickover, Erle R., on earthquake in Japan, 366
Dickson, David, description of Texas, 93–94
Dien Bien Phu, 430–431
Dillon, Romaine, on death of Camillo di Cavour, 148–149
diplomat, office of
  description, 4
  duties, 287
  insufficient funding of, 31
  ranking of, 10
  reporting by, 17–20
  women, 6
Dorsz, Edmund J., on Mau Mau revolt in British Kenya, 427–430
Douglas, Lewis Williams, on Winston Churchill's views on the Soviet Union, 407–408
Douglass, Frederick, 6, 281
  on political situation in Haiti, 282
Dulles, John Foster, on Marshal Tito's views on Communist China, 433–434
Duncan, Enoch S., on establishment of mission in Kuwait, 426–427
Dutch East Indies. *See* Indonesia

Earthquakes
  Ecuador (1868), 199-200
  Japan (1923), 366
  Peru (1868), 199
  San Salvador (1873), 210-212
Ecuador, 94
  earthquake (1868), 199–200
Egan, Patrick, on civil war in Chile (1891), 283–284
Eggleston, Mrs. Ebenezer, 6
Egypt, 221
  discovery of source of Nile River, 170
  gift of obelisk to New York City, 228–229
  Suez crisis, 436–437
Eisenhower, Dwight D., 399–400, 430, 437
Elmslie, James, on Dutch capitulation of Cape of Good Hope to British, 68–69
El Salvador, 261–262
  communist uprising (1932), 373–374
  revolution (1890), 279–281
Emancipation Proclamation, 165
Engert, Cornelius Van H., on audience with Emperor Haile Selassie of Ethiopia, 387–388
Erwin, John D., on President Carías and political stability in Honduras, 405–406
Ethiopia, 233
  invasion by Italy, 387–388
Europe
  Chinese resentment of European presence, 255–256. *See also* China, Boxer rebellion
  Chinese trade with, 40–41
  influence of French July 1830 revolution on, 98
  looming of general war in, 231–232
  Napoleonic Wars and United States trade relations with, 66–67, 73
  in prewar Europe (1914), 347–349
  reactions to American Civil War, 143–149, 151, 161, 165
  recognition of independent United States, 32–33
  shah of Persia's visit (1873), 212–213
  unrest in (1776), 26–27
  U.S. mediation among warring nations (1914), 357
  views of Pope Pius IX on, 178–179
Eve, Joseph, on Texans' reaction to Mexican incursion (1842), 108–109

Farman, Elbert E.
  on freedom for an Egyptian slave, 221
  on Egypt's gift of obelisk to New York City, 228–229
Fascists. *See* Franco, Francisco; Mussolini, Benito
Faulkner, Charles J., on French reaction to American Civil War, 143–144
Ferdinand VII (King of Spain), 83
fishing, 74
Flack, Joseph, on assassination of Major Villaroel and hope for democracy in Bolivia, 406–407
Florida, acquisition from Spain, 83–84

foreign service, U.S. *See also* ambassador, office of; consul, office of; State Department
   conditions of early years, 7–9
   creation of, 12
   diplomatic usage, 9–11
   fatalities, 7–8
Forsyth, John, on acquisition of Florida from Spain, 83
Fort George, Ore., 79
Foster, John W.
   on assassination of Czar Alexander II, 237–238
   on pogroms in Russia, 242–244
Foulk, George C., on execution of dissidents in Korea, 260
France, 35. *See also* Charles X; Kellogg-Briand Pact; Napoleon; Nasser, Gamal Abdel; Syria
   Algiers and, 39, 97–98
   colonization of Africa, 233–236
   defeat at Dien Bien Phu, 430–431
   dire military situation (1940), 394–395
   establishment of protectorate over Tahiti, 110
   French human shields used in Gallipoli, 353
   French Revolution, 42–44, 46–50. *See also* Bastille prison
   involvement in Mexico, 188
   July Revolution, 98–100
   Louisiana and, 55
   political and military assistance to colonies, 25–27
   purchase of Louisiana from, 60–66
   reaction to American Civil War, 143–144
   recognition of United States of America, 28. *See also* Statue of Liberty
   role in Pope's control of Rome, 178–179
   seeming imminent fall of (1940), 392
   tension between United States and (1797), 52–54
   war with Prussia, 202
Francis, Charles S., on riots in Athens over translation of Bible, 323–325
Franco, Francisco, 389–390
Franklin, Benjamin, 4, 17, 25, 30, 31–34
   on recognition of independent United States, 32–33
   request for mission funding, 31
   views on peace, 33–34
freedom, 43
Frias, Thomas, 218

Gallatin, Albert, 73
Gallipoli Campaign, 352–353
Gandhi, Mohandas, 398
Garfield, James, 244–245
Garibaldi, Giuseppe, 160–162
Geneva Convention (1864), 273
George, Reuben D., on problems at U.S. border with Mexico, 299–300
George III (King of England), reception of John Adams, 36–37
Gerard, James W.
   on effect of early World War I victories on German population, 356
   on German victories over European armies (1914), 350–351
   on prewar Europe (1914), 347
Germany, 183. *See also* Austria; Bismarck, Otto von
   Belgium and British ultimatum to (1914), 348
   Berlin airlift, 403, 413
   Berlin Wall, 449–451
   colonization of Africa, 233, 267
   deciphering of Zimmermann telegram, 357–358
   early World War I victories of, 349–351
   effect on population of early World War I victories, 356
   Hitler's intimidation campaign after Reichstag fire, 374–377
   Nazi banning of American movie in, 370–372
   Nazi methods and policies (1933), 377–378
Gero, Erno, 439–440
Gerry, Elbridge, on French bribery for reconciliation with United States, 52–54
Goebbels, Joseph, 371, 376
Goering, Hermann, 375–376
Graham, Walter, on arrival of *Alabama* to Cape Town, 157–158
Grant, James, 170–171
Grant, Ulysses S., 15
Great Britain, 67, 396. *See also* India; Jerusalem; Nasser, Gamal Abdel; William IV; Zimmermann telegram
   British human shields used in Gallipoli, 353
   challenge to John Adams, 34–35
   colonization of Africa, 233
   conflict with Kingdom of Burma, 121–122
   death of Queen Victoria, 322–323
   effect of French Revolution on, 47

effect of Napoleonic Wars on U.S. relations, 73
establishment of the Rhodes Scholarship Program, 328
ignorance of U.S. politics, 130
move into the Cape of Good Hope, 68–69. *See also* Boer War
naval tensions between U.S. and, 57. *See also* War of 1812
reaction to American Civil War, 146
reception of John Adams by King George III, 36–37
relations between China and, 105
seeming imminent fall of (1940), 391–393
suppression of slave trade, 90–91
treaty with United States, 32
ultimatum to Germany from (1914), 348
U.S. neutrality in conflict between France and (1797), 52
Greater Colombia, 95–96
Greece, 167, 217, 220
riots over translation of Bible, 323–325
Greener, Richard, 7
Gregg, David L., on U.S. attempt at annexation of Hawaii, 127
Grew, Joseph C., on early warning of Japanese attack on Pearl Harbor, 397–398
Griffis, Stanton, on Juan Perón's government in Argentina, 420–421
Guadalupe Hidalgo, Treaty of, 77, 116–117
Guatemala, 261–262
revolution in, 279–281
Gulf of Tonkin, 456

Haiti, 6, 282
unstable political system in, 351–352
Haldeman, J.S., on Swedish reaction to naval warfare in Hampton Roads, 152
Halderman, John A.
description of early Vladivostok, 257–258. *See also* Denby, Charles, Jr.
on Royal Elephant Hunt in Siam, 251–253
Hale, Charles, on arrest of John Surrat in Alexandria, 186–187
Hale, John P., on insurrection in Madrid, 182–183
Hall, Henry C., on demise of Central American Union, 262
Hanna, Philip C., on occupation of U.S. consulate in Monterey, 343–344
Hanson, Abraham, on Liberian reaction to Abraham Lincoln's assassination, 175

Hare, Raymond A., on Gamal Abdel Nasser's assessment of Suez crisis, 438–439
Harriman, W. Averell, on concern about situation in Vietnam, 452
Harrison, Benjamin, 281
Harrison, William Henry, 4, 94
on José Paez and Simon Bolívar, 96–97
on revolt in Greater Columbia, 95–96
Harte, Bret, 6
on launching of revolutionary steamship in Glasgow, 249
Hartley, David, 33
Harvey, James E., on ravages of *Alabama*, 156
Hatfield, Stewart, Jr., on eruption of the Krakatau volcano, 253–254
Havana, Cuba, 57, 442, 305–308
Hawaii
early warning of Japanese attack on Pearl Harbor, 397–398
immigration to and epidemic in 241–242
negotiations for statehood of, 127
U.S protectorate on, 289–290
Hawthorne, Nathaniel, 6, 8
on seamen's problems in Liverpool, 131–134
Haynes, John Henry, 294
Heco, Joseph, 7
Hernández Martínez, Maximiliano, 373
Herrick, Myron Timothy, on prewar Europe (1914), 347
Herzegovina, 346
Hicks, John, on anti-American riots in Peru, 291–292
Higinbothom, W. R., on assistance to American seaman stranded in Bermuda, 82
Himmler, Heinrich, 399–400
Hitler, Adolf, 374, 376, 377, 380, 399–400
Hoffman, Wickham, 237
on plague of grasshoppers in the Caucasus, 229
Hogan, Michael, on surrender of Lima to José de San Martín, 84–85
Holland, 30, 35. *See also* Indonesia
Cape of Good Hope, 68. *See also* Boer War
Napoleonic Wars and, 68
Hollis, W. Stanley, on the Boer War, 315–318
Honduras, 88, 261–262
President Carías and political stability in, 405–406

Hovey, Alvin P., on earthquake in Ecuador (1868), 199–200
Hubbard, Richard B., on new constitution for Japan, 274–276
Huerta, Victoriano, 342
Huffnagle, Charles
  on British invasion of Burma, 121–122
  on Indian mutiny against British (1857), 135–136
Humphreys, David, 50–51
  on release of American captives in Algiers, 51
Hungary, uprising against Soviet Union (1956), 440

immunity, diplomatic, 11
independence
  of American colonies, 26
  Declaration of, 28
India
  British expansion to, 121, 134
  civil disobedience against British colonial rule, 398–399
  mutiny against British (1857), 135–136
Indians, American. See Native Americans
Indonesia
  eruption of Krakatau volcano, 253–254
  independence of, 417–418
Iraq. See Baghdad, Iraq
Irving, Washington, 6
  on siege and capture of Madrid, 111–112
Israel. See Jerusalem; Palestine
Italy, 117–118, 396. See also Garibaldi, Giuseppe; Pius IX
  colonization of Africa, 233
  death of Camillo di Cavour, 148–149
  invasion of Ethiopia by, 387–388
Iturbide, Agustin de, 85–89

Jackson, Andrew, 100–101
  on transfer of Florida from Spain to United States, 83–84
Jackson, Henry, on Napoleon's defeat at Waterloo, 75–76
Japan, 153, 278
  American bombs dropped on Hiroshima and Nagasaki, 399
  destruction of American legation in, 168–169
  earthquake (1923), 366
  expansion in eastern Asia, 397
  influence over Korea, 260
  invasion of Manchuria, 372–373
  new constitution for, 274–276
  offer to accept Potsdam declaration to surrender, 401
  opening to foreigners of, 195
  Soviet government and, 384–385
  war between China and, 298
Jarvis, Thomas J., on abolition of slave trade in Brazil, 270–271
Jay, John, 30
Jefferson, Thomas, 4, 13, 17, 42
  on storming of Bastille prison, 44–46
  views on war against Barbary States, 38–39
Jerusalem
  assassination of United Nations mediator on Palestine in, 412
  proclamation of State of Israel, 409–411
Jesuits, in Argentina, 215–217
Joffre, J. J. C., 349
Johnson, Herschel V.
  on Fascist revolutionary movement in Spain, 389
  on Himmler's peace proposal, 400–401
  on Japanese proposal to surrender, 401
Johnson, Lyndon B., 457
Johnson, Nelson T., on Japanese invasion of Manchuria, 372–373

Kearsarge, fight between *Alabama* and, 158–159
Keeley, James Hugues, on Syrian nationalists' revolt against French occupation of Damascus, 367
Keim, DeBenneville, 8–9, 15
Kellogg, Frank, 369
Kellogg-Briand Pact, 369–370, 372–373
Kennedy, John F., 451
Kennedy, Joseph P., 6
  plea that United States not enter war against Germany, 393
  on Winston Churchill's request for United States assistance, 391–392
Kenya, British, emergence of Mau Mau in Nairobi, 427–430
Khruschev, Nikita, 441, 449
King, Rufus, on Pope Pius IX's evaluation of world affairs, 178–179
Korea, 197, 260, 269
  Sino-Japanese war over, 298
  war between North and South, 424–425
Krakatau, volcano eruption, 253–254
Kuwait, establishment of United States mission in, 426–427

Lafayette, Marquis de, 29, 45, 50, 76
Lamar, Mirabeau B., 5
  on harassment of U.S. citizen in Nicaragua, 138–139
Laurens, Henry, 32
  biographical background, 29–30
  capture by British, 30
  confinement to Tower of London, 31
Lawson, Edward B., on conversation with David Ben-Gourion on Israeli mobilization, 437–438
Lawton, Alexander R., on admission of Rothschilds to Austro-Hungarian court, 269–270
League of Nations, 369, 372, 385, 387–388
Lear, Tobias, on threat by dey of Algiers, 69–71
Lebanon, lack of safety in Beirut, 329–330
Lee, Fitzhugh, on riots in Havana and sinking of *Maine*, 305–308
Lee, Henry, 97
  on attack on French commander in Algiers, 97–98
Leishman, John G.A., on establishment of constitutional government in Turkey, 341–342
Lenin, V. I., 358, 383
Lewis, Meriwether, 79
Liberia, 233
Liebknecht, Karl, 375
Liedesdorff, William, 6
Lightner, Edwin A., on Berlin Wall, 449–451
Lima, Peru, 84–85
Lincoln, Abraham, 14, 160, 163, 173
  assassination of, 175–176, 186
  Karl Marx congratulation on reelection, 173–174
  Union generals and, 141
Livingston, Robert R., 13
  on Napoleon's government, 59
  on negotiations with France for purchase of Louisiana, 61–64
Livingstone, David, 193
  death of, 201
Lodge, Henry Cabot
  on coup against Diem, 455
  on plan to overthrow Ngo Dinh Diem in Vietnam, 453–454
  on success of coup against Diem, 456
Long, James de, 149–152
Louisiana, 54
  purchase from France, 60–66
Louis-Phillipe (Duc d'Orléans), 98

Louis XVI (King of France), 43–45
  execution of, 47
Lowell, James Russell, 6
  on death of Queen Mercedes of Spain, 226–227
  on marriage of King Alfonso XII of Spain, 223–226

MacArthur, Douglas, 424–425
Macdonald, John J., on assassination in Jerusalem of United Nations mediator on Palestine, 412
MacMurray, John Van A., on American consulate attack in Peking, 368
Madagascar, French protectorate, 235–236
Madrid, Spain, 111–112
Malan, Daniel F., 422–423
Mao Tse-tung, 417, 432–433
Marie-Antoinette (Queen of France), 43, 46
  execution of, 48
Marshall, Humphrey, on visit to China, 122–126
Marshall, John, on XYZ affair, 52–54
Martí, Farabundo, 373
Marx, Karl, 173–174
Mason, John, on Ostend Manifesto, 128–129
Mathews, Felix A., on Berber terror in Morocco, 230
Mau Mau revolt, British Kenya, 427–430
Maximilian (Archduke of Austria)
  as emperor of Mexico, 188
  execution of, 191
Maynard, Horace, on lunar eclipse in Constantinople, 222
McCafferty, William J., on communist uprising in El Salvador, 373–374
McClintock, Robert, on account of Dien Bien Phu by French general, 431
McCook, James, 5
  on gold rush in Yukon territory and Alaska, 312–314
McDonald, Alexander, on assassination of shah of Persia (1896), 300–301
McKinley, William, 308
McLane, Robert, on French protectorate in Madagascar, 235–236
Merrell, George R., on Mohandas Gandhi's plan to launch civil disobedience against British, 398–399
Messersmith, George S.
  on assassination of Austrian chancellor Dollfuss by Nazis, 385–386
  on Nazi methods and policies, 377–380

Mexican War, 114, 116, 128
Mexico. *See also* Zimmermann telegram
    American relations with, 113–114,
        342–343, 343–345
    French involvement in, 188
    independence from Spain, 85–89
    problems at the U.S. border with,
        208–210, 99–300
    reaction to American Civil War, 147
    siege of Mexico city, 189–190
military supplies for American colonies,
    25–27
Miller, Douglas, on Nazi methods and policies, 379–380
Mizner, Lansing B., on revolution and wars
    in Central America, 279–281
Moerenhaut, Jacob Antoine, 103
    on attack in Tahiti, 104–105
Monroe, James, 4, 17, 42, 61–64
    on American security and Napoleonic
        Wars in Europe, 66–67
    on fall of Maximilien Robespierre,
        49–50
Montgomery, Robert, 51
Morgan, George W., on Portuguese reaction
    to American Civil War, 144–145
Morgenthau, Henry, 6
    on Armenian genocide in Turkey during
        World War I, 353–355
    on Turkish involvement in World War I
        and use of human shields in Gallipoli,
        352–353
Morocco, 230
Morris, Edward Joy
    on cholera and fire in Constantinople,
        177
    on murder of American missionary in
        Turkey, 163
Morris, Gouverneur, 42
    on beginning of French Revolution, 43
    on execution of Louis XVI, 47
    on execution of Marie Antoinette, 48
    on terror during French Revolution, 46
Morse, Samuel, 185
Morton, George C., on American fleet captured off Havana, 57
Morton, Levi P., 247
    on French expansion into Central
        Africa, 234–235
    on French gift of Statue of Liberty,
        258–259
Mosby, John Singleton, on corruption in
    American consulate in Bangkok, 238–239

Motley, John Lothrop
    on defeat of Austrian army by Prussia,
        184
    evaluation of situation in Balkans,
        166–168
Muccio, John J.
    on invasion of South Korea by North
        Korea, 424
    on martial law in Seoul, 425
Murphy, Robert Daniel, on Berlin airlift,
    413
Mussolini, Benito, 386–387

Nagy, Imre, 439–440
Naples, Italy, 39
Napoleon, 59–60
    Battle of Waterloo, 75–76
    campaigns in Europe, 66–67
    negotiations for purchase of Louisiana,
        62–64
    retreat from Moscow, 71–72
    return of remains to France, 107
Narváez, Ramón María, 111–112
Nasser, Gamal Abdel, 436,
    438–439
National Socialist German Workers' Party
    (Nazis), 370–372, 374–377
Native Americans
    in New Mexico, 115
    problems along Mexican border,
        209–210
Nazis. *See* Germany; National Socialist
    German Workers' Party
Nehru, Jawaharlal, 399, 432
Netherlands. *See* Holland
New Mexico, 114–115
New Orleans, La. 55–56, 61, 65. *See also*
    Louisiana
    trade between Texas and, 94
Ngo Dinh Diem, 451–453
Nicaragua, 88, 138–139, 292
    "Mosquito Reservation," 293
    United States intervention in (1922),
        364–365
Nile River, discovery of source,
    170–171
Nobel, Alfred, 325–326
Nobel Prize, 325–326

Opium War, 105, 255
Osborn, Thomas O., on anti-Jesuit riots in
    Argentina, 215–217
Ostend Manifesto, 128–129

Otterbourg, Marcus, on siege of Mexico, 189–190
Owen, Ruth Bryan, 6

Paez, José, 94, 96–97
Page, Walter Hines
 on British ultimatum to Germany, 348
 on early World War I British condemnation of Germany, 349–350
 on prewar Europe (1914), 348
 on Zimmermann telegram, 357–358
Paine, Thomas, 13
Palestine, 408–409
Palfrey, William, 7
Paris, France, 52–54, 202
 entry of Prussian troops into (1871), 203–204
 government of the Commune and insurrectionary movements in, 204–208
 Napoleon's return to, 72
 reaction to execution of Louis XVI, 47
 storming of Bastille prison, 44–46
Parson, Richmond, on Kurdish attacks on foreigners in Teheran, 330–331
peace, 33–34, 116–117
 with Algiers. See Jefferson, Thomas
 spirit after World War I, 369
 William IV's interest in, 101–102
Penfield, Frederic Courtland
 on assassination of Archduke Franz Ferdinand, 346
 on prewar Europe (1914), 347
Perón, Juan, 420–421
Perry, Amos, on civil unrest in Tunisia, 171–172
Pershing, John, 342
Persia. See also Teheran
 shah's visit to Europe (1873), 212–213
Peru, 96
 anti-American riots in (1893), 291–292
 capture of Lima by Chilean forces, 239–241
 earthquake (1868), 199
Pétain, Henri-Philippe, 394, 396–397
Philippines, battle of Manilla Bay, 310–311
Pierce, Franklin, 128
Pierce, Herbert H.S., on Theodore Roosevelt's acceptance of Nobel Prize, 336–338
Pike, James S., on European reaction to Emancipation Proclamation, 165
Pinckney, Charles Cotesworth, on XYZ affair, 52–54
Pius IX (Pope), 178–179

Plumb, E.L., on execution of Archduke Maximilian, 191
Polk, James K., 114, 116
Portugal, 39. See also Brazil
 colonization of Africa, 233
 reaction to American Civil War, 144–145
Preston, William, on Spanish reaction to American Civil War, 146–147
Prevost, John B., description of Oregon and California, 79–81
Price, Ernest B., on election of Sun Yat-sen as President of China, 363–364
Prussia, 26–27, 183–184. See also Germany
 reaction to American Civil War, 147
 war with France, 202–204
Pruyn, Robert H.
 on bureaucratic changes in Japan, 153
 on destruction of American legation in Japan, 168–169

Ramer, John Edward, on U.S. intervention in Nicaragua (1922), 365–366
Randall, Thomas, on pirates' attacks off Caribbean coast, 92–93
Rankin, Karl L., on military tensions in China, 435–436
Ravndal, G. Bie, on unsafe conditions in Beirut, 329–330
Read, George Meredith
 on festivities at Greek court, 217
 on unearthing of arms of Venus de Milo, 220
Red Cross, International, 273
Reynolds, Robert M., on attempted revolution in Bolivia (1875), 218–219
Rhee, Syngman, 424–425
Rhodes, Cecil, 328
Rhodes Scholarship Program, 328
Rives, William G., 98
 on France's July 1830 revolution, 99–100
Robespierre, Maximilien, 42
 fall of, 49–50
Rogers Act, 12
Roosevelt, Franklin D., 382, 384
Roosevelt, Theodore, 303, 364
 as Nobel Prize recipient, 336
Ropes, E.D., on German colonization in East Africa, 267
Rush, Richard, on negotiations for British suppression of slave trade, 90–91
Russell, Jonathan, on government under Napoleon, 59–60

Russia, 167. *See also* Hungary
  assassination of Czar Alexander II, 236–238
  Berlin airlift and, 413
  Churchill's views on United States relations with, 407–408
  designs upon United States, 81
  emancipation of serfs by Czar Alexander II, 137, 172, 236
  establishment of U.S. relations with Soviets, 382–385
  famine in, 286–287
  founding of Vladivostok, 257–258. *See also* Denby, Charles, Jr.
  launching of *Sputnik* by, 441–442
  Napoleonic Wars in, 72
  plague of grasshoppers in Caucasus, 229
  pogroms in, 242–244
  progress in, 172–173
  reaction to American Civil War, 145
  relations with Prussia, 231
  revolution (1917), 358–360
  Trans-Siberian Railroad and effect on China, 268
  United States purchase of Alaska from, 187–188
  workers' insurrection in Moscow (1906), 332–335
Russo-Japanese War, 303, 332, 336

Sackett, Frederic Mosley
  on Nazi banning of American film in Germany, 370–372
  on Nazi repressive measures after Reichstag fire, 374–377
Saint Petersburg, Russia, 71–72
San Francisco, Calif., 81
San Martín, Jose de, role in South American revolutions, 84
San Salvador, earthquake in, 210–212
Santa Ana, Antonio Lopez de, 85, 88
Schuchardt, William, on problems along Mexican border, 209–210
Scott, Winfield, 114, 116
Selassie, Haile, 387–388
Serbia, 346
Seward, George F., on trial of American looter in Shanghai, 197–199
Seward, William H., 175
  on dismissal and reinstatement of consul to Vienna, 162
Seymour, Charles, on antiforeign riots in Canton, 255–256
Shaw, Samuel, on China, 40–42

Siam. *See* Thailand
slave trade, 90–91, 129, 165. *See also* Claxton, Francis S.
  Brazil abolition of, 271–272
  in China, 270–271
  in Turkey, 296–297
  between Turkey and the Levant, 213–215
Smith, Charles Emory, on famine in Russia, 286–287
Smith, James A., on atrocities against natives in Congo, 339–340
Smith, Samuel, on workers' insurrection in Moscow (1906), 332–335
Smyth, John, on French colonization of West Africa, 233–234
Snow, Peter W., on arrival of British fleet in Macao, 106
Soulé, Pierre, 5, 128
  on Ostend Manifesto, 128–129
South Africa, 102. *See also* Rhodes, Cecil
  Boer War, 315–318
  Cape Town, 68–69
  riots in (1950), 422–423
Soviet Union. *See* Russia
Spain, 67, 111–112
  anti-American riots (1898), 308–309
  battle of Manilla Bay, 310–311
  Civil War in, 389–390
  Cuba and, 128
  death of Queen Mercedes, 226–227
  effect of Napoleonic Wars on American provinces governed by, 84, 85
  independence of Mexico from, 85–89
  insurrection in Madrid (1868), 182–183
  Louisiana and, 55–56
  marriage of King Alfonso XII to Queen Mercedes, 223–226
  negotiations for purchase of Louisiana and, 61, 64–65
  reaction to American Civil War, 146–147
  signature of Transcontinental Treaty between United States and, 82–83
  surrender of Lima to José de San Martín, 84
  transfer of Florida to United States, 82–83
Sparks, William, 12
  recognition of Republic of Venice, 118–119
Speke, John, 170–171
Sperry, Watson R., on protection of American citizen insulted in Persia, 288
Sputnik, 441-442

Stalin, Joseph, 384
Stanley, Henry Morton, 193, 201, 338
  role in colonization of Africa, 233, 235, 263
Stapp, Walter, 7
State Department
  development of reporting, 16–20
  establishment and growth, 13–14
  expansion of duties and responsibilities, 16
  spoils system, 15, 238
Statue of Liberty, 247, 258–259
Stevens, John L., on U.S. protectorate of Hawaii, 289–290
Stuart, John Leighton, on violation of U.S. ambassador's residence in Nanking, 414–415
Suez Canal, 436–439
Sundberg, John C.
  on epidemic in Baghdad, 294–296
  on Persian rugs as health hazard, 297–298
  on slavery in Turkey, 296–297
Sun Yat-sen, 363–364, 368
Sweden, 152
  award of first Nobel Prizes, 325–326
Swift, John F., on Japanese gift to Smithsonian Institution, 278
Switzerland, 35
  birth of international organizations in, 272–274
Syria, 437
  nationalist revolt against French occupation of Damascus, 367

Tahiti, 5, 103–105
  French protectorate over, 109–110
Taiwan, 432, 435
Talleyrand, Marquis de, 52–54, 61–62
Taylor, Maxwell D., 451
  urging for American response to attack of *Maddox*, 457
Teheran
  assassination of Persian shah in, 300–301
  Kurdish attacks on foreigners in Teheran, 330–331
Telegraph Union, International, 273
Texas, 93–94, 113
  Mexican incursions into (1842), 107–108
  Mexican raids on (1916), 344–345
Thailand
  corruption in American consulate in Bangkok, 238–239
  Royal Elephant Hunt in, 251–253
Thayer, William S., on discovery of source of Nile River, 170–171
Thomas, William W., on award of the first Nobel Prizes, 325–326
Thompson, Llewellyn E., Jr., on launching of *Sputnik* by Soviet Union, 441–442
Tisdel, W.P., on conditions in Central Africa, 263–266
Tito, Joseph Broz, 418–419, 432, 433–434
Tower of London, 31
Townsend, Lawrence, on universal suffrage and riots in Belgium, 327
trade
  from American colonies, 26, 28
  with China, 40–42, 105
  consul's role in foreign, 14, 17–18
  establishment of U.S.-Soviet relations and boost to, 382
  German colonization of Zanzibar and threat to American, 267
  maritime, 249–251, 257–258
  nascent American, 41–42
  in Nicaragua by Americans, 292–294
  suppression of slave. *See* slave trade
  with the Vatican, 33
  from West Africa, 264–266
Transcontinental Treaty, 82–84
Trans-Siberian Railroad, 268
Treaty of Ghent, 73–75, 79. *See also* War of 1812
Treaty of Guadalupe Hidalgo, 77, 116–117
Treaty of Lausanne, 330
Treaty of Sèvres, 330
Tripoli, 58
Trist, Nicholas, 77
  negotiation of Treaty of Guadalupe Hidalgo, 116
Truman, Harry S., 424
Tunisia, revolt against increased taxation, 171–172
Turkey, 222
  Armenian genocide during World War I, 353–355
  cholera and fire in Constantinople, 177
  decay of empire, 167
  establishment of constitutional government (1908), 340–342
  involvement in World War I and Gallipoli campaign, 352–353
  memorial service for President Garfield, 244–245
  murder of American Christian missionary, 163
  reaction to American Civil War, 148

slave trade between the Levant and, 213–215
war with Russia (1879), 231
Tyler, John, 5

Valkenburgh, Robert B. van, on hara-kiri of Japanese official, 195–197
Van Buren, Martin, 4, 100–101
on King William IV's interest in peace, 101–102
Venezuela, 94, 96–97
Venice, establishment of republic in, 117–119
Venus de Milo, 220
Veragua, 88
Vichy government. *See* Pétain, Henri-Philippe
Victoria (Queen of England), 322–323
Vietnam
Gulf of Tonkin incident, 457
U.S. plans to overthrow Diem and coup, 453–456
warning against American involvement in, 451–452
Villa, Francisco "Pancho," 342–343, 345
Villarroel, Gualberto, 406–407

Wailes, Edward T., on Hungarian uprising in Budapest, 440
Wallace, Lew, 6
on memorial service for President Garfield in Constantinople, 244–245
War of 1812, 73
Washburne, Elihu B., 6, 202
on the Commune and insurrectionary movements in Paris, 205–208
on Prussian troops' entry into Paris, 203–204
Washington, George, 13
Wasson, Thomas C.. *See also* Burdett, William C.
on Arabs' anticipation of proclamation of Jewish State in Palestine, 409–410
Waterloo, Battle of, 75–76

Waters, Richard P., gift of Arabian horses to President Tyler, 113
Webb, Francis R.
on death of David Livingstone, 201
on Stanley's expedition to Central Africa, 201
Welles, Benjamin Sumner, on proclamation of Batista's revolutionary government in Cuba, 381–382
White, Andrew D., on German-Austrian alliance, 231–232
Whitehouse, H. Remsen, on proclamation of Central American Union, 261–262
Whitehouse, Sheldon, on French expectation of bilateral convention with the United States, 370
Whitlock, Brand, on German occupation of Brussels (1914), 349
Wilcocks, James Smith, on independence of Mexico, 85–89
William IV, 101–103
Williams, James H., on gold and natural resources in Australia, 119–121
Williams, Oscar F., on battle of Manilla Bay, 310–311
Williams, S. Wells, on Peking reaction to Lincoln's assassination, 176
Wilson, Huntington, on prewar Europe (1914), 348
Wilson, Woodrow, 336
Winchester, Boyd, on birth of international organizations in Switzerland, 272–274
Winship, North, on Russian revolution (1917), 358–360
women diplomats, 6. *See* diplomat, office of
Wright, Joseph A., Prussian reaction to American Civil War, 147

XYZ affair, 52–54

Yugoslavia, 418–419, 432–434

Zapata, Emiliano, 342
Zimmermann telegram, 357–358

WITHDRAWN